Census Substitutes
&
State Census Records

♦ ♦ 3rd Edition ♦ ♦

Volume 1
Northeastern States & U.S. Territories

by
William Dollarhide

Published by Family Roots Publishing Co., LLC
PO Box 1682
Orting, WA 98360-1682
www.familyrootspublishing.com

Library of Congress Control Number: 2020934867

ISBN (Paperback): 978-1-62859-284-9
ISBN (eBook): 978-1-62859-285-6

Recommended Citation:
Census Substitutes & State Census Records, 3rd Edition,
Volume One – Northeastern States & U.S. Territories,
by William Dollarhide, publ. Family Roots Publishing Co., LLC,
Orting, WA, 2020, 271 pages. Updated May 2021.

Printed in the United States of America

Contents – Vol. 1
Northeastern States & U.S. Territories

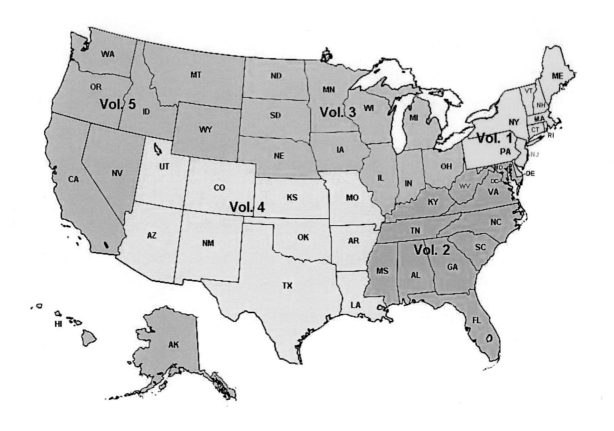

State Finder, Vols. 1-5

States	Vol.	Page
Alabama	2	233
Alaska	5	19
Arizona	4	213
Arkansas	4	75
California	5	57
Colorado	4	239
Connecticut	1	145
Delaware	1	223
District of Columbia	2	58
Florida	2	277
Georgia	2	193
Hawaii	5	37
Idaho	5	163
Illinois	3	119
Indiana	3	91
Iowa	3	179
Kansas	4	41
Kentucky	2	113
Louisiana	4	123
Maine	1	19
Maryland	2	19
Massachusetts	1	91

States	Vol.	Page
Michigan	3	43
Minnesota	3	225
Mississippi	2	259
Missouri	4	19
Montana	5	189
Nebraska	3	243
Nevada	5	107
New Hampshire	1	63
New Jersey	1	191
New Mexico	4	191
New York	1	173
North Carolina	2	145
North Dakota	3	273
Ohio	3	19
Oklahoma	4	101
Oregon	5	121
Pennsylvania	1	205
Rhode Island	1	133
South Carolina	2	177
South Dakota	3	261
Tennessee	2	161
Texas	4	169

States	Vol.	Page
Utah	4	261
Vermont	1	77
Virginia	2	79
Washington	5	141
West Virginia	2	97
Wisconsin	3	159
Wyoming	5	205

US Territories	Vol.	Page
Caribbean Region	1	245
Puerto Rico	1	246
US Virgin Islands	1	251
Panama Canal Zone	1	256
Pacific Region	1	259
Guam	1	260
No. Mariana Islands	1	262
American Samoa	1	264
The Philippines	1	268

US Nationwide	Vol.	Page
1790-1950 Maps / Descr.	5	217
US Census Substitutes	5	259

Foreword

by Leland K. Meitzler

In late 2003 Bill Dollarhide came by my office and asked if I had any ideas for *Genealogy Bulletin* articles. As it turned out, I had just finished organizing materials for a lecture on state and territorial census records and had a file folder full of data I had collected over the years on my desk. I suggested he put something together on that subject and gave him the file to review. After looking through my file, Bill decided that we needed to identify the many substitutes to censuses (statewide tax lists, voter registration lists, and such), as he quickly noted that a number of states didn't take any state or territorial censuses at all. Bill began compiling a bibliography of not only extant state and territorial censuses, but substitute lists as well.

Researched and compiled by region, he added timelines of historical references to show the jurisdictions in place at the time of each census. Compiling the material by region was a logical way to go, as we quickly realized that in most cases, it would have been difficult to write about one state without writing about those surrounding it. So, if you start with Maine, for example, the adjoining state of New Hampshire would be the next chapter, then Vermont, Massachusetts, and so on.

Much of the data found in the two-volume First Edition (2008) was initially published in serial form in the old *Genealogy Bulletin (1983-2006).* That said, the District of Columbia, for which there are many excellent sources, was never published. Also never published was The Oregon Country chapter. However, both chapters were included in the First Edition.

In the three-volume Second Edition (2016), numerous online sources were added, reflecting the ongoing efforts of both public and private companies to digitize relevant records.

In this new five-volume Third Edition (2020), the *Northeastern States* (Volume 1) adds seven (7) U.S. Territories for the first time. In addition, the *Western & Pacific States* (Volume 5) has an all-new *Maps, Descriptions, and Internet Access for the U.S. Federal Censuses, 1790-1950;* followed by an updated *U.S. Census Substitutes* chapter. Each of the 50 states & DC in this 3rd Edition has many more citations for newly added online databases and recently digitized microfilm collections – in just three years, the number went from 3,865 to 8,067 hyperlinks.

Bill also spent countless hours compiling tabulated charts that may be worth the cost of this book all by themselves. The first, found on page 13, is a chart for the non-state census states. There happens to be 13 of them (including the District of Columbia). This chart lists the states and the years covered by census substitutes. The second chart, found on pages 14-15, lists the 38 states that have extant colonial, pre-statehood, territorial, and state censuses, complete with the census year, and an indication if the census is available online as of the date of publication. The third chart, found on page 16, shows in graphic form the states that had censuses taken in common years – "on the fives." Census dates for some states are within a range. The fourth chart, on page 17, shows the availability of federal censuses for all states, 1790-1950.

Note that the title of this series of volumes is *Census Substitutes & State Census Records,* which reflects the fact that the volumes really contain a list of census substitutes, with state censuses turning out to be in the minority. Substitutes outnumber censuses by a factor of ten to one! However, the state censuses identified in this series are by far the most complete lists of Colonial, Territorial, or State Censuses published to date.

State and Territorial Censuses have long fascinated me. Many were taken in order to get congress to allow statehood. Some territories would take censuses on a nearly annual basis, in the attempt to show that they had the population base necessary to justify statehood.

Other states, like New York, had authorization of non-federal censuses written into their state constitutions. New York was one of the most prolific when it came to state censuses, as it produced numerous schedules, most falling on the ubiquitous "fives." Today we have extant New York censuses for 1825, 1835, 1845, 1855, 1865, 1875, 1892, 1905, 1915, and 1925. Some of the early years are not complete, but what is available is certainly useful. The 1925 New York census was taken as well as any other, and the population returns are largely legible and complete. However, the census was wrought with scandal, leaving New Yorkers with a taste of bitterness for such things. To make a long story short, it seems that the New York Secretary of State, a former Dean of Home Economics at Syracuse University, Florence Elizabeth Smith Knapp, took nepotism to a whole new level. As the state official in charge of the 1925 census, she put family and friends on the payroll, and while this wasn't illegal, most of these folks did little or nothing to earn their salaries. Even her 74-year old mother, Ella Smith, enjoyed a non-working stint as an assistant supervisor. Florence's stepdaughter, Clara Blanche Knapp, a professor at Middlebury College in Vermont, was on the payroll for over $5,000 in income, while never leaving the state of Vermont. Moreover, checks written to both Ella and Blanche seemed to have been endorsed into Florence E.S. Knapp's bank account. Numerous other family members and friends were paid substantial sums for non-work. In 1928, Mrs. Knapp finally went on trial for her misdeeds, and found guilty of first-degree grand larceny for misappropriation of state funds. She served 30 days in the Albany Jail. She could have gotten 10 years. So ended the brief political career of the first woman ever to be elected to state-wide office in New York. So also ended the state censuses of New York State.

Iowa, Kansas, Rhode Island, Florida, North Dakota, and South Dakota also took censuses up through 1925. South Dakota and Florida even took censuses in 1935 and 1945! The real value of state censuses is found in the numerous schedules enumerated in the mid-nineteenth century. Thirty-eight states took non-federal censuses that are still extant today.

And then there are the substitutes. They are of prime importance, since 12 states, as well as the District of Columbia, took no state censuses at all. And even if your ancestors lived in a state where censuses were taken "on the fives," census substitutes are helpful, especially if the family was on the move.

Although Mr. Dollarhide has used all kinds of substitutes throughout this volume, more attention has been given to tax lists, voter registration rolls, vital records, directories, statewide probate indexes, land records, and even military censuses, than most others. These records are often easily accessible and using this guide, you will be able to quickly find them for your own use. You are in for a treat, so sit back and look up the states of your ancestors. You will find information on records you never knew existed. Then... go get the records, and happy hunting!

- Leland K. Meitzler
Publisher

Introduction

Census Substitutes & State Census Records

Census Substitutes are those name lists derived from tax lists, directories, military lists, land ownership lists, voter registrations, and other compilations of names of residents for an entire state, or part of a state. A census substitute can be used to determine the names of residents in a given area when a federal or state census is missing. Moreover, a census substitute can be used as an alternative name list; confirming, contradicting, or adding to information found in a federal or state census.

This book identifies at least ten times the number of Census Substitute titles than any previous work ever published. All states are represented with significant alternative name lists – name lists that stop time for a certain year and place and name the residents of a certain place. Since all of these name lists are specific to a certain year, they are listed within each state category in chronological order. Incorporated into the lists are any State Census titles – a reference to a state census taken for a specific year.

Federal vs. State Censuses

Federal Censuses have their origins in the constitutional provision for apportionment of the U.S. House of Representatives. The first federal census was taken in 1790, and beginning about the same time, state censuses were conducted for the same reason, that is, apportionment of the various state legislatures.

Although the primary purpose of all censuses was to simply count the population, beginning with the first federal census of 1790, more information than a simple tally was added. This included the name and age of a person and progressively more details about a household for each subsequent census year. State censuses followed this same pattern.

State censuses usually add even more information than the federal censuses, and as a result, they are premier genealogical resources. Except in cases where a federal census is lost, state census records are not substitutes for the federal censuses – state censuses were almost always taken between federal census years, and usually add unique information and details about a household not found in a federal census. If a state census exists between federal census years, it may add marginally to the knowledge one gains about a family. But, more often, it will add critical information, such as more exact dates of birth, marriages, deaths; plus, additional children, different residences, other relatives living with a family; and more.

Non-State Census States

Thirteen (13) states (including DC) have never conducted a state-sponsored census. For these Non-State Census States, this review attempts to identify as many census substitutes as possible. In some cases, the census substitutes are for a single county within a state, and by listing multiple county name lists for about the same time period, regional coverage is achieved.

For an overview of the Non-State Census States, see Table 1 (page 13) showing the years for which census substitutes exist. More detail for each census substitute year indicated on the table is covered in the bibliographic sections.

State Census States

Thirty-eight (38) states have conducted censuses separate from the federal censuses. The number of censuses taken by each of the State Census States ranges from one (1) census year, e.g., the 1852 California; to twenty-four (24) census years, e.g., the 1792-1866 Mississippi territorial/state censuses. For this review, all of the state-sponsored censuses are identified, plus, to a lesser degree than the non-state census states, census substitutes available. See Table 2 (pages 14-15) for an overview of the State Census States, the year for each surviving census for a state; and an indication of which specific years are now available online as digitized databases.

Locating the Extant State Census Records

Generally, state censuses were conducted from the time of territorial status or early statehood up until about 1905, but a few continued until 1925, 1935, or 1945. The last state censuses taken by any of the states was in 1945 (Florida and South Dakota). Due to budget restraints, the Depression Era of the 1930s was a contributing factor to states ending their census-taking endeavors. Eventually, all states of the Union stopped using the population figures from state censuses and began using the federal census figures for apportionment of their state legislatures.

While the surviving federal census manuscripts are all located mostly in one repository (the National Archives), state census manuscripts are spread across the country in the various state archives or local repositories. The accessibility of state censuses may be just as good as federal censuses – but one needs to know where they are located first.

Beginning in 1941, the U.S. Bureau of the Census issued a bibliographic report attempting to identify all known state censuses, those undertaken by the various states separate from the federal censuses since 1790.[1] Prepared by Henry J. Dubester of the Library of Congress, the report was the first known attempt to research all of the state constitutions and subsequent laws related to state censuses for all of the states. The Dubester report sought, first, to identify what state censuses had ever been authorized by a state constitution or legislature; and second, to identify what census manuscripts still survive. The identification of extant state censuses was very incomplete, due to the war and under-funding of the project.

However, Dubester's review of each state's constitutional provisions for taking state censuses still stands as the best overview of what state censuses were ever authorized. The report cites the specific articles of the state constitutions or the actual state laws relating to censuses for all states.

Unfortunately, the fact that a state legislature authorized a state census does not mean one was actually taken. For example, the State Constitution of California of 1849 authorized a census in the years 1852 and 1855 and each ten years thereafter, all for the purpose of apportionment of its state legislature. Yet, only one was ever taken, that for 1852. Later, the California Constitution of 1879 provided that the decennial national census serve as the basis for legislative apportionment.[2]

This was fairly typical of all states. Even in those states for which several decades of state censuses now survive, they eventually got out of the census business, turning to the federal decennial censuses to determine apportionment. For example, New York took state censuses from 1825 and every ten years thereafter until 1925, yet, in 1938, New York decided to use the federal decennial censuses thereafter.[3]

Since the Dubester report, there have been several attempts to list all known state censuses, where they are located, and the contents of the census name lists. All of these attempts differ dramatically, because some of the lists rely on the Dubester report, which may have been accurate in identifying which state censuses were ever authorized but was not nearly complete in identifying the extant manuscripts of state census records. For example, Table 4-8 of *The Source,*[4] seems to use the census years cited in the Dubester report for "authorized state censuses" rather than those actually extant. There are lists of state censuses for each state in *The Red Book,*[5] but are only a slight improvement over those found in *The Source.* And, several Internet sites offer lists of state censuses, all of which seem to take data previously published in the *Source* or *The Red Book,* and similar publications.

Based on survey results from all states, the Family History Library prepared a two-volume publication, *U.S. State and Special Census Register: A Listing of Family History Library Microfilm Numbers,* compiled by G. Eileen Buckway and Fred Adams, a revised edition published by the FHL in 1992 (FHL book 973 X2 v. 1 & 2, and fiche #6104851 (vol. 1) and #6104852 (vol. 2). This is a very good guide to military censuses, school censuses, and special censuses of American Indian tribes. As a guide to state censuses, however, the list is incomplete. Since the results of the surveys from each of the states were only partially successful, there are many omissions.

Clearly, the best list of state censuses to date is Ann S. Lainhart, *State Census Records,* published by Genealogical Publishing Co., Inc., Baltimore, in 1992. The book identifies state censuses in 43 states, including 5 states without state censuses (but have major state-wide census substitutes available). For the 38 state census states, the lists generally do not include colonial or pre-territorial censuses. With a few exceptions, census substitutes such as those compiled from tax lists, voter registration lists, military lists, or other name sources, are also not included. Still, Lainhart's book stands as the most complete list ever done.

At the time when most of the previous state census lists were put together, there were some research tools unavailable to the authors. Today, the Internet as a resource for finding place-specific records is overwhelming. And, special tools such as the Periodical Source Index (PERSI)[6] which indexes articles in over 11,000 different genealogical periodicals (by subject, place, and surname) gives a big boost to the task of finding references to relevant articles using keywords such as "state census," "territorial census," or "tax list." In addition, the State Archives and/or State Libraries where obscure census originals and substitute name lists reside often have a website with an online searchable catalog.

For any genealogical research project, it helps to be close to the Family History Library (FHL) in Salt Lake City. But from any place where a researcher has access to the Internet, the FamilySearch[TM] online catalog as a genealogical research tool has no equal. Searching for published state censuses and census substitutes in the FHL catalog will not bring up every extant resource, but it is more complete than any other library in the world.

The Evolution of Regional Chapters to State Chapters

In the 2008 First Edition of this work, the two volumes had chapters for six (6) Eastern Regions and five (5) Western Regions of the United States.

For the 2016 Second Edition, the three volumes included an Eastern volume with five (5) regions; the Central Volume had three (3) regions; and the Western volume had four (4) regions; plus, an all-new Nationwide Chapter was added to the Western volume. A timeline for each region was prepared to put the area into a historical perspective from a genealogist's point of view.

This 2020 Third Edition was expanded to five volumes, each volume a region of the United States. Therefore, the content of each state's review now includes much of the content that was done at the regional level in the earlier editions, e.g., there is now a Timeline specific to each state.

The organization of the state bibliographic lists has changed as well. The Second Edition had several category listings for bibliographic entries, including State Resource Centers, Ancestry.com, FamilySearch.org, and others. This Third Edition has just one (1) listing where all databases from any provider are presented in chronological order.

About PERSI

PERSI (PERiodical Source Index) is a digitized database project of the Allen County Public Library (ACPL), Fort Wayne, IN. Since 1986, the PERSI extractors have indexed article titles, places, and surnames from over 11,000 genealogical & historical periodicals. The PERSI database is currently available online through the FindMyPast.com subscription website.

A number of printed articles found in periodicals were included in the state bibliography listings that follow. The Fort Wayne library has an online order form for requesting a printed copy of any article indexed in the PERSI database, see **http://genealogycenter.org/docs/default-source/resources/articlerequest.pdf?sfvrsn=2**.

Federal Censuses

Since the Second Edition was published in 2016, the digital images of all federal censuses 1790-1940 became accessible to the public via the Family History Library online catalog. It is now possible to view the digital images for any state's federal censuses separate from the various indexed databases at FamilySearch.org, Ancestry.com, My Heritage.com, et al. This meant adding the URL link for each state's digitized federal censuses in this Third Edition.

The Nationwide Chapter (Vol. 5) was completely reorganized into Part 1: *Maps, Descriptions, and Internet Access for the U.S. Federal Censuses, 1790-1950;* and Part 2: *U.S. Census Substitutes.* To review the federal censuses in more detail, refer to *The Census Book*[7] for each census year. The new 2019 *Census Book* has a detailed review of published federal censuses online, 1790-1950.

The maps of the changing county boundaries for all of the states shown in *Map Guide to the U.S. Federal Census, 1790-1920*[8] should also be helpful for reviewing substitute or state census years between federal census years.

- bill$hide

Notes:

1. *State Censuses: An Annotated Bibliography of Censuses of Population Taken After the Year 1790 by States and Territories of the United States*, prepared by Henry J. Dubester, Chief, Census Library Project, Library of Congress, published Washington, DC, by United States Department of Commerce, Bureau of the Census, 1941, rev. 1948.

2. Dubester, *State Censuses*, p. 3.

3. Dubester, *State Censuses*, p. 50.

4. *The Source: A Guidebook of American Genealogy*, first edition, edited by Arlene Eakle and Johni Cerny, published by Ancestry, Inc., Salt Lake City, 1984.

5. *The Red Book: American State, County & Town Sources*, edited by Alice Eichholz, rev. ed., published by Ancestry, Inc., Salt Lake City, UT, 1992.

6. Allen County Public Library, *Periodical Source Index (PERSI)*, updated semi-annually. [database online at various contracted websites] Original data: Allen County Public Library. Periodical Source Index, Fort Wayne, IN: Allen County Public Library Foundation, 1985- .

7. *The Census Book: Facts, Schedules & Worksheets for the U.S Federal Censuses,* by William Dollarhide, publ. Family Roots Publishing Co., Orting, WA, 2019, 245 pages. See **www.familyrootspublishing.com/store/product_view.php?id=3643**.

8. *Map Guide to the U.S. Federal Censuses, 1790-1920,* by William Thorndale and William Dollarhide, published by Genealogical Publishing Co., Inc., Baltimore, 1987-2016, 445 pages. See **www.familyrootspublishing.com/store/product_view.php?id=67**.

Table 1 – Non-State Census States • **13**

Table 1 – Non-State Census States. The following 13 states (including DC) have never conducted a state-sponsored census (or no state census survives). Census Substitutes for each state are shown for a range of years. Refer to the bibliographic listings for details about each.

State	Terr.	State	Years for which Census Substitutes are Available
Alaska	1912	1959	1870, 1873, 1878, 1885, 1887, 1890-1895, 1902-1912, 1905, 1908-1914, 1910- 1929, 1913-1916, 1917-1918, 1947, 1950, 1959-1986, and 1960-1985.
Delaware	—	1787	1609-1888, 1646-1679, 1680-1934, 1682-1759, 1684-1693, 1726, 1755, 1759, 1779, 1782, 1785, 1790, 1800, 1807, 1850-1860, and 1862-1872.
District* of Columbia	1801	1871*	1803, 1807, 1818, 1867, 1878, 1885, 1888, 1894, 1897, 1905-1909, 1912-1913, 1915, 1917, 1919, and 1925.
Idaho	1863	1890	1863, 1865-1874, 1871-1881, 1880, 1890, 1911-1937, 1911-1950, and 1930.
Kentucky	—	1792	1773-1780, 1774-1796, 1780-1909, 1781-1839, 1782-1787, 1782-1875, 1787, 1787-1811, 1787-1875, 1788-1875, 1789-1882, 1792-1830, 1792-1913, 1792-1796, 1793-1836, 1794-1805, 1794-1817, 1795, 1796-1808, 1797-1866, 1800, 1820-1900, 1851-1900, 1859-1860, 1860-1936, 1861-1865, 1862-1866, and 1895- 1896.
Montana	1864	1889	1860, 1856-1993, 1864-1872, 1868-1869, 1868-1929, 1870, 1880, 1870-1957, 1872- 1900, 1879-1880, 1881-1928, 1881-2000, 1891-1929, 1894, 1913, 1906- 1917, 1909- 1910, 1917-1918, 1921, and 1930-1975.
New Hampshire	—	1788	1648, 1709. 1723, 1736, 1740, 1763, 1767, 1775, 1776, 1779, 1789, 1795-1816, 1797, 1802, 1803, 1821, 1826, 1833, 1836, 1838, 1849, 1855 & 1865 MA, 1860, 1862-1866, 1903, and 1902-1921
Ohio	1787	1803	1787-1840, 1787-1871, 1788-1799, 1788-1820, 1790, 1800-1803, 1801-1814, 1801-1824, 1802, 1803-1827, 1804, 1807, 1810, 1812, 1816-1838, 1816-1838, 1825, 1827, 1832-1850, 1833-1994, 1835, 1846-1880, 1851-1900, 1851-1907, and 1907.
Pennsylvania	—	1787	1682-1950, 1759, 1680-1938, 1680s-1900s, 1760s-1790s, 1700s, 1780, 1798, 1740- 1900, 1887-1893, and 1870.
Texas	—	1845	1736-1838, 1700s-1800s, 1756-1830s, 1782-1836, 1809-1836, 1814-1909, 1821-1846, 1826, 1826-1835, 1820s-1846, 1820-1829, 1826-1836, 1829-1836, 1830-1839, 1835, 1835-1846, 1836, 1836-1935, 1837-1859, 1840-1849, 1840, 1846, 1837-1910, 1851-1900, 1858, 1861-1865, 1863, 1865-1866, 1867, 1874, 1882-1895, 1884, 1889-1894, 1890, 1914, 1917-1918, 1896-1948, and 1964-1968.
Vermont	—	1791	1770s-1780s, 1700s-1800s, 1654-1800, 1710-1753, 1721-1800, 1770-1832, 1771, 1782, 1788, 1793, 1796-1959, 1800s-1870, 1807, 1813, 1815, 1816, 1827-1833, 1828, 1832, 1843, 1852-1959, 1855-1860, 1861-1866, 1865, 1869, 1871-1908, 1874, 1880-1881, 1881-1882, 1882-1883, 1883-1884, 1884, 1887-1888, 1888, 1889, and 1895-1924.
Virginia	—	1788	1600s-1700s, 1600s, 1619-1930, 1623-1990, 1623-1800, 1632-1800, 1654-1800, 1704-1705, 1720, 1736-1820, 1740, 1744-1890, 1760, 1769-1800, 1779, 1779-1978, 1779-1860, 1782-1785, 1785, 1787, 1809-1848, 1810, 1815, 1828-1938, 1835, 1835-1941, 1840, 1861, 1861-1865, 1852, 1853-1896, and 1889-1890.
West Virginia	—	1863	1600s-1900s, 1777-1850, 1787, 1782-1907, 1782-1850, 1782-1860, 1782, 1783-1900, 1783-1850, 1785-1850, 1787,1850, 1789-1850, 1792-1850, 1797-1899, 1797-1851, 1799-1850, 1800, 1801-1850, 1810, 1811-1850, 1862-1866, 1863-1900, and 1899-1900.

From *Census Substitutes & State Census Records* by William Dollarhide, publ. Family Roots Publishing Co., Orting WA

Table 2 – State Census States – Alabama to Michigan

The following 38 states have state-sponsored censuses available:

State	Year a Terr.	Year a State	Years for which State Censuses are available (underlined year = an online database is available)	Notes
Alabama	1817	1819	**Colony:** 1706 1721 1764 1785 1786-1803 **AL Territory:** 1801* 1808* 1809* 1810* 1816* 1818 **State:** <u>1820</u>** 1821 1823 1832 1838 1844 <u>1850</u>** <u>1855</u> <u>1866</u>.	* as part of MS Terr. ** separate from federal.
Arizona	1863	1912	**AZ Territory:** 1831 <u>1864</u> <u>1866</u> <u>1867</u>* <u>1869</u>* <u>1874</u>* <u>1876</u>* <u>1882</u>*	*1-2 counties only
Arkansas	1819	1836	**Colony:** 1686-1791 **AR Territory:** <u>1814</u>* <u>1823</u> <u>1827</u> <u>1829</u> 1833 1835 **State:** 1838 1854 1865	* as part of MO Terr.
California	—	1850	**Colony:** <u>1790</u> <u>1790-1796</u> 1822 1834 1836 1837 **State:** <u>1852</u> only	
Colorado	1861	1876	**CO Territory:** 1861 1866* **State:** <u>1885</u>	* 2 counties only
Connecticut	--	1788	**Colony:** 1762 **State:** <u>1917</u>*	* Military census, males over 16
Florida	1822	1845	**Colony:** 1759 1763-1779 1783-1814 **FL Territory:** <u>1825</u> 1838 **State:** 1845** 1855 1864* <u>1867</u> <u>1875</u> <u>1885</u> 1895 <u>1935</u> <u>1945</u>	* Military census ** Statehood census
Georgia	—	1788	<u>1800</u> federal* **State:** Partial lists only: 1827 <u>1838</u> <u>1845</u> 1852 1859 1879 1890 federal** <u>1890</u> (statewide reconstruction).	* Oglethorpe Co only ** Washington Co only
Hawaii	1900	1959	**Kingdom of Hawaii:** 1840-1866 1878 1890 1896	
Illinois	1809	1818	**IL Territory:** <u>1810</u> **State:** <u>1818</u> <u>1820</u>* 1825 <u>1830</u>* 1835 <u>1840</u>* 1845 1855 1865.	* separate from federal
Indiana	1800	1816	**IN Territory:** <u>1807</u>. **State:** A few townships only: 1857 1871 1877 1883 1889 1901 1913 1919 1931	
Iowa	1838	1846	As part of **WI Territory:** <u>1836</u> **IA Territory:** <u>1838</u> **State:** <u>1844</u> <u>1845</u> <u>1847</u> <u>1849</u> <u>1851</u> <u>1852</u> <u>1853</u> <u>1854</u> <u>1856</u> <u>1859</u> <u>1873</u> <u>1875</u> <u>1885</u> <u>1888</u> <u>1893</u> <u>1895</u> <u>1896</u> <u>1897</u> <u>1905</u> <u>1915</u> <u>1925</u>	
Kansas	1854	1861	**KS Territory:** <u>1855</u> <u>1856</u> <u>1857</u> <u>1858</u> <u>1859</u> **State:** <u>1865</u> <u>1875</u> <u>1885</u> <u>1895</u> <u>1905</u> <u>1915</u> <u>1925</u>	
Louisiana	1809	1812	**Orleans District:** 1804 **State:** 1833 1837 1890 federal*	*Ascension Parish only
Maine	—	1820	<u>1837</u> only.	
Maryland	—	1788	<u>1776</u> <u>1778</u> <u>1783</u>*	* Tax list
Massachusetts	—	1788	<u>1855</u> <u>1865</u>	
Michigan	1805	1837	**MI Territory:** <u>1827</u> <u>1834</u> **State:** <u>1837</u> <u>1845</u> <u>1854</u> <u>1864</u> <u>1874</u> <u>1884</u> <u>1894</u>	

From *Census Substitutes & State Census Records* by William Dollarhide, publ. Family Roots Publishing Co., Orting WA

Table 2 – State Census States   •   15

Table 2 – State Census States – Minnesota to Wyoming

Continuation of states with state-sponsored censuses available:

State	Year a Terr.	Year a State	Years for which State Censuses are available (underlined year = an online database is available)	Notes
Minnesota	1849	1858	MN Territory: 1849 1853 1855 1857* State: 1865 1875 1885 1895 1905	* special federal
Mississippi	1798	1817	Colony: 1792** MS Territory: 1801 1805 1809 1810 1813 1815 1816 1817 State: 1818 1820* 1822 1823 1824 1825 1830* 1837 1840* 1841 1845 1850* 1853 1857 1866	˙ separate from federal ** Natchez District only
Missouri	1805	1821	Colony: 1752 1791 1797 MO Territory: 1817 1818 1819 State: 1844* 1845* 1846* 1852* 1856* 1864* 1868* 1876**	* 1-2 counties only ** 28 counties
Nebraska	1854	1867	NE Territory: 1854 1855 1856 1865 State: Lancaster & Cass Co Only: 1874 1875 1876 1877 1878 1881 1882 1883 1884 1885	
Nevada	1861	1864	NV Territory: 1861 1862 1863 State: 1864 1875	
New Jersey	—	1787	1855 1865 1875* 1885 1895 1905 1915	* a few townships only
New Mexico	1850	1912	Colony: 1600 1750 1790 NM Territory: 1885	
New York	—	1788	1825 1835 1845 1855 1865 1875 1892 1905 1915 1925	
North Carolina	—	1789	Pre-statehood: 1784 -1787.	
North Dakota	1861*	1889	Dakota Territory: 1885 State: 1905 (statistics only) 1915 1925	* Dakota Territory
Oklahoma	1890	1907	OK Territory: 1890* State: 1907 federal (Seminole Co. only)	* separate from federal
Oregon	1848	1859	OR Provisional Territory: 1842 1843 1845 1846 OR Territory: 1849 1853 1854 1855 1856 1857 1858 1859 State: 1865* 1875* 1885* 1895* 1905	* indexes for a few counties only
Rhode Island	—	1790	1865 1875 1885 1905 1915 1925 1935	
South Carolina	—	1788	1829 1839 1869 1875	
South Dakota	1861*	1889	Dakota Territory: 1885 State: 1895 1905 1915 1925 1935 1945	* Dakota Territory
Tennessee	1790*	1796	Southwest Territory: 1790 (Reconstructed) State: 1891 (partial)	
Utah	1850	1896	UT Territory: 1856 only.	
Washington	1853	1889	WA Territory: 1851* 1856 1857 1858 1859 1861 1871 1879 1881 1883 1885 1887 State: 1891 1892 1894 1898	* As part of Oregon Territory.
Wisconsin	1836	1848	WI Territory: 1836 1838 1842 1846 1847 State: 1855 1865 1875 1885 1895 1905	
Wyoming	1868	1890	WY Territory: 1869 1885* .	*1 county only

From *Census Substitutes & State Census Records* by William Dollarhide, publ. Family Roots Publishing Co., Orting, WA

Table 3 – State Censuses Taken in Common Years. As a means of comparing state censuses taken by the 8 state census states, this table shows the common years for which many states conducted a state census. Many were done in years ending in "5." Census dates for some states are within a range, e.g., within 3 years of 1825, are indicated in the 1825 column.

	1815	1825	1835	1845	1855	1865	1875	1885	1895	1905	1915	1925	1935	1945
Alabama	•	•	•	•	•	•								
Arizona						•								
Arkansas	•	•	•		•	•								
California					•									
Colorado						•		•						
Connecticut											•			
Florida		•			•		•	•	•			•	•	•
Georgia		•	•	•	•		•							
Hawaii				•		•		•	•					
Illinois		•	•	•	•									
Indiana					•			•	•		•			
Iowa				•	•		•	•	•	•	•	•		
Kansas					•	•	•	•	•	•	•	•		
Louisiana		•												
Maine		•												
Maryland														
Massachusetts					•	•								
Michigan			•	•	•	•	•	•	•					
Minnesota				•	•	•	•	•	•	•				
Mississippi	•	•	•	•	•	•								
Missouri					•	•	•	•						
Nebraska					•	•	•	•						
Nevada						•	•							
New Jersey					•	•	•	•	•	•	•			
New Mexico								•						
New York		•	•	•	•	•	•		•	•	•	•		
No. Carolina														
No. Dakota								•			•	•	•	
Oklahoma										•	•			
Oregon				•	•	•	•	•	•	•				
Rhode Island						•	•	•	•	•	•	•	•	
So. Carolina		•	•			•	•							
So. Dakota									•	•	•	•	•	•
Tennessee										•				
Utah					•									
Washington					•		•	•	•					
Wisconsin			•			•	•	•	•	•				
Wyoming						•								
No. of States:	3	8	12	11	21	20	17	16	16	11	9	7	3	2

From *Census Substitutes & State Census Records* by William Dollarhide, publ. Family Roots Publishing Co., Orting WA

Table 4 - Availability of Federal Censuses for each State • 17

State	Year a Terr	Year a State	Federal Census Years 1790	1800	1810	1820	1830	1840	1850	1860	1870	1880	1890	1900	1910	1920	1930	1940	1950
Alabama	1817	1819				lost	●	●	●	●	●	●	lost	●	●	●	●	●	●
Alaska (to US 1867)	1912	1959	No census taken, District of Alaska, 1870, 1880, or 1890 →								--	--	--	●	●	●	●	●	●
Arizona	1863	1912									●	●	lost	●	●	●	●	●	●
Arkansas	1819	1836				lost	●	●	●	●	●	●	lost	●	●	●	●	●	●
California (to US 1848)	—	1850							●	●	●	●	lost	●	●	●	●	●	●
Colorado	1861	1876										●	lost	●	●	●	●	●	●
Connecticut	—	1788	●	●	●	●	●	●	●	●	●	●	lost	●	●	●	●	●	●
Delaware	—	1787	●	●	●	●	●	●	●	●	●	●	lost	●	●	●	●	●	●
Distr. of Columbia	1801	—		●	●	●	●	●	●	●	●	●	lost	●	●	●	●	●	●
Florida	1822	1845							●	●	●	●	lost	●	●	●	●	●	●
Georgia	—	1788	lost	lost	lost	●	●	●	●	●	●	●	lost	●	●	●	●	●	●
Hawaii (to US 1898)	1900	1959												●	●	●	●	●	●
Idaho	1863	1890									●	●	lost	●	●	●	●	●	●
Illinois	1809	1818			part	●	●	●	●	●	●	●	lost	●	●	●	●	●	●
Indiana	1800	1816		lost	lost	●	●	●	●	●	●	●	lost	●	●	●	●	●	●
Iowa (* part of WI Terr.)	1838	1846						●*	●	●	●	●	lost	●	●	●	●	●	●
Kansas	1854	1861								●	●	●	lost	●	●	●	●	●	●
Kentucky (*Distr. of VA)	—	1791	lost*	lost	●	●	●	●	●	●	●	●	lost	●	●	●	●	●	●
Louisiana (*OrleansTer)	1809	1812			●*	●	●	●	●	●	●	●	lost	●	●	●	●	●	●
Maine (*Distr. of MA)	—	1820	●*	●*	●*	●	●	●	●	●	●	●	lost	●	●	●	●	●	●
Maryland	—	1788	●	●	●	●	●	●	●	●	●	●	lost	●	●	●	●	●	●
Massachusetts	—	1788	●	●	●	●	●	●	●	●	●	●	lost	●	●	●	●	●	●
Michigan	1805	1837			lost	●	●	●	●	●	●	●	lost	●	●	●	●	●	●
Minnesota	1849	1858	MN Terr. had a special federal census in 1857 →						●	●	●	●	lost	●	●	●	●	●	●
Mississippi	1798	1817		lost	lost	●	●	●	●	●	●	●	lost	●	●	●	●	●	●
Missouri	1805	1821			lost	lost	●	●	●	●	●	●	lost	●	●	●	●	●	●
Montana	1864	1889									●	●	lost	●	●	●	●	●	●
Nebraska	1854	1867								●	●	●	lost	●	●	●	●	●	●
Nevada	1861	1864									●	●	lost	●	●	●	●	●	●
New Hampshire	—	1788	●	●	●	●	●	●	●	●	●	●	lost	●	●	●	●	●	●
New Jersey	—	1787	lost	lost	lost	lost	●	●	●	●	●	●	lost	●	●	●	●	●	●
New Mexico	1850	1912							●	●	●	●	lost	●	●	●	●	●	●
New York	—	1788	●	●	●	●	●	●	●	●	●	●	lost	●	●	●	●	●	●
North Carolina	—	1789	●	●	●	●	●	●	●	●	●	●	lost	●	●	●	●	●	●
North Dakota*	1861	1889	*1860, 1870, 1880 as part of Dakota Territory →							●	●	●	lost	●	●	●	●	●	●
Ohio (*NW Terr.)	1787	1803		* lost	lost	●	●	●	●	●	●	●	lost	●	●	●	●	●	●
Oklahoma	1890	1907	1 month prior to statehood in 1907, Oklahoma Territory had a special federal census										lost	●	●	●	●	●	●
Oregon	1848	1859							●	●	●	●	lost	●	●	●	●	●	●
Pennsylvania	—	1787	●	●	●	●	●	●	●	●	●	●	lost	●	●	●	●	●	●
Rhode Island	—	1790	●	●	●	●	●	●	●	●	●	●	lost	●	●	●	●	●	●
South Carolina	—	1788	●	●	●	●	●	●	●	●	●	●	lost	●	●	●	●	●	●
South Dakota*	1861	1889	*1860, 1870, 1880 as part of Dakota Territory →							●	●	●	lost	●	●	●	●	●	●
Tennessee (*SW Terr)	1790	1796	* tally	lost	lost	part	●	●	●	●	●	●	lost	●	●	●	●	●	●
Texas (to US 1845)	—	1845							●	●	●	●	lost	●	●	●	●	●	●
Utah	1850	1896							●	●	●	●	lost	●	●	●	●	●	●
Vermont	—	1791	●	●	●	●	●	●	●	●	●	●	lost	●	●	●	●	●	●
Virginia	—	1788	lost	lost	●	●	●	●	●	●	●	●	lost	●	●	●	●	●	●
Washington	1853	1889									●	●	lost	●	●	●	●	●	●
West Virginia	—	1863	Part of Virginia, 1790-1860								●	●	lost	●	●	●	●	●	●
Wisconsin	1836	1848						●	●	●	●	●	lost	●	●	●	●	●	●
Wyoming	1868	1890									●	●	lost	●	●	●	●	●	●

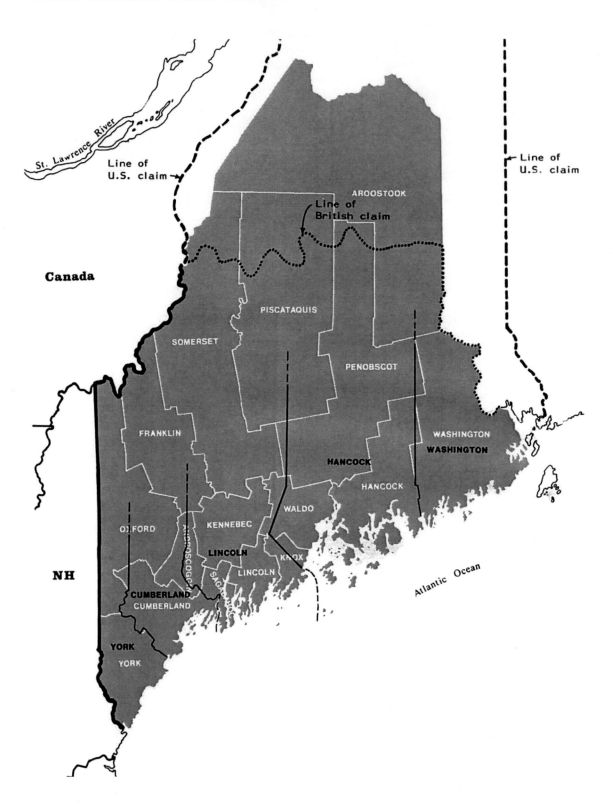

Maine • 1790 (as part of Massachusetts). The five counties within the district of Maine at the time of the August 1790 Federal Census are shown in black. The current sixteen counties of Maine are shown in white. The 1790 county lines, by statute, all extended to the Canadian border, which was in dispute. The U.S. and British lines of claims were settled by treaty in 1842 (to the gray footprint of present Maine). **Map Source:** Page 144, *Map Guide to the U.S. Federal Censuses, 1790-1920*, by William Thorndale and William Dollarhide.

Maine
Censuses & Substitute Name Lists

Historical Timeline of Maine, 1524-1863

1524. Italian Giovanni da Verrazzano sailed up the Atlantic coast in sight of present New York, Connecticut, Rhode Island, Massachusetts, and Maine, and wrote of his travels to his sponsor, King Francis I of France. While he encountered mostly friendly natives at his stops, Maine's natives were less welcoming. They greeted Verrazzano's men from the height of a cliff, refused to approach the shore, and would only trade by lowering items on a rope. When they were finished trading, Verrazzano wrote that they "showed their buttocks and laughed immoderately." For this, Verrazzano named the area, *terra onde la mala gente*, or "the land of the bad people."

1558. Elizabeth I became Queen of England. The first explorations of North America took place during her 45-year reign, the Elizabethan Era, or "Golden Age." When Elizabeth I was crowned, England was nearly bankrupt, but during her reign, the English Empire expanded and thrived, and English culture flourished in Literature, Theatre, Music, and Architecture.

1559. Norumbega. Englishman David Ingram claimed to have traveled the length of the Atlantic seaboard from Florida to Maine, and on his return, told stories that he had visited the wealthy city of Norumbega, somewhere near present Maine, where the streets were "far broader than any street in London... the men were bedecked with gold and silver bracelets, and the women with gold plates and pearls as big as thumbs." Though Ingram may have exaggerated a bit, he did spark an interest in the New England region.

1603 England. James I became King of England, the first monarch to rule both England and Scotland. (He was James VI of Scotland since 1566), He was also the first English monarch to publicly assert that he was blessed with "the divine right of Kings," meaning he was the voice of God on earth, at least in England, Scotland, or Ireland. Although James I was most remembered for commissioning a Bible translation, during his reign, the first permanent English colonies were established in Virginia and New England. James I was in power when England acquired possession of Northern Ireland and was an advocate for the transportation of thousands of clan people living along the Scottish-English border to Ulster Province.

1603. English Captain Martin Pring led an expedition to present Maine, New Hampshire, and Massachusetts. He was the first European to ascend the Piscataqua River. Pring was sponsored by Bristol businessmen looking for potential sites for commercial ventures in North America.

1603. French nobleman Pierre DuGua (Sieur DeMonts) was granted exclusive rights to colonize the area he had named l'Acadie (Acadia), granted by French King Henry IV. The area of Acadia included all of present Nova Scotia, New Brunswick, and most of Maine.

1604. Acadia. DeMonts established a French colony on St. Croix Island, at the mouth of the St. Croix River, now Maine. After surviving a bad Winter, the entire colony was moved across the Bay of Fundy to Port-Royal, now Nova Scotia.

1605. Samuel de Champlain, DeMonts' navigator and cartographer, explored and mapped the Penobscot River and adjoining coastline of present Maine.

Champlain's maps reflected the claims France held in Acadia that extended well into present Maine.

1605. English Captain George Weymouth visited an island he named Saint George, near present Monhegan, Maine. Weymouth was sponsored by Sir Ferdinando Gorges, a wealthy English nobleman who was intent on starting a commercial venture/colony in present Maine.

1606. Two joint stock companies were founded in 1606, both with royal charters issued by King James I for the purpose of establishing colonies in North America. The Virginia Company of London was given a land grant between Latitude 34° (Cape Fear) and Latitude 41° (Long Island Sound). The Virginia Company of Plymouth was founded with a similar charter, between Latitude 38° (Potomac River) and Latitude 45° (St. John River), which included a shared area with the London Company between Latitude 38° and 41°. The first leader of the Plymouth Company was Sir Ferdinando Gorges, who now had official sanction for starting colonies in North America.

1606. English Captain Martin Pring returned to the Maine coast, where he prepared maps detailing the locations of the Saco, Kennebunk, York, and Piscataqua rivers.

1607. In May 1607, the London Company established the first permanent English settlement in North America – the Jamestown Colony. It was followed in August 1607 by the Sagadahoc Colony (also called the Popham Colony), established by the Plymouth Company, near the mouth of the Kennebec River (present Phippsburg, Maine). The Sagadahoc colony was abandoned after just one year, due to a lack of confidence in a change of leadership. Thereafter, the Plymouth Company dissolved until it was revived in 1620 as the Plymouth Council for New England.

1609. The 2nd Virginia Charter of 1609 extended the jurisdiction of the London Company to include the former shared area with the defunct Plymouth Company, and the language of the new charter now included the words, "sea to sea." (James I was assured that the Pacific Ocean was just a bit west of the Appalachian Mountains).

1611. From his base in Port-Royal, Acadia (now Nova Scotia), French Jesuit Priest Pierre Baird, crossed the Bay of Fundy to an island on the Penobscot River of present Maine, where he established an Indian mission.

1613. Father Baird and others attempted a new French mission on Mount Desert Island (present Maine), but soon after their arrival, they were arrested by English Captain Samuel Argall of the Jamestown Colony.

1614-1615. English Captain John Smith, leader of the Jamestown Colony, visited the coast of Connecticut, Massachusetts, and Maine; then wrote his *Description of New England*, which encouraged Englishmen to settle there. Smith was credited as the first to call the area New England. Back in England, Christopher Jones was one seafarer who was known to have read Smith's *Description of New England*, and often remarked that he would like to go there. He got his wish as the master of the *Mayflower* in 1620.

1620. Plymouth Colony. A new Royal Charter was issued by King James I to the Plymouth Council for New England (formerly the Virginia Company of Plymouth) to establish colonial settlements in New England. The area was from Latitude 40° to Latitude 45° ("sea to sea"). In that same year, the *Mayflower* dropped anchor off Cape Cod, and Plymouth Colony was founded by a small group of Separatists/Pilgrims, who had fled England for Holland a few years earlier. Unlike the Puritans, the Pilgrims did not want to purify the Church of England, they just wanted to get away from the church's Prayer Book and have their own method of worship.

1622. Province of Maine. In 1622, the Plymouth Council of New England granted rights of lands to Sir Ferdinando Gorges and Captain John Mason. The lands were between the Merrimack and Kennebec rivers, an area which included parts of present New Hampshire and Maine. Gorges was the first to use the name *Maine* to describe the area.

1623. First Maine Settlements. English Captain Christopher Levett obtained grants of land from the Plymouth Council to establish colonies in New England. Levett's first Casco Bay settlement was the Colony of York, at the site of present Portland, Maine, but the small group of people Levett had left there were gone when he returned a few months later. Later, the 1623 Levett colony at the mouth of the Piscataqua River (now Kittery) was successful, as was a second York colony on the York River. Piscataqua/Kittery and York[2] were the first permanent English settlements in the Province of Maine.

1625. England. Charles I became King of England, Scotland, and Ireland. Charles believed in the same principles his father, James I had espoused, i.e., that as King, he was the infallible interpreter of God's will on earth. Soon after taking office, Charles began to note a large number of non-conformists among his subjects. Along with his Archbishop, William Laud, the King began a campaign to purge his church of the largest group of non-conformists, the so-called Puritans, a militant Calvinist religious sect attempting to purify the Church of England. Unfortunately, Charles I took on a job that led to civil war in England as well as the loss of his head. But, his campaign can be credited as the main cause for the founding of significant English settlements in New England.

1628. The **Massachusetts Bay Company** was granted a royal charter for an English colony to be established in North America within the bounds of the Plymouth Council of New England. It is said that King Charles I was misled as to the religious leanings of the Massachusetts Bay Company leaders, all prominent Puritans, not Pilgrims, as he had surmised.

1629. Sir Ferdinando Gorges and Captain John Mason agreed to split their grants at the Piscataqua River, with Mason retaining the land west of the river as the Province of New Hampshire.

1629. The "Great Migration" to New England began. As a result of the Charles I campaign to purge non-conformists from the Church of England, 1629-1640, large groups of people were disenfranchised. Charles I disbanded Parliament and ruled England alone for eleven years. The Puritans referred to this era as "the eleven years of tyranny." It was during these eleven years that about 80,000 Puritans felt compelled to leave England. About a fourth of them moved to Holland; another fourth of them to Ireland; a fourth to the West Indies, particularly the islands of Barbados, Nevis, and St. Kitts; and the final group, some 21,000 Puritan immigrants, established the Massachusetts Bay Colony of North America.

1630. Massachusetts Bay Colony. The colony government was organized with the first three counties of Norfolk, Suffolk, and Essex. They happened to be the same names as the three East Anglia counties of England from whence the majority of the Puritans had lived before coming to America.

1639. Sir Ferdinando Gorges obtained a renewed patent to the area between the Piscataqua and Kennebec Rivers, in the form of a Royal Charter from Charles I of England. As a result, his ability to attract colonists to the province of Maine was enhanced.

1641. The "Great Migration" to New England ended. It was also the beginning of the Civil War in England, and by 1649, Charles I and William Laud were beheaded; Oliver Cromwell, a Puritan, became Lord Protectorate, ruling England for the next decade. The group of Royalists who supported Charles I were now out of power, the Puritans were in control (and there was no need to send any more Puritans to New England, in fact many of the "purged" Puritans returned to England). Instead of Puritans to New England, another English migration began, this time to Virginia by the opponents of the Puritans—Loyalists of the king who were known as Cavaliers.

1658. Since the 1630s, Massachusetts had expressed a claim to Maine, based on the language of their Royal Charter. The Massachusetts Colony was interested in Maine's natural resources, which were more abundant than their own. After several land grabs beginning in the late 1640s, all of Maine was annexed as a frontier territory by the Massachusetts Bay Colony. Most of the affected communities of Maine had voted in favor of the take-over, the final acquisition taking place in 1658.

1660. England. Charles II was restored to the throne as King of England, Scotland, and Ireland. He had lived in exile after the execution of Charles I. In 1649, the Scots had proclaimed Charles the King of Scotland. But the Puritan leader Oliver Cromwell defeated his army in 1651, and Charles fled to France. After Cromwell died in 1658, the English people became increasingly dissatisfied with the government that Cromwell had established. In 1660, Parliament invited Charles to return and declared him king. He ruled until his death in 1685, and during his reign, the English colonials forced out the remaining pockets of Atlantic settlements made earlier by the Dutch, Swedes, and Danes. Charles II saw the Atlantic colonies as a source of trade and commerce, supported development, and granted several more charters for settlement (including one to William Penn in 1681). All of the English colonies thrived as a result. He was the first monarch to recognize the potential for the North American colonies to become a contiguous, viable commonwealth. He encouraged the development of post roads, and a regular communication between the Governors. Charles II was responsible for setting the tone of self-government, religious tolerance, and individual freedoms in the English colonies that were to become American institutions.

1675. King Philip's War began. It was a bloody battle between the English colonists of New England and a confederation of Indian tribes for control of the New England areas. The war was named for the main leader of the Native Americans, Metacomet, known to the English as "King Philip." The Northern Theatre of King's Philip's War was fought along the New England/Acadia border (the Kennebec River of Maine). The Indians were nearly liquidated, and the conflict ended with the Treaty of Casco in 1678.

1686. Dominion of New England. After Charles II died without issue in 1685, his brother, the Duke of York, was crowned King of England as James II. As the original Royal Charter holder of the New York Colony, James was familiar with the English colonies. In 1686, he established the *Dominion of New England.* This was an administrative union of English colonies, encompassing the areas from the Delaware River to the Penobscot River. The *Dominion* managed to install some religious reforms in the English colonies, allowing Catholics to hold office. After James II had declared his Catholic beliefs, he was deposed in the "Glorious Revolution" of 1689. Soon after, the *Dominion of New England* disappeared, and the English colonies all went back to denying Catholics the right to hold any office.

1689. After James II was deposed, his Protestant daughter, Mary, was declared the legal heir to the throne. She had married her cousin, William of Orange, the Stadtholder/Ruler of Holland, and Europe's most staunch Protestant leader. Because of William's stature, and his role in the "Glorious Revolution" which had overthrown the Catholic James II, Parliament asked both William and Mary to rule England jointly.

1689-1690. King William's War. Soon after they were crowned, William III and Mary II joined a European alliance against France, and the subsequent battles became known as King William's War. In 1689, several battles took place, including the French attack on Saco, Maine; followed by the English attack and destruction of the French Acadia capital of Port-Royal in 1690.

1691. Province of Massachusetts Bay. The province was formed after merging the Plymouth Colony and the Massachusetts Bay Colony. The district of Maine was now part of the Province of Massachusetts Bay.

1696. During King Williams's War, French forces from Pentagouet (present Castine, Maine) attacked and destroyed the English settlement at Pemaquid (present Bristol, Maine). Pemaquid was the northernmost community of New England, lying on the border with French Acadia. The French community of Pentagouet was the southernmost settlement of French Acadia. After the Siege of Pemaquid, the French forces continued north and destroyed virtually every English settlement in Newfoundland and deported over 500 people back to England. In retaliation, the English attacked and destroyed more Acadian communities, including present Fredericton, New Brunswick.

1702. Queen Anne's War. This was a decisive war in the series of conflicts between France and England. Battles took place in New England, Newfoundland, Québec, and Acadia. One notable event was the brutal French/Indian raid on Deerfield, Massachusetts in 1704, where the surviving English colonists were forced to march to Québec as hostages. The English Queen Anne succeeded to the throne after the death of Mary II, her older sister, and William III, who died in 1702 without issue. Queen Anne's reign of 1702-1714 was about the same duration as the war that took her name. The English prevailed in most of the battles, and the war marked a turning point for the success of English interests over the French in North America.

1707. During the reign of Queen Anne, the **United Kingdom of Great Britain** was established after the *Union with Scotland Act* passed the English Parliament in 1706; and the *Union with England Act* passed the Parliament of Scotland in 1707. The English Colonies were now the British Colonies.

1713. The Peace of Utrecht ended Queen Anne's War. France ceded to Great Britain its claims to Newfoundland, Hudson's Bay, and the peninsular part of French Acadia, which the British renamed Nova Scotia. The British took possession of the peninsula area and required the Acadians to swear allegiance to Britain or leave. The continental part of Acadia (including areas of present Maine and New Brunswick) remained in French control and a number of displaced Acadians from the British side moved across the Bay of Fundy to lands near the St. John and St. Croix rivers.

1714. After Queen Anne died without issue, her 2nd cousin, George I was crowned King of Great Britain and Ireland. Although there were several English heirs closer to Queen Anne than George I, he was the closest Protestant heir, a great-grandson of the English King James I. George I was the first of the House of Hanover to rule Great Britain. He left his palace in Hanover infrequently, never learned to speak English, and sanctioned the creation of the first Prime Minister and Cabinet Government in Great Britain.

1718. The arrival of the first Scots-Irish immigrants to New England was via Boston Harbor. The so-called Scots-Irish (or Ulster Scots) were former border clan people who had lived near the Scottish-English border for centuries. A good number of them had moved into areas of Northern Ireland in the early 1600s, and a mass migration to most of the British colonies of America began in about 1717. Generally, the Scots-Irish did not care for civilization that much, and usually leap-frogged over any Atlantic settlements en route to the higher, wilderness areas of America. They did this in New England, New York, Pennsylvania, Virginia, the Carolinas, and Georgia. The first Scots-Irish who came to New England were to immediately head west into central Massachusetts or north into New Hampshire. Soon after the first New England arrivals, a number of Scots-Irish discovered the coastal areas of Maine. Their first settlement in Maine was in 1718 on Casco Bay, near the present city of Portland. Several more Scots-Irish settlements were established, notably the 1736 founding of the Upper Town of St. Georges Plantation (now Warren, Maine) by a group of Scots-Irish from Londonderry, New Hampshire. They had purchased part of the Waldo Patent. In 1759, that same group settled the plantation that became the town of Belfast, Maine.

1727. With the death of George I, his son, George II became King of Great Britain and Ireland. By this time, the Parliament of Great Britain was in control of much of the government, and the King had fewer responsibilities. George II spent more time in Hanover than he did in Great Britain. As the Duke of Brunswick-Lüneburg (Hanover), he had a more active governing role. George II was the last British monarch born outside of Great Britain. During his reign, the largest group of immigrants to America were the Scots-Irish, who overtook the other British immigrants in numbers by about four to one.

1755-1758. Expulsion of the Acadians. At the beginning of the French and Indian War, the British completed their conquest of Acadia, and in 1755, began forcibly removing Acadians from their homes. (The British remembered the forced deportations imposed by the French against the English in Newfoundland back in 1696). The first expulsions were to the lower British colonies, but in 1758 they began transporting Acadians back to France. Those Acadians who avoided deportation made their way to other French-speaking areas, such as present Québec, present New Brunswick, or parts of present Maine. For an historical reference to the era, re-read Longfellow's poem, *Evangeline*, which was based on the events of the Acadian expulsions.

1760. At the age of 22 years, King George III began a reign that would last over 60 years. He was a son of Frederick, Prince of Wales, heir apparent of George II who had died before his father. Although George III was also the Duke of Brunswick-Lüneburg, he never visited Hanover. He was crowned while the Seven Years War was in progress, and after that war the British Empire reached its greatest influence in North America.

1763. The Treaty of Paris of 1763 ended the French and Indian War (it was called the Seven Years War in Canada and Europe). France was the big loser and lost virtually all of its remaining North American claims. The areas east of the Mississippi and all of Acadia/Nova Scotia and Québec were lost to Britain; the areas west of the Mississippi went to Spain. After the Treaty of Paris, George III issued a proclamation renaming the Province of Québec as the Province of Canada. He also issued the *Proclamation Line of 1763*, in which Indian Reserves were established west of the Appalachian Mountain Range, limiting western migrations by all of the British colonies. The proclamation had the intent of forcing any future expansion of the British colonies into Florida recently acquired from Spain, or into Nova Scotia. Instead, the proclamation became one of the Acts of Tyranny perceived by Americans that would lead to the Revolutionary War.

1764. Per terms of the Treaty of Paris, the British were given the right to remove the remaining French Acadians but agreed to provide resettlement assistance. The destinations were not always clear, and the displaced Acadians were sometimes loaded onto ships headed to Boston, New York, Baltimore, Norfolk, Charleston, Savannah, or Mobile. In early 1765, several shiploads of Acadians arrived in New Orleans. For the next several years, thousands of Acadians, including those who had first been deported to the Atlantic colonies or France, were finally drawn together in French-speaking Louisiana (actually Spanish Luisiana), where they received land grants and assistance in starting a new life.

1765. Stamp Act. The 1765 Stamp Act was the hated tax levied against the British colonies that led to active acts of rebellion.

1773. Boston Tea Party. One of the last of these acts of rebellion before actual shots were fired was the Boston Tea Party. The British reaction to the Boston Tea Party was Parliament's series of punitive laws called the *Coercive Acts*, which took away Massachusetts' rights to self-government. In Massachusetts, they were called the *Intolerable Acts*, and fueled even more rebellion.

1774. Québec Act. The British reacted to the increased American rebellions by solidifying British loyalty in the Province of Canada. They enacted the Québec Act, which reversed the long-standing British policy against Catholic governments in all of their colonies. The Québec Act, just a few years after the forced deportations of Catholic Acadians, restored the name Province of Québec and granted Québec residents full British citizenship, allowed Québec to retain their Catholic churches and parish taxing systems, and to keep their established French Laws and Customs. The Act also expanded the physical area of Québec to include a huge area of western lands claimed by the Thirteen Colonies: including much of the Great Lakes and former French lands east of the Mississippi River. The Thirteen Colonies viewed the Québec Act as one of the *Intolerable Acts* that made the impeding war justifiable.

1775. Revolutionary War Begins. The first naval battle of the Revolutionary War occurred off the coast of Maine. During the war, British warships would attack various port cities, and in 1775, Portland, Maine was attacked and burned. Also in 1775, Benedict Arnold marched a band of American revolutionaries through Maine in an attempt to capture British strongholds in Québec City and Montreal. He failed. A year later, turncoat Arnold, now with the British Army, was doing the same thing against the Americans in Connecticut.

1783. U.S.-British Boundary. The Treaty of Paris of 1783 first recognized the United States as an independent nation, with borders from the Atlantic Ocean to the Mississippi River, and from present Maine to Georgia. The U.S.–British boundary for the Maine region was not defined precisely at the Treaty of Paris and the boundary remained in dispute for nearly 60 years. See the Maine 1790 map on page 18 showing the conflicting lines claimed by the U.S. and Britain.

1790. Aug 2nd. The **1790 Federal Census** was taken in the 13 original states, plus the 14th state of Vermont (with a census day of 4 April 1791). The 1790 census divisions were based on the 16 US Circuit Courts, one for each state except Massachusetts and Virginia, both having two US court districts. Massachusetts had a second US Court district with boundaries that matched the present state of Maine (a state in 1820). Virginia had a second US Court district with boundaries that matched the present state of Kentucky (a state in 1792). The 1790 population of the Maine district of Massachusetts was 96,540 people.

1800. Aug 4th. The **1800 Federal Census** was taken in the district of Maine, part of the State of Massachusetts. The population of Maine was 151,719 people.

1810. Aug 6th. The **1810 Federal Census** was taken in the district of Maine, part of the State of Massachusetts. The population of Maine was 228,705 people.

1813-1815. During the War of 1812, British naval forces and troops occupied a large portion of the Maine coast, including Machias, Blue Hill, Castine, and Belfast. American resistance managed to keep the British from advancing further south, but the British remained in their captured territories until the Treaty of Ghent of 1815 ended the war.

1819. Jun. The voters of Maine approved a proposal for the separation of Maine from Massachusetts.

1820. Mar 3rd. The *Missouri Compromise* in Congress allowed Missouri to enter the Union as a slave state and Maine as a free state, thus keeping the balance of slave and free states equal in Congress.

1820. Mar 15th. Maine was admitted to the Union as the 23rd state. Soon after statehood, Maine began issuing land grants in areas near the St. Croix River, in defiance of the British claims to the region. The first state capital of Maine was the city of Portland.

1820. Aug 7th, the **1820 Federal Census** was taken for the new state of Maine, with a population of 298,335 people.

1827. A compromise offer to settle the border issue between New Brunswick and Maine went to an international arbiter in 1827. The offer was accepted by the British, but rejected by the U.S.

1838-1842. Aroostook War. This was a bloodless, but politically intense battle between the State of Maine and the Province of New Brunswick. In 1838, Canadian logging crews began crossing into areas claimed by Maine, where they were met by armed Americans intent on going to war over the intrusion. After the New Brunswick Governor authorized military intervention in 1839, Maine Governor John Fairfield declared war on England over the boundary dispute between the U.S. and Britain. (This was the first and only time a state had declared war on a foreign power). In 1842, The Webster-Ashburton Treaty settled the border dispute as both sides compromised on a new boundary between the two territories. That ended the Aroostook War.

1851. Harriet Beecher Stowe began writing *Uncle Tom's Cabin* in Brunswick, Maine. This novel would later serve as a source of inspiration for abolitionists prior to the Civil War.

1851. The state capital of Maine was moved from Portland to Augusta.

1860. Hannibal Hamlin, a Paris, Maine native, was named Abraham Lincoln's Vice President.

1863. Joshua Chamberlain, a Brunswick, Maine native, successfully defended Little Round Top against confederate troops at the Battle of Gettysburg in the Civil War. Col. Chamberlain commanded the 20th Maine Regiment, and was awarded a Medal of Honor for his heroism. Historians credit Chamberlain's actions as the turning point of that battle. And, Gettysburg turned out to be the turning point of the Civil War. After the war, Chamberlain returned to his home in Brunswick, Maine, and was elected the Governor of Maine in 1866, serving three terms.

Accounts of the First Europeans to Visit Present Maine

Several items in the Historical Timeline for Maine were derived from the following resources:

1602-1658. See *The Beginnings of Colonial Maine* **[Online Database],** complete text from a published book by Henry S. Burrage, D.D., State Historian, printed for the state, 1914, Marks Printing House, Portland, ME. The chapters begin with the early English voyages to the American Coast: Gosnold and Pring, The DeMonts Colony, Waymouth's Voyage of

1605, Hanham and Pring, the Popham Colony, the French Colony at Mount Desert, and the Voyages of Captain John Smith and Others. The history continues to the time of the 1658 Massachusetts takeover of Maine. The original book was digitized at the Maine GenWeb site. See **http://files.usgwarchives.net/ma/mastate/colonialmaine.txt.**

1603-1820. See *The Maine Book* **[Printed Book & Digital Version],** by Henry E. Dunnack, Librarian of the Maine State Library. Publ. Augusta, ME, 1920, 338 pages. A narrative timeline of historical events for Maine begins on page 42. The original book was digitized by the Genealogical Society of Utah, 2009. For access to the digital version, see the online FHL catalog page: **https://familysearch.org/search/catalog/1709230.**

1604. See "DeMont Voyages: 1604, Calais; 1605, Pt. Royal" **[Printed Article],** in *Maine Historical Magazine* (Joseph W Porter, Bangor, ME), Vol. 7, No. 10 (Apr 1892).

1604. See "Champlain Visit (to Maine), 1604" **[Printed Article],** in *Sprague's Journal of Maine History* (John F Sprague, Foxcroft, ME), Vol. 1, No. 2 (Jul 1913).

1605. See "Capt. George Waymouth's Voyage (to Penobscot River)" **[Printed Article],** in *Bangor Historical Magazine / Maine Historical Magazine* (Joseph W Porter, Bangor, ME), Vol. 2, No. 11 (May 1887).

1607. See "Popham Colony of 1607" **[Printed Article],** in *Historical Magazine* (Henry B Dawson, Morrisania, NY), Vol. 10, No. 3 (1866).

1607. See "Settlement of Maine, 1607" **[Printed Article],** in *Historical Magazine* (Henry B Dawson, Morrisania, NY), Vol. 7, No. 1 (Jan 1863).

1607-1608. See "Early Account, Sagadahoc Plantation" **[Printed Article],** in *Winthrop Society Quarterly* (Winthrop Society, Carmel, CA), Vol. 2, No. 4 (2003).

Things to Know About Maine's Censuses & Substitutes

Maine Prior to Statehood. Surviving colonial name lists for the Maine region are from town or local jurisdictions only. Any colonial name lists found in published articles or online databases were included in the bibliography – the earliest was for 1623. The first federal direct tax was levied in 1798 against individual property owners in all states. There are only a handful of name lists that have survived, but one complete set is for Massachusetts/Maine.

State of Maine. The only state census taken in Maine was authorized by the state legislature in January 1837 to determine disbursement of a federal surplus from the sale of public lands. The 1837 name lists were compiled for local Maine jurisdictions, e.g., the original name lists for Bangor, Portland, and most towns, townships, and plantations are at the Maine State Archives in Augusta, except the town of Eliot, York County, at the Maine Historical Society in Portland. None have been microfilmed. A few of the town-wide state census name lists were published in various periodicals, and a project of the Maine GenWeb has indexed most of the 1837 locations with online name lists. The name lists were digitized by FamilySearch International in 2011.

Civil War Tax. During the Civil War Era, the creation of the Internal Revenue Service was for collecting the "Civil War Tax.," as locals called it. Maine's name lists are for 1862-1866. After the Civil War, Congress levied the tax against all of the former Confederate states, where the tax was often referred to as "Abraham Lincoln's Tax.

Maine's Federal Censuses, 1790-1940 are noted in the bibliography, including microfilmed originals and printed indexes. Federal censuses taken for Maine, 1790 through 1810, were separate from Massachusetts because the area of Maine was a district of the Federal Circuit Court system. As the district and state of Maine, federal censuses for 1790-1880 are complete. The 1890 was lost in a fire (like all other states), and the 1900 thru 1940 federal censuses are also complete for Maine. The 1950 will open to the public in 2022.

Federal Censuses Online. All federal census years are identified in the Nationwide Censuses & Substitutes chapter in great detail, with a list of recommended websites for all federal censuses, 1790 through 1940.

Genealogy Resources at the Maine State Archives & Maine State Library

Information from the "Genealogy" webpage at the Maine State Archives website is reproduced below. See **www.maine.gov/sos/arc/research/genealogy.html**.

The Maine State Archives has many record groups containing information which can be of use to those pursuing family history. These records, many of them on microfilm, can be viewed by the public in our Research Room.

The registration of vital records in the State of Maine dates back, in some towns, to the Seventeenth Century. When seeking records for family research in Maine, the important date to remember is 1892. This was the year in which a comprehensive state-wide system of vital records registration was incorporated. Not only were more records kept from that time on, but records began to bear more information, such as parent's names, occupation, and places of birth.

Before 1892, with a few exceptions, vital records registration occurred and remained on the town level, and the information on the records was generally sparse. Marriages and death records, for example, rarely listed parent's names or the party's place of birth. Some towns kept good records, some kept no records, and some kept adequate records, only to have them lost to fire, flood, or storage in private homes.

In the 1920's, the State requested copies of pre-1892 vital records from the towns, to which only about 20 percent responded. The Archives has these town records on the Delayed Vital Records Microfilm.

The Maine State Archives has become one of the centers to which the state's vital records, both originals and copies, have been gathered. See **www.maine.gov/sos/arc/research/geniebrochure2017.doc.** – (a download) gives a list of some of the types of records available for genealogical research."

Online Resources: Maine State Archives Digital Records at **FamilySearch.org.** To access these records: create a free account; click Search, then Catalog; search by Last Names, Titles, Subjects or Keywords.

Family Search's Maine resources include: Military Records, Maine Naturalization Records by County 1800-1990, and Court Records…"

Civil War Records: See the following links:
• **Civil War Sesquicentennial** - stories and primary source records of Maine Civil War soldiers. See www.maine.gov/sos/arc/sesquicent/civilwarwk.html.
• **Civil War Officer Photos** - CDVs currently available to view on MSL/Digital Commons. See http://digitalmaine.com/arc_civilwarportraits.
• **Other Civil War Records** - information available from our website." See www.maine.gov/sos/arc/research/civilwar.html.

Professional Genealogists: "Due to limited resources, Maine State Archives staff cannot undertake genealogical research for patrons. The incomplete, unindexed nature of pre-1892 vital records does not allow us to search them for specific information. A list of local **Professional Genealogists**, not connected with the Maine State Archives, will do more extensive research for a fee."

The Maine State Library has a substantial collection of genealogies; town histories and published vital records for towns in Maine and a large part of New England; plus materials on the Maritime Provinces of Canada; and genealogy handbooks and other helpful tools. For a review of the Genealogy webpage, see www.state.me.us/msl/services/genealogy/index.shtml.

MSL Online Resources:
- Ancestry (in library only)
- Heritage Quest (w/MSL card barcode)
- Genealogy Resources on the Web
- FamilySearch
- Obituary Search (Maine Newspapers)
- Tips for finding genealogy material

MSL Catalog. There is a keyword search box at the Genealogy webpage.
MSL Links to Specific Resources at
- Maine State Archives Research
- Maine Historical Society
- Maine Genealogical Society

MSL Guides to Available Materials
- City Directories (by city)
- Microfilm Availability List
- Town Reports

Maine State Genealogical Researcher Card. Any genealogical researcher who can prove their membership in a genealogical society can apply for a Maine CDC Vital Records Researcher Card. Card holders are allowed access to Maine Vital Records normally closed to the public. There is a $50.00 fee for the researcher card. The application form is accessible at the Genealogy webpage of the Maine State Library's website.

Online Genealogy Research at the Maine Historical Society

The Maine Historical Society in Portland has one of the largest collections of genealogy material in Maine. Collections include published and compiled genealogies, town histories, vital records, census records, city directories, town reports, maps, photographs, manuscripts, journals, and many other resources. For the Online Resources webpage, see www.mainehistory.org/online_resources.shtml#public.

Online Resources – Public MHS Databases. Included are the Book & Manuscript Catalog, Museum Collections Catalog, Maine Memory Network (digital museum), *Maine History* Index, and the Online Maine Genealogy Forum.

Online Maine Genealogy Forum is an electronic bulletin board. Someone asks a question such as "Looking to find marriage records or other information on Joshua Prescott of Williamsburg, ME, born circa 1830." Someone else can read the message (either right away or anytime in the future) and reply with an answer or a suggestion for a resource. Discussion often goes back and forth, with people sharing information, giving tips, trading experiences, and helping each other with Maine–related genealogy issues. To review the Genealogy Discussion Forum, see www.mainehistory.org/cgi-bin/discus/discus.pl.

Online Resources – Members Only Databases. For active members of the Maine Historical Society, the databases include, *Maine History, Publication of the Maine Historical Society*, Naturalization Petitions of U.S. District Court (Portland, Maine), 1912-1929; Portland Voter Registrations 1891-1902; and Town of Deering, Record of Naturalization Papers, 1873-1898.

Bibliography
Maine Censuses & Substitutes

This bibliography identifies the available censuses and substitutes for the province, district, and state of Maine. The region of Maine was an independent colony/province from 1622 until 1658, when it joined the Province of Massachusetts. Through the Revolutionary War and the formation of the United States, Maine was a district of the Commonwealth of Massachusetts until its separation and statehood in 1820. The Massachusetts Archives still has original documents with lists of Maine residents, from the colonial period up to 1820 – they are identified in the bibliography. In addition to Maine's federal censuses, there are many census substitute name lists that fill out the bibliography.

The first citations in the bibliography are some of the most comprehensive genealogical name lists ever compiled anywhere. Fortunately for genealogists, Maine is part of New England, where the study of genealogy is as American as apple pie (or lobsters). Virtually all of Maine's earliest settlers have been bred, wed, and laid to rest in numerous books, articles, microfilm, and digital images.

After the first New England compilations, the name lists may include Local Census Records, Court Records, Directories, Histories, Militia Lists, Tax Lists, Vital Records, or Voter Lists.

1620-2014. See **Maine,** *Tombstone Inscriptions, Surname Index, 1620-2014* **[Online Database],** digital images of index cards located at the Maine State Library, Augusta, ME. Married women are generally indexed twice, once under their maiden name and once under their married surname. See **www.familysearch.org/search/collection/2523434.**

◆ ◆ ◆ ◆ ◆

1623-1660. *Pioneers of Maine and New Hampshire, 1623-1660: A Descriptive List, Drawn From Records of the Colonies, Towns, Churches, Courts and Other Contemporary Sources* **[Printed Book],** by Charles Henry Pope. Includes genealogical notices on 1,000 early settlers of Maine and New Hampshire, a revision and supplement to the Maine/New Hampshire entries in Savage's *Genealogical Dictionary of the First Settlers of New England,* compiled from public and private archives as well as ship passenger lists.

Originally publ. C.H. Pope, Boston, 1908, reprinted 2013, New England Historic Genealogical Society, Boston, 252 pages, FHL book 974 D2po 2013.

1623-1660. *Maine Pioneer Settlements* **[Printed & Digitized Book],** by Herbert Milton Sylvester, publ. W.B. Clarke, Boston, 1909, 5 vols: Vol. 1: Olde Casco, ye romance of Casco Bay; Vol. 2: Old York; Vol. 3: The Sokoki Trail; Vol. 4: Olde Pemaquid; and Vol. 5: The Land of St. Castin, FHL book 974.1 H2sh v.1-5. For an online digital version of this title, see the Ancestry.com website. See **http://search.ancestry.com/search/db.aspx?dbid=21989.**

1623-1692. *A Genealogical Dictionary of the First Settlers of New England: Showing Three Generations of Those Who Came Before May 1692, on the Basis of Farmer's Register* **[Printed Book],** by James Savage, originally publ. Little, Brown and Co., Boston, 1860-1862, 4 vols., 2,541 pages, reprinted (with a cross-index at the end of Vol. 4) by Genealogical Publishing Co, Baltimore, 1969, FHL book 974 D2s. Also on CD-ROM, FHL CD No. 9 pt. 169.

1623-1699. *Genealogical Dictionary of Maine and New Hampshire* **[Printed & Digitized Book],** by Sybil Noyes and Charles T Libby, originally publ. 1928-1929 in five parts, reprinted by Genealogical Publishing Co, Baltimore, 1979, 795 pages. This comprehensive reference work is offered in a combined one-volume form. It contains extensive biographical and genealogical data on every family established in Maine and New Hampshire before 1699. Listed are the births, marriages, and deaths of the settlers through the third generation, and sometimes into the fourth. Also included are data on places of origin, residences, wills and deeds, court cases, and highlights of lives and careers. See FHL book 974 D2. Also on CD-ROM, FHL CD No. 2607. For an online digital version of this title, see the Ancestry.com website. See **http://search.ancestry.com/search/db.aspx?dbid=3166.**

1623-1700. *New England Marriages Prior to 1700* **[Printed & Digitized Book],** by Clarence A Torrey. This work, compiled over a period of thirty years from about 2,000 books and manuscripts, is a comprehensive listing of the 37,000 married couples who lived in New England between 1620 and 1700. Listed are the names of virtually every married couple living in New England before 1700, their marriage date or the birth year of a first child, the maiden names of 70% of the wives, the birth and death years of both partners, mention of earlier or later marriages, book 974 V2t.

- A digitized version of this book is available at the Ancestry.com website. See **http://search.ancestry.com/search/db.aspx?dbid=3824.**

- **NOTE:** There are three *Supplements to Torrey's New England Marriages*, each a separate book, as well as a separate database at the Ancestry.com website.

1623-1775. *Piscataqua Pioneers: Register of Members and Ancestors* **[Microfilm & Digitized Book],** from the original book edited by John Scales. The *Piscataqua Pioneers* organization was a hereditary society for descendants of the first settlers along the New Hampshire/Maine border formed by the Piscataqua River. This name list of members in 1919 is enhanced with genealogical biographies of each of the original pioneers from as early as 1623, a valuable genealogical resource. Book publ. C.F. Whitehouse, Dover, NH, 1919, 212 pages, filmed by the Genealogical Society of Utah, 1973, 1 roll, FHL film #928026. To access the digital images, see the online FHL catalog:
https://familysearch.org/search/catalog/157726.

1623-2000s. *Maine GenWeb (MEGenWeb) Archives* **[Online Databases].** MEGenWeb, of the USGenWeb Project, is hosted by Ancestry's free RootsWeb system. The MEGenWeb offers free genealogical databases on the Internet, and searchable name lists are available for all Maine counties. Typical county records include Bibles, Biographies, Cemeteries, Censuses, Court, Death, Deeds, Directories, Histories, Marriages, Military, Newspapers, Obituaries, Photos, Schools, Tax Lists, Wills, and more. The MEGenWeb Welcome page has links to a webpage for each of these categories: County Selection Options, Books & Diaries; Cemeteries, Court & Probate; Genealogical & Historical Societies; Libraries & State Archives; Mailing Lists; Maps; Military; Newspapers & Periodicals; Query Resources; Religious Societies; Resources; Vital Records; Volunteer!; USGenWeb Project; About ME GenWeb Web Project; About USGenWeb; and Search This Site. Visit the MEGenWeb welcome page. See
www.rootsweb.ancestry.com/~megenweb.

1623-2000s. *Free Search for Maine Items in the Library Catalog of the New England Historic Genealogical Society* [Online Database]. Non-members of NEHGS may search the library catalog

for free. The library holdings relate mostly to New England states, but include surrounding areas, such as New York and Eastern Canada; as well as databases related to the British Isles. A search of the library catalog using the keyword "Maine" returned a list of 3,258 publications, including many original manuscripts, unpublished family histories, and genealogical compilations found in no other library in the world. See **http://library.nehgs.org.**

1623-2000s. *Member Databases (for Maine) at the New England Historic Genealogical Society* **[Online Databases],** indexed at the NEHGS membership website (AmericanAncestors.org). This is one of the most widely used online genealogical resources in the world, with over 400 million names accessible to members of NEHGS. A search of the digital Library & Archives requires a membership log-in. Databases specific to Maine include:

- *Hollis, ME: Tax List of Hollis, Maine - 1862*
- *Maine Deaths Index, 1960-1996*
- *Maine Genealogist, The*
- *Maine Marriages Index, 1892-1966, 1977-1996*
- *Maine Marriages Performed by Rev. Enoch M. Fowler*
- *Maine Soldiers in World War I - (1917-1919)*
- *Maine: Early Wills & Deeds*
- *Marriages and Marriage Intentions in the State of Maine*
- *Massachusetts and Maine 1798 Direct Tax*
- *Norridgewock, ME: Tax List of Norridgewock, Maine - 1803*

For membership information, library catalog search, and member database search, visit the American Ancestors website. See
http://library.nehgs.org/screens/mainmenu.html.

1623-2000s. *Linkpendium – Maine: Family History & Genealogy, Census, Birth, Marriage, Death Vita Records & More* **[Online Databases].** Linkpendium is a genealogical portal site, with links to state, county, town, and local databases. Currently listed are selected sites for Maine statewide resources (617), Androscoggin County (532), Aroostook County (663), Cumberland County (1,348), Franklin County (552), Hancock County (634), Kennebec County (1,060), Knox County (492), Lincoln County (550), Oxford County (779), Penobscot County (981), Piscataquis County (409), Sagadahoc County (501), Somerset County (627), Waldo County (494), Washington County (644), and York County (1,087). See
www.linkpendium.com/genealogy/USA/ME/.

1625-1892. *Gardiner, Maine Biographical Resources from Illustrated History of Kennebec County Maine* **[Online Database],** indexed at the RootsWeb site for Kennebec Co ME:
www.rootsweb.ancestry.com/~megardin/biographies.html.

1636. See **"Inhabitants of Saco Bay, 1636, York County, Maine" [Printed Article],** in *York County Genealogical Society Journal* (YCGS, Eliot, ME), Vol. 1, No. 4 (Oct 1986).

1638. See **"Early Settlers of Wells, York County, Maine, 1638" [Printed Article],** in *York County Genealogical Society Journal* (YCGS, Eliot, ME), Vol. 16, No. 2 (Apr 2001).

1640-1649. See **"Maine Provincial Records Extracts, 1640-1649" [Printed Article],** in *Massachusetts Historical Society Collections* (MHS, Boston, MA), Vol. 1, No. 1 (1792).

1640-1760. *Maine Wills* **[Online Database],** digitized and OCR indexed at the Ancestry.com website. Source: book, same title, orig. publ. 1887, Portland, reprinted by Genealogical Publishing Co., 1996. This database has 962 pages. See
https://search.ancestry.com/search/db.aspx?dbid=48210

1642-1905. See *Deeds, York County, Maine, 1642-1904; Index to Deeds, 1647-1905* **[Microfilm & Digital Capture],** from the original records at the York County Courthouse, Alfred, ME. Includes indexes to early records. Filmed by the Genealogical Society of Utah, 1953, 2003, 237 rolls, beginning with FHL film # 12627 (Index to early records, vol. 1-2, 1647-1768). To access the digital images, and contents of each roll, see the online FHL catalog page:
https://familysearch.org/search/catalog/123968.

1644-1885. See **"Hangings in Maine, 1644-1685" [Printed Article],** in *York County Genealogical Society Journal* (YCGS, Eliot, ME), Vol. 19, No. 1 (Jan 2004).

1646-1770. See **"Court Record Extracts, York County, Maine, 1646-1770" [Printed Article],** in *Maine Historical and Genealogical Recorder* (Recorder Publishing, Portland, ME), Vol. 4, No. 3 (Jul 1887).

1647-1675. See **"Vital Records, York County, Maine, 1647-1675" [Printed Article],** in *Maine Historical and Genealogical Recorder* (Recorder Publishing, Portland, ME), Vol. 4, No. 1 (Jan 1887).

1647-1721. See **"Abstracts of Marriages Taken from Court Records in York County, Maine for the years 1647-1721" [Digitized Article],** from an article in the *York County Genealogical Society Journal* (YCGS, Eliot, ME), Vol. 22, No. 1 (Jan 2007). For access to a digital version of this article, see the FHL catalog:
https://familysearch.org/search/catalog/1843840

1648-1659. See **"Selectmen, York County, Maine, 1648-1659" [Printed Article],** in *Old Eliot* (J.L.M. Willis, Eliot, ME), Vol. 7, No. 1 (Jan 1906).

1649-1650. See **"Early Records, Georgeana, York County, Maine, 1649-1650" [Printed Article],** in *New England Historical and Genealogical Register* (NHGS, Boston, MA), Vol. 35, No. 1 (Jan 1881).

1650-1697. See **"Essex County (MA) Connections Found in Maine Deeds, 1650-1697" [Printed Article],** in *Essex Genealogist* (Lynnfield, MA), Vol. 29, No. 3 (Aug 2009).

1652-1892. See *Marriage Returns of York County, Maine: Prior to 1892* **[Printed Book],** edited by John Eldridge Frost and Joseph Crook Anderson II, publ. Picton Press, Camden, ME, 1993, 566 pages, FHL book 974.195 V2m.

1653-1741. See **"Vital Records, Biddeford-Saco, York County, Maine, 1653-1741" [Printed Article],** in *New England Historical and Genealogical Register* (NEHGS, Boston, MA), Vol. 71, No. 2 (Apr 1917).

1653-1786. *Transcript of the Early Records of Biddeford From 1653-1786* **[Microfilm & Digital Capture],** contains minutes of town meetings, families of Saco and Biddeford as births; deaths 1653-1743, intentions of marriage 1731-1780; lists of jurors; ear marks; boundary lines and land grants. Filmed by the Genealogical Society of Utah, 1956, 1 roll, FHL film #10600. To access the digital images, see
www.familysearch.org/search/catalog/134868.

1657-1710. See **"Court Record Extracts, York County, Maine, 1657-1710" [Printed Article],** in *Maine Historical and Genealogical Recorder* (Recorder Publishing, Portland, ME), Vol. 4, No. 4 (Oct 1887).

1658. See "Inhabitants, 1658, Blue Point/Casco Bay, Cumberland County, Maine" [Printed Article], in *New England Historic and Genealogical Register* (NEHGS, Boston, MA), Vol. 39, No. 3 (Jul 1885).

1661-1900. *The History of Sanford, Maine* [Printed Book], by Edwin Emery and his son, William Morrell Emery, publ. W.M. Emery, Fall River, MA, 1901, 559 pages, FHL book 974.195/S2 H2e.
- See also, *Index of Names in the History of Sanford, Maine, 1661-1900 by Edwin Emery* [Printed Book], by Rachel Bean Perkins, publ. Sanford-Alfred Historical Society, Sanford, ME, 1985, 60 pages, FHL book 974.195/S2 H2e index.

1663. See "Declaration, Inhabitants of Scarborough, Cumberland County, Maine, 1663" [Printed Article], in *New England Historical and Genealogical Register* (NEHGS, Boston, MA), Vol. 5, No. 2 (Apr 1851).

1665-1717. See "Court Record Extracts, York County, Maine, 1665-1717" [Printed Article], in *Maine Historical and Genealogical Recorder* (Recorder Publishing, Portland, ME), Vol. 3, No. 4 (Oct 1886).

1670-1907. *Maine, Vital Records* [Online Database], digitized and indexed at the FamilySearch.org website. Name index and images of birth, marriage and death returns acquired from the State Board of Health, Division of Vital Statistics and the state archives. Records are organized alphabetically, then chronologically within a name. The collection is divided into three parts, Vital Records Prior to 1892, 80 towns, Vital Records, 1892-1907, and Delayed returns for births, deaths, and marriages, 1670-1891. This database has 1,841,454 images, see https://familysearch.org/search/collection/1803978.

1670-1921. *Maine, Marriage Index* [Online Database], indexed at the Ancestry.com website. Source: Ancestry extractions from various county marriage collections. Each record may include: Name, Gender, Marriage Date, Marriage Place, Father, Mother, Spouse, and File Number. This database has 1,173,492 records. See https://search.ancestry.com/search/db.aspx?dbid=61373.

1670s-1875. *Partial Index to Biographical Sketches Found in Wheeler's History of Castine, Penobscot, and Brooksville, Maine* [Online Database], indexed at the RootsWeb site for Hancock Co ME. See www.rootsweb.ancestry.com/~mecpenob/bio.html.

1676. "Inhabitants, 1676, Blackpoint Garrison" {Printed Article], in *New England Historical and Genealogical Register* (NEHGS, Boston, MA), Vol. 43, No. 1 (Jan 1889).

1676-1918. *Maine, Veterans Cemetery Records* [Online Database], indexed at the FamilySearch.org website. Index and images of a card file of veteran cemetery records located at the Maine State Archives. Cards are arranged by war then alphabetical by surname. The index cards may contain dates of birth, death and place of death and burial. The Index covers King Philip's War through World War I. This database has 51,541 records. See https://familysearch.org/search/collection/1985567.

1683-1701. See "Essex County (MA) Connections to York County, Maine, 1683-1701" [Printed Article], in *Essex Genealogist* (Lynnfield, MA), Vol. 30, No. 1 (Feb 2010).

1687. See "1687 Town Rate, Jamestown, now Newton, York County" [Printed Article], in *New England Historical and Genealogical Register* (NEHGS, Boston, MA), Vol. 32, No. 3 (Jul 1878).

1690-1917. *Maine, York County, Probate Estate Files* [Online Database], digitized at the FamilySearch.org website. From the original records at the York County Courthouse, Alfred, ME. This database has 508,689 records. See https://familysearch.org/search/collection/2094226.

1690. See "Petition of Kittery, York County, Maine, 1690" [Printed Article], in *Old Eliot* (J.L.M. Willis, Eliot, ME), Vol. 2, No. 5 (May 1898).

1696-1854. *Maine Court Records* [Online Database], indexed at the Ancestry.com website. Source: Maine State Archives. These records came from the York County Court of Common Pleas (1696-1760); the Kennebec County Supreme Court (1799-1854); and the Washington County District Court (1839-1846). Each record may include a Name, Plaintiff/Defendant, Court, Date, Cause, and Vol./page. This database has 55,254 records. See https://search.ancestry.com/search/db.aspx?dbid=6888.

1704. See "Petition of Kittery, York County, Maine, 1704" [Printed Article], in *Maine Historical* *and Genealogical Reorder* (Recorder Publishing, Portland, ME), Vol. 9, No. 3 (Mar 1898).

1709-1917. See *Maine (Marriages), 1743-1891* **[CD-ROM],** from Broderbund's Family Tree Maker family archives marriage index. From back of case: "Contains information of approximately 230,000 individuals who were married between 1709 and 1917 in select Maine counties. The date range for this title was chosen to reflect the range in which most marriages fall. Some marriages included on this CD occurred before the dates listed, and some occurred after those dates. Information was collected from the following Maine counties and time periods Androscoggin (1789-1898), Cumberland (1709-1901), Franklin (1784-1879), Hancock, (1788-1875), Kennebec (1742-1893), Knox (1835-1888), Lincoln (1756, 1818-1829), Penobscot (1794-1889), Piscataquis (1801-1892), Sagadahoc (1688-1917), Somerset (1822-1863), Waldo (1774-1892), Washington (1772-1891), York (1714-1891). For each listed individual, you can generally obtain the individual's name, his or her spouse's name, the marriage date, and the county where the marriage was recorded." See FHL CD No. 404.

1712-1892. See *Portland, Maine, Records of Births, V. 4-10, 1782-1892; Index to Births, 1712-1891* [Microfilm & Digital Capture], from the originals at the City Clerk's Office, Portland, ME. Filmed by the Genealogical Society of Utah, 1956, 4 rolls, beginning with FHL film #12012 (Index to births, 1712-1910). To access the digital images, see the online FHL catalog page: **https://familysearch.org/search/catalog/302343.**

1713-1922. *Maine, Marriage Records* **[Online Database],** indexed at the Ancestry.com website, from data obtained from the Maine State Archives. Each record may include: Name, Maiden Name, Gender, Age, Birth Date, Birthplace, Marriage Date, Marriage Place, and Spouse. This database has 1,322,469 records. See **http://search.ancestry.com/search/db.aspx?dbid=1961.**

1715-1922. *Maine Birth Records* [Online Database], indexed at the Ancestry.com website. Source: Maine State Archives. Each record includes the Child's Name, Birth Date, Birthplace, Father's Name, and Mother's Name. This database has 2,166,136 records: **https://search.ancestry.com/search/db.aspx?dbid=1960.**

1718-1957. *Maine, State Archives Collections* **[Online Database],** digitized at the FamilySearch.org website. Includes images of collections from the Maine State Archives consisting of court, military, naturalization, land, and other record sets. This collection is being published as images become available. The index at present covers two military collections; the Civil War Soldiers and Sailors Card Index, 1861-1865 and World War I Card Index to Soldiers by Town, 1917-1919. This database has 1,656,347 images. See **https://familysearch.org/search/collection/1877829.**

1720-1910. See *Portland, Maine, Records of Deaths, Vol.. 4-10, 1800-1910; Index to Deaths, Vol. 1-3, 1720-1910* **[Microfilm & Digital Capture],** from the originals at the City Hall, Portland, ME. Filmed by the Genealogical Society of Utah, 1956, 4 rolls, beginning with FHL film #12016 (Index to deaths, Vol. 1-3 1720-1910). To access the digital images, see the online FHL catalog page: **https://familysearch.org/search/catalog/641411.**

1722. See "1722 Census, Garrison at Kittery, York County" **[Printed Article],** in *Old Eliot,* (J.L.M. Willis, Eliot, ME), Vol. 1, No. 9 (1897).

1722. See "Order for Defensible Houses, Kittery, York County" **[Printed Article],** in *Maine Historical and Genealogical Recorder* (S. M. Warren, Portland, ME), Vol. 3, No. 3 (Jul 1886).

1730-1891. *Vital Records, Town of Greene, Androscoggin County, Maine* **[Online Database],** indexed at the TownofGreene.net website. Archived at **https://web.archive.org/web/20190120115508/http://www.townofgreene.net/Vital%20records.html.**

1733-1749. See "Genealogical Records from Court Sessions, 1733-1749, York County, Maine" **[Printed Article],** in *York County Genealogical Society Journal* (YCGS, Eliot, ME), Vol. 3, No. 4 (Oct 1988).

1733-1891. See *Portland, Maine, Records of Intentions of Marriage, 1837-1891; Index of Intentions of Marriage, 1733-1886* **[Microfilm & Digital Capture],** from the originals at the city hall, Portland, ME. Filmed by the Genealogical Society of Utah, 1956, 4 rolls, beginning with FHL film #12020 (Index to intentions of marriage A-Z 1733-1886. To access the digital images, see the online FHL catalog: **https://familysearch.org/search/catalog/249281.**

1734-1907. *Maine, Church Records* **[Online Database]**, digitized and indexed from records compiled by the DAR, Washington, DC. , see www.familysearch.org/search/collection/2787824.

1736-1763. *List of Grantees of Narragansett No. 7 (now Gorham, Maine)* **[Online Database]**, at the RootsWeb site for Cumberland Co ME. See www.rootsweb.ancestry.com/~megotham/grantee.htm.

1737. See **"Quakers in Kittery, York County, Maine, 1737"** **[Printed Article]**, in New England Historical and Genealogical Register (NEHGS, Boston, MA), Vol. 30, No. 1 (Jan 1876).

1739-1900. *Maine, Births and Christenings* **[Online Database]**, indexed at the FamilySearch.org website, a name index to microfilmed birth, baptism, and christening records at the Family History Library, Salt Lake City. This database has 940,649 records. See https://familysearch.org/search/collection/1674856.

1742. See **"1742 Tax List, Lincoln County"** **[Printed Article]**, in *Old Broad Bay Bund und Blatt* (A Newsletter about the German Colony Established at Broad Bay, Maine, 1740-1753, W.W. Whitaker, Murray, UT), Vol. 3, No. 4 (Oct 1994).

1743-1892. *Waldo County, Maine Births: Belfast* **[Online Database]**, indexed at the Ancestry.com website. Compiled by James Flint. Original data: Vital Records of Belfast, ME. Boston, MA, Alfred Johnson of the New England Historic Genealogical Society, Boston, MA. See http://search.ancestry.com/search/db.aspx?dbid=5298.

1743-1892. *Waldo County, Maine Deaths: Belfast* **[Online Database]**, indexed at the Ancestry.com website. Compiled by James Flint. Original data: Vital Records of Belfast, ME. Boston, MA, Alfred Johnson of the New England Historic Genealogical Society, Boston, MA. See http://search.ancestry.com/search/db.aspx?dbid=5283.

1748. See **"1748 Providence & Town Rate (Falmouth), Cumberland County"** **[Printed Article]**, in *Maine Seine / Maine Genealogist* (Maine Genealogical Society, Farmington, ME), Vol. 8, No. 3 (Summer 1986).

1748-1875. *Maine, Compiled Marriages for Belfast, Hallowell and Pittsdon* **[Online Database]**, indexed at the Ancestry.com website. This database is a collection of marriage records from three towns in Maine. Currently, the collection includes Belfast (Waldo County), 1774-1875; Hallowell (Kennebec County), 1748-1875; and Pittsdon (Kennebec County), 1771-1875; with periodic updates to come in the future. Researchers may find names of both the bride and groom, the date of the marriage, and the place of the marriage. This database has 11,046 records. See http://search.ancestry.com/search/db.aspx?dbid=5266.

1755. See **"1755 Tax List, Saco, York County"** **[Printed Article**, in *Bangor Historical Magazine / Maine Historical Magazine* (Joseph W Porter, Bangor, ME), Vol. 2, No. 10 (Apr 1887).

1756-1760. See **"Genealogical Records from Court Sessions, 1756-1760, York County, Maine"** **[Printed Article]**, in *York County Genealogical Society Journal* (YCGS, Eliot, ME), Vol. 5, No. 3 (Jul 1990).

1756-1790. See **"1756, 1758, 1770 Tax Lists, Kittery, York County, Maine"** **[Printed Article]**, in *New England Historical and Genealogical Register* (NEHGS, Boston), Vol. 55, No. 3 (Jul 1901).

1757. See **"Militia Company, Georgetown, Sagadahoc County, Maine, 1757"** **[Printed Article]**, in *Bangor Historical Magazine / Maine Historical Magazine* (Joseph W Porter, Bangor, ME), Vol. 4, No. 7 (Jan 1889).

1759. See **"1759 Tax List, New Marblehead, Cumberland County, Maine"** **[Printed Article]**, in *Maine Historical and Genealogical Recorder* (S. M. Warren, Portland, ME), Vol. 4, No. 4 (Oct 1887).

1759. See **"1759 Tax List, North Yarmouth, Cumberland County"** **[Printed Article]**, in *Old Times – North Yarmouth Maine / Westcustogo Chronicle* (Augustus W Corliss, Yarmouth, ME), Vol. 1, No. 2 (Mar 1877), and Vol. 1, No. 3 (Jul 1877).

1760. See **"1760 Valuation List, Kittery, York County"** **[Printed Article]**, in *York County Genealogical Society Journal*, (YCGS, Eliot, ME),Vol. 15, No. 1 (Jan 2000).

1760. See **"1760 Perfecting or Valuation List, Kittery, York County"** **[Printed Article]**, in *York County Genealogical Society Journal*, (YCGS, Eliot, ME),Vol. 14, No. 4 (Oct 1999).

1760-1808. *Earliest Records of the Settlement of Washington County, Maine* **[Online Database],** a narrative that presents the earliest known records beginning with the 1760-1762 Petitions for Land Grants through a dozen more events, all interspersed with the names of the earliest settlers in each location, ending with the 1808 Deeds Granted in Eastport & Lubec. This great site contains many census and genealogy records for Addison, Beddington, Centerville, Cherryfield, Columbia, Columbia Falls, Harrington, Jonesboro, Jonesport, Machias, Machiasport, Milbridge and Steuben, located at the Downeast Genealogy site. See the archived file: **https://web.archive.org/web/20151002092601/http://home.comcast.net/~downeastgenealogy/History/EarliestRecords.htm.**

1760-1814. See **"Marriages, Births, Deaths, Ear Marks, Strays, Pew Deeds, Voting, Real Estate Records, 1760-1814, Wiscasset, Lincoln County, Maine" [Printed Article],** in *Tri-City Genealogical Society Online Bulletin* (Richland, WA), Vol. 52, No. 1 (Mar 2012).

1760-1892. *Marriage Returns of Cumberland County, Maine: Prior to 1892* **[Printed Book],** edited by Judith Holbrook Kelly and Clayton Rand Adams, published as Maine Genealogical Society Publication, No. 29, Publ. Picton Press, Rockport, ME, 1998, 1,041 pages, FHL book 974.191 V2k.

1760s-1890s. *Vital Records of the Town of Wales (now Androscoggin County), Maine* **[Online Database],** indexed at the USGenWeb archives for Kennebec Co ME. See **http://files.usgwarchives.net/me/kennebec/wales/cem/cemvr.txt.**

1760-1979. *Maine, County Probate Records* **[Online Database],** digitized at the FamilySearch.org website. Includes images from the original records and represents all sixteen counties of Maine, Androscoggin to York. At each county heading, the record types and descriptions vary, and may include accounts, administrations, bonds, wills, dockets, petitions, probate record indexes, or general probate records. This database has 504,141 records. See **https://familysearch.org/search/collection/2040534.**

1761-1912. See *Land Records, Lincoln County, Maine, 1761-1912; Indexes to Land Records, 1761-1901* **[Microfilm & Digital Capture],** from the originals at the Lincoln County Courthouse, Wiscasset, ME. Filmed by the Gen. Soc. of Utah, 1954-1991, 144 rolls, beginning with FHL film #11355 (Index to Vol. 1-7, 1761-1848). To view the digital images, see the online FHL catalog page: **https://familysearch.org/search/catalog/352440.**

1761-1922. *Maine, Death Records* **[Online Database],** indexed at the Ancestry.com website. Source: Maine State Archives. Each record may include: Name, Gender, Age, Birth Date, Birthplace, Death Date, Death Place, Father, Mother, and Spouse. This database has 1,287,277 records. See **https://search.ancestry.com/search/db.aspx?dbid=1962.**

1762. See **"Petition of Inhabitants, 1762, Deer Island, Hancock County, Maine" [Printed Article],** in *Bangor Historical Magazine / Maine Historical Magazine* (Joseph W Porter, Bangor, ME), Vol. 1, No. 11 (May 1886).

1762-1790s. *First Book of Records of the Town of Pepperellborough, Now the City of Saco* **[Microfilm & Digital Capture],** from a book publ. Thurston Print, Portland, ME, 1896, 299 pages. Filmed by the Genealogical Society of Utah, 1956, 1 roll, FHL film #12243. To access a digital version of this book, see the FHL catalog page: **www.familysearch.org/search/catalog/140573.**

1764-1889. *Vital Records, Lewiston, Maine* **[Microfilm & Digital Capture],** from the originals created by the Lewiston Town Clerk, now located at the Androscoggin Historical Society, Auburn, ME. Contains family records giving births and deaths, deaths 1847-1852, marriage records 1847-1854, intentions of marriage 1764-1889. Filmed by the Genealogical Society of Utah, 1960, 1 roll, FHL film #223931. To access the digital images, see the online FHL catalog: **www.familysearch.org/search/catalog/317449.**

1767-1801. *Early Birth Records of Poland, Maine* **[Online Database],** name list extracted from an article published in the *New England Genealogical & Historical Register* (Jan 1934). The town of Poland was in Cumberland Co ME during the period of these records, and is now in Androscoggin Co ME. This database was indexed at the RootsWeb site for Cumberland Co ME. See **http://freepages.genealogy.rootsweb.ancestry.com/~susan/POLANDV.htm.**

1769-1892. *Sanford Town and Vital Records* **[Microfilm & Digital Capture],** from the originals at the Town Hall, Sanford, Maine. Typescript material includes an index. Besides births, marriages, and deaths, the town records contain minutes of various town meetings, ear marks of farm animals, deeds and other land records, boundaries and roads, certificates of members of First Baptist Society, agreements, lists of jurors, treasurer's notices, election results, oaths of office from the town officers, and other miscellaneous information. Filmed by the Genealogical Society of Utah, 1956, 3 rolls, beginning with FHL film #12233 To access the digital images, see the online FHL catalog page: https://familysearch.org/search/catalog/138041.

1770. See **"1770 Tax Assessment, Gorham, Cumberland County"** [Printed Article], in *Sprague's Journal of Maine History* (John F. Sprague, Foxcroft, ME), Vol. 14, No. 1 (Jan 1926).

1770. See **"Petition of Inhabitants, 1770, Kennebec, Maine"** [Printed Article], in *Maine Historical and Genealogical Recorder* (Recorder Publishing, Portland, ME), Vol. 8, No. 3 (Jul 1895).

1771. See **"1771 List of Inhabitants, Pownalboro, Cumberland County"** [Printed Article], in *Maine Seine / Maine Genealogist* (Maine Genealogical Society, Farmington, ME), Vol. 9, No. 4 (Nov 1987).

1771. See **"1771 Polls and Estates of Boothbay, Lincoln County"** [Printed Article], in *Downeast Ancestry* (News-Journal, Machias, ME), Vol. 4, No. 3 (Oct 1980).

1771-1791. *Early Settlers & Incorporation, Town of Readfield, Kennebec County, Maine* [Online Database], indexed at the RootsWeb site for Kennebec Co ME. See www.rootsweb.ancestry.com/~mecreadf/rdfldset.htm.

1771-1794. *York County, Maine, Marriage Returns* [Printed Book & Digital Version), compiled and publ. by George Walter Chamberlain, Malden, MA, 1909, 14 pages, FHL book 974.195 V2y. To access the digital version of this book, see the online FHL catalog page for this title, see https://familysearch.org/search/catalog/559567.

1771-1907. *Maine, Marriages* [Online Database], indexed at the FamilySearch.org website. This is a name index to microfilmed marriage records at the Family History Library, Salt Lake City. This database has 597,621 records. See https://familysearch.org/search/collection/1674915.

1775. See **"Patriotism of Inhabitants, Bagaduce-Castine, 1775, Hancock County, Maine"** [Printed Article], in *Bangor Historical Magazine / Maine Historical Magazine* (Joseph W Porter, Bangor, ME), Vol. 1, No. 10 (Apr 1886).

1775. *The Families of Early Greene, Kennebec County, Maine* [Online Database], a list of the first settlers of the town of Greene at the RootsWeb site for Kennebec Co ME. See www.rootsweb.ancestry.com/~mecgrene/families/families.htm.

1775-1786. *Missing Records of Portland, Maine* [Online Database], extracts from a document recovered from a city clerk's copy of records that had escaped a fire in 1849. The document contained miscellaneous family information. Indexed and abstracted at the USGenWeb site for Cumberland Co ME. See http://files.usgwarchives.net/me/cumberland/sources/a-k.txt.

1775-1818. *Births, Intentions and Marriages of Monmouth, Kennebec County, Maine* [Online Database], indexed at the USGenWeb site for Kennebec Co ME. See http://files.usgwarchives.net/me/kennebec/monmouth/vitals/vr1.txt.

1776. See **"1776 Tax List, Families on Penobscot River"** [Printed Article], name list in *Bangor Historical Magazine / Maine Historical Magazine* (Joseph W Porter, Bangor, ME), Vol. 4, No. 7 (Jan 1889).

1776. See **"1776 Valuation List, Kittery, York County"** [Printed Article], in *Old Eliot* (Quarterly-History & Biography of the Upper Parish of Kittery now Eliot), Vol. 3, No. 8 (Aug 1899).

1776-1780. *Maine, Revolutionary War Land Grants [Online Database],* indexed at the Ancestry.com website. Original data: Maine State Archives. Revolutionary War Land Grants and Pension Applications Index. Augusta, ME. See http://search.ancestry.com/search/db.aspx?dbid=2411

1776-1780. See **"Revolutionary Soldiers Pension Applications, York County, Maine"** [Printed Article], in *New England Historical and Genealogical Register* (Boston, MA), Vol. 65, No. 1 (Jan 1911) thru Vol. 65, No. 3 (Jul 1911).

1776-1780. See **"Revolutionary War Pensioners, Maine" [Printed Article]**, in *Sprague's Journal of Maine History* (John F Sprague, Foxcroft, ME), Vol. 5, No. 4 (Dec 1917) thru Vol. 8, No. 5 (Nov 1920).

1776-1780. *An Alphabetical Index of Revolutionary Pensioners Living in Maine* **[Printed Book]**, by Charles Alcott Flagg, provides information in tabular form on some 5,000 Maine Revolutionary pensioners. Arranged alphabetically, the pensioners are identified by name, rank, service, age, county of residence, remarks such as date of death or town of residence, and source of the information. Originally published 1929; reprinted 2005, Genealogical Publishing Co, Baltimore, 91 pages, FHL book 974.1 M22f.

1777. See **"Male Inhabitants, 1777, Blue Hill, Hancock County" [Printed Article]**, in Bangor *Historical Magazine / Maine Historical Magazine* (Joseph W Porter, Bangor, ME), Vol. 4, No. 9-10 (Apr 1889).

1777. See **"Male Inhabitants, 1777, Plantation of Gardinerston, Lincoln County, Maine" [Printed Article]**, in *Maine Genealogist* (Maine Genealogical Society),Vol. 13, No. 3 (Aug 1991).

1777-1866. *Marriage Returns of Lincoln, County, Maine to 1866* **[Printed Book]**, publ. as Maine Genealogical Society Special Publications No. 39. Compiled and edited by Judith Holbrook Kelley and Clayton Rand Adams. Contains marriage records for: 1777-1810, 1828-1847, 1848-1866, and 1804-1837. Includes every name index. Publ. Picton Press, Rockport, ME, 2002, 538 pages, FHL book 974.157 V2k.

1778. See **"1778 Pleasant River Inhabitants, Town of Addison, Washington County, Maine" [Printed Article]**, in Bangor *Historical Magazine / Maine Historical Magazine* (Joseph W Porter, Bangor, ME), Vol. 10 (April 1886).

1779. See **"Petition of Inhabitants, 1779, Lincoln County, Maine" [Printed Article]**, in *Maine Historical and Genealogical Register* (Recorder Publishing, Portland, ME), Vol. 3, No. 3 (Jul 1886).

1779-1780. See **"Artificers and Inhabitants Who Built Fort George, Penobscot County, Maine" [Printed Article]**, in *Old Broad Bay Family History Association Newsletter* (Waldoboro, ME), Vol. 1, No. 3 (Summer 2004). See the same title in *Maine Genealogist* (Maine Genealogical Society, Farmington, ME), Vol. 26, No. 2 (May 2004).

1779-1782. See **"1779-1782 Tax Lists, Shapleigh, York County" [Printed Article]**, in *York County Genealogical Society Journal* (YCGS, Ogunquit, ME), Vol. 7, No. 2 (Apr 1992).

1779-1892. *Illustrated History of Kennebec County, Maine* **[Printed Book]**, edited by Henry D Kingsbury and Simeon L Deyo, publ. H.W. Blake, New York, 1892, 2 vols., 1,273 pages, 139 plates, FHL book 974.16 H2k v. 1-2. Also on microfilm, 2 rolls, FHL film #599182 (vol. 1) and FHL film #599183 (Vol. 2). For access to a digital version of this book, see the online FHL catalog page:
https://familysearch.org/search/catalog/177625.
- See also *Index to Kingsbury and Deyo's Illustrated History of Kennebec County, Maine* **[Printed Book]**, compiled by Cynthia and Robert McCausland, publ. Picton Press, 1996, 265 pages, FHL book 974.16 H2k v. 1-2 index.

1779-1895. *Biddeford, Maine Vital Records* **[Microfilm & Digital Capture]**, from the originals at Biddeford, ME. Includes marriage records 1779-1818, 1836-1844; births; deaths 1805-1843; intentions of marriage 1815-1844; births 1855-1890; depositions of births; marriage records 1854-1895; and deaths 1855-1895. Filmed by the Genealogical Society of Utah, 1956, 2 rolls, FHL film #10601-10602. To access the digital images, see the online FHL catalog page:
www.familysearch.org/search/catalog/134877.

1779-1915. *Maine, Kennebec County Probate Estate Files* **[Online Database]**, digitized at the FamilySearch.org website. From the original records at the Kennebec County Courthouse, Augusta, ME. This database has 271,532 records. See
https://familysearch.org/search/collection/1386085.

1780-1781. See **"1780-1781 Taxpayers, Winslow, Clinton, Kennebec County" [Printed Article]**, in *Bangor Historical Magazine / Maine Historical Magazine*, Joseph W Porter, Bangor, ME), Vol. 7, No. 1-3 (Jul 1891).

1780-1811 Valuations (Tax Lists) **[Microfilm & Digital Capture]**, from the originals for the Maine District of Massachusetts, located at the State House, Boston, MA. Filmed by the Genealogical Society of Utah, 1974, 8 rolls, as follows:
- Tax lists for 1780 Cape Elizabeth; 1783 Scarborough; 1784 Arundel, York & Plantation of Wales, FHL film #959904

- Tax lists for 1784, Plantation of Walpole; 1791 Ballstown, York. FHL film #959905
- Tax lists for 1792 Ballstown & Woolwich. FHL film #959907
- Tax lists for 1800 Augusta – Woolwich, FHL film #959906.
- Tax lists for 1801 Anson – Lewiston, FHL film #959909
- Tax lists for 1801 Medumcook – Woolwich, FHL film #959908
- Tax lists for 1811 Bangor – Windham, etc., FHL film #959910
- Tax lists for Bangor – Wiscasset, and summaries of miscellaneous towns, FHL film #9599911

To access the digital images, see the online FHL catalog page: www.familysearch.org/search/catalog/293490.

1780-1980. *Maine, Nathan Hale Cemetery Collection* **[Online Database],** digitized and indexed at the FamilySearch.org website. This is a digitized version of the Nathan Hale cemetery card file at the Maine State Library. This database has 356,698 records. See https://familysearch.org/search/collection/2241461.

1780-1990. *Maine, Faylene Hutton Cemetery Collection* **[Online Database],** indexed at the FamilySearch.org website. Source: Maine State Library, Augusta. Includes transcripts of tombstones from various Maine cemeteries. There are some additional family members listed on some cards whose names are not indexed. This database has 297,412 records. See www.familysearch.org/search/collection/2242151.

1780-1999. *Maine, J. Gary Nichols Cemetery Collection* **[Online Database],** indexed at the FamilySearch.org website. Source: Maine State Library, Augusta. Includes transcripts of tombstones from various Maine cemeteries. This database has 181,059 records. See www.familysearch.org/search/collection/2242146.

1781. See "**1781 Partial Census, Lincoln County, Maine**" **[Printed Article]**, in *Downeast Ancestry* (Biddeford, ME), Vol. 7, No. 4 (Dec 1983).

1781. See "**1781 Settlers at Pittston, Kennebec County, Maine**" **[Printed Article]**, in *Maine Historical and Genealogical Recorder* (Recorder Publishing, Portland, ME), Vol. 7, No. 3 (Jul 1893).

1782. See "**1782 Penobscot Journal (List of Inhabitants)**" **[Printed Article]**, in *Downeast Ancestry* (Biddeford, ME), Vol. 7, No. 4 (Dec 1983).

1783. See "**Penobscot Inhabitants Certified Loyal, 1783, Hancock County, Maine**" **[Printed Article]**, in *Downeast Ancestry* (Biddeford, ME), Vol. 6, No. 1 (Jun 1982), and Vol. 7, No. 4 (Dec 1983).

1784. See "**Petition of Inhabitants, 1784, Union River (Hancock County, Maine)**" **[Printed Article]**, in *Bangor Historical Magazine / Maine Historical Magazine* (Joseph W Porter, Bangor, ME), Vol. 4, No. 12 (Jul 1889).

1784 List of Penobscot Settlers **[Online Database],** extracted at the RootsWeb site for Hancock Co ME: www.rootsweb.ancestry.com/~mecpenob/settlers.html.

1784-1831. *Marriages in Hollis, Lyman, Kennebunkport and Adjoining Towns of York County, Maine* **[Microfilm & Digital Capture],** from an original manuscript compiled by Rev. Simon Locke, copied by Miss Emma Gould, at the Maine Historical Society, Portland, 2 vols. Title on Vol. 2: "A copy of the marriage records of the Rev. Simon Lock[e] of Lyman, Me. between 1784-1831 in Lyman, Hollis, Biddeford and other York Co. towns."
Another title: "Marriages solemnized in Lyman, Me. and neighboring towns of York Co., between 1784 and 1831 by the Rev. Simon Lock, the second Baptist minister in Maine/copied by Emma Gould from the original records, now in the possession of John Locke of Saco, Me." Filmed by the Genealogical Society of Utah, 1956, 1 roll, FHL film #12834. To access the digital images, see the online FHL catalog page: www.familysearch.org/search/catalog/142055.

1784-1840. *Massachusetts, Marriage Index* **[Online Database],** indexed at the Ancestry.com website. This database contains marriage notices from *The Massachusetts Centinal*, beginning in 1784. In 1790 its name changed to the *Columbian Centinel* and publication ceased in 1840. The marriages are arranged in alphabetical order, under the name of both husband and wife, and comprise over 34,000 names. Because it was an area newspaper, researchers can find marriage notices for persons living in the surrounding states of Rhode Island, Connecticut, New Hampshire, and Maine. See http://search.ancestry.com/search/db.aspx?dbid=3393.

1785. See "Sedgwick, Hancock County, Settlers" [Printed Article], in *Bangor Historical Magazine / Maine Historical Magazine* (Joseph W Porter, Bangor, ME), Vol. 9, No. 7-9 (Jul 1894).

1785. See "Petition, 1785, Bagaduce Inhabitants, Penobscot County, Maine" [Printed Article], in *Bangor Historical magazine / Maine Historical Magazine* (Joseph W Porter, Bangor, ME), Vol. 3, No. 4 (Oct 1887).

1785-1835. *Index to Portland Newspapers* [Printed index], by William B. Jordan, Jr., publ. Heritage Books, Bowie, MD, 1994, 398 pages, FHL book 974.1191/Ps B32j.

1785-1950. *Maine, Washington County Courthouse Records* [Online Database], digitized at the FamilySearch.org website. Records from the Washington County Courthouse including revolutionary war, probate and census records. Indexes to these records are included. This database has 99,893 records. See https://familysearch.org/search/collection/1930294.

1785-1903. See *Deeds, Washington County, Maine, 1785-1903; Index 1785-1895* [Microfilm & Digital Capture], from the originals at the Washington County Courthouse, Machias, ME (1956). Filmed by the Genealogical Society of Utah, 1956, 110 rolls, beginning with FHL film #12462 (Index 1785-1840). To access the digital images, see the online FHL catalog page: https://familysearch.org/search/catalog/122803.

1785-1950. *Maine Newspaper Archives* [Online Database], digitized and indexed newspapers at the GenealogyBank website for the following cities: Augusta, Bangor, Bath, Belfast, Biddeford, Brunswick, Bucksport, Castine, Dover-Foxcroft, Eastport, Falmouth, Farmington, Fryeburg, Gardiner, Hallowell, Kennebunk, Lewiston, Limerick, Norridgewock, North Yarmouth, Paris, Portland, Richmond, Saco, Sanford, Skowhegan, Waterville, Winthrop, and Wiscasset. See www.genealogybank.com/gbnk/newspapers/explore/USA/Maine/.

1786. See "Penobscot Region Tax List, Hancock County, Maine" [Printed Article] in *Downeast Ancestry* (Biddeford, ME), Vol. 7, No. 4 (Dec 1983).

1786-1760. County *Court Records, York County, Maine* [Online Database], files arranged alphabetically by surname. See the parent directory for each database (A to Y) at the USGenWeb site for York Co ME. See http://files.usgwarchives.net/me/york/court/index/.

1786-1814. *Vital Records of Portland, Maine: Births, Marriages and Deaths* [Printed Book], compiled by Angela M Foster, publ. Picton Press, Rockport, ME, 2005, 260 pages, FHL book 974.191/P1 V2f.

1786-1843. See "Births & Deaths, Alfred, York County, Maine, 1786-1843" [Printed Article], in Maine Historical and Genealogical Recorder (Recorder Publishing, Portland, ME), Vol. 8, No. 3 (Jul 1896).

1786-1852. *Early Grants and First Settlers, Town of Norway, Oxford County, Maine* [Online Database], from Noyes' *History of Norway*, published in 1852. For the online extracted text, see http://files.usgwarchives.net/me/oxford/norway/history/early/file1.txt.

1786-1882. *City of Portland Records* [Microfilm & Digital Capture], from the originals at the City Clerk's Office, Portland, ME. Each volume is individually indexed by subject. These records contain proceedings of meetings, elections, roads and streets, school matters, weights, money matters, militia, invoices, cemeteries, land and property, hospital, taxes, jurors, licenses, cases of insanity, and other miscellaneous matters. Filmed by the Genealogical Society of Utah, 1956, 11 rolls, beginning with FHL film #12028 (City Records, Vol. 1-2, 1786-1827). To access the digital images, see the online FHL catalog page: https://familysearch.org/search/catalog/303112.

1786-1954. *Auburn, Maine, General Index to Vital Records: Births* [Microfilm & Digital Capture], from the originals at the City Clerk's Office, Auburn, ME. Includes certificates of births registered outside the Town of Auburn of children whose parents resided in Auburn. Filmed by the Genealogical Society of Utah, 1955, 5 rolls, beginning with FHL film #10409 (Births: A-Crocket). To access the digital images, see the online FHL catalog page: https://familysearch.org/search/catalog/279765.

1787-1922. *New England, Select United Methodist Church Records* [Online Database], indexed at the Ancestry.com website. This database has 374,894 records. See https://search.ancestry.com/search/db.aspx?dbid=9134.

1787-1952. *Maine, Federal Naturalization Records* **[Online Database],** indexed at the Ancestry.com website. National Archives microfilm. Each record may include: Name, Gender, Record Type, Birth Date, Birthplace, Arrival Date, Arrival Place, Spouse, and Petition Number. This database has 139,387 records: https://search.ancestry.com/search/db.aspx?dbid=2899.

1788. See "St. Georges Island Inhabitants, 1788, Knox County, ME" [Printed Article], in *Bangor Historical Magazine / Maine Historical Magazine* (Joseph W Porter, Bangor, ME), Vol. 2, No. 3 (Sep 1886).

1789-1819. *Deaths, Town of Norway, Oxford County, Maine* **[Online Database],** indexed at the USGenWeb site for Oxford Co ME. See http://files.usgwarchives.net/me/oxford/norway/deaths/file1.txt.

1789-1850. See *Hancock Records, Waldo Lands, 1791-1850; Index, 1789-1827* **[Microfilm & Digital Capture],** from the originals located at the Waldo County Courthouse, Belfast, ME (1954). Contains copies of deeds for the areas of Waldo County originally part of Hancock County, Maine. (Waldo was created in 1827, taken from Hancock). Filmed by the Genealogical Society of Utah, 1954, 13 rolls, beginning with FHL film #12329 (Grantor Index, 1789-1827. To access the digital images, see the online FHL catalog page: https://familysearch.org/search/catalog/73592.

1789-1892. See *Marriage Records of Hancock County, Maine, Prior to 1892* **[Printed Book],** edited by Alice MacDonald Long, publ. as Maine Genealogical Society Special Publication No. 9, Picton Press, Camden, ME, 1992, 570 pages, FHL book 974.145 V2m.

1789-1892. See *Marriage Returns of Washington County, Maine: Prior to 1892* **[Printed Book],** edited by Alice MacDonald Long, publ. as Maine Genealogical Society Special Publications No. 15, Picton Press, Camden, ME, 1993, 118 pages, FHL book 974.142 V2m.

1790. See **"Prescots and Whitchers Plantation, Maine" [Printed Article],** in *New Hampshire/Maine Connection* (Paula Kane, Editor, Litchfield, NH), Vol. 2, No. 4 (Summer 1999).

1790. See **"1790 Valuation, Blue Hill, Hancock County" [Printed Article],** in *Bangor Historical Magazine / Maine Historical Magazine*, Joseph W Porter, Bangor, ME), Vol. 9, No. 4-6 (Apr 1894).

1790. *Heads of Families at the First Census of the United States Taken in the Year 1790, Maine* **[Printed Book & Digital Capture],** originally published by the Bureau of the Census, 1908. Includes a full name index. Reprinted by various publishers, including Accelerated Indexing Systems, Bountiful, UT, 1978, 105 pages, FHL book 974..1X2b. To access the digital images, see the online FHL catalog: www.familysearch.org/search/catalog/287260.
- Refer to the ME 1790 map on page 18,

1790-1840. *Maine, 1790 thru 1840 Federal Census: Population Schedules* **[Microfilm & Digital Capture],** from the originals at the National Archives, Washington, DC. The 1790, 1800, 1810, 1820, 1830, and 1840 censuses were filmed by the National Archives in one series, 1938-1969, 29 rolls, beginning with FHL film #568142 (Maine 1790). To access the digital images, see the online FHL catalog page: https://familysearch.org/search/catalog/745492.

1790-1933. See *Old Hancock County Families: Containing Genealogies of Families Resident in Hancock County in 1933, Whose Ancestors of Their Surnames Settled in the Town in Which They Live in or Before 1790* **[Printed & Digitized Book],** by William Macbeth Pierce, publ. Hancock Co Publishing Co, 1933, 133 pages, FHL book 974.145 D2p. For access to a digital version of this book, see the online FHL catalog page for this title. See https://familysearch.org/search/catalog/214444.

1790-2000. *Hancock County Probate Index* **[Online Database],** originally indexed at the Registry of Probate website. See the archived database: https://web.archive.org/web/20160907163234/http://www.registryofprobate.com/ProbateIndex1.html.

1791-1864. See *Deeds, Hancock County, Maine, 1791-1861; Index 1791-1864* **[Microfilm & Digital Capture],** from the originals at the Hancock County Courthouse, Ellsworth, ME (1955). Filmed by the Genealogical Society of Utah, 1955, 60 rolls, beginning with FHL film #10944 (Index to Grantors and Grantees 1791-1824). To access the digital images, see the online FHL catalog page: https://familysearch.org/search/catalog/334690.

1791-1906. *New England Petitions for Naturalization Index* **[Online Database],** indexed at the FamilySerch.org website. This is an index to photocopies of naturalization documents filed in courts in Connecticut, Maine, Massachusetts, New Hampshire, Rhode Island, and Vermont from 1791 to 1906. The photocopies and the index are in the National Archives-New England Region. The index consists of 3x5 inch cards arranged by state and thereunder by name of petitioner, arranged according to the Soundex system. The index refers to the name and location of the court that granted the certificate of naturalization, and to the volume and page/certificate number. This database has 26,959 records. See https://familysearch.org/search/collection/1840474.

1793-1849. *Births, Town of New Sharon, Franklin County, Maine* **[Online Database],** indexed at the RootsWeb site for Franklin Co ME. See www.rootsweb.ancestry.com/~mefrankl/nsbirths.htm.

1794. See **"Census, Bridgton, Farnsworth (Dr.), 1794, Cumberland County, Maine"** **[Printed Article],** in *Connections* (Bridgton Historical Society, Bridgton, ME), (Apr 2000).

1794. See **"1794 Tax List, Rustfield (Norway), Oxford County [Printed Article]**, in *Maine Historical and Genealogical Recorder* (S. M. Warren, Portland, ME), Vol. 9, No. 11 (Nov 1898).

"1794 Parish Tax List, Wells, York County" **[Printed Article],** in *Sprague's Journal of Maine History*, Vol. 5, No. 1 (Jul 1917).

1794-1834. *Early Settlers of Barnard, Piscataquis County, Maine* **[Online Database],** at the USGenWeb site for Piscataquis Co ME. See http://files.usgwarchives.net/me/piscataquis/barnard/settlers/sj3p220.txt.

1796-1891. *Augusta, Maine Vital Records* **[Microfilm & Digital Capture],** from the original records at Augusta, ME. Includes Index of marriages Vol.1-3, 1796-1891; Intentions & marriages Vol.1-3, 1796-1891; Deaths 1814-1891; Births and some deaths prior to 1890; and Deaths of soldiers 1863-1864. Filmed by the Genealogical Society of Utah, 1953, 2 rolls, FHL film #10402-10403. To access the digital images, see the online FHL catalog page: www.familysearch.org/search/catalog/294241.

1797. See **"Tax List, Eden, Hancock County, Maine"** **[Printed Article],** in *Bangor Historical Magazine / Maine Historical Magazine* (Joseph W Porter, Bangor, ME),Vol. 5, No. 7-9 (Jan 1890).

1797-1913. *Vital Records, Town of Guilford, Piscataquis County, Maine* **[Online Database],** indexes to births and marriages at the USGenWeb site for Piscataquis Co ME. See http://files.usgwarchives.net/me/piscataquis/guilford/vitals/.

1798. *Massachusetts and Maine Direct Tax of 1798* **[Microfilm]** from the original records at the New England Historic Genealogical Society, Boston, MA. Indexes are included with first 3 volumes. Filmed by the NEHGS with a published index and guide, 18 rolls, beginning with FHL film #940072 (Hancock, Washington, Lincoln, Cumberland, and York counties, Maine). For a complete list of roll numbers and contents of each roll, see the online FHL catalog page for this title. See https://familysearch.org/search/catalog/46827.

1798. *An Index and Guide to the Microfilm Edition of the Massachusetts and Maine Direct Tax Census of 1798* **[Printed Book],** by Michael H. Gorn, published by the New England Historic Genealogical Society, Boston, 1979, 98 pages. FHL book 974.R42i.

1798. See **"1798 Owners of Taxable Land, Poland, Androscoggin County"** **[Printed Article],** in *Maine Historical and Genealogical Recorder* (Recorder Publishing, Portland, ME), Vol. 1, No. 3 (Jul 1884).

1798. See **"1798 Taxpayers, Bristol, Lincoln County, Maine"** **[Printed Article],** in *Genealogical Advertiser* (Lucy Hall Greenlaw, Cambridge, MA), Vol. 3, No. 3 (Sep 1900) and Vol. 3, No. 4 (Dec 1900).

1798. See **"1798 Taxpayers, Medumcook (Friendship), Knox County, Maine"** **[Printed Article],** in *Genealogical Advertiser* (Lucy Hall Greenlaw, Cambridge, MA), Vol. 4, No. 5 (1901).

1798. See **"1798 Taxpayers, Waldoborough, Lincoln County, Maine"** **[Printed Article],** in *Genealogical Advertiser* (Lucy Hall Greenlaw, Cambridge, MA), Vol. 3, No. 4 (Dec 1900), thru Vol. 4, No. 5 (1901).

1798. See "**1798 List of Freeholders, Northerly Eliot, York County, Maine**" **[Printed Article]**, in *Old Eliot* (J.L.M. Willis, Eliot, ME), Vol. 6, No. 4 (Dec 1903).

1798-1806. *Index to Death Notices, Jenks's Portland Gazette* **[Printed Book]**, compiled by David Colby Young, publ. Danville, ME, 1983. From intro: "Includes over 1,400 death and obituary notices of York and Cumberland counties in the district of Maine." See FHL book 974.19 V42y.

1798-1819. *Early Settlers of Weld (Franklin County, Maine)* **[Online Database]**, narrative at the RootsWeb site for Franklin Co ME. See www.rootsweb.ancestry.com/~mecweld/EarlySettlersof Weld.htm.
- See also *First Families of Weld,* see www.rootsweb.ancestry.com/~mefrankl/WELDONE.htm.

1798-1891. *Maine, Divorce Records* **[Online Database]**, indexed at the Ancestry.com website. The details in this index were extracted by the Maine State Archives from divorce proceedings heard by County Supreme Judicial Courts in Maine. Details included are plaintiff's name, defendant's name, term/date, docket number, county, court, and volume & page number. This index does not include records for Lincoln County or cases heard in District Courts or Courts of Common Pleas. See http://search.ancestry.com/search/db.aspx?dbid=1656.

1799. See "**1799 Families, Clinton, Formerly Hancocktown, Kennebec County, Maine**" **[Printed Article]**, in *New England Historical and Genealogical Register* (NEHGS, Boston, MA), Vol. 111, No. 1 (Jan 1957), and Vol. 111, No. 2 (Apr 1957).

1799. See "**Tax List, 1799, Gorham, Cumberland County, Maine**" **[Printed Article]**, in *Maine Historical and Genealogical Recorder* (Recorder Publishing, Portland, ME), Vol. 1, No. 4 (Oct 1884).

1799. See "**Piscataqua Harbour Inhabitants Object to Road Tax Labor, 1799, York County, Maine**" **[Printed Article]**, in *York County Genealogical Society Journal* (YCGS, Eliot, ME), Vol. 21, No. 1 (Jan 2006).

1799-1835. *Deed Books, Oxford County, Maine* **[Microfilm & Digital Capture]**, from the originals at the Register of Deeds, Fryeburg, Maine. Filmed by the Genealogical Society of Utah, 2004, 5 rolls, beginning with FHL film #1221088 (Deed books, Vol. 1-3 (1799-1805). To access the digital images, see the online FHL catalog page: https://familysearch.org/search/catalog/1202649.

1799-1850. *Index to Kennebec County Probate* **[Microfilm & Digital Capture]**, from the original typescript by Georgiana Lilly and Mary Kelton, Dummer Chapter, DAR, Hallowell, ME. Filmed by the Genealogical Society of Utah, 1971, 1 roll, FHL film # 859058. To access the digital images, see the online FHL catalog page: www.familysearch.org/search/catalog/274836.

1799-1865. *Kennebec County, Maine Probate* **[Online Database]**, index for towns of Greene, Leeds, Wales & Livermore (now Androscoggin Co ME). Indexed at the RootsWeb site for Kennebec Co ME: www.rootsweb.ancestry.com/~meandrhs/probate/kenne bec/179965/kennbec.html.

1799-1899. *Birth Records, Town of Oxford, Oxford County, Maine* **[Online Database]**, indexed at the RootsWeb site for Oxford Co ME. See www.rootsweb.ancestry.com/~mecoxfor/births_alpha.htm.

1799-1906. See *Land Records, 1799-1906, Kennebec County, Maine; Indexes to Land Records, 1799-1900* **[Microfilm & Digital Capture]**, from the originals at the Kennebec County Courthouse, Augusta, ME. Filmed by the Genealogical Society of Utah, 1954, 1993, 197 rolls, beginning with FHL film #11065 (Grantor Index 1799-1830). To access the digital images, see the online FHL catalog page: https://familysearch.org/search/catalog/323983.

1800. *U.S. Federal Census Index Maine 1800* **[Printed Index]**, edited by Ronald Vern Jackson, publ. Accelerated Indexing, Bountiful, UT, 1979, 107 pages, FHL book 974.1 X22j.

1800-1835. *Early Records of the Town of Monson, Piscataquis County, Maine* **[Online Database]**, vital statistics originally published in *Sprague's Journal of Maine History*, 1913, text at the USGenWeb site for Piscataquis Co ME. See http://files.usgwarchives.net/me/piscataquis/monson/vit al/spraguej/file123.txt.

1800-1890. *Maine, Compiled Census and Census Substitutes Index, 1800-1890* **[Online Database]**, indexed at the Ancestry.com website from data obtained from Accelerated Indexing Systems,

from microfilmed schedules of the U.S. Federal Decennial Census, territorial/state censuses, and/or census substitutes. This collection contains the following indexes: 1800 Federal Census Index; 1810 Federal Census Index; 1820 Federal Census Index; 1830 Federal Census Index; 1840 Federal Census Index; 1840 Pensioners List; 1850 Federal Census Index; 1860 Federal Census Index; 1870 Federal Census Index; 1890 Veterans Schedules; Early Census Index. See
http://search.ancestry.com/search/db.aspx?dbid=3551.

1800-1892. *Gardiner, Kennebec County Maine, Birth & Death Records* **[Online Database],** indexed at the Ancestry.com website. From data compiled by James Flint. Original data: Vital Records of Gardiner, Kennebec County, ME, Vol. 1, by Henry Sewall Webster of the New England Historic Genealogical Society, Boston, 1914. See
http://search.ancestry.com/search/db.aspx?dbid=5529.

1800-1990. *Maine, County Naturalization Records, 1800-1990* **[Online Database],** digitized at the FamilySearch.org website. Naturalization records and digitized indexes acquired from Androscoggin, Cumberland, Franklin, Hancock, Kennebec, Knox, Oxford, Penobscot, Piscataquis, Sagadahoc, Waldo, & York counties. This database has 207,883 records. See
https://familysearch.org/search/collection/2040046.

1800-2007. *Maine, Knox County Cemetery Records* **[Online Database],** digitized at the FamilySearch.org website. Includes images from several cemeteries of Knox County, Maine. This database has 3,878 records. See
https://familysearch.org/search/collection/1766753.

1801. See "**1801 Tax List, Gouldsborough, Hancock County, Maine**" **[Printed Article],** in *Downeast Ancestry* (Biddeford, ME), Vol. 6, No. 3 (Oct 1982).

1802. See *The Massachusetts Register and United States Calendar for the Year of our Lord 1802* **[Printed Book],** originally printed in 1802 by Manning & Loring, Boston. Reprinted 1978 with all the names listed in the original book, with an index added. Contains civil, ecclesiastical, judicial, and military lists in Massachusetts; associations and corporate institutions for literary, agricultural, and charitable purposes; also catalogues of the officers of the general government. In addition, there is information on Maine people. See FHL book 974.4 N2m.

1802. *Vienna, Kennebec County, Maine-Landowners at Time of Incorporation in 1802* **[Online Database],** indexed at the RootsWeb site for Kennebec Co ME:
www.rootsweb.ancestry.com/~mecreadf/vienlots.htm.

1802-1887. *Waldo County, Maine Marriage Records, Vols. 1-3, 1802-1887* **[Microfilm & Digital Capture],** from the original records at the Waldo County Courthouse, Belfast, ME (1954). Filmed by the Genealogical Society of Utah, 1954, 1 roll, FHL film #12415. To access the digital images, see the online FHL catalog page:
www.familysearch.org/search/catalog/91337.

1803-2003. *Otisfield (Oxford County) Maine Vital Statistics* **[Online Database],** includes indexes from the town registers of births, deaths, marriages, and miscellaneous (wills, obits, etc.). Indexed at the RootsWeb site for Cumberland Co ME. See
www.rootsweb.ancestry.com/~mecotisf/otis2.htm.

1810-1852. *Lewiston, Maine, Valuations* **[Microfilm & Digital Capture],** from the originals created by the Lewiston Town Assessors, now located at the Androscoggin Historical Society, Auburn, ME. Filmed by the Genealogical Society of Utah, 1960, 1962, 3 rolls, beginning with FHL film #223928 (Valuations 1801-1846). To access the digital images, see the online FHL catalog page:
https://familysearch.org/search/catalog/189252.

1804-1838. *Book of Record in the Office of Justice of the Peace for the County of Lincoln, Maine* **[Microfilm & Digital Capture],** from the originals at the Lincoln County Courthouse, Wiscasset, ME (1991). Includes records of complaints, warrants, oaths, marriages, and other miscellaneous records. Filmed by the Genealogical Society of Utah, 1991, 1 roll, FHL film #1765239. To access the digital images, see the online FHL catalog page:
www.familysearch.org/search/catalog/580961.

1803. See "**Taxpayers, 1803, Norridgewock, Somerset County, Maine**" **[Printed Article],** in *New England Historical and Genealogical Register* (NEHGS, Boston, MA), Vol. 97, No. 4 (Oct 1943).

1805-1892. See *Marriage Returns of Oxford County, Maine: Prior to 1892* **[Printed Book],** as Maine Genealogical Society Special Publication No.

16, edited by Donald L. McAllister and Lucille E. Naas, publ. Picton Press, Camden, ME, 1993, 345 pages, FHL book 974.175 V2m.

1805-1915. *Maine, Oxford County, Probate Estate Files* **[Online Database]**, digitized at the FamilySearch.org website. From the original records at the Oxford County Courthouse, South Paris, ME. This database has 177,447 records. See **https://familysearch.org/search/collection/2040540.**

1807. Blue Hill Families, 1807, Hancock County, Maine" **[Printed Article]**, in *Bangor Historical Magazine / Maine Historical Magazine* (Joseph W Porter, Bangor, ME), Vol. 1, No. 6 (Dec 1885).

1808. See **"Tax List, 1808, Kittery, York County, Maine"** **[Printed Article]**, in *Old Eliot* (J.L.M. Willis, Eliot, ME), Vol. 1, No. 10 (Oct 1897).

1809. See **"Taxpayers, 1809, Otisfield, Cumberland County, Maine"** **[Printed Article]**, in *Maine Historical and Genealogical Recorder* (Recorder Publishing, Portland, ME), Vol. 8, No. 4 (Oct 1895).

1809-1915. *Maine, Somerset County, Probate Estate Files* **[Online Database]**, digitized at the FamilySearch.org website. From the originals located at the Maine State Archives, Augusta, ME. This database has 162,928 records. See **https://familysearch.org/search/collection/2094263.**

1810. *Maine 1810 Census Index, A-Z* **[Printed Index]**, by Heritage Quest, Bountiful, UT, 2000, 214 pages, FHL book 974.1 X22h.

1810. See **"Highway List, 1810, Kittery, York County, Maine"** **[Printed Article]**, in *Old Eliot* (J.L.M. Willis, Eliot, ME), Vol. 3, No. 1 (Jan 1899).

1810. See **"Tax List, 1810, Kittery, York County, Maine"** **[Printed Article]**, in *Old Eliot* (J.L.M. Willis, Eliot, ME), Vol. 1, No. 10 (Oct 1897).

1810. See **"First Town Meeting, Eliot, York County, Maine, 1810"** **[Printed Article]**, in *Old Eliot* (J.L.M. Willis, Eliot, ME), Vol. 2, No. 8 (Aug 1898).

1810-1868. See **"Births and Deaths, Charlotte, Washington County, Maine, 1810-1868"** **[Printed Article]**, in *New England Historical and Genealogical Register* (NEHGS, Boston, M), Vol. 101, No. 4 (Oct 1947).

1811. See **"Inhabitants & Residents in Town of Lubeck, Washington County, Maine"** **[Printed Article]**, in *Downeast Ancestry* (Biddeford, ME), Vol. 10, No. 2 (Aug 1986); Vol. 10, No. 3 (Oct 1986); and Vol. 10, No. 4 (Dec 1986).

1812. See **"Tax List, 1812, Poland, Androscoggin County, Maine [Printed Article]**, in *Rota-Gene* (Rotary Club, Sarasota, FL), Vol. 4, No. 5 (Dec 1983).

1812-1865. See *Maine Militia Records, 1812-1814, 1820-1850; the Civil War Soldiers Card Index, 1861-1865; and World War I Card Index to Solders* **[Online Database]**, indexed at the FamilySearch.org website, images as part of the Maine State Archives Collections. This military database has 101,580 records. The entire collection consists of court, military, naturalization, land and other record sets; part of **1718-1958 Maine State Archives Collections**, the parent database with 1,656,347 records. See **https://familysearch.org/search/collection/1877829.**

1812-1865. *Maine, Compiled Military Records* **[Online Database]**, indexed at the Ancestry.com website. This index provides numerous details extracted from records on three different groups of men: soldiers from Maine who served in the War of 1812, Maine sailors who enlisted in the Navy primarily in the years 1861–1865, and men from New England who served in CCC camps in Maine and New Hampshire in 1937. Index entries can include a name, residence, rank, unit, age, birthplace, occupation, years of service, place and date of enlistment, company location, company number, eye color, hair color, complexion, and comments. This database has 8,268 records. See **http://search.ancestry.com/search/db.aspx?dbid=1667.**

1814. See **"Parole of Inhabitants, 1814, Bangor, Penobscot County, Maine" [Printed Article]**, in *Bangor Historical Magazine / Maine Historical Magazine* (Joseph W Porter, Bangor, ME), Vol. 4, No. 9-10 (Apr 1889).

1814-1860. See *Deeds 1814-1860: Indexes 1814-1859 – Penobscot County (Maine)* **[Microfilm & Digital Capture]**, from the originals at the Penobscot County Courthouse, Bangor, ME (1955). Filmed by the Genealogical Society of Utah, 1955, 162 rolls, beginning with FHL film #11786 (Grantor Index, A-

E, 1814-1844). To access the digital images, see the online FHL catalog page: https://familysearch.org/search/catalog/351868.

1814-1897. *Death Records, Town of Oxford, Oxford County, Maine* **[Online Database],** indexed at the RootsWeb site for Oxford Co ME. See www.rootsweb.ancestry.com/~mecoxfor/deaths_alpha.htm

1815. See **"Direct Tax, 1815, Hancock County" [Printed Article],** in *Bangor Historical Magazine / Maine Historical Magazine* (Joseph W Porter, Bangor, ME), Vol. 4, No. 1-2 (Jul 1888).

1814-1892. *Westbrook (Maine) Vital Records to 1892* **[Microfilm & Digital Capture],** from the records originally at the Town Clerk's office. Westbrook was part of Portland, ME from 1814 to 1891. The original records before 1891 are located at the Maine Historical Society, Portland, ME. The records include births to 1881 in Westbrook and Falmouth; family records, deaths mixed in with births, and births 1881-1891, marriages 1873-1892; marriages 1814-1846, 1851; lists of town clerks and treasurers; Westbrook family records giving births to ca.1855; and Westbrook town officials. Filmed by the Genealogical Society of Utah, 1956, 2 rolls, FHL film #12615-12616. To access the digital images, see the online FHL catalog page: www.familysearch.org/search/catalog/306378.

1815. See **"Tax List, 1815, North Yarmouth, Cumberland County, Maine" [Printed Article],** in *Old Time-North Yarmouth, Maine* (Augustus W Corliss, Yarmouth, ME), Vol. 1, No. 1 (Jan 1877); thru Vol. 1, No. 4 (Oct 1877).

1815, *Unpaid Direct Tax of Leeds, Kennebec County, District of Maine* **[Online Database],** indexed at the Leeds, Maine Genealogy & History Page. See www.rootsweb.ancestry.com/~meandrhs/taxlists/leeds/1815tax.html.

1815-1916. *Westbrook [Maine] Assessors Valuations* **[Microfilm & Digital Capture],** from the original assessor records now located at the Walker Memorial Library, Westbrook, ME. Includes an index for the period 1891-1915. Filmed by the Genealogical Society of Utah, 1992, 21 rolls, beginning with FHL film #1845594 (Valuations 1815, 1824-1825). To access the digital images, see the online FHL catalog page: https://familysearch.org/search/catalog/580266.

1816. See **"Direct Tax List, 1816, Penobscot County, Maine" [Printed Article],** in *Hermon Roots News* (Kopy Eyes County, Waterville, ME), Vol. 2, No. 3 (May 1984).

1816-1892. See *Marriage Returns of Penobscot County, Maine: Prior to 1892* **[Printed Book],** edited by Ruth Gray, publ. as Maine Genealogical Society Special Publication No. 17, Picton Press, Camden, ME, 1994, 2 vols., FHL book 974.13 V2m v. 1-2.

1817. See **"Tax Bills, 1817, Dexter, Penobscot County, Maine" [Printed Article],** in *Dexter Historical Society Newsletter* (Dexter, ME), (Summer 1997).

1817. See **"Tax List, 1817, Dixmont, Penobscot County, Maine" [Printed Article],** in *Maine Seine / Maine Genealogist* (Maine Genealogical Society, Farmington, ME), Vol. 12, No. 4 (Nov 1990).

1817. See **"Ratable Polls, Friendship, Knox County, Maine" [Printed Article],** in *New England Historical and Genealogical Register* (NEHGS, Boston, MA), Vol. 83, No. 3 (Jul 1929).

1818, 1831, 1836 Taxpayers, Stetson Plantation, Penobscot County, Maine **[Online Database],** archived at the Wayback Machine site. See http://web.archive.org/web/20060718014029/http://www.feliixplace.com/maine/stetsonfamilies.html.

1818-1850s. *Tax Lists & Birth Records, Town of Sangerville, Piscataquis County, Maine* **[Online Database],** includes a name list for the taxpayers in 1819, and birth records for the period 1818 to about 1855. Indexed at the USGenWeb site for Piscataquis Co ME. See http://files.usgwarchives.net/me/piscataquis/sangerville/vital/spraguej/births.txt.

1818-1900. *Vital Records from the Eastport Sentinel of Eastport, Washington County, Maine* **[Printed Book],** publ. as Maine Genealogical Society Special Publication No. 24. Edited by Kenneth L Willey, publ. Picton Press, Camden, ME, 1996, 884 pages, FHL book 974.142/E1 V2w.

1819. See **"Taxpayers, 1819, Sangerville, Piscataquis County, Maine" [Printed Article],** in *Downeast Ancestry*, Vol. 1, No. 1 (Jun 1977) and in *Sprague's Journal of Maine History*, Vol. 3, No. 3 (Jul 1914).

1819-1891. *Town and Vital Records, Bangor, Maine* [**Microfilm & Digital Capture**], from the original records at Bangor. ME, Includes index to marriages in town records; births prior to 1833; intentions of marriage and marriage records 1819-1854; licenses to retailers and inn holders; and marriages records, 1843-1846. Filmed by the Genealogical Society of Utah, 4 rolls, beginning with FHL film #10583 (Deaths 1834-1891, births prior to 1891). For a complete list of roll numbers and contents of each roll, see the online FHL catalog page for this title. See https://familysearch.org/search/catalog/352954.

1820. *Maine 1820 Census Index* [**Printed Index**], edited by Ronald Vern Jackson, publ. Accelerated Indexing Systems, Bountiful, UT, 1976, 118 pages, FHL book 974.1 X2j.

1820. *The 1820 US Census of Matawasca (Madawaska) Parish-Penobscot County, Maine and York County, New Brunswick* [**Online Database**]. Includes communities on both banks of the Upper St. John River Valley in what are today Aroostook Co ME and Madawaska Co NB. Transcription at the UpperStjohn.com website. See www.upperstjohn.com/1820/index.htm.

1820. See **"Militia Rolls, Cumberland County, Maine, 1820"** [**Printed Article**], in *Old Times-North Yarmouth Maine / Westcustogo Chronicle* (Augustus W Corliss, Yarmouth, ME), Vol. 4, No. 3 (Jul 1880).

1820-1852. *Death Records, Town of Norway, Oxford County, Maine* [**Online Database**], indexed at the USGenWeb site for Oxford Co ME. See http://files.usgwarchives.net/me/oxford/norway/deaths/file2.txt.

1821. See **"Tax List, 1821, Pownal, Cumberland County, Maine"** [**Printed Article**], in *Old Times-North Yarmouth, Maine*, Vol. 4, No. 3 (Jul 1880).

1821. *List of Inhabitants of Peru at time of Incorporation, February 5, 1821* [**Online Database**], indexed at the RootsWeb site for Oxford Co ME. See www.rootsweb.ancestry.com/~mecperu/peru1821.html.

1823. See **"Tax List, 1823, North Yarmouth, Cumberland County, Maine"** [**Printed Article**], in *Old Times-North Yarmouth, Maine*, Vol. 1, No. 3 (July 1877) thru Vol. 1, No. 4 (Oct 1877).

1823-1893. *Portland (Maine) City Directories* [**Microfilm**], from originals by various publishers. FHL has: 1823, 1827, 1830, 1831, 1834, 1837, 1841, 1844, 1846-1848, 1850-1853, 1856-1860, 1863-1864, 1866-1869, 1871, 1873, 1875, 1877, 1879, and 1881-1893. Filmed by Research Publications, Woodbridge, CT, 1980-1984, 44 microfiche & 29 microfilm rolls, beginning with FHL fiche #6044325 (1823-1826 Portland directories). For a complete list of roll numbers and contents of each roll, see the online FHL catalog page for this title. Under "Contains," click on a year to see details. See https://familysearch.org/search/catalog/538612.

1824. See **"Danville School Districts, 1824 Census, Danville, Androscoggin County"** [**Printed Article**], in *Downeast Ancestry* (Biddeford, ME), Vol. 6, No. 5 (Feb 1983).

1824-1842. *Births, Berlin, Franklin County, Maine* [**Online Database**], indexed at the RootsWeb site for Franklin Co ME. See www.rootsweb.ancestry.com/~mefrankl/berlinbir.htm.

1824-1842. *Deaths, Berlin, Franklin County, Maine* [**Online Database**], indexed at the RootsWeb site for Franklin Co ME. See www.rootsweb.ancestry.com/~mefrankl/berlindeaths.htm.

1824-1870. *Early Settlers, Greenville, Piscataquis County, Maine* [**Online Database**], history text at the USGenWeb site for Piscataquis Co ME. See http://files.usgwarchives.net/me/piscataquis/history/loring/chap23.txt.

1824-1915. *Maine State Prisoners* [**Printed Book**], by Lewis Bunker Rohrbach, publ. Picton Press, Rockport, ME, 2001, 252 pages, FHL book 974.1 J6m.

1825-1970. *Hancock County, Maine Cemetery Index* [**Online Database**], indexed at the Ancestry.com website. Source: Book, same title, by Elizabeth Prather Ellsberry. Each record includes a Name, Gender, Death Age, Birth Date, Cemetery, Burial Place, Cemetery Notes, and Spouse. This database has 1,645 records. https://search.ancestry.com/search/db.aspx?dbid=5598.

1827-1881. See *Returns of Marriages, Androscoggin County, Maine, 1827-1881* [**Microfilm & Digital Capture**], from the originals at the Androscoggin

County Courthouse, Auburn, ME. Filmed by the Genealogical Society of Utah, 1956, 1 roll, FHL film #10520. To access the digital images, see the online FHL catalog:
www.familysearch.org/search/catalog/282960.

1827-1888. *Record of Marriages in Penobscot County, Maine* **[Microfilm & Digital Capture],** from the originals at the Penobscot County Courthouse, Bangor, ME. Filmed by the Genealogical Society of Utah, 1955, 3 rolls, beginning with FHL film #11948 (Marriage records, Vo. 1-3, 1827-1857). To access the digital images, see the online FHL catalog page:
https://familysearch.org/search/catalog/18172.

1827-1900. See *Records of Deeds, Waldo County, Maine, 1828-1896; Indexes to Deeds, 1827-1900* **[Microfilm & Digital Capture],** from the originals at the Waldo County Courthouse, Belfast, ME (1954). Filmed by the Genealogical Society of Utah, 1954, 65 rolls, beginning with FHL film #12342 (Index to Grantors, 1827-1839). For a complete list of roll numbers and contents of each roll, see the online FHL catalog page for this title. See
https://familysearch.org/search/catalog/73890.

1827-1892. *Marriage Records of Waldo County, Maine, Prior to 1892* **[Printed Book],** transcribed by Elizabeth M Mosher and Isabel Morse Maresh, publ. Picton Press, Camden, ME, 1990, 634 pages, FHL book 974.152 V2me.

1828-1866. *Record of Marriages, Lincoln County, Maine* **[Microfilm & Digital Capture],** from the originals at the Lincoln County Courthouse, Wiscasset, ME (1991). Includes a partial index. Filmed by the Genealogical Society of Utah, 1991, 1 roll, FHL film #1765239. To access the digital images, see the online FHL catalog page:
www.familysearch.org/search/catalog/580958.

1828-1873. *Notes From History of Patten, Penobscot County, Maine* **[Online Database],** text at the RootsWeb site for Penobscot ME. See
www.rootsweb.ancestry.com/~usgenweb/me/penobscot/towns/patten.html.

1828-1887. See *Marriage Records, Kennebec County, Maine, ca1828-1887 and Birth Records 1876-1879* **[Microfilm & Digital Capture],** from the originals at the Kennebec County Courthouse, Augusta, MD (1955). Filmed by the Genealogical Society of Utah, 1954, 2 rolls, FHL film #11314 film #11315 (Marriage ca 1839-1887). To access the digital images, see the online FHL catalog page:
www.familysearch.org/search/catalog/333238.

1829. See **"Poll Tax, 1829, Lincoln County, Maine"** **[Printed Article],** in *Mattanawcook Observer* (Alan H Hawkins, Null, ME), Vol. 1, No. 1 (Apr 1982).

1829-1831. See **"Tax and Census Records, Orono, Penobscot County, Maine, 1829-1831"** **[Printed Article],** in *Downeast Ancestry* (Biddeford, ME), Vol. 10, No. 3 (Oct 1986).

1830. *Maine 1830 Census Index* **[Printed Index],** edited by Ronald Vern Jackson, publ. Accelerated Indexing Systems, Bountiful, UT, 1977, 170 pages, FHL book 974.1 X2j.

1830. *The 1830 US Census of the Madawaska Settlements, Penobscot County, Maine (and areas of present New Brunswick)* **[Online Database],** lists names from communities on both banks of the Upper St. John River Valley in what are today Aroostook Co Maine and Madawaska Co New Brunswick. Extracted at the US-census.org site. See
http://us-census.org/pub/usgenweb/census/me/penobscot/1830/pg0374.txt.

1830. *Names in the 1830 Census for Aroostook, Washington County, Maine* **[Online Database],** listed at the RootsWeb site. See
http://freepages.genealogy.rootsweb.ancestry.com/~lallen/1830_census.htm.

1830. See **"Single Poll Tax, 1830, Lincoln County, Maine"** **[Printed Article],** in *Missing Links -Genealogical Clues* (Chedwato Service, Burlington, VT), Issue No. 35 (Jun 1965).

1830-1892. See *Waterville (Maine) Vital Records, 1830-1892; Index 1830-1843* **[Microfilm & Digital Capture],** from originals of the Waterville Town Clerk, Waterville, ME. Contains intentions of marriage 1830-1892; marriage records 1830-1891; deaths 1831-1855, 1865-1888; births 1861, 1870-1891; Filmed by the Genealogical Society of Utah, 1953-1954, 22 rolls, beginning with FHL film #12277 (Index to Births, A-Bri). To access the digital images, see the online FHL catalog page:
https://familysearch.org/search/catalog/50942.

1831. See **"Voter List, Berlin, Franklin County, Maine"** **[Printed Article],** in *Sprague's Journal of Maine History* (John F. Sprague, Foxcroft, ME), Vol. 7, No. 1 (May 1919).

1831. *The Deane and Kavanagh Report, July-August 1831: Survey of the Madawaska Settlement, Penobscot and Washington Counties (now Aroostook County), Maine; and Carleton County (now Madawaska Co.), New Brunswick* [Online Database]. From the introduction: "The Deane and Kavanagh report is an invaluable source of information on the people who lived on both the north and the south banks of the upper St. John River, as well as in the Aroostook River valley, in 1831, a time when this whole region was disputed territory. Not only does it give the names of heads of households, it also gives where many of them were from, how much land they owned and any improvements on the land, and occasionally other information. This report is therefore an incredibly important source for anyone working on history or genealogy in this region, on both sides of the river. Because the north bank of the upper St. John River was at that time claimed by the United States, this survey also includes communities that are now in New Brunswick." A name index and details on the surveys, grants, and background information on the Deane and Kavanagh Report are all at the Upperstjohn.com website. See www.upperstjohn.com/aroostook/deane-kavanagh.htm.

1831-1965. *Maine City Directories* [Online Database], indexed at the Ancestry.com website. This is a collection of over 300 city directories from Maine Counties, Towns, and Cities. *Browse this Collection* to find a locality and year. Based on the run of directories for the city of Portland, the earliest start with 1831 and go through 1965 or so. There may be some cities with earlier and later years in the collection. Most of the images have OCR indexes. This database has 170,315 records. See https://search.ancestry.com/search/db.aspx?dbid=8774.

1833 New Brunswick Special Census of the Madawaska Settlement: Carleton County, New Brunswick and Penobscot County, Maine [Online Database]. From intro: "This is a transcription of a special census of the Madawaska Settlement undertaken by the Province of New Brunswick in late 1833. The census is very interesting for several reasons. First, like many of the censuses and surveys undertaken in this area, which was in dispute between Great Britain and the United States, it covered communities on both sides of the Upper St. John River, in communities that are now in both Madawaska Co NB and Aroostook Co ME. It is thus an invaluable resource for information on

the population of Madawaska, especially when compared to other contemporary documents such as the 1820 US Census of Matawascah Parish, the 1830 US Census of Madawaska, the 1831 Deane and Kavanagh Survey of Madawaska, and the 1840 US Census of Madawaska, all of which survey both north and south banks of the St. John River." Indexed at the UpperStjohn.com website. See www.upperstjohn.com/1833/index.htm.

1833-1868. *Maine, Bath, Seaman's Proofs of Citizenship* [Online Database], indexed at the FamilySearch.org website. Source: National Archives microfilm M1825. Includes proofs of citizenship used to apply for Seamen's Protection Certificates at the ports of Bath, Maine in 1833, 1836, 1839-50, 1853-65, 1867-68; and at Portsmouth, New Hampshire in 1857-58. This database has 3,473 records. See www.familysearch.org/search/collection/2300674.

1834-1890. *Records, Somerset County, Maine* [Microfilm & Digital Capture], from the originals at the Somerset County Courthouse, Skowhegan, ME (1954). Contains commissioner's records 1833-1846; marriages, 1834-1861; and marriages, 1860-1890. Filmed by the Genealogical Society of Utah, 1954, 2 rolls, FHL film #12210 & #12211. To access the digital images, see the online FHL catalog page: www.familysearch.org/search/catalog/73110.

1834. See **"Taxpayers, 1834, Vienna, Kennebec County, Maine** [Printed Article], in *Sprague's Journal of Maine History* (John F. Sprague, Foxcroft, ME), Vol. 14, No. 1 (Jan 1926).

1834-1935. See *Bangor (Maine) City Directories* [Microfilm], from various publishers. FHL has directories for 1834, 1843, 1846, 1848, 1851, 1855, 1859, 1864, 1867-1880, 1882, 1884-1885, 1887-1888,1891-1895, 1897, 1899, 1901, 1903, 1905, 1907, 1909, 1914, 1919, 1921-1935. Filmed by Research Publications, Woodbridge, CT, 45 rolls/fiche, beginning with FHL fiche #6043602 (1834 Bangor Directory). For a complete list of roll/fiche numbers and contents of each, see the online FHL catalog page for this title. See https://familysearch.org/search/catalog/512786.

1834-1984. *Days Before Yesterday in Springfield, Maine* [Printed Book], by Leona Frances Brown and Frances Webster, Includes index, publ. The Calais Press, 1984, 180 pages, FHL book 974.13/S1 H2b.

1835. See "Census, Passadumkeag, Penobscot County, Maine" [Printed Article], in *Bangor Historical Magazine / Maine Historical Magazine* (Joseph W Porter, Bangor, ME), Vol. 2, No. 3 (Sep 1886).

1835-1836. *Maine Revolutionary War Bounty Applications* [Online Database], indexed at the Ancestry.com website. Original data: *Names of Soldiers of the American Revolution Who Applied for State Bounty under Resolves of March 17, 1835, March 24, 1836, and March 20, 1836, as Appears of Record in Land Office, 1893*. This database has 4,952 records. See http://search.ancestry.com/search/db.aspx?dbid=4461.
- This database is also available at the FamilySearch.org website. See www.familysearch.org/search/collection/1881491.

1837 Maine State Census (aka Maine, Surplus Revenue Census, 1837) [Original Records & Digital Capture]. This census was conducted for the purpose of distributing a surplus of revenue from the sale of public lands to the US federal government. The original name lists for Bangor, Portland, and most towns, townships, and plantations are at the Maine State Archives in Augusta. The originals for the town of Eliot, York County, are at the Maine Historical Society in Portland. Some of the towns identified the number of school age children in a household, thus the lists were sometimes referred to as "School Censuses." The name lists were digitized by FamilySearch International in 2011. To access the digital images, see the online FHL catalog page: www.familysearch.org/search/catalog/1923492.
A few of the 1837 town name lists have been published in periodicals, as follows:
- "1837 Census, Gray Surplus & 80 Rod Strip," in *Maine Genealogist*, Vol.. 12, No. 2 (May 1990).
- "1837 State Census, Mount Desert, Hancock County," in *Maine Genealogist*, Vol. 11, No. 2 (May 1989). See also "1837 State Census, Mount Desert," compiled by Alice MacDonald Long, in *The Maine Seine*, Vol. 11 (1989).
- "1837-1847 South Berwick Persons in Great Works Vicinity, York County," in *Downeast Ancestry*, Vol. 13, No. 5 (Feb 1990).
- "Township Nineteen and the 1837 Census," in *A-CHSs Newsletter / Alexander-Crawford Historical Society Newsletter*, Issue 129 (May 2006).

1837. *Special Maine 1837 Census* [Online Database], indexed at the RootsWeb site by locality (No 1. Adamstown, Oxford Co to No. 99 Wyman, Franklin Co) w/added townships and separate 1837 county indexes accessible from the same page. See www.rootsweb.ancestry.com/~meandrhs/history/usdebt/census/maine/1837.html.

1837 Maine State Census (with Index) [Online Database], indexed at the USGenWeb site for Maine, 5 files by county/town: 2 files of an alpha index.
- For the index, part 1 (A-J) see www.usgwcensus.org/cenfiles/me/1837/index/index1.txt
- For the index, part 2 (K-Z) See www.usgwcensus.org/cenfiles/me/1837/index/index2.txt
- For the parent directory of all online censuses at the USGenWeb site, see www.usgwcensus.org/cenfiles/me/

1837. *Special Maine 1837 Census: Aroostook County* [Online Database], indexed by census districts. See www.rootsweb.ancestry.com/~mearoost/1837census.html.

1837 Census of Upton (Township Letter B), Oxford County, Maine [Online Database], indexed at the David Colby Young/RootsWeb site. See www.rootsweb.ancestry.com/~meandrhs/census/maine/upton/1837.html.

1837. *Special 1837 Census of Unincorporated Townships and Plantations of Penobscot County* [Online Database], originally indexed at the Penobscot County Megen.info website. See the archived database: https://web.archive.org/web/20170927130523/www.penobscotcountymegen.info/med_1837_cen.htm.

1837. *Lewiston, Maine Tax Records* [Online Database], records of the County and Town Tax for 1837 (as part of Kennebec Co ME). Since 1854, Lewiston now part of Androscoggin County. Indexed at the RootsWeb site for Kennebec Co ME: www.rootsweb.ancestry.com/~meandrhs/taxlists/lewiston/1837/countytx.html.

1837-1965. *Maine & Massachusetts, Case Files of Deceased and Deserted Seamen* [Online Database], indexed at the FamilySearch.org website. This collection contains three NARA collections: Case Files of Deceased and Deserted Seamen, compiled 1912-1965; Case Files of Deceased and Deserted Seamen, compiled 1873-1911; and Case Files of Deceased and Deserted Seamen, compiled 1909-1951. For the most part, the records are arranged by case number and contain an assortment of details including personal information, death details, wages etc. about deceased and deserted sailors and others who worked on board ships. This database has 16,231 records. See www.familysearch.org/search/collection/2303027.

1837-2007. *Maine, Aroostook County, Probate Records* **[Online Database],** digitized at the FamilySearch.org website. From the original records at the Aroostook County Courthouse, Houlton, ME. Includes indexes, books, dockets and estate files. This database has 116,427 records. See https://familysearch.org/search/collection/1415491.

1838 Militia Roll for Town of Mexico, Oxford County, Maine **[Online Database],** indexed at the USGenWeb site for Oxford Co ME. See http://files.usgwarchives.net/me/oxford/mexico/company/soldiers.txt.

1838-1902. *Maine, Piscataquis County, Deed Books* **[Online Database],** digitized at the FamilySearch.org website. From the original records at the Piscataquis County Courthouse, Dover-Foxcroft, ME. Includes images from deed books & indexes, vol. 1-131. This database has 56,970 records. See https://familysearch.org/search/collection/1447336.

1838-1939. See **Deeds, Mortgages, and Executions, Franklin** *County, Maine, 1838-1939; Indexes 1838-1884, 1884-1903* **[Microfilm & Digital Capture],** from the original records at the Franklin County Registry of Deeds, Farmington, ME (1954). Filmed by the Genealogical Society of Utah, 1954, 65 rolls, beginning with FHL film #10871 (Index A-B, 1838-1884). To access the digital images, see the online FHL catalog page: https://familysearch.org/search/catalog/334379.

1839. See **"Eliot Militia, Aroostook War, York County, Maine, 1839" [Printed Article],** in *Old Eliot* (J.L.M. Willis, Eliot, ME), Vol. 8, No. 4 (Oct 1908).

1839. See *Aroostook War: Historical Sketch and Roster of Commissioned Officers and Enlisted Men Called Into Service for the Protection of the Northeastern Frontier of Maine From February to May 1839* **[Printed Book & Digital Version],** originally printed 1903, reprinted 1989, Genealogical Publishing Co, Baltimore, 95 pages, FHL book 974.1 M2m. To access the digital version, see the online FHL catalog: http://search.ancestry.com/search/db.aspx?dbid=4518.

1839-1845. See *Court Indexes, Washington County, Maine* **[Online Database],** files arranged alphabetically by surname. See the parent directory for each database (A to Y) at the USGenWeb site for Washington Co ME. See http://files.usgwarchives.net/me/washington/court/index/.

1839-1891. *Marriage Records, Piscataquis County, Maine* **[Microfilm & Digital Capture]** from the original records at the County Courthouse, Dover-Foxcroft, ME (1955). Includes marriage records from the various town clerks and ministers in the county. Filmed by the Genealogical Society of Utah, 1955, 1 roll, FHL film #11785. To access the digital images, see the online FHL catalog page: www.familysearch.org/search/catalog/43754.

1839-1892. *Record of Marriages of Aroostook County, Vol. 1-2* **[Microfilm & Digital Capture],** from the originals at the Aroostook County Courthouse, Houlton, ME. Filmed by the Genealogical Society of Utah, 1954, 1 roll, FHL film #10450. To access the digital images, see the online FHL catalog page: www.familysearch.org/search/catalog/287787.

1840. *Maine 1840 Census Index* **[Printed Index],** edited by Ronald Vern Jackson, publ. Accelerated Indexing Systems, North Salt Lake, UT, 1978, 210 pages, FHL book 974.1 X2j index.

1840 Census of Pensioners Revolutionary or Military Service, Maine **[Online Database],** indexed at the US-Roots.org website. This tabular index includes the names, ages, and place of residences for all military pensioners, taken from the special census schedules, part of the 1840 federal census: www.us-roots.org/colonialamerica/census/1840/1840me_a.html.

1840-1900. *Saco (Maine) Vital Records* **[Microfilm & Digital Capture],** from the originals at Saco, Maine. Many records are indexed. Contains deaths 1840-1891; family records listing births and deaths; adoption of a child; marriage records 1851-1867, 1881; intentions of marriage 1851-1891; births ca.1865-1900; and delayed births. Filmed by the Genealogical Society of Utah, 1956, 1 roll, FHL film #12243. To access the digital images, see the online FHL catalog page: www.familysearch.org/search/catalog/140646.

1841-1910. *Maine, Deaths and Burials* **[Online Database],** indexed at the FamilySearch.org website, a name index to microfilmed death and burial records at the Family History Library. This database has 172,879 records. See
https://familysearch.org/search/collection/1674914.

1844. See **"1844 Taxpayers in Townsend (Southport), Lincoln County, Maine"** [Printed Article], in *Downeast Ancestry* (Biddeford, ME),Vol. 5, No. 4 (Dec 1981).

1846-1891. See *Vital Records Published in Rockland (Knox County), Maine Prior to 1892* [Printed Book], transcribed by Charles Samuel Candage and Ruth Louise Pittman Candage. Includes a record of birth, marriage, and death notices which appeared in Rockland newspapers from 1846 to 1891.
Includes notices for Rockland and the surrounding area. Publ. Picton Press, Camden, ME, 1989, 2 vols, FHL book 974.153/R1 V2c v.1-2.

1847-2011. *The New England Historical & Genealogical Register* **[Online Database],** digitized and indexed at the Ancestry.com website. This database contains volumes of the *New England Historical and Genealogical Register*, a quarterly publication. The New England Historic Genealogical Society (NEHGS) was formed in 1845, and in 1847, they published the first issue of the *Register*. The NEHGS is the oldest genealogical society in the United States, and the *Register*, likewise, is the country's oldest genealogical journal. The database is searchable by name, birth, death, marriage, and any event and any keyword found in the articles. This database has 300,569 records. See
http://search.ancestry.com/search/db.aspx?dbid=2129.

1848-1917. *Town and Vital Records, Sagadahoc County, Maine* **[Microfilm & Digital Capture],** from the originals at the Division of Vital Statistics, Augusta, ME. Contains deaths 1848-1917, births from early to 1914, intentions of marriage and marriage records 1856-1909, bills of sale, list of people liable for military duty, and dog licenses. Filmed by the Genealogical Society of Utah, 1953, 1 roll, FHL film #11544. To access the digital images, see the online FHL catalog page: **www.familysearch.org/search/catalog/36341.**

1850. *Maine, 1850 Federal Census: Population Schedules* **[Microfilm & Digital Capture],** from the originals at the National Archives, Washington, DC.

Filmed by the National Archives, 1964, series M432, 29 rolls, beginning with FHL film #9718 (Aroostook Co). To access the digital images, see the online FHL catalog page:
https://familysearch.org/search/catalog/744482.

1850 Federal Census, Waldo County, Maine - County Copy **[Microfilm Only],** from the county's original copy at the Waldo County Courthouse, Belfast, ME. Organized by the towns of Appleton, Belfast, Belmont, Brooks, Burnham, Camden, Frankfort, Freedom, Hope, North Haven, Islesboro, Jackson, Liberty, Knox, Montville, Palermo, Montville, Monroe, Northport, Islesboro, Prospect, Searsport, Searsmont, Swanville, Lincolnville, Thorndike, Troy, Unity, Vinal Haven, and Waldo. Filmed by the Genealogical Society of Utah, 1954, 2 rolls, FHL film #12408-12409.

1850. *Maine 1850 Census Index* **[Printed Index],** edited by Ronald Vern Jackson, et al, publ. Accelerated Indexing Systems, Salt Lake City, UT, 1978, 404 pages, FHL book 974.1 X22j 1850.

1850. See **"Census, 1850, New Englanders in Florida"** [Printed Article], in *New England Historical and Genealogical Register* (NEHGS, Boston, MA), Vol. 76, No. 1 (Jan 1922).

1850. *Military Information Found in Old Ledgers in the town of Farmington, Franklin County, Maine* **[Online Database],** a request to the governor for the organization of a company of artillery, listing names of persons involved. List at the RootsWeb site for Franklin Co ME. See
www.rootsweb.ancestry.com/~mefrankl/Farmmil.htm.

1850-1870. See *Maine Census Indexes, 1850-1870* **[Microfilm & Digital Capture],** from the original records at the Maine Division of Vital Statistic, Augusta, ME. This card index to Maine's federal censuses for 1850, 1860, and 1870 were the first statewide indexes ever done by any state, executed by the Maine Vital Statistics Division in the early 1950s. Filmed by the Genealogical Society of the Utah, 1953, 5 rolls, beginning with FHL film #9734 (Census indexes for Auburn, Baldwin, Belgrade, Bridgton, Brunswick, Gardiner, Hallowell, Harpswell, Harrison, Lewiston, Litchfield, Portland and Waterville, 1850-1870). To access the digital images of completed rolls, see the online FHL catalog page:
https://familysearch.org/search/catalog/78880.

1851-1955. *Indexes to Naturalization Records of Federal Courts, Portland, Maine* [Microfilm & Digital Capture], from the originals at the National Archives branch, Waltham, MA. Filmed by the Genealogical Society of Utah, 2004, 6 rolls, beginning with FHL film #2371828 (Index to Declarations of Intention, 1906-1955). For a complete list of roll numbers and contents of each roll, see the online FHL catalog page for this title. See https://familysearch.org/search/catalog/1201478.

1852. See "1852 Census, Siskiyou County, California, Primarily People From Maine" [Printed Article], in *Pinecone and Tassel* (Deborah Roberge, Waterville, ME), Vol. 3, No. 6 (Mar 2006).

1854-1855. *Abstracts of Records at Androscoggin County, Maine Probate Court* [Online Database], indexed at the RootsWeb site. See www.rootsweb.ancestry.com/~meandrhs/probate/proba te.html.

1854-1869. See *Deeds, Sagadahoc County, Maine, 1854-1863; Index 1854-1869* [Microfilm & Digital Capture], from the originals at the Sagadahoc County Courthouse, Bath, ME (1954). Filmed by the Genealogical Society of Utah, 1954, 10 rolls, beginning with FHL film #12106 (Index to deeds, 1854-1869). To access the digital images, see the online FHL catalog page: https://familysearch.org/search/catalog/65949.

1854-1918. *Maine, Androscoggin County, Probate Estate Files* [Online Database], digitized at the FamilySearch.org website. From the original records at the Androscoggin County Courthouse in Auburn, ME. The probate estate files are arranged by case number. The docket index books are arranged by case number and date. Included is an alphabetical card index to the probate cases. This database has 258,605 records. See https://familysearch.org/search/collection/2037995.

1854-1923. See *Land Records (Androscoggin County, Maine), 1854-1923; Indexes to Land Records, 1854-1909* [Microfilm & Digital Capture], from the originals at the Androscoggin County Building, Auburn, ME. Filmed by the Genealogical Society of Utah, 1956-1992, 62 rolls, beginning with FHL film #10472 (Index to records, 1854-1876). To access the digital images, see the online FHL catalog: https://familysearch.org/search/catalog/332172.

1855-1865. See "People from Maine in 1855 and 1865 Massachusetts State Census" [Printed Article], in *Maine Seine / Maine Genealogist*, (Maine Genealogical Society (Farmington, ME), Vol. 11, No. 4 (Aug 1989).

1856-1934. *Biddeford (Maine) City Directories* [Microfilm], by various publishers. FHL has 1856-1857, 1882, 1884, 1886, 1888, 1890, 1894, 1896, 1900, 1902, 1904, 1907, 1911, 1913, 1916, 1920-1921, 1922-1923, 1929-1930, 1932, and 1934 (film only). Filmed by Research Publications, Woodbridge, CT, 1980-1990, 20 films/fiche, beginning with FHL fiche #6043611 (1856-1857 Directory of Biddeford and Saco). For a complete list of rolls/fiche numbers and contents of each, see the online FHL catalog page for this title. Under "Contains," click on a year to see details. See https://familysearch.org/search/catalog/530397.

1859. See "Pensioners Alive in 1859 (in Maine)" [Printed Article], in *Historical Magazine* (Henry B Dawson, Morrisania, NY), Vol. 8, No. 12 (Dec 1864).

1860. *Maine, 1860 Federal Census: Population Schedules* [Microfilm & Digital Capture], from the originals at the National Archives, Washington, DC. Filmed twice by the National Archives, 1950, 1967, 31 rolls, beginning with FHL film #803432 (2nd filming: Androscoggin Co). To access the digital images, see the online FHL catalog: https://familysearch.org/search/catalog/704928.

1860. *Maine 1860 Federal Census Index* [Printed Index), edited by Ronald Vern Jackson. Contents: Vol. 1: Cumberland Co; Vol. 2: Androscoggin Co – Kennebec Co (except Cumberland), Vol. 3: Lincoln Co – Penobscot Co; and Vol. 4, Sagadahoc Co – York Co. Publ. Accelerated Indexing Systems, 1991, FHL book 974.1 X22j 1860.

1860. *Maine 1860 Federal Census, Androscoggin County, Maine* [Microfilm], from the county's original manuscript, located at the Androscoggin County Building, Auburn, ME (1991). Contains census schedules for the towns of Leeds, Greene, Lewiston, Auburn, Danville, Durham, East Livermore, and Livermore. Includes population, mortality, agricultural, industrial, and social statistics schedules. This set was the original (county) copy, from which a (federal) copy was made and sent to Washington, DC. (The federal copy is the one that was digitized and indexed at FamilySearch.org, Ancestry.com, et al). In comparing any two "duplicate" sets, there are always copying errors, i.e., different spellings of names, different ages, places of birth, or missing names altogether. Filmed by the Genealogical Society of Utah, 1991, 1 roll, FHL film #1753452.

1860. See *1860 Federal Census, Waldo County, Maine* **[Microfilm Only],** from the county's original copy at the Waldo County Courthouse, Belfast, ME (1954). Organized by the towns of Belfast, Belmont, Morrill, Burnham, Knox, Freedom, Unity, Liberty, Searsmont, Lincolnville, Montville, Monroe, Brooks, Northport, Islesboro, Palermo, Prospect, Stockton, Swanville, Thorndike, Jackson, Troy, Waldo, Winterport, and Frankfort. This set was the original (county) copy, from which a (federal) copy was made and sent to Washington, DC. (The federal copy is the one that was digitized and indexed at FamilySearch.org, Ancestry.com, et al). In comparing any two "duplicate" sets, there are always copying errors, i.e., different spellings of names, different ages, places of birth, or missing names altogether. Filmed by the Genealogical Society of Utah, 1954, 2 rolls, FHL film #12410-12411.

1861. See *Maine at Work in 1861: A Directory to 17,000 Maine Residents and Their Occupations & Businesses* **[Printed Book],** by Robert Moseley Jackson, publ. Higginson Book Co, Salem MA, 1999, 334 pages, FHL book 974.1 E4j.

1861-1865. *Index to Compiled Service Records of Volunteer Union Soldiers Who Served in Organizations From the State of Maine* **[Microfilm & Online Database],** from originals at the National Archives, Washington, DC. Filmed by the National Archives, 1964, series M543, 23 rolls, beginning with FHL film #881847 (Index, A-Ba). For a complete list of roll numbers and contents of each roll, and access to the National online database, see the online FHL catalog page:
https://familysearch.org/search/catalog/293443.

1861-1865. *Military Records of the Civil War, Androscoggin Historical Society* **[Microfilm],** from the originals at the Androscoggin Historical Society, Auburn, Maine. Contains military discharge papers; newspaper clippings of soldiers, from the Lewiston journal; pension claims papers; letters from soldiers; regimental roster of the 15th Maine, June 1863; other

miscellaneous papers. Filmed by Genealogical Society of Utah, 1991, 1 roll, FHL film #1753680.

1861-1865. *Civil War Soldiers, Town of Peru, Oxford County, Maine* **[Online Database],** indexed at the RootsWeb site for Oxford Co ME. See **www.rootsweb.ancestry.com/~mecperu/civilwar.html.**

1861-1865. *Portland Soldiers and Sailors: A Brief Sketch of the Part They Took in the War of the Rebellion* **[Printed Book],** originally published by B. Thurston & Co, Portland, ME, 1884; reprinted by Heritage Books, Westminster, MD, 2005, 56 pages, FHL book 974.1191/P1 M2p.

1861-1915. *Maine, Knox County, Probate Estate Files* **[Online Database],** digitized at the FamilySearch.org website. From the original records at the Knox County Courthouse, Rockland, ME. This database has 58,109 records. See **https://familysearch.org/search/collection/1931808.**

1861-2012. *Penobscot County, Maine, Mount Hope Burial Index* **[Online Database],** indexed at the Ancestry.com website. The Mount Hope Cemetery is located at Bangor, Maine. The interment list shows over 28,000 burials. See **http://search.ancestry.com/search/db.aspx?dbid=9161.**

1862-1865. *Maine, Civil War Enlistment Papers* **[Online Database],** digitized and indexed at the FamilySearch.org website. Source: ME State Archives, Augusta. Each record includes a Name, Event type, Event date, Event place, Age, Birth year, and Birthplace. This database has 34,697 records. See **www.familysearch.org/search/collection/1881486.**

1862-1866 Internal Revenue Assessment Lists for Maine **[Microfilm & Digital Capture],** from the original records at the National Archives, Washington, DC, series M770, 15 rolls, beginning with FHL film #1534403 (District 1- 1864 lists). To access the digital images, see the online FHL catalog: **www.familysearch.org/search/catalog/577884.**

1863-1877. See *Aroostook County, Maine, Births, Marriages, Obituaries and Death Notices: Extracted from the Loyal Sunrise, 1863-1865, 1877, the Fort Fairfield Aurora 1875-1876, and the Presque Isle Sunrise 1876-1877* **[Printed Book],** transcribed by Linda J. Zapatka, publ. 2000, 60 pages, FHL book 974.11 B38z.

FORM.

CHECK LIST of the town of *Albany* in the County of *Oxford*

Names of Voters.	September 12, 1864.	November 8, 1864.
A ——— B ———	Voted	Voted
C ——— D ———	Voted	Absent
E ——— F ———	Absent	Voted
G ——— H ———	Absent	Absent
Calvin B Abbot	voted	voted
Luther M Albot	absent	voted
John Aspinwall	voted	voted
Edgar T Andrews	absent	voted
Luther Bisbee	voted	voted
Byron Bisbee	voted	voted
Enoch Bunker	voted	voted
Solomon I. Bunker	voted	voted
James M. Bunker	absent	voted
Ephraim H Bean	absent	absent
Andrew I. Bean	absent	voted
John C. Buckler	voted	absent
Isaac T. Buckler	voted	absent
George W. Buckler		

1864 Maine Poll List [Original Manuscripts & Digital Capture], for most towns/counties of Maine. According to the Maine State Archives, the 1864 Poll List is organized by town. The list includes all men who were eligible to vote and then indicates whether they voted or were absent on the two voting dates for that year. These documents were digitized by FamilySearch International in 2011. To access the digital images, see the online FHL catalog page: www.familysearch.org/search/catalog/1923493.

1864. See "**Voters List, Harmon, Penobscot County, Maine**" **[Printed Article]**, in *Harmon Roots News* (Kopy Eyes County, Waterville, ME), Vol. 1, No. 5 (Sep 1983).

1864-1866. *Civil War Tax Lists, Hancock County, Maine* **[Online Database]**, extracted name lists from the Hancock County towns of Brooklin, Brooksville, Castine, Deer Isle, Penobscot, and Sedgewick. Indexed at the RootsWeb site for Hancock Co ME: **www.rootsweb.ancestry.com/~mecpenob/taxes.html**.

1865. See "**Maine Natives in 1865 Census, Charlestown, MA**," **[Printed Article]**, in *Maine Genealogist* (Maine Genealogical Society, Farmington, ME), Vol. 15, No. 1 (Feb 1993).

1865. See "**1865 Census, Fourth school, Penobscot, Maine**" **[Printed Article]**, in *Mattanawcook Observer* (Alan H Hawkins, Null, ME), Vol. 2, No. 3-4 (Oct 1984).

1865-1866. See "**Births, Deaths, and Marriages, Penobscot County, Maine, 1865-1866**" **[Printed Article]**, in *Mattanawcook Observer* (Alan H Hawkins, Null, Me), Vol. 3 (1989).

1865-1900. *Maine, Aroostook County Deed Books* **[Online Database]**, digitized at the FamilySearch.org website. From the original records at the Aroostook County Courthouse, Houlton, ME. Includes Grantor and Grantee Indexes, and Deed Books for the Northern District and Southern District of Aroostook County. This database has 116,427 records. See **https://familysearch.org/search/collection/1447693**.

1866. See *Annual Report of the Adjutant General of the State of Maine: For the Year Ending December 31, 1866* **[Printed Book]**, by the Adjutant General, John L Hodsdon. Includes name lists of all Maine soldiers of the Civil War, organized by regiment. Publ. Stevens & Sayward, Augusta, ME, 1867, 588 pages, FHL book 974.103 M29hjl .

1866-1880. See "**Great Register, 1866-1880, Siskiyou County, California-People from Maine**" **[Printed Article]**, in *Pinecone and Tassel* (Deborah Roberge, Waterville, ME), Vol. 3, No. 6 (Mar 2006).

1866-1890. *Records of Soldiers Discharge, Lincoln County, Maine* **[Microfilm & Digital Capture]**, from the originals at the Lincoln County Courthouse,

Wiscasset, ME (1991). Filmed by the Genealogical Society of Utah, 1991, 1 roll, FHL film #1765239. To access the digital images, see the online FHL catalog page: **www.familysearch.org/search/catalog/580939**.

1866-1961. *Maine, Kennebec County, Togus National Cemetery Records* **[Online Database]**, digitized and indexed at FamilySearch.org, includes cemetery records for the Togus National Cemetery in Kennebec County, Maine. Digitized from microfilm held by the Maine State Archives, Augusta, ME. See **www.familysearch.org/search/collection/3246495**.

1867-1932. *Bath (Maine) City Directories* **[Microfilm]**, from various publishers. FHL has 1867-1868, 1871-1872, 1874, 1876-1877, 1880, 1883-1884, 1887, 1900-1902, 1905-1907, 1912, 1914, 1919-1920, 1922-1929, and 1931-1932. The directories may include Brunswick, Richmond, Arrowsic, Phipsburg, West Bath, Woolwich, and other surrounding areas. Filmed by Research Publications, Woodbridge, CT, 1980-1984, 6 rolls, beginning with FHL film #1930440 (1867-1868 Directory). For a complete list of rolls numbers and contents of each roll, see the online FHL catalog page for this title. See **https://familysearch.org/search/catalog/728759**.

1867-1935. **Augusta (Maine) City Directories** **[Microfilm]**, from various publishers. FHL has 1867-1868, 1871, 1873-1874, 1876-1877, 1880, 1882, 1886-1889, 1892-1895, 1897-1898, 1901-1902, 1909-1910, 1915-1920, 1923-1927, 1929, 1931, and 1933-1935. Filmed by Research Publications, Woodbridge, CT, 1980-1984, 1995, 7 rolls, beginning with FHL film #1844146 (1867-1868 directories). For a complete list of rolls numbers and contents of each roll, see the online FHL catalog page for this title. See **https://familysearch.org/search/catalog/721721**.

1870. *Maine, 1870 Federal Census: Population Schedules* **[Microfilm & Digital Capture]**, from the originals at the National Archives, Washington, DC. Film twice by the National Archives, 1962, 1968, 51 rolls, beginning with FHL film #552035 (2nd filming: Androscoggin Co). To access the digital images, see the online FHL catalog: **https://familysearch.org/search/catalog/698900**.

1870 Federal Census, Waldo County, Maine **[Microfilm only]**, from the county's original copy at the Waldo County Courthouse, Belfast, ME (1954).

Organized by the towns of Swanville, Prospect, Monroe, Searsport, Islesboro, Lincolnville, Northport, Thorndike, Jackson, Brooks, Knox, Belmont, Morrill, Waldo, Stockton, Burnham, Troy, Unity, Freedom, Montville, Liberty, Searsmont, and Palermo. This set was the original (county) copy, from which a (federal) copy was made and sent to Washington, DC. (The federal copy is the one that was digitized and indexed at FamilySearch.org, Ancestry.com, et al). In comparing any two "duplicate" sets, there are always copying errors, i.e., different spellings of names, different ages, places of birth, or missing names altogether. Filmed by the Genealogical Society of Utah, 1954, 2 rolls, FHL film #12412-12413.

1870. *Maine 1870 Census Index* **[Printed Index],** edited by Raeone Christensen Steuart, publ. Heritage Quest, Bountiful, UT, 2000, 2 vols., FHL book 974.1 X22m.

1871. See **"Non-resident Taxpayers, Dayton, York County, Maine" [Printed Article]**, in *Genealogist's Post* (Richard T Williams, Danboro, PA), Vol. 4, No. 8 (Aug 1967).

1879. See **"1879 Tax List, Farmingdale, Kennebec County, Maine" [Printed Article]**, in *Living Tree News* (Harris County Genealogical Society, Pasadena, TX), Vol. 2, No. 3 (Spring 1976) and Vol. 2, No. 4 (Summer 1976).

1880. *Maine, 1880 Federal Census: Soundex and Population Schedules* **[Microfilm & Digital Capture],** from the originals at the National Archives, Washington, DC (ca1985). After filming, the originals were transferred to the Maine Division of Vital Statistics, Augusta, ME. Filmed on 47 rolls, beginning with FHL film #447186 (1880 Soundex: A000 thru B242); and FHL film #1254475 (1880 Population Schedules: Androscoggin Co). To access the digital images (Population Schedules, see the online FHL catalog: **https://familysearch.org/search/catalog/673562.**

1880 Federal Census (Short Form), Androscoggin County, Maine **[Microfilm & Digital Capture]**, from the county's original volumes of the 1880 name list, located at the Androscoggin County Courthouse, Auburn, ME (1956). Filmed by the Genealogical Society of Utah, 1956,1991, 3 rolls, as follows:
- Towns of Auburn, Durham, East Livermore, Greene, Leeds, Lewiston, Lisbon, Livermore, Minot, Turner, Wales, and Webster. FHL film #10521. (1956 filming)
- Towns of Auburn, Durham, East Livermore, Greene, Leeds, Lisbon, Minot, Poland, Turner, Wales, Webster, Lewiston (ward 5 A-B). FHL film #1753452 (1991 filming)

- Town of Lewiston (ward 5, B-Z). FHL film #1753453 (1991 filming)
To access the digital images of certain rolls, see the online FHL catalog: **www.familysearch.org/search/catalog/571052.**

1880 Federal Census (Short Form), Kennebec County, Maine **[Microfilm & Digital Capture]**, from the county's original volumes of the 1880 name list, located at the Kennebec County Courthouse, Augusta, ME (1987). See the 1880 note for information. Filmed by the Genealogical Society of Utah, 1987, 2 rolls, FHL film #11316 (Surnames A-R) and FHL film #11317 (Surnames S-Z). To access the digital images, see the Online FHL catalog page: **www.familysearch.org/search/catalog/233154.**

1880 Federal Census (Short Form), Waldo County, Maine **[Microfilm & Digital Capture]**, from the county's original volumes of the 1880 name list, located at the Waldo County Courthouse, Belfast, ME (1954). Organized by the towns of Belfast, Belmont, Brooks, Burnham, Freedom, Frankfort, Islesboro, Jackson, Knox, Liberty, Lincolnville, Morrill, Montville, Monroe, Northport, Prospect, Palermo, Searsmont, Searsport, Stockton, Swanville, Thorndike, Troy, Unity, Waldo, and Winterport. Filmed by the Genealogical Society of Utah, 1954, 1 roll, FHL film #12414. To access the digital images, see the Online FHL catalog page: **www.familysearch.org/search/catalog/90941.**

✓ **1880 NOTE.** The 1880 "Short Form" was a county copy of the 1880 federal census. The full schedules were transferred to the Census Bureau in Washington, DC. The 1880 "Short Form" was retained at the county courthouse in every county of the U.S. Extant manuscripts of the county copies are very rare. The Short Form name list is not by family, but as an index to the full schedules with all names arranged by the first letter of their surname. By law, the Short Form was to remain at a county courthouse for one month after the 1880 census was taken, allowing for public inspection of the data. The data was brief, including just a person's name, color, age, and sex. Only in 1880 did the Census Bureau ask for a county copy to be made that was different than the full schedules.

1882. See *Directory of the City of Portland: And of the Towns of Cape Elizabeth, Deering, Westbrook and Falmouth for A.D. 1882; Being the 250th Anniversary of the Settlement of Those Towns Which Comprise the Territory of "Ancient Falmouth,"* **[Microfilm]**, from the original book prepared and published by John T. Hull. Reprinted 1974, W.C. Cox, Tucson, AZ, 1 roll, FHL film #1000781.

1883-1935. *Lewiston and Auburn (Maine) City Directories* **[Microfilm],** from the originals by various publishers. This series includes directories for Lewiston, Auburn, Lisbon, Mechanic Falls, and Turner, Androscoggin County, Maine. Filmed by Research Publications, Woodbridge, CT, 1995, 4 rolls, beginning with FHL film #2156616 (1883 Lewiston and Auburn Directory). For a complete list of roll numbers and contents of each roll, see the online FHL catalog page for this title. See https://familysearch.org/search/catalog/984094.

1885-1934. *Waterville (Maine) City Directories* **[Microfilm],** from various publishers. The FHL has 1885, 1887, 1891-1892, 1925-1926, 1927, 1929, 1931, 1932, and 1934. Filmed by Research Publications, Woodbridge, CT, 1995, 9 rolls, beginning with FHL film #2258186 (1885 Directory). For a complete list of roll numbers and contents of each roll, see the online FHL catalog page for this title. See https://familysearch.org/search/catalog/1026651.

1888. *Warren History: Census, History, Statistics, Business Directory, Etc., Etc.* **[Printed Book & Digital Version],** originally published by Union Publishing Co., Union, ME, 1888, 44 pages. For access to a digital version of this book, see the online FHL catalog page for this title, see https://familysearch.org/search/catalog/2106851.

1890 Maine Census Index of Civil War Veterans or Their Widows **[Printed Index],** compiled by Bryan Lee Dilts, Publ. Index Publishing, Salt Lake City, UT, 1984, 156 pages, FHL book 974.1 X22d.

1890-1899. *Information From an Old Ledger in the Farmington (Franklin County, Maine) Town Office* **[Online Database],** includes petitions, licenses, reburials, business licenses, etc., and includes names of all persons involved listed at the RootsWeb site for Franklin Co ME. See www.rootsweb.ancestry.com/~mefrankl/miscledger.htm

1891 History. See *History of Androscoggin County, Maine* **[Microfilm & Digital Capture],** from the original book edited by Georgia Drew Merrill, publ. W.A. Fergusson, Boston, 1891, 879 pages. Book and separate index filmed by the Genealogical Society of Utah, 1976, 1 roll, FHL film #908964. For access to a digital version of this book, see the online FHL catalog page for this title. See https://familysearch.org/search/catalog/183142.

- See also, *Index to Georgia Drew Merrill's History of Androscoggin County* **[Printed Index & Microfilm],** by volunteers of the Genealogical Society, LDS Church, 1975, 187 pages, FHL book 974.182 H2m index. Also on microfilm, FHL film #908964.

1891-1892 Directory, Wales, Androscoggin County, Maine [Online Database], indexed at the RootsWeb website. See www.rootsweb.ancestry.com/~mecwales/directory1891-1892.html.

1892. See **"Voter List, Easton, Aroostook County, Maine" [Printed Article]**, in *Downeast Ancestry* (Biddeford, ME), Vol. 3, No. 1 (Jun 1979).

1892. See **"Great Register, 1892, Siskiyou County, California–People from Maine" [Printed Article],** in *Pinecone and Tassel* (Deborah Roberge, Waterville, ME), Vol. 3, No. 6 (Mar 2006).

1892-1996. See *Maine, Marriage Index, 1892-1966, 1977-1996* **[Online Database],** indexed at the FamilySearch.org website, a name index from the Maine State Archives. This database has 1,714,258 records. See https://familysearch.org/search/collection/2077670.
- Another version of this database is at the Ancestry.com website. See http://search.ancestry.com/search/db.aspx?dbid=6904.

1892-1954. *Vital Records, Town of Upton, Oxford County, Maine* **[Online Database],** includes birth records, death records, marriage intentions by groom, marriage intentions by bride, marriages by bride, and marriages by groom. Indexed at the RootsWeb site for Oxford Co ME. See www.rootsweb.ancestry.com/~mecupton/VR/vr_index.htm.

1892-1996. *Maine, Marriage Index* **[Online Database],** indexed at the Ancestry.com website. This database is an index to Maine marriages that occurred between 1892 and 1996. However, it excludes the years 1967-1976. Information provided in the index includes bride's name, bride's town and state of residence, groom's name, groom's town and state of residence, date of marriage, and marriage certificate number, if known. This database has 1,714,258 records. See https://search.ancestry.com/search/db.aspx?dbid=6904.

1892-2000s. *Death Records, Town of Andover, Oxford County, Maine* **[Online Database],** indexed at the AndoverMaine.com website. See www.andovermaine.com/deathstoc.html.

1893-1954. See *Passenger Lists of Vessels Arriving at Portland, Maine, 1893-1943; Index, 1893-1954* **[Microfilm & Digital Capture],** from the originals at the National Archives, Washington, DC. The index includes all individuals on the passenger lists, with an indication of head of household, age, sex, name of ship, date of arrival, page and line numbers. Filmed by the National Archives, 1944, 1986, series T524, 36 rolls, beginning with FHL film #1412619 (Index, 1893-1954. To access the digital images, see the online FHL catalog page: https://familysearch.org/search/catalog/341267.

1894-1925. *Androscoggin County (Maine) Directories* **[Microfilm],** from the originals by various publishers. This series includes Auburn, Lewiston, East Livermore, Livermore, Durham, Greene, Leeds, Lisbon, Mechanic Falls, Minot, Poland, Turner, and Wales, Androscoggin County, Maine. Filmed by Research Publications, Woodbridge, CT, 1990, 8 rolls, as follows:

- 1894-1895 & 1896-1897, FHL film #2156607
- 1898-1899 & 1900-1901, FHL film #2156608
- 1902-1903 & 1904-1905, FHL film #2308913
- 1906-1906 & 1908-1909, FHL film #2308914
- 1910-1911 & 1912-1913, FHL film #2308915
- 1914-1915 & 1916-1917, FHL film #2308916
- 1918-1919 & 1920-1921, FHL film #2308917
- 1922-1923 & 1924-1925, FHL film #2308918

For a complete list of roll numbers and contents (cities, towns) on each roll, see the online FHL catalog page for this title See https://familysearch.org/search/catalog/983961.

1894-1962. *Maine, Passenger Lists* **[Online Database],** indexed at the Ancestry.com website. Original data: Selected Passenger Lists, Crew Lists and Manifests. National Archives, Washington, DC. These passenger and crew lists from both ships and aircraft were recorded on a variety of forms that were then turned over to the Immigration and Naturalization Service. Details requested on the forms varied, but they typically include the name of the vessel and arrival date, ports of departure and arrival (as well as future destinations on a ship's itinerary), dates of departure and arrival, shipmaster, full name, age, gender, physical description, military rank (if any), occupation, birthplace, citizen of what country,

and residence. For military transports, you may find the next of kin, relationships, and address listed as well. Later manifests may include visa or passport numbers. This database has 17,086 records. See http://search.ancestry.com/search/db.aspx?dbid=9033.

1895-1942. *Directory of Portland: Including the City of South Portland and the Town of Cape Elizabeth* **[Printed Books & Microfilm],** publ. Portland Directory Company, Portland, ME. FHL has: 1895, 1912 (also on film), 1939 (film only), 1940, 1941 (film only), and 1942. See FHL book 974.1.191/Ps E4d (year). The 1912, 1939, and 1942 directories were filmed by the Genealogical Society of Utah, 2 rolls, FHL film #1415259 (1912 & 1939 Portland directories); and FHL film #1697769 (1941 Portland directory).

1897-1944. *Births From Town of Standish, Cumberland County, Maine* **[Online Database],** from annual town reports, indexed at the USGenWeb site for Cumberland Co ME. See http://files.usgwarchives.net/me/cumberland/standish/birth.txt.

1897-1947. *Record of Deaths, Town of Gray, Cumberland County, Maine* **[Online Database],** indexed at the USGenWeb site for Cumberland Co ME. See http://files.usgwarchives.net/me/cumberland/gray/townreport/deaths/grayvr.txt.

1899-1917. *Vital Records of Hancock County, Maine* **[Typescript, Microfilm & Digital Capture],** compiled by Linnie L Howard. Contains various records of births, marriages, deaths, obituaries for the approximate years of 1899 to 1917. Typed by the Genealogical Society of Utah, 1949, 112 pages, FHL book 974.145 V2h. Also on microfilm, FHL film #855272. To access the digital images, see the online FHL catalog: www.familysearch.org/search/catalog/279279.

1900. *Maine, 1900 Federal Census: Soundex and Population Schedules* **[Microfilm & Digital Capture],** from the originals held by the Bureau of the Census in the 1940s. After microfilming, Congress allowed the Census Bureau to destroy the originals to free up space for WWII-related files. Filmed on 97 rolls, beginning with FHL film #1244397 (Soundex: A000 thru A430); and FHL film #1240587 (Population Schedules: Androscoggin Co). To access the digital images, see the online FHL catalog: https://familysearch.org/search/catalog/655732.

1900. *Maine 1900 Census Index* **[Printed Index],** compiled and published by Heritage Quest, North Salt Lake, UT, 2 vols., 1,442 pages, FHL book 974.1 X22m.

1900. See **"City Directory, 1900, Biddeford, York County, Maine" [Printed Article],** in *Maine's Franco-American Heritage* (Franco-American Genealogical Society, Biddeford, ME), Vol. 7 (Nov 1990).

1900. See **"City Directory, 1900, Presque Isle, Aroostook County, Maine" [Printed Article],** in *Connecticut Maple Leaf* (French-Canadian Genealogical Society of Connecticut, Tolland, CT), Vol. 5, No. 2 (Winter 1991).

1900. See **"City Directory, 1900, Fort Fairfield, Aroostook County, Maine" [Printed Article],** in *Connecticut Maple Leaf* (French-Canadian Genealogical Society of Connecticut, Tolland, CT), Vol. 5, No. 2 (Winter 1991).

1902-1934. *Westbrook (Maine) City Directories* **[Microfilm],** from various original publishers. The FHL has 1902-1905, 1909-1910, 1915-1916, 1919, 1921, 1923-1926, 1928, 1930, and 1934. Some directory years include the towns of Gorham and Windham. Filmed by Research Publications, Woodbridge, CT, 1980-1984, 12 rolls, beginning with FHL film #1841751 (1902-1903 directory). For a complete list of roll numbers and contents of each roll, see the online FHL catalog page for this title. See **https://familysearch.org/search/catalog/741863.**

1903. See **"Voters List, 1903, Waterboro, York County, Maine" [Printed Article],** in *York County Genealogical Society Journal* (YCGS, Eliot, ME), Vol. 20, No. 3 (Jul 2005).

1903-1924. *Kennebec County (Maine) Directories* **[Microfilm],** from various publishers. FHL has directories for Augusta, Gardiner, Hallowell, and Waterville. Directory years 1903-1904, 1905-1906, 1907-1908, 1909-1910, 1911-1912, 1913-1914, 1915-1916, 1917-1918, 1919-1920, 1921-1922, and 1923-1924. Filmed by Research Publications, Woodbridge, CT, 1995, 6 rolls, beginning with FHL film #2308928 (1903-1904 and 1905-1906 Directories). For a complete list of roll numbers and contents of each roll, see the online FHL catalog page for this title. See **https://familysearch.org/search/catalog/1045033.**

*1904 Census, Town of Winslow, North Vassalboro P.O., Kennebec County, Main*e **[Online Database],** indexed at the USGenWeb site for Kennebec Co ME: **http://files.usgwarchives.net/me/kennebec/winslow/register/nvassalboro/nvfile1.txt.**

*1904 Census, Town of Winslow, Waterville P.O., Kennebec County, Main*e **[Online Database],** indexed at the USGenWeb site for Kennebec Co ME: **http://files.usgwarchives.net/me/kennebec/waterville/register/c1904r1.txt.**

*1904 Census, Town of Winslow, Winslow P.O., Kennebec County, Main*e **[Online Database],** indexed at the USGenWeb site for Kennebec Co ME: **http://files.usgwarchives.net/me/kennebec/winslow/register/p54to63.txt.**

1905. See **"Census, Town of Lincoln, Penobscot County, Maine" [Printed Article],** in *Mattanawcook Observer* (Alan H Hawkins, Null, ME) Vol. 2, No. 3-4 (Oct 1984).

1905. See **"Births, Marriages, Deaths, Hiram, Oxford County, Maine, 1905" [Printed Article],** in *Pinecone and Tassel* (Deborah Roberge, Waterville, ME), Vol. 5, No. 4 (Nov 2007).

1905-1906 Aroostook County (Maine) Directories **[Microfilm],** from the original records published by Newton Journal Publishing Co. Includes directory listings for Ashland, Blaine, Caribou, Fort Fairfield, Fort Kent, Houlton, Island Falls, Limestone, Mars Hill, New Sweden, Presque Isle, Van Buren, and Washburn, Aroostook County, Maine. See FHL film #2310324.

1906 Saco Register, with Old Orchard (York County) **[Printed Book],** compiled by Mitchell, Daggett, Holt, Lawton, and Sawyer. Published Brunswick, Maine, 1906. FHL book 974.195/S1 H2.

1906. *Town Register: Waterford, Albany, Greenwood, E. Stoneham, Oxford County, Maine* **[Printed Book],** compiled by Mitchell and Davis, publ. H.E. Mitchell Co, Brunswick, ME, 1906, 136 pages, FHL book 974.175 H2m.

1906-1929. *Maine, Naturalization Records* **[Online Database],** indexed at the Ancestry.com website. Original data: Naturalization Petitions of the United States District Court, Portland, Maine, 1912-1929. Part of the 1787-1952 series. See **http://search.ancestry.com/search/db.aspx?dbid=2899.**

1907. *Directory: Greenville and Lily Bay, Piscataquis County, Maine* [Online Database], indexed at the USGenWeb site for Piscataquis Co ME. See http://files.usgwarchives.net/me/piscataquis/greenville/directory/1907/pcd1907.txt.

1907-1930. *Book Indexes, Portland, Maine, Passenger Lists* [Microfilm & Digital Capture], from the originals at the National Archives, Washington, DC. Filmed by the National Archives, 1944, series T793, 12 rolls, beginning with FHL film #1375989 (1907-1910). To access the digital images, see the online FHL catalog page: https://familysearch.org/search/catalog/341129.

1910. *Maine, 1910 Federal Census: Population Schedules* [Microfilm & Digital Capture], from originals held by the Bureau of the Census in the 1940s. After microfilming, Congress allowed the Census Bureau to destroy the originals to free up space for WWII-related files. Filmed on 13 rolls, beginning with FHL film #1374549 (Androscoggin Co). To access the digital images, see the online FHL catalog: https://familysearch.org/search/catalog/637199.

1910. *Register of the Towns of Sedgwick, Brooklin, Deer Isle, Stonington (Hancock County) and Isle au Haut (Knox County), 1910* [Printed Book], compiled by Chatto and Turn, publ. Lawton Register Co, Auburn, ME, 1910, 245 pages, FHL book 974.145 H2r. Also on microfilm, see FHL film #1033879.

1913-1935. *Sanford (Maine) City Directories* [Microfilm], from various publishers. Directories may include Springvale and Alfred. FHL has 1913-1927, 1932, and 1935. Filmed by Research Publications, Woodbridge, CT, 2 rolls, FHL film #2308939-2308940.

1914-1950. *Maine, State Archives, World War I (WWI) Grave Cards* [Online Database], digitized and indexed at FamilySearch.org. This is a card index of WWI soldiers from the ME State Archives, see www.familysearch.org/search/collection/2968248.

1915. See **Voter List, 1915, Medford, Piscataquis County, Maine"** [Printed Article], in *Tri-City Genealogical Society Bulletin* (Richland, WA), Vol. 19, No. 1 (Jan 1979).

1915-1928. *Oxford County (Maine) Directories* [Microfilm], from various publishers. Directories may include the following: Albany, Andover, Bethel, Buckfield, Canton, Dixfield, Greenwood, Hartford, Hebron, Mexico, Newry, Norway, Oxford, Paris, Peru, Roxbury, Rumford, Sumner, Waterford, and Woodstock. FHL has directories for 1915, 1916-1917, 1918-1919, 1920-1921, 1922-1923, 1925-1926, and 1927-1928. Filmed by Primary Source Microfilm, Woodbridge, CT, 2 rolls, FHL film #2308936 (1915-1921 Directories) and FHL film #238937 (1922-1928 Directories).

1917. *To The Voters of Franklin County,* [Online Database], a list of names (from a newspaper ad?) with "We, the undersigned, women of voting age, respectfully petition you to vote in favor of Woman Suffrage at the Special Election September 10, 1917." The names are listed by the towns of Avon, Carthage, Chesterville, Farmington, Freeman, Industry, Jay, Kingfield, Madrid, New Sharon, New Vineyard, Phillips, Rangeley, Salem, Strong, Temple, Weld, and Wilton. Listed at the RootsWeb site for Franklin Co ME. See www.rootsweb.ancestry.com/~mefrankl/sufraglist.htm.

1917-1918. *Maine, World War I Selective Service System Draft Registration Cards* [Microfilm & Digital Capture], from the originals at the National Archives, Washington, DC. Filmed by the National Archives, 1987-1988, 29 rolls, beginning with FHL film #1653898 (Maine: Androscoggin Co, A-Pinard). To access the digital images, see the online FHL catalog: https://familysearch.org/search/catalog/747005.

1917-1919. *Maine, World War I Draft Registration Index* [Online Database], indexed at the FamilySearch.org website. This is a card index to draft registrations in Maine during World War I acquired from the Maine State Archives. The index includes Name, Age, Marital status, Residence, Place of birth, Date of birth, Nationality, Race, Occupation, Local board, and the name of a Relative, relationship and address. This database has 162,613 records. See www.familysearch.org/search/collection/1807269.

1917-1919. *Roster of Maine in the Military Service of the United States and Allies in the World War* **[Printed Book],** by the Adjutant General of Maine, publ. Augusta, ME, 1929, 2 vols: Vol. 1: Army, A-M; Vol. 2: Army N-Z, Army Nurse Corps, Navy Nurse Corps and Yeomen, Navy, Marine Corps, and Coast Guard. See FHL book 974.1 M2ma v.1-2. Also on microfilm, FHL film #1036025 (Vol. 1) and FHL film #1036049 (Vol. 2).

1917-1920. *Maine, Military Index* **[Online Database],** indexed at the Ancestry.com website. Source: Ancestry's digital copy of *Roster of Maine in the Military Service of the United States...* Each record includes a Name, Birth Date, Military Roster, Residence Place, and Comments. This database has 36,325 records. See https://search.ancestry.com/search/db.aspx?dbid=4619.

1918-1991. *Maine, United States Naturalization Records* **[Online Database],** digitized and indexed at the FamilySearch.org website. Source: National Archives microfilm of the district courts of Maine. Each records includes a Name, Event type, Event place, Relationship to head of household, Birthdate, and Affiliate record identifier. This database has 6,762 records. See www.familysearch.org/search/collection/2613134.

1920. *Maine, 1920 Federal Census: Soundex and Population Schedules* **[Microfilm & Digital Capture],** from the originals held by the Bureau of the Census in the 1940s. After microfilming, Congress allowed the Census Bureau to destroy the originals to free up space for WWII-related files. Filmed on 82 rolls, beginning with FHL film #1825655 (Soundex: A000 thru A450); and FHL film #1820637 (Population Schedules: Androscoggin Co). To access the digital images, see the online FHL catalog: https://familysearch.org/search/catalog/571885.

1922 History. See *History of Aroostook* **[Printed Book],** by Edward Wiggin, publ. Star-Herald Press, Presque Isle, ME, 1922, 428 pages, FHL book 974.11 H2w. Indexed in *Index to Hon. Edward Wiggin's History of Aroostook* **[Printed Book],** by volunteer workers of the Genealogical Society, LDS Church, 1975, 31 pages, FHL book 974.11 H2w index.

1926. *Franklin County (Maine) Directories* **[Microfilm],** from Strout's Franklin County Directory, publ. by Franklin M Strout. FHL film #2310324.

1926-1927. *Brief Biographies, Maine: A Biographical Dictionary of Who's Who in Maine, Vol. 1* **[Microfilm],** from an original book edited and compiled by Theodore Roosevelt Hodgkins, publ. Lewiston Journal, Lewiston, ME, 1926-1927, 284 pages. Filmed for the FHL by the Library of Congress, Photoduplication Service, Washington, DC, 1989, FHL film #1654724.

1927-1930. *Knox County (Maine) Directories* **[Microfilm],** by various publishers. FHL has 1927 directory and 1929-1930 directory. Contains the following locations: Rockland, Rockport, Camden, Thomaston, Appleton, Cushing, Friendship, Hope, Isle Au Haut, North Haven, Owl's Head, St. George, South Thomaston, Union, Vinalhaven, Warren, Washington, Criehaven Plantation and Matinicus Isle Plantation. Filmed by Research Publications, Woodbridge, CT, 1990, 1 roll, FHL film #2310453.

1930. *Maine, 1930 Federal Census: Population Schedules* **[Microfilm & Digital Capture],** from originals held by the Bureau of the Census in the 1940s. After microfilming, Congress allowed the Census Bureau to destroy the originals to free up space for WWII-related files. Filmed on 16 rolls, beginning with FHL film #2340562 (Androscoggin Co). To access the digital images, see the online FHL catalog: https://familysearch.org/search/catalog/1036356.

1930. *Directory of Bangor, Brewer, Hampden, Old Town, Orono and Veazie: Combining Five Separate and Distinct Directories* **[Printed Book],** compiled and published by Fred L Tower Companies, 1930, Portland, ME, 780 pages, FHL book 974.13 E4.

1931. *Manning's Waterville, Skowhegan, Fairfield, Oakland and Winslow, Maine, Directory: Containing General Directories of Citizens, Classified Business Directories, Street Directories, Record of the City and Village Governments, Society, Churches...* **[Printed Book],** compiled and published by H.A. Manning Company, Springfield, MA, 1931, 583 pages, FHL book 974.1 E4.

1932-1965 Vital Records, Town of Lebanon, York County, Maine **[Online Database],** links by year are noted at the USGenWeb site for Lebanon, ME. Archived at https://web.archive.org/web/20150608215327/http://www.raynorshyn.com/megenweb/york/lebanon.

1934. *Mt. Vernon, Kennebec County, Maine Town officers & Taxpayers List* [Online Database], indexed at the RootsWeb site for Kennebec Co ME: www.rootsweb.ancestry.com/~mecreadf/mtvn1934.htm.

1940. *Maine, 1940 Federal Census: Population Schedules* [Digital Capture], from the original records held by the Bureau of the Census in the 1940s. After microfilming, Congress allowed the Census Bureau to destroy the originals to free up space for WWII-related files. Filmed on 29 rolls, beginning with FHL film #5462013 (Androscoggin Co). The Family History Library (FHL) has the microfilm archived at their Granite Mountain Record Vault. They are not available for viewing but the entire digital collection is available online at several sites (noted at the National Name Lists chapter). To access the digital images, see the online FHL catalog: https://familysearch.org/search/catalog/2057759.

1941-1945. *Deaths of World War II Veterans of Maine* [Microfilm & Digital Capture], from the originals at the Vital Statistics Office, Augusta, ME. Filmed by the Genealogical Society of Utah, 1954, 1 roll, FHL film #10216. To access the digital images, see the online FHL catalog page: www.familysearch.org/search/catalog/292609.

1943-1944. *Service Roll, Town of Lebanon, York County, Maine* [Online Database], includes alpha lists for Army, Navy, Waves, Wacs, and Merchant Marines. Indexed at the USGenWeb site for York Co ME. Archived at https://web.archive.org/web/20150608211907/http://www.raynorshyn.com/megenweb/york/lebanon/ServiceRoll1944.htm.

1947-1954. *Maine, Crew Lists Arriving at Robbinston* [Online Database], indexed at the FamilySearch.org website. Source: National Archives microfilm A3424. This collection contains Crew Lists of Vessels Arriving at Robbinston, Maine, August 1947-June 1954. The records are in chronological order and usually contain Name, Citizenship, Position in crew, Identification number, Discharge information, and details about the medical examination. This database has 3,025 records. See www.familysearch.org/search/collection/2427242.

1949-1958. *Maine, Crew List Arriving at Eastport* [Online Database], indexed at the FamilySearch.org website. Source: National Archives microfilm A3457. This collection contains crew lists for vessels arriving at Eastport, Maine from 1949-1958. The crew members were primarily U.S. or Canadian citizens. The records usually contain particulars about the vessel and the following personal information about the crew members: Full Name, Citizenship, Position, etc. This database has 4,774 records. See www.familysearch.org/search/collection/2426337.

1960-1996. *Maine, Death Index* [Online Database], indexed at the FamilySearch.org website, a name index from the Maine State Archives. This database has 401,960 records. See https://familysearch.org/search/collection/2046945.
- This database (thru 1997) is available from Ancestry.com: http://search.ancestry.com/search/db.aspx?dbid=6703.

1992 - Current. See *Maine Recent Newspaper Obituaries)* [Online Database], digitized and indexed newspaper obituaries at the GenealogyBank website, including newspapers from these cities: Augusta, Bangor, Biddleford, Biddleford/Saco, Brunswick, Kennebunk, Lewiston, Madawaska, Portland, Sanford, Scarborough. South Portland/Cape Elizabeth, and Waterville. See www.genealogybank.com/gbnk/obituaries/explore/USA/Maine.

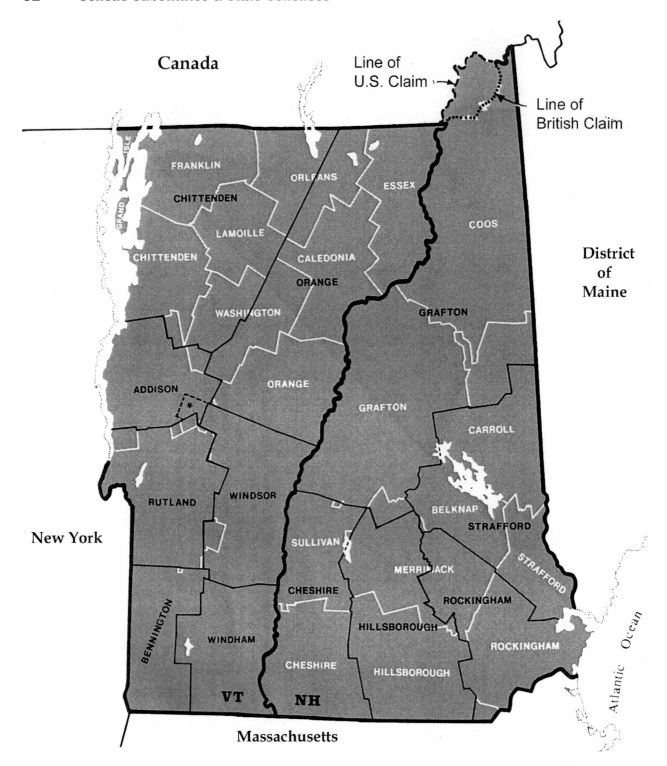

Vermont & New Hampshire ● **1790.** The current counties of both states are shown in white. Shown in black are the counties at the time of the 1790 Federal Census. As one of the original thirteen states, New Hampshire was included in the first census with a census day of 2 Aug 1790, and nine months to complete the door-to-door enumeration. But in August 1790, Vermont was still claimed by both New Hampshire and New York until the U.S. Congress arbitrated the dispute and made Vermont the 14th state on 4 March 1791. By a special Act of Congress, the new state of Vermont was then included in the 1790 census, and with its own census day of 4 April 1791. Another dispute at the time was over the northern border areas of New Hampshire and Maine with British Canada. That dispute was not resolved until the Webster-Ashburton Treaty of 1842.

New Hampshire
Censuses & Substitute Name Lists

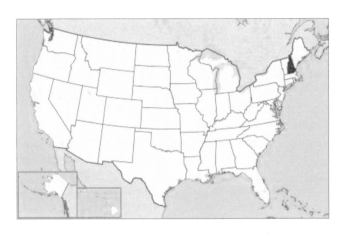

Historical Timeline
of New Hampshire, 1603-1791

1603. English Captain Martin Pring led an expedition to present Maine, New Hampshire, and Massachusetts. He was the first European to ascend the Piscataquis River and was the first to erect a small fort on Cape Cod (now Truro, MA).

1606. Two joint stock companies were founded in 1606, both with royal charters issued by King James I for the purpose of establishing colonies in North America. The Virginia Company of London was given a land grant between Latitude 34° (Cape Fear) and Latitude 41° (Long Island Sound). The Virginia Company of Plymouth was founded with a similar charter, between Latitude 38° (Potomac River) and Latitude 45° (St. John River), which included a shared area with the London Company between Latitude 38° and 41°..

1620. Plymouth Colony. A new Royal Charter was issued by King James I to the Plymouth Council for New England (formerly the Virginia Company of Plymouth) to establish colonial settlements in New England. The area was from Latitude 40° to Latitude 45° ("sea to sea"). In that same year, the *Mayflower* dropped anchor off Cape Cod, and Plymouth Colony was founded by a small group of Separatists/Pilgrims, who had fled England for Holland a few years earlier.

1622. Province of Maine. In 1622, the Plymouth Council of New England granted rights of lands to Sir Ferdinando Gorges and Captain John Mason. The lands were between the Merrimack and Kennebec rivers, an area which included parts of present New Hampshire and Maine. Gorges was the first to use the name Maine to describe the area.

1623. New Hampshire. Dover, the first permanent settlement in present New Hampshire was founded.

1625. England. Charles I became King of England, Scotland, and Ireland. Soon after taking office, Charles began to note a large number of non-conformists among his subjects. Along with his Archbishop, William Laud, the King began a campaign to purge his church of the largest group of non-conformists, the so-called "Puritans," a militant Calvinist religious group attempting to purify the Church of England. Unfortunately, Charles I took on a job that led to civil war in England as well as the loss of his head. But, his campaign can be credited as the cause for the founding of English settlements in New England.

1628. The **Massachusetts Bay Company** was granted a royal charter for an English colony to be established in North America within the bounds of the Plymouth Council of New England. It is said that King Charles I was misled as to the religious leanings of the Massachusetts Bay Company leaders, all prominent Puritans, not Pilgrims, as he had surmised. The language of the Royal Charter essentially removed the Plymouth Council from the picture, and the Massachusetts Bay Company managed to acquire legal interest in the area from Latitude 41° to Latitude 45°, except for any previous grants in the same area.

1629. Sir Ferdinando Gorges and Captain John Mason agreed to split their grants at the Piscataqua River, with Mason retaining the land west of the river as the Province of New Hampshire.

1629. The Great Migration to New England Begins. As a result of the Charles I campaign to purge non-conformists from the Church of England, large groups of people were disenfranchised. Charles I disbanded Parliament and ruled England alone for eleven years. The Puritans referred to this era as "the eleven years of tyranny." It was during these eleven years that 80,000 Puritans felt compelled to leave England. About a fourth of them moved to Holland, a fourth of them to Ireland, mostly around County Dublin; another fourth to the West Indies, particularly the islands of Barbados, Nevis, and St. Kitts; and the final group, some 21,000 Puritan immigrants, were to establish the Massachusetts Bay Colony of North America.

1629. New Hampshire. John Mason received a grant of that portion of the Province of Maine which lay between the Merrimac and the Piscataqua River, under the name of New Hampshire.

1641. New Hampshire. The Massachusetts Bay Colony gained control of the New Hampshire settlements.

1642. The English Civil War Begins. Since taking the throne in 1625, King Charles I had purged most of the Puritans from the Church of England. To deal with a Parliament opposing his every move, in 1629, Charles disbanded Parliament and ruled England on his own. That action canceled over 400 years of liberties gained by Parliament since the Magna Carta. When Parliament was restored in 1640, it quickly became dominated by the same Puritans who Charles had removed from the Church of England. Beginning in 1642, Royalist supporters were forced to fight the armies of the Puritan Parliament in the English Civil War. The Great Migration to New England ended about this time.

1645-1651. England. After his defeat and capture in 1645, Charles I refused to accept his captors' demands for a constitutional monarchy, and briefly escaped captivity in 1647. While recaptured, his son, Prince Charles, was able to marshal Scottish forces for the king. However, by 1648, Oliver Cromwell had consolidated the English opposition. King Charles I was tried, convicted, and executed for high treason in January 1649. The Civil War continued until 1651, when Oliver Cromwell, a Puritan, became Lord Protectorate, ruling the Commonwealth of England for the next seven years.

1660. England. Charles II was restored to the throne as King of England, Scotland, and Ireland. In 1649, the Scots had proclaimed Charles the king of Scotland. But the Puritan leader Oliver Cromwell defeated his army in 1651, and Charles fled to France. After Cromwell died in 1658, the English people became increasingly dissatisfied with the government that Cromwell had established. In 1660, Parliament invited Charles to return and declared him king. He ruled until his death in 1685, and during his 25-year reign, the English colonies forced out the remaining pockets of Atlantic settlements made earlier by the Dutch, Swedes, Danes and French. Charles II saw the colonies as a source of trade and commerce, supported development, and granted several more charters for settlement (including one to William Penn in 1681). All of the English colonies thrived as a result. He was the first monarch to recognize the potential for the North American colonies to become a contiguous, viable commonwealth. He encouraged the development of post roads, and a regular communication between the Governors. Charles II was responsible for setting the tone of self-government, religious tolerance, and individual freedoms in the English colonies that were to become American institutions.

1679. New Hampshire. The English Crown formed New Hampshire as a separate royal colony.

1686. Dominion of New England. After Charles II died without issue in 1685, his brother, the Duke of York, was crowned King of England as James II. As the original Royal Charter holder of the New York Colony, James was familiar with the English colonies. In 1686, he established the Dominion of New England. This was an administrative union of English colonies, encompassing the areas from the Delaware River to the Penobscot River. The Dominion managed to install some religious reforms in the English colonies, allowing Catholics to hold office.

1689. King James II Deposed. After James II had declared his Catholic beliefs, he was deposed in the "Glorious Revolution" of 1689. Soon after, the Dominion of New England disappeared, and the English colonies all went back to denying Catholics the right to hold any office. After James II was deposed, his Protestant daughter, Mary, was declared the legal heir to the throne. She had married her cousin, William of Orange, the Stadtholder/Ruler of Holland, and Europe's most staunch Protestant leader. Because of

William's stature, and his role in the "Glorious Revolution" which had overthrown the Catholic James II, Parliament asked both William and Mary to rule England jointly.

1707. During the reign of Queen Anne, the **United Kingdom of Great Britain** was established after the Union with Scotland Act passed the English Parliament in 1706; and the Union with England Act passed the Parliament of Scotland in 1707.

1718. The arrival of the first Scots-Irish immigrants to New England was via Boston Harbor. The so-called Scots-Irish (or Ulster Scots) were former border clan people who had lived near the Scottish-English border for centuries. A good number of them had moved into areas of Northern Ireland in the early 1600s, and a mass migration to most of the British colonies of America began in about 1717. The first Scots-Irish who came to New England were to immediately head west into central Massachusetts or north into New Hampshire.

1741. New Hampshire vs New York. When Benning Wentworth became royal governor of New Hampshire, according to his commission, New Hampshire extended west across the Merrimack River until it met "with our other Governments." Since the English crown had never publicly proclaimed the eastern limits of the colony of New York, this vague description bred considerable confusion.

1749. The New Hampshire Grants. Governor Wentworth, assuming that New York's modified boundary with Connecticut and Massachusetts (20 miles east of the Hudson River) would be extended even farther north, made the first of the *New Hampshire Grants* to a group that included his relatives and friends. However, New York claimed that its boundary extended as far east as the Connecticut River, and Gov. George Clinton of New York promptly informed Governor Wentworth that he had no authority to make such a grant. Wentworth thereupon suggested that the dispute between New York and New Hampshire over control of Vermont be referred to the crown. The outbreak of the French and Indian War in 1754 briefly suspended interest in the area, but after the British captured Ticonderoga and Crown Point in 1759, Wentworth resumed granting land in the area of present Vermont.

1775. Revolutionary War Begins. In April, the battles of Lexington and Concord were the first military engagements of the Revolutionary War. Both battles took place near Boston, where the British had sent an armed force to repel the American rebels. In June, the Battle of Bunker Hill was a defeat for the Americans, but the loss of life on the British side was so great that British General Clinton later remarked in his diary, "A few more such victories would have shortly put an end to British dominion in America." After Bunker Hill, the focus of the Revolutionary War shifted to areas around New Jersey and New York.

1777. Vermont declared itself an independent republic, and it was the first time the name was used. However, both New York and New Hampshire still claimed the area. Vermont's independence was basically ignored by the other colonies, but Vermont did its share to help in fighting the British.

1788. New Hampshire Statehood, 21 June, the 9th state, with the same boundaries as today. Concord was the state capital.

1791. Vermont Statehood, 4 March, the 14th state. The compromise admission of Vermont as a state was the first successful arbitration between the states by the U.S. Congress. Montpellier was the state capital.

New Hampshire State Archives

This facility in Concord, NH is home to many materials of value to genealogists, including probates, land title deeds, military records, census records, photographs, portraits, prints, naturalizations records, voter lists, prisoner indexes, marriage records, paupers' indexes, court records, and more. This is a genealogy-friendly place to visit in person, but a welcome page at the Secretary of State/Archives website states, "Genealogical & Vital Records are not available online."

New Hampshire's Censuses and Substitutes

There were no official province-wide or state-wide censuses taken by New Hampshire before or after statehood. Censuses of the entire province for 1767 and 1775 were found and published, but they were most likely a list of names taken from tax lists. A 1776 "census" exists but was actually a list of those males over 21 loyal to the Patriot cause.

The first recorded name lists began after the 1629 grant to John Mason for lands between the Merrimac and Piscataqua Rivers. The name lists continued after the Massachusetts Bay Colony took control of the New Hampshire settlements in 1641; and they continued after the English Crown formed New Hampshire as a separate royal colony in 1679.

New England Name Indexes

The following important resources relate to all of the New England states, including, Connecticut, Maine, Massachusetts, New Hampshire, Rhode Island, and Vermont. These name indexes are the major compilations of the first settlers of New England

1620-1635. See *The Great Migration Begins: Immigrants to New England, 1620-1635* [Printed Book & Online Database], by Robert Charles Anderson, F.A.S.G., 7 vols., publ. New England Historic Genealogical Society, Boston, 1999-. This classic anthology features comprehensive biographical sketches of the earliest New Englanders. The project continues, with the goal of providing authoritative and detailed biographical sketches of the approximately 21,000 original immigrants to New England from 1620 to 1641. Each immigrant is identified with details concerning parents, spouse(s), and children. See FHL book 974.W2aa v.1-7. The Great Migration volumes were digitized and indexed at the Ancestry.com website. See
http://search.ancestry.com/search/db.aspx?dbid=2496.
For more information about the status of the project, visit the NEHGS's Great Migration Newsletter site at **www.greatmigration.org**.

1620-1692. See *A Genealogical Dictionary of the First Settlers of New England: Showing Three Generations of Those Who Came Before May 1692, on the Basis of Farmer's Register* [Printed Book & CD-ROM], by James Savage, originally publ. Little, Brown and Co., Boston, 1860-1862, 4 vols., 2,541 pages, reprinted (with a cross-index at the end of Vol. 4) by Genealogical Publishing Co, Baltimore, 1969, FHL book 974 D2s. Also on CD-ROM, FHL CD No. 9 pt. 169.

1620-1700. See *New England Marriages Prior to 1700* [Printed & Digitized Book], by Clarence A Torrey. This work, compiled over a period of thirty years from about 2,000 books and manuscripts, is a comprehensive listing of the 37,000 married couples who lived in New England between 1620 and 1700.

Listed are the names of virtually every married couple living in New England before 1700, their marriage date or the birth year of a first child, the maiden names of 70% of the wives, the birth and death years of both partners, mention of earlier or later marriages, the residences of every couple and an index of names. The provision of the maiden names make it possible to identify the husbands of sisters, daughters, and many granddaughters of immigrants, and of immigrant sisters or kinswomen. Publ. Genealogical Publishing Co, Baltimore, MD, 1985, 2004, 1,009 pages, FHL book 974 V2t. A digitized version of this book is available at the Ancestry.com website. See
http://search.ancestry.com/search/db.aspx?dbid=3824.
Note: There are three Supplements to Torrey's *New England Marriages*, each a separate book, as well as a separate database at the Ancestry.com website.

1620-1850. See *Early New England Settlers, 1600s-1800s* [CD-ROM], from a series of published guides by Genealogical publishing Co, Baltimore, publ. as part of Family Tree Maker's Family Archives, FHL CD No. 9 pt. 504. Contents:

- *Chronicles of the first planters of the colony of Massachusetts Bay from 1623 to 1636,* by Alexander Young
- *Peirce's colonial lists: civil, military, and professional lists of Plymouth and Rhode Island colonies,* by Ebenezer W. Peirce
- *The Colonial clergy and colonial churches of New England,* by Frederick Lewis Weis
- *Directory of the ancestral heads of New England families, 1620-1700,* compiled by Frank R. Holmes
- *Genealogical guide to the early settlers of America: with a brief history of those of the first Generation,* by Henry Whittemore
- *Genealogical notes, or, Contributions to the family history of some of the first settlers of Connecticut and Massachusetts,* by Nathaniel Goodwin
- *Genealogical notes on the founding of New England: my ancestors' part in that undertaking,* by Ernest Flagg
- *Genealogical notes of New York and New England families,* compiled by S.V. Talcott
- *A Genealogical register of the first settlers of New England,* by John Farmer
- *The History of New England from 1630 to 1649,* by John Winthrop (vols. I-II)
- *Immigrants to New England, 1700-1775,* compiled by Ethel Stanwood Bolton
- *Marriage notices, 1785-1794 for the whole United States, copied from the Massachusetts Centinel and the Colombian Centinel,* by Charles Knowles Bolton
- *One hundred and sixty allied families,* by John Osborne Austin

- *The Real founders of New England: stories of their life along the coast, 1602-1628,* Charles Knowles Bolton
- *Result of some researches among the British Archives for information relative to the founders of New England: made in the years 1858, 1859 and 1860,* by Samuel G. Drake
- *Soldiers in King Phillips War: being a critical account of that war with a concise history of the Indian Wars of New England from 1620-1677,* by George Madison Bodge
- *The Pioneers of Maine and New Hampshire: a descriptive list drawn from records of the colonies, towns, churches, courts, and other contemporary sources,* by Charles Henry Pope
- *The English ancestry and homes of the pilgrim fathers: who came to Plymouth on the 'Mayflower' in 1620, the 'Fortune' in 1621, and the 'Anne' and 'Little James' in 1623,* by Charles Edward Banks
- *The Planters of the Commonwealth: a study of the emigrants and emigration in colonial times, 1620-1640,* by Charles Edward Banks
- *Topographical dictionary of 2,885 English emigrants to New England, 1620-1650,* Charles Edward Banks
- *The Winthrop fleet of 1630: an account of the vessels, the voyage, the passengers and their English homes, from original authorities,* by Charles Edward Banks.

Note: Virtually all of the titles shown above in the CD-ROM for Early New England Settlers are available at the Ancestry.com website as separate online databases. Ancestry's Online Card Catalog shows 159 databases with the keywords "New England" as part of the title. See the list of titles at **http://search.ancestry.com/search/cardcatalog.aspx#cc at=hc=25&dbSort=1&sbo=1&title=new%20england&key word=&.**

1704-1930. See *U.S., Newspaper Extractions from the Northeast, 1704-1930* **[Online Database].** Digitized and indexed at the Ancestry.com website. Source: American Antiquarian Society, Worcester, MA. This collection contains marriage and death details extracted from various newspapers from Massachusetts, Connecticut, and New York. Details may include names, event dates, ages, family relationships, and other facts of interest. The collection includes 3 volumes of deaths compiled from various Boston papers, 1704–1800, and excerpts from the following newspapers:

- *The American Mercury* (Connecticut), Deaths and Marriages, 1784–1832
- *Christian Secretary* (Connecticut), Deaths and Marriages, 1823–1867
- *The Hartford Times* (Connecticut), Deaths and Marriages, 1817–1866
- *The New York Evening Post* (New York), Deaths, 1801–1885, and Marriages, 1801–1890

- *Columbian Centinel* (Massachusetts), Deaths and Marriages, 1784–1840
- *The Boston Transcript*, Deaths, 1875-1930 (broken into ranges of 1875–1899 and 1900–1930)
- *New Haven Columbian Register*, Deaths and Marriages, 1812–1836

This database has 833,843 records. See **http://search.ancestry.com/search/db.aspx?dbid=50015.**

1787-1906. See *United States, New England, Petitions for Naturalization, 1787-1906* **[Online Database],** digitized at the FamilySearch.org website. This is the collection of images of the petitions. Browse the records. Use the digitized card index to find specific records. This database has 41,694 records. See **https://familysearch.org/search/collection/2064580.**

Index to New England Naturalization Petitions, 1791-1906 **[Online Database],** digitized and indexed at the FamilySearch.org website. Original card index by the United States Immigration and Naturalization Service, on microfilm at the National Archives, series M1299. This is an index to naturalization documents in courts in Connecticut, Maine, Massachusetts, New Hampshire, Rhode Island and Vermont. Index cards are organized by state and then by name of petitioner, arranged according to the Soundex system. Index gives name and location of the court that granted the naturalization, date of naturalization, and volume and page (or certificate) number of the naturalization record. With this information, the digitized images of the petitions can be searched. See **https://familysearch.org/search/collection/1840474.**

1787-1922. See *New England, Select United Methodist Church Records, 1787-1922* **[Online Database],** digitized and indexed at the Ancestry.com website. These records are from the New England Methodist Church Commission on Archives and History and include baptism, marriage, death, membership, and other religious records from congregations throughout New England. See the browse feature on this collection to identify which congregations are included. This database has 72,850 records. See **http://search.ancestry.com/search/db.aspx?dbid=9134.**

Pre-1700-Present. See **AmericanAncestors.org Databases.** Visit the *Browse Databases* webpage of the AmericanAncestors.org website. (New England Historic Genealogical Society, Boston). This is the online presence of the largest genealogical society in America. A membership is required to see the individual records, but a search of the 456 database titles is free. The AmericanAncestors.org site now has over one billion records online. See www.americanancestors.org/browse-database.

Bibliography
New Hampshire Censuses & Substitutes

1623. See "New Hampshire Land Grants to Boston Men" [Printed Article], in *Colonial Society of Massachusetts Publications,* Vol. 25 (Mar 1922).

1623-1848. *First Settlers of New Hampshire* [Online Database], a narrative history. Source: Historical and Genealogical Registers, New England Historic Genealogical Society, Boston, Samuel G. Drake, Publisher, Vols 1-50 (Jan 1848 p37-39). See http://files.usgwarchives.net/nh/strafford/history/earlynh.txt.

1623-1900. *New Hampshire Birth Records, Early to 1900* [Online Database], digitized and indexed at the FamilySearch.org website. Source: NH Bureau of Vital Statistics. Name index and images of New Hampshire birth records. Records consist of index cards that give the town and date of the event and often much more information. This database has 480,354 records. See https://familysearch.org/search/collection/1542861. NOTE: See samples from this database on page 75.

1623-1938. *Index to Divorces and Annulments Prior to 1938* [Microfilm & Digital Capture], from the originals at the NH State Archives, Concord, NH. The records are indexed by surname. Filmed by the Genealogical Society of Utah, 1975, 8 rolls, beginning with FHL film #1001323 To access the digital images, see the online FHL catalog page for this title. See https://familysearch.org/search/catalog/310806.

1623-1975. *Card Index to Genealogies, Published and Manuscript* [Microfilm & Digital Capture], from the original card file at the New Hampshire Historical Society. Filmed by the Genealogical Society of Utah, 1975, 2 rolls, FHL film #1001440 (Genealogies, A-M) & FHL film #1001441 (Genealogies, N-Z). To access the digital images, see the online FHL catalog page: www.familysearch.org/search/catalog/312172.

1623-1988. *New Hampshire Notables Card File* [Microfilm*], from the original card file at the New

Hampshire Historical Society, Concord, NH. An index to biographical sketches of people who were born in New Hampshire or spent a large portion of their lives there. Also serves as an index to a collection of obituaries and other brief biographies from New Hampshire newspapers. Filmed by the Genealogical Society of Utah, 1988, 8 rolls, beginning with FHL film #1570255 (Abbott, Abiel – Andrews, Elisha). For a complete list of roll numbers and contents of each roll, see the online FHL catalog page for this title. See https://familysearch.org/search/catalog/488390.

1623-1988. *Index to Genealogies in New Hampshire Town Histories* [Printed Book & Digital Capture], by William Copeley, publ. NH Hist. Soc., 1988, 103 pages, FHL book 974.2 D22c. For a digital version of this book, see the online FHL catalog page for this title. https://familysearch.org/search/catalog/400390.

1623-1900. *New Hampshire Genealogical Digest* [Printed Book], by Glenn C. Towle, an index to biographies published in various New Hampshire histories, publ. Heritage Books, Bowie, MD, 1986, 333 pages, FHL book 974.2 D32t.

1623-2000s. *New Hampshire GenWeb Archives* [Online Database]. The NHGenWeb site offers free genealogical databases with searchable name lists for all New Hampshire counties, which may include Bibles, Biographies, Cemeteries, Censuses, Court, Death, Deeds, Directories, Histories, Marriages, Military, Newspapers, Obituaries, Photos, Schools, Tax Lists, Wills, and more. See http://usgwarchives.net/nh/nhfiles.htm.

1623-2000s. *Linkpendium – New Hampshire: Family History & Genealogy, Census, Birth, Marriage, Death Vita Records & More* [Online Databases]. Linkpendium is a genealogical portal site, with links to state, county, town, and local databases. Currently listed are selected sites for New Hampshire statewide resources (601), Belknap County (454), Carroll County (485), Cheshire County (1,115), Coos County (588), Grafton County (1,216), Hillsborough County (1,424), Merrimack County (1,281), Rockingham County (2,197), Strafford County (689), and Sullivan County (1,115) See www.linkpendium.com/nh-genealogy.

1623-1861. See *Military History of the State of New Hampshire, from its Settlement in 1623 to the Rebellion in 1861 by Chandler E. Potter, Vol. II* [Online Database], indexed at the Ancestry.com website. This database has 452 images. See http://search.ancestry.com/search/db.aspx?dbid=48212.

1635-1753. *New Hampshire Probate Records* [Online Database], indexed at the Ancestry.com website. Source: NH State Papers series. Includes mostly wills and inventories. This database has 3,242 records. See http://search.ancestry.com/search/db.aspx?dbid=7089.

1637-1947. *New Hampshire Marriage Records* [Online Database], indexed at the FamilySearch.org website. Source: NH Bureau of Vital Records. These records consist of cards giving the names of the bride and groom with the town and date of the marriage and often much more information. This database has 501,128 records. See https://familysearch.org/search/collection/1520640.

1636-1947. *New Hampshire, Town Clerk, Vital and Town Records* [Online Database], digitized at the FamilySearch.org website. Records from local town clerk offices, extracted by FamilySearch. Browse the records. No index yet. This database has 402,443 images. See https://familysearch.org/search/collection/1987741.

1637-1947. *New Hampshire, Marriage Records Index* [Online Database], indexed at the Ancestry.com website. Source: NH Bureau of Vital Records, Concord, NH (extracted from the microfilm by FamilySearch). Details may include: name, date of marriage, place of marriage, birth date, birthplace, age, marital status, race, gender, father's name, mother's name, paternal grandparent, maternal grandparent, previous spouse, spouse's birth date, birthplace, age, race, gender, marital status, previous spouse, spouse's father, spouse's mother, spouse's paternal grandparent, spouse's maternal grandparent, and FHL film number. This database has 990,291 records. See http://search.ancestry.com/search/db.aspx?dbid=2554.

1643-1982. *New Hampshire, Wills and Probate Records* [Online Database], digitized and indexed at the Ancestry.com website. Includes probate court and district court records from all counties of New Hampshire. There may be wills, letters of administration, inventories of estates, administrators'

bonds, or guardianships. This database has 195,097 records. See http://search.ancestry.com/search/db.aspx?dbid=8996.

1643-1948. *New Hampshire Naturalization and Probate Records* [Online Database], digitized at the FamilySearch.org website. Images of naturalization and probate records for Belknap, Grafton, Hillsborough, Merrimack, Rockingham and Sullivan counties. The records were acquired from the state archives in Concord. Browse the images. No index yet. This database has 444,393 images. See https://familysearch.org/search/collection/2138472.

"1648 Dover Taxpayers, Strafford County" [Printed Article], in *New England Historical and Genealogical Register,* Vol. 4, No. 1 (Jan 1850).

1654-1947. *New Hampshire Death Records* [Online Database], digitized and indexed at the FamilySearch.org website. Source: NH Bureau of Vital Records. Name index and images of New Hampshire death records. Records consist of index cards that give the name of the deceased, date and place of death, plus often much more information, such as age, place of birth and names of parents. This database has 581,056 records. See https://familysearch.org/search/collection/1601211.

1654-1949. See *New Hampshire, Death and Burial Records Index7* [Online Database], indexed at the Ancestry.com website. Source: NH Bureau of Vital Records, Concord, NH (extracted from the microfilm by FamilySearch). Details in the index may include: name, date of death, place of death, age, birth date, birthplace, occupation, marital status, burial date, burial place, cemetery, father's name and birthplace, mother's name and birthplace, spouse's name, gender, estimated birth year, father, mother, previous spouse, informant's name and residence, and FHL film number. This database has 825,529 records. See http://search.ancestry.com/search/db.aspx?dbid=2555.

1656-1938. *New Hampshire, Vital and Town Records Index* [Online Database], digitized and indexed at FamilySearch.org, an index to selected births, marriages, and deaths. See www.familysearch.org/search/collection/2366595.

1659-1947. See *New Hampshire, Marriage and Divorce Records, 1659-1947* [Online Database], digitized and indexed at the Ancestry.com website.

This database originated from the NH Vital Records Bureau, Concord, NH. There are two card images for each record. The cards include the following: Groom's name, age, residence, color, occupation, and birthplace. Bride's name, age, residence, color, occupation, and birthplace. Number of marriage for each and whether widowed or divorced. Date of intent to marry. Name and residence of the official performing the marriage. The marriage date and place. Groom's parents' names, residences, ages, colors, occupations, and birthplaces. Bride's parents' names, residences, ages, colors, occupations, and birthplaces. This database has 2,545,835 records. See
http://search.ancestry.com/search/db.aspx?dbid=5241.

1659-1900. *New Hampshire, Birth Records* **[Online Database],** indexed at the Ancestry.com website. Source: NH Bureau of Vital Records, Concord, NH (Extracted from the microfilm by the New England Historic Genealogical Society). Details typically include the following: child's name, date of birth, place of birth, gender and color, living or stillborn, number of child (1st child, 2nd, etc.), father's name, birthplace, color, age, residence, and occupation, mother's maiden name, birthplace, color, age, and occupation, and name and address of physician or person reporting the birth. This database has 478,413 records. See
http://search.ancestry.com/search/db.aspx?dbid=4582.

1660-1973. *New Hampshire, County Probate Records* **[Online Database],** digitized at the FamilySearch.org website. Probate records from Belknap, Carroll, Cheshire, Grafton, Hillsborough, Merrimack, Rockingham, Strafford, and Sullivan counties. Browse the images. No index yet. This database has 524,272 images. See
https://familysearch.org/search/collection/2040537.

1690-1992. *New Hampshire Newspaper Archives* **[Online Databases],** digitized and indexed newspapers at the GenealogyBank website for the following cities: Amherst, Concord, Dover, Exeter, Hanover, Haverhill, Keene, Laconia, Manchester, Portsmouth, and Walpole. See
www.genealogybank.com/explore/newspapers/all/usa/n ew-hampshire.

1694-1994. *The Vital Records of Kingston, New Hampshire* **[Online Database],** indexed at the FamilySearch.org website. Source: Book, same title, compiled by Judith A. Arseneault, publ. 2002. The book is divided into two parts: vital records from 1694 through 1900, which were abstracted from the original records, and vital records from 1901 through 1994, which are based on Kingston Town Reports for those years. Within each half of the book, births are followed by marriages, which are, in turn, followed by deaths. The births and marriages are arranged alphabetically according to the name of the father or husband, while the deaths are arranged alphabetically by the name of the deceased. Fully searchable text, with an OCR index. This database has 25,000 records. See
http://search.ancestry.com/search/db.aspx?dbid=49394

"1709 Hampton Falls Taxpayers, Rockingham County" [Printed Article], in *New England Historical and Genealogical Register,* Vol. 28, No. 4 (Oct 1874).

1714-1904. *New Hampshire Births and Christenings* **[Online Database],** indexed at the FamilySearch.org website. Name index to birth, baptism and christening records from New Hampshire extracted from microfilm copies of these records at the Family History Library, Salt Lake City, UT. This database has 401,037 records.
https://familysearch.org/search/collection/1680836.

1714-1904. *New Hampshire, Births and Christenings Index* **[Online Database],** indexed at the Ancestry.com website. Source: extractions from microfilm at the Family History Library, Salt Lake City, UT. Details in the entries may include name, gender, race, birthplace, birth date, christening place, christening date, death date, age at death, father's name, age, birthplace, mother's name, age, birthplace, paternal grandparents, maternal grandparents, and FHL film number. This database has 595,665 records. See
http://search.ancestry.com/search/db.aspx?dbid=2559.

1720-1920. New Hampshire Marriages [Online Database], indexed at the FamilySearch.org website. Name index to marriage records, extracted from microfilm copies at the Family History Library, Salt Lake City, UT. This database has 442,376 records. See
https://familysearch.org/search/collection/1680841.

1722-1910. *Londonderry, New Hampshire, Vital Records* **[Online Database],** indexed at the Ancestry.com website. Source: Vital Records of Londonderry, New Hampshire, by Daniels, Annis, publ. 1914. This database is a collection of vital records for town residents from its creation to 1910. Compiled from old town records, gravesites and family records, it contains birth, marriage intention, marriage, and death information. In addition, researchers will find detailed information, such as military service, occupation, and progenitors regarding important town residents. This database has 9,556 records. See http://search.ancestry.com/search/db.aspx?dbid=3710.

1727-1788. Tax Books [Microfilm & Digital Capture], from the originals at the NH State Archives, Concord, NH. Contains inventories of taxes assessed and received from the towns. First volume of set has title: *Inventories of the polls and estates in the province of New Hampshire, 1727-1773.* Filmed by the Genealogical Society of Utah, 1975, 1 roll, FHL film #983686. To access the digital images, see the online FHL catalog page: www.familysearch.org/search/catalog/7291.

"1723 Greenland Parish Rate, Rockingham County" [Printed Article], in *New England Historical and Genealogical Register,* Vol. 22, No. 4 (Oct 1868).

1732. *New Hampshire 1732 Census* [Printed Book], by Jay Mack Holbrook, compiled from lists of ratables, land ownership lists, town records and petitions. publ. Holbrook Research Institute, Oxford, MA, 1981, 75 pages, FHL book 974.2 X4.

"1736 Census, Hillsboro County" [Printed Article], in *Ventura County Genealogical Society Quarterly,* (Dec 1996).

"1740 Parish Taxpayers, Hillsboro County" [Printed Article], in *New England Historical and Genealogical Register,* Vol. 28, No. 1 (Jan 1874).

1748. See *Sanbornton, NH Petition for Land Grant, 1748* **[Online Database],** indexed at the Sanbornton RootsWeb site. See www.rootsweb.ancestry.com/~nhcsanbo/petition1748.htm.

1748-1846. *Proprietors' Records* [Microfilm & Digital Capture], from the originals at the NH State Archives, Concord, NH. Filmed by the Genealogical Society of Utah, 1975, 1 roll, FHL film #983688. Partial indexes are found at the beginning of volumes 1-3. To access the digital images, see the online FHL catalog page: www.familysearch.org/search/catalog/5428.

1754-1947. *New Hampshire, Death and Disinterment Records* [Online Database], indexed at the Ancestry.com website. Source: NH Bureau of Vital Records, Concord, NH (Extracted from the microfilm by the New England Historic Genealogical Society). The death records in this database may include the following details: decedent's name, date and place of death, age, place of birth, gender, color and marital status, occupation, cause of death, burial place, father's name and birthplace, mother's maiden name and birthplace, father's occupation, and name and address of physician or informant. This database has 659,426 records. See http://search.ancestry.com/search/db.aspx?dbid=5242.

"1763 New Castle Tax List, Rockingham County" [Printed Article], in *New England Historical and Genealogical Register,* Vol. 105, No. 2 (Apr 1951).

1767 & 1775. *Census of New Hampshire, for the Years 1767 and 1775* [Microfilm & Digital Capture], from the original records at the NH State Archives, Concord, NH. Filmed by the Genealogical Society of Utah, 1975, 1 roll, FHL film #983687. To access the digital images, see the online FHL catalog page: www.familysearch.org/search/catalog/5404.

1769-1936. *New Hampshire, County Probate Estate Files* [Online Database], digitized at the FamilySearch.org website. County probate estate files for Carroll, Cheshire, Coos, and Rockingham counties. Browse the images. No index yet. This database has 877,366 images. See https://familysearch.org/search/collection/2040042.

1771-1905. *New Hampshire, Church Records* [Online Database], digitized and indexed at FamilySearch.org. This collection contains Church records from various denominations, see www.familysearch.org/search/collection/2787826.

1771-2001. *New Hampshire, County Naturalization Records* [Online Database], digitized at the FamilySearch.org website. Naturalization records from all ten NH counties: Belknap, Carroll, Cheshire, Coos, Grafton, Hillsborough, Merrimack, Rockingham, Strafford, and Sullivan counties. Some of the record books include indexes. Browse the images. No complete digitized index yet. This database has 173,600 images. See https://familysearch.org/search/collection/2040051.

"1775 Hawke Census, Rockingham County" [Printed Article], in *Reminiscences,* Vol. 1 No. 4 (Sep 1995).

1776. *New Hampshire 1776 Census* **[Printed Book],** by Jay Mack Holbrook. This is an alphabetized list from the "New Hampshire Association Test of 1776" found in Miscellaneous Revolutionary Documents of New Hampshire, published in Manchester, New Hampshire, 1910
Publ. Holbrook Research Institute, Oxford, MA, 1976. See FHL Book 974.2 X2h.

1776. *Inhabitants of New Hampshire, 1776* **[Online Database],** indexed at the Ancestry.com website. Source: *Inhabitants of New Hampshire, 1776,* by Emily S. Wilson. In 1776, at the outset of the American Revolution, the New Hampshire Committee of Safety directed that all males over the age of twenty-one sign the Association Test – a kind of loyalty oath to the Patriot cause. This database has over 9,000 names. See http://search.ancestry.com/search/db.aspx?dbid=49199.

"1779 Hudson Tax List, Hillsboro County" **[Printed Article],** in *Pennsylvania Traveler-Post,* Vol. 8, No. 2 (Feb 1972).

1784-1949. *New Hampshire Deaths and Burials* **[Online Database],** indexed at the FamilySearch.org website. Name index to death and burial records from New Hampshire, extracted from microfilm copies at the Family History Library, Salt Lake City, UT. This database has 248,856 records. See https://familysearch.org/search/collection/1680840.

"1789 Conway Tax List, Carroll County" **[Printed Article],** in *Nexus,* Vol. 6, No. 2 (Apr 1989).

1790-1890. *New Hampshire, Compiled Census and Census Substitute Index* **[Online Database],** this is one of the first census databases acquired from Accelerated Indexing to launch Ancestry.com online in 1999. It is still useful as a means of comparing different databases for the same census years for common errors in spelling, omissions, etc. See https://www.ancestry.com/search/collections/nhcen.

"1795-1816 Tax Lists, Effingham, Carroll County" **[Printed Article],** in *New Hampshire Genealogical Record,* Vol. 7, No. 3 (Jul 1990).

"1797 Highway Taxpayers List, Rockingham County" **[Printed Article],** in *Reminiscences,* Vol. 2, No. 10 (Dec 2000).

1800-2007. *New Hampshire, Hillsborough County, Manchester, Cemetery Records* **[Online Database],** digitized at the FamilySearch.org website. Cemetery records from the Pine Grove, Valley and other cemeteries in the Manchester area. Browse the records. No index yet. This database has 50,399 images. See https://familysearch.org/search/collection/1930346.

"1802 Cheshire Highway Tax Bill" **[Printed Article],** in *New Hampshire Genealogical Record,* Vol. 10, No. 4 (Oct 1993.

"1803 Delinquent Taxpayers from Dover Sun, Strafford County" **[Printed Article],** in *Genealogical Record of Strafford County,* Vol. 23, No. 4 (Jul 2000).

1812-1883. *Register of Convicts Committed to the State Prison in Concord, New Hampshire, 1812-1883* **[Microfilm & Digital Capture],** from the originals at the NH State Archives, Concord, NH. Includes names, ages, birthplaces, when convicted, crime, when committed, term of confinement, and when discharged. Filmed by the Genealogical Society of Utah, 1975, 1 roll, FHL film #980930. To access the digital images, see the online FHL catalog page: www.familysearch.org/search/catalog/7801.

1813. *Revolutionary War Pensioners for 1813* **[Online Database],** indexed at the Genealogy-trails.com website. Source: Revolutionary Pensioners, A Transcript of the Pension List of the US for 1813, Baltimore, Southern Book Company, 1953. See http://genealogytrails.com/newham/1813revwarpensioners.html.

"1821 Portsmouth Register and Directory" **[Printed Article],** names published in *Kinship Kronicle,* Vol. 4, No. 3 (Fall 1981) through Vol. 5, No. 1 (Mar 1982).

"1826 Highway Tax List, Rockingham County" **[Printed Article],** in *Detroit Society for Genealogical Research Magazine,* Vol. 35, No. 2 (Winter 1971).

1832-1945. See *New Hampshire, State and Federal Naturalization Records, 1832-1945* **[Online Database],** digitized and indexed at Ancestry.com. The webpage for this database has extensive search aids. www.ancestry.com/search/collections/naranatsnewhampshire.

"1833 Danville Voter List, Rockingham County" [Printed Article], in *Reminiscences,* Vol. 1, No. 9 (Dec 1996).

"1836 Census, Meredith Bridge, Belknap County" [Printed Article], in *New Hampshire Genealogical Record,* Vol. 9, No. 2-3 (Apr 1992).

"1836 Middleton Voters, Strafford County" [Printed Article], in *Genealogical Record of Strafford County*, NH, Vol. 23, No. 2 (Mar 2000).

"1838 Danville Voter List, Rockingham County" [Printed Article], in *Reminiscences,* Vol. 1, No. 9 (Dec 1996).

1847-2011. *The New England Historical & Genealogical Register* [Online Database], digitized and indexed, every page of every quarterly issue of the oldest genealogical publication in America. See www.ancestry.com/search/collections/negenreg.

1849-1874. *Non-Resident Tax Lists* [Microfilm & Digital Capture], from the originals at the NH Historical Society, Concord, NH. Filmed by the Genealogical Society of Utah, 1975, 9 rolls, beginning with FHL film #983573 (Non-resident tax lists, 1849-1850). To access the digital images, see the online FHL catalog page:
https://familysearch.org/search/catalog/133016.

1849-1921. *New Hampshire (State) Directories* [Microfilm*], from the originals by various publishers. Filmed by Research Publications, Woodbridge, CT, 1980-1984, 5 rolls, 2 fiche, beginning with FHL fiche #6044224 (1849 New England Mercantile Union Business Directory). For a complete list of fiche/roll numbers, visit the online FHL catalog page for this title. See https://familysearch.org/search/catalog/534777.

"1855 and 1865 Massachusetts State Census (New Hampshire People)" [Printed Article], published serially in *New Hampshire Genealogical Record,* beginning with Vol. 10, No. 4 (Oct 1993).

"1860 Milford Taxpayers, Hillsboro County" [Printed Article], in *Genealogist's Post,* Vol. 6, No. 2 (Jun 1969).

1861-1865. *Revised Register of the Soldiers and Sailors of New Hampshire in the War of the Rebellion* [Online Database], indexed at the Ancestry.com website. This database has 1,355 records. See http://search.ancestry.com/search/db.aspx?dbid=30133.

1861-1865. *New Hampshire, Civil War Service and Pension Records* [Online Database], Index and images of Civil War enlistment papers, muster in and out rolls of New Hampshire Regiments and pension records acquired from the New Hampshire state archives. The pension records are arranged by town with indexes arranged by name and town. The enlistment papers are arranged by military unit, volume and year range. The muster rolls are arranged by unit name and folder number. See www.familysearch.org/search/collection/2127318.

1862-1866. *Internal Revenue Assessment Lists for New Hampshire* [Microfilm & Digital Capture], from the original records at the National Archives, Washington, D.C. District 1 includes: Belknap, Carroll, Rockingham, and Strafford counties; District 2: Hillsborough and Merrimack counties; and District 3: Cheshire, Coos, Grafton, and Sullivan counties. Filmed by the National Archives, series M780, 10 rolls, beginning with FHL film #1534780 (District 1, 1862-1864). For a complete list of roll numbers and access to the National online database, see the online FHL catalog page:
https://familysearch.org/search/catalog/577882.

1869-1904. *The New Hampshire Register, Farmers' Almanac and Business Directory* [Printed Book & Microfilm], from the originals publ. Claremont Manufacturing, Claremont, NH, 1869-. Library has registers for 1869-1904. Registers for 1869-1870, 1878-1880, 1892-1904 are on film only. FHL book 974.2 E4ne. Filmed by the Genealogical Society of Utah, 1965-1978, 8 rolls, beginning with FHL film #1036188 (Registers 1869-1877). For a complete list of roll numbers and contents of each roll, see the online FHL catalog page for this title. See
https://familysearch.org/search/catalog/772961.

1870s-1960. New *Hampshire City Directories* [Online Database], digitized and OCR indexed directories from dozens of New Hampshire places, courtesy of the New England Historic Genealogical Society. Use the Browse this Collection feature to find a city and range of years available. This database at Ancestry.com may be the best census substitute available – if one knows the exact place of residence in New Hampshire. See www.ancestry.com/search/collections/nhnehgs.

1880. *Clarke's Manchester Directory, Political Manual, and Hotel Register* **[Printed Book & Digital Version],** by John B. Clarke Co., Manchester, NH, 1880, FHL book removed to storage. For an online digital version of this book, see the online FHL Catalog page for this title. See **https://familysearch.org/search/catalog/2311869.**

1883-1893. *Dover, New Hampshire City Directories* **[Online Database],** indexed at the Ancestry.com website. This database has 36,318 records. Archived at **https://web.archive.org/web/20160621130226/http://search.ancestry.com/search/db.aspx?dbid=4459.**

1886-1900. *New Hampshire, Cheshire County, Probate Estate Files* **[Online Database],** digitized at the FamilySearch.org website. Images of probate estate case files located at the 8th Circuit Court, Probate Division in Keene, NH. Browse the images. No index yet. This database has 100,767 images. See **https://familysearch.org/search/collection/2103496.**

1890 Census Substitute **[Online Database],** indexed at the Ancestry.com website. This is nationwide collection of city directories for the time of the 1890 federal census (lost in a fire in Washington DC in 1921). A global search includes directories from several New Hampshire cities. See **http://search.ancestry.com/search/group/1890census.**

1895-1956. *United States Border Crossings from Canada to United States* **[Online Database],** digitized and indexed at FamilySearch.org. This database contains an index of aliens and citizens crossing into the U.S. from Canada via various ports of entry along the U.S.-Canadian border between 1895 and 1956. Data courtesy of Ancestry.com. See **www.familysearch.org/search/collection/1803785.**

1900s-1930s. *New Hampshire City Directories* **[Online Database],** indexed at the Ancestry.com website. To see the list of cities and years of publications, use the "Browse this Collection" search box for locality and year. This database has 102,687 records. See **http://search.ancestry.com/search/db.aspx?dbid=8775.**

1901-1915. *New Hampshire Birth Certificates* **[Online Database],** digitized and indexed at the FamilySearch.org website. Includes index and images of birth certificates from the New Hampshire Division

of Vital Records in Concord. Records are arranged by year, certificate number, and name of child. This database has 104,327 records. See **https://familysearch.org/search/collection/1876928.**

"1903 Sandwich Local Returns, Carroll County" **[Printed Article],** in *Sandwich Historical Society, Annual Excursion Publication*, No. 76 (1995).

1906-1993. *New Hampshire, United States Naturalization Records* [Online Database]. This collection contains United States Naturalization records from New Hampshire that are housed by the National Archives and Records Administration in Boston, Massachusetts. This is a collaboration with the National Archives and Records Administration and Ancestry. See **www.familysearch.org/search/collection/2632083.**

1921-1922. *New Hampshire Register and Business Directory* **[Microfilm & Digital Capture],** from the originals publ. Eastman Co., Concord, NH, 340 pages. Filmed by W.C. Cox, Tucson, AZ, 1974, 1 roll, FHL film #1000207. To access the digital images, see the online FHL catalog page: **www.familysearch.org/search/catalog/106824.**

1938-1959. *New Hampshire Death Certificates* **[Online Database],** digitized and indexed at the FamilySearch.org website. Images of death certificates from the New Hampshire Division of Vital Records in Concord. The Collection is arranged by year, by certificate number, or by surname letter. This database has 80,720 records. See **https://familysearch.org/search/collection/1876925.**

1946-1977. *Nashua Telegraph (Nashua, New Hampshire)* **[Online Database],** indexed at the Ancestry.com website. Source: *Nashua Telegraph*, Nashua, New Hampshire. This is a fully searchable text version of the newspaper, with an OCR index. This database has over 180,000 records. See **http://search.ancestry.com/search/db.aspx?dbid=6931.**

1948-1959. *New Hampshire Marriage Certificates* **[Online Database],** digitized and indexed at the FamilySearch.org website. Source NH Div. of Vital Records. The Collection is arranged by year, by certificate number, and by name. This database has 96,665 records. See **https://familysearch.org/search/collection/1876926.**

1989-Current. *New Hampshire Recent Newspaper Obituaries* **[Online Database],** digitized and indexed newspaper obituaries at the GenealogyBank website, including newspapers from Bedford, Candia, Auburn, Chester/ Hampstead/Sandown, Claremont, Derry, Dover, Exeter, Goffstown, Hooksett, Kingston, Londonderry, Manchester, Nashua, Newport/New London/Sunapee, Portsmouth, Rochester, Salem, State-Wide County, and Taylorton. See **www.genealogybank.com/explore/obituaries/all/usa/new -hampshire.**

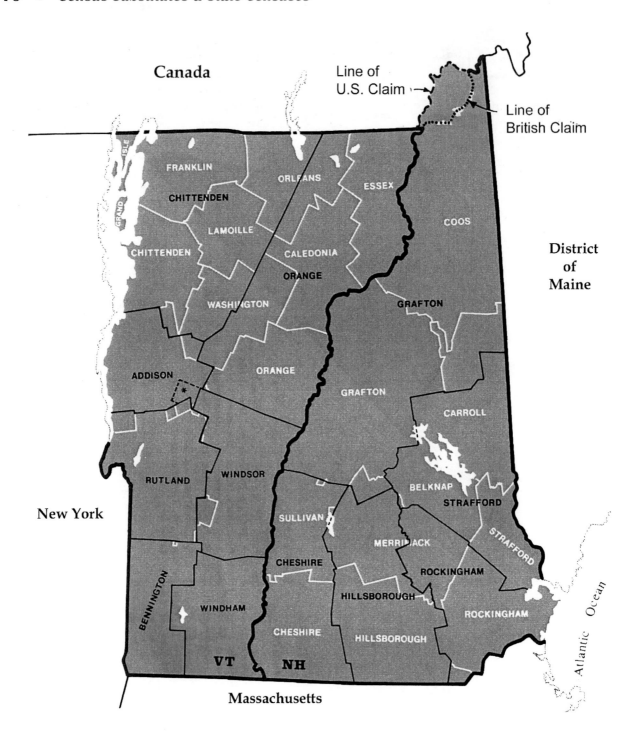

Vermont & New Hampshire • 1790/1791. The current counties of both states are shown in white. Shown in black are the counties at the time of the 1790 Federal Census. As one of the original thirteen states, New Hampshire was included in the first census with a census day of 2 Aug 1790, and nine months to complete the door-to-door enumeration. In August 1790, Vermont was still claimed by both New Hampshire and New York until the U.S. Congress arbitrated the dispute and made Vermont the 14th state on 4 March 1791. By a special Act of Congress, the new state of Vermont was then included in the 1790 census, and with its own census day of 4 April 1791.

* Notes: Vermont's county boundaries were the same for 1790 and 1791, except that the town of Hancock – shown by dashed lines and an asterisk – was in Windsor County in 1790; transferred to Addison County in Jan 1791. **Map Source:** Page 216, *Map Guide to the U.S. Federal Censuses, 1790-1920*, by William Thorndale and William Dollarhide.

Historical Timeline
of Vermont, 1603-1791

1603. England. James I became King of England, the first monarch to rule both England and Scotland. (He was James VI of Scotland since 1566). During his reign, the first permanent English colonies were established in Virginia and New England. James I was also an advocate for the transportation of thousands of clan people living along the Scottish-English border to Ulster Province, Northern Ireland.

1606. Two joint stock companies were founded in 1606, both with royal charters issued by King James I for the purpose of establishing colonies in North America. The Virginia Company of London was given a land grant between Latitude 34° (Cape Fear) and Latitude 41° (Long Island Sound). The Virginia Company of Plymouth was founded with a similar charter, between Latitude 38° (Potomac River) and Latitude 45° (St. John River), which included a shared area with the London Company between Latitude 38° and 41°.

1614. Connecticut. Dutchman Adriaen Block sailed up the present Connecticut River and claimed the region as part of the New Netherland colony.

1614-1615. New England. English Captain John Smith, a leader of the Jamestown Colony, visited the coast of present Connecticut, Rhode Island, Massachusetts, and Maine; then wrote his *Description of New England*, which encouraged Englishmen to settle there. Smith was credited as the first to call the area New England.

1620. Plymouth Colony. A new Royal Charter was issued by King James I to the Plymouth Council for New England (formerly the Virginia Company of Plymouth) to establish new colonial settlements in New England. The area was from Latitude 40° to Latitude 45° ("sea to sea"). In that same year, the *Mayflower* dropped anchor off Cape Cod, and Plymouth Colony was founded by a small group of Separatists/Pilgrims, who had fled England for Holland a few years earlier.

1625. England. Charles I became King of England, Scotland, and Ireland. Soon after taking office, Charles began to note a large number of non-conformists among his subjects. Along with his Archbishop, William Laud, the King began a campaign to purge his church of the largest group of non-conformists, the so-called "Puritans," a militant Calvinist religious group attempting to purify the Church of England. Unfortunately, Charles I took on a job that led to civil war in England as well as the loss of his head. But, his campaign can be credited as the cause for the founding of English settlements in New England.

1628. The **Massachusetts Bay Company** was granted a royal charter for an English colony to be established in North America within the bounds of the Plymouth Council of New England. It is said that King Charles I was misled as to the religious leanings of the Massachusetts Bay Company leaders, all prominent Puritans, not Pilgrims, as he had surmised.

1629. Sir Ferdinando Gorges and Captain John Mason agreed to split their grants at the Piscataqua River, with Mason retaining the land west of the river as the Province of New Hampshire.

1629. The Great Migration to New England Begins. As a result of the Charles I campaign to purge non-conformists from the Church of England, large groups of people were disenfranchised. Charles I disbanded

Parliament and ruled England alone for eleven years. The Puritans referred to this era as "the eleven years of tyranny." It was during these eleven years that some 21,000 Puritan immigrants, were to establish the Massachusetts Bay Colony of North America.

1629. New Hampshire. John Mason received a grant of that portion of the Province of Maine which lay between the Merrimac and the Piscataqua River, under the name of New Hampshire.

1642. The English Civil War Begins. Since taking the throne in 1625, King Charles I had purged most of the Puritans from the Church of England. To deal with a Parliament opposing his every move, in 1629, Charles disbanded Parliament and ruled England on his own. That action canceled over 400 years of liberties gained by Parliament since the Magna Carta. When Parliament was restored in 1640, it quickly became dominated by the same Puritans who Charles had removed from the Church of England. Beginning in 1642, Royalist supporters were forced to fight the armies of the Puritan Parliament in the English Civil War. The Great Migration to New England ended about this time.

1645-1651. England. After his defeat and capture in 1645, Charles I refused to accept his captors' demands for a constitutional monarchy, and briefly escaped captivity in 1647. While recaptured, his son, Prince Charles, was able to marshal Scottish forces for the king. However, by 1648, Oliver Cromwell had consolidated the English opposition. King Charles I was tried, convicted, and executed for high treason in January 1649. The Civil War continued until 1651, when Oliver Cromwell, a Puritan, became Lord Protectorate, ruling the Commonwealth of England for the next seven years.

1660. England. Charles II was restored to the throne as King of England, Scotland, and Ireland. He had lived in exile after the execution of his father, King Charles I. In 1649, the Scots had proclaimed Charles the king of Scotland. But the Puritan leader Oliver Cromwell defeated his army in 1651, and Charles fled to France. After Cromwell died in 1658, the English people became increasingly dissatisfied with the government that Cromwell had established. In 1660, Parliament invited Charles to return and declared him king. He ruled until his death in 1685, and during his 25-year reign, the English colonies forced out the remaining

pockets of Atlantic settlements made earlier by the Dutch, Swedes, Danes, and French. Charles II saw the colonies as a source of trade and commerce, supported development, and granted several more charters for settlement (including one to William Penn in 1681). All of the English colonies thrived as a result. He was the first monarch to recognize the potential for the North American colonies to become a contiguous, viable commonwealth. Charles II was responsible for setting the tone of self-government, religious tolerance, and individual freedoms in the English colonies that were to become American institutions.

1679. New Hampshire. The English Crown formed New Hampshire as a separate royal colony.

1707. During the reign of Queen Anne, the **United Kingdom of Great Britain** was established after the Union with Scotland Act passed the English Parliament in 1706; and the Union with England Act passed the Parliament of Scotland in 1707. The English Colonies were now the British Colonies.

1724. Vermont Area. Fort Dummer, built by the English near the site of Brattleboro, was the first permanent settlement in what is now Vermont.

1741. New Hampshire vs New York. When Benning Wentworth became royal governor of New Hampshire, according to his commission, New Hampshire extended west across the Merrimack River until it met "with our other Governments." Since the English crown had never publicly proclaimed the eastern limits of the colony of New York, this vague description bred considerable confusion.

1749. Early Lands Grants in the Vermont Area. New Hampshire's Governor Wentworth, assuming that New York's modified boundary with Connecticut and Massachusetts (20 miles east of the Hudson River) would be extended even farther north, made the first of the *New Hampshire Grants*. (The first grant was named Bennington). However, New York claimed that its boundary extended as far east as the Connecticut River, and Gov. George Clinton of New York promptly informed Governor Wentworth that he had no authority to make such a grant. Wentworth thereupon suggested that the dispute between New York and New Hampshire over control of Vermont be referred to the crown. The outbreak of the French and Indian War in 1754 briefly suspended interest in the area, but after the British captured Ticonderoga and Crown Point in 1759, Wentworth resumed granting land in the area of present Vermont.

1754. The French and Indian War. France and Britain fought for control of the territory of Canada, the Great Lakes, and the Mississippi River Basin. In Europe it was called the Seven Years War. After conquering the peninsular part of Acadia, the British renamed it Nova Scotia and began transporting Acadians back to France. By 1765, many of the deported Acadians had made their way to the French-speaking areas of Spanish Louisiana

1763. Treaty of Paris was signed by France, Spain, and Britain, ending the French and Indian War. France was the loser. England now owned all the territory east of the Mississippi River. Spain took everything west of the Mississippi. The British area became known officially as *British North America.*

1764. Vermont Area. The British government upheld New York's territorial claim to Vermont. New York immediately tried to assert its jurisdiction— Wentworth's grants were declared void, and new grants (for the same lands) were issued by New York.

1765. Stamp Act. This was the first tax levied directly against the inhabitants of the British colonies (without the approval of their own legislatures) and led to vigorous acts of rebellion. In protest over the stamp tax, American colonists sacked and burned the home of Massachusetts governor Thomas Hutchinson. In 1774 he was exiled to Britain. The hated Stamp Act led to the organization of one of the first anti-British groups, The Sons of Liberty, who coined the rallying cry, "No Taxation Without Representation."

1767. Townshend Acts. Charles Townshend, the British Chancellor of the Exchequer, proposed a program to levy new taxes in the colonies to raise funds to pay the salaries of the governors and judges so that they would remain loyal to Great Britain. Six different acts were meant to establish a precedent that the British Parliament had the right to tax the colonies. In Massachusetts, the Townshend Acts were met with a public outrage and extreme resistance.

1768. The British government responded to the protests to the Townshend Acts by sending an occupation force of 4,000 British troops to Boston. With a population of about 15,000, it meant there was one British soldier for every Boston household.

1774. June. Québec Act. The British reacted to the increased American rebellions by solidifying British loyalty in the Province of Canada. They enacted the Québec Act, which reversed the long-standing British policy against Catholic governments in all of their colonies. The Québec Act, just a few years after the forced deportations of Catholic Acadians, restored the name Province of Québec and granted Québec residents full British citizenship, allowed Québec to retain their Catholic churches and parish taxing systems, and to keep their established French Laws and Customs. The Act also expanded the physical area of Québec to include a huge area of western lands claimed by the Thirteen Colonies: including the lands north of the Ohio River, encompassing the entire Great Lakes region. The Thirteen Colonies viewed the Québec Act as one of the Intolerable Acts that made the impending war justifiable.

1775. Revolutionary War Begins. In April, the battles of Lexington and Concord were the first military engagements of the Revolutionary War. Both battles took place near Boston, where the British had sent an armed force to repel the American rebels. In June, the Battle of Bunker Hill was a defeat for the Americans, but the loss of life on the British side was so great that British General Clinton later remarked in his diary, "A few more such victories would have shortly put an end to British dominion in America." After Bunker Hill, the focus of the Revolutionary War shifted to areas around New Jersey and New York.

1777. June. Vermont declared itself an independent republic. It was the first time the name was used. However, both New York and New Hampshire still claimed the area. Vermont's independence may have been ignored by the other colonies, but Vermont did its share in fighting the British. For the next fourteen years, Vermont continued to govern itself as a sovereign state, issued its own coinage, and operated a statewide postal service. Thomas Chittenden was the Governor of the independent state of Vermont for most of that era.

1777. August. The **Battle of Bennington** was fought in an area near Bennington in the Vermont Republic. This decisive battle was the first major defeat of the British Army by American forces. The anniversary of the battle is still celebrated in Vermont as a legal holiday.

1779. The Republic of Vermont divided itself into two counties. Windham was on the east side of the Green Mountains; Bennington was on the west side.

1781. October. **Siege of Yorktown.** In six years of war, Commanding General George Washington won very few battles with the British. He had learned how to fight the British by avoiding direct frontal attacks at all costs. Washington's greatest success, however, was his last great battle, the Siege of Yorktown. His brilliant handling of the final battle of the war was credited as the basis for the founding of the America republic. At Yorktown, the British Commanding General Charles Cornwallis surrendered and prompted the British government to negotiate an end to the conflict.

1783. Sept 3rd. **Treaty of Paris.** This was the official end of the Revolutionary War, as well as the first recognition of the United States of America as an independent nation. The treaty defined the limits of the U.S. to be from the Atlantic Ocean to the Mississippi River; and from Massachusetts/Maine to Georgia. But the northern boundary between the U.S. and British North America was not defined precisely at the Treaty of Paris and the boundary remained in dispute for nearly 60 years.

1791. March 4th. **Vermont** became the 14th state. From 1787 to 1791, Vermont's admission was held up by New Hampshire. Vermont's statehood was subject to a provision of the U.S. Constitution where adjoining states whose territory might be impacted had to vote in favor of the proposed state. New Hampshire claimed all of Vermont, but finally gave its blessing to Vermont's statehood (as long as they paid New Hampshire for the loss of improved properties). Since its days as an independent state, Vermont's capital cities rotated between eastern and western sides of the Green Mountains, a system they referred to as "Mountain Rule." In 1805, that system was replaced with a permanent state capital at Montpelier.

About Vermont's Censuses

The area that became known as Vermont was long in dispute between the New Hampshire and New York colonies. Some of the earliest settlements in the area were initiated by New Hampshire's colonial Governor Benning Wentworth, beginning in 1749. After the British government upheld New York's claim to the Vermont area, Wentworth's land grants were voided and replaced by New York's Governor George Clinton in 1764. The first use of the name came when the Vermont Republic was declared in 1777, which remained until Vermont became the 14th state of the Union in March 1791, a compromise facilitated by the new United States Congress.

During the time of cross-claims between New York and New Hampshire, a number of census-like name lists were created. Any name lists from the colonial period are included in the bibliography that follow.

There were no official state-wide censuses taken in Vermont. However, there are extant tax lists for virtually every town in Vermont, many taken annually. Often called "Grand Lists," the tax lists are sometimes hard to find, since they may appear in town records, proprietor meeting records, town clerk's offices, or at the VT State Archives.

Vermont was included in the 1790 federal census (with a census day of 4 April 1791), and has complete federal censuses open to the public from 1790 through 1940 (except for the 1890, lost for all states).

Resources at the Vermont State Archives

This facility in Montpelier has limited online databases at their website. But the VT State Archives has allowed several databases to be available to the public through the Ancestry.com and FamilySearch.org websites. Use the main VT State Archives website for general information. See **https://sos.vermont.gov/vsara/research.**

Digital State Archives (Under Development). "Born-digital" public records are now being transferred to the VT Digital State Archives. The website is available for exploring, see **https://vermont.access.preservica.com.**

Vital Records: Vermont has no restrictions on access to vital records, and full details from birth, death, marriage, and divorce records are available to the public. The desired dates of the vital records dictates whether the records are available at a town clerk's office, the state Department of Health office, or the VT State Archives.

The Archival Records Database is an index to records in the Vermont State Archives. The records are organized based on the agency or department that created or received the records, and then by record series.

The Nye Index. The index to the *Manuscript Vermont State Papers* (c. 1760-1860) and other early Vermont records, better known as the Nye Index, was originally created as a personal name card file by Mary Greene Nye, the Editor of State Papers (1927–1950). The entire card file is located in the Reference Room and is open to the public.

Bibliography
Vermont Censuses & Substitutes

1749-1760s. *Grants of Vermont Territory by the Government of New Hampshire* **[Printed Book & Digital Version].** Author/publisher not noted, 788 pages. Copy of book located at the Mesa Arizona Family Search Library, FHL book 974.3 R2n. Digitized by the Genealogical Society of Utah, 2008. To view a digital version, see the online FHL catalog page for this title. See
https://familysearch.org/search/catalog/1920048.

1749-1908. *Vermont, Vital Records* **[Online Database],** indexed at the Ancestry.com website. Source: Microfilm of VT Vital Records, early to 1870; and VT Vital Records, 1871-1908, both series located at the New England Historic Genealogical Society in Boston. Records may contain some of the following information: name, birth date, birthplace(s), parents' names, maiden name, occupation, residence, bride, groom, marriage date, age, color, date of death, and cause of death. This database has 1,426,900 records:
http://search.ancestry.com/search/db.aspx?dbid=4661.

1749-1999. *Vermont, Wills and Probates* **[Online Database],** digitized and indexed at the Ancestry.com website. Source: County, district, and probate court records. Includes probate court and district court records from over half of the counties of Vermont. There may be wills, letters of administration, inventories of estates, administrators' bonds, or guardianships. This database has 98,222 records. See
http://search.ancestry.com/search/db.aspx?dbid=9084.

1749-2005. *Vermont, Town Clerk, Vital and Town Records* **[Online Database],** digitized and indexed at the FamilySearch.org website. This database consists of vital records and other town records acquired from local town clerk offices. This database has 6,910 records. See
https://familysearch.org/search/collection/1987653.

1749-2008. *Vermont GenWeb Archives* **[Online Database].** The VTGenWeb site offers free genealogical databases with searchable name lists for all Vermont counties, which may include Bibles, Biographies, Cemeteries, Censuses, Court, Death, Deeds, Directories, Histories, Marriages, Military, Newspapers, Obituaries, Photos, Schools, Tax Lists, Wills, and more. See
http://usgwarchives.net/vt/vtfiles.htm.

1749-2008. *Linkpendium – Vermont: Family History & Genealogy, Census, Birth, Marriage, Death Vita Records & More* **[Online Databases].** Linkpendium is a genealogical portal site, with links to state, county, town, and local databases. Currently listed are selected sites for Vermont statewide resources (539), Addison County (853), Bennington County (863), Caledonia County (741), Chittenden County (1,034), Essex County (342), Franklin County (864), Grand Isle County (273), Lamoille County (365), Orange County (658), Orleans County (861), Rutland County (1,345), Washington County (681), Windham County (880), and Windsor County (1,001) See
www.linkpendium.com/vt-genealogy.

1760-1954. *Vermont Vital Records* **[Online Database],** digitized and indexed at the FamilySearch.org website. Name index and images (3x5 index cards) of town clerk transcriptions of births, marriages and deaths, 1760-1954. A sample index card is shown above. See
https://familysearch.org/search/collection/1784223.

1760-2008. *Vermont Vital Records* **[Online Database],** digitized and indexed at the FamilySearch.org website. Name index and images from microfilm of births, marriages and deaths. This collection includes images for the years 1955-2003.

The records for 1955-1979 are arranged alphabetically. Index and images courtesy of Ancestry.com and the Vermont State Archives. This database has 1,974,198 records. See https://familysearch.org/search/collection/2075288.

"1761 Cornwall Grantees" [Printed Article], in *Missing Links-Genealogical Clues*, No. 12 (Jul 1963).

"1761 Leicester Land Grantees" [Printed Article], in *Missing Links-Genealogical Clues*, No. 12 (Jul 1963).

"1761 Peru Original Grantees" [Printed Article], in *Missing Links-Genealogical Clues*, No. 61 (Aug 1967).

"1761 Addison's Original Grantees" [Printed Article], in *Missing Links-Genealogical Clues*, No 56 (Mar 1967).

1760s-1870. *General Index to Vital Records of Vermont, Early to 1870* **[Microfilm & Digital Capture],** from the original records at the VT State Archives. Coverage for every town of Vermont. Index includes births, deaths and marriages. With the lack of census records for Vermont, this index provides an outstanding substitute. Filmed by the Genealogical Society of Utah, 1951, 287 rolls, beginning with film #27455 (A – Adams, C.). To access the digital images, see the online FHL catalog page: https://familysearch.org/search/catalog/279437.

1761-1999. *Bennington, Vermont Cemetery Inscriptions* **[Online Database],** indexed at the Ancestry.com website. Each record includes the name of the deceased, sex, birth date, death date, age at death, and location of death. This database has 14,883 records. See http://search.ancestry.com/search/db.aspx?dbid=3990.

"1763 Jericho Original Grantees" [Printed Article], in *Missing Links-Genealogical Clues*, No. 47 (Jun 1966).

1765-1908. *Vermont Births and Christenings* **[Online Database],** indexed at the FamilySearch.org website. Source: extraction from microfilm of the Vermont records at the Family History Library, Salt Lake City, UT. Includes birth, baptism and christening records. This database has 221,5459 records. See https://familysearch.org/search/collection/1675544.

1770-1832. *Orange County Tax Records; Miscellaneous Records* **[Microfilm & Digital Capture],** from the original records at Chelsea, Vermont. Includes record of taxes paid and land sold, peddlers licenses, licenses to preach, clergyman's appointments, deputations and recognizances, and docket and records referred to in the Judicial history of Vermont. Filmed by the Genealogical Society of Utah, 1952, FHL film #28622. To access the digital images, see the online FHL catalog page: www.familysearch.org/search/catalog/291312.

1770s-1860s. *Index to State of Vermont Military Records: Revolutionary War, Civil War, War of 1812: Salvaged From the State Arsenal Fire, September 1, 1945* **[Printed Book & Microfilm],** author/publisher not stated, 65 pages. FHL Book 974.3 M22i. Also on microfilm. Filmed by the Genealogical Society of Utah, 1971. 1 roll, film #824107.

1771. *Vermont 1771 Census* **[Printed Book],** by Jay Mack Holbrook, publ. Oxford, MA, 1982, 102 pages, FHL book 974.3 X3h.

"1771 Census, Windham, Vermont" [Printed Article], name list from unknown sources in *Branches and Twigs*, Vol. 8, No. 3 (Summer 1979).

1779-1935. *Vermont, Bennington County, Manchester District Estate Files* **[Online Database],** digitized at the FamilySearch.org website. Index and images of probate estate files. Each estate file consists of multiple images. This database has 119,038 records. See https://familysearch.org/search/collection/1935045.

1780-1815, *Vermont, Orange County, Bradford District Estate Files* **[Online Database],** digitized at the FamilySearch.org website. Images of probate estate files from the Supreme Court of Vermont. The files are located at the VT State Archives in Montpelier, VT. The collection is divided into multiple parts, 1780-1800, 1800-1847, 1800-1810 and 1820-1830. This database has 75,694 records. See https://familysearch.org/search/collection/1807377.

1781-1921. *Vermont, Windham County, Westminster District, Probate Records* **[Online Database],** digitized at the FamilySearch.org website. Images of probate records located at the Vermont Public Records

Office in Middlesex. Records are bundled together by year. This database has 21,168 records. See https://familysearch.org/search/collection/1879202.

1781-1960. *General Alphabetical Card Index to Court Records, Rutland County, Vermont* [Microfilm & Digital Capture], from the
originals at the VT Public Records Commission, Montpelier, VT. Filmed by the Genealogical Society of Utah, 2005, 7 rolls, as follows:
  ● Card index, 1781-1960, A to Goodspeed, FHL film #1913874
  ● Card index, 1781-1960, Goodwin to Preybyto, FHL film #1913875
  ● Card index, 1781-1960, Price to Z, FHL film #1913876
  ● Card index, Abbiati, Steven D. - Devers, Charles, et al., FHL film #1838276
  ● Card index, Devers, Charles, et al. - Matthias, Christopher, FHL film #1838277
  ● Card index, Manchester, Fred A. - Wetherbee, Charles A., FHL film #1838278
  ● Card index, Wetherbee, Charles A. - Zyrambi, Eva, FHL film #1838327
To access the images, see the online FHL catalog page: https://familysearch.org/search/catalog/1192384.

1781-2006. *Vermont Newspaper Archives* [Online Databases], digitized and indexed newspapers at the GenealogyBank website for the following cities: Bellows Falls, Bennington, Brattleboro, Burlington, Chelsea, Chester, Danville, Middlebury, Montpelier, Peacham, Putney, Randolph, Royalton, Rutland, St. Albans, St. Johnsbury, Vergennes, Westminster, Windsor, and Woodstock See www.genealogybank.com/explore/newspapers/all/usa/vermont.

"1782 Wells Poll List, Rutland County" [Printed Article], in *Detroit Society for Genealogical Research Magazine*, Vol. 13, No. 5 (Jun 1950).

1785 Vermont Early Census Head of House Addison County [Online Database], indexed at the USGenWebArchives website. See http://files.usgwarchives.net/vt/addison/census/1785/1785ferri.txt.

1785 Vermont Early Census Head of House Bennington County [Online Database], indexed at the USGenWebArchives website. See http://files.usgwarchives.net/vt/bennington/census/1785/1785dorse.txt.

1785 Vermont Early Census Head of House Orange County [Online Database], indexed at the USGenWebArchives website. See http://files.usgwarchives.net/vt/orange/census/1785/1785bradf.txt.

1785-1941. See *Land Records, Chittenden County, Vermont, 1785-1905; Index, 1785-1941* [Microfilm & Digital Capture], from the originals at the Vermont Public Records Division, Montpelier, VT. Filmed by the VT Public Recds Div., 1974, 5 rolls, as follows:
  ● Index to land records 1785-1941; and Land records, Vol. 1-3, 1785-1810, FHL film #847974
  ● Land records, Vol. 4-5, 1791-1800, FHL film #847975
  ● Land records, Vol. 6-7, 1800-1811, FHL film #847976
  ● Land records, Vol. 8-9, 1813-1852; and Land records, Vol. 11, 1852-1905, FHL film #847977 .
  ● Land records, Vol. 10, 1849-1893, FHL film #847978 .
To access the digital images, see the online FHL catalog page: www.familysearch.org/search/catalog/360141.

"1788 Starsborough Road Tax" [Printed Article], name list in *Missing Links-Genealogical Clues*, No. 22 (May 1964).

"1788 Addison Tax for Roads and Bridges" [Printed Article], in *Missing Links-Genealogical Clues*, No. 12 (Jul 1963).

1790-1860. *Vermont, Compiled Census and Census Substitute Index, 1790-1860* [Online Database], this is one of the first census databases acquired from Accelerated Indexing to launch Ancestry.com online in 1999. It is still useful as a means of comparing different databases for the same census years for common errors in spelling, omissions, etc. See www.ancestry.com/search/collections/vtcen.

1790-1935. *Vermont, Orange County, Randolph District Probate Records* [Online Database], digitized at the FamilySearch.org website. Images of prob ate estate files for Orange County, Randolph District located at the Division of Public Records in Middlesex. Each estate file consists of multiple images. The files are arranged by folder number then name. Folders 1-8 cover 1790-1890, folders 9-30 cover 1800-1840, etc. This database has 65,929 records. See https://familysearch.org/search/collection/1453983.

1791-1974. *Vermont Marriages* **[Online Database],** indexed at the FamilySearch.org website. Name index to marriage records from microfilm at the Family History Library, Salt Lake City, UT. This database has 9,235 records. See
https://familysearch.org/search/collection/1675550.

"1793 Chittenden Delinquent Tax Records" [Printed Article], Rutland County, in *Rooted in the Green Mountains,* Vol. 2, No. 2 (Jul 1998).

"1793 Rutland Delinquent Tax Records" [Printed Article], in *Rooted in the Green Mountains*, Vol. 2, No. 3 (Jul 1998).

"1793 Brattleboro Tax List, Windham County" [Printed Article], in *Vermont Genealogy*, Vol. 5, No. 4 (Oct 2000).

1796-1921. *Vermont, Franklin County Probate Records* **[Online Database],** digitized at the FamilySearch website. Probate papers at the Public Records Office, Middlesex, VT. This database has 235,834 records. See
https://familysearch.org/search/collection/1921463.

1796-1959. *General Alphabetical Card Index to Estate Files, Chittenden County, Vermont* **[Microfilm & Digital Capture],** from the originals at the VT Public Records Division. Filmed by the VT Public Records Commission, Montpelier, VT, 1959, 3 rolls, as follows:
- Card index to estate files, A-G, 1796-1959, FHL film #1913864
- Card index to estate files, H-S, 1796-1959, FHL film #1913865
- Card index to estate files, S-Z, 1796-1959, FHL film #1913866

To access the images, see the online FHL catalog page:
https://familysearch.org/search/catalog/1052845.

1800-1921. *Vermont Probate Files* **[Online Database],** digitized and indexed at the FamilySearch.org website. Index and images of probate estate files. Each estate file consists of multiple images. Currently images are available for Chittenden and Essex Counties. This database has 10,225 records:
https://familysearch.org/search/collection/1435692.

1802-1965. Addison County, Vermont, Cemetery Index [Online Database], indexed at the Ancestry.com website. Source: book by Elizabeth

Ellsberry, 1965. The following cemeteries are included in the database: West Cemetery: New Haven, VT; Riverside Cemetery, New Haven, VT; Munger Street Cemetery, The Old Abandoned Cemetery: in South Western Part of New Haven, VT; Sunset View Cemetery, Waltham, VT; Chipman Private Cemetery, Waltham School District, No. 1, Ward Private Cemetery; and Waltham School District No. 1, Cornwall and Weybridge Parish, Located on Route 30 in Cornwall, VT. This database has 1,870 records. See
http://search.ancestry.com/search/db.aspx?dbid=5734.

"1807 Cavendish Legal Voters, Windsor County" [Printed Article], in *Branches and Twigs,* Vol. 21, No. 3 (Summer 1992).

"1807 Poultney Grand List, Rutland County" [Printed Article], in *Rooted in the Green Mountains*, Vol. 2, No. 1 (Jan 1998).

1811-1959. *General Alphabetical Card Index to Guardianships, Chittenden County, Vermont* **[Microfilm & Digital Capture],** from the originals at the Public Records Commission, Montpelier, VT. Filmed by the commission, 1959, 2 rolls, as follows:
- General Alphabetical Card Index to Guardianships, A-I, 1811-1959, FHL film #1913866
- General Alphabetical Card Index to Guardianships, J-W, 1811-1959, FHL film #1913867

To access the digital images, see the online FHL catalog page:
https://familysearch.org/search/catalog/1175711.

1812-1815. *A List of Vermont Pensioners of the War of 1812* **[Online Database],** from the book of the same name by Byron Clark, 1969. The book begins with an alphabetically arranged series of abstracts of the evidence presented by the claimants to a pension agent, in most cases indicating the veteran's unit, dates and places of service, and relationship to the claimant. This is followed by lists of some 200 Vermonters who volunteered to serve at Plattsburgh. The Appendix to the book, consists of yet other lists and various accounts of the conflict. See
http://search.ancestry.com/search/db.aspx?dbid=49226.

"1813, 1815, 1816 Williston Federal District Tax, Chittenden County" [Printed Article], in *Vermont Genealogy*, Vol. 6, No. 2 (Apr 2001).

"1815 Grand List for New Haven, Addison County" [Printed Article], in *Vermont Genealogy*, Vol. 6, No. 1 (Jan 2001).

"1827-1833 Rutland Freemen" [Printed Article], in *Missing Links-Genealogical Clues*, No. 41 (Dec 1965).

"1828 Windsor Tax Rates" [Printed Article], in *Vermont Historical Society Proceedings*, Vol. 23, No. 2 (Apr 1955).

"1832 Brattleboro Voters List" [Printed Article], in *Missing Links-Genealogical Clues,* No. 42 (Jan 1966).

1840 Census of Pensioners Revolutionary or Military Services [Online Database], indexed at the Roots.org website. See www.us-roots.org/colonialamerica/census/1840.

1840s-1960s. *School Lists, Caledonia, Orleans, and Essex Counties, Vermont* **[Online Database],** indexed at the Vermont NorthEast Kingdom Genealogy website. See www.nekg-vt.com/submenu-schools.php.

"1843 Derby Census, Orleans County" [Printed Article], in *Vermont Genealogy*, Vol. 4, No. 4 (Oct 1999).

1845-1915. *Vermont, Addison County and District Probate Files* **[Online Database],** digitized at the FamilySearch.org website. Probate estate files of the Addison District located at Administrator Services, Montpelier, Vermont. This database has 54,451 records. See https://familysearch.org/search/collection/1879935.

1847-2011. *The New England Historical & Genealogical Register* **[Online Database],** digitized and indexed, every page of every quarterly issue of the oldest genealogical publication in America. See www.ancestry.com/search/collections/negenreg.

1850-2005. *Vermont, Town Records* **[Online Database],** digitized at the FamilySearch.org website. Images of Vermont vital records from various counties and towns. Currently includes only records from the following counties: Bennington, Caledonia, Chittenden, Essex, Franklin, Grand Isle, Lamoille, Orange, Orleans, and Washington. This database has 75,597 records. See https://familysearch.org/search/collection/1627819.

1850-1900. *Vermont Land Records, Early to 1900* **[Online Database],** digitized at the FamilySearch.org website. Land records give the locations and dates for land transactions with the names of buyers and sellers.

Most volumes of land records have indexes of buyers and sellers. Look in the indexes first to find the volumes and page numbers where the actual land records can be found. Then look in the appropriate land records volumes to see the images of the deeds. This database has 169,270 records. See https://familysearch.org/search/collection/1409123.

1852-1959. *General Alphabetical Card Index to Case Files, Addison District, Vermont* **[Microfilm & Digital Capture],** from the original records in the Probate Court, Middlebury, Vermont. FHL film #1913861-191382. To access the digital images, see the online FHL catalog page: www.familysearch.org/search/catalog/1052790.

1855-1860. *Statewide Directories for Vermont,* **[Microfilm],** from the originals of various publishers, filmed by Research Publications, Woodbridge, Conn., 1980-1984. These directories are essentially heads of household censuses for the entire state of Vermont. There are microfilm copies for this series of directories at the FHL, for the following years:
- **1855** Vermont Directory, by W. W. Atwater, FHL film # 6044609, 6044610.
- **1856** Vermont Directory, by W. W. Atwater, FHL film # 6044611.
- **1857** Vermont Directory, by W. W. Atwater, FHL film #6044612.
- **1858** The Vermont Directory, by W. W. Atwater, FHL film #6044613.
- **1859** Vermont Directory, by W. W. Atwater, published by G. A. Tuttle & Co., FHL film #6044614.
- **1860** Vermont Directory, by W. W. Atwater; published by G. A. Tuttle & Co., FHL film # 6044615.

1861-1865. *Index to Compiled Service Records of Volunteer Union Soldiers Who Served in Organizations from the State of Vermont* **[Microfilm & Digital Capture],** from the originals at the National Archives, Washington, DC. Filmed by the National Archives, 1964, series M557, 14 rolls, beginning with FHL film #882472 (A-Be). To access the digital images, see the online FHL catalog: https://familysearch.org/search/catalog/313424.

1861-1866. *Internal Revenue Tax Assessment Lists for Vermont* **[Microfilm & Online Database],** from the original records at the National Archives, Washington, DC, series M792, 7 rolls, beginning with

FHL film #1578444 (District 1, 1862-1864). To access the digital images, see the online FHL catalog: **https://familysearch.org/search/catalog/577870**

1861-1867. *Vermont, Enrolled Militia Records* **[Online Database],** digitized and indexed at the FamilySearch.org website. Index and images of Vermont enrolled militia records that identify thousands of young men who served in the military or who were eligible for service. Includes some corrected entries. This collection currently includes only enrolled militia records from the following counties: Addison, Bennington, Chittenden, Franklin, Lamoille, Orange, Orleans, and Rutland. Also included are burial records and personal war sketches for the town of Cambridge, Lamoille County. This database has 4,350 records. See **https://familysearch.org/search/collection/1483040.**
- See also, *Vermont, Enrolled Militia Records, 1861-1867* **[Online Database],** indexed at the Ancestry.com website. Source: FamilySearch extractions from microfilm of original Vermont military records. The record was created to provide a list of those men in the state of Vermont who were eligible to serve in the military. This database has 4,350 records. See **http://search.ancestry.com/search/db.aspx?dbid=60208.**

1862-1915. *Vermont, Washington County, Probate Estate Files* **[Online Database],** digitized at the FamilySearch.org website. Probate estate files located at the Washington District Probate Court in Montpelier, Vermont. This database has 35,679 records. See **https://familysearch.org/search/collection/1419704.**

1863-1866. *Report of the Adjutant General & Inspector General of the State of Vermont* **[Online Database],** digitized and indexed at the Ancestry.com website. Names of all soldiers from all Vermont militia units. This database has 1,074 records. See **http://search.ancestry.com/search/db.aspx?dbid=31405.**

1865 Vermont Directory **[Printed Book & Microfilm],** prepared by Alice I. Noble. Reproduction of original book published 1865, 144 pages, FHL book 974.3 E4. Also on microfilm, roll #1440652.

1865-1910. *Burlington (Vermont) City Directories* **[Microfilm],** from the originals of various publishers. This series includes a run of 35 annual city directories, 1865 through 1910, filmed by Research Publications, Woodbridge, CT, 1980-1984, 7 rolls, beginning with

FHL film #1376640 (1865/1866 Burlington City Directory). For a complete list of roll numbers and contents of each roll, see the online FHL catalog page for this title. See **https://familysearch.org/search/catalog/532468.**

1871-1908. *General Index to Vital Records of Vermont* **[Microfilm & Digital Capture],** from the original records at the VT State Archives. Index includes births, deaths and marriages. Some cards filmed out of sequence – re-filmed cards are on the end of some rolls. Filmed by the Genealogical Society of Utah, 1967-1995, 122 rolls, beginning with FHL film #540051 (Aabin, Louise – Albee, William Taylor0. To access the digital images, see the online FHL catalog page: **https://familysearch.org/search/catalog/313352.**

1871-1965. *Vermont Deaths and Burials* **[Online Database],** indexed at the FamilySearch.org website. Name index to death and burial records from microfilm copies at the Family History Library, Salt Lake City, UT. This database has 74,098 records. See **https://familysearch.org/search/collection/1675549.**

"1874 Newfane Grand List, by School Districts, Windham County" **[Printed Article],** in *Branches and Twigs,* Vol. 23, No. 2 (Spring 1994).

1880-1881 Gazetteer and Business Directory of Bennington County, Vermont **[Printed Book],** compiled and published by Hamilton Child, 1880, Syracuse, NY, 500 pages. FHL film #1486499.
- See also *Index of Gazetteer of Bennington County, Vt., 1880-81* **[Printed Book],** compiled by Charles D. Townsend, Sarasota, FL, Aceto Bookmen, 1989, 41 pages. FHL book 974.38 E42c.

1881-1882 Gazetteer and Business Directory of Rutland County, Vermont **[Printed Book],** compiled and published by Hamilton Child, 1882, 642 pages. Includes historical notes of the county and the towns. FHL book 974.37 E4c.

1881-1882 Gazetteer and Business Directory of Addison County, Vermont **[Printed Book],** compiled and published by Hamilton Child, Syracuse, N.Y., 1882, 541 pages. FHL film #1415262. See also, Index of Gazetteer of Addison County, Vermont, 1882. FHL book 974.35 E4c.

1882-1883 Gazetteer and Business Directory of Chittenden County, Vermont **[Printed Book]**, compiled and published by Hamilton Child, Syracuse, N.Y., 1882, 584 pages. FHL book 974.317 E4c.

1882-1883 Gazetteer and Business Directory of Franklin and Grand Isle Counties, Vermont **[Printed Book]**, compiled and published by Hamilton Child, Syracuse, NY, 1883, 612 pages. Includes a history of the counties with biographical sketches. FHL film #1000626.

1883-1884 Gazetteer and Business Directory of Windsor County, Vermont **[Printed Book]**, compiled and published by Hamilton Child, Syracuse, NY, 1884, 664 pages. FHL book 974.365.
- See also *Index, Gazetteer of Windsor County, VT, for 1883-84* **[Printed Book]**, compiled by Charles D. Townsend, publ. 1999, Sarasota, FL, Aceto Bookmen, 63 pages. FHL book 974.365 E5.

1883-1884 Gazetteer and Business Directory of Lamoille and Orleans Counties, Vermont **[Printed Book]**, compiled and published by Hamilton Child, Syracuse, NY, 1884, 658 pages. FHL film #1000626.

1884 Gazetteer and Business Directory of Windham County, Vermont **[Printed Book]**, compiled and published by Hamilton Child, Syracuse, NY, 1884, 600+ pages. Includes a history of the county, with biographical sketches. FHL book 974.39 E4c.
- See also, *Index of Gazetteer of Windham County, Vermont, Hamilton Child, 1884* **[Printed Book]**, compiled by Charles D. Townsend, Sarasota, FL, Aceto Bookmen, 1987, 203 pages. FHL book 974.39 E4c index.

1886 History. *History of Chittenden County, Vermont: With Illustrations and Biographical Sketches of Some of its Prominent Men and Pioneers* **[Microfilm & Digital Capture]**, from the book edited by W. S. Rann, publ. Syracuse, NY, D. Mason and Co., 1886, 867 pages. Filmed by the Genealogical Society of Utah, 1976, 1 roll, FHL film #928117. Another filming, Tucson, AZ: W.C. Cox, 1974, 1 rolls, FHL film #1000626. See also *Index to History of Chittenden County, Vermont,* compiled by the LDS Research Dept, 7 pages, FHL book 974.317 H2r index. To access a digital version of this book, see the FHL catalog page: **https://familysearch.org/search/catalog/228046**.

1887-1888 Gazetteer of Caledonia and Essex Counties, Vermont, Part 2 **[Printed Book]**, compiled and published by Hamilton Child, Syracuse, NY, 1888. Part 1 includes a history of the counties with biographical sketches. FHL book 974.3 E4c.

1888 Gazetteer of Orange County, Vermont **[Microfilm & Digital Capture]**, from a book compiled and published by Hamilton Child, Syracuse, NY, 1888. Includes a history of the county with biographical sketches. Filmed by the Genealogical Society of Utah, 1974, FHL film #962543. To access a digital version of Part 1 of this book, see the online FHL catalog page: **www.familysearch.org/search/catalog/155591**.

1889 Gazetteer of Washington County, Vermont **[Printed Book]**, compiled and published by Hamilton Child, Syracuse Journal Company, 1889. Includes a history of the county with biographical sketches. FHL book 974.34 E4c.

1894. See *Vermont Men, 1894* **[Online Database]**, Indexed at the Ancestry.com website. Source: *Men of Vermont: An Illustrated Biographical History of Vermonters and Sons of Vermont*, by Jacob G. Ullery, Brattleboro, VT, 1894. This collection of biographical sketches covers natives of Vermont from the state's early history through the close of the 19th Century. Rich in detail, this database includes information on prominent Vermonters such as profession, children, and some genealogies. See **http://search.ancestry.com/search/db.aspx?dbid=3337**.

1895-1954. *St. Albans District Manifest Records of Aliens Arriving From Foreign Contiguous Territory: Records of Arrivals Through Small Ports in Vermont* **[Microfilm & Digital Capture]**, from originals at the National Archives. This six-roll series is for Vermont only. Records include Primary Inspection Memorandum cards, Card Manifests, Record of Registry cards, and Resident Aliens Border Crossing Cards (from Canada to the U.S.). The records are arranged alphabetically for each port of entry in Vermont. Filmed by the National Archives, series M1462, 6 rolls. beginning with FHL film #143098. To access the digital images, see the online FHL catalog page: **https://familysearch.org/search/catalog/452594**.

1895-1954. *Vermont, St. Albans Canadian Border Crossings* [Online Database], digitized and indexed at the FamilySearch.org website. Source: National Archives microfilm series M1461, M1463, M1464, and M1465. This collection contains an index to Canadian border entries through the St. Albans, Vermont, District (and many, many more crossings). There are dozens of entry points from Canada into the U.S., and virtually all of them had their records filed at the St. Albans, Vermont customs house. The records are from crossings in Washington, Idaho, Montana, North Dakota, Minnesota, New York, Vermont, and Maine. This database has 6,288,677 records. See https://familysearch.org/search/collection/2185163.

1908-1987. *Vermont Naturalization Records* [Online Database], digitized and indexed at FamilySearch.org. Records of Naturalization from Vermont. These records were captured in Boston at the National Archives and Records Administration. This is a collaboration with Ancestry.com and the National Archives and Records Administration. his database has 71,835 images, see www.familysearch.org/search/collection/2625097.

1909-2008. *Vermont, Marriage Records* [Online Database], indexed at the Ancestry.com website. Source: VT Dept of Health, Burlington, VT. The records consist of 1) Certificate of Marriage, 2) Amended Certificate of Marriage, 3) Certificate of Civil Union, and 4) Amended Certificate of Civil Union. Generally, the following information is listed: Names of bride and groom, Age, Birth date, Parents' names, Marriage date, and place of marriage. This database has 1,382,965 records. See http://search.ancestry.com/search/db.aspx?dbid=1606.

1909-2008. *Vermont, Birth Records* [Online Database], indexed at the Ancestry.com website. Source: VT State Archives (1909-2003) and VT Dept of Health (2004-2008). The records consist of 1) Certificate of Birth, 2) Amended Certificate of Birth, 3) Delayed Certificate of Birth, and 4) Certificate of Birth for Foreign Born Child. Generally, the following information is listed: Child's name, Gender, Date and time of birth, Birthplace, Parents' names (including mother's maiden name), and Residence of parents. This database has 960,913 records. See http://search.ancestry.com/search/db.aspx?dbid=1605.

1909-2008. *Vermont, Death Records* [Online Database], indexed at the Ancestry.com website. Source: VT State Archives (1909-2003) and VT Dept of Health (2004-2008). Generally, the following information is listed: Name of deceased, Gender, Death date and place, Birth date and place, Residence, Spouse's name, Parents' names, and cause of death. This database has 506,711 records. See http://search.ancestry.com/search/db.aspx?dbid=1607.

1981-2001. *Vermont Marriage Index, 1981-1984 and 1989-2001* [Online Database], indexed at the Ancestry.com website. Source: VT Vital Records Office, Burlington, VT. Included for each record, at least, is a marriage date, groom, bride, place of marriage, place of birth of bride and groom, and their ages at time of marriage. This database has 200,633 records. See http://search.ancestry.com/search/db.aspx?dbid=8956.

1981-2001. *Vermont Birth Index* [Online Database], indexed at the Ancestry.com website. Source: VT Vital Records Office, Burlington, VT. Includes child's name, birthdate, place of birth, sex of the child, mother's name, and father's name. This database has 152,062 records. See http://search.ancestry.com/search/db.aspx?dbid=8957.

1981-2001. *Vermont Death Index* [Online Database], indexed at the Ancestry.com website. Source: VT Dept of Health, Burlington, VT. Information provided in this index may include the full name of the deceased, age, date of death, town and state of death, sex, race, marital status, birth date, state of birth, town and state of residence. This database has 101,438 records. See http://search.ancestry.com/search/db.aspx?dbid=3269.

1981-2001. *Vermont Divorce Index* [Online Database], indexed at the Ancestry.com website. Source: VT Vital Records Office, Burlington, VT. Each record contains, at least, the husband's name, wife's name, their state of birth, county of divorce degree, and their ages at the time of divorce. This database has 88,920 records. See http://search.ancestry.com/search/db.aspx?dbid=8954.

Sample Divorce Record, page 89 →

1999-Current. See *Vermont Recent Newspaper Obituaries (1999-Current)* [Online Database], digitized and indexed newspaper obituaries at the GenealogyBank website, including newspapers from Barre, Bennington, Brattleboro, Burlington, Chester, Colchester County, Essex Junction, Manchester, Middlebury, Milton, Newport, Northfield, Rutland, Springfield, St. Albans, and St. Johnsbury. See www.genealogybank.com/explore/obituaries/all/usa/vermont.

DH-PHS-DIV-89

102028

412-10-02 Worden.

COURT DOCKET NUMBER

02002064

STATE FILE NUMBER

DEPARTMENT OF HEALTH

VERMONT RECORD OF DIVORCE OR ANNULMENT

HUSBAND		
1. HUSBAND'S NAME (First, Middle, Last) Henry North Parker		
2a. RESIDENCE—STATE Vermont	2b. CITY OR TOWN Norwich	3. MAILING ADDRESS (Street and Number or Rural Route Number, City or Town, State, Zip Code) P.O. Box 26, Norwich, VT 05055
4. BIRTHPLACE (State or Foreign Country) North Carolina	5. DATE OF BIRTH (Month, Day, Year) 9-10-48	

WIFE		
6a. WIFE'S NAME (First, Middle, Last) Virginia Louise Beggs		6b. MAIDEN SURNAME Beggs
7a. RESIDENCE—STATE New Hampshire	7b. CITY OR TOWN Hanover	8. MAILING ADDRESS (Street and Number or Rural Route Number, City or Town, State, Zip Code) 57 E. Wheelock Street
9. BIRTHPLACE (State or Foreign Country) Massachusetts	10. DATE OF BIRTH (Month, Day, Year) 1-5-54	Hanover, NH 03755

MARRIAGE		
11a. PLACE OF THIS MARRIAGE (State or Foreign Country) Massachusetts	11b. CITY TOWN OR LOCATION Osterville	11c. DATE OF THIS MARRIAGE (Month, Day, Year) 3/19/77
12a. DATE COUPLE LAST RESIDED IN SAME HOUSEHOLD (Month, Day, Year) 6/30/00	12b. NUMBER OF CHILDREN UNDER 18 IN THIS HOUSEHOLD AS OF THE DATE IN ITEM 12a. Number ___ [X] NONE	13. PETITIONER ☐ Husband [X] Wife ☐ Both ☐ Other (Specify) ___
14a. NAME OF PETITIONER'S ATTORNEY (Type/Print) SUSAN M. BUCKHOLZ ☐ NO ATTORNEY		14b. ADDRESS (Street and Number or Rural Route Number, City or Town, State, Zip Code) P.O. Box 1221 Quechee, VT 05059

DECREE		
15. I CERTIFY THAT THIS DECREE BECAME ABSOLUTE (FINAL) ON (Month, Day, Year) NOV 5 02	16. TYPE OF DECREE—Absolute Divorce or Annulment (Specify) Absolute	17. COUNTY OF DECREE Windsor
18. NUMBER OF CHILDREN UNDER 18 WHOSE PHYSICAL CUSTODY WAS AWARDED TO: Husband ___ Wife ___ Joint (Husband/Wife) ___ Other ___ [X] No Children	19. LEGAL GROUNDS FOR DECREE (Specify) Lived separate and apart for a period in excess of six consecutive months.	
20. SIGNATURE OF COURT OFFICIAL	21. TITLE OF COURT OFFICIAL Court officer	22. DATE SIGNED (Month, Day, Year) 11/05/02

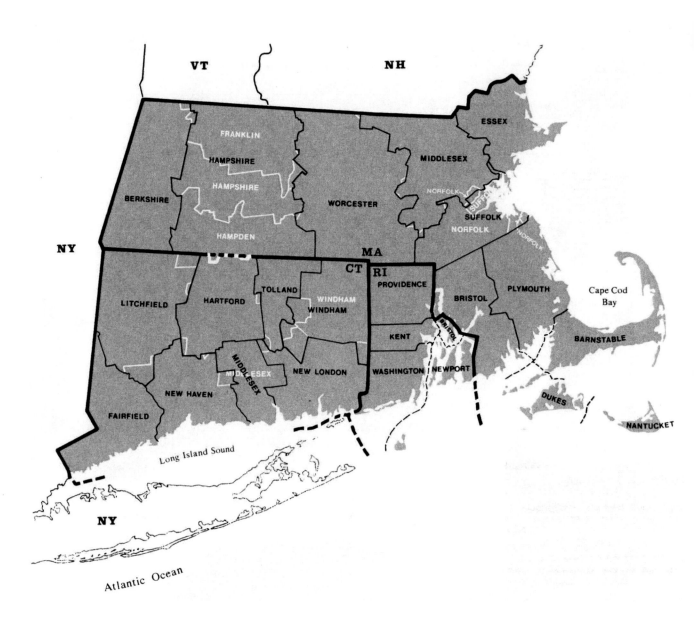

1790 Massachusetts Counties (with Connecticut & Rhode Island). Shown in black are the eleven Massachusetts counties at the time of the August 1790 Federal Census. The current fourteen counties, where different, are shown in white. Not shown on this map is the District of Maine. Although part of Massachusetts in 1790, the Maine area was a separate court district of the U.S. Circuit Court System and had its own 1790 census taken. Neither Connecticut nor Rhode Island were ever organized as part of Massachusetts, but they were both colonized first by Massachusetts people. The area below the dashed state line was claimed by Massachusetts, but the dispute was not settled until 1804. **Map Source:** Page 60, *Map Guide to the U.S. Federal Censuses, 1790-1920,* by William Thorndale and William Dollarhide.

Massachusetts
Censuses & Substitute Name Lists

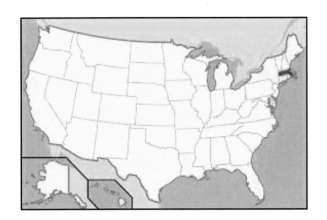

Historical Timeline of Massachusetts, 1524-1820

1524. Italian Giovanni da Verrazzano sailed up the Atlantic coast in sight of present New York, Connecticut, Rhode Island, Massachusetts, and Maine, and wrote of his travels to his sponsor, King Francis I of France.

1558. Elizabeth I became Queen of England. The first explorations of North America took place during her 45-year reign, the Elizabethan Era, or "Golden Age." When Elizabeth I was crowned, England was nearly bankrupt, but during her reign, the English Empire expanded and thrived, and English culture flourished in Literature, Theatre, Music, and Architecture.

1559. Norumbega. Englishman David Ingram claimed to have traveled the length of the Atlantic seaboard from Florida to Maine, and on his return, told stories that he had visited the wealthy city of Norumbega, somewhere near present Massachusetts, where the streets were "far broader than any street in London…the men were bedecked with gold and silver bracelets, and the women with gold plates and pearls as big as thumbs." Though Ingram may have exaggerated a bit, he did spark an interest in the New England region.

1602 Cape Cod & Martha's Vineyard. English Privateer Bartholomew Gosnold led an expedition to present Massachusetts, named Cape Cod and discovered an island south of Cape Cod, which he named Martha's Vineyard. Gosnold had planned on planting a small settlement in the Cape Cod area, but the settlers chose to return to England due to a lack of provisions. Gosnold went on to become one of the founders of the Jamestown Colony.

1603. England. James I became King of England, the first monarch to rule both England and Scotland. (He was James VI of Scotland since 1566). He was also the first English monarch to publicly assert that he was blessed with "the divine right of Kings," meaning he was the voice of God on earth, at least in England, Scotland, or Ireland. Although James I was most remembered for commissioning a Bible translation, during his reign the first permanent English colonies were established in Virginia and New England. James I was also an advocate for the transportation of thousands of clan people living along the Scottish-English border to Ulster Province, Northern Ireland.

1603. English Captain Martin Pring led an expedition to present Maine, New Hampshire, and Massachusetts. He was the first European to ascend the Piscataqua River and was the first to erect a small fort on Cape Cod (now Truro, MA).

1603. French nobleman Pierre DuGua (Sieur DeMonts) was granted exclusive rights to colonize the area he had named l'Acadie (Acadia), granted by French King Henry IV. The area of Acadia included all of present Nova Scotia, New Brunswick, and most of Maine.

1604. Acadia. DeMonts established a French colony on St. Croix Island, at the mouth of the St. Croix River, now Maine. After surviving a bad Winter, the entire colony was moved across the Bay of Fundy to Port-Royal, now Nova Scotia.

1606. Two joint stock companies were founded in 1606, both with royal charters issued by King James I for the purpose of establishing colonies in North America. The Virginia Company of London was given a land grant between Latitude 34° (Cape Fear) and Latitude 41° (Long Island Sound). The Virginia Company of Plymouth was founded with a similar charter, between Latitude 38° (Potomac River) and Latitude 45° (St. John River), which included a shared area with the London Company between Latitude 38° and 41°.

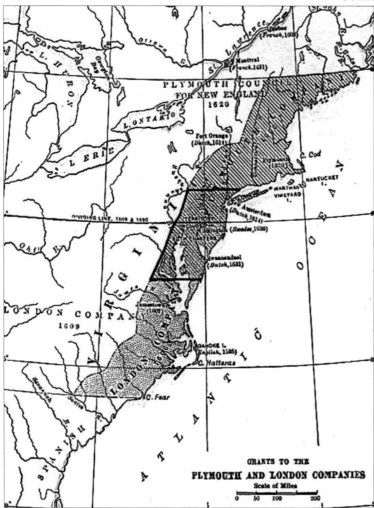

GRANTS TO THE
PLYMOUTH AND LONDON COMPANIES
Scale of Miles
0   50   100   200

1607. May. Led by John Smith , the London Company established the first permanent English settlement in North America – the Jamestown Colony. It was followed in August by the Sagadahoc Colony, a settlement led by George Popham, established by the Plymouth Company, near present Phippsburg, Maine. The Sagadahoc/ Popham colony was abandoned after just one year, due to a lack of confidence in a change of leadership.

Thereafter, the Plymouth Company dissolved until it was revived in 1620 as the Plymouth Council for New England.

1609. The 2nd Virginia Charter of 1609 extended the jurisdiction of the London Company to include the former shared area with the original Plymouth Company.

1614-1615. English Captain John Smith, leader of the Jamestown Colony, visited the coast of present Connecticut, Massachusetts, and Maine; then wrote his *Description of New England*, which encouraged Englishmen to settle there. Smith was credited as the first to call the area New England. Back in England, Christopher Jones was one seafarer who was known to have read Smith's *Description of New England* and remarked that he would like to go there. He got his wish as the master of the *Mayflowe*r in 1620.

1620. Plymouth Colony. A new Royal Charter was issued by King James I to the Plymouth Council for New England (formerly the Virginia Company of Plymouth) to establish colonial settlements in New England. The area was from Latitude 40° to Latitude 45° ("sea to sea"). In that same year, the *Mayflower* dropped anchor off Cape Cod, and Plymouth Colony was founded by a small group of Separatists/Pilgrims, who had fled England for Holland a few years earlier. Unlike the Puritans, the Pilgrims did not want to purify the Church of England, they just wanted to get away from the church's Prayer Book and have their own method of worship.

1625 England. Charles I became King of England, Scotland, and Ireland. Charles believed, like his father, that as King, he was the infallible interpreter of God's will on earth. Soon after taking office, Charles began to note a large number of non-conformists among his subjects. Along with his Archbishop, William Laud, the King began a campaign to purge his church of the largest group of non-conformists, the so-called Puritans, a militant Calvinist religious sect attempting to purify the Church of England. Unfortunately, Charles I took on a job that led to civil war in England as well as the loss of his head. But, his campaign can be credited as the main cause for the founding of significant English settlements in New England.

1628. The **Massachusetts Bay Company** was granted a royal charter for an English colony to be established in North America within the bounds of the Plymouth Council of New England. It is said that King Charles I was misled as to the religious leanings of the Massachusetts Bay Company leaders, all prominent Puritans, not Pilgrims, as he had surmised. The Massachusetts Bay Company managed to acquire legal interest in the area from Latitude 41^0 to Latitude 45^0, except for any previous grants in the same area.

1629. Sir Ferdinando Gorges and Captain John Mason agreed to split their grants at the Piscataqua River, with Mason retaining the land west of the river as the Province of New Hampshire.

1629. The "Great Migration" to New England began. As a result of the Charles I campaign to purge non-conformists from the Church of England, 1629-1640, large groups of people were alienated. Charles I disbanded Parliament and ruled England alone for eleven years. The Puritans referred to this era as "the eleven years of tyranny." It was during these eleven years that about 80,000 Puritans felt compelled to leave England. About a fourth of them moved to Holland; another fourth of them to Ireland; a fourth to the West Indies, particularly the islands of Barbados, Nevis, and St. Kitts; and the final group, some 20,000 Puritan immigrants, established the Massachusetts Bay Colony of North America.

1630. Massachusetts Bay Colony. The colony government was organized, with the first General Court at Charlestown and the creation of the first three counties of Norfolk, Suffolk, and Essex. They happened to be the same names as the three East Anglia counties of England from whence the majority of the Puritans had lived before coming to America.

1631. The General Court of the Massachusetts Bay Colony gave voting rights only to Freemen landowners who were Puritan church members.

1632. The General Court of Plymouth Colony gave voting rights to any Freeman/landowner if elected by the General Court.

1634. The Massachusetts Bay colony began annexing areas of present Maine. The original grants issued to Sir Ferdinand Gorges and Captain Christopher Levett were overlapped by grants of the Massachusetts Bay Colony, which began selling land in any unsettled areas just across the Piscataqua River in present Maine. As soon as settlements were established, Massachusetts Bay formally annexed those areas as part of their territory.

1635-1637. In 1635, religious dissident Roger Williams was banished from the Massachusetts Bay Colony. In 1637, Anne Hutchinson, a charismatic religious leader opposed to the Puritans, was put on trial (in the Church Court), excommunicated, and banished.

1636. Connecticut Colony. The English settlements of Hartford, Wethersfield, and Windsor were formed as the Connecticut Colony. First known as the River Colony, it was a recognized organization for a Puritan congregation established by the Massachusetts Bay Colony.

1637. King Charles I, now keenly aware of the fact that the Massachusetts Bay Colony was an enclave of non-conformist Puritans, turned their charter over to Sir Ferdinand Gorges, a loyal supporter of the king, and the original leader of the Plymouth Company. However, the official transfer document with the king's seal was on board a ship that sank en route to Boston. The Puritans, believing it to be an Act of Providence, ignored the king's edict.

1638. Roger Williams, Anne Hutchinson, and more dissidents, founded the **Providence Plantations** (later Rhode Island and Providence Plantations).

1638-1643. In 1638, **New Haven Colony** was formed as an independent colony, separate from Connecticut Colony. In 1643, the coastal settlements of Branford, Guilford, Milford, Stamford, plus Southold (on Long Island), all joined the New Haven Colony.

1642. English Civil War. Since taking the throne in 1625, King Charles I had purged most of the Puritans from the Church of England. To deal with a Parliament opposing his every move, in 1629, Charles disbanded Parliament and ruled England on his own. That action canceled over 400 years of liberties gained by Parliament since the Magna Carta. When Parliament was restored in 1640, it quickly became dominated by the same Puritans who Charles had removed from the Church of England. Beginning in 1642, Royalist supporters were forced to fight the armies of the Puritan Parliament in the English Civil War. The supporters of Charles I did not fare well against them.

1645-1651. England. After his defeat and capture in 1645, Charles I refused to accept his captors' demands for a constitutional monarchy, and briefly escaped captivity in 1647. While recaptured, his son, Prince Charles, was able to marshal Scottish forces for the king. However, by 1648, Oliver Cromwell had consolidated the English opposition. King Charles I was tried, convicted, and executed for high treason in January 1649. The Civil War continued until 1651.

1649-1651. New England, Virginia & Maryland. The English colonies were still divided between the Puritans/Parliamentarians and the Royalists/Cavaliers. The New England colonies were 85-90% Puritan, and the Virginia colony was 60-65% Royalist. The Maryland colony was about 55% Puritan.

1651-1658. Commonwealth of England. Prince Charles had lived in exile after the execution of his father, Charles I. In 1649, the Scots had proclaimed Charles the King of Scotland. But, the Puritan leader, Oliver Cromwell, defeated his army in 1651, and Charles fled to France. Cromwell was to become the Lord Protectorate of the Commonwealth of England, with a Puritan-controlled Parliament. After Cromwell died in 1658, the English people became dissatisfied with the government that Cromwell had established.

1656. The first Quakers in New England, Mary Fisher and Ann Austin, arrived at Boston Harbor and were immediately arrested.

1658. Massachusetts had always expressed a claim to Maine, based on the language of their 1628 Royal Charter (which had defined their northern bounds as the St. John River). The Massachusetts Colony was also interested in Maine's natural resources, which were more abundant than their own. After several partial annexations beginning in 1634, all of Maine was annexed as frontier territory by the Massachusetts Bay Colony in 1658. Several of the Maine communities were allowed to vote on the final annexations, and all were in favor of joining Massachusetts.

1659. After being convicted by the Church Court in Salem, Mary Dyer was hanged for the crime of being a Quaker.

1660. England. In 1660, Parliament invited Prince Charles to return and declared him king. Charles II was restored to the throne as King of England, Scotland,

and Ireland. He was to become one of the most effective English monarchs of all time. He ruled until his death in 1685, and during his reign, the English colonials forced out the remaining pockets of Atlantic settlements made earlier by the Dutch, Swedes, and Danes. Charles II saw the Atlantic colonies as a source of trade and commerce, supported development, and granted several more charters for settlement. All of the English colonies thrived as a result. He was the first monarch to recognize the potential for the North American colonies to become a contiguous, viable commonwealth. He encouraged the development of post roads, and a regular communication between the Governors. Charles II was responsible for setting the tone of self-government, religious tolerance, and individual freedoms in the English colonies that were to become American institutions.

1661. March. The last Quaker was hanged in Boston. In April, King Charles II ordered the Massachusetts Bay Colony to end the practice.

1664-1665. New York and New Jersey. In 1664, King Charles II granted to his brother, James, the Duke of York (of England) and the Duke of Albany (of Scotland), all of the territory between the Delaware and Connecticut Rivers. The area had recently been relieved from the Dutch and carried the name New Netherlands. James immediately renamed it the Province of New York. In 1665, James granted to Sir George Carteret and Lord Berkley of Stratton, a part of the New York colony between the Hudson River and the Delaware River. Carteret's portion was named West New Jersey, Berkley's portion was named East New Jersey. The two Proprietors appointed a governor for the Province of New Jersey, with land sales by both East New Jersey and West New Jersey.

1665 Connecticut Colony. New Haven Colony and Connecticut Colony merged into one chartered colony, retaining the name Connecticut.

1675-1678. King Philip's War. This was a bloody battle between the English colonists of New England and a confederation of Indian tribes for control of the New England areas. The war was named for the main leader of the Native Americans, Metacomet, known to the English as "King Philip." The Northern Theatre of King's Philip's War was fought along the New England/Acadia border (the Kennebec River of Maine). The Indians were nearly liquidated, and the conflict ended with the Treaty of Casco in 1678.

1681. Pennsylvania. Charles II granted to William Penn a land charter to repay a debt owed to William's father, Admiral William Penn. This was the largest English land grant to an individual, and William Penn became the sole owner and proprietor, with allegiance to the English Crown.

1682. Delaware. The area of present Delaware was transferred from James, the Duke of York, proprietor of New York to William Penn, proprietor of Pennsylvania. The area became known as the "Lower Counties on the Delaware."

1686. Dominion of New England. After Charles II died without issue in 1685, his brother, the Duke of York, was crowned King of England as James II. As the original Royal Charter holder of the New York Colony, James was familiar with the English colonies. In 1686, he established the *Dominion of New England.* This was an administrative union of English colonies, encompassing the areas from the Delaware River to the Penobscot River. The *Dominion* managed to install some religious reforms in the English colonies, allowing Catholics to hold office.

1688. The Glorious Revolution. After James II had declared his Catholic beliefs, he was deposed in 1688. His Protestant daughter, Mary, was declared the legal heir to the throne. She had married her cousin, William of Orange, the Stadtholder/Ruler of Holland, and Europe's most staunch Protestant leader. Because of William's stature as the leader of the Protestant insurrection which had overthrown the Catholic James II, Parliament asked both William and Mary to rule England jointly. The Protestant-controlled Parliament considered the skirmish a holy war, and later gave the insurrection the name of *Glorious Revolution.* The Dominion of New England was dissolved in 1689, and the concept of religious tolerance reverted back to the prohibition of Catholics to hold public office in all of the English colonies. James was exiled to France, where he died in 1701.

1689-1690. King William's War. Soon after they were crowned, William III and Mary II joined a European alliance against France, and the subsequent battles became known as King William's War. In 1689, several battles took place, including the French attack on Saco, Maine; followed by the English attack and destruction of the French Acadia capital of Port-Royal in 1690.

1691. Province of Massachusetts Bay. The province was formed after merging the Plymouth Colony and the Massachusetts Bay Colony. About this time, the term "District of Maine," was used to describe that area as part of the Province of Massachusetts Bay.

1692. The Salem Witch Trials took place, culminating in over 170 arrests and 20 executions.

1696. During King Williams's War, French forces from Pentagouet (present Castine, Maine) attacked and destroyed the English settlement at Pemaquid (present Bristol, Maine). Pemaquid was the northernmost community of New England, lying on the border with French Acadia. The French community of Pentagouet was the southernmost settlement of French Acadia. After the Siege of Pemaquid, the French forces continued north and destroyed virtually every English settlement in Newfoundland and deported over 500 people back to England. In retaliation, the English attacked and destroyed more Acadian communities, including present Fredericton, New Brunswick.

1702-1713. Queen Anne's War. This was a decisive war in the series of conflicts between France and England. Battles took place in New England, Newfoundland, Québec, and Acadia. Notable events were the brutal French/Indian raid on Deerfield, Massachusetts in 1704, where 40 were killed and over 100 surviving English colonists were forced to march to Québec as hostages; and, the 1708 French/Indian raid on Haverhill, MA, where 16 settlers were killed. The English Queen Anne succeeded to the throne after the death of Mary II, her older sister, and William III, who died in 1702 without issue. The English prevailed in most of the battles – Queen Anne's War marked a turning point for the success of English interests over the French in North America.

1707. During the reign of Queen Anne, the **United Kingdom of Great Britain** was established, a merger of Scotland and England-Wales-Ireland. The English Colonies now became the British Colonies.

1713. The Peace of Utrecht ended Queen Anne's War. France ceded to Great Britain its claims to Newfoundland, Hudson's Bay, and the peninsular part of French Acadia, which the British renamed Nova Scotia. The British took possession of the peninsula area and required the Acadians to swear allegiance to Britain or leave. The continental part of Acadia (including areas of present Maine and New Brunswick) remained in French control and a number of displaced Acadians from the British side moved across the Bay of Fundy to lands near the St. John and St. Croix rivers, putting them in the Province of Massachusetts Bay.

1714. After Queen Anne died without issue, her 2nd cousin, George I was crowned King of Great Britain and Ireland. Although there were several English heirs closer to Queen Anne than George I, he was the closest Protestant heir, a great-grandson of English King James I. George I was the first of the House of Hanover to rule Great Britain. He left his home in Hanover infrequently, never learned to speak English, and sanctioned the creation of the first Prime Minister and Cabinet Government in Great Britain. During the reign of a mostly absent George I, the British Colonies were invaded by the first wave of Scots-Irish immigrants.

1718. The arrival of the first Scots-Irish immigrants to New England was via Boston Harbor. The so-called Scots-Irish (or Ulster Scots) were former border clan people who had lived near the Scottish-English border for centuries. A good number of them had moved into areas of Northern Ireland in the early 1600s, and a mass migration to most of the British colonies of America began in about 1717. Generally, the Scots-Irish did not care for civilization that much, and usually leap-frogged over any Atlantic settlements en route to the higher, wilderness areas of America. They did this in New England, New York, Pennsylvania, Virginia, the Carolinas, and Georgia. The first Scots-Irish who came to New England were to immediately head west into central Massachusetts or north into New Hampshire. Soon after the first New England arrivals, a number of Scots-Irish discovered the coastal areas of Maine.

1727. With the death of George I, his son, George II became King of Great Britain and Ireland. By this time, the Parliament of Great Britain was in control of much of the government, and the King had fewer responsibilities. During his reign, the largest group of immigrants to America were the Scots-Irish, who overtook the other British immigrants in numbers by about three to one.

1755-1758 Expulsion of the Acadians. At the beginning of the French and Indian War, the British completed their conquest of Acadia, and in 1755, began forcibly removing Acadians from their homes. (The British remembered the forced deportations imposed by the French against the English in Newfoundland back in 1696). The first expulsions were to the lower British colonies, but in 1758 they began transporting Acadians back to France.

1760. At the age of 22 years, **King George III** began a reign that would last over 60 years. He was a grandson of George II, and a son of Frederick, Prince of Wales (died 1751) the first heir apparent of George II. He was crowned while the Seven Years War was in progress, and after that war the British Empire reached its greatest influence in North America.

1763. The Treaty of Paris of 1763 ended the French and Indian War (it was called the Seven Years War in Canada and Europe). France was the big loser and lost virtually all of its remaining North American claims. The areas east of the Mississippi and all of Acadia/Nova Scotia and Québec were lost to Britain; the areas west of the Mississippi went to Spain. After the Treaty of Paris, George III issued a proclamation renaming the Province of Québec as the Province of Canada. He also issued the *Proclamation Line of 1763*, in which Indian Reserves were established west of the Appalachian Mountain Range, limiting western migrations by all of the British colonies. The *Proclamation Line* had the intent of forcing any future expansion of the British colonies into Florida (recently acquired from Spain), or into Nova Scotia. Instead, the proclamation became one of the *Intolerable Acts* perceived by Americans that would lead to the Revolutionary War.

1764-1765. Per terms of the Treaty of Paris, the British were given the right to remove the remaining French Acadians but agreed to provide resettlement assistance. The destinations were not always clear, and the displaced Acadians were sometimes loaded onto ships headed to Boston, New York, Baltimore, Norfolk, Charleston, Savannah, or Mobile. In early 1765, several shiploads of Acadians arrived in New Orleans. For the next several years, thousands of Acadians, including many of those who had first been deported to the Atlantic colonies or France, were finally drawn together in French-speaking Louisiana, where they received land grants and assistance in starting a new life.

The British conquest of North America during the French and Indian War was an expensive victory, putting the British government in debt greater than any other time in its history. By 1765, the maintenance of thousands of British army and naval forces in British North America was a serious drain on the British economy.

1765. Stamp Act. This was one of the first taxes levied directly against the inhabitants of the British colonies (without the approval of their own legislatures) and led to vigorous acts of rebellion. In protest over the stamp tax, American colonists sacked and burned the home of Massachusetts governor Thomas Hutchinson. In 1774 he was exiled to Britain. The hated Stamp Act led to the organization of one of the first anti-British groups, The Sons of Liberty, who coined the rallying cry, "No Taxation Without Representation."

1767. Townshend Acts. Named after Charles Townshend, the British Chancellor of the Exchequer, who first proposed a program to levy new taxes in the colonies to raise funds to pay the salaries of the governors and judges so that they would remain loyal to Great Britain. Six different acts were meant to establish a precedent that the British Parliament had the right to tax the colonies. In Massachusetts, the Townshend Acts were met with a public outrage, extreme resistance. and a formal demand to repeal the taxes.

1768. The British government responded to the protests to the Townshend Acts by sending an occupation force of 4,000 British troops to Boston. With a population of about 15,000, it meant there was one British soldier for every Boston household.

1770. March. Boston Massacre. A mob formed around a single British sentry, who was bombarded with verbal abuse and harassment. The sentry was soon joined by eight additional soldiers. After being subjected to thrown objects, the soldiers opened fire on the mob, killing three people instantly and wounding several others. Two more died later of wounds sustained in the shootings. The incident became a rallying point for the radical Sons of Liberty – including men such as Samuel Adams and Paul Revere.

1773. Boston Tea Party. One of the last of the acts of rebellion credited to the Sons of Liberty before American shots were fired was the Boston Tea Party. Apparently, the resistance to a tax on tea imports was more than the British could abide, because the British reaction to the Boston Tea Party was Parliament's series of punitive laws called the *Coercive Acts*, and the *Massachusetts Government Act,* which took away Massachusetts' rights to self-government. In Massachusetts, they were called the *Intolerable Acts*, and fueled even more rebellion.

1774. June. **Québec Act.** The British reacted to the increased American rebellions by solidifying British loyalty in the Province of Canada. They enacted the Québec Act, which reversed the long-standing British policy against Catholic governments in all of their colonies. The Québec Act, just a few years after the forced deportations of Catholic Acadians, restored the name Province of Québec and granted Québec residents full British citizenship, allowed Québec to retain their Catholic churches and parish taxing systems, and to keep their established French Laws and Customs. The Act also expanded the physical area of Québec to include a huge area of western lands claimed by the Thirteen Colonies: including much of the Great Lakes and former French lands east of the Mississippi River. The Thirteen Colonies viewed the Québec Act as one of the *Intolerable Acts* that made the impending war justifiable.

1774. September. **The Suffolk Resolves** was a declaration by the leaders of Suffolk County, Massachusetts, of which Boston was the major city. The declaration rejected the *Massachusetts Government Act* and resolved to boycott any imported goods from Britain unless the *Intolerable Acts* were repealed. The declaration was immediately heard and endorsed by the First Continental Congress in Philadelphia, which had convened specifically to address "the passage of the Coercive Acts" imposed on the colonies by Great Britain. But, the lack of retraction and the continued show of force by the British was to escalate rapidly into an armed rebellion. The first armed militia drawn to oppose the British took place in and around Boston.

1775. Revolutionary War Begins. In April, the battles of Lexington and Concord were the first military engagements of the Revolutionary War. Both battles took place near Boston, where the British had sent an armed force to repel the American rebels. In June, the Battle of Bunker Hill was a defeat for the Americans, but the loss of life on the British side was so great that British General Clinton later remarked in his diary, "A few more such victories would have shortly put an end to British dominion in America." After Bunker Hill, the focus of the Revolutionary War shifted to areas around New Jersey and New York.

1781. October. **Siege of Yorktown.** In six years of war, Commanding General George Washington won very few battles with the British. He had learned how to fight the British by avoiding direct frontal attacks at all costs. Most of his few successes came with sneak attacks or tactics learned in the French and Indian War, where the Indians hid behind trees and fired on the British redcoats marching to war at four abreast. Washington's greatest success, however, was his last great battle, the Siege of Yorktown. His brilliant handling of the final battle of the war was credited as the basis for the founding of the America republic. At Yorktown, the British Commanding General Charles Cornwallis surrendered and prompted the British government to negotiate an end to the conflict.

1783. September 3rd. **Treaty of Paris.** This was the official end of the Revolutionary War, as well as the first recognition of the United States of America as an independent nation. The treaty defined the limits of the U.S. to be from the Atlantic Ocean to the Mississippi River; and from Massachusetts/Maine to Georgia. But, the northern boundary between the U.S. and British North America was not defined precisely at the Treaty of Paris and the boundary remained in dispute for nearly 60 years.

1788. February 6th. Upon adoption of the Constitution of the United States, the Commonwealth of Massachusetts became the 6th state in the Union. Its area included the District of Maine.

1790. August 2nd. The **1790 Federal Census** was taken in the 13 original states, plus the 14th state of Vermont (with a census day of 4 April 1791). The 1790 census divisions were based on the 16 US Circuit Courts, one for each state except Massachusetts and Virginia, both having two US court districts. Massachusetts had a second US Court district with boundaries that matched the present state of Maine (a state in 1820). Virginia had a second US Court district with boundaries that matched the present state of Kentucky (a state in 1792). The 1790 population of the Maine district was 96,540 people. The population of the Massachusetts district was 376,787 people.

1800. August 4th. The **1800 Federal Census** was taken in the district of Maine and the district of Massachusetts. The population of the Maine district was 151,719 people. The population of the Massachusetts district was 422,845 people.

1810. August 6th. The **1810 Federal Census** was taken in the district of Maine and the district of Massachusetts. The population of the Maine district was 228,705 people. The population of the Massachusetts district was 472,040 people.

1819. June. The voters of Maine approved a proposal for the separation of Maine from Massachusetts.

1820. March 3rd. The *Missouri Compromise* in Congress allowed Missouri to enter the Union as a slave state and Maine as a free state, thus keeping the balance of slave and free states equal in Congress.

1820. March 15th. Maine was admitted to the Union as the 23rd state.

1820. August 7th. The **1820 Federal Census** was taken for the state of Massachusetts. The population was 523,287 people.

About New England's Towns and Counties

There are currently 50 cities and 301 towns in Massachusetts, grouped into 14 counties. The history and function of the Massachusetts towns and counties derives from the system brought to New England by East Anglian Puritans. In 1643, four original counties of the Massachusetts Bay Colony were named and organized similar to their counterparts of Middlesex, Norfolk, Suffolk, and Essex counties, England.

A Town in East Anglia was the basic unit of government, and a number of towns made up a County. Individual land ownership in East Anglia predated most other parts of England. With land ownership came voting rights and a male landowner was often called a Freeman. Voting took place in town hall meetings, a practice still used in many New England towns today. Land divisions in the towns were usually long, narrow parcels connecting to a water source at one end, usually used exclusively for furrow crop farming. Central to a number of land parcels was a common grazing area, used freely by any landowner with contact to it.

All six of the New England states began with the county/town system, but there were some differences in their functions. Generally, births, marriages, and deaths, were recorded at the Town level in all six states. Certain courts were held at the Town level as well as the County level; but land sales (deeds) were recorded at the county level in Massachusetts, Maine, and New Hampshire; and recorded at the Town level in Connecticut, Rhode Island, and Vermont.

Years ago, Connecticut (1960) and Rhode Island (1846) both abolished county government for all functions except for judicial administration, and for colleting statistics by geographic areas. From 1997 to 2000, Massachusetts essentially abolished eight of their fourteen counties. Each of the abolished counties of Massachusetts still have elections for a Sherriff and a Registrar of Deeds, both offices now part of the state government.

In all of the New England states, the counties are still geographic divisions on maps and remain essential for understanding the origin of historical resources. For a list of all of the 351 city and town clerks in Massachusetts, with contact information and websites, see *www.sec.state.ma.us/ele/eleclk/clkidx.htm.*

Resources at the Massachusetts Archives

Introduction. The Archives, a division of the Office of the Secretary of the Commonwealth, is the repository for Massachusetts records generated by state government. Archives holdings date from the beginning of the Massachusetts Bay Colony in 1628 and document the settlement of lands in Maine and Massachusetts, the arrival of immigrants, and the development of state government. Specific collections with great value to genealogical researchers are described briefly below.

Boston Passenger Lists: Over one million immigrants came through the Port of Boston between 1848 and 1891. A project to digitize and index the records by volunteers may take several years to complete. To search the available lists online, see *www.sec.state.ma.us/arc/arcsrch/PassengerManifestSearchContents.html.*

City and Town Vital Records, 1841-1920: The Archives holds vital records covering the years 1841-1920. The vital records cover births, marriages, and deaths that occurred in Massachusetts. The Archives also has an online index to these records. For more information on vital records and access to the search screen, see *www.sec.state.ma.us/arc/arcsrch/VitalRecordsSearchContents.html.*

Massachusetts State Censuses: Massachusetts state censuses were taken every ten years, from 1855 through 1945. The Massachusetts Archives holds the original state census schedules for 1855 and 1865, the only two census years that have survived. The MA State Censuses for 1855 and 1865 are available online at both the FamilySearch.org and Ancestry.com websites. See the bibliography for details.

Military Records: Conflicts date from the seventeenth through the twentieth centuries; those most useful to genealogists are from 1643 to 1865. The records can be used to identify the service of particular individuals but provide little background on the person's family or life. Information can be gleaned from legislative records, military rolls, payroll accounts, pensions, bounties, and land grants. Adjutant General records are still held at the Massachusetts National Guard Museum & Archives, Concord, MA.

The Massachusetts Archive Collection (or Felt Collection) is an important source of records for early Massachusetts, Maine, and New Hampshire families. The records were originally bound into 328 volumes, generally arranged by topic. An online database provides name, location, and subject access for eighteen volumes. See *www.sec.state.ma.us/arc/arcsrch/RevolutionarySearchContects.html.*

For more details, visit the Massachusetts Archives webpage, *Researching Your Family's History.* See *www.sec.state.ma.us/arc/arcgen/genidx.htm.* There are descriptions of the following:
- Vital Records: Pre-1841
- Vital Records: Post 1920
- Papers Relating to Maine
- Plymouth Colony Records
- Records of State Institutions
- Massachusetts Supreme Judicial Court Archives
- The Suffolk Files
- Naturalizations
- Divorces
- Probates
- Name Changes
- Adoptions
- Suffolk County Deeds
- African-American and Native American Resources
- Additional Collections

Resources at the Massachusetts State Library

Introduction. The State Library has an extensive collection of materials dealing with the history of Massachusetts and its cities and towns. Resources include papers and photographs of political figures, historical newspapers, maps, and other historical documents dating back to the 1800s. For a review of the State & Local History collections, see *www.mass.gov/anf/research-and-tech/research-state-and-local-history.*

Massachusetts Historical Resources. The State Library's holdings include an extensive and unique collection of Massachusetts historical, cultural, and legislative material.

City, Town, and County Resources. The State Library has a vast collection of local histories in its research collection, as well as city and town directories, town reports, and tax valuations.

Maps, Atlases, and Plans. This collection holds more than 430 atlases and 3,400 maps covering most Massachusetts communities. It is particularly strong in 19th and 20th century materials. The collection includes panoramic maps, railroad maps, county atlases, and topographic maps.

Genealogical Resources. The State Library's holdings include materials useful for genealogical research. Among these are city and town directories, town histories, family histories, and tax valuations.

Massachusetts Political Figures. The State Library has a substantial collection of digital and print materials relating to Massachusetts public officials and legislative districts. These include photographic and manuscript collections for state political figures.

Bibliography
Massachusetts Censuses & Substitutes

This bibliography identifies censuses and substitute name lists available from the Plymouth Colony beginning in 1620; the Massachusetts Bay Colony from 1628; the Province of Massachusetts Bay from 1691; and the Commonwealth of Massachusetts from 1788.

MA State Censuses. The 1855 and 1865 MA State Censuses are extant, the only two census years that have survived. The originals are located at the Massachusetts Archives in Boston. The contents of the MA state censuses are similar to the 1850-1860 federal censuses. There are printed indexes and microfilm at the NEHGS in Boston and the FHL in Salt Lake City. Digitized-indexed versions are online at the AmericanAncestors.org, FamilySearch.org and Ancestry.com websites.

MA Federal Censuses. The 1790-1880 and 1900-1940 federal censuses for Massachusetts are complete for all towns and counties. The 1890 was lost in a fire in 1921 (like all other states). The 1950 will open to the public in 2022. For Massachusetts, printed indexes to the federal censuses are identified in the bibliography; as well as the microfilm, 1880-1940.

Substitute Name Lists. In addition to state and federal censuses, there are many Substitute Name Lists unique to Massachusetts, including Town or County Censuses, Court Records, Directories, Histories, Militia Lists, Tax Lists, Vital Records, or Voter Lists. - In the U.S. Census Substitutes chapter (Vol. 5), examples include Federal Censuses for all states, Find A Grave, or the Social Security Death Index.
- The published and online databases with name lists specific to areas of Massachusetts begin below in chronological order:

◆ ◆ ◆ ◆ ◆

1620-1635. *New England, The Great Migration and The Great Migration Begins* **[Online Database],** digitized and indexed at the Ancestry.com website. Robert Charles Anderson's *The Great Migration Begins* includes more than 1,100 sketches of immigrants or immigrant families that arrived in New England between 1620 and 1633. Each sketch contains information on the immigrant's migration dates and patterns, various biographical matters (such as occupation, church membership, education, offices, and land holdings), and genealogical details (birth, death, marriages, children, and other associations by blood or marriage), along with detailed comments, discussion, and bibliographic information on the family. This database has 62,840 records. See *http://search.ancestry.com/search/db.aspx?dbid=2496.*

1620-1640. *The Planters of the Commonwealth in Massachusetts* **[Online Database],** digitized and indexed at the Ancestry.com website. This is a complete digital version of the book by Charles Edward Banks. This database has 238 pages. See *http://search.ancestry.com/search/db.aspx?dbid=48127.*

1620-1691. *Index to Plymouth Colony Land Records* **[Printed Book & Digital Capture],** by Mabel W. Mayer, publ. c1955, Flint, MI, 64 pages. Digitized by the Genealogical Society of Utah, 2009. To access the digital version, see the online FHL catalog page: *www.familysearch.org/search/catalog/1717303.*

1620-1691. *Records of the Colony of New Plymouth, in New England* **[Printed Book & Digital Capture]**, edited by Nathaniel B. Shurtleff and David Pulsifer, 12 vols., publ. 1855-1861, Boston. For access to digital version of all 12 volumes, see the online FHL catalog page: *www.familysearch.org/search/catalog/344454*.

1620-1692. *A Genealogical Dictionary of the First Settlers of New England: Showing Three Generations of Those Who Came Before May 1692, on the Basis of Farmer's Register* **[Printed Book]**, by James Savage, originally publ. Little, Brown and Co., Boston, 1860-1862, 4 vols., 2,541 pages, reprinted (with a cross-index at the end of Vol. 4) by Genealogical Publishing Co, Baltimore, 1969, FHL book 974 D2s. Also on CD-ROM, FHL CD No. 9 pt. 169.

1620-1700. *New England Marriages Prior to 1700* **[Printed Book & Online Database]**, by Clarence A Torrey. This work, compiled over a period of thirty years from about 2,000 books and manuscripts, is a comprehensive listing of the 37,000 married couples who lived in New England between 1620 and 1700. Listed are the names of virtually every married couple living in New England before 1700, their marriage date or the birth year of a first child, the maiden names of 70% of the wives, the birth and death years of both partners, mention of earlier or later marriages, the residences of every couple and an index of names. The provision of the maiden names make it possible to identify the husbands of sisters, daughters, and many granddaughters of immigrants, and of immigrant sisters or kinswomen. Publ. Genealogical Publishing Co, Baltimore, MD, 1985, 2004, 1,009 pages, FHL book 974 V2t. A digitized version of this book (with 95,807 records) is available at the Ancestry.com website. See *http://search.ancestry.com/search/db.aspx?dbid=3824*.

1620-1800. *Index of Surnames in Early Massachusetts (From Printed Sources)* **[Microfiche]**, from a 1,673-page manuscript donated by Evelyn C. Kane, Gloucester, MA, filmed by the Genealogical Society of Utah, c1990, 30 fiche, FHL fiche #6334440 (Index).

1620-1800. *Early Massachusetts Marriages Prior to 1800, Vols. 1-4* **[Online Database]**, indexed at the Ancestry.com website. Book, same title, 4 vols. (See Contents page for each volume for marriage places).
- For vol. 1, see
https://search.ancestry.com/search/db.aspx?dbid=48585.

- For vol. 2, see
https://search.ancestry.com/search/db.aspx?dbid=48190.
- For vol. 3, see
https://search.ancestry.com/search/db.aspx?dbid=48586.
- For vol. 4, see
https://search.ancestry.com/search/db.aspx?dbid=48191.

1620-1839. *Historical Collections: Being a General Collection of Interesting Facts, Traditions, Biographical Sketches, Anecdotes, Etc., Relating to the History and Antiquities of Every Town in Massachusetts, With Geographical Descriptions* **[Printed Book & Online Database]**, by John Warner Barber, publ. Dorr, Howland, Worcester, MA, 1839, 624 pages, FHL book 974.4 H2b. To view a digital version of this book, visit the online FHL catalog page for this title. See
https://familysearch.org/search/catalog/119726.

1620-1850. *Mayflower Deeds and Probates* **[Online Database]**, digitized and indexed at the Ancestry.com website. George Ernest Bowman, founder of the Massachusetts Society of Mayflower Descendants in 1896, compiled more than 20,000 pages of research on descendants of the original Mayflower colonists. In 1994, Susan E. Roser extracted the deed and probate details contained in the database from Bowman's files. This database has 18,601 records. See
http://search.ancestry.com/search/db.aspx?dbid=3223.

1620-1850. *Consolidated Index to the Early Vital Records of Commonwealth of Massachusetts to About 1850* **[CD-ROM]**, by Search & ReSearch, Wheat Ridge, CO, 2001, FHL CD No. 1292.

1620-1850. *Early Vital Records of Barnstable, Dukes, and Nantucket Counties, Massachusetts to About 1850* **[CD-ROM]**, by Search & ReSearch, Wheat Ridge, CO, 1999, 2003, FHL CD No. 2655.

1620-1850. *Early New England Settlers* **[CD-ROM]**, from a series of published guides by Genealogical publishing Co, Baltimore, publ. as part of Family Tree Maker's Family Archives, FHL CD No. 9 pt. 504. Contents: *Chronicles of the first planters of the colony of Massachusetts Bay from 1623 to 1636* / by Alexander Young – *Peirce's colonial lists: civil, military, and professional lists of Plymouth and Rhode Island colonies* / by Ebenezer W. Peirce – *The Colonial clergy and colonial churches of New England* / by Frederick Lewis Weis – *Directory of the ancestral heads of New England families, 1620-1700* / compiled by Frank R. Holmes – *Genealogical guide to the early settlers of America : with a brief history of those of the first generation* / by Henry Whittemore – *Genealogical notes, or, Contributions to the family history of some of the first settlers of Connecticut and Massachusetts* / by Nathaniel Goodwin – *Genealogical notes on the founding of New England: my ancestors part in that undertaking* / by Ernest Flagg – *Genealogical notes of New York and New England families* / compiled by S.V. Talcott – *A Genealogical register of the first settlers of New England* / by John Farmer – *The History of New England from 1630 to 1649* / by John Winthrop (vols. I-II) – *Immigrants to New England, 1700-1775* / compiled by Ethel Stanwood Bolton – *Marriage notices, 1785-1794 for the whole United States* / copied from the Massachusetts Centinel and the Colombian Centinel by Charles Knowles Bolton – *One hundred and sixty allied families* / by John Osborne Austin – *The Real founders of New England: stories of their life along the coast, 1602-1628* / Charles Knowles Bolton – *Result of some researches among the British Archives for information relative to the founders of New England: made in the years 1858, 1859 and 1860* / by Samuel G. Drake – *Soldiers in King Phillips War: being a critical account of that war with a concise history of the Indian Wars of New England from 1620-1677* / by George Madison Bodge – *The Pioneers of Maine and New Hampshire: a descriptive list drawn from records of the colonies, towns, churches, courts, and other contemporary sources* / by Charles Henry Pope – *The English ancestry and homes of the pilgrim fathers: who came to Plymouth on the 'Mayflower' in 160, the 'Fortune' in 1621, and the 'Anne' and 'Little James' in 1623* / by Charles Edward Banks – *The Planters of the Commonwealth: a study of the emigrants and emigration in colonial times, 1620-1640* / by Charles Edward Banks – *Topographical dictionary of 2885 English emigrants to New England, 1620-1650* / Charles Edward Banks – *The Winthrop fleet of 1630: an account of the vessels, the voyage, the passengers and their English homes, from original authorities* / by Charles Edward Banks.

1620-1850. *Massachusetts, Town Birth Records* **[Online Database],** digitized and indexed at the Ancestry.com website. Extracted birth records from the published vital records, towns of Bellingham, Granville, Lawrence, Lincoln, Richmond, Shirley, and Chelmsford. This database has 230,797 records. See *http://search.ancestry.com/search/db.aspx?dbid=4094.*

1620-1850. Massachusetts, Town Marriage Records [Online Database], digitized and indexed at the Ancestry.com website. Extracted marriage records from the published vital records, towns of Abington, Acton, Andover, Ashburnham, Ashfield, Billerica, Brimfield, Brockton, Carver, Chelmsford, Chester, Dartmouth, Dover, Dracut, Essex, Framingham, Gill, Granville, Holden, Holliston, Hummards, Lawrence, Lexington, Lynn, Medford, Medway, Middlefield, New Ashford, New Bedford, New Braintree, Pembroke, Shirley, Shrewsbury, Sturbridge, Taunton, Templeton, Tisbury, Tyringham, Wayland, Washington, Westford, Westminster, Westport, West Springfield, Winchendon, Windsor, Worthington, and Wrentham. This database has 124.918 records. See *http://search.ancestry.com/search/db.aspx?dbid=4079.*
- For **Town Death Records, 1620-1850**, see *http://search.ancestry.com/search/db.aspx?dbid=4080.*

1620-1890. *History of Barnstable County, Massachusetts* **[Microfilm & Online Database],** from the book edited by Simeon L. Deyo, publ. H.W. Blake, New York, 1890, 1,010 pages. Filmed by W.C. Cox Co., 1974, 1 roll, FHL film #1000064. To view a digital version of this book, visit the online FHL catalog page for this title. See *https://familysearch.org/search/catalog/205627.*
- See also, **Index to History of Barnstable County [Printed Index],** compiled by Charles A. Holbrook, Jr., publ. Holbrook, Yarmouth, MA, 1984, 174 pages, FHL book 974.492 H2d index.

1620-1900. *Bibliography of Massachusetts Vital Records: an Inventory of the Original Birth, Marriage, and Death Volumes* **[Microfiche],** by Jay Mack Holbrook, This fifth edition of the *Bibliography of Massachusetts Vital Records* lists 472 collections of town records, some dating as early as 1620 and most continuing until about 1900, publ. Holbrook Research Institute, Oxford, MA, 1994-1995, 2 fiche, FHL fiche #6344488.

1620-1937. *The Mayflower Descendant, Index of Persons* **[Printed Book & Online Database],** by the Society of Mayflower Descendants, 1959-1962, 2 vols., Vol. 1: A-G; Vol. 2: H-Z), FHL book 974.4 D25md v.1-2. To view a digital version of this book, visit the online FHL catalog page: *https://familysearch.org/search/catalog/556930.*

1620-1986. *Massachusetts, Land Records* **[Online Database].** Digitized at FamilySearch.org. Includes

Land and Property records from the Massachusetts Land Office and county courthouses. Records include land grants, patents, deeds, and mortgages. This database includes all counties in Massachusetts and has 5,766,135 images. Browse through the images, organized by County, Record Type, Year Range, and Volume. See *https://familysearch.org/search/collection/2106411*.

1620-1988. *Massachusetts, Town and Vital Records* **[Online Database]**, digitized and indexed at the Ancestry.com website. Includes records filmed by the Holbrook Research Institute. Records may include birth and baptismal registers, intention of marriage and marriage records, courthouse records, death registers, account books, almshouse records, aids to soldiers and veterans, assessments and tax records (lists, collections, invoices, valuations), cemetery records, censuses, church and parish records, school records, town meeting records, pew sales, deeds, dog licenses, minutes, militia lists and military records, indexes, fishing permits, land grants, voters lists and registers, mortgage records, and selectmen's records. This database has 23,159,802 records. See *http://search.ancestry.com/search/db.aspx?dbid=2495*.

1620-2000s. *Massachusetts Databases at FamilySearch* **[Online Databases]**, digitized at the FamilySearch.org website. Data collections are listed by *Image Only Historical Records* (Land Records, Crew Lists, Mortality Schedules, Vital and Town Records) and *Digitized and Indexed Historical Records* (Births and Christenings, Births, Crew Lists, Passenger Lists, Death Index, Marriages, Naturalizations, Vital Records, 1855 State Census, 1865 State Census, and State Vital Records, 1841-1920). All individual databases specific to Massachusetts are identified in chronological order, beginning with 1620-1986 (MA Land Records). See *https://familysearch.org/search/collection/location/52*.

1620-2000s. *Massachusetts Databases at Ancestry.com* **[Online Databases]**, indexed at the Ancestry.com website. Massachusetts data collections are organized by Census & Voter Lists; Birth, Marriage & Death; MA Military; Immigration & Travel; MA Newspapers & Publications; Pictures; Schools, Directories & Church Histories; Tax, Criminal, Land & Wills; Reference, Dictionaries & Almanacs; Maps, Atlases & Gazetteers; and Stories, Memories & Histories. Or, search the entire Ancestry Massachusetts collection by county. Counties and (No. of Databases):

Barnstable (2), Berkshire (63), Bristol (90), Dukes (5), Essex (197), Franklin (50), Hampden (39), Hampshire (47), Middlesex (285), Nantucket (28), Norfolk (119), Plymouth (109), Suffolk (156), and Worcester (211). See the website for the complete list of titles available. The 50 largest individual databases specific to Massachusetts are identified in chronological order, beginning with 1620-1635 (Great Migration). See *http://search.ancestry.com/Places/US/Massachusetts/Default.aspx*.

1620-2000s. *Massachusetts GenWeb (MAGenWeb) Archives* **[Online Databases].** The MAGenWeb offers free genealogical databases on the Internet, and searchable name lists are available for all Massachusetts counties. Typical county records include Bibles, Biographies, Cemeteries, Censuses, Court, Death, Deeds, Directories, Histories, Marriages, Military, Newspapers, Obituaries, Photos, Schools, Tax Lists, Wills, and more. The MAGenWeb Table of Contents page has links for each of the counties. To visit the MEGenWeb Archives. See *http://usgwarchives.net/ma/mafiles.htm*.

1620-2000s. *Free Search for Massachusetts Items in the Library Catalog of the New England Historic Genealogical Society* **[Online Database].** Non-Members of NEHGS may search the library catalog for free. The library holdings relate mostly to New England states, but include surrounding areas, such as New York and Eastern Canada; as well as databases related to the British Isles. Categories include Vital Records, Census Records, Tax and Voter Lists; Court, Land and Probate Records; Journals and Periodicals, and Military Records. A search of the library catalog using the keyword "Massachusetts" returned a list of 10,614 publications, including many original manuscripts, unpublished family histories, and genealogical compilations found in no other library in the world. See *http://library.nehgs.org*.

1620-2000s. *Member Databases (for Massachusetts) at the New England Historic Genealogical Society* **[Online Databases],** indexed at the NEHGS membership website. This is one of the most widely used online genealogical resources in the world, with over 400 million names accessible to members of NEHGS. This huge database is searchable by name, date, place, keyword or type of record. As an example, a Database Search for keywords, "Massachusetts" returned 21.8 million hits. A search of the digital Library & Archives requires a membership log-in. See *www.americanancestors.org/search/advanced-search*.

1620-2000s. *Linkpendium – Massachusetts: Family History & Genealogy, Census, Birth, Marriage, Death Records & More* **[Online Databases].** Linkpendium is a genealogical portal site, with links to state, county, town, and local databases. Currently listed are selected sites for Massachusetts Statewide Resources (741), Barnstable County (1,984), Berkshire County (1,574), Bristol County (2,240), Dukes County (476), Essex County (3,635), Franklin County (1,227), Hampden County (1,529), Hampshire County (1,905), Middlesex County (4,278), Nantucket County (298), Norfolk County (1,738), Plymouth County (2,950), Suffolk County (4,291), and Worcester County (3,302). See *www.linkpendium.com/genealogy/USA/MA.*

1620–2000s. **Massachusetts Collections at MyHeritage [Online Database],** over 533 collections with 21,112,773 records can be searched at the Massachusetts – Collections Catalog (databases of the former World Vital Records website). Databases include censuses, directories, family histories, town histories, military rosters, college/school year books, and more. This is a subscription site, but all initial searches are free. A free search can be done for a name, place, year, or keyword. See *www.myheritage.com/records/Massachusetts/all-records.*

"1623-1650 Given Names in Plymouth Records" **[Printed Article],** in *Mayflower Quarterly,* Vol. 67, No. 1 (Mar 2001).

1626-1806. See *Massachusetts State Archives Collection, Colonial and Post-Colonial Period, 1626-1806* **[Microfilm & Digital Capture],** from the originals at the MA State Archives, Boston. Includes a myriad of papers relating to the operation of the colonial government of Massachusetts. Review the contents of each roll of film for details. Filmed by the Genealogical Society of Utah, 2002, 74 rolls, beginning with FHL film #2318834 (Hutchinson papers, 1626-1771). For a complete list of roll numbers, roll contents, and the digital images of each roll, see the online FHL catalog page: *www.familysearch.org/search/catalog/1050952.*

1627-2001. *Massachusetts, Town Clerk, Vital and Town Records* **[Online Database],** digitized and indexed at the FamilySearch.org website. Includes vital and town records acquired from local town clerk offices. Each index record, e.g., marriages, includes: Name, Event type, Event date, Event place, Gender, Marital status, Spouse's name, and Spouse's gender.

The document image has more information. This database has 2,608,950 records. See *https://familysearch.org/search/collection/2061550.*

1629-1799. *Card Index to the Massachusetts Archives* **[Microfilm & Digital Capture],** from the original index cards at the Massachusetts State Archives, Boston, MA. The Massachusetts Archives is a series of volumes containing documents of Massachusetts from its founding in 1629 to the year 1799. There are 328 volumes in the series. They are housed in the Massachusetts State Archives. Filmed by the Genealogical Society of Utah, 1972-1973, 57 rolls, beginning with FHL film #543878 (Aa-Annapolis). For a complete list of roll numbers and contents of each roll, visit the online FHL catalog page for this title. See *https://familysearch.org/search/catalog/285054.*
• An online MA Archives database provides name, location, and subject access for eighteen volumes. See *www.sec.state.ma.us/arc/arcsrch/RevolutionarySearchContects.html.*

1630. *The Winthrop Fleet of 1630* **[Online Database],** digitized and indexed at the Ancestry.com website. For a complete digital version of the book, *The Winthrop Fleet of 1630: An Account of the Vessels, the Voyage, the Passengers and their English Homes from Original Authorities,* by Charles Edward Banks, publ. 1930, Boston. Reprinted GPC, Baltimore, 1961-1999. See *http://search.ancestry.com/search/db.aspx?dbid=48245.*

1630-1691. *List of Freemen, Massachusetts Bay Colony from 1630 to 1691, with Freeman's Oath, the First Paper Printed in New England* **[Online Database],** digitized at the FamilySearch.org website. From a book by H.F. Andrews, publ. Exira Printing Co, Exira, IA, 1906. To view this digital book, visit the online FHL catalog page: *https://familysearch.org/search/catalog/2175860.*
- For the Ancestry.com database, *Applications of Freemen, 1630-1691,* see *http://search.ancestry.com/search/db.aspx?dbid=4296.*
- See also, *List of Freeman of Massachusetts, 1630-1691* **[Online Database],** digitized and OCR indexed at the Ancestry.com website. Source: Book, same title (see the title page image for details). This database has 59 pages. See *https://search.ancestry.com/search/db.aspx?dbid=48187.*
- See also, *The Founders of the Massachusetts Bay Colony* **[Printed Essay & Digital Capture],** a presentation to the Old Planters Society, originally

publ. Salem, MA, 1908, 13 pages. To access a digital version, see the online FHL catalog page: *www.familysearch.org/search/catalog/2175887*.

1630-1699. *Boston Births, Baptisms, Marriages, and Deaths* [**Online Database**], digitized and OCR indexed at the Ancestry.com website. Source: Book, *Report of the Record Commissioners*. See the title page image for details. This database has 287 pages: *https://search.ancestry.com/search/db.aspx?dbid=48165*.

1630-1877. *History of Cambridge, Massachusetts; With a Genealogical Register, by Lucius R. Paige: Comprising a Biographical and Genealogical Record of the Early Settlers and Their Descendants; With References to Their Wills and the Administration of Their Estates in the Middlesex County Registry of Probate* [**Printed Book & Digital Capture**], by Mary Isabella Gozzaldi, publ. Cambridge Historical Society, 1930, 860 pages, FHL 974.4 H2c. To view a digital version of this book, visit the online FHL catalog page: *https://familysearch.org/search/catalog/2030583*.

1630-1943. *Massachusetts, Church Records* [**Online Database**], digitized and indexed at FamilySearch, this collection contains church vital records from different denominations located in several counties in Massachusetts. see *www.familysearch.org/search/collection/2787822*.

1630-1992. *A Surname Guide to Massachusetts Town Histories* [**Printed Book**], by Phyllis O. Longver & Pauline J. Oesterlin, a master guide to the surnames to be found in 128 volumes of Massachusetts town histories, publ. Heritage Books, Bowie, MD, 1993, 425 pages, FHL book 974.4 H22Lp.

"1632-1634 Tax Lists, Plymouth" [**Printed Article**], in *New England Historical and Genealogical Register,* Vol. 4, No. 4 (Jul 1850).

1633-1850. *Massachusetts, Compiled Marriages* [**Online Database**], digitized and indexed at the Ancestry.com website. From Liahona Research. Includes a name, sex, spouse's name, marriage date and location, and source. This database has 820,711 records. See *http://search.ancestry.com/search/db.aspx?dbid=7853*.

1633-1895. See *Histories and Genealogies of Essex County, Massachusetts: Containing Town Histories of Amesbury, Andover, Haverhill, Ipswich, Lawrence, Lynn, Lynnfield, Methuen, Nahant, North Andover, Saugus, Swampscot, and Merrimac; Plus Biographical Sketches of Leading Citizens* [**CD-ROM**], by Heritage Books, Bowie, MD, 1996. Contains: *Historical sketches of Andover (comprising the present towns of North Andover and Andover), Massachusetts,* by Sarah Loring Bailey – Life sketches of leading citizens of Essex County, Massachusetts, by Biographical Review Pub. Co. – *The Hammatt papers: early inhabitants of Ipswich, Massachusetts, 1633-1700,* by Abraham Hammatt – *History of the city of Lawrence [Massachusetts],* by J.F. C. Hayes – *A Short history of the first church and parish of Methuen, Massachusetts, 1729-1929,* by Frederick D. Hayward – *Lynn and surroundings,* by Clarence W. Hobbs – *Celebration of the two hundred and fiftieth anniversary of the town of Ipswich,* compiled by Ipswich Committee – *History of Lynn, Essex County, Massachusetts,* by Alonzo Lewis and James R. Newhall – *History of Amesbury and Merrimac, Massachusetts,* by Joseph Merrill – *The History of Haverhill, Massachusetts,* by B.L. Mirick –
Some old puritan love- letters: John and Margaret Winthrop, 1618-1638, edited by Joseph Hopkins Twichell – *A Sketch of the life of John Winthrop the younger, founder of Ipswich, Massachusetts in 1633 (2nd ed.),* by Thomas Franklin Waters – *History of the town of Lynnfield, Mass, 1635-1895,* by Thomas B. Wellman. See FHL CD No. 80.

1633-1967. *Massachusetts, Plymouth County, Probate Records* [**Online Database**], digitized at the FamilySearch.org website. Includes probate estate files of Plymouth County from two different sources: the Secretary of the Commonwealth and the archive of the Supreme Judicial Court of Massachusetts. This database has 302,640 images. See *https://familysearch.org/search/collection/2018320*.

1635-1681. *Essex County, Massachusetts Probate Records* [**Online Database**], digitized and OCR indexed at the Ancestry.com website. Original data: George Francis Dow, ed. *The Probate Records of Essex County, Massachusetts. Vol. I-II.* Salem, MA, USA: Essex Institute, 1916-1920. This database has 1,570 records. See *https://search.ancestry.com/search/db.aspx?dbid=6593*.
- See also *Essex County, Massachusetts Probate Records, Part 1* [**Online Database**], indexed at the

Ancestry.com website. This database has 1,176 records. See *https://search.ancestry.com/search/db.aspx?dbid=3361.*

1635-1991. *Massachusetts, Wills and Probate Records* [Online Database], digitized and indexed at the Ancestry.com website. Source: MA County, District and Probate Courts. Probates include Wills, Letters of Administration, Inventories, Distributions and Accounting, Bonds, and Guardianships. Each index record includes: Name, Probate date, Probate place, Inferred death year, Inferred death place, and Item Description. The document image has more information. Some records with multiple pages have a Table of Contents, listing the number of pages within each category or records. This database has 607,745 records. See *https://search.ancestry.com/search/db.aspx?dbid=9069.*

1636-1686. *Essex County, Massachusetts Depositions* [Online Database], indexed at the Ancestry.com website. Includes names of deponents and their ages. This database has 5,431 records. See *http://search.ancestry.com/search/db.aspx?dbid=5342.*

1636-1886. See *Springfield, 1636-1886: History of Town and City, Including an Account of the Quarter-Millennial Celebration at Springfield, Mass., May 25 and 26, 1886* [Printed Book], by Mason Arnold Green, publ. C.A. Nichols, Springfield, MA, 1888, 645 pages, FHL book 974.426/S1 H2g.
- See also *Index to Springfield, History of Town and City, 1636-1886, by Mason A,. Green, 1888* [Printed Index], prepared by the Berkshire Genealogist Indexing Committee, publ. Berkshire Family History Assoc., Pittsfield, MA, 1997, 26 pages, FHL book 974.425/S1 H2g index.

1636-1893. *Index to the Probate Records of the County of Suffolk, Massachusetts, From the year 1636 to and Including the Year 1893* [Printed Book], edited by Elijah George, publ. Rockwell and Churchill, Boston, 1895, 3 vols. Contents: Vol. 1: A-F; Vol. 2: G-O; Vol. 3: P-Z., FHL book 974.46s2g.

1638-1887. *Massachusetts, Springfield Vital Records* [Online Database], digitized and indexed at the FamilySearch.org website. Includes an index and images of birth, marriage, and death records recorded by the town clerk of Springfield. This database has 68,176 records. See *https://familysearch.org/search/collection/1865477.*

1638-1840. See *Essex, Massachusetts Probate Records, 1638-1840* [Online Database], indexed at the Ancestry.com website. Each entry shows the name of the person, date of probate, and type of record (will, inventory, etc.). It also provides a brief description of the record that may include the individual's profession, town of residence, and record number. This database has 5,431 records. See *http://search.ancestry.com/search/db.aspx?dbid=4592.*

1638-1961. *Massachusetts Town Records* [Online Database], digitized and indexed at the FamilySearch.org website. Includes Index to various town vital records from the following counties: Berkshire, Bristol, Dukes, Essex, Franklin, Hampden, Hampshire, Norfolk, Plymouth, Suffolk, and Worcester. Each index record includes: Name, Event type, Event date, Event place, Gender, Marital status, Birthplace, Father's name, Mother's name, Spouse's name, Spouse's gender, Spouse's age, Spouse's marital status, Spouse's birth year, Spouse's birthplace, Spouse's father's name, and Spouse's mother's name. **Note:** to view the images you must access the site at a Family History Center or FamilySearch Affiliate Library. This database has 252,581 records. See *www.familysearch.org/search/collection/2285844.*

1639-1915. *Massachusetts, Births and Christenings* [Online Database], indexed at the FamilySearch.org website. These records were extracted from the microfilmed county and town records at the Family History Library, Salt Lake City. Each index record includes: Name, Gender, Birth date, Birthplace, Father's name, and Mother's name. This database has 4,175,660 records. See *https://familysearch.org/search/collection/1675197.*

1640-1793. *Records of the Town of Braintree* [Online Database], digitized and OCR indexed at the Ancestry.com website. Source: Book, same title, author unknown, publ. 1886. This database has 942 pages. See *https://search.ancestry.com/search/db.aspx?dbid=10036.*

1640-1880. *History of Framingham, Massachusetts: Early Known as Danforth's Farms; With a Genealogical Register* [Microfilm & Digital Capture], from book publ. by the town of Framingham, 1887, 794 pages. Filmed by the Genealogical Society of Utah, 1967, 1 roll, FHL film #476875. To view a digital version of this book, visit the online FHL catalog page: *https://familysearch.org/search/catalog/269364.*

1643-1765. See *Early Census Making in Massachusetts, 1643-1765: With a Reproduction of the Lost Census of 1765 (Recently Found) and Documents Relating Thereto* [Printed Book & Digital Capture], by Josiah Henry Benton, publ. C.E. Goodspeed, 1905, 104 pages. To access a digital version, see the online FHL catalog page: *www.familysearch.org/search/catalog/2558797.*

1643-1799. *Card Index to Births, Deaths, Wills, and Miscellaneous Court Records, Middlesex County, Massachusetts* [Microfilm], from the handwritten card index at the Clerk of Courts Office, Middlesex County Courthouse, Cambridge, MA. Filmed by the Genealogical Society of Utah, 1986, 1 roll, FHL film #1420474.

1643-1800. See *Probate and Deed Indexes, Suffolk County, Massachusetts* [Microfilm & Digital Capture], from the typescript at the New York Genealogical and Biographical Society, New York City, 111 pages, filmed by the Genealogical Society of Utah, 1949, 1 roll, FHL film #14786. Another copy, FHL film #1421101. To access the digital images, see the online FHL catalog page: *www.familysearch.org/search/catalog/506672.*

1643-1850. *Early Vital Records of Suffolk County, Massachusetts to About 1850* [CD-ROM], by Search & ReSearch, Wheat Ridge, CO, 2002, FHL CD No. 1208.

1644-1691. *Essex County, Massachusetts Probate Records Supplement* [Online Database], indexed at the Ancestry.com website. Original data: Records and Files of the Quarterly Courts of Essex County, Massachusetts Peabody Essex Museum, Salem, MA, USA. Each index record includes: Name, Death year, Death place, Probate date, Probate place, and Record type. This database has 1,988 records. See *https://search.ancestry.com/search/db.aspx?dbid=3357.*

1645-1686. *Essex County, Massachusetts Depositions* [Online Database], indexed at the Ancestry.com website. Source: Original records at the MA Archives. Compiled by Melinde Lutz Sanborn for Ancestry. The database includes names of deponents and their ages, which were required at the time of the deposition. This database has 5,413 records. See *https://search.ancestry.com/search/db.aspx?dbid=5342.*

1648-1840. See *Essex, Massachusetts Probate Records, 1648-1840* [Online Database], indexed at the Ancestry.com website. Source: Book, same title, by Melinde Lutz Sanborn. Each entry shows the name of the person, date of probate, and type of record (will, inventory, etc.). It also provides a brief description of the record that may include the individual's profession, town of residence, and record number. This database has 39,555 records. See *https://search.ancestry.com/search/db.aspx?dbid=4592.*

1648-1870. *Middlesex County, Massachusetts Probate Index* [Online Database], indexed at the FamilySearch.org website. From the book compiled by James Flint, publ. 1912. This database has 60,184 records. See *https://search.ancestry.com/search/db.aspx?dbid=4775.*

1648-1871. *Index to the Probate Records of the County of Middlesex, Massachusetts: First Series, From 1648 to 1871* [Printed Book & Digital Capture], from the book edited by Samuel H. Folsom and William E. Rogers, registers of probate and insolvency for the county of Middlesex, publ. Cambridge, MA, 1914, 552 pages, FHL book 974.44 P22m ser.1. To view a digital version of this book, visit the online FHL catalog page for this title. See *https://familysearch.org/search/catalog/161764.*

1649-1700. *Middlesex County, Massachusetts Deponents* [Online Database], indexed at the Ancestry.com website. Includes names of deponents and their ages. This database has 3,083 records. See *http://search.ancestry.com/search/db.aspx?dbid=5233.*

"1650 Salisbury Tax List, Essex County" [Printed Article], in *New England Historical and Genealogical Register,* Vol. 3, No. 1 (Jan 1849).

1650-1800. *Folio Index Cards, Middlesex County, Massachusetts* [Microfilm & Digital Capture], from the original index cards at the Clerk of Courts, Middlesex County Courthouse, Cambridge, MA. Filmed by the Genealogical Society of Utah, 1986, 3 rolls: FHL film #1420472 (Abbi, Joshua – Gill, John); FHL film #1420473 (Gill, Michael – Smith, John); and FHL film #1420474 (Smith, John – Younge, William). To access the digital images of these rolls, see the online FHL catalog page for this title: *www.familysearch.org/search/catalog/487256.*

1656-1877. *Fall River and its Industries: An Historical and Statistical Record of Village, Town, and City, From the Date of the Original Charter of the Freeman's Purchase in 1656 to the Present Time, With Valuable Statistical Tables, Family*

Genealogies, Etc., Illustrated by Views and Portraits on Steel **[Printed Book & Digital Capture],** by Frederick M. Peck and Henry H. Earl, publ. by Atlantic Publ. and Engraving Co., New York, 1877, 280 pages, FHL book 974.485/F1 H2e. To view a digital version of this book, visit the online FHL catalog page for this title. See *https://familysearch.org/search/catalog/243727.*

1656-1894. *History of Brockton, Plymouth County, Massachusetts, 1656-1894* **[Printed Book],** by Bradford Kingman, publ. D. Mason, Syracuse, NY, 1895, 814 pages, FHL book 974.482/B1 H2kb.
- See also *A Genealogist's Index of Bradford Kingman's History of Brockton, Plymouth County, Massachusetts, 1656-1894* **[Printed Index & Digital Capture],** compiled by Elizabeth Hayward, publ. Chedwato Service, West Hartford, CT, 1957, 15 pages, FHL book 974.482/B1 H2kb index. To view a digital version of this index, visit the online FHL catalog page for this title. See *https://familysearch.org/search/catalog/246833.*

1657-1892. *Epitaphs from Burial Hill, Plymouth, Massachusetts, from 1657 to 1892* **[Online Database],** digitized and OCR indexed at the Ancestry.com website. Source: Book, same title (see the title page image for details). This database has records. See *https://search.ancestry.com/search/db.aspx?dbid=48178.*

1659 Rate List, Taunton, Bristol County, Massachusetts **[Online Database],** from an extraction taken from *A Descriptive & Biographical Record of Bristol County, Massachusetts,* 1899. Names listed at the dunhamwilcox.net site for Taunton, MA. See *http://dunhamwilcox.net/ma/taunton_ma_1659_ratelist.htm.*

1662-1855. *History of Western Massachusetts: the Counties of Hampden, Hampshire, Franklin, and Berkshire, Embracing an Outline or General History of the Section, an Account of its Scientific Aspects and Leading Interests, and Separate Histories of its One Hundred Towns* **[Printed Book],** by Josiah Gilbert Holland, 2 vols., full name index in each volume, originally publ. Springfield, MA, Samuel Bowles & Co, 1855; reprinted by Heritage Books, Bowie, MD, 1994, 2 vols., FHL book 974.4 H2hj 1994.

"Pre-1660 Tax List, Rowley, Essex County" **[Printed Article],** in *New England Historical and Genealogical Register,* Vol. 15, No. 3 (Jul 1861).

1660-1988. *Index to Estate Files, Hampshire County, Massachusetts* **[Microfilm & Digital Capture],** from the original index cards at the Registrar of Probate, Northampton, MA. Filmed by the Genealogical Society of Utah, 1989, 38 rolls, beginning with FHL film #1558627 (A & W Apartments – Austin, Wayne G.). To access the digital images, visit the online FHL catalog page: *https://familysearch.org/search/catalog/487026.*

"1664, 1681 Topsfield Tax List, Essex County" **[Printed Article],** in *Topsfield Historical Collections,* Vol. 2 (1896).

1666-1682. *List of Freemen (Plymouth Colony)* **[Microfilm & Digital Capture],** from the originals at MA State Archives, Boston. Filmed by the Genealogical Society of Utah, 1968. FHL film #567791. To access the digital images, see the online FHL catalog page: *www.familysearch.org/search/catalog/136735.*

1671-1680. *Records of the Suffolk County Court: 1671-1680* **[Online Database],** digitized and OCR indexed at the. Ancestry.com website. Source: Book, same title, publ. Colonial Society of Massachusetts, 1933. This database has 1,328 records: *https://search.ancestry.com/search/db.aspx?dbid=21521.*

"1673 Ipswich Voters, Essex County" **[Printed Article],** in *Essex Institute Historical Collections,* Vol. 45, No. 4 (Oct 1909).

1675 Householders, Taunton, Bristol County, Massachusetts **[Online Database],** name list at the dunhamwilcox.net website. See *http://dunhamwilcox.net/ma/taunton_ma_1675_householder.htm.*

"1679 Billerica Tax List, Middlesex County" **[Printed Article],** in *New England Historical and Genealogical Register,* Vol. 5, No. 2 (Apr 1851).

"1679 Hatfield Tax List, Hampshire County" **[Printed Article],** in *Missing Links-Genealogical Clues,* No. 35 (Jun 1965).

1679-1779. *Newton, Massachusetts: A Biographical Directory* **[Printed Book],** compiled by Priscilla R. Ritter and Thelma Fleishman, publ. New England Historic Genealogical Society, Boston, 1982, 152 pages, FHL book 974.44/N1 D3r.

"1683 Salem Tax List, Essex County" [Printed Article], in *Genealogical Quarterly Magazine,* Vol. 2, No. 3 (1901).

1686-1859. *An Index to Plymouth County, Massachusetts, Warnings Out from the Plymouth Court Records* [Printed Book], by Ruth Wilder Sherman, Robert M. Sherman, and Robert S. Wakefield, publ. General Society of Mayflower Descendants, Plymouth, MA, 2003, 95 pages, FHL book 974.482 P22s.
- NOTE: The term "Warning out" or "Warning out of town" refers to the practice of asking certain residents to leave. For example, the first warning out in Plymouth Colony was recorded on June 6, 1654 in the village of Rehoboth. Robert Titus was called into town court and told to take his family out of Plymouth Colony for allowing "persons of evil fame" to live in his home. (His wife was a Quaker).

1686-1915. *Massachusetts, Plymouth County, Probate Estate Files* [Online Database], digitized at the FamilySearch.org website. The files are arranged by number then alphabetical by surname. This database has 819,700 images. See
https://familysearch.org/search/collection/1918549.

"1687 Boston Tax List' [Printed Article], in *New England Historical and Genealogical Register,* Vol. 55, No. 32 (Apr 1901).

"1687 Boxford Tax List, Essex County" [Printed Article], in *Essex Institute Historical Collections,* Vol. 56, No. 4 (Oct 1920).

"1688 Billerica Town Rate, Middlesex County" [Printed Article], in *New England Historical and Genealogical Register,* Vol. 31, No. 3 (Jul 1877).

"1688 Charles Town Rate, Suffolk County" [Printed Article], in *New England Historical and Genealogical Register,* Vol. 34, No. 3 (Jul 1880).

"1688 Marlborough Town Rate, Middlesex County" [Printed Article], in *New England Historical and Genealogical Register,* Vol. 36, No. 2 (Apr 1882).

"1688 Medford Town Rate, Middlesex County" [Printed Article], in *New England Historical and Genealogical Register,* Vol. 32, No. 3 (Jul 1878).

"1688 Newton Town Rate, Middlesex County" [Printed Article], in *New England Historical and Genealogical Register,* Vol. 31, No. 3 (Jul 1877).

"1688 Stow Town Rate, Middlesex County" [Printed Article], in *New England Historical and Genealogical Register,* Vol. 32, No. 1 (Jan 1878).

1690-1938. *Probate Records, Dukes County, Massachusetts* [Microfilm & Digital Capture], from the originals at the Dukes County Courthouse, Edgartown, MA. Filmed by the Genealogical Society of Utah, 1972, 14 rolls, beginning with FHL film #911746 (1700-1870). To access the digital images, visit the FHL catalog page:
https://familysearch.org/search/catalog/323854.

1690-1992. See *Massachusetts Newspaper Archives* [Online Databases], digitized and indexed newspapers at the GenealogyBank website for the following cities: Barre, Belchertown, Beverly, Boston, Brookfield, Cambridge, Charlestown, Concord, Dedham, Gloucester, Greenfield, Haverhill, Lenox, Leominster, Lowell, Nantucket, New Bedford, Newburyport, Northampton, Pittsfield, Plymouth, Quincy, Salem, Springfield, Stockbridge, Stoughton, Taunton, Vineyard Grove, Watertown, West Springfield, and Worcester. See
www.genealogybank.com/explore/newspapers/all/usa/massachusetts.

"1695 Tax List, Bristol" [Printed Article], in *New England Historical and Genealogical Register,* Vol. 123, No. 3 (Jul 1969).

1695-1910. *Massachusetts, Marriages* [Online Database], indexed at the FamilySearch.org website. Includes marriage records extracted from the microfilmed marriages of Massachusetts filmed on site by the Genealogical Society of Utah. Each index record includes: Name, Spouse's name, Event date, Father's name, Mother's name, Spouse's father's name, and Spouse's mother's name. This database has 949,293 records. See
https://familysearch.org/search/collection/1675351.

1695-1924. *The History of Nantucket: County, Island and Town, Including Genealogies of the First Settlers* [Printed Book & Online Database], from the book by Alexander Starbuck, publ. Goodspeed, Boston, 1924, 871 pages, FHL book 974.497 H2s.

Also on microfiche, FHL fiche #6046898. To view a digital version of this book, visit the online FHL catalog page for this title. See
https://familysearch.org/search/catalog/76960.

"1700 Salem Tax Lists, Essex County" [Printed Article], in *Genealogical Quarterly Magazine,* Vol. 4, No. 1 (Apr 1903).

1700-1751. *Boston Marriages from 1700 to 1751* **[Online Database],** digitized and OCR indexed at the Ancestry.com website. Source: Book, same title (See the title page image for details). This database has 476 pages. See
https://search.ancestry.com/search/db.aspx?dbid=48163.

1700-1800. *Boston Births, 1700-1800* **[Online Database],** digitized and OCR indexed at the Ancestry.com website. Source: *Report of the Record Commissioners of the City of Boston* (See the title page image for details). This database has 381 pages:
https://search.ancestry.com/search/db.aspx?dbid=48166.

1700-1817. See *Bristol County, Massachusetts, Marriages, 1700-1799, 1817* **[Microfilm & Digital Capture],** from the originals at the Bristol County Courthouse, Taunton, MA. Contains marriages from the towns of Norton, 1725-1794; Rayham, 1731-1764; Rehoboth, 1717-1795; Somerset, 1790-1794; Swansea, 1716-1795; Taunton, 1700-1795; Tiverton, 1729-1930; Warren, 1761; Westport, 1789-1795, 1817; Attleboro, 1717-1795; Barrington, 1778; Berkley, 1736-1791; Bristol, 1725-1746; Dartmouth, 1730-1794; Dighton, 1768-1795; Easton, 1726-1799; Freetown, 1734- 1795; Little Compton, 1725-1749; Mansfield, 1771-1794; New Bedford, 1790-1795; and Norton, 1734-1793. Filmed by the Genealogical Society of Utah, 1972, 1 roll, FHL film #905545. To access the digital images of this roll, see the online FHL catalog page:
www.familysearch.org/search/catalog/294583.

1700-1850. *Massachusetts, Compiled Birth, Marriage, and Death Records* **[Online Database],** indexed at the Ancestry.com website. Source: NEHGS copies of MA Town Vital Records. The complete list of sources is at the Ancestry title page. This collection consists of birth, marriage, and death records The birth records in this collection typically include the following information: Name of child, Gender and birthplace of child, Date of birth, Date of baptism, Parents' names, Some birth records may also have the spouse of the primary person's name recorded. The

marriage records in this collection typically include the following information: Marriage date, Name of Groom, Age and birthplace of Groom, Groom's parents' names, Name of Bride, Age and birthplace of Bride, Bride's parents' names. The death records in this collection typically include the following information: Name of deceased, Date of death, Date of burial, Age and birthplace of deceased, as well as Parents' names, and Spouse's name. This database has 1,309,951 records.
https://search.ancestry.com/search/db.aspx?dbid=61401.

1700-1850. *Deaths to 1850, Tisbury, Dukes County, Massachusetts* **[Online Database],** name list at the history.vineyard.net website. See
http://history.vineyard.net/tvr.htm.

1700-1909. *Report of the Record Commissioners of the City of Boston* **[Printed Book & Online Database],** this is a 39-volume set of official historical records from various city functions, including selectmen's minutes, censuses, tax lists, and many other documents. The volumes are not obviously in any order by date, as Vol. 1 seems to start with 1876, while Vol. 39 starts with 1818. The FHL catalog gives the inclusive publication dates as 1876-1909, but the volume issued in 1876 may have documents relating to the early 1800s. Fortunately, each volume has been digitized separately at the FHL catalog page, see
https://familysearch.org/search/catalog/51395.
- View any of the 39 volumes to look at the Table of Contents page to see the inclusive dates for each volume. The FHL's "Title Also Known As: A report of the Record Commissioners Twenty-First Report of the record commissioners. Dorchester births, Marriages, and Deaths. to the end of 1825. Twenty-Eighth Report of the Record Commissioners. Boston Marriages 1700-1751. City document no. 90. City document no. 147. Twenty-Second Report of the Record commissioners. United States Direct Tax of 1798. United States Census of 1790. For Boston Only."

"1704 Raid on Deerfield" [Printed Article], in *Links* (Vermont French-Canadian Genealogical Society, Burlington, VT), Vol. 4, No. 2 (Spring 2000).

1704-1800. *Index of Obituaries in Boston Newspapers* **[Printed Book & Digital Capture],** publ. G.K. Hall, Boston, MA, 1968, 3 vols. Contents: Vol. 1: Deaths within Boston, A-Z; Vol. 2: Deaths outside Boston, A-Johnson, Chloe; Vol. 3: Deaths outside Boston, Johnson, Daniel-Z., FHL book 974.461 V4b. Also on microfilm, FHL film #823596.

- To view a digital version of Vol. 1, visit the online FHL catalog page for this title. See *https://familysearch.org/search/catalog/230790.*

1706-1867. *Probate Records, Nantucket County, Massachusetts* **[Microfilm & Digital Capture],** from the originals the Nantucket County Courthouse, Nantucket, MA. Filmed by the Genealogical Society of Utah, 1972, 9 rolls, beginning with FHL film #906832 (probate Records, 1706-1789). For a complete list of roll numbers, roll contents, and the digital images of each roll, visit the online FHL catalog page for this title: *https://familysearch.org/search/catalog/300798.*

1707. *Boston, Massachusetts, Census, 1707* **[Online Database],** digitized and indexed at the Ancestry.com website. Includes information such as the names of the residents, if they are widowed, how many Negroes they own, and the name of their landlord. Part of *A Report of the Record Commissioners of the City of Boston Containing Miscellaneous Papers.* This database has 344 records. See *http://search.ancestry.com/search/db.aspx?dbid=6363.*

"1711-1744 Boxford Tax Lists, Essex County" **[Printed Article],** in *Essex Institute Historical Collection,* Vol. 57, No. 3 (Jul 1921).

1714-1799. See *The New North Church, Boston, 1714-1799* **[Online Database],** digitized and OCR indexed at the Ancestry.com website. Source: Book, same title (see Ancestry's title page for details). This database has 138 pages. See *https://search.ancestry.com/search/db.aspx?dbid=49272.*

"1723-1725 Topsfield Tax List, Essex County" **[Printed Article],** in *Topsfield Historical Collections,* Vol. 3 (1897).

"1725-1729 Salem Village Tax Lists" **[Printed Article],** in *Danvers Historical Collections,* Vol. 24 (1936).

1725-1885. *Gazetteer of Berkshire County, Mass.* **[Microfilm & Digital Capture],** from the book compiled by Hamilton Child, publ. Syracuse, NY, 1885. Filmed by the Genealogical Society of Utah, 1985, 1 roll, FHL film #1425650. To view a digital version of this book, visit the online FHL catalog page for this title. See *https://familysearch.org/search/catalog/213890.*

"1729-1732 Salem Village Tax Lists" **[Printed Article],** in *Danvers Historical Collections,* Vol. 25 (1937).

"1730 Inhabitants, Sandwich" **[Printed Article],** in *New England Historical and Genealogical Register,* Vol. 13, No. 1 (Jan 1859).

1731-1850. *Early Vital Records of Worcester County, Massachusetts to About 1850* **[CD-ROM],** by Search & ReSearch, Wheat Ridge, CO, 2001, FHL CD No. 2646.

1731-1906. *Historic Homes and Institutions and Genealogical and Personal Memoirs of Worcester County, Massachusetts: With a History of Worcester Society of Antiquity* **[Printed Book & Online Database],** edited by Ellery Bicknell Crane, publ. Lewis, New York, 1907, 4 vols., FHL book 974.43 D2c v.1-4. To view a digital version of this book, Vol. 1-4, visit the online FHL catalog page. See *https://familysearch.org/search/catalog/246007.*
- See also *Master Index of Persons in Genealogical and Personal Memoirs of Worcester County, Massachusetts Volumes 1-4: by Ellery Bicknell Crane* **[Printed Index],** prepared by Berkshire Genealogist Indexing Committee, publ. Berkshire Family History Association, 2004, 362 pages, FHL book 974.43 D2c index.

1731-1925. *Massachusetts, Worcester County, Probate Files* **[Online Database],** digitized at the FamilySearch.org website. Probate estate files of Worcester County arranged by number then alphabetical by surname. This database has 513,629 images. See *https://familysearch.org/search/collection/2102083.*
- See also the Ancestry.com database, with an index, 1731-1881. See *http://search.ancestry.com/search/db.aspx?dbid=5189.*

1733-1900. *Massachusetts, Mason Membership Cards* **[Online Database],** digitized and indexed at the Ancestry.com website. From the *Massachusetts Grand Lodge of Masons* publication at the NEHGS, Boston. This database has 336,033 records. See *http://search.ancestry.com/search/db.aspx?dbid=5061.*

"1734 Rate List, Concord, Middlesex County" **[Printed Article],** in *New England Historical and Genealogical Register,* Vol. 12, No. 1 (Jan 1858).

"**1735-1748 Boxford Tax Lists, Second Parish, Essex County**" **[Printed Article],** in *Essex Institute Historical Collections,* Vol. 57, No. 4 (Oct 1921).

1737-1788. *Worcester County, Massachusetts Warnings* **[Printed Book],** by Francis E. Blake, an every-name index by Mary Peters, originally printed Worcester, MA, Systematic History Fund, 1899; reprinted Picton Press, Camden, ME, 1992, 126 pages, FHL book 974.43 N2w.

"**1738-1752 Omes Ledger of Salem People, Essex County**" **[Printed Article],** in *Essex Institute Historical Collections,* Vol. 47, No. 3 (Jul 1911).

"**1744-1752 Northborough Taxpayers, Worcester County**" **[Printed Article],** in *Worcester Magazine and Historical Journal,* Vol. 2, No. 3 (Jul 1926?).

"**1748 Marblehead Tax Lists, Essex County**" **[Printed Article],** in *Essex Institute Historical Collections,* Vol. 43, No. 3 (Jul 1907).

"**1750 Brookfield Tax List, Worcester County**" **[Printed Article],** in *New England Historical and Genealogical Register,* Vol. 20, No. 2 (Apr 1866).

"**1752 Danvers Tax List, Essex County**" **[Printed Article],** in *Danvers Historical Collections,* Vol. 3 (1915).

1752-1809. *Boston Marriages from 1752 to 1809* **[Online Database],** digitized and OCR indexed at the Ancestry.com website. Source: Book, same title (see title page for details). This database has 716 pages: *https://search.ancestry.com/search/db.aspx?dbid=48164.*

"**1753 Danvers Voters List, Essex County**" **[Printed Article],** in *Danvers Historical Collections,* Vol. 37 (1949).

"**1753 Danvers Tax Lists, Essex County**" **[Printed Article],** in *Danvers Historical Collections,* Vol. 39 (1951).

1753-1900. *Massachusetts, Delayed and Corrected Vital Records* **[Online Database],** digitized and indexed at the FamilySearch.org website. Source: Birth, Marriages, and Death Registers at the MA State Archives, Boston. Each index record includes: Name, Event type, Event date, Event place,, Gender, Father's name, Father's birthplace, Mother's name, and Mother's birthplace. The document image may include more information. This database has 31,696 records. See *www.familysearch.org/search/collection/2268583.*

"**1754 Poll Records, Carlisle, Middlesex County, Massachusetts**" **[Printed Article],** in *New England Historical and Genealogical Register,* Vol. 62, No. 1 (Jan 1908).

1755-1775. See *Soldiers in the French War from Essex County, 1755-1761: Militia Officers, Essex Co., Mass., 1761-1771; Danvers Tax List, 1775, District Covered by Amos Trask, Collector* **[Microfiche & Digital Capture],** from a book by Eben Putnam, publ. Historical Collections of the Essex Institute, 1892, 15 pages. Filmed by the Genealogical Society of Utah, 1983, 1 microfiche, FHL fiche #6019250. To view a digital version of this book, visit the online FHL catalog page for this title: *https://familysearch.org/search/catalog/50012.*

"**1754 Rockport Tax List, Essex County**" **[Printed Article],** in *New England Historical and Genealogical Register,* Vol. 137, No. 2 (Apr 1983).

"**1754 Sandy Bay Taxpayers, Essex County**" **[Printed Article],** in *Missing Links-Genealogical Clues, N*o. 24 (Jul 1964).

"**1756-1760 Acadians on Cape Cod**" **[Printed Article],** in *Acadian Genealogy Exchange,* Vol. 33, No. 2 (Oct 2004).

"**1757 Coach Excise Taxpayers, Worcester County**" **[Printed Article],** in *Genealogical Quarterly Magazine,* Vol. 3, No. 4 (Dec 1902).

"**1757 Coach Excise Taxpayers, Plymouth County**" **[Printed Article],** in *Genealogical Quarterly Magazine,* Vol. 3, No. 4 (Dec 1902).

"**1760 Muster Roll (French and Indian War), Essex County, Massachusetts**" **[Printed Article],** in *Essex Institute Historical Collections,* Vol. 88, No. 3 (Jul 1952).

1760-1771. *Massachusetts Property Valuations and Taxes* **[Microfilm & Digital Capture],** from originals at the MA Archives, Boston. Contains property valuations and taxes from various counties and towns of Massachusetts Colony. Filmed by the MA Archives, ca1975, 4 rolls, beginning with FHL film #926471

(1760-1770). For a complete list of roll numbers, roll contents, and the digital images of each roll, see the online FHL catalog page: *https://familysearch.org/search/catalog/316720.*

"1761-1778 Norfolk Assessment Roll Family Names" [Printed Article], in *New England Historical and Genealogical Register,* Vol. 36, No. 4 (Oct 1882).

"1764 Rehoboth Tax Return, Bristol County" [Printed Article], in *American Genealogist,* Vol. 64, No. 1 (Jan 1989).

1765-1790. *Divided Hearts, Massachusetts Loyalists: A Biographical Directory* [Microfilm & Digital Capture], from a book publ. 1980 by the NEHGS, Boston, 189 pages. Digitized by the Genealogical Society of Utah, 2016. To access the digital images of the microfilm roll, see the online FHL catalog page: *www.familysearch.org/search/catalog/2612846.*

1766-1909. *Early Records of Great Barrington, Berkshire County, Massachusetts* [Online Database], links to Births, Marriages, Deaths, and Cemeteries. For an archived database, see *https://web.archive.org/web/20160103210457/http://www.rootsweb.ancestry.com/~maberksh/towns/greatbarr/greatbarrington.htm.*

1766-1775. *Boston, The Redcoats, and the Homespun Patriots* [Printed Book], compiled by Armand Francis Lucier. This is a collection of newspaper articles transcribed from colonial newspapers for the years 1766-1775. Publ. Heritage Books, Bowie, MD, 1998, 460 pages, FHL book 974.461 H29L.

1767-1833. *Muster Rolls (Index File Cards) of the Revolutionary War (Massachusetts)* [Microfilm & Digital Capture], from the original card file at the MA State Archives, Boston. Filmed by the Genealogical Society of Utah, 1995-1996, 259 rolls, beginning with FHL film #2020564 (Atwood, Jess to Bacon, Abijah). For a complete list of roll numbers, roll contents, and the digital images of each roll, see the online FHL catalog page: *https://familysearch.org/search/catalog/746935.*

1770-1773. *The Historic Boston Tea Party of December 16, 1773: its Men and Objects: Incidents Leading to, Accompanying, And Following the Throwing Overboard of the Tea; Including a Short Account of the Boston Massacre of March 5, 1770;* *with Patriotic Lessons Therefrom Adapted to the Present Time* [Printed Book], by Caleb A. Wall, publ. F.S. Blanchard, Worcester, MA, 1896, 87 pages, FHL book 974.461 H2w. Also on microfilm, FHL film #564396.

1771 Massachusetts Tax Valuations [Printed Book], name lists indexed in the Massachusetts Tax Valuation List of 1771, edited by Bettye Hobbs Pruitt, published by Picton Press, Camden, ME, 1998, 945 pages. FHL book 974.4 R4p.

1771. See *Tax Valuation List of 1771, Tisbury, Dukes County, Massachusetts* [Online Database], alpha name list at the history.vineyard.net website. See *http://history.vineyard.net/1771sttx.htm.*

"1775 Known Taxpayers, Franklin County" [Printed Article], in *Missing Links-Genealogical Clues,* Vol. 19 (Feb 1964).

1775-1781. *Massachusetts Soldiers and Sailors in the Revolutionary War* [Online Database], digitized at the Ancesry.com website. This database has 17,026 images. See *http://search.ancestry.com/search/db.aspx?dbid=7726.*

1775-1783. *Massachusetts, Revolutionary War, Index Cards to Muster Rolls* [Online Database], digitized and indexed at the FamilySearch.org website. Source: MA State Archives, Boston. Each index record includes: Name, Event type, Event date, Event place, Residence place, and Military rank. The document image may have much more information. This database has 605,085 records. See *www.familysearch.org/search/collection/2548057.*

1780-1811. See *Massachusetts General Court Valuation Committee Tax Lists, 1780-1792, 1810-1811* [Microfilm & Digital Capture]. Includes index to taxpayers for all counties and towns of Massachusetts. Filmed by the Genealogical Society of Utah, 1974, 19 rolls, as follows:
- Valuations, (arranged by county) 1780-1841, FHL film #954452.
- Valuations, (arranged by county) 1850-1860, FHL film #954453.
- Amherst to Deerfield 1780, FHL film #953995.
- Dighton to Wilbraham 1780, FHL film #953996.
- Abington to Lynn 1783, FHL film #954454.
- Marshfield to Yarmouth 1783, FHL film #954455.
- Abington to Braintree 1784, FHL film #954458.

● Bridgewater to Foxborough 1784, FHL film #954459.
● Framingham to Lunenburg, 1784, FHL film #954460.
● Lynn to Whately 1784, FHL film #954498.
● Raynham to Warwick 1784, FHL film #954499.
● Watertown to Yarmouth 1784, FHL film #954500.
● Ashburnham to Weymouth 1791, FHL film #953997.
● Ashburnham to Colrain 1792, FHL film #953998.
● Deerfield to Lancaster 1792, FHL film #953999.
● Lee to Sandwich 1792, FHL film #954000.
● Sharon to Williamstown 1792, FHL film #955501.
● Ashfield to Heath 1810-1811, FHL film #959902.
● Leverett to Whately 1811, FHL film #959903.

To access the digital images of each of the above rolls, see the online FHL catalog page:
www.familysearch.org/search/catalog/75570.

1780-1892. *Massachusetts Name Changes* **[Online Database],** digitized and indexed at the Ancestry.com website. This collection of court records originally published in 1893 contains changes of names approved by the courts of Massachusetts between 1780 and 1892. Each entry includes the original name and the new name. In addition, most entries contain information on family relatives and the person's residence at the time of court action. This database has 7,975 records. See *http://search.ancestry.com/search/db.aspx?dbid=3280.*

"1781 Northborough Assessment, Worcester County" [Printed Article], in *Hourglass,* Vol. 64 (Jun 1997).

1783-1790s. *Revolutionary War Bounty Land Grants* **[Online Database],** indexed at the Ancestry.com website. Source: Book, same title, by Lloyd DeWitt Bockstruck, publ. 1998. Includes grants made in Massachusetts for areas in military reserves in the area northwest of the River Ohio. Typically, each entry contains the name of the claimant, who is usually the veteran, the state of service, the rank held, the date of the records, and the acreage. This database has 636 pages. See *https://search.ancestry.com/search/db.aspx?dbid=49315.*

"1783 Brookfield Assessors List, Worcester County" [Printed Article], in *Rota-Gene,* Vol. 5, No. 4 (Oct 1984).

1784-1840. *Massachusetts, Marriage Index* **[Online Database],** indexed at the Ancestry.com website. The *Massachusetts Centinel* began publication in 1784, its name changed to the *Columbian Centinel* and publication ceased in 1840. This database is one of four volumes covering marriage notices from this newspaper throughout its printing. It contains persons whose last name begins with A-D. The marriages are arranged in alphabetical order, under the name of both husband and wife, and comprise over 34,000 names. Because it was an area newspaper, researchers can find marriage notices for persons living in the surrounding states of Rhode Island, Connecticut, New Hampshire, and Maine. This database has 31,687 records. See *https://search.ancestry.com/search/db.aspx?dbid=3393.*

1784-2009. *MyHeritage.com Newspaper Archives Collection for Massachusetts* **[Online Database],** links to newspaper sites with images, newspapers published in Acton, Ashfield, Pittsfield, Boston, Brookfield, Edgartown, Fitchburg, Lowell, and North Adams. See *www.myheritage.com/research/catalog?q=Massachusetts.*

1787-1892. *History of New Bedford and its Vicinity* **[Printed Book & Digital Capture],** by Leonard Bolles Ellis, publ. D. Mason, Syracuse, NY, 1892, 906 pages, FHL book 974.485/N2 H2e. To view a digital version of this book, visit the online FHL catalog page for this title. See *https://familysearch.org/search/catalog/240311.*

1787-1906. *United States, New England, Petitions for Naturalization* **[Online Database],** digitized at the FamilySearch.org website. From the National Archives microfilm publication. Includes naturalization documents filed for Maine, Massachusetts, New Hampshire, Rhode Island, and Vermont. This database has 954,378 images. See *https://familysearch.org/search/collection/2064580.*

1789-1900. *Massachusetts, Boston Archdiocese Roman Catholic Sacramental Records* **[Online Database],** digitized and indexed at the Ancestry.com website. Source: Boston Archdiocese records. Each index record includes: Name, Record type, Marriage date, Marriage place, Father, Mother, and Spouse. This database has 771,876 records. See *https://search.ancestry.com/search/db.aspx?dbid=61585.*

"1789 Tax Assessors List, Berkshire County" **[Printed Article]**, in *Missing Links-Genealogical Clues,* No. 30 (Jan 1965).

"1789 Boston City Directory" [Printed Article], in *New England Historical and Genealogical Register,* Vol. 140, No. 2 (Apr 1986) and No. 3 (Jul 1986).

"1789 Pittsfield Assessors List, Berkshire County" **[Printed Article]**, in *Missing Links-Genealogical Clues,* No. 28 (Nov 1964).

1789-1842. See *Boston, Massachusetts City Directories, Citizens of Boston, 1789, 1816, 1825, 1835, 1842* **[CD-ROM]**, by Burke Publishing, Craig, CO, 2000, FHL CD No. 430.

1789-1935. See *Boston, Massachusetts City Directories* **[Microfilm]**, from the originals by various publishers. FHL has 1789, 1796, 1798, 1800, 1803, 1805, 1807, 1809, 1810, 1813, 1816, 1818, 1820-1823, and 1825-1935. Filmed by Research publications, Woodbridge, CT, 1980-1984, 334 microfiche and 84 rolls, beginning with FHL fiche #6043615 (1789 Boston Directory). For a complete list of fiche/roll numbers, visit the online FHL catalog page for this title. See *https://familysearch.org/search/catalog/512794.*

1790. *Heads of Families at the First Census of the United States Taken in the Year 1790, Massachusetts* **[Printed Book & Online Database]**, publ. for the Census Bureau by the Government Printing Office, Washington, DC, 1908, 363 pages, FHL book 974. X2. The Census Office of 1850 became the Bureau of the Census in 1905, promoted to a full-time federal agency for the first time. The Census Bureau's first project was to compile an extract and index to the 1790 federal census. See the Nationwide chapter for references to the 1790 federal census, online at several major genealogical websites. A digital version of this Massachusetts book is at the Ancestry.com website: *http://search.ancestry.com/search/db.aspx?dbid=48173.*

1790-1840. See *Massachusetts, 1790 Thru 1840 Federal Census: Population Schedules* **[Microfilm & Digital Capture]**, from the originals at the National Archives, Washington, DC. Filmed by the National Archives as one series, 1938-1969, 42 rolls, beginning with FHL film #568144 (Massachusetts, 1790). For a complete list of roll numbers, roll contents, and the digital images of each roll, see the online FHL catalog page: *www.familysearch.org/search/catalog/745494.*

1790-1890. *Massachusetts, Compiled Census and Census Substitutes Index* **[Online Database]**. Indexed at the Ancestry.com website. The census indexes were originally compiled by Accelerated Indexing Systems, Salt Lake City, UT and acquired by Ancestry, Inc., which has these lists: 1790 Federal Census Index; 1800 Federal Census Index; 1810 Federal Census Index; 1820 Federal Census Index; 1830 Federal Census Index; 1840 Federal Census Index; 1840 Pensioners List; 1850 Federal Census Index; 1860 Federal Census Index; 1890 Veterans Schedule; Early Census Index. *http://search.ancestry.com/search/db.aspx?dbid=3553.*

1790-1926. *Naturalization Index Cards, Massachusetts* **[Microfilm & Digital Capture]**, from the originals at the U.S. District Court, Boston, MA. An index to naturalization records of the U.S. District Court and U.S. Circuit Court for Massachusetts. A letter "M" beside the petition number indicates that it is a military naturalization. Filmed by the Genealogical Society of Utah, 1985, 17 rolls, beginning with FHL film #1420205 (Aaron – Bzurowsky). For a complete list of roll numbers, roll contents, and the digital images of each roll, see the online FHL catalog page: *www.familysearch.org/search/catalog/393728.*

1791-1884. *Massachusetts, Land Deeds* **[Microfilm & Digital Capture]**, microfilm now located at the Granite Mountain Record Vault. Digitized by the Genealogical Society of Utah, 2009, 7 rolls, beginning with FHL film #5656090 (Land deeds, Revolutionary War Soldiers, Massachusetts, Mars Hill, Book 1, 1829-1884). To access the digital images of all 7 rolls, see the online FHL catalog page: *www.familysearch.org/search/catalog/1881411.*

1791-1906. *United States, New England Petitions for Naturalization Index* **[Online Database]**, digitized and indexed at the FamilySearch.org website. Source: National Archives microfilm series M1299. This is an index to photocopies of naturalization documents filed in courts in Connecticut, Maine, Massachusetts, New Hampshire, Rhode Island and Vermont from 1791 to 1906. The photocopies and the index are in the National Archives, New England Region. The index consists of 3x5 inch cards arranged by state and thereunder by name of petitioner, arranged according to the Soundex system. The index refers to the name and location of the court that granted the certificate of naturalization, and to the volume and page number (or certificate number) of the naturalization record. NARA publication title: This database has 635,867 images (index cards). See *www.familysearch.org/search/collection/1840474.*

"1792 Danvers Assessors List, Essex County" **[Printed Article],** in *Danvers Historical Collections,* Vol. 32, (1944).

"1792 Tax Valuation List, Stockbridge, Berkshire County" [Printed Article], in *Berkshire Genealogist,* Vol. 6, No. 2 (Spring 1985).

1792-1894. *Town Records, Quincy, Massachusetts* **[Microfilm & Digital Capture],** from the original records at the Quincy City Hall. Quincy became a town in 1792, a city in 1888. Town (and city) records filmed by the Genealogical Society of Utah, 1970, 4 rolls, FHL film #845726 (Index to town records 1792-1879; town records to 1826); FHL film #845727 (Town records to 1879); FHL film #845728 (Town minutes, 1792-1826; town officers, 1846-1888; fence boundaries, 1824-1894; and rebellion records, 1861), and FHL film #845687 (Tax Records 1792-1821). To access the digital images of these rolls, see the online FHL catalog page: *www.familysearch.org/search/catalog/275192.*

1793-1900. *Norfolk County, Massachusetts Probate Index* **[Online Database],** indexed at Ancestry.com website. This database gives a listing of wills, administration of wills, guardianships, adoptions, etc. Information includes names, residence, nature of document, and date. This database has 43,646 records: *http://search.ancestry.com/search/db.aspx?dbid=5656.*

1794-1847. *Tax Records, Cambridge, Massachusetts* **[Microfilm & Digital Capture],** from originals at the Cambridge City Hall, Cambridge, MA. Filmed by the Genealogical Society of Utah, 1972, 12 rolls, beginning with FHL film #902086 (Tax Records, 1794-1807). For a complete list of roll numbers, roll contents, and the digital images of each roll, see the online FHL catalog page: *https://familysearch.org/search/catalog/304631.*

1795-1910. *Massachusetts, Deaths and Burials* **[Online Database],** indexed at the FamilySearch.org website. This name index to death and burial records is from the microfilm at the Family History Library, filmed in the state of Massachusetts. Each index record includes: Name, Gender, Death date, age, and Birth date. This database has 1,324,801 records. See *https://familysearch.org/search/collection/1675350.*

"1796-1797 Harwich Tax Books, Barnstable County" [Printed Article], in *Cape Cod Genealogical Society Bulletin,* Vol. 24, No. 3 (Winter 1998).

"1797 Voter List, Berkshire County, Massachusetts" [Printed Article], in *Berkshire Genealogist,* Vol. 27, No. 4 (Fall 2006).

1797-1934. *Massachusetts, Salem and Beverly Crew Lists and Shipping Articles* **[Online Database],** digitized and indexed at the FamilySearch.org website. From three National Archives microfilm publications. Each index record includes: Name, Event type, Event date, Event place, Age, Birth year, Birth country, and Ship name. The document image may have more information. This database has 215,124 records. See *https://familysearch.org/search/collection/2302948.*

"1798 Boston Taxables" [Printed Article], in *Pennsylvania Traveler-Post,* Vol. 8, No. 2 (Feb 1972).

1798. *Massachusetts and Maine Direct Tax of 1798* **[Microfilm],** from the original records at the New England Historic and Genealogical Society, Boston, MA. Film includes a published index and guide (FHL book 974.R42i). Filmed by NEHGS, 1978, 18 rolls, beginning with FHL film #940072 (Maine counties: Hancock, Washington, Lincoln, Cumberland). For a complete list of roll numbers and contents of each roll, see the online FHL catalog page: *https://familysearch.org/search/catalog/46827.*

1798. *An Index and Guide to the Microfilm Edition of the Massachusetts and Maine Direct Tax Census of 1798* **[Printed Book],** by Michael H. Gorn, published by the New England Historic Genealogical Society, Boston, 1979, 98 pages. FHL book 974.R42i.

1798-1950. *Massachusetts, State and Federal Naturalization Records* **[Online Database],** digitized and indexed at Ancestry.com. Source: National

Archives microfilm and textual records. Each index record includes: Name, Petition age, Record type, Birth date, Birthplace, Arrival date, Arrival place, Petition date, and Petition place. The document image has more information. This database has 3,113,455 records. See *https://search.ancestry.com/search/db.aspx?dbid=2361*.

"1799 Savoy Tax List, Berkshire County" [Printed Book], in *Berkshire Genealogist*, Vol. 8, No. 4 (Fall 1987).

1799-1930. *Suffolk County, Massachusetts Sheriff's Records* **[Microfilm & Digital Capture],** from the original records at the MA State Archives, Boston. The records appear to relate to debtors or criminal jail sentences. Each person's entry contains amount of bail, birthplace, residence, color, age, sex, height, occupation or condition, when committed, offence, authority, sentence or otherwise, when discharged, how discharged, and length of sentence. Filmed by the Genealogical Society of Utah, 2002, 31 rolls, beginning with FHL film #2295040 (Debtor calendar: 1799-1829 and Criminal calendar 1810-1814). For a complete list of roll numbers, roll contents, and the digital images of each roll, see the online FHL catalog page: *https://familysearch.org/search/catalog/1058281*.

1800. *Index to the 1800 Census of Massachusetts* **[Online Database],** indexed at the Ancestry.com website. Source: Book, same title, compiled by Elizabeth Petty Bentley, publ. Genealogical Publishing Co., 1978. This database has 315 pages. See *https://search.ancestry.com/search/db.aspx?dbid=48161*.

1800. *Massachusetts 1800 Census Index* **[Printed Index],** edited by Ronald Vern Jackson, publ. Accelerated Indexing Systems, Salt Lake City, UT, 1985, 56 pages, FHL book 974.4 X22ja 1800.

"1802, 1809-1810 Voter Lists, Pittsfield, Berkshire County" [Printed Article], in *Berkshire Genealogist*, Vol. 20, No. 2 (Spring 1999).

1805-1845. *Massachusetts Revolutionary War Bounty Land Applications* **[Online Database],** digitized and indexed at the FamilySearch.org website. Source: Maine State Archives, Augusta. Each index record includes: Name, Event type, Event date, Event place, and Relative's name. The document image may have more information. This database has 616 records. See *www.familysearch.org/search/collection/1881492*.

"1806 Tax Valuation List, Washington, Berkshire County" [Printed Article], in *Berkshire Genealogist*, Vol. 5, No. 3 (Summer 1984).

1806-1958. *Naturalization Records and Index Cards, Norfolk County, Massachusetts* **[Microfilm & Digital Capture],** from the originals at the Superior Courts in Dedham and Quincy, Norfolk Co MA. Filmed by the Genealogical Society of Utah, 1987, 15 rolls, beginning with FHL film #1522670 (Index to Naturalization Records, alphabetically, 1806-1906). For a complete list of roll numbers, roll contents, and the digital images of certain rolls, see the online FHL catalog page: *https://familysearch.org/search/catalog/479889*.

"1808 Tax Document, Worcester County" [Printed Article], in *Rota-Gene*, Vol. 13, No. 1 (Apr 1992).

1810. *Massachusetts 1810 Census Index, A-Z* **[Printed Index],** publ. Heritage Quest, Bountiful, UT, 2000, 461 pages, FHL book 974.4 X22m 1810.

1811-1921. *Massachusetts, Boston, Crew Lists* **[Online Database],** digitized and indexed at the FamilySearch.org website. Includes crew lists of ships arriving at Boston, 1811-1921, from the National Archives publication. Each index record include: Name, Event type, Event date, Event place, Gender, Age, Birth year, Birth country, and Ship name. The document image may have more information. This database has 355,821. See *https://familysearch.org/search/collection/2216301*.

"1814 Windsor Town Tax List, Berkshire County" [Printed Article], name list published in *Berkshire Genealogist*, beginning with Vol. 6, No. 1 (Winter 1985) through Vol. 7, No. 1 (Winter 1986).

1817-1915. *Massachusetts Military Records* **[Microfilm & Digital Capture],** from the originals at the Massachusetts National Guard Supply Depot, Natick, MA. Includes enlistments, enrollments, medical examinations, detachments, oaths, rosters, election returns, discharges, desertions, and resignations. Some lists include name, rank, company, regiment, enlistment, and discharge dates. Filmed by the Genealogical Society of Utah, 1988-1991, 148 rolls, beginning with FHL film #1562394 (General Service – Regular Army and Cavalry 1863-1864).

Certain rolls were digitized for Enlistments 1861-1865; Enlistments, 1863-1864; and Muster-in rolls, Mexican Border Service, 1916. For a complete list of roll numbers, roll contents, and the digital images for certain rolls, see the online FHL catalog page: *www.familysearch.org/search/catalog/486195.*

1818-1834. *Tax Records, Lynn, Massachusetts* **[Microfilm & Digital Capture],** from the original records at the Lynn City Hall. Filmed by the Genealogical Society of Utah, 1971, 1 roll, FHL film #877733. To access the digital images, see the online FHL catalog page: *www.familysearch.org/search/catalog/417915.*

1820. *Massachusetts 1820 Census Index* **[Printed Index],** edited by Ronald Vern Jackson, et al, publ. Accelerated Indexing Systems, Bountiful, UT, 1976, 222 pages, FHL book 974.4 X2j 1820.

1820-1891. *Massachusetts, Boston Passenger Lists* **[Online Database],** digitized and indexed at the FamilySearch.org website. From the National Archives microfilm publication. Each index record includes: Name, Event type, Event date, Event place, Gender, Nationality, Birth country, and Ship name. The document image has more information. This database has 903,407 records. See *https://familysearch.org/search/collection/1860873.*

1820-1963. *Massachusetts, Passenger and Crew Lists* **[Online Database],** digitized and indexed at the Ancestry.com website. Source: National Archives microfilm. Each index record includes: Name, Gender, Age, Birth date, Departure place, Arrival date, and Arrival place. This document image may have more information. This database has 6,850,802 records. See *https://search.ancestry.com/search/db.aspx?dbid=8745.*

1821. *Boston Taxpayers in 1821* **[Printed Book],** edited by Lewis Bunker Rohrbach, originally published Boston, True & Greene, 1822 (with the title, *At a legal meeting of the freeholders and other inhabitants of the town of Boston, holden on the 14th day of January, A.D. 1822);* reprinted with added introduction and index, Picton Press, Camden, ME, 1988, 256 pages, FHL book 974.461 R4b.

1822-1918. *Massachusetts, Boston Tax Records* **[Online Database],** digitized at the FamilySerch.org website. Contains tax records, transfer books, tax

books, and assessor's lists from the Boston City Archives. This database has 586,834 images. Browse through the images, organized by Record Type, Year Range, and Volume. See *https://familysearch.org/search/collection/2125599.*

"1823-1824 Salem Village Tax Lists, Essex County [Printed Article], in *Danvers Historical Collections,* Vol. 23 (1935).

1823-1981. *Massachusetts City Directories* **[Online Database],** indexed at the Ancestry.com website. Source: NEHGS Collection. This database is a collection of 554 city/county/town directories for various years and places in Massachusetts. Generally a city directory will contain an alphabetical list of its citizens, listing the names of the heads of households, their addresses, and occupational information. Sometimes the wife's name will be listed in parentheses or italics following the husbands. Often, dates of deaths of individuals listed in the previous year's directory are listed as well as the names of partners of firms, and when possible, the forwarding addresses or post offices of people who moved to another town. In addition to the alphabetical portion, a city directory may also contain a business directory, street directory, governmental directory, and listings of town officers, schools, societies, churches, post offices, and other miscellaneous matters of general and local interest. To see what cities and years are currently available, view the *Browse this Collection* feature. Begin by selecting a city, then choose a year. This MA database has 698,392 records. See *https://search.ancestry.com/search/db.aspx?dbid=8779.*

1823-1981 Massachusetts Directories, as part of *U.S. City Directories, 1822-1995* **[Online Database],** digitized and OCR indexed at the Ancestry.com website. See each directory title page image for the full title and publication information. This collection is one of the largest single databases on the Internet. All states are represented (except Alaska) with a total of 1.56 billion names, all indexed from scanned images of the city directory book pages. 184 Massachusetts directories are listed here for a **City/Town/County** (No. of years), and Date-Range: **Abington** (4) 1872-1892, **Acton** (3) 1883-1936, **Boston** (121) 1823-1981, **Charlestown** (22) 1831-1871, and 180 more cities. Use Ancestry's *Browse this Collection* feature to choose a state, choose a city, and choose a directory year available for that city. This U.S. database has 1,560,284,702 records. See *https://search.ancestry.com/search/db.aspx?dbid=2469.*

1826-1850. *Valuation Books, Lowell, Massachusetts* **[Microfilm & Digital Capture],** from originals at the Lowell City Hall, City Clerk's Office, Lowell, MA. Filmed by the Genealogical Society, 1973, 7 rolls, beginning with FHL film #930921 (Valuations, 1826-1836). To access the digital images, visit the online FHL catalog page:
https://familysearch.org/search/catalog/398988.

1829-1935. *Worcester, Massachusetts City Directories* **[Microfilm],** from originals by various publishers. FHL has 1829, 1842-1856, and 1856-1935. Filmed by Research Publications, Woodbridge, CT, 1980-1984, 53 fiche and 29 rolls, beginning with FHL fiche #6044654 (1829 Village Register). For a complete list of fiche/roll numbers, visit the online FHL catalog page for this title. See
https://familysearch.org/search/catalog/538718.

1830. *Massachusetts 1830 Census Index* **[Printed Index],** edited by Ronald Vern Jackson, et al, publ. Accelerated Indexing Systems, Bountiful, UT, 274 pages, FHL book 974.4 X22j 1830.

"1830 Voters List, Pittsfield, Berkshire County" **[Printed Article],** in *Berkshire Genealogist,* Vol. 17, No. 3 (Summer 1996).

1831-1936. *Divorce Index Cards to Hampden County Superior Court Records* **[Microfilm],** from the original records at the Hampden County Courthouse, Springfield, MA. Filmed by the Genealogical Society of Utah, 1986, 4 rolls, beginning with FHL film #1464363 (Aarons, Anna J. Hurley – Beebe, Albert A.). For a complete list of roll numbers and contents of each roll, visit the online FHL catalog page for this title. See
https://familysearch.org/search/catalog/591602.

1832-1935. *Lowell, Massachusetts City Directories* **[Microfilm],** from originals by various publishers. Filmed by Research Publications, Woodbridge CT, 1980-1984, 75 fiche, 26 rolls. FHL has 1832-1842, 1844-1845, 1847, 1849, 1851, 1853, 1855, 1858, 1860, 1861, 1864-1866, 1868, 1870, 1872, 1874-1876, 1878, 1880, 1881, and 1883-1935, beginning with FHL fiche #6044048 (1832 Lowell Directory). For a complete list of fiche/roll numbers, visit the online FHL catalog page for this title. See
https://familysearch.org/search/catalog/530551.

1832-1935. *Lynn, Massachusetts City Directories* **[Microfilm],** from originals by various publishers. Filmed by Research Publications, Woodbridge CT,

1980-1984, 34 fiche/rolls. FHL has 1832, 1841, 1851, 1854, 1856, 1858, 1860, 1863, 1865, 1867, 1869, 1871, 1873, 1876, 1878-1879, 1880, and 1882-1935, beginning with FHL fiche #6044071 (1832 The Lynn Directory and Town Register). For a complete list of fiche/roll numbers, visit the online FHL catalog page for this title. See
https://familysearch.org/search/catalog/530363.

"1832 Rowe Valuation List, Franklin County" **[Printed Article],** in *Rowe Historical Society Bulletin,* Vol. 21, No. 4 (Fall 1984).

1836-1934. *New Bedford, Massachusetts City Directories* **[Microfilm],** from originals by various publishers. Filmed by Research Publications, Woodbridge, CT, 1980-1984, 32 fiche/rolls. FHL has 1836, 1838, 1839, 1841, 1845,1849, 1852, 1856, 1859, 1865, 1867-1883, 1885,1887, 1890-1919, 1921, 1923-1928, 1930-1932, and 1934, beginning with FHL fiche #6044199 (1836 New Bedford Directory). For a complete list of fiche/roll numbers, visit the online FHL catalog page for this title. See
https://familysearch.org/search/catalog/544377.

1837 Census, Town of Danvers, Essex County **[Microfilm],** a manuscript name list was microfilmed for the Genealogical Society of Utah by Reproduction Systems, 1971. See FHL film #876100, item 9.

"1837 Tax Bills, North Ward, Plymouth County" **[Printed Article],** in *Scituate Historical Society Bulletin,* Vol. 8, No. 3 (Sep 1956).

1840. *Massachusetts 1840 Census Index* **[Printed Index],** edited by Ronald Vern Jackson, publ. Accelerated Indexing Systems, Salt Lake City, UT, 1978, 344 pages, FHL book 974.4 X22j 1840.

1841-1915. *Massachusetts, Birth Records* **[Online Database],** digitized and indexed at the FamilySearch.org website. From the Massachusetts Archives. Includes name index and images of state birth records from 1841-1915. The registers of births are first arranged in volumes by year. Within the volumes the birth entries are arranged by town then numerically by the number it was entered into the registers. This database has 3,817,626 records. See
https://www.familysearch.org/search/collection/1536925.

1840-1915. *Massachusetts, Marriages* **[Online Database],** digitized and indexed at the FamilySearch.org website. From the Massachusetts Archives. Includes a name index and images of

statewide marriage registers in numbered volumes arranged by year then by individual town. This database has 18,537,430 records. See *https://familysearch.org/search/collection/1469062.*
- For the Ancestry.com database, see *http://search.ancestry.com/search/db.aspx?dbid=2511.*

1841-1915. *Massachusetts, Death Records* **[Online Database],** digitized and indexed at the FamilySearch.org website. From the Massachusetts Archives. Includes name index and images of Massachusetts statewide death registers and certificates. The death registers and certificates are in numbered volumes arranged by year then by individual town. This database has 2,739,146 records. See *https://familysearch.org/search/collection/1463156.*
- For the Ancesstry.com database, see *http://search.ancestry.com/search/db.aspx?dbid=2101.*

1841-1920. *Massachusetts, State Vital Records* **[Online Database],** digitized and indexed at the FamilySearch.org website. This is a collection of births, marriages and deaths, 1916-1920 and state amendments to vital records, 1841-1920 located at the state archives in Boston. This collection is being published as images become available. This database has 1,141,063 records. See *https://familysearch.org/search/collection/1928860.*

1842-1900. *New Ashford, Massachusetts Landowners* **[Online Database],** indexed at the Ancestry.com website. Source: Landowners/Poll Tax, compiled for Ancestry by Edward J. LeFebvre, 1998. This database is a listing of persons who owned land in the town between 1842 and 1900. Also included in this collection is a list of males eligible to vote and were thus assessed a poll tax, the amount of which settled at two dollars. An asterisk following the name indicates the landowner did not live within the town; however, most lived within the county. Due to missing records, landowners between 1870-1873 are not recorded. This database has 4,448 records. See *https://search.ancestry.com/search/db.aspx?dbid=3453.*

1842-1912. *Somerville, Mass: The Beautiful City of Seven Hills, its History and Opportunities* **[Online Database],** from the book by the Somerville Board of Trade, publ. A. Martin & Sons, 1912, 200 pages, digitized by the Genealogical Society of Utah from a copy at the Allen County Public Library, Ft. Wayne, IN. To view a digital version of this book, visit the online FHL catalog page for this title. See *https://familysearch.org/search/catalog/2181226.*

1843-1917. *Registers of Patients in Private Hospitals (Massachusetts)* **[Microfilm & Digital Capture],** from records at the MA State Archives. Filmed by the Genealogical Society of Utah, 1997, 1 roll, FHL film #2080271 (Vol. 1, 1884-1910; Vol. 2, 1867-1917; Vol. 3, 1843-1912 (McLean Asylum, Massachusetts). To access the digital images of this roll, see the online FHL catalog page: *www.familysearch.org/search/catalog/691202.*

1844-1920. *Index to Births in Tisbury, Dukes County, Massachusetts* **[Online Database],** indexed at the history.vineyard.net website. See *http://history.vineyard.net/birthsi.htm.*

1845-1895. *Lawrence Up to Date 1845-1895: Illustrated* **[Microfilm & Digital Capture],** from a book publ. Rushforth and Donoghue, 1895, 172 pages. Filmed by the Genealogical Society of Utah, 1990, 1 roll, FHL film #1697267. To view a digital version of this book, see the online FHL catalog page: *https://familysearch.org/search/catalog/466949.*

1845-1935. *Springfield, Massachusetts City Directories* **[Microfilm],** from originals by various publishers. Filmed by Research publications, Woodbridge CT, 1980-1984, 54 fiche/rolls. FHL has a complete run, 1845 through 1935, beginning with FHL fiche #6044502 (1845 Directory). For a complete list of fiche/roll numbers, visit the online FHL catalog page for this title. See *https://familysearch.org/search/catalog/546220.*

1846-1932. *Plymouth, Massachusetts City Directories* **[Microfilm & Microfiche],** by various publishers, filmed by Research Publications, Woodbridge, CT, 1995. FHL has directories for 1846, 1860, 1887, 1891-1892, 1893-1894, 1896, 1899, 1899-1900, 1901, 1903, 1905, 1907, 1909, 1911, 1913, 1915, 1917, 1919, 1921, 1924, and 1932, beginning with FHL fiche #6044322 (1846 Plymouth directory). For a complete list of fiche/roll numbers, visit the online FHL catalog page for this title. See *https://familysearch.org/search/catalog/534622.*

1847-1851. *A List of Alien Passengers Bonded from January 1, 1847, to January 1, 1851* **[Online Database],** digitized and OCR indexed at the Ancestry.com website. Source: Book, same title, by the Superintendent of Alien Passengers for the Port of Boston, 1851. This database has 99 pages. See *https://search.ancestry.com/search/db.aspx?dbid=48061.*

1847-1931. *Cambridge, Massachusetts City Directories* [Microfilm], from the originals by various publishers, filmed by Research Publications, Woodbridge CT, 1980-1984, 35 fiche/rolls. The FHL has 1847-1854, 1856-1857, 1859-1861, 1863-1923, 1925-1928, and 1930-1931, beginning with FHL fiche #6043749 (1847 Cambridge Almanac). For a complete list of fiche/roll numbers, visit the online FHL catalog page for this title. See *https://familysearch.org/search/catalog/533001.*

1847-1935. *Fitchburg, Massachusetts City Directories* [Microfilm], from the originals by various publishers. The FHL has annual directories starting with 1847 through 1860; and 1882 through 1935. Filmed by the Research Publications, Woodbridge, CT, 1995, 32 fiche/rolls, beginning with FHL fiche #6043902 (1847 Directory). For a complete list of fiche/roll numbers, visit the online FHL catalog page: *https://familysearch.org/search/catalog/542369.*

1847-1935. *Lawrence, Massachusetts City Directories* [Microfilm], from the originals by various publishers. The FHL has annual directories starting with 1847-1848, 1850-1851, 1853-1855, 1857, 1859-1861, 1883, 1885-1925, and 1927-1935. Filmed by Research Publications. Woodbridge, CT, 1980-1984, 31 fiche/rolls, beginning with FHL fiche #6044031 (1847 Directory). For a complete list of fiche/roll numbers, visit the online FHL catalog page: *https://familysearch.org/search/catalog/530166.*

1847-1940. *Divorce Record Indexes, Berkshire County, Massachusetts* [Microfilm & Digital Capture], from the originals at the Berkshire County Courthouse, Pittsfield, MA, filmed by the Genealogical Society of Utah, 1986, 6 rolls, beginning with FHL film #1450561 (Abbe, Roselle – Duquette, Helen R). For a complete list of roll numbers, roll contents, and the digital images of certain rolls, see the online FHL catalog page. *https://familysearch.org/search/catalog/592685.*

1847-2011. *The New England Historical & Genealogical Register* [Online Database], indexed at the Ancestry.com website. The New England Historic Genealogical Society (NEHGS) was formed in 1845, and in 1847, they published the first issue of the *New England Historical and Genealogical Register.* The NEHGS is the oldest genealogical society in the United States, and the Register, likewise, is the country's oldest genealogical journal. The *Register* includes histories, compiled genealogies, indexes, biographical

sketches, abstracts of wills, birth records, marriage records, death records, lists of early settlers, memoirs and remembrances, pedigrees, entries from journals, letters, descendant reports, copied church records, inscriptions from headstones, proceedings of historical societies, and notifications of books recently published on genealogy, among other items. These records may include a name, birth date, father's name, mother's name, death date, age at death, residence, spouse, marriage date, and spouse's father. This database has 300,565 records. See *https://search.ancestry.com/search/db.aspx?dbid=2129.*

1848-1891. *Massachusetts, Index to Boston Passenger Lists* [Online Database], digitized and indexed at the FamilySearch.org website. From the National Archives microfilm publication, this database has 1,139,732 records. See *https://familysearch.org/search/collection/2304666.*

1849-1859. *Massachusetts (State) Directories* [Microfilm], from the originals by various publishers, filmed by Research Publications, Woodbridge, CT, 1980-1984, 61 microfiche, beginning with FHL fiche #6044103 (1849 New England Mercantile Union Business Directory). For a complete list of fiche numbers and contents of each, visit the online FHL catalog page for this title. See *https://familysearch.org/search/catalog/535744.*

1850. *Massachusetts, 1850 Federal Census: Population Schedules* [Microfilm & Digital Capture], from the originals at the National Archives, Washington, DC. Filmed by the National Archives, 1964, 43 rolls, beginning with FHL film #14697 (Massachusetts: Barnstable Co-Part). To access the digital images, see the online FHL catalog: *www.familysearch.org/search/catalog/744484.*

1850. *Massachusetts 1850 Census Index* [Printed Index], edited by Ronald Vern Jackson, publ. Accelerated Indexing Systems, Salt Lake City, UT, 1978, 934 pages, FHL book 974.4 X2j 1850.

1850-1875. *Deaths in Tisbury, Dukes County, Massachusetts* [Online Database], name list at the history.vineyard.net website. See *http://history.vineyard.net/index1.htm.*

1851-1933. *Somerville, Massachusetts City Directories* [Microfilm], from originals by various publishers. The FHL has 1851, 1869-1881, 1883-1885, 1887, 1889-1890, 1890, 1892-1920, 1924-1925, 1927,

1929-1930, and 1933. Filmed by Research Publications, Woodbridge, CT, 15 fiche/rolls, beginning with FHL fiche #6044494 (1851 - The Somerville Directory). For a complete list of fiche/roll numbers, visit the online FHL catalog page: *https://familysearch.org/search/catalog/534140.*

"1853 Plymouth Tax List" [Printed Article], in *Scituate Historical Society Bulletin,* Vol. 14, No. 3 (Sep 1962).

1853-1935. *Fall River, Massachusetts City Directories* **[Microfilm],** from originals by various publishers, filmed by Research Publications, Woodbridge CT, 1980-1984, 27 fiche/rolls. The FHL has 1853, 1855, 1857, 1859, 1861, 1864, 1866, 1869, 1870-1871, 1873, 1874, 1876, 1878, 1880, 1882, 1884, 1885, 1887, 1888, 1889, 1890-1905, 1906-1907, and 1908-1935, beginning with FHL fiche #6043898 (1853 Fall River Directory). For a complete list of fiche/roll numbers, visit the online FHL catalog page: *https://familysearch.org/search/catalog/542187.*

1853-1935. *Haverhill, Massachusetts City Directories* **[Microfilm],** from originals by various publishers. FHL has 1853, 1857, 1859-1861, 1865, 1867, 1869-1870, 1872, 1874, 1876, 1878, 1880, 1889, 1891, 1894-1896, 1898-1911, 1913-1924, 1926-1928, 1930, 1932, and 1935. Filmed by Research Publications, Woodbridge, CT, 1980-1984, 16 fiche/rolls, beginning with FHL fiche #6043977 (1853 Haverhill Directory). For a complete list of fiche/roll numbers, visit the online FHL catalog page: *https://familysearch.org/search/catalog/527459.*

1855 & 1865 Massachusetts State Censuses **[Microfilm & Digital Capture],** from the originals at the Massachusetts Archives, Boston. Filmed and cataloged as one series by the Genealogical Society of Utah, 1974, 68 rolls, beginning with FHL film #953973 (1855 Barnstable Co – Barnstable to Yarmouth) and FHL film #953966 (1865 Barnstable Co – Barnstable to Yarmouth). For a complete list of roll numbers, roll contents, and the digital images of each roll, visit the online FHL catalog page for this title. See *https://familysearch.org/search/catalog/293408.*

1855. *Massachusetts, State Census, 1855* **[Online Database],** digitized and indexed at the FamilySearch.org website. This database has 1,202,234 records. See *https://familysearch.org/search/collection/1459985.*
- For the Ancestry.com database, see *http://search.ancestry.com/search/db.aspx?dbid=4472.*

1856-1870. *Case Histories and Commitment Register of Boys (Massachusetts State Nautical School), 1856-1870* **[Microfilm & Digital Capture],** filmed by the Genealogical Society of Utah, 1997, 1 roll, FHL film #2080409 (Vol. 1 Case Histories, 1856-1865; Vol. 2 case histories, 1865-1870; Commitment Register, 1860-1869). For access to the digital images of this roll, see the online FHL catalog page: *www.familysearch.org/search/catalog/691735.*

1857-1920. *Massachusetts, City of Boston Voter Registers* **[Online Database],** digitized and indexed at FamilySearch.org. This collection includes voter registration records for men from 1857-1900, women from 1920-1940 and men from 1921-1940. The registers are not a comprehensive listing of all registered voters. The period 1857-1895 includes only naturalized males and for the period 1920-1940 other sets of registers were used to register voters. The collection has been divided into four series: Naturalized male voter indexes; Naturalized male voter registers; Naturalized and Native male voter registers; and Women voter registers. The fourth series is labeled "Women voters" because the books were initially used to register women in 1920 and are labeled as such. These 4th series volumes do include men after 1920. See *www.familysearch.org/search/collection/3159283.*

1859-1996. *Naturalization Index, Hampshire County, Massachusetts, 1859- Present* **[Microfilm & Digital Capture],** from the originals at the MA State Archives, Boston. Filmed by the Genealogical Society of Utah, 1996, 5 rolls, beginning with FHL film #2057085 (Abarno, Elizabeth Vickers to Corbitt, Daniel). For a complete list of roll numbers, roll contents, and the digital images of each roll, visit the online FHL catalog page: *https://familysearch.org/search/catalog/781623.*

1860. *Massachusetts, 1860 Federal Census: Population Schedules* **[Microfilm & Digital Capture],** from the originals at the National Archives, Washington, DC. Filmed twice by the National Archives, 1950 & 1967, total of 63 rolls, beginning with FHL film #803486 (Massachusetts, 2nd filming, Barnstable Co). For a complete list of roll numbers, roll contents, and the digital images of each roll, see the online FHL catalog page: *www.familysearch.org/search/catalog/705076.*

1860. *Massachusetts 1860 North Federal Census Index* **[Printed Index],** edited by Ronald Vern Jackson, publ. Accelerated Indexing Systems, Salt

Lake City, UT, 1992, 2 vols., 1,403 pages, FHL book 974.4 X2mn 1860.

1860. *Massachusetts, 1860, South, Federal Census Index: Barnstable, Bristol, Dukes, Essex, Middlesex, Nantucket, Norfolk, Plymouth* **[Printed Index],** edited by Ronald Vern Jackson, publ. Accelerated Indexing Systems, Salt Lake City, UT, 1992, 905 pages, FHL book 974.4 X2ms 1860.

1860 Mortality Schedules. See *Schedule 3. Persons Who Died During the Year Ending 1st June 1860: Federal Nonpopulation Census Schedules for Massachusetts* **[Microfilm & Digital Capture],** from the originals at the National Archives, Kansas City, MO. Filmed by the National Archives, series T1204, 1975, 1 roll, FHL film #1421017. To access the digital images, see the online FHL catalog:
www.familysearch.org/search/catalog/565573.

1860-1970. *Massachusetts, Birth Index* **[Online Database],** digitized and indexed at the Ancestry.com.org website. Source: MA Dept of Health. This database is from a computer print-out index, which Ancestry scanned with character recognition software to compile its own index. Each index record includes Name, Birth date, Birthplace, Volume number, Page number, Index vol. no., and Reference number. This database has 5,270,346 records. See
https://search.ancestry.com/search/db.aspx?dbid=3928.

1861-1865. *Index to Compiled Service Records of Volunteer Union Soldiers Who Served in Organizations from the State of Massachusetts* **[Microfilm & Digital Capture],** from the originals at the National Archives, Washington, DC. Filmed by the archives, 1965, Series M544, 44 rolls, beginning with FHL film #881870 (A). For a complete list of roll numbers, roll contents, and the digital images of each roll, visit the online FHL catalog page:
https://familysearch.org/search/catalog/320457.

1861-1865. *History and Complete Roster of the Massachusetts Regiments: Minute Men of '61 who Responded to the First Call of President Abraham Lincoln, April 15, 1861, to Defend the Flag and Constitution of the United States Together with Photographs and Biographical Sketches of Minute Men of Massachusetts* **[Printed Book, Microfilm & Digital Capture],** by Georg W. Nason, publ. Smith &

McCance, Boston, 1910, 413 pages, FHL book 974.4 M2n. Also on microfilm, FHL film #1425662. For access to a digital version of this book, see the online FHL catalog page:
www.familysearch.org/search/catalog/86401.

1861-1865. *Massachusetts Army & Navy* **[Online Database],** indexed at the Ancestry.com website. This database lists Massachusetts officers and soldiers who were killed in action. Each entry includes the following information: name and rank of the individual, command, engagement, and date of death. This database has 8,089 records. See
http://search.ancestry.com/search/db.aspx?dbid=3082.

1861-1865. *Massachusetts Soldiers, Sailors, and Marines in the Civil War* **[Online Database],** digitized and indexed at the Ancestry.com website. This is the official Massachusetts Adjutant General's report, published 1931-1935. This database has 6,852 records. See
http://search.ancestry.com/search/db.aspx?dbid=29987.
- See also *Massachusetts in the Army and Navy During the War of 1861-1865* **[Online Database],** book, OCR indexed at the Ancestry.com website. This database has 744 pages. See
https://search.ancestry.com/search/db.aspx?dbid=31417.

1861-1865. *Record of the Massachusetts Volunteers* **[Online Database],** digitized and indexed at the Ancestry.com website. From the Massachusetts Adjutant General's report of 1868. This database has 1,885 records. See
http://search.ancestry.com/search/db.aspx?dbid=28893.

1861-1865. *United States Civil War Soldiers Index* **[Online Database],** an index to soldiers who served in the Civil War, culled from 6.3 million soldier records in the General Index Cards to the Compiled Military Service Records in the National Archives. This index was a joint project of the U.S. National Park Service, the Federation of Genealogical Societies (FGS), and the Genealogical Society of Utah (GSU). Each record provides the full name of the soldier, state, regiment, whether Union or Confederate, the company, the soldier's rank, sometimes alternate names, the NARA publication and roll numbers. Massachusetts supplied a total of 164,434 soldiers to the Union forces. It is possible to search for Massachusetts regiments and see complete rosters of the soldiers. See
https://familysearch.org/search/collection/1910717.

1861-1865. See *Soldiers and Sailors Database* **[Online Database],** indexed at the National Park Service website. This is the original database containing information about the men who served in the Union and Confederate armies during the Civil War. Other information on the site includes histories of Union and Confederate regiments, links to descriptions of significant battles, and selected lists of prisoner-of-war records and cemetery records, which will be amended over time. This database has 6.3 million records. See
www.nps.gov/civilwar/soldiers-and-sailors-database.htm.

1861-1917. *Military Records, Massachusetts* **[Microfilm & Digital Capture],** from the originals at the Massachusetts State Archives, Boston. This series includes U.S. Navy enlistments, U.S. Marine Corps enlistments, Transfers from Army to Navy, Returns of Naval enlistments from towns, lists of seamen from various place, and many more details related to naval activities in Massachusetts. Filmed by the Genealogical Society of Utah, 1997-1998, 7 rolls, beginning with FHL film #2108352. To access the digital images, see the online FHL catalog:
www.familysearch.org/search/catalog/721401.

1863-1865. See *Annual Report of the Adjutant General of the Commonwealth of Massachusetts* **[Online Database],** digitized and indexed at the Ancestry.com website. From the Adjutant General's report of 1863-1866. This database has 1,628 records:
http://search.ancestry.com/search/db.aspx?dbid=31406.

1864-1872. *Case Histories of Boys for the School Ship George M. Bernard (Massachusetts State Nautical School)* **[Microfilm & Digital Capture],** filmed by the Genealogical Society of Utah, 1997, 2 rolls, FHL film #2080272 (Vol. 1, 1864-1869; Vol. 2, 1869-1871) & FHL film #2080409 (Vol. 2 (Cont.), 1872). To access the digital images of these rolls, see the online FHL catalog page:
www.familysearch.org/search/catalog/691717.

1865. *Massachusetts, State Census, 1865* **[Online Database],** digitized and indexed at the FamilySearch.org website. This database has 1,352,857 records. See
https://familysearch.org/search/collection/1410399.
- For the Ancestry.com database, see
http://search.ancestry.com/search/db.aspx?dbid=9203.

1866-1888. *Massachusetts Military Company History, Vol. 4* **[Online Database],** digitized and indexed at the Ancestry.com website. This is a history of the Military Company of Massachusetts, known as The Ancient and Honorable Artillery Company of Massachusetts. Volume 4 begins with the establishment of peace in 1866 and covers the history until the year 1888. The database contains many facts concerning births, marriages, and occupations. This database has 5,914 records. See
http://search.ancestry.com/search/db.aspx?dbid=3100.

1867. *The Plymouth County Directory, and Historical Register of the Old Colony: Containing an Historical Sketch of the County and of Each Town in the County: A Roll of Honor, With the Names of all Soldiers of the Army and Navy from this County who Lost their Lives in Service: An Alphabetical List of the Voters: A Complete Index to the Mercantile, Manufacturing, and Professional Interests of the County, Together With Much Valuable Miscellaneous Matter* **[Microfiche],** from the original book publ. Middleboro, MA, S.B. Pratt & Co., 1867, 400 pages, filmed by University Microfilms International, 1989, 6 fiche, FHL fiche #6078749.

1868-1901. *Newton, Massachusetts City Directories* **[Microfilm],** from the originals by various publishers. The FHL has directories for 1868, 1871, 1873, 1875, 1877, 1879, 1881, 1883-1885, 1887, 1889, 1891, 1893, 1895, 1897, 1899, and 1901. Filmed by Research Publications, Woodbridge CT, 1980-1984, 12 rolls, beginning with FHL film #1930454 (1868 The Newton Directory). For a complete list of roll numbers and contents of each roll, visit the online FHL catalog page for this title. See
https://familysearch.org/search/catalog/728137.

1868-1935. *Quincy, Massachusetts City Directories* **[Microfilm],** from the originals by various publishers. The FHL has directories for 1868-1871, 1873-1874, 1876-1885, 1888, 1891, 1893-1904, 1906, 1908-1916, 1918, 1920, 1922, 1924, 1926, 1927, and 1929-1935. Filmed by Research Publications, 1980-1984, 10 rolls, beginning with FHL film #1930462 (1868-1869 – The Dorchester and Quincy directory). For a complete list of roll numbers and contents of each roll, visit the online FHL catalog page for this title. See
https://familysearch.org/search/catalog/728156.

1870. *Massachusetts, 1870 Federal Census: Population Schedules* **[Microfilm & Digital Capture],** from the originals at the National Archives, Washington, DC. Filmed twice by the National

Archives, 1962 & 1968, total of 79 rolls, beginning with FHL film #552099 (Massachusetts, 2nd filming, Barnstable Co). For a complete list of roll numbers, roll contents, and the digital images of each roll, see the online FHL catalog page: *www.familysearch.org/search/catalog/698902.*

1870. *Massachusetts 1870 Census Index* **[Printed Index],** edited by Raeone Christensen Steuart, publ. Heritage Quest, Bountiful, UT, 2000, 4 vols., Contents: Vol. 1: A-C; Vol. 2: D-J; Vol. 3: K-P; and Vol. 4: Q-Z. FHL book 974.4 X22sr v.1-4.

1870 Social Statistics & Mortality Schedule. See *Schedule 5. Social Statistics for the Year Ending June 1, 1870. Schedule 2. Persons Who Died During the Year Ending 1st June, 1870: Federal Nonpopulation Census Schedules for Massachusetts* **[Microfilm & Digital Capture],** from the originals at the National Archives, Kansas City, MO. Filmed by the National Archives, series T1204, 2 rolls, FHL film #1421018 (Social Statistics, Barnstable Co MA) and FHL film #142109 (Mortality schedules, Nantucket-Worcester counties). For access to the digital images of each roll, see the online FHL catalog page: *www.familysearch.org/search/catalog/565601.*

1870. *Massachusetts, Federal Census Mortality Schedule* **[Online Database],** digitized at the FamilySearch.org website. This is an image-only database. Lists the names of persons who died during the year ending June 1, 1870. This database has 657 images. See *www.familysearch.org/search/collection/2311325.*

1871-1909. *Middlesex County, Massachusetts Probate Index (Part A-K)* **[Online Database],** indexed at the Ancestry.com website. These records include wills, administrations of wills, change of name documents, commitment papers, sales of estates, permissions to marry, guardianships, adoptions, and partitions. This database has 101,796 records. See *http://search.ancestry.com/search/db.aspx?dbid=4892.*
- **NOTE:** A search of this Middlesex County Probate Index for the surname "Alcott" revealed that a will for Louisa M. Alcott of Concord, MA, was recorded in 1888, file No. 23711.

1871-1991. *Massachusetts, United States Naturalization Records* **[Online Database],** indexed at the FamilySearch.org website. Source: National Archives records. The records include Petitions, Declarations, and Certificates. Each index record

includes: Name, Event type, Event date, Event place, Age, Birth date, Birthplace, Spouse's name, and Spouse's birth date. The document image may have much more information. This database has 474,126 records. See *www.familysearch.org/search/collection/2632082.*

"1872 List of Taxpayers, Franklin County" [Printed Article], in *Rowe Historical Society Bulletin,* Vol. 9, NO. 4 (Fall 1972).

1872-1897. *Massachusetts, Seamen's Records: Returns From U.S. Consuls Relating to Wages and Effects of Deceased Seamen* **[Microfilm & Digital Capture],** from original records at the National Archives, Waltham, MA. Digitized by the Genealogical Society of Utah, 2017, 2 rolls. To access the digital images of the rolls, see the online FHL catalog page for this title: *www.familysearch.org/search/catalog/2822371.*

1872-1917. *Chelsea, Massachusetts, Navy General Register of Patients* **[Online Database],** digitized and indexed at the Ancestry.com website. This database has 13,154 records. See *http://search.ancestry.com/search/db.aspx?dbid=3657.*

1872-1933. *Franklin County, Massachusetts, Divorce Records* **[Microfilm & Digital Capture,** from the originals at the MA State Archives, Boston, filmed by the Genealogical Society of Utah, 2000, 2 rolls, FHL film #2196180 (Records books, 1872-1887) and FHL film #2196181 (Record books, 1888-1933). To access the digital images, see the online FHL catalog page: *www.familysearch.org/search/catalog/973594.*

1873-1965. *Maine & Massachusetts, Case Files of Deceased and Deserted Seamen* **[Online Database],** indexed at the FamilySearch.org website. Source: National Archives microfilm. Generally, the records are arranged numerically by case number and contain an assortment of details including personal information, death details, wages etc. about deceased and deserted sailors and others who worked on board ships. This database has 16,231 records. See *www.familysearch.org/search/collection/2303027.*

1874-1935. *Brockton, Massachusetts City Directories* **[Microfilm],** from the originals by various publishers, filmed by Research Publications, Woodbridge, CT, 1980-1984, 16 rolls. FHL has 1874-1880, 1882, 1884-1885, 1887, 1889-1890, 1892, 1894, 1896, 1898-1919, 1921, 1922, 1924-1927, 1929, 1930, 1932, 1933, and 1935, beginning with FHL film #1930442 (1874-1875

Directory of Brockton, Bridgewater, East and West Bridgewater, and Abington). For a complete list of roll numbers, visit the online FHL catalog page for this title. See *https://familysearch.org/search/catalog/721719*.

1877. *Directory of Danvers, Marblehead, Peabody, Beverly, Manchester, Essex, Wenham, Topsfield – 1877* [Printed Book & Digital Version], digitized by the Genealogical Society of Utah, 2011. To view the digital version, visit the online FHL catalog page: *https://familysearch.org/search/catalog/1880663*.

"1877-1882 Voter Lists, Washington, Berkshire County" [Printed Article], in *Berkshire Genealogist,* Vol. 9, No. 3 (Summer 1988).

1880. *Massachusetts, 1880 Federal Census: Soundex and Population Schedules* [Microfilm & Digital Capture], from the originals at the National Archives, Washington, DC (ca1985). After filming, the originals (40 volumes) were transferred to the Massachusetts Archives, Boston, MA. Filmed on 120 rolls, beginning with FHL film #447262 (1880 Soundex: A000 thru A450); and FHL film #1254519 (1880 Population Schedules: Barnstable Co). To access the digital images, see the online FHL catalog: *https://familysearch.org/search/catalog/673568*.

1880 Mortality Schedules. See *Schedule 5. Persons Who Died During the Year Ending May 31, 1880: Federal Nonpopulation Census Schedules for Massachusetts* [Microfilm & Digital Capture]**, from the originals at the National Archives, Kansas City, MO. Filmed by the National Archives, series T1204, 4 rolls, beginning with FHL film #1421020 (Barnstable Co – Newburyport, Essex Co). For a complete list of roll numbers, roll content, and the digital images of each roll, see the online FHL page: *www.familysearch.org/search/catalog/565641*.

1880. *Massachusetts, Federal Census Mortality Schedule, 1880* [Online Database], digitized at the FamilySearch.org website. This is an image-only database. Lists the names of persons who died during the year ending June 1, 1880. This database has 2,423 images. See *www.familysearch.org/search/collection/2315101*.

1880. See *List of Persons, Hampden County, Massachusetts, 1880* [Microfilm & Digital Capture], a title given to this original record by the film crew of the Genealogical Society of Utah in 1986. The record is actually from the county's four original volumes of

the 1880 federal census, a "Short Form" name list, located at the Office of the Court Clerk, Superior Court, Springfield, Hampden County, MA. Filmed by the Genealogical Society of Utah, 1986, FHL film #1451427 (Vol. 1: Towns of Chicopee, Brimfield, Hampden, Holland, Monson, Longmeadow, Ludlow, Palmer, Wales, and Wilbraham, and Vol. 2: Town of Holyoke); and FHL film #1451428 (Vol. 3: Towns of Blandford, Chester, Granville, Montgomery, Russell, Southwick, Tolland, Westfield, and West Springfield. Vol. 4: Towns of Springfield and Holyoke). To access the digital images, see the online FHL catalog: *www.familysearch.org/search/catalog/484045*.

✓ **1880 NOTE.** The 1880 "Short Form" was an official county copy of the 1880 federal census. The full schedules were transferred to the Census Bureau in Washington, DC. The 1880 "Short Form" was created for each town/subdivision of a county, then gathered together and retained at the county courthouse in every county of the U.S. Extant manuscripts of the county copies are very rare (Hampden County has the only surviving manuscripts from any Massachusetts county). By law, the Short Form was to remain at a county courthouse for one month after the 1880 census was taken, allowing for public inspection of the data. The Short Form name list is not by family, but as an index to the full schedules with all names arranged by the first letter of their surname. The data was brief, including just a person's name, color, age, and sex. Only in 1880 did the Census Office ask for a county copy to be made that was different than the full schedules.

"1881 Concord Voter List, Middlesex County" [printed Article], in *New England Historical and Genealogical Register,* Vol. 38, No. 4 (Oct 1884).

1882-1890. *Middlesex County, Massachusetts Directories* [Microfilm], from the Middlesex County Directory for 1882-1883, 1884-1885, and 1890, & Co., publishers. Filmed by Research Publications, Woodbridge, CT, 1995, 1 roll, FHL film #2258180.

1883-1896. *Essex County, Massachusetts Directories* [Microfilm], from various publishers, filmed by Research Publications, Woodbridge, CT, 1995, 3 rolls, FHL film #2156645 (1883-1887); FHL film #2156646 (1888-1889), and FHL film #2156647 (1891-1896).

1887-1936. *Worcester County, Massachusetts, Divorce Records Index* [Microfilm & Digital Capture], from originals at the MA State Archives,

Boston, filmed by the Genealogical Society of Utah, 2000, 3 rolls, FHL film #2196342 (A - Bryce); FHL film #2200026 (Bryce – McGann); and FHL film #2200027 (McGann – Z). To access the digital images, see the online FHL catalog:
www.familysearch.org/search/catalog/973538.

1889. *Tax Record, New Bedford, Massachusetts* [Microfilm & Digital Capture], from the original manuscript at the New Bedford City Hall. Filmed by the Genealogical Society of Utah, 1969, 1 roll, FHL film #574897. To access the digital images of this roll, see the online FHL catalog page:
www.familysearch.org/search/catalog/192255.

"1890 Register of Voters, Pittsfield, Berkshire County" [Printed Article], name list published in *Berkshire Genealogist,* beginning with Vol. 10, No. 1 (Winter 1989) through Vol. 14, No. 3 (Summer 1993).

1890 Massachusetts Census Index of Civil War Veterans or Their Widows **[Printed Index],** compiled by Bryan Lee Dilts, publ. Index Publishing, Salt Lake City, UT, 1985, 222 pages, FHL book 974.4 X22d 1890.

1891-1943. *Massachusetts, Boston Passenger Lists* [Online Database], digitized and indexed at the FamilySearch.org website. From the National Archives microfilm publication, this database has 2,913,815 records. See
https://familysearch.org/search/collection/1923995.

"1892 Webster Poll Tax List, Worcester County" [Printed Article], in *Connecticut Maple Leaf,* Vol. 5, No. 1 (Summer 1991).

1893-1905. *Register of the Massachusetts Society of Colonial Dames of America* [Online Database], digitized and OCR indexed at the Ancestry.com website. Source: Book, same title, publ. by the Society, 1905. This database has 426 pages:
https://search.ancestry.com/search/db.aspx?dbid=30208. -
- See also, *Supplement to the Register of the Massachusetts Society of Colonial Dames of American, 1905-1909* **[Online Database],** digitized and OCR indexed at the Ancestry.com website. This database 119 pages. See
https://search.ancestry.com/search/db.aspx?dbid=30209.

1894. See *Men of Progress: One Thousand Biographical Sketches and Portraits of Leaders in Business and Professional Life in the Commonwealth of Massachusetts* **[Printed Book, Microfilm & Digital Version],** compiled by Richard Herndon, edited by Edwin M. Bacon, publ. by the New England

Magazine, Boston, 1894, 1,027 pages, FHL book 974.4 D3hr. Also on microfilm, FHL film #1425549. For access to the digital images of this roll, see the online FHL catalog page:
www.familysearch.org/search/catalog/213845.

1896-1941. *Boston Transcript Genealogy Newspaper Columns, June 6, 1896 – April 30, 1941* [Microfiche], compiled by Carlos Parsons Darling, this is a collection of genealogical queries and answers clipped from the Boston Evening Transcript. Clippings from 1896 contain also general queries and notes. The clipping collection resides at the Godfrey Memorial Library, Middletown, CT. This collection was indexed in the Godfrey Library's *American Genealogical & Biographical Index.* The Boston Transcript clippings were filmed by the Godfrey Library, c1975, on 682 microfiche, beginning with FHL fiche #6011001. For a complete list of fiche and contents of each, visit the online FHL catalog page:
https://familysearch.org/search/catalog/27402.
- See also, *Index to Boston Evening Transcript Genealogy – Newspaper Columns, ca. 1900-1941* **[Microfilm & Digital Capture],** from a typewritten and handwritten card file at the Buffalo/Erie County Public Library, Buffalo, NY. Filmed by the Genealogical Society of Utah, 1984, 5 rolls, beginning with FHL film #1381674 (Aaron-Clark). For a complete list of roll numbers, roll contents, and the digital images of each roll, see the online FHL catalog page: *https://familysearch.org/search/catalog/39033.*

1897 Vineyard Haven and Tisbury Resident Directory (Martha's Vineyard, Dukes County, Massachusetts) **[Online Database],** indexed at the history.vineyard.net website. See
http://history.vineyard.net/td1897.htm.

1898. *Massachusetts Spanish American War Records* [Online Database], indexed at the Ancestry.com website. From 1908 book, *Twelve Months with the Eighth Massachusetts Infantry in the Service of the United States,* by Harry E. Webber. This database has 1,490 records. See
http://search.ancestry.com/search/db.aspx?dbid=5070.

1899-1940. *Massachusetts, Boston Passenger Lists Index* [Online Database], digitized and indexed at the FamilySearch.org website. This database has 2,913,815 records. See
https://familysearch.org/search/collection/2173946.
- See also *Book Indexes to Boston Passenger Lists, 1899-1940* **[Online Database],** indexed at the Ancestry.com website. This database has 1,498,736 records. See
http://search.ancestry.com/search/db.aspx?dbid=1909.

1900. *Massachusetts, 1900 Federal Census: Soundex and Population Schedules* **[Microfilm & Digital Capture],** from originals held by the Census Bureau in the 1940s. After microfilming, Congress allowed the Census Bureau to destroy the originals to free up space for WWII-related files. Filmed on 386 rolls, beginning with FHL film #1244604 (1900 Soundex: A000 thru A234); and FHL film #1240631 (1900 Population Schedules: Barnstable and Berkshire Cos). To access the digital images, see the online FHL catalog: *https://familysearch.org/search/catalog/655929.*

1901. See *Biographical Sketches of Representative Citizens of the Commonwealth of Massachusetts* **[Printed Book & Digital Capture],** publ. by Graves & Steinbarger, Boston, 1901, 1,093 pages. To access a digital version, see the online FHL catalog page: *www.familysearch.org/search/catalog/2634657.*

1901-1970. See *Massachusetts, Marriage Index, 1901-1955 and 1966-1970* **[Online Database],** digitized and indexed at the Ancestry.com website. From the MA Registry of Vital Records and Statistics. Entries typically include names, town, year of marriage, and a volume and page number for the original. This database has 6,704,282 records. See *http://search.ancestry.com/search/db.aspx?dbid=2966.*

1901-1970. See *Massachusetts, Birth Index, 1901-1955 and 1966-1970* **[Online Database],** digitized and indexed at the Ancestry.com website. From the MA Registry of Vital Records and Statistics. Entries will typically include a name, town, birth year, and volume and page where original record is located. This database has 6,704,633 records. See *https://www.ancestry.com/search/collections/2966.*

1901-1980. See *Massachusetts, Death Index, 1901-1980* **[Online Database],** digitized and indexed at the Ancestry.com website. From the MA Registry of Vital Records and Statistics. Entries typically include a name, town, date of death, birth year, and a certificate number or a volume and page number for the original record. This database has 4,509,751 records. See *http://search.ancestry.com/search/db.aspx?dbid=3659.*

"1902 Poll Tax List, Southbridge, Worcester County" **[Printed Article],** in *Connecticut Maple Leaf,* Vol. 4, No. 3 (Summer 1990) through Vol. 4, No. 4 (Winter 1990).

"1902 Southbridge Poll Tax List, Worcester County **[Printed Article],** in *Connecticut Maple Leaf,* Vol. 5, No., 1 (Summer 1991).

"1902 Southbridge Poll Tax List, French-Canadian Surnames, Worcester County" **[Printed Article],** in *Connecticut Maple Leaf,* Vol. 4, No. 2 (Winter 1989) thru Vol. 4 (Winter 1990).

"1905 Hopkinton Tax List, Middlesex County" **[Printed Article],** in *Massog,* Vol. 17, No. 1 (Jan 1993) thru No. 4 (Oct 1993).

1905-1933. See *Lowell, Massachusetts Suburban Directories* **[Microfilm],** from the original Lowell suburban directory for Billerica, Chelmsford, Dracut, Tewksbury, Tyngsboro, and Westford, 1905-1933, by the Henry M. Meek Publishing Co, et al. Filmed by Primary Source Microfilm, Woodbridge, CT, 1995, 2 rolls, FHL film #2309051 (1905, 1913-1914, 1917-1918) and FHL film #2309052 (1917-1918 (cont.), 1927, 1930-1931, and 1932-1933).

1905-1951. See *Boston, Suffolk County, Massachusetts City Directory: Including Allston, Brighton, Charlestown, Dorchester, East Boston, Hyde Park, Jamaica Plain, Mattapan, Readville, Roslindale, Roxbury, South Boston, and West Roxbury* **[Microfilm],** from the originals of various publishers. The FHL has 1905, 1909, 1912, 1917, 1941, 1947, and 1951. Filmed by Genealogical Society of Utah, 1992, 4 rolls, beginning with FHL film #1697675 (1905). For a complete list of roll numbers and contents of each roll, see the online FHL catalog page:: *https://familysearch.org/search/catalog/224762.*

1905-2007. *The Boston Jewish Advocate Wedding Announcements* **[Online Database],** indexed at the Ancestry.com website. Includes the full names of the bride and groom, the date of the announcement, names of the parents, and hometowns. This database has 54,810 records. See *http://search.ancestry.com/search/db.aspx?dbid=1358.*

1906-1917. *Massachusetts, Naturalization Records* **[Online Database],** digitized and indexed at the FamilySearch.org website. Source: National Archives microfilm publications of U.S. District and Circuit Courts of Massachusetts. The records include Petitions,

Declarations, and Certificates. Each index record includes: Name, Event type, Event date, Event place, Birth date, Birthplace, Certificate number, and Volume number. The document image includes more information. This database has 92,745 records. See *www.familysearch.org/search/collection/2140604.*

1906-1935. See *Framingham, Massachusetts City Directories* [Microfilm], from originals by various publishers. FHL has 1906, 1908, 1911, 1912, 1914, 1916, 1918, 1920, 1924, 1926, 1930, 1933, and 1935. Filmed by Research Publication, Woodbridge, CT, 1995, 2 rolls, FHL film #2309013 (1906-1924), and FHL film #2309014 (1924-1935).

1906-1986. See *Naturalization Index Cards, 1906-1986, to Hampden County Superior Court, Massachusetts* [Microfilm & Digital Capture], from a typescript at the Hampden County Courthouse, Springfield, MA. Filmed by the Genealogical Society of Utah, 1986, 16 rolls, beginning with FHL film #1464331 (Aato, Anna – Bergeron, Suk Cha). For a complete list of roll numbers, roll contents, and the digital images of each roll, see the online FHL catalog page for this title: *www.familysearch.org/search/catalog/591530.*

1906-1966. See *Massachusetts, Naturalization Index* [Online Database], digitized and indexed at the FamilySearch.org website. Includes petitions and naturalization records from National Archives microfilm publications. This database has 388,086 records. See *https://familysearch.org/search/collection/1834334.*

1907 Directory of Chilmark & Gay Head, Dukes County, Massachusetts [Online Database], name list at the history.vineyard.net website. See *http://history.vineyard.net/dukes/chilgh1907.htm.*

1907 Directory of Oak Bluffs, Dukes County, Massachusetts [Online Database], name list at the history.vineyard.net website. See *http://history.vineyard.net/dukes/ob1907.htm.*

1907 Resident Directory of Vineyard Haven (Tisbury, Martha's Vineyard, Dukes County, Massachusetts) [Online Database], indexed at the History vineyard.net website. See *http://history.vineyard.net/vh1907.htm.*

1907-1921. *Inheritance Tax Records, Berkshire County, Massachusetts, Vol. 1-2* [Microfilm & Digital Capture], from the original records at the Berkshire Probate Court, Pittsfield, MA. Indexes in each volume. Filmed by the Genealogical Society of Utah, 1991, 1 roll, FHL film #1750275. To access the digital images of this roll, see the online FHL catalog page: *www.familysearch.org/search/catalog/494593.*

1907-1934. *Berkshire County (Massachusetts) Directories* [Microfilm], from the originals by various publishers. The FHL has 1907-1908, 1910-1911, 1913-1914, 1916-1918, 1920-1921, 1923-1925, 1926-1928, 1929-1931, 1929, 1931, and 1932-1934. Filmed by Research Publications, Woodbridge, CT, 1995, 4 rolls, beginning with FHL film #2309120 (1907-1908 Resident and Business Directory of Southern Berkshire County, Mass., including the towns of Great Barrington, Sheffield, Stockbridge, Alford, Egremont, Monterey, New Marlboro, and West Stockbridge). For a complete list of roll numbers, see the online FHL catalog page: *https://familysearch.org/search/catalog/1056648.*

1910. *Massachusetts, 1910 Federal Census: Population Schedules* [Microfilm & Digital Capture], from originals held by the Bureau of the Census in the 1940s. After microfilming, Congress allowed the Census Bureau to destroy the originals to free up space for WWII-related files. Filmed on 62 rolls, beginning with FHL film #1374584 (Barnstable & Berkshire Cos). To access the digital images, see the online FHL catalog: *https://familysearch.org/search/catalog/637204.*

1910. *Genealogical and Personal Memoirs Relating to the Families of the State of Massachusetts* [Printed Book and Digital Capture], by Richard Cutter and William Frederick Adams, 4 vols., publ. Lewis Historical Publ. Co., New York, 1910. For access to all four volumes, plus a separate index, see the online FHL catalog page for this title: *www.familysearch.org/search/collection/2303027.*

"1910 Medway Assessors Report of Valuation and Taxes, Norfolk Count" [Printed Article], in *Massog,* Vol. 18, No. 1 (Jan 1994) thru No. 4 (Oct 1994).

1912. *Register of the Towns of Manchester, Essex, Hamilton and Wenham, Essex County, Massachusetts* **[Printed Book],** publ. by the Lawton Register, Auburn, ME, 1912. List includes name of every person, wife's maiden name, street address, residence, occupation, and other remarks. See FHL book 974.45 X2r.

1912-1916. *Franklin County, Massachusetts Directories* **[Microfilm],** from original of various publishers. Suburban directories of Hampden, Franklin and Worcester Counties, MA for 1912-1916. The 1913 Franklin County suburban directory includes the towns of Ashfield, Bernardston, Buckland, Charlemont, Chesterfield, Colrain, Conway, Cummington, Deerfield, Erving, Gill, Goshen, Hawley, Heath, Leyden, Millers Falls, Monroe, Montague City, Montague Center, New Salem, Shelburne, Shelburne Falls, Northfield, Rowe, Sunderland, Turners Falls, Warwick, Wendell and Whatley. Filmed by Research Publications, Woodbridge, CT, 1995, 1 roll, FHL film #2309016.

1915. *The Decennial Census, 1915* **[Microfilm],** from a book by Charles F. Gettemy. State Censuses were taken in Massachusetts beginning in 1855, and every ten years thereafter through 1945. Only the original manuscripts for 1855 and 1865 survive. This is a comprehensive demographic analysis of the 1915 MA State Census. There are no names listed, but it does provide useful historical information about the nature of the population by race, ages, places of birth, value of property, etc. Publ. Boston, 1918, 749 pages, filmed by the Genealogical Society of Utah, 1 roll, FHL film #908760; and FHL fiche #6051394.

1915-1918. *Hampshire County, Massachusetts Suburban Directories* **[Microfilm],** from the originals publ. by H.A. Manning Co., 1 roll, FHL film #2310325 (1915 & 18918, Tows of Hatfield, Hadley, Williamsburg, Haydenville, Chesterfield, Cummington, Goshen, Sunderland, Leverett, Southampton, Westhampton, Whately, Deerfield,

South Deerfield, Pelham, Belchertown, South Hadley, and Granby).

1917-1918. *Massachusetts, World War I Selective Service System Draft Registration Cards, 1917-1918* **[Microfilm & Digital Capture],** from the original records at the National Archives. Filmed by the National Archives, series M1509, 162 rolls, beginning with FHL film #1684875 (MA North Adams City, Draft Board No. 1, A-V). For a complete list of roll numbers, roll contents, and the digital images of each roll, see the online FHL catalog page: *www.familysearch.org/search/catalog/746980.*
- See also *Selective Service Records, and, Exemptions as Aliens for 1917-1918 (Massachusetts)* **[Microfilm & Digital Capture],** from the originals at the Clerk of Courts, Superior Court, Barnstable, MA. Filmed by the Genealogical Society of Utah, 1992, 1 roll, FHL film #1846563. To access the digital images of this roll, see the online FHL catalog for this title: *www.familysearch.org/search/catalog/585815.*

1917-1943. *Massachusetts, Boston Crew Lists* **[Online Database],** digitized and indexed at the FamilySearch.org website. From the National Archives microfilm publication T938. This database has 1,570,299 records. See *https://familysearch.org/search/collection/2173944.*
- For the Ancestry.com database, see *http://search.ancestry.com/search/db.aspx?dbid=1071.*

1920. *Massachusetts, 1920 Federal Census: Soundex and Population Schedules* **[Microfilm & Digital Capture],** from the originals held by the Bureau of the Census in the 1940s. After microfilming, Congress allowed the Census Bureau to destroy the originals to free up space for WWII-related files. Filmed on 400 rolls, beginning with FHL film #1825848 (Soundex: A000 thru A213); and FHL film #1820679 (Population Schedules: Barnstable and Berkshire Cos). To access the digital images, see the online FHL catalog: *https://familysearch.org/search/catalog/572641.*

1920-1960. *Index to Deaths in Tisbury, Dukes County, Massachusetts* **[Online Database],** indexed at the history.vineyard.net website. See *http://history.vineyard.net/deaths2i.htm.*

1922-1985. *Massachusetts, Order Sons of Italy in America (OSIA), Lodge Records* [Online Database], digitized and indexed at the Ancestry.com website. This database contains documents from the Grand Lodge of Massachusetts of the OSIA from 1922 to 1985. This database has 18,428 records. See *http://search.ancestry.com/search/db.aspx?dbid=1887.*

1925-1955. *Massachusetts, Order Sons of Italy in America (OSIA), Membership Applications* [Online Database], digitized and indexed at the Ancestry.com website. This database contains application forms for membership in a Massachusetts lodge of OSIA. The forms vary somewhat, but they may include residence, age, name, birth date, birth country, father's name, occupation, marital status, spouse's name, and whether a U.S. citizen. This database has 29,298 records. See *http://search.ancestry.com/search/db.aspx?dbid=1665.*

1930. *Massachusetts, 1930 Federal Census: Population Schedules* [Microfilm & Digital Capture], from originals held by the Bureau of the Census in the 1940s. After microfilming, Congress allowed the Census Bureau to destroy the originals to free up space for WWII-related files. Filmed on 89 rolls, beginning with FHL film #2340618 (Barnstable and Berkshire Cos). To access the digital images, see the online FHL catalog: *https://familysearch.org/search/catalog/1036358.*

1930-1931. *Polk's Worcester Suburban, Massachusetts, Directory: For the Towns of Auburn, Boylston, Grafton, Holden, Leicester, Millbury, Paxton, Shrewsbury and West Boylston; Also a Buyers' Guide and a Complete Classified Business Directory* [Printed Book], by R.L. Polk, 1930-1931, Boston, MA, FHL book 974.43 E4pw.

1940. *Massachusetts, 1940 Federal Census: Population Schedules* [Microfilm & Digital Capture], from the original records held by the Bureau of the Census in the 1940s. After microfilming, Congress allowed the Census Bureau to destroy the originals to free up space for WWII-related files. Filmed on 155 rolls, beginning with FHL film #5460837 (Barnstable Co). For a complete list of roll numbers, roll contents, and the digital images of each roll, visit the online FHL catalog page: *https://familysearch.org/search/catalog/2057761.*

1940 Federal Census Finding Aids [Online Database]. The National Archives prepared a special website online with a detailed description of the 1940 federal census. Included at the site are descriptions of location finding aids, such as Enumeration District maps, Geographic Descriptions of Census Enumeration Districts, and a list of 1940 City Directories available at the National Archives. See *www.archives.gov/research/census/1940/general-info.html#questions.*

1940-1963. See *Index to Boston Evening Transcript Genealogy Columns – Newspaper Columns, 1940-1963, with Some Entries ca.1900-1939* [Microfilm & Digital Capture], from a typewritten and handwritten card file at the Buffalo/Erie County Public Library, Buffalo, NY. Filmed by the Genealogical Society of Utah, 1984, 4 rolls, beginning with FHL film #1381679 (Aaba-Hoyt). To access the digital images of certain rolls, visit the online FHL catalog page: *https://familysearch.org/search/catalog/39374.*

1943-1945. See *Overseas Military Naturalization Petitions, 1943-1945* [Microfilm & Digital Capture], from the originals at the National Archives, Waltham, MA. From the intro: " Lists name, place of residence, date and place of birth, physical description, marital and family status, date and place of arrival in the United States, name of the vessel on which they arrived, branch of military service, military serial number, character witnesses, oath of renunciation and allegiance, and overseas location where naturalization petition was filed." Filmed by the Genealogical Society of Utah, 2007, 1 roll, FHL film #2416218. To access the digital images of this roll, see the online FHL catalog page: *www.familysearch.org/search/catalog/1376357.*

1949-1957. See *Massachusetts, Passenger and Crew Lists, 1949-1957* [Online Database], digitized and indexed at the Ancestry.com website. From the National Archives publication. This database has 76,343 records. See *http://search.ancestry.com/search/db.aspx?dbid=9215.*

1952-1970. See *Massachusetts, Divorce Index, 1952-1970* [Microfilm & Digital Capture], from the originals at the MA State House, Boston, filmed by the Genealogical Society of Utah, 1974, 2 rolls, FHL film #959804 (1952-1963) & FHL film #959805 (1964-1970). To access the digital images on these rolls, see the online FHL catalog page: *www.familysearch.org/search/catalog/76413.*

"1958 Rowe List of Voters" [Printed Article], in *Rowe Historical Society Bulletin,* Vol. 20, No. 3 (Summer 1983).

1970-2003. See *Massachusetts, Death Index, 1970-2003* **[Online Database],** digitized and indexed at the FamilySearch.org website. Index of deaths from the Commonwealth of Massachusetts Department of Health Services in Boston. Index by Ancestry.com. This database has 2,037,185 records. See *https://familysearch.org/search/collection/1949332.*

- For the Ancestry.com database, see *http://search.ancestry.com/search/db.aspx?dbid=7457.*

1988-Current. See *Massachusetts Recent Newspaper Obituaries (1988-Current)* **[Online Database],** digitized and indexed newspaper obituaries at the GenealogyBank website, including newspapers from Acton, Amesbury, Andover, Arlington, Ashburnham, Ashland, Attleboro, Auburn, and 165 more Massachusetts places. See *www.genealogybank.com/explore/obituaries/all/usa/massachusetts.*

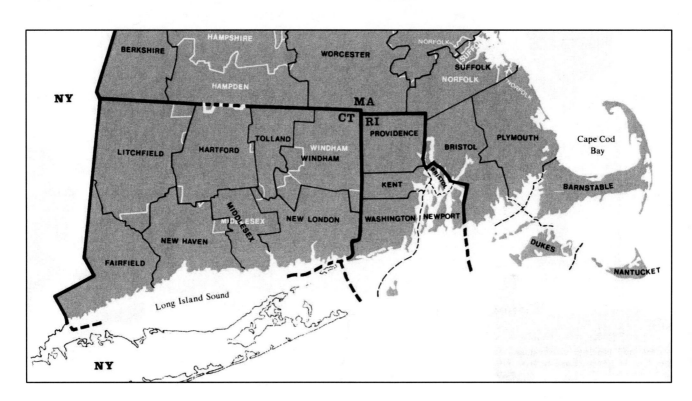

Rhode Island and Providence Plantations (with Connecticut & Massachusetts) ● Aug 1790. This map shows the counties of Rhode Island at the time of the 1790 Federal Census (and today). The modern counties of Connecticut and Massachusetts are shown in white. The area of Bristol County, RI was gained from Massachusetts in 1747 after resolution of a boundary dispute. Kent County was created in 1750, the last of the five counties. Rhode Island counties have not had any county government since 1846. County boundaries are still used as state divisions for sheriff districts, court districts, and for the gathering of statistics (such as censuses). **Map Source:** Page 60, *Map Guide to the U.S. Federal Censuses, 1790-1920,* by William Thorndale and William Dollarhide

Rhode Island (and Providence Plantations)
Censuses & Substitute Name Lists

Historical Timeline
of Rhode Island, 1497-1790

1614. Dutchman Adriaen Block sailed up the Connecticut River and claimed the region as part of the New Netherland colony. He also was credited as the first European to discover an island off Rhode Island now called Block Island. Block was also the first to give a name to Aquidneck Island.

1614-1615. New England. English Captain John Smith, a leader of the Jamestown Colony, visited the coast of present Connecticut, Rhode Island, Massachusetts, and Maine; then wrote his *Description of New England*, which encouraged Englishmen to settle there. Smith was credited as the first to call the area New England.

1620. Plymouth Colony. A new Royal Charter was issued by King James I to the Plymouth Council for New England (formerly the Virginia Company of Plymouth) to establish colonial settlements in New England. The area was from Latitude 40° to Latitude 45° ("sea to sea"). In that same year, the *Mayflower* dropped anchor off Cape Cod, and Plymouth Colony was founded by a small group of Separatists/Pilgrims, who had fled England for Holland a few years earlier.

1625. England. Charles I became King of England, Scotland, and Ireland. Soon after taking office Charles began to note a large number of non-

conformists among his subjects. Along with his Archbishop, William Laud, the King began a campaign to purge his church of the largest group of non-conformists, the so-called "Puritans," a militant Calvinist religious group attempting to purify the Church of England. Unfortunately, Charles I took on a job that led to civil war in England as well as the loss of his head. But, his campaign can be credited as the cause for the founding of English settlements in New England.

1628. The **Massachusetts Bay Company** was granted a royal charter for an English colony to be established in North America within the bounds of the Plymouth Council of New England. It is said that King Charles I was misled as to the religious leanings of the Massachusetts Bay Company leaders, all prominent Puritans, not Pilgrims, as he had surmised.

1629. The Great Migration to New England Begins. As a result of the Charles I campaign to purge non-conformists from the Church of England, large groups of people were disenfranchised. Charles I disbanded Parliament and ruled England alone for eleven years. The Puritans referred to this era as "the eleven years of tyranny." It was during these eleven years that 21,000 Puritan immigrants were to establish the Massachusetts Bay Colony of North America.

1635. Roger Williams, a religious dissident, was put on trial (in the Church Court), excommunicated, and banished from the Massachusetts Bay Colony.

1637. Anne Hutchinson, a charismatic religious leader opposed to the Puritans, was put on trial, excommunicated, and banished from the Massachusetts Bay Colony.

1637. August. **Providence Plantations.** Roger Williams, with a small band of followers, founded the Providence Plantations.. A document was signed, "We whose names are hereunder, desirous to inhabit in the town of Providence, do promise to subject ourselves in active and passive obedience to all such orders or agreements as shall be made for the public good of the body in an orderly way, by the major consent of present inhabitants, masters of families, incorporated together in a Towne fellowship, and others whom they shall admit unto them only in civil things."

1638. March. **Portsmouth Compact.** The document was written and signed by a group of followers of Anne Hutchinson. She was a banished dissident from Massachusetts, seeking religious freedom, and a desire to form a new colony on Aquidneck Island. The Compact was to set up an independent colony that was Christian in character but non-sectarian in its government.

1638. New Haven Colony was formed as an independent colony, separate from Connecticut Colony.

1641. New Hampshire. The Massachusetts Bay Colony gained control of the New Hampshire settlements.

1642. The English Civil War Begins. Since taking the throne in 1625, King Charles I had purged most of the Puritans from the Church of England. To deal with a Parliament opposing his every move, in 1629, Charles disbanded Parliament and ruled England on his own. When Parliament was restored in 1640, it quickly became dominated by the same Puritans who Charles had removed from the Church of England. Beginning in 1642, Royalist supporters were forced to fight the armies of the Puritan Parliament in the English Civil War. The Great Migration to New England ended about this time.

1643. Massachusetts. County government was established, with the first three counties of Essex, Middlesex, and Suffolk. It was no coincidence that these three counties had the same names as the East Anglia counties where the majority of the Puritans had lived back in England.

1643. New Haven Colony. The coastal settlements of Branford, Guilford, Milford, Stamford, plus Southold (on Long Island), all joined the New Haven Colony.

1644. Providence Plantations. Roger Williams of Providence, Rhode Island, was issued a charter in the name of King Charles I, which connected the towns of Providence, Portsmouth, and Newport under the title,

"Incorporation of Providence Plantations in the Narragansett Bay in New England."

1660. England. Charles II was restored to the throne as King of England, Scotland, and Ireland. He had lived in exile after the execution of his father, King Charles I. In 1649, the Scots had proclaimed Charles the king of Scotland. But the Puritan leader Oliver Cromwell defeated his army in 1651, and Charles fled to France. After Cromwell died in 1658, the English people became increasingly dissatisfied with the government that Cromwell had established. In 1660, Parliament invited Charles to return and declared him king. He ruled until his death in 1685, and during his 25-year reign, the English colonies forced out the remaining pockets of Atlantic settlements made earlier by the Dutch, Swedes, Danes, and French.

1663. Rhode Island and Providence Plantations. In 1663, King Charles II of England granted John Clarke a charter for the colony of Rhode Island and Providence Plantations, giving the colony an elected governor and legislature. Roger Williams (1603-1683) authored the Rhode Island and Providence Plantation Charter, which stated that religion and conscience should never be restrained by civil supremacy. NOTE: the name *Rhode Island and Providence Plantations* of 1663 remained unchanged until shortened to *Rhode Island* in 2020.

1665. Connecticut. New Haven Colony and Connecticut Colony merged into one chartered colony, retaining the name Connecticut.

1674. The English asked the Dutch to leave New York and Connecticut. But after swearing allegiance to the English Crown, the Dutch simply transferred control of their local governments to the English, maintained their farming communities, and continued their Dutch language, religion, and culture.

1679. New Hampshire. The English Crown formed New Hampshire as a separate royal colony.

1686. Dominion of New England. After Charles II died without issue in 1685, his brother, the Duke of York, was crowned King of England as James II. As the original Royal Charter holder of the New York Colony, James was familiar with the English colonies. In 1686, he established the Dominion of New England., replacing all of the Royal Charters in the New England colonies. This was an administrative union of English

English colonies, encompassing the areas from the Delaware River to the Penobscot River. The Dominion managed to install some religious reforms in the English colonies, allowing Catholics to hold office.

1689. King James II Deposed. After James II had declared his Catholic beliefs, he was deposed in the "Glorious Revolution" of 1689. Soon after, the Dominion of New England disappeared, and the English colonies all went back to denying Catholics the right to hold any office. After James II was deposed, his Protestant daughter, Mary, was declared the legal heir to the throne. She had married her cousin, William of Orange, the Stadtholder/Ruler of Holland, and Europe's most staunch Protestant leader. Because of William's stature, and his role in the "Glorious Revolution" which had overthrown the Catholic James II, Parliament asked both William and Mary to rule England jointly.

1689. William and Mary restored all of the New England Royal Charters, including Rhode Island's.

1691. Province of Massachusetts Bay. A new charter merged the old Plymouth Colony into the Massachusetts Bay Colony with the new name, Province of Massachusetts Bay.

1703. Rhode Island created two counties, Providence and Rhode Island counties. Rhode Island county was renamed Newport in 1729.

1707. During the reign of Queen Anne, the **United Kingdom of Great Britain** was established after the Union with Scotland Act passed the English Parliament in 1706; and the Union with England Act passed the Parliament of Scotland in 1707. The English colonies were now British colonies.

1729. Rhode Island created Kings County as its 3rd county. Kings was renamed Washington in 1781.

1747. Rhode Island's claim to areas of Massachusetts was settled with a compromise. Several East Bay Towns and the port of Bristol were transferred from Massachusetts to Rhode Island, who created the county of Bristol for the acquired areas as its 4th county.

1750. Rhode Island created Kent County as its 5th and last county.

1755-1762. French and Indian War. See *A Prelude to the French and Indian Wars,* a good review of the events of the era. See also *A List of Rhode Island*

Soldiers in the Old French and Indian War 1755-1762. See *www.rootsweb.ancestry.com/~rikent/george/french.html#A 04.*

1772. June. The first naval attack of the Revolutionary War took place when rebels of Providence, RI, stormed the British revenue cutter HMS Gaspee, burned it to the waterline and shot the captain.

1776. Rhode Island and Providence Plantations was the first of the thirteen colonies to declare independence from Great Britain.

1777-1778. Revolutionary War. British forces occupied Newport; colonial forces fled to Bristol.

1778. The Battle of Rhode Island was a partial victory, but the Americans failed to oust the British Army.

1779. British forces evacuated Rhode Island.

1790. May 29th. Statehood, 13th State: The official name: **State of Rhode Island and Providence Plantations.** The city of Providence was the capital.

2020. Nov 3. Question 1 on the statewide ballot was a proposed constitutional amendment to change the name of "State of Rhode Island and Providence Plantations" to "State of Rhode Island." The measure passed with "yes" votes accounting for 53.12% of the total votes cast.

Rhode Island Censuses and RI State Archives

Colonial Era. Censuses were taken in Rhode Island for several years, but except for the statistics of the population figures, the name lists for only a few exist today – those that survive are identified in the bibliography that follows.

State Censuses. More than any other New England state, the several state censuses taken for Rhode Island provide many census options between federal census years. Rhode Island began taking state censuses in 1865 and every ten years thereafter, the last in 1935. Most all of the name lists are extant, except that no record of the 1895 RI State Census can be found. All seven extant census years, 1865-1935, are available on microfilm at the Family History Library. The online versions at

Ancestry.com include all of the extant RI State Censuses except for the 1905; while online versions at FamilySearch.org includes the 1905 but not the 1865 or 1875.

Rhode Island State Archives. This Providence facility holds many original records of value to genealogists, but their online genealogical databases range from few to none. The Digital Content list shows a few sample census pages, tax lists, and perhaps more, but the collection is mostly limited to one or two pages of documents, rather than any large name lists. Review the Digital Contents page at **http://sos.ri.gov/archon/?p=digitallibrary/digitallibrary&browse.**

Bibliography
Rhode Island Censuses & Substitutes

1630-1945 Rhode Island, Town Clerk, Vital and Town Records [Online Database], digitized and indexed at FamilySearch.org. Includes vital and town records acquired from local town clerk offices. Additional images and indexed records will be published as they become available. Some of these records have been indexed and are searchable. *www.familysearch.org/search/collection/2146229.*

1636-1792 Records of the Colony of Rhode Island and Providence Plantations in New England [Printed Book, Microfilm, Digital Capture & Online Database], printed extracts of the *Rhode Island Colonial Record*, printed by order of the legislature, transcribed and edited by John Russell Bartlett, 10 vols., publ. Providence: A.C. Green, 1856-1865. Title also known as *Rhode Island Records*. This is an excellent source for finding a reference to a resident of Rhode Island during the Colonial period. Includes a name index, and includes statistics from censuses taken in 1698, 1708 (+ name list), 1730, 1747, 1748-9, 1754, 1776, 1777, and 1782. FHL book 974.5 N29. Also on microfilm, filmed by the Genealogical Society of Utah, 1966, 1971. 7 rolls, beginning with FHL film #496842. To access the digital images, see the online FHL catalog page: *https://familysearch.org/search/catalog/291706.*
- This collection is also online at the Ancestry.com website. See *http://search.ancestry.com/search/db.aspx?dbid=3897.*

1636. See **"Rhode Island Deed Abstracts"** [Printed Article], names of land buyers and sellers, in *Rhode Island Historical Magazine,* Vol. 2, No. 3 (Jan 1882).

1636-1850. *Vital Records of Rhode Island, First Series, Births, Marriages and Deaths: A Family Register for the People* [Online Database], digitized and indexed at the Ancestry.com website. Source: *Vital Records of Rhode Island 1636-1850, first series...* by James N. Arnold, 1891-1912. This 2-vol. set includes town by town records of births, marriages, and deaths. This database has 12,913 records. Archived at *https://web.archive.org/web/20121123131233/http://search.ancestry.com/search/db.aspx?dbid=15395.*

1636-1899. *Rhode Island, Vital Extracts* [Online Database], digitized and indexed at the Ancestry.com website. Source: a series of 21 volumes compiled by James N. Arnold, 1891-1912, with digitized images taken from the microfilm at the New England Historic Genealogical Society. These volumes of extracted vital records for the state of Rhode Island include birth, marriage, death, baptism, church, and military records. Military records include both Revolutionary War service records and pension records. This database has 501,177 records. See *http://search.ancestry.com/search/db.aspx?dbid=3897.*

1636-1930. *Rhode Island, Births* [Online Database], indexed at the Ancestry.com website. Source: extractions from the published county records. Each record provides the child's name, parents' names, and birth date. This database has 273,579 records. See *http://search.ancestry.com/search/db.aspx?dbid=4262.*

1636-1930. *Rhode Island, Deaths* [Online Database], indexed at the Ancestry.com website. Source: extractions from the published county records. Each record provides, at least, the name of the deceased, date of death, and place of death. This database has 261,974 records. See *http://search.ancestry.com/search/db.aspx?dbid=4264.*

1636-1932. *Rhode Island, Wills and Probate Records* [Online Database], digitized and indexed at the Ancestry.com website. Source: extractions from district and probate courts of Rhode Island. The details found in most probates, in most cases, include the names and residences of beneficiaries and their relationship to the decedent. There may also be a reference to debts, deeds, and other documents related to the settling of the estate. This database has 106,591 records. See *http://search.ancestry.com/search/db.aspx?dbid=9079.*

1636-1914. *Rhode Island Births and Christenings* **[Online Database],** indexed at the FamilySearch.org website. Source: extractions from microfilm of Rhode Island records at the Family History Library, Salt Lake City, UT. Name index to birth, baptism and christening records from Rhode Island compiled from a variety of sources including family and church and civil records. This database has 896,289 records. See *https://familysearch.org/search/collection/1675525.*

1636 – 2000s. *Rhode Island GenWeb Archives* **[Online Database].** The RIGenWeb site offers free genealogical databases with searchable name lists for all Rhode Island counties, which may include Bibles, Biographies, Cemeteries, Censuses, Court, Death, Deeds, Directories, Histories, Marriages, Military, Newspapers, Obituaries, Photos, Schools, Tax Lists, Wills, and more. See *http://usgwarchives.net/ri/rifiles.htm.*

1636-2000s. *Linkpendium – Rhode Island: Family History & Genealogy, Census, Birth, Marriage, Death Vita Records & More* **[Online Databases].** Linkpendium is a genealogical portal site, with links to state, county, town, and local databases. Currently listed are selected sites for Rhode Island statewide resources (545), Bristol County (291), Kent County (355), Newport County (948), Providence County (1,535), and Washington County (574) See *www.linkpendium.com/ri-genealogy.*

1639-1916 Rhode Island Town Marriages Index **[Online Database],** indexed at FamilySearch.org. Index only to various town and vital marriages from all the counties: Bristol, Kent, Newport, Providence, and Washington. The collection includes some church records. See *www.familysearch.org/search/collection/2301760.*

1647-1662. *Rhode Island Court Records: Records of the Court of Trials of the Colony of Providence Plantations* **[Online Database],** digitized and indexed at the Ancestry.com website. Source: 2 vol. publication of the Rhode Island Historical Society, 1920. There is an index at the end of each volume, and the entire database is indexed by Ancestry. See *http://search.ancestry.com/search/db.aspx?dbid=17373.*

1647-2008. *Rhode Island, Historical Cemetery Commission Index* **[Online Database],** a third-party database obtained from the Rhode Island Historical Cemetery Commission. Indexed at the Ancestry.com website, with a link to the RI Historical Cemetery Commission website, which adds photos to some records. Each record contains, at least, the name of the deceased, birthdate, death date, and name of the cemetery. This database has 436,160 records. See *http://search.ancestry.com/search/db.aspx?dbid=70671.*

"1649 Providence Tax List" [Printed Article], in *Rhode Island Historical Society Proceedings* (1893).

"1659 Rhode Island Deeds" [Printed Article], names of land buyers and sellers in *Narragansett Historical Register,* Vol. 3, No. 1 (Jul 1884).

"1668-1759 Rhode Island Freemen" [Printed Article], in *Genealogical Reference Builders Newsletter,* Vol. 5, No. 2 (May 1971) and No. 3 (Aug 1971).

"1676-1695 Newport Will List and Witnesses" [Printed Article], in *Newport Historical Magazine,* Vol. 3, No. 1 (Jul 1882).

"1687 Rochester Town Rate, Kingston" [Printed Article], in *New England Historical and Genealogical Register*, Vol. 35, No. 2 (Apr 1881).

"1687 Providence Militia List" [Printed Article], in *Rhode Island Historical Publications*, Vol. 7, No. 4 (Jan 1900).

"1688-1689 Bristol Census" [Printed Article], name list in *The American Genealogist*, Vol. 68, No. 3 (Jul 1993); and in *New England Historical and Genealogical Register,* Vol. 34 (1880), p. 404-5.

"1692, 1698 Tiverton Inhabitants" [Printed Article], name lists in *Newport Historical Magazine,* Vol. 1, No. 4 (Apr 1881

"1695 Bristol Tax List" [Printed Article], in *New England Historical and Genealogical Register,* Vol. 123, No. 3 (Jul 1969).

"1711-1717 Rhode Island Freemen" [Printed Article], in *Genealogical Reference Builders Newsletter*, Vol. 5, No. 4 (Nov 1971).

"1719-1738 Rhode Island Freemen" [Printed Article], in *Genealogical Reference Builders Newsletter,* Vol. 6, No. 1 (Feb 1972).

1724-1916. *Rhode Island Marriages* **[Online Database]**, indexed at the FamilySearch.org website. Source: extractions from microfilm of Rhode Island records at the Family History Library, Salt Lake City, UT. Includes, at least, name of bride, groom, date and place of marriage. This database has 208,653 records. See *https://familysearch.org/search/collection/1675538*.

"1730-1738 Rhode Island Freemen" [Printed Article], in *Genealogical Reference Builders Newsletter*, Vol. 6, No. 2 (May 1972).

"1730 Rhode Island Colonial Census, Portsmouth" [Printed Article], transcribed by Mildred Mosher Chamberlain in *Rhode Island Roots*, Vol. 7, No. 2 (Jun 1981).

"1730 Rhode Island Colonial Census, South Kingstown, Washington County" [Printed Article], in *Rhode Island Roots*, Vol. 10, No. 1 (Mar 1984).

1731-1773 *Accounts of the Agents of the Colony of Rhode Island* **[Microfilm & Digital Capture]**, from the original manuscripts at the Rhode Island Archives, Providence. This is the written accounts of agents Richard Partridge, 1731-1759; and Joseph Sherwood, 1760-1773, who were London-based agents of the Rhode Island Colony. Includes many names of people coming to Rhode Island from England during the 18th century. Filmed by the Genealogical Society of Utah, 1974, 1 roll, FHL film #954960. To access the digital images, see the online FHL catalog page: *www.familysearch.org/search/catalog/838531*.

1732-1921. *Rhode Island Newspaper Archives* **[Online Databases]**, digitized and indexed newspapers at the GenealogyBank website for the following cities: Bristol, Newport, Pawtucket, Providence, Warren, and Woonsocket. See *www.genealogybank.com/explore/newspapers/all/usa/rhode-island*.

"1738-1760 Rhode Island Freemen" [Printed Article], in *Genealogical Reference Builders Newsletter*, Vol. 6, No. 3 (Nov 1972).

1740-1762. *Rhode Island Colonial War Servicemen* **[Online Database]**, indexed at Ancestry.com. This database is a listing of men called into service by Rhode Island in two conflicts between France and Great Britain, 1) King George's War, 1740-1748; and 2) the French and Indian War, 1755-1762. Each record provides the soldier or sailor's name, and the war in which they served. Also included are notes regarding the branch of service, wounding or death information, and battles in which the individual was involved. It contains the names of over 3,800 men. See *http://search.ancestry.com/search/db.aspx?dbid=4055*.

1740-1890. *Rhode Island, Compiled Census and Census Substitutes Index* **[Online Database]**, indexed at the Ancestry.com website. Originally edited by Ron Jackson, Accelerated Indexing, Salt Lake City, acquired by Ancestry in 1999. This collection contains the following indexes: 1740-1743 Colonial Census Index; 1747 Colonial Census Index; 1777 Military Census Index; 1782 Census Index; 1790 Federal Census Index; 1800 Federal Census Index; 1810 Federal Census Index; 1820 Federal Census Index; 1830 Federal Census Index; 1840 Federal Census Index; 1840 Pensioners List; 1850 Federal Census Index; 1860 Federal Census Index; 1870 Federal Census Index; 1890 Veterans Schedules; and Early Census Index. This database has 28,815 records: *http://search.ancestry.com/search/db.aspx?dbid=3571*.

1742 Rhode Island Census [Printed Index], edited by Ronald Vern Jackson, Accelerated Indexing, North Salt Lake, 1988. See FHL book 974.5 X22r.

1747. *A Census of the Freeman of 1747 as Found in the Supplement to the Rhode Island Colonial Records* **[Microfilm & Digital Capture]**, from a book by Frank T. Calef, filmed by the Genealogical Society of Utah, 1950, 1 roll. See FHL film #22390 Item 2. To access the digital images, see the online FHL catalog page: *www.familysearch.org/search/catalog/299411*.
- The Calef book was indexed as *Rhode Island, 1747,* edited by Ronald Vern Jackson, Accelerated Indexing, North Salt Lake, UT, 1988, FHL book 974.5 X22r.
- See also *Supplement to the Rhode Island Colonial Records Comprising a List of the Freemen Admitted from May 1747 to May 1754* [Microfilm & Digital Capture], from the originals filmed by the Genealogical Society of Utah, 1950, 1 roll, film #22393. To access the digital images and a digital version of the Supplement, see the online FHL catalog page: *www.familysearch.org/search/catalog/299469*.

"1747 Warren, Male Inhabitants" [Printed Article], in *Rhode Island Historical Magazine*, Vol. 6, No. 2 (Oct 1885).

1747-1755 Rhode Island Freemen: A Census of Registered Voters **[Printed Book],** compiled by Bruce C. MacGunnigle, published by Genealogical Publishing Co., Inc., 1977, 49 pages. FHL book 974.5 A1 No. 7. Taken from the index cards at the Rhode Island State Archives, the Freemen lists comprise a record of the men eligible to vote in Rhode Island for this period, and thus, a fairly complete listing of the head of households of Rhode Island.

1755-1762. *A List of Rhode Island Soldiers in the Old French and Indian War.* Archived at *https://web.archive.org/web/20150310090650/http://www.rootsweb.ancestry.com/~rikent/george/french.html.*

"1760-1762 Freemen, Smithfield" [Printed Article], in *Rhode Island Roots*, Vol. 12, No. 3 (Sep 1986).

"1760-1762 Freemen, South Kingstown & Westerly" [Printed Article], in *Rhode Island Roots*, Vol. 12, No. 4 (Dec 1986).

"1760-1762 Freemen, Tiverton" [Printed Article], in *Rhode Island Roots*, Vol. 12, No. 4 (Dec 1986).

"1760-1762 Freemen, Warwick & W. Greenwich, Kent County" [Printed Article], in *Rhode Island Roots,* Vol. 12, No. 4 (Dec 1986).

"1763 Warwick Voters, Kent County" [Printed Article], in *American Monthly Magazine*, Vol. 82, No. 2 (Feb 1948).

1774. *Census of the Colony of Rhode Island* **[Microfilm & Digital Capture],** from manuscripts at the Rhode Island State Archives. Filmed by the Genealogical Society of Utah, 1973. See FHL film #947359 item 1. To access the digital images, see the online FHL catalog page: *www.familysearch.org/search/catalog/299563.* - See also, *Census of the Inhabitants of the Colony of Rhode Island and Providence Plantations 1774, Rhode Island Secretary of State, reprint of the 1858 edition* **[Printed Book],** arranged by John R. Bartlett, published Hunterdon House, Lambertville, NJ, 1984, 243 pages. FHL book 974.5 X2pb.

1774. *Rhode Island Census, 1774* **[Online Database],** indexed at the Ancestry.com website. Source: *Census of the State of Rhode Island 1774*, by John R. Bartlett, publ. Providence, 1858. This index to the census returns of 1774 for the State of Rhode Island is categorized by each town. There are over 9,000 records which contain the following information: family surname, name of the male head of the family, number of white males both above and under age 16, the number of white females above age 16, and the number of Indians and Blacks. All towns are complete, except for the town of Shoreham. This database has 9,289 records. See *http://search.ancestry.com/search/db.aspx?dbid=3081.*

1774-1805 Card Index to Rhode Island Military and Naval Records **[Microfilm & Digital Capture],** from the originals at Rhode Island State Archives, Providence. Filmed by the Genealogical Society of Utah, 1974, 1980, 19 rolls, beginning with film #934758 (Aaron-Babcock, Joshua). To access the digital images, see the online FHL catalog page: *https://familysearch.org/search/catalog/277354.*

1776 Rhode Island Military **Census [Printed Index],** edited by Ronald Vern Jackson, Accelerated Indexing, North Salt Lake, UT, 1988, 66 pages. FHL book 974.5 X22j.

1777. *The Rhode Island 1777 Military Census* **[Printed Book, Microfilm & Digital Capture],** compiled by Mildred M. Chamberlain. Published under the direction of the Rhode Island Genealogical Society, originally published in installments in *Rhode Island Roots* between December 1981 and September 1984. Reprinted with an added index by Genealogical Publishing Co., Inc., Baltimore, 1985, 181 pages. Originals cataloged as *List of all male persons 16 years of age and upwards, 1777, Rhode Island. General Assembly,* microfilm of manuscripts in the National Archives in Washington. Includes a list of men on the alarm list of Westerly, and signers of the Test Act. A letter by the State Record Commissioner of 1916 reads "I have examined with great care the original manuscripts of the census for 1777 and I find that the following towns are omitted: Exeter, Little Compton, Middletown, Newport, New Shoreham and Portsmouth. Undoubtedly this was due to the occupation of the British." Filmed by the Genealogical Society of Utah, 1973, 1 roll. FHL film #947359. To access the digital images, see the online FHL catalog page: *www.familysearch.org/search/catalog/299443.* - See also *Rhode Island 1777 State Census Index* (Running title: *Rhode Island Military Census 1777*), edited by Ronald Vern Jackson, Accelerated Indexing, North Salt Lake, UT, 1988. FHL book 974.5 X22.

- See also, *The Rhode Island 1777 Military Census* [Online Database], indexed at the Ancestry.com website. Source: book of the same title by Mildred M. Chamberlain, 1985. This military census of Rhode Island was an enumeration of all males over sixteen both able and unable to bear arms. In addition, the census was to provide the names of men already in the state militia or in Continental battalions, and to identify transients, Indians, Negroes, and Quakers. The result is a town-by-town list of about 8,500 Rhode Island men. See
http://search.ancestry.com/search/db.aspx?dbid=49316.

"1778 Gloucester Tax List" [Printed Article], in *Rhode Island Roots*, Vol. 19, No. 4 (Dec 1993) through Vol. 20, No. 4 (Dec 1994).

"1778 Smithfield Tax List" [Printed Article], in *Rhode Island Roots*, Vol. 21, No. 1 (Mar 1995) through Vol. 23, No. 1 (Mar 1997).

"1779 Scituate Census" [Printed Article], in *National Genealogical Society Quarterly*, Vol. 14, No. 2 (Jun 1925).

"1780 Newport Strangers Tax" [Printed Article], in *Newport Historical Magazine*, Vol. 2, No. 1 (Jul 1881).

1798-1872. *Rhode Island Passenger Lists, Port of Providence, 1798-1808, 1820-1872; Ports of Bristol and Warren, 1820-1871* [Printed Book], compiled by Maureen A. Taylor, published by Genealogical Publishing Co., Inc., Baltimore, 245 pages. FHL book 974.5 W3t. Compiled from the Custom House Papers in the Manuscript Department of the Rhode Island Historical Society and supplemented by a National Archives microfilm publication containing copies of passenger arrival lists.

1798-1872. *Rhode Island Passenger Lists* [Online Database], indexed at the Ancestry.com website. Source: *Rhode Island Passenger Lists*, by Maureen A. Taylor, 1995. The information in this volume was compiled from the little-known Custom House Papers in the Manuscript Department of the Rhode Island Historical Society and was supplemented by a National Archives microfilm publication containing copies of passenger arrival lists. The Providence lists from 1798 to 1808 are actually extremely rare Alien Registration Lists, kept in compliance with the Alien Act of 1798.

They contain the name of the alien, his age, place of birth, the country he came from, the nation he belonged to and owed allegiance to, his occupation, and a physical description. The 1820-1872 passenger lists for Providence and Bristol/Warren are Customs Passenger Lists in the possession of the Rhode Island Historical Society – a large percentage of which are actually missing from the National Archives microfilm for the same period of coverage. These lists give the name of the passenger, his age, sex, occupation, the name of the country to which he belonged, and the country which he intended to inhabit. Altogether about 4,000 persons are listed. See
http://search.ancestry.com/search/db.aspx?dbid=49318.

1802-1950. *Rhode Island Deaths and Burials* [Online Database], indexed at the FamilySearch.org website. Source: extractions from microfilm of Rhode Island records at the Family History Library, Salt Lake City, UT. Includes name of deceased, date of death, and place of death. This database has 838,777 records. See
https://familysearch.org/search/collection/1675536.

1822-1995. See *U.S. City Directories (Rhode Island)* [Online Database], indexed at the Ancestry.com website. This major database for the entire U.S. includes city directories for several cities of Rhode Island. To find the list, go to "Browse this Collection," then type Rhode Island as the state, and expand the list of cities. Select any city to see an expanded list of years of publication of city directories. See
http://search.ancestry.com/search/db.aspx?dbid=2469.

"1830 West Greenwich Town Tax Bill, Kent County" [Printed Article], in *Rhode Island Roots*, Vol. 6, No. 2 (Summer 1980).

1846-1953. *Rhode Island, Vital records, 1846-1898, 1901-1953* [Online Database], digitized and indexed at FamilySearch.org. Includes Certificates and Registers of Births, 1846-1898 & 1901-1903; Marriages 1901-1903; and Deaths, 1901-1953, acquired from the State Archives in Providence. See
www.familysearch.org/search/collection/1935767.

1847-2011. *The New England Historical & Genealogical Register* [Online Database], indexed at the Ancestry.com website. The New England Historic Genealogical Society (NEHGS) was formed in 1845, and in 1847, they published the first issue of the *New England Historical and Genealogical Register*. The

NEHGS is the oldest genealogical society in the United States, and the Register, likewise, is the country's oldest genealogical journal. The *Register* includes histories, compiled genealogies, indexes, biographical sketches, abstracts of wills, birth records, marriage records, death records, lists of early settlers, memoirs and remembrances, pedigrees, entries from journals, letters, descendant reports, copied church records, inscriptions from headstones, proceedings of historical societies, and notifications of books recently published on genealogy, among other items. These records may include a name, birth date, death date, age at death, residence, spouse, marriage date, and spouse's father. This database has 300,565 records. See *https://search.ancestry.com/search/db.aspx?dbid=2129*.

1851-1920. *Rhode Island, Marriages* **[Online Database],** indexed at the Ancestry.com website. Source: extractions from the published county records. Each record provides, at least, the name of the bride, name of the groom, marriage date, and the place of the marriage. This database has 215,283 records. See *http://search.ancestry.com/search/db.aspx?dbid=4263*.

"1855 New York State Census (Rhode Island People)" [Printed Article], name lists for people born in Rhode Island, in *Rhode Island Roots*, Vol. 21, No. 1 (Mar 1995) and No. 2 (Jun 1995).

"1855 & 1865 Massachusetts State Census Rhode Island People)" [Printed Article], name lists for people born in Rhode Island, in *Rhode Island Roots*, Vol. 19, No. 1 (Mar 1993) through Vol. 20, No. 4 (Dec 1994).

1856-2013. *Providence County, Rhode Island, St. Ann Cemetery Index* **[Online Database],** a third-party database obtained from the St. Ann Cemetery, Cranston, RI. Indexed at the Ancestry.com website and also linked to the St. Ann Cemetery website, where another search can be made. This database has 79,694 records. See *http://search.ancestry.com/search/db.aspx?dbid=9258*.

1862-1866. *Internal Revenue Tax Assessment Lists for Rhode Island, 1862-1866.* **[Microfilm & Digital Capture],** from the original records at the National Archives, Washington, D.C., 7 rolls. FHL film #1299309 (District 1, 1862-1863). To access the digital images, see the online FHL catalog page: *https://familysearch.org/search/catalog/314277*

1865-1935. Rhode Island, State Censuses [Online Database], digitized and indexed at the Ancestry.com website. Source: digitized from the microfilm held by the New England Historic Genealogical Society. This collection includes the 1865, 1875, 1885, 1915, 1925, and 1935 RI State Censuses. This Ancestry set is missing the census years of 1895 (lost) and 1905 (available at the FamilySearch.org site). Rhode Island took statewide censuses beginning in 1865 and continuing through 1935. This collection includes images and an every-name index to six of these censuses. The censuses may include the following details: location, often including street address, names of everyone in the household, the relationship to the head of household, age, gender, color, place of birth, occupation, and for some years, parents' birthplace. Other details you may find include military service (in 1865), literacy, whether in school (1865 and 1875 asked for the type of school, and 1935 asked for the name of the school), and disabilities. In 1935, the state even asked whether your relative had had the measles, scarlet fever, diphtheria or a "Schick test" (Schick tests determined whether you were susceptible to diphtheria). This database has 2,643,678 records. See *http://search.ancestry.com/search/db.aspx?dbid=4721*.

1865 Rhode Island State Census and Index **[Microfilm & Digital Capture],** from the original manuscript records at the Rhode Island State Archives, Providence. The census schedules and a card index compiled by the archives was filmed together in one series by the Genealogical Society of Utah, 1998, 29 rolls, beginning with FHL film #2135474 (Index, Baillayon to Boardman) through #2115175 (Index, Wood to Zuel); followed by the census schedules, Vol. 1 (#2130153) through Vol. 23 (#2130267). Contents: name of all members of a household, age, sex, color, place of birth, nativity of parents, whether a person over 15 could read or write, occupation, naturalization info, if attended school, deaf and dumb, blind, insane or idiotic; employment in military or navy since 1860. It should be noted that for those persons born in Rhode Island, this census listing gives their exact Rhode Island Town of birth. To access the digital images for certain rolls, see the online FHL catalog page: *www.familysearch.org/search/catalog/740180*.

1875. *Census of the State of Rhode Island, 1875* **[Microfilm & Digital Capture],** from the original manuscripts at the Rhode Island State Archives, Providence. Contents: name of each member of a household, age, sex, color, relationship to head of household, marital status, nativity of parents, read/write, occupation, voter info, number of months in school (whether Public, Select or Catholic school). Filmed by the Genealogical Society of Utah, 1973, 9 rolls, beginning with FHL film #947361 (Bristol, Warren, Barrington, Pawtucket). To access the digital images of certain rolls, see the online FHL catalog page: *https://familysearch.org/search/catalog/299578.*

- See also, *Rhode Island 1875 State Census Index Cards* **[Microfilm & Digital Capture],** from the original cards prepared by the Rhode Island State Archives. Filmed by the Genealogical Society of Utah, 2000, 48 rolls, beginning with FHL film #2223509 (A to Andrews, Ellen M.). To access the digital images of certain cards, see the online FHL catalog page: *https://familysearch.org/search/catalog/989045.*

1885. *Rhode Island State Census, 1885* **[Online Database],** digitized and indexed at the FamilySearch.org website. Source: RI State Archives. This project was indexed in partnership with the New England Historic Genealogical Society. Name index and images of census population schedules of the population of the state of Rhode Island as of June 1, 1885. Contents: name of each member of a household, sex, relationship to head of household, color/race, age, marital status, place of birth, nativity of parents, occupation, read/write, number of months in school, whether blind, deaf and dumb, idiotic, or insane; voting info for males over 21, and naturalization info. This database has 321,999 records. See *https://familysearch.org/search/collection/1794115.*

- See also, *Rhode Island State Census, 1885* **[Printed Book, Microfilm & Digital Capture],** printed book by E.L. Freeman, Printers to the State, Providence, 1887, 660 pages. Includes a name index for each town, one for males, another for females. See FHL book 974.5 X2. Microfilm of the original manuscripts at the Rhode Island State Archives, Providence. Contents: name of each member of a household, sex, relationship to head of household, color/race, age, marital status, place of birth, nativity of parents, occupation, read/write, number of months in school, whether blind, deaf and dumb, idiotic, or insane; voting info for males over 21, and naturalization info. Filmed by the Genealogical Society of Utah, 1975, 13 rolls, beginning with FHL film #953910 (Providence, Wards 1-3). To access the digital images, see the online FHL catalog page: *https://familysearch.org/search/catalog/293179.*

1890-1992. *Rhode Island, Indexes to Naturalization Records* **[Online Database],** indexed at the Ancestry.com website. Source: National Archives microfilm series M2084. This database contains an index to petitions for naturalization from 1906-1991 filed in various federal courts in Rhode Island. Information that may be found in this database for each individual includes: Given name and surname, Court where petitioned, Naturalization date, Birth date, Nationality, Arrival port, Arrival date, and a reference to the location of the original record including a volume number, page number and record number. This database has 120,719 records. See *http://search.ancestry.com/search/db.aspx?dbid=2897.*

1905. *State Census of 1905* **[Microfilm & Digital Capture],** from the original records at the Rhode Island State Archives, Providence. The name lists are organized by town, with separate alphabetized listing of males and females. Contents: name of all members of a household, relationship to head of household, color/race, age, marital status, date of birth, number of children, place of birth, read/write, year of immigration to the U.S., number of years in the U.S., number of years a resident of Rhode Island, number of months (of the census year) a resident of the Town, birthplace of father and mother, occupation, number of months unemployed, whether a Union soldier, sailor or marine during Civil War/Spanish American War, pension, and religion. Filmed by the Genealogical Society of Utah, 1997-1999, 445 rolls, beginning with film #2070397 (Burrillville (males) Acheson, John to Darby, Thomas E). To access the digital images, see the online FHL catalog page: *https://familysearch.org/search/catalog/654813.*

- See also, *Rhode Island State Census, 1905* **[Online Database].** Indexed at the FamilySearch.org website. Source: RI State Archives. Each resident is listed on a single form. The forms are arranged in order by place of residence (county, town or city, ward, enumeration district), then by gender, and then alphabetically by surname. This database has 950,314 images. See *https://familysearch.org/search/collection/1542866.*

- See also, *1905 Rhode Island State Census Index* **[Online Database],** digitized and indexed at the FamilySearch.org website. Source: RI State Archives, Providence, RI. Name index to the population schedule of the census taken by the state in 1905. The name lists are organized by town, with separate alphabetized listing of males and females. Contents: name of all members of a household, relationship to head of household, color/race, age, marital status, date of birth, number of children, place of birth, read/write, year of immigration to the U.S., number of years in the U.S.,

number of years a resident of Rhode Island, number of months (of the census year) a resident of the town, birthplace of father and mother, occupation, number of months unemployed, whether a Union soldier, sailor or marine during Civil War/Spanish American War, pension, and religion. This database has 474,152 records. See
https://familysearch.org/search/collection/1542866.

1907-1991 Rhode Island Naturalization Records [Online Database], digitized and indexed at FamilySearch.org. Source: National Archives, Records of U.S. District Court for the District of Rhode Island, 1790 – Present. This database has 5,753 images, see *www.familysearch.org/search/collection/2622566.*
- See also, *Rhode Island, District Court Naturalization Indexes, 1906-1991* [Online Database], digitized and indexed at the FamilySearch.org website. Source: National Archives microfilm series M2084. Card index of naturalizations in the U.S. District Courts in Rhode Island. Cards arranged alphabetically. This database has 128,766 records. See
https://familysearch.org/search/collection/2141014.

1915. *Rhode Island State Census, 1915* [Microfilm & Digital Capture], from the original manuscripts at the Rhode Island State Archives, Providence. Contents: names of all members of a household, relationship to head of household, sex, color, age, place of birth, place of birth of father and mother, whether alien or naturalized, occupation, nature of business; employer, employee, or working on own account; and whether out of work. Filmed by the Genealogical Society of Utah, 1991, 25 rolls, beginning with film #1763723 (Providence County: Providence Enumeration districts 214-224). The census schedules are organized by enumeration districts. An index to the districts, Barrington to Westerly, is on the last roll (#1769155). To access the digital images, see the online FHL catalog page:
https://familysearch.org/search/catalog/467796.
- See also, *Rhode Island State Census, 1915* [Online Database], digitized and indexed at the FamilySearch.org website. Source: RI State Archives. Name index to population schedule of the census of Rhode Island taken by the state in 1915. Contents: names of all members of a household, relationship to head of household, sex, color, age, place of birth, place of birth of father and mother, whether alien or naturalized, occupation, nature of business; employer,

employee, or working on own account; and whether out of work. This database has 540,589 records. See
https://familysearch.org/search/collection/1532188.

1925. *Rhode Island State Census, 1925* [Microfilm & Digital Capture], from the original manuscripts at the Rhode Island State Archives, Providence. The census schedules are organized by enumeration districts. Contents: names of all members of a household, relationship to the head of household, sex, color, age, place of birth, and citizenship. Filmed by the Genealogical Society of Utah, 1991, 1997, 20 rolls, beginning with film #1769232 (Providence County: Providence Enumeration districts : 175-190). To access the digital images, see the online FHL catalog page for this title. See
https://familysearch.org/search/catalog/483580.
- See also, *Rhode Island State Census, 1925* [Online Database], digitized and indexed at the FamilySearch.org website. Source: RI State Archives. The census lists residents of the state as of April 15, 1925 by household. Contents: names of all members of a household, relationship to the head of household, sex, color, age, place of birth, and citizenship. This database has 684,447 records. See
https://familysearch.org/search/collection/1532195.

1935. *Rhode Island 1935 Census* [Microfilm & Digital Capture], from the original manuscripts at the Rhode Island State Archives, Providence. (Although referred to officially as the "1935 census," the schedules are dated January 1936). Names from the census schedules are in alphabetical order for each town. Contents: names of all members of a household, sex, race, place of birth, date of birth, marital status, read/write, citizenship, if at school, name of school, grade, any physical handicaps, occupation, whether unemployed and how long.
Filmed by the Genealogical Society of Utah, 1991, 132 rolls, beginning with film #1753773 (Bristol County Barrington: Abatantuano-Zwicker).
To access the digital images, see the online FHL catalog page:
https://familysearch.org/search/catalog/436182.
- See also, *Rhode Island State Census, 1935* [Online Database], digitized and indexed at the FamilySearch.org website. Source: RI State Archives. Name index to population schedule of the census of Rhode Island taken by that state in 1935. Contents: names of all members of a household, sex, race, place of birth, date of birth, marital status, read/write,

citizenship, if at school, name of school, grade, any physical handicaps, occupation, whether unemployed and how long. This database has 693,472 records. See *https://familysearch.org/search/collection/1529126.*

1981-Current. See *Rhode Island Recent Newspaper Obituaries* **[Online Database],** digitized and indexed newspaper obituaries at the GenealogyBank website,

including newspapers from Charlestown, Coventry, Cumberland, East Greenwich, Hopkinton, Narragansett, South Kingstown, North Kingstown, Newport, North Providence, Pawtucket, Providence, Smithfield, Wakefield, West Warwick, Westerly, Woonsocket, and Wyoming. See *www.genealogybank.com/explore/obituaries/all/usa/rhode-island.*

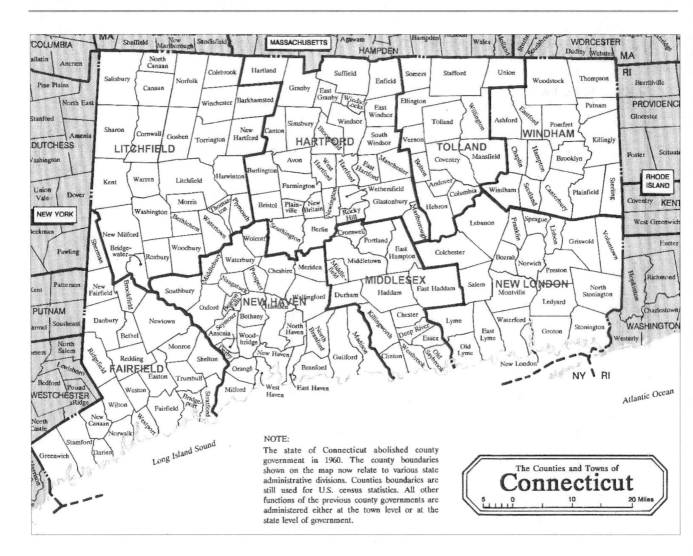

The Counties and Towns of Connecticut. Map source: Dollarhide's base map for Connecticut modified for this publication. (An earlier version was used for *Ancestry's Red Book: American State, County & Town Sources*).

Connecticut
Censuses & Substitute Name Lists

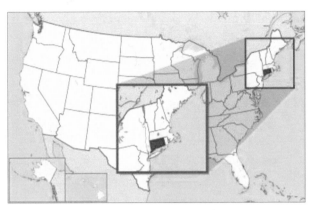

Historical Timeline of Connecticut, 1524 -1788

1524. Italian Giovanni da Verrazzano sailed up the Atlantic coast in sight of present New York, Connecticut, Rhode Island, Massachusetts, and Maine, and wrote of his travels to his sponsor, King Francis I of France.

1558. Elizabeth I became Queen of England. All of the great explorations of North America took place during her 45-year reign, the Elizabethan Era. When Elizabeth I was crowned, England was nearly bankrupt, but during her reign, the English Empire expanded and thrived, and English culture flourished in Literature, Theatre, Music, and Architecture.

1603. England. James I (James VI of Scotland since 1566), became King of England, the first monarch to rule both England and Scotland. He was also the first English King to publicly assert that he was blessed with "the divine right of Kings," meaning he was the voice of God on earth, at least in England and Scotland. Although James I was most remembered for commissioning a Bible translation, during his reign, the first permanent British colonies of North America were established in Virginia and New England. James I was in power when England acquired possession of Northern Ireland and was an advocate for the transportation of thousands of clan people living along the Scottish-English border to Ulster Province. After about 120 years in Ireland, many of these "Scots-Irish"

were to migrate to the interior of New England via the Connecticut River.

1614. English Captain John Smith (of the Jamestown Colony) visited the shores of present Connecticut to Maine, then wrote his *Description of New England*, which encouraged Englishmen to settle there. Smith was credited as the first to call the area New England, which had previously been known as Norumbega. Back in England, Christopher Jones was one seafarer who was known to have read Smith's description of New England, and often remarked that he would like to go there. He got his wish as the master of the *Mayflower* in 1620.

1614. Connecticut. Dutchman Adriaen Block sailed up the present Connecticut River and claimed the region as part of the New Netherland colony. He named the river "Fresh River," The Dutch were famous for trading a few beads and baubles for large tracts of land from the natives.

1620. Plymouth Colony. The *Mayflower* dropped anchor off Cape Cod, and soon after Plymouth Colony was founded by a small group of Pilgrims/Separatists, who had fled England for Holland a year earlier. Unlike the Puritans, the Pilgrims did not want to purify the Church of England, they just wanted to get away from the church's Prayer Book and have their own method of worship.

1623. Fort House of Good Hope. The Dutch built a fortified trading post on the present site of Hartford, but the Dutch were asked to leave by the English in a few years.

1625. England. Charles I became King of England, Scotland, and Ireland. Charles believed in the same principles his father, James I had espoused, i.e., that as King, he was the infallible interpreter of God's will on earth. Soon after taking office, Charles began to note a large number of non-conformists among his subjects. Along with his Archbishop, William Laud, the King began a campaign to purge his church of the largest group of non-conformists, the so-called Puritans, a militant Calvinist religious sect attempting to purify the Church of England. Unfortunately, Charles I took on a job that led to civil war in England as well as the loss of his head. But, his campaign can be credited as the main cause for the founding of English settlements in New England.

1629. The Great Migration to New England Begins. As a result of the Charles I campaign to purge non-conformists from the Church of England, 1629-1640, large groups of people were disenfranchised. Charles I disbanded Parliament and ruled England alone for eleven years. The Puritans referred to this era as "the eleven years of tyranny." It was during these eleven years that about 80,000 Puritans felt compelled to leave England. About a fourth of them moved to Holland; another fourth of them to Ireland; a fourth to the West Indies, particularly the islands of Barbados, Nevis, and St. Kitts; and the final group, some 21,000 Puritan immigrants, established the Massachusetts Bay Colony of English North America.

1632. Edward Winslow of the Plymouth Colony visited the Connecticut River, and noted a point on the river as a good place for a settlement.

1633. Plymouth Colony sent William Holmes to establish the settlement at Windsor, the first permanent settlement in present Connecticut.

1634. Puritans from the Massachusetts Bay Colony founded Wethersfield in present Connecticut.

1636. Connecticut Colony. The English settlements of Hartford, Wethersfield, and Windsor were formed as the Connecticut Colony. The name was based on Mohegan/Algonquin Indian words for a "long tidal river," which the French had earlier corrupted into Quinetucket.

1637. The Pequot War. The Pequot Indians of Connecticut were defeated by the Connecticut colonists in alliance with the Narragansetts and Mohegans.

1638. New Haven Colony was formed as an independent colony, separate from Connecticut Colony.

1641. The "Great Migration" to New England ended. It was also the beginning of the Civil War in England, and by 1649, Charles I and William Laud were beheaded; Oliver Cromwell, a Puritan, became Lord Protectorate,

ruling England for the next decade. The group of Royalists who supported Charles I were now out of power, the Puritans were in control (and there was no need to send any more Puritans to New England, in fact many of the "purged" Puritans returned to England). Instead of Puritans to New England, another English migration began, this time to Virginia by the opponents of the Puritans – Loyalists of the king who were known as Cavaliers.

1643 New Haven Colony. The coastal settlements of Branford, Guilford, Milford, Stamford, plus Southold (on Long Island), all joined the New Haven Colony.

1646. The settlement of New London was founded by John Winthrop, Jr.

1660 England. Charles II was restored to the throne as King of England, Scotland, and Ireland. He had lived in exile after the execution of his father, Charles I. In 1649, the Scots had proclaimed Charles the king of Scotland. But the Puritan leader Oliver Cromwell defeated his army in 1651, and Charles fled to France. After Cromwell died in 1658, the English people became increasingly dissatisfied with the government that Cromwell had established. In 1660, Parliament invited Charles to return and declared him king. He ruled until his death in 1685, and during his reign, the English colonials forced out the remaining pockets of Atlantic settlements made earlier by the Dutch, Swedes, Danes, and French. Charles II saw the Atlantic colonies as a source of trade and commerce, supported development, and granted several more charters for settlement (including one to William Penn in 1681). All of the British colonies thrived as a result. He was the first monarch to recognize the potential for the North American colonies to become a contiguous, viable commonwealth. He encouraged the development of post roads, and a regular communication between the Governors. Charles II was responsible for setting the tone of self-government, religious tolerance, and individual freedoms in the English colonies that were to become American institutions.

1665 Connecticut Colony. New Haven Colony and Connecticut Colony merged into one chartered colony, retaining the name Connecticut.

1666. The four original counties of Connecticut were established: **Fairfield, Hartford, New Haven**, and **New London** counties.

1674. The English asked the Dutch to leave New York and Connecticut. Outnumbered, the Dutch complied, not by leaving, but by moving out of their town halls and political offices. The Dutch communities remained, kept their own churches and culture, and continued to be a factor in the development of the Hudson and Connecticut River valleys.

1701-1718. The Collegiate School was authorized by the Connecticut General Assembly. In 1717, the school was moved to New Haven, and became Yale College the following year.

1707. During the reign of Queen Anne, the **United Kingdom of Great Britain** was established, a merger of Scotland and England. The English Colonies now became the British Colonies.

1726. Windham County was formed, taken from parts of New London and Hartford counties.

1751. Litchfield County was formed, taken from parts of Fairfield, Hartford, and New Haven counties.

1754. French and Indian War began. France and Britain fought for several years over the territory of Canada, the Great Lakes, and the Mississippi River Valley down to New Orleans. In Europe it was called the Seven Years War.

1763. The **Treaty of Paris** was signed by France, Spain, and Britain, ending the French and Indian War. France was the loser and was divested of virtually all of its North American claims. The British now held all the territory east of the Mississippi River, and from Florida to the Great Lakes; plus the Hudson's Bay Company's "Rupert's Land;" the Province of Quebec; and all lands of the present Maritime Provinces of Canada. The British areas became known officially as *British North America.* Spain took from France all of Louisiana west of the Mississippi, and added to its previous possession of Mexico, now claimed all North American lands west of the Mississippi.

1775-1781 Revolutionary War. Several thousand Connecticut men rushed to answer the "Lexington Alarm." Connecticut troops were also instrumental in the planning and seizure of Ft. Ticonderoga. British raids in Connecticut included New Haven, Fairfield, and Norwalk, and turncoat Benedict Arnold led British attacks on New London and Groton.

1785. Middlesex County was formed, taken from parts of Hartford and New London counties. At the same time, **Tolland County** was formed, taken from parts of Hartford and Windham counties. These two counties brought the final total to eight counties.

1788. Jan. 9th. Connecticut ratified the U.S. Constitution and became the 5th state formed from the original 13 colonies.

Connecticut's Colonial, Pre-Statehood, and Statewide Name Lists

1614-1775. Colonial Era. The first surviving name lists from the Colonial Era were lists of landowners from the 1630s. From the 1700s through 1750s, various town name lists have survived as well. A census of the entire colony for 1762 was found, published in 1979.
- The best resource for locating an ancestor from colonial Connecticut is the State Library/Archives, where some outstanding finding aids are available, including card indexes of town records, microfilmed versions, or online databases.

1775-1787. Revolutionary War and Pre-Statehood Era. The name lists of Connecticut during the Revolutionary War and just prior to statehood, were mostly those related to town tax lists and military rosters but include some lists of the loyalists in Connecticut who supported the British during the war.

1787- Present. State of Connecticut Era. Although the State of Connecticut has never conducted a census of the general population, a Military Census was taken in 1917, mainly to determine the manpower available for war.
- The federal censuses from 1790 forward are complete, and well before the current Internet databases were created, the Connecticut State Library/Archives created card indexes to all CT federal censuses, 1790-1850, as well as some outstanding vital records indexes.
- There are several national name lists for the entire U.S. that may include Connecticut residents. A researcher should check the *Nationwide Censuses & Substitutes* chapter (Vol. 5). Examples of national name lists include Military Rosters, Army, Navy, and Widow's Pensions, Find a Grave, and the Social Security Death Index.

Bibliography
Connecticut Censuses & Substitutes

The most important genealogical resource center in Connecticut is the State Library/Archives in Hartford. This is where the major indexes to censuses, vitals, and other records were created. All of these great resources have been microfilmed. Many of the records microfilmed by the Family History Library of Salt Lake City are now available as digital images online via the FamilySearch.org website. Since the 2016 2nd Edition, there have been numerous Connecticut county records digitized. Look for "Microfilm & Digital Capture" in the title to see which original documents can now be accessed from your home computer. The bibliography begins with name lists from the 1630s, as shown below:

◆ ◆ ◆ ◆ ◆

1630-1799. *Early Connecticut Marriages as Found on Ancient Church Records Prior to 1800* [Printed Book & Online Database], compiled by Frederic W. Bailey, published by the Bureau of American Ancestry, New Haven, CT, 1896-1906, 7 vols. This classic work contains the complete marriage records of Connecticut from the creation of the colony through 1800. The records were taken from the books at Congregational church parishes throughout the state from the years 1630 to 1800. Prior to 1659, there were eleven organized parishes. Between 1660 and 1800 this number increased to 200. See FHL book 974.6 K2. See also ***Master Index to Early Connecticut Marriages Books 1-7,*** FHL book 974.6 K2bf index. An online digital version (images only) of the 7-vol. set with the title, ***Connecticut Marriages to 1800*** is located at the Ancestry.com website. See
http://search.ancestry.com/search/db.aspx?dbid=1044.
- A fully digitized and indexed version of Bailey's ***Early Connecticut Marriages*** is also online at the Ancestry.com website. See
https://search.ancestry.com/search/db.aspx?dbid=3719.

1630-1920. *Connecticut, Church Record Abstracts* [Online Database], indexed at the Ancestry.com website. Original data: *Connecticut. Church Records Index.* CT State Library, Hartford. Each index record includes names, event, dates, places, and a reference to the volume title. Many of the records are typescripts from various churches, and include such things as admissions, communicants, baptisms, deaths, dismissals, marriages, memberships, members of committee, pledges, and recommends. People transferring to or from one church will be named and the places involved. Information in Connecticut's church records have often been found to be more informative and more complete than the town vital records. This database has 761,979 records. See
https://search.ancestry.com/search/db.aspx?dbid=3032.

1630s-1849. *Connecticut Vital Records Prior to 1850 – Barbour Collection* [Microfilm & Digital Capture], from the original records at the Connecticut State Library, Hartford, CT. Vital records alphabetically arranged by towns, with a general index arranged under surnames. Filmed by the Genealogical Society of Utah, 1949, 98 rolls, beginning with FHL film #2887 (General Index: Aa – Alk). To access the digital images, see the online FHL catalog page:
www.familysearch.org/search/catalog/295370.

1630s-1870s. *The Barbour Collection of Connecticut Town Vital Records* [Printed Extract & Index], from the original records at the Connecticut State Archives, Hartford, CT, compiled for publication by Lorraine Cook White, published by Genealogical Publishing Co., Baltimore, MD, 1994-2001, 55 vols, FHL book 974.6 V2wL v.1-55.

1630s-1869. *Connecticut Town Birth Records (Barbour Collection), Pre-1870* [Online Database], a digitized birth index to the 55-volume Barbour Collection set is available online at the Ancestry.com website. Information in the index contains 1) Name of child, 2) Relationship (son or daughter), 3) birth date, 4) Birth location, and 5) Parents' names. The volumes are arranged in alphabetical order according to surname. A link to the image of the record within the book is also provided with each search result, and because the collection is arranged so that all of the vital information for an individual is in one location within a volume, marriage and death information may also be found with this database. This birth index has 252,432 records. See
http://search.ancestry.com/search/db.aspx?dbid=1034.

1630s-1869. *Connecticut Town Marriage Records, Pre-1870 (Barbour Collection)* **[Online Database],** a digitized marriage index to the 55-volume Barbour Collection set is available online at the Ancestry.com website. Information in the index contains 1) Name, 2) Spouse's name, 3) Birth location, 4) Spouse's birth location, 5) age, 6) Spouse's age, 7) Place of residence, 8) Spouse's place of residence, 9) Marriage date, and 10) parents' names. The volumes are arranged in alphabetical order according to town name. Within each town, the records are arranged in alphabetical order according to surname. A link to the image of the record within the book is also provided with each search result. Because this collection is arranged so that all of the vital information for an individual is in one location within a book, birth and death information may also be found within this database. This database has 218,569 records. See
http://search.ancestry.com/search/db.aspx?dbid=1062.

1630s-1869. *Connecticut Town Death Records (Barbour Collection), Pre-1870* **[Online Database],** a digitized death index to the 55-volume Barbour Collection set is available online at the Ancestry.com website. Information in the index contains 1) Name, 2) age, 3) Death date, and 4) Death place. The volumes are arranged in alphabetical order according to town name. Within each town, the records are arranged in alphabetical order according to surname. A link to the image of the record within the book is also provided with each search result. Because this collection is arranged so that all of the vital information for an individual is in one location within a book, birth and marriage information may also be found within this database. This death index has over 56,000 records. See
http://search.ancestry.com/search/db.aspx?dbid=1063.

1630s-1934. *Hale Collection* **[Microfilm & Digital Capture],** from the typescript at the Connecticut State Library. The Charles R. Hale Collection of Vital Records includes newspaper notices and cemetery inscriptions with a surname index referring to places and newspapers; an index to death notices from newspapers (not included above); an index to marriages by newspapers; a general index to marriage notices arranged alphabetically; and indexes to cemeteries and newspapers, by location. Filmed by the Genealogical Society of Utah, 1949-1950, 360 rolls, beginning with FHL film #3076 (Surname index, Death and Inscriptions, AA-ALB). To access the digital images, see the online FHL catalog page:
www.familysearch.org/search/catalog/18917.

1630s-1934. *Hale Collection of Cemetery Inscriptions and Newspaper Notices* **[Online Database],** digitized and indexed at the Ancestry.com website. Original data: The Charles R. Hale Collection. CT State Library, Hartford. Images were taken from the 360-roll microfilm set, described above. This database has 1,995,633 records. See
https://search.ancestry.com/search/db.aspx?dbid=2900.

1630s-1800s. *Index Cards to Vital Records of Connecticut Churches* **[Microfilm & Digital Capture],** from the original cards at the Connecticut State Library, Hartford, CT. Filmed by the Genealogical Society of Utah, 1949, 69 rolls, beginning with FHL film #2806 (A – Ay). For a complete list of roll numbers and contents of each roll, see the online catalog page for this title:
www.familysearch.org/search/catalog/19954.

1630s-1800s. *New London County, Connecticut USGenWeb Research Website* **[Online Databases],** transcriptions of Vital Records, Wills, Obituaries, Deeds, Histories, Biographies, and Links to Related Sites. See
www.ctgenweb.org/county/conewlondon/research.html.

1630s-1800s. *Cutter Index: A Consolidated Index of Cutter's 9 Genealogy Series* **[Photocopy of Original & Digital Version],** by Norma Olin Ireland and Winifred Irving. Includes an index to several books with a Connecticut theme. Published by Ireland Indexing Service, Fallbrook, CA, 1975, 88 pages, FHL book 974.D22i. To access the digital version, see the online FHL catalog page:
www.familysearch.org/search/catalog/75530.

1630s-1800s. *The First Puritan Settlers of Connecticut* **[Printed Book],** by Royal R. Hinman, publ. New England Historical Genealogical Society, 2015, 367 pages, FHL book 974.6 D2hr.
- See also *Index to First Puritan Settlers: Catalog of the Names of the First Puritan Settlers of the Colony of Connecticut by R.R. Hinman* **[Printed Index],** indexed by Elva Smallwood Wilson and Vera Meek Wimberly, published Conroe, TX, 1992, 77 pages, FHL book 974.6 D2hr index.

1630s-1997 Connecticut Marriages **[Online Database],** indexed at the FamilySearch.org website, a name index to marriage records from the state of Connecticut, originally microfilmed by the Genealogical Society of Utah for the Family History Library in Salt Lake City, Utah. The database contains 444,458 records. See **www.familysearch.org/search/collection/1674749.**

1630s-1999. *Connecticut, Wills and Probate Records* **[Online Database],** indexed at the Ancestry.com website. This database includes records from all counties of Connecticut, and includes Wills, Letters of Administration, Inventories, Distribution and Accounting, Bonds, and Guardianships. Each index record includes: Name, Probate Date, Probate Place, Inferred Death Year, Inferred Death Place, and Item Description. The useful Table of Contents indicates the number of image for each record, listing types of papers included. The image document may have much more information than the index. This database has 327,896 records. See **https://search.ancestry.com/search/db.aspx?dbid=9049.**

1630s-2000s. *Connecticut Collections at MyHeritage.com* **[Online Database],** over 700 databases can be searched at the Connecticut – Collections Catalog at the former World Vital Records website. Databases include censuses, family histories, town histories, military rosters, and more. A search can be done for a name, place, year, or keyword. See **www.myheritage.com/records/Connecticut/all-records.**

1630s-1699. *U.S. New England Marriages Prior to 1700* **[Online Database],** indexed at the Ancestry.com website. Original data: Torry, Clarence A.: *New England Marriages Prior to 1700*, Genealogical Publishing Co., Baltimore, 2004. This work, compiled over a period of thirty years from about 2,000 books and manuscripts, is a comprehensive listing of the 37,000 married couples who lived in New England between 1620 and 1700 (Connecticut marriages from the 1630s). Listed are the names of most married couples living in New England before 1700, their marriage date or the birth year of a first child, the maiden names of 70% of the wives, the birth and death years of both partners, mention of earlier or later marriages, the residences of every couple and an index of names. This database has 95,807 records. See **https://search.ancestry.com/search/db.aspx?dbid=3824.**

1630s-1699. See **"Divisions of Land, Valuations & Taxes, 1600s," [Printed Article],** in *Windsor Historical Society Annual Reports*, Vol. 29 (1950).

1631-1794. *Robert C. Winthrop Collection: Connecticut Manuscripts* **[Microfilm & Digital Capture],** from originals at the Connecticut State Library, Hartford, CT. Includes jurisdiction and land titles 1631-1716, documents no. 1-123; Indians, military and foreign affairs, 1651-1712, documents no. 124-251; council, churches, shipping and miscellaneous 1650-1784, documents no. 252-350; index. Filmed by the Genealogical Society of Utah, 1954, 1 roll, FHL film #3644. To access the digital images, see the online FHL catalog page: **www.familysearch.org/search/catalog/100443.**

1635-1850. *Judd Manuscripts (Connecticut)* **[Microfilm & Digital Capture],** from original manuscripts at Forbes Public Library, Northampton, Hampshire Co, MA, compiled by Sylvester Judd (1789-1860). Includes land, vital, and town records. Filmed by the Genealogical Society of Utah, 1960, 5 rolls, FHL film #234515-234517 (Vols. 1-10); alpha index to names, vol. 1-10, FHL film #250287; and Misc. MA Town records, FHL film #234518. To access the digital images, see the online FHL catalog page: **www.familysearch.org/search/catalog/119583.**

1635-1860. *The Vital Records of Saybrook Colony: Including the Towns of Chester, Deep River, Essex, Old Saybrook, and Westbrook, Connecticut* **[Printed Book],** by Elizebeth B. Plimpton, published by the Connecticut Valley Shore Research Group, 1985, 705 pages, FHL book 974.66V2.

1635-1860. *Marriage Index: Connecticut, 1635-1860* **[CD-ROM],** published by the Learning Company, 1999, FHL CD No. 9 pt. 397.

1636 "Original Proprietors of Hartford, 1636," [Printed Article], in *McHenry County Illinois Connection Quarterly*, Vol. 7, No. 4 (Oct 1989).

1636-1677. *List of Officials, Civil, Military and Ecclesiastical of Connecticut Colony: From March 1636 through 11 Oct 1677, and of New Haven Colony throughout its Separate Existence, Also Soldiers in the Pequot War who then or Subsequently Resided within the Present Bounds of Connecticut* **[Printed**

Book], compiled by Donald Lines Jacobus, published by R.M. Hooker, New Haven, CT, 1935, 65 pages, FHL book 974.D3j.

1636-1776. *History of Taxation in Connecticut* **[Book, Microfilm & Digital Capture]**, from a book by Frederick Robertson Jones, originally published by Johns Hopkins Press, 1896, reprint by Johnson Reprint Corp., New York, 1973, filmed by the Genealogical Society of Utah, 1997, 1 roll, FHL film #2055359. To access the digital version, see the online FHL catalog page: **www.familysearch.org/search/catalog/561215.**

1637-1820 Tax Guidebook [Printed Book], see *As True as Taxes: An Historian's Guide to Direct Taxation and Tax Records in Connecticut, 1637-1820,* by Diana Ross McCain, a 1981 Master's Thesis on file at Wesleyan University, Middletown, CT. See FHL book 974.6 R4m.

1639-1700. *Hartford, Connecticut Probate Records* **[Online Database]**, indexed at the Ancestry.com website. Original data: *A Digest of the Early Connecticut Probate Records, Hartford District, 1635-1700. Vol. I.* publ. 1906. Each probate record contains the filing individual's name, date of probate, and location of filing. Entries often reveal the person's close family relations such as spouse, heirs, and siblings, along with the names of witnesses. Additionally, marriage, burial, and death dates are provided when relevant to the document. This database has 990 records. See **https://search.ancestry.com/search/db.aspx?dbid=4337.**

1639-1750. See *Early Records of Hartford, Connecticut: Land Records, 1639-1688; Vital Records, 1644-1730; Probate Records, 1635-1750; Plus Genealogical Notes and a Manual of the First Church in Harford* **[CD-ROM]**, a publication of Heritage Books, Bowie, MD, 1995. See FHL CD No. 98.

1640. *First Settlers of Windsor, Connecticut* **[Online Database]**, indexed at the USGenWeb site for Hartford CT. See **http://files.usgwarchives.net/ct/hartford/history/settlers.txt.**

1640-1752 Early Greenwich Landowners, Fairfield County, Connecticut [Online Database], indexed at the USGenWeb site for Fairfield Co CT. See **www.ctgenweb.org/county/cofairfield/pages/greenwich/grnwich_landowners01.htm.**

1640-1846. *Colonial Land Records of Connecticut* **[Microfilm & Digital Capture]**, from originals at the Connecticut State Library, Hartford, CT. Includes index. Filmed by the Genealogical Society of Utah, 1954, 3 rolls, FHL film #3656 (1640-1673), FHL film #3657 (1671-1674), and FHL film #3658 (1723-1846). To access the digital images, see the online FHL catalog page: **www.familysearch.org/search/catalog/84462.**

1640-1926. *Connecticut, Marriage Index* **[Online Database]**, indexed at the Ancestry.com website. Original data: Marriage Records. Connecticut Marriages. Various Connecticut County collections. The date of 1620 was for Tolland Co marriages, but is not a realistic. The earliest date noted was for Hartford Co in 1640. This index may be related to the 1640-1949 CT Marriages at the FamilySearch.org site. This database has 67,802 records. See **https://search.ancestry.com/search/db.aspx?dbid=61367.**

1640-1949. *Connecticut Marriages* **[Online Database]**, indexed at the FamilySearch.org website. Source: CT State Library, Hartford, CT. Each index record includes: Name, Event Type, Event Date, Event Place, Gender, Marital Status, Spouse's Name, and Spouse's Gender. This database has 557,526 records. See **www.familysearch.org/search/collection/2448940.**

1641-1948. *General Index to Probate Records, all Districts of Connecticut* **[Microfilm & Digital Capture]**, from the original records at the Connecticut State Archives, Hartford, CT. Filmed by the Genealogical Society of Utah, 1957-1958, 67 rolls, beginning with FHL film #166000 (Aal, Abraham – Amidon, Raymond). To access the digital images, see the online FHL catalog page: **www.familysearch.org/search/catalog/354857.**

1642-1845 Register of Marriages, Births & Deaths, Simsbury, Hartford County, Connecticut [Online Database], indexed at the DunhamWilcox.net site: **http://dunhamwilcox.net/ct/simsbury_ct_mbd.htm.**

1648-1757. *Abstract of Probate Records at Fairfield, County of Fairfield, and State of Connecticut* **[Microfilm & Digital Capture]**, from a typescript original at the New York Genealogical & Biographical Society, New York City, by Spencer P. Mead. Filmed by the Genealogical Society of Utah, 1 941, 1 roll,

FHL film #4197. To access the digital images, see the online FHL catalog page: www.familysearch.org/search/catalog/38660.
- See also, *Abstract of Probate Records at Fairfield, County of Fairfield, and State of Connecticut, 1648-1757* [Online Database], indexed at the USGenWeb Site for Fairfield Co CT. See www.ctgenweb.org/county/cofairfield/pages/probate/vol _1-6/ctfairfi_probate.indexv1.html.

1649-1906. *Connecticut Births and Christenings* [Online Database], digitized and indexed at the FamilySearch.org website, this is a name index to births, baptisms, and christening records from the state of Connecticut, originally microfilmed by the Genealogical Society of Utah for the Family History Library in Salt Lake City, Utah. The database contains 506,665 records. See www.familysearch.org/search/collection/1674736.

1649-1932 Probate Records, Hartford County, Connecticut [Microfilm & Digital Capture], from the original records in Hartford, CT. Hartford probate district included the towns of Hartford, Bloomfield, Glastonbury, Newington, Rocky Hill, West Hartford, Wethersfield, and Windsor Locks. Indexes are found within each volume. Filmed by the Genealogical Society of Utah, 1949-1954, 1982, 52 rolls, beginning with FHL film #4572 (Probate records, vol. 2, 1649-1663; Vol. 3, 1663-1677). To access the digital images, see the online FHL catalog page: www.familysearch.org/search/catalog/247486.

1650-1934. *Connecticut, Death and Burials Index* [Online Database], a searchable index at the Ancestry.com website. The source of this database is from the FamilySearch series, entitled "1772-1934," which Ancestry has chosen to rename "1650-1934," but the indexes are probably identical. This database has 1,904,722 records. See http://search.ancestry.com/search/db.aspx?dbid=2557.

1656-1700 "Register of Voters, 1656-1700, Norwalk," [Printed Article], in *Car-Del Scribe,* Vol. 12, No. 4 (Jul 1975).

1658-1884 Early Militia, Hartford County, Connecticut [Online Database], indexed at the DunhamWilcox.net site. See http://dunhamwilcox.net/ct/hartford_military_1658.htm.

1660 Names of the First Settlers of Norwich, New London County [Online Database], indexed at the DunhamWilcox.net site. See http://dunhamwilcox.net/ct/norwich_ct_settlers.htm.

1660-1955 Connecticut Church Records [Online Database], digitized and indexed at FamilySearch.org. Contains Church records from several counties in Connecticut. Source: CT State Library, Hartford, CT. See www.familysearch.org/search/collection/2658799.

1661-1835. See *William F. J. Boardman Collection of Manuscripts 1661-1835: Land Transfers, Estates, Legal Papers, Accounts and Correspondence of the Boardman and Seymour Families, and Miscellaneous Papers Related to Colonial and Revolutionary Wars Militia, Schools and Ecclesiastical Matters Principally in Hartford and Wethersfield* [Microfilm & Digital Capture], from originals at the Connecticut State Library. Filmed by the Genealogical Society of Utah, 1954, 6 rolls, beginning with FHL film #3650 (Index). To access the digital images, see the online FHL catalog page: www.familysearch.org/search/catalog/100469.

1668 Inhabitants of Stratford, Fairfield County, Connecticut [Online Database], indexed at the USGenWeb site for Fairfield Co CT. See www.ctgenweb.org/county/cofairfield/pages/stratford/st ratford_residents1668.htm.

1669 List of Freemen of Windsor, Connecticut [Online Database], indexed at the DunhamWilcox.net site. See http://dunhamwilcox.net/ct/windsor_freemen1669.htm.

1669-1670. See "**The Wyllys papers: Correspondence and Documents Chiefly of Descendants of Gov. George Wyllys of Connecticut, 1590-1796,**" [Printed Article], by Lemuel A. Welles, in *Collections of the Connecticut Historical Society,* vol. 21, 1870. FHL book 974.B4.

1670 Connecticut Census: A Reconstructed Listing found in Household, Estate, Tax, Landowner, Church and Freeman Lists Between 1660 and 1673 [Printed Book] compiled by Jay Mack Holbrook (Oxford, MA, Holbrook Research Institute, 1977), 74 pages. FHL book 974.6 X2h.

1670 Inhabitants, Stonington, New London County, Connecticut [Online Database], indexed at the DunhamWilcox.net site. See http://dunhamwilcox.net/ct/stonington_ct_residents167 0.htm.

1670 List of Householders and Proprietors, Middletown, Middlesex County, Connecticut [Online Database], indexed at the DunhamWilcox.net site: http://dunhamwilcox.net/ct/middletown-1670.htm.

1672 Proprietors of Greenwich, Connecticut [Online Database], indexed at the USGenWeb site for Fairfield Co CT. See www.ctgenweb.org/county/cofairfield/pages/greenwich/ grnwich_27Proprietors.htm.

1677-1781 Early Proprietors, Waterbury, New Haven County, Connecticut [Online Database], indexed at the DunhamWilcox.net site. See http://dunhamwilcox.net/ct/waterbury_early_settlers.htm.

1685 Names of the Proprietors, New Haven, Connecticut [Online Database], indexed at the DunhamWilcox.net site. See http://dunhamwilcox.net/ct/new_haven_proprietors.htm.

1686-1850. *Connecticut Marriages to 1850* [Online Database], indexed at the Ancestry.com website. Two published indexes were used for this database: 1) Mansfield, Tolland Co CT Marriages, 1686-1850 and 2) Redding, Fairfield Co CT Marriages, 1767-1850. The index has 2,311 records. http://search.ancestry.com/search/db.aspx?dbid=5318.

1688-1709. See "Proprietors, 1688-1709, East Haddam," [Printed Article], in *New England Historical and Genealogical Register*, Vol. 13, No. 1 (Jan 1859).

1688. See "Tax List, Saybrook, 1688," [Printed Article], in *Hear-Save*, Vol. 2, No. 1 (Dec 1987).

1694-1695 Greenwich Tax List [Online Database], indexed at the USGenWeb site for Fairfield Co CT: www.ctgenweb.org/county/cofairfield/pages/greenwich/ grnwich_twnlst.htm.

1694-1701. *Tax Lists for Simsbury, Hartford County, Connecticut* [Online Database]. Indexed at the DunhamWilcox.net site. See http://dunhamwilcox.net/ct/simsbury_ct_tax.htm.

1698-1968. *New London County, Connecticut, Cemetery Index* [Online Database], indexed at the Ancestry.com website. Original data: Ellsberry, Elizabeth Prather, comp. *Cemetery Records of New London County, Connecticut.* Vol. I-II. This database has 3,594 records. See https://search.ancestry.com/search/db.aspx?dbid=5564.

1698-1968. *Windham County, Connecticut, Cemetery Index* [Online Database], indexed at the Ancestry.com website. Original data: Ellsberry, Elizabeth Prather, comp. *Cemetery Records of Windham County, Connecticut.* Vol. I. This database has 2,783 records. See https://search.ancestry.com/search/db.aspx?dbid=5576.

1700-1729. *Hartford, Connecticut Probate Records* [Online Database], indexed at the Ancestry.com website. Original data: *A Digest of the Early Connecticut Probate Records, Hartford District, 1700-1729. Vol. II.* Publ. 1906. Each probate record contains the filing individual's name, date of probate, and location of filing. Entries often reveal the person's close family relations such as spouse, heirs, and siblings, along with the names of witnesses. This database has 1,057 records. See https://search.ancestry.com/search/db.aspx?dbid=4355.

1700-1775. *Immigrants to New England* [Printed Book], compiled by Ethel Stanwood Bolton, a reprint of the 1931 edition, published Salem, MA. Includes index. Reprint by Genealogical Publishing Co., 1966, 236 pages, FHL book 974.W2b.

1700s-1800s. *Family Secrets: 18th & 19th Century Birth Records in the Windham County, CT, County Court House & Files at the CT State Library Archives, Hartford* [Printed Book], by Marcella Houle Pasay, published by Heritage Books, Bowie, MD 2000, 101 pages, FHL book 974.645 V2p.

1700s-1800s. *Connecticut Officers & Soldiers* [CD-ROM], Contents: Rolls of Connecticut men in the French and Indian War, 1755-1762 (vols. 1-2); Rolls and lists of Connecticut men in the Revolution, 1775-783 (vols. 1-2); Connecticut Revolutionary pensioners, compiled by The Connecticut Daughters of the American Revolution; Record of service of Connecticut men in the War of the Revolution, War of 1812, Mexican War (vols. 1-2), edited by Henry P. Johnston. Published by Broderbund/Genealogical Publishing Co, 2000, FHL CD No. 9 pt.120.

1710-1711. *Roll and Journal of Connecticut Service in Queen Anne's War [Printed Book]*, Morehouse & Taylor Press, 1916, 62 pages. See FHL film #6019415.

1712-1899 Divorce Papers, New Haven County, Connecticut [Microfilm & Digital Capture], from the originals at the Connecticut State Archives, Hartford, CT. Filmed by the Genealogical Society of Utah, 1989, 56 rolls, beginning with FHL film #1672069 (Divorce Papers, A-Z, 1712-1773). To access the digital images, see the online FHL catalog page: www.familysearch.org/search/catalog/577900.

1713 Petition, Tolland County, Connecticut [Online Database], indexed at the Dunham Wilcox.net site: http://dunhamwilcox.net/ct/tolland_petition_1713.htm.

1719-1910. *Connecticut Divorces: Superior Court Records for the Counties of New London, Tolland & Windham* [Printed Book], compiled by Grace Louise Knox and Barbara B. Ferris, published by Heritage Books, Bowie, MD, 1987, 452 pages, FHL book 974.6 P2k.

1720-1799 Divorce Papers, Fairfield County, Connecticut [Microfilm & Digital Capture], from the originals at the Connecticut State Archives, Hartford, CT. Filmed by the Genealogical Society of Utah, 1990, 2 rolls, FHL film #1673219 (Divorce Papers, 1720-1769), and FHL film #1673220 (Divorce Papers, 1770-1799). To access the digital images, see the online FHL catalog page: www.familysearch.org/search/catalog/611841.

1721 Land Allotments, Bristol, Hartford County, Connecticut [Online Database], indexed at the DunhamWilcox.net site. See http://dunhamwilcox.net/ct/bristol_ct_land.htm.

1722 Land Division, Waterbury, New Haven County, Connecticut [Online Database], indexed at the Dunham/Wilcox.net site. See http://dunhamwilcox.net/ct/waterbury_ct_land.htm.

1725-1849 Divorce Papers, Hartford County, Connecticut [Microfilm & Digital Capture], from the originals at the Connecticut State Archives, Hartford, CT. Filmed by the Genealogical Society of Utah, 1989, 4 rolls, beginning with FHL film #1637917 (Divorce Papers, 1725-1772). To access the digital images, see the online FHL catalog page: www.familysearch.org/search/catalog/614982.

1726-1907 Divorce Papers, Windham County, Connecticut [Microfilm & Digital Capture], from the originals at the Connecticut State Library, Hartford, CT. Arranged in alphabetical order. Filmed by the Genealogical Society of Utah, 1990, 27 rolls, beginning with FHL film #1638582 (Abbe-Adams). To access the digital images, see the online FHL catalog page: www.familysearch.org/search/catalog/599011.

1729-1750. *Hartford, Connecticut Probate Records* [Online Database], indexed at the Ancestry.com website. Original data: *A Digest of the Early Connecticut Probate Records, Hartford District, 1729-1750. Vol. III.* Publ. 1906. Each probate record contains the filing individual's name, date of probate, and location of filing. Entries often reveal the person's close family relations such as spouse, heirs, and siblings, along with the names of witnesses. Additionally, marriage, burial, and death dates are provided when relevant to the document. This database has 1,515 records. See https://search.ancestry.com/search/db.aspx?dbid=4376.

1730-1783 List of Tax Paying Inhabitants, Town of Waterbury, New Haven County, Connecticut [Online Database], indexed at the DunhamWilcox.net site: http://dunhamwilcox.net/ct/waterbury_ct_taxlist.htm.

1730 Land Inventory, Waterbury, New Haven County, Connecticut [Online Database], indexed at the Dunham/Wilcox.net site. See http://dunhamwilcox.net/ct/waterbury_ct_land_1730.htm.

1738 Freemen of Coventry, Tolland County [Online Database], indexed at the USGenWeb site for Coventry, CT. See www.ctgenweb.org/town/ctccoventry/freemen.html.

1739-1748 Early Inhabitants and Tax Lists, Cornwall, Litchfield County, Connecticut [Online Database], indexed at the DunhamWilcox.net site: http://dunhamwilcox.net/ct/cornwall_ct.htm.

1740. See "Election of 1740 in CT," [Printed Article]. Name list in *Connecticut History*, No. 22 (Jan 1981).

1740-1922. See *Connecticut Divorces: Superior Court Records for the Counties of Litchfield, 1752-1922 and Hartford 1740-1849* [CD-ROM], compiled by Barbara B. Ferris and Grace Louise Knox, a 2000 reproduction by Heritage Books on CD-ROM of original published by Heritage Books, Bowie, MD, 1989, 299 pages. See FHL CD No. 2630.

1741 Rate Bill, North Parish of Lebanon (Now Columbia), New London County, Connecticut [Online Database], indexed at the DunhamWilcox.net site. See http://dunhamwilcox.net/ct/lebanon_tax_1741.htm.

1741–1748 Probate Records at Fairfield, County of Fairfield, and State of Connecticut [Online Database], indexed at the USGenWeb site for Fairfield Co CT: www.ctgenweb.org/county/cofairfield/pages/probate/vol_7-11/ctfairfi_probate.indexv9.html.

1741. See **"Rate Bill, 1741, Lebanon,"** [Printed Article], in *New England Historical and Genealogical Register*, Vol. 20, No. 1 (Jan 1866).

1742-1748 Tax Lists, Cornwall, Litchfield County, Connecticut [Online Database], indexed at the DunhamWilcox.net site. See http://dunhamwilcox.net/ct/cornwall_ct.htm.

1744. See **"Tax List, 1744, Kent,"** [Printed Article], in *American Genealogist*, Vol. 11, No. 1 (Jul 1934).

1744 List of Names of the Original Proprietors, Winchester, Litchfield County, Connecticut [Online Database], indexed at the DunhamWilcox.net site: http://dunhamwilcox.net/ct/winchester_ct_proprietors.htm.

1746-1760. See **"Taxpayers, 1746, 1756, 1760, Salisbury,"** [Printed Article], in *National Genealogical Society Quarterly*, Vol. 71, No. 2 (Jun 1983).

1747 Grand Levy, Middlefield, Middlesex County, Connecticut [Online Database], indexed at the DunhamWilcox.net site. See http://dunhamwilcox.net/ct/middlefield_levy_1747.htm.

1748–1755 Probate Records at Fairfield, County of Fairfield, and State of Connecticut [Online Database], indexed at the USGenWeb site for Fairfield Co CT. See www.ctgenweb.org/county/cofairfield/pages/probate/vol_7-11/ctfairfi_probate.indexv10.html.

1750. See **"Tax List, circa 1750, Brookfield,"** [Printed Article], in *New England Historical and Genealogical Register*, Vol. 20, No. 2 (Apr 1866).

1750-1775. *Connecticut Taxation* [Printed Book], by Lawrence Henry Gipson. Includes two essays: 1) Essays in Colonial History, Yale University Press, 1931; and 2) The American Historical Review, XXXVI, pp721-739. Includes bibliographic notes. Published by Yale University Press, New Haven, CT, 1933, 41 pages, FHL book 974.6 H2c No. 10.

1750-1903. *Sharon, Connecticut and Northeast New York, Cemetery Index* [Online Database], indexed at the FamilySearch.org website. Original data: Van Alystyne, L. Burying Grounds of Sharon, Connecticut, Amenia and North East New York: Being an Abstract of Inscriptions from Thirty Places of Burial in the Above-Named Towns. 1903. This database has 13,082 records. See https://search.ancestry.com/search/db.aspx?dbid=4823.

1752-1922 Divorce Papers, Litchfield County, Connecticut [Microfilm & Digital Capture], from the originals at the Connecticut State Archives, Hartford, CT. Filmed by the Genealogical Society of Utah, 1989-1900, 26 rolls, beginning with FHL film #1664674 (Divorce Papers, Abbott-Barnard). To access the digital images, see the online FHL catalog page: www.familysearch.org/search/catalog/578335.

1755-1762. *Rolls of Connecticut Men in the French and Indian War* [CD-ROM], a reproduction of a facsimile reprint by Heritage Books, Bowie, MD, 1984, 2 vols. Includes indexes. The original 2-vol. set was published by the Connecticut Historical Society, 1903-1905. See FHL CD No. 2612.

1755-1762. *Miscellaneous French and Indian War Records* [Microfilm], from originals at the Connecticut State Library, Hartford, CT. Includes partial index. Filmed by the Genealogical Society of Utah, 1954, 2 rolls, FHL film #3626-3627.

1755-1762. *Connecticut Soldiers in the French and Indian War: Bills, Receipts and Documents Printed from Original Manuscripts* [Printed Book], with and introduction by Frank D. Andrews, published Vineland, NJ, 1925, 41 pages, FHL book 974.6 M2cst.

1755-1762. *Connecticut Soldiers, French and Indian War* **[Online Database],** indexed at the Ancestry.com website. Original data: Connecticut Historical Society, *Rolls of Connecticut Men in the French and Indian War, 1755-1762.* Vol. I-II. Hartford, CT. This database is a listing of over 29,000 men who served in the colonial militia between 1755 and 1762. It reveals the soldier's name, rank, location of enlistment, regiment, and company. Additionally, researchers will find the regimental and company commanders, with accompanying rank, listed with each record. This database has 29,722 records. See **https://search.ancestry.com/search/db.aspx?dbid=3983.**

1755-1789. *Land Lotteries and Divorces of Connecticut, With Index* **[Microfilm & Digital Capture],** arranged by Sylvester Judd and Connecticut State Library, from originals at the Connecticut State Library, Hartford, CT. Includes index. Filmed by the Genealogical Society of Utah, 1954, 2 rolls, FHL film #3617 (Index) & FHL film #3618 (Lotteries & Divorces). To access the digital images, see the online FHL catalog page: **www.familysearch.org/search/catalog/441667.**

1755-2004. *Connecticut Newspaper Archives* **[Online Database],** digitized and indexed at the GenealogyBank.com website. One search screen for names and keywords in the following city newspapers: Bridgeport, Brooklyn, Danbury, Danielson, Derby, Fairfield, Falls Village, Hartford, Killingly, Litchfield, Middletown, Mystic, New Canaan, New Haven, New London, Norwalk, Norwich, Sharon, Stamford, Stonington, Stonington- Port, Suffield, Waterbury, Willimantic, and Windham. **www.genealogybank.com/gbnk/newspapers/explore/USA/Connecticut/.**

1756-1774. See **"1756-74 Town Populations," [Printed Article],** in *Historical Footnotes,* Vol. 11, No. 4 (Aug 1974).

1758 Military Roll, Tolland County, Connecticut **[Online Database],** indexed at the Dunham-Wilcox.net site. See **http://dunhamwilcox.net/ct/tolland_military_1758.htm.**

1762. See **"Lost Census of 1762 Found," [Printed Articles],** in *Notes and News,* Vol. 3, No. 3 (Jan 1978); - see also, **"Census, 1762, Found at New Haven,"** in *Connecticut Historical Society Bulletin,* Vol. 44, No. 2 (Apr 1979).

1772 Tax List, Farmington, Hartford County, Connecticut **[Online Database],** indexed at DunhamWilcox.net site. See **http://dunhamwilcox.net/ct/farmington_ct_tax_1772.htm.**

1772-1891 Records of Executions of Court Judgments, A-Z, Tolland County Superior Court **[Microfilm & Digital Capture],** from the original records at the Connecticut State Archives, Hartford, CT. Filmed by the Genealogical Society of Utah, 1989, 1 roll, FHL film #1637443 (Executions, A-Z). To access the digital images, see the online FHL catalog page: **www.familysearch.org/search/catalog/576810.**

1772-1934. *Connecticut Deaths and Burials* **[Online Database],** indexed at the FamilySearch.org website, a name index to death and burial records from the state of Connecticut, originally microfilmed by the Genealogical Society of Utah for the Family History Library in Salt Lake City, Utah. The database contains 2,010,979 records. See **www.familysearch.org/search/collection/1674748.**

1775 Names of all Taxpayers in the North Society of Preston and the Amount of their Property **[Online Database],** extracted from *Griswold, A History: Being a History of the Town of Griswold, Connecticut..* by Daniel L. Phillips. The "Grand List" indexed at the Dunham/Wilcox.net site. See **http://dunhamwilcox.net/ct/preston_ct_n_society.htm.**

1775-1783. *Connecticut Revolutionary War Military Lists* **[Online Database],** indexed at the Ancestry.com website. Original data: Johnston, Henry P., ed.. *Collections of the Connecticut Historical Society Revolution Rolls and Lists, 1775-1783.* Vol. VIII. Hartford, CT, 1999. Among the most comprehensive volumes on Connecticut Revolutionary War soldiers, this collection provides the name, residence, rank, and unit information. This database has 12,896 records: **https://search.ancestry.com/search/db.aspx?dbid=3779.**

1775-1783. *Connecticut Men in the Revolutionary War* **[Online Database],** indexed at the Ancestry.com website. Original data: Johnston, Henry P., ed.. *The Record of Connecticut Men in the Military and Naval Service During the War of the Revolution 1775-1783.* Vol. I-III. Hartford, CT, 1889. This database has 971 records. See **https://search.ancestry.com/search/db.aspx?dbid=7426.**

1775-1783 Connecticut Line (Revolutionary War), Those Receiving Supplies, Middlesex County, Connecticut **[Online Database]**, indexed at the DunhamWilcox.net site. See http://dunhamwilcox.net/ct/middlesex_ct_rev_war1775.htm

1776. *A Census of Newington, Connecticut* **[Printed Book]**, compiled by Frederic B. Hartranft, published Hartford, 1909. Includes name of every person in a household, plus place of birth, and remarks. See FHL book 974.62/N2 X2p. Also online at the DunhamWilcox.net site. See http://dunhamwilcox.net/ct/newington_census_1776.htm.

1776-1783. See **"Connecticut Loyalists List, Revolution,"** **[Printed Article]**, in *Generations*, Vol. 20 (Jun 1984).

1776-1783. *Connecticut Loyalists: An Analysis of Loyalist Land Confiscations in Greenwich, Stamford, and Norwalk* **[Printed Book]**, by John W. Tyler. Includes index of personal names & bibliographical references. Published by Polyanthos, New Orleans, LA, 1977, 135 pages, FHL book 974.69 R2t.

1777-1850 List of Freemen, Torrington, Litchfield County, Connecticut **[Online Database]**, indexed at the DunhamWilcox.net site. See http://dunhamwilcox.net/ct/torrington_ct_freemen.htm.

1779 Businesses in Hartford County, Connecticut **[Online Database]**, indexed at the USGenWeb site for Hartford Co CT. See http://files.usgwarchives.net/ct/hartford/history/directories/business/hartford60gms.txt.

1779 Residents of Hartford County, Connecticut **[Online Database]**, indexed at the USGenWeb site for Hartford Co CT. See http://files.usgwarchives.net/ct/hartford/history/directories/business/resident61gms.txt.

1780-1788 see **"Tax List, circa 1780-88, Brookfield,"** **[Printed Article]**, in *New England Historical and Genealogical Register*, Vol. 28, No. 1 (Jan 1874).

1781 Connecticut Line (Revolutionary War), Those Receiving Supplies, Middlesex County, Connecticut **[Online Database]**, indexed at the DunhamWilcox.net site. See http://dunhamwilcox.net/ct/rev_war_midsex_1781.htm.

1784-1867. *U.S., Newspaper Extractions from the Northeast* **[Online Database]**, indexed at the Ancestry.com website. Original data: Newspapers and Periodicals, American Antiquarian Society, Worcester, MA. Included in this collections are these Connecticut newspapers: 1) *American Mercury* (Deaths/Marriages, 1784-1832); 2) *Christian Secretary* (Deaths/Marriages, 1823-1867); 3) *New Haven Columbian* (Deaths / Marriages, 1812-1865); and *The Hartford Times* (Deaths / Marriages, 1817-1866). This database has 833,843 records. See https://search.ancestry.com/search/db.aspx?dbid=50015.

1786-1797 Divorce Papers, Middlesex County, Connecticut **[Microfilm & Digital Capture]**, from the originals at the Connecticut State Archives, Hartford, CT. Filmed by the Genealogical Society of Utah, 1989, 1 roll, FHL film #1639454 (Divorce Papers, 1786-1797). To access the digital images, see the online FHL catalog page: www.familysearch.org/search/catalog/616280.

1786-1797 Court Records, Middlesex County, Connecticut **[Microfilm & Digital Capture]**, from the originals at the Connecticut State Archives, Hartford, CT. Includes miscellaneous, partition of land, jurors, court expense, costs, travel, and inquest records. Filmed by the Genealogical Society of Utah, 1989, 1 roll, FHL film #1639454 (Court Records, 1786-1797). To access the digital images, see the online FHL catalog page: www.familysearch.org/search/catalog/616283.

1787-1910 Tolland County Divorce Papers **[Microfilm & Digital Capture]**, from original records at the Connecticut State Archives, Hartford, CT. Records are in approximate alphabetical order. Filmed by the Genealogical Society of Utah, 1989, 16 rolls, beginning with FHL film #1637443 (Abbott-Avery). To access the digital images, see the online FHL catalog page: www.familysearch.org/search/catalog/576645.

1787-1922. *New England, Select United Methodist Church Records* **[Online Database]**, indexed at the Ancestry.com website. These records are from the New England Methodist Church Commission on Archives and History and include baptism, marriage, death, membership, and other religious records from New England, including Connecticut churches in Hartford, Middlesex, New Long, Tolland, and Windham counties. This database has 374,894 records, see https://search.ancestry.com/search/db.aspx?dbid=9134.

1790. See *Heads of Families at the First Census of the United States Taken in the year 1790 - Connecticut* [Printed Book & Digital Version]. Originally printed for the U.S. Census Bureau by the Government Printing Office, Washington, DC, 1908, 227 pages, FHL Book 974.6 X2b. To access a digital version of this book, see the online FHL catalog page: www.familysearch.org/search/catalog/244344.

1790-1840. See *Connecticut, 1790 thru 1840 Federal Census: Population Schedules* [Microfilm & Digital Capture[, from originals at the National Archives in Washington, DC. Filmed by the National Archives, 1938-1969, 22 rolls, beginning with FHL film #5157133 (Connecticut). To access the digital images, see the online FHL catalog page: www.familysearch.org/search/catalog/745482.

1790-1850 Index of Connecticut Federal Census Records [Microfilm & Digital Capture]. This is a filmed copy of the special card index created by the Connecticut State Library in Hartford, CT. The residents of cities beginning with the letters A to New Haven are alphabetically indexed by name. The residents of the remaining cities are indexed alphabetically by city. Some surname variations are alphabetized together. Example: Buckley, Bulkley, Bulckley are all found under Buckley. Filmed by the Genealogical Society of Utah, 1950, 95 rolls of microfilm, beginning with FHL film #3434. To access the digital images of certain rolls, see the online FHL catalog page: www.familysearch.org/search/catalog/332021.

1790-1890. *Connecticut, Compiled Census and Census Substitute Index* [Online Database], originally compiled and indexed by Ronald Vern Jackson, the first CT database acquired by Ancestry.com. This collection contains the following indexes: 1790 Federal Census Index; 1800 Federal Census Index; 1810 Federal Census Index; 1820 Federal Census Index; 1830 Federal Census Index; 1840 Federal Census Index; 1840 Pensioners List; 1850 Federal Census Index; 1860 Federal Census Index; 1890 Veterans Schedule; and Early Census Index. See http://search.ancestry.com/search/db.aspx?dbid=3537.

1790-1855. *Marriages and Deaths (Not Taken From Cemetery or Tombstone Records), Fairfield County, Connecticut* [Microfilm & Digital Capture], from an original (1934) typescript at the New York Genealogical and Biographical Society, New York City, by Lester Card. Includes index. Death info was taken from the Norwalk Gazette. Filmed by the Genealogical Society of Utah, 1941, 1 roll, FHL film #4197. Another filming, FHL film #1405480. To access the digital images, see the online FHL catalog page: www.familysearch.org/search/catalog/31721.

1790-1973 Index to Naturalization Petitions, Litchfield County, Connecticut [Microfilm & Digital Capture], from the original records now located at the National Archives, Waltham, MA. Filmed by the Genealogical Society of Utah, 3 rolls, beginning with FHL film #2369711 (1790-1906: A to Roy, Eugene Francis). To access the digital images, see the online FHL catalog page: www.familysearch.org/search/catalog/1154805.

1790-1996. *Connecticut, Federal Naturalization Records* [Online Database], digitized and indexed at the Ancestry.com website. Source: Naturalization records at the National Archives branch, Waltham, MA. Includes Petitions, Intentions, and Certificates. Each index record includes: Name, Gender, Record type, Birth date, Birthplace, Arrival date, and Arrival place. The document image may have much more information. This database has 983,483 records. See https://search.ancestry.com/search/db.aspx?dbid=61195.

1790s to late 1800s. See *Bowman Collection: Connecticut Vital Records in Massachusetts* [Microfilm & Digital Capture], from the original card file in the Connecticut State Library, Hartford, CT. Contains abstracts of death notices from newspapers and Massachusetts vital records. Filmed by the Genealogical Society of Utah, 1949, 2 rolls, FHL film #2884 (A – Hy) and #2885 (I – Z). To access the digital images, see the online FHL catalog page: www.familysearch.org/search/catalog/19994.

1799 See **"Taxpayers, New Britain, 1799,"** [Printed Article]. in *Genealogy*, Vol. 1, No. 14 (Apr 1912).

1800. *Connecticut 1800 Census Index* **[Printed Index]**, edited by Ronald Vern Jackson, published by Accelerated Indexing Systems, Bountiful, UT, 1977, 167 pages, FHL book 974.6 X2.

1800. See "**East Guilford Voters, 1800 & CT Property Test,**" **[Printed Article]**. Names listed in *Connecticut Historical Society Bulletin,* Vo. 19, No. 4 (Oct 1954).

1808-1900 Divorce Papers, No Appearance Files, New Haven County, Connecticut **[Microfilm & Digital Capture]**, from the originals at the Connecticut State Archives, Hartford, CT. A record of divorce cases which were withdrawn or discontinued. Filmed by the Genealogical Society of Utah, 1990, 9 rolls, beginning with FHL film #1673026 (A-Salter 1808-1865). To access the digital images, see the online FHL catalog page: **www.familysearch.org/search/catalog/611734.**

1810. *Connecticut 1810 Census Index* **[Printed Index]**, edited by Ronald Vern Jackson, et al, published by Accelerated Indexing systems, Bountiful, UT, 1976, 109 pages, FHL book 974.6 X2j.

1810. *Connecticut 1810 Census Index, A-Z* **[Printed Index]**, compiled and published by Heritage Quest, Bountiful, UT, 2000, 257 pages, FHL book 974.6X22h.

1817 See "**Tax List, 1817, Branford,**" **[Printed Article]**. in *Connecticut Nutmegger*, Vol. 26, No. 3 (Dec 1993).

1820. *Connecticut 1820 Census Index* **[Printed Index]**, edited by Ronald Vern Jackson, published by Accelerated Indexing Systems, Bountiful, UT, 1977, 124 pages, FHL book 974.6 X2j 1820.

1828 City Directory, Hartford, Connecticut **[Online Database]**, originally indexed at the Distant-Cousin.com site. For an archived database, see **https://web.archive.org/web/20160426053009/http://distantcousin.com/Directories/CT/Hartford/1828/.**

1830. *Connecticut 1830 Census Index* **Printed Index]**, edited by Ronald Vern Jackson, published by Accelerated Indexing Systems, Bountiful, UT, 977, 138 pages, FHL book 974.6 X2j 1830.

1833 Citizens of Hartford County, Connecticut **[Printed Book]**, originally printed as a memorial of citizens, addressed to Congress, document No. 508, 23rd Congress, 1st Session, House of Representatives,

reprinted by Mountain Press, Signal Mountain, TN, 1999, 25 pages, FHL book 974.62 X4c.

1834-1906 Naturalization Records, Hartford County, Connecticut [Microfilm & Digital Capture], from the originals at the Superior Court Building, Hartford, CT. Filmed by the Genealogical Society of Utah, 1983, 11 rolls, beginning with FHL film #1319703. To access the digital images, see the online FHL catalog page: **www.familysearch.org/search/catalog/570010.**

1838 See "**New Canaan Town Tax, 1838,**" **[Printed Article]**, in *New Canaan Historical Society Annual*, Vol. 3, No. 3 (Jun 1953).

1839-1955 Naturalization Records, Fairfield County, Connecticut **[Microfilm & Digital Capture]**, from the originals now located at the National Archives, Waltham, MA. Includes all petitions for citizenship along with papers created during the naturalization process. Included are petitions for naturalization filed by aliens serving in the Armed forces during World War I, wherein the requirements for citizenship was reduced from five years to one year of residency. Includes indexes. Filmed by the Genealogical Society of Utah, 2003-2207, 155 rolls, beginning with FHL film #2368899. (Petitions index, 1839-1955, Aabye – Atamian). To access the digital images, see the online FHL catalog page: **www.familysearch.org/search/catalog/1147528.**

1840. *Connecticut 1840 Census Index* **[Printed Index]**, edited by Ronald Vern Jackson, published by Accelerated Indexing Systems, Bountiful, UT, 977, 138 pages, FHL book 974.6 X2j 1940.

1841-1945 Naturalization Records, Middlesex County, Connecticut **[Microfilm & Digital Capture]**, from the original records in Middleton, CT. Includes Declarations of Intention and Petitions. Filmed by the Genealogical Society of Utah, 1984-2008, 12 rolls, beginning with FHL film #1398618 (Declarations of intent, 1841-1843). To access the digital images, see the online FHL catalog page: **www.familysearch.org/search/catalog/403937.**

1844-1927. See *Index to James N. Arnold Tombstone Records Collection* **[Microfilm & Digital Capture]**, from the original index cards at Knight Memorial Library, Providence, RI. The date range shown is for the author's life span, the tombstone records probably date much earlier. The records are alphabetized for tombstones combined with several New England states, including Connecticut. Filmed by the Genealogical Society of Utah, 1992, 12 rolls, beginning with FHL film #1819819 (A to Arnold, Phebe). To access the digital images, see the online FHL catalog page: **www.familysearch.org/search/catalog/641346.**

1844-1955 Naturalization Index, Middlesex County, Connecticut **[Microfilm & Digital Capture]**, from the original card file in the Superior Court, Middleton, CT. Filmed by the Genealogical Society of Utah, 1984, 5 rolls, beginning with FHL film #1398614 (Naturalization Index – Abair-Bartolotta, 1844-1955). To access the digital images, see the online FHL catalog page: **www.familysearch.org/search/catalog/402829.**

1845 see **"Tax Records, 1845, Hamonsette,"** **[Printed Article],** in *Connecticut Nutmegger*, Vol. 27, No. 3 (Dec 1994).

1845 see **"Borough Tax Rolls, 1845, New London,"** **[Printed Article],** in *Historical Footnotes*, Vol. 25, No. 2 (May 1988).

1847-2011. *The New England Historical & Genealogical Register* **[Online Database],** digitized and indexed at the Ancestry.com website. This database contains volumes of the *New England Historical and Genealogical Register*, a quarterly publication. The New England Historic Genealogical Society (NEHGS) was formed in 1845, and in 1847, they published the first issue of the *Register*. The NEHGS is the oldest genealogical society in the United States, and the *Register*, likewise, is the country's oldest genealogical journal. The database is searchable by name, birth, death, marriage, and any event and any keyword found in the articles. This database has 300,569 records. See **http://search.ancestry.com/search/db.aspx?dbid=2129.**

1849-1858. *Connecticut (State) Directories* **[Microfilm],** from originals published by various publishers. Filmed by Research Publications, Woodbridge, CT, 1980-1984, 16 microfiche. The FHL has the following:
- **1849** New England Mercantile Union Directory. Part 6: Connecticut, by Pratt & Co., 3 fiche, FHL fiche #6043845.
- **1851** The Connecticut Business Directory, by J. Benham, 6 fiche FHL fiche #6043846.
- **1856** The Connecticut Business Directory, by George Adams, 2 fiche, FHL fiche #6043847.
- **1857/58** The Illustrated Commercial, Mechanical,

Professional and Statistical Gazetteer and Business Book of Connecticut, by A.D. Jones, 5 fiches, FHL fiche #6043848.

1850. *Connecticut, 1850 Federal Census: Population Schedules* **[Microfilm & Digital Capture],** from the originals at the National Archives, Washington, DC. Filmed by the National Archives, 1964, 15 rolls, beginning with FHL film #3065 (Connecticut: Fairfield Co, part). To access the digital images, see the online FHL catalog page: **www.familysearch.org/search/catalog/744472.**

1850. *Connecticut 1850 Census Index* **[Printed Index],** edited by Ronald Vern Jackson, published by Accelerated Indexing Systems, Bountiful, UT 1978, 339 pages, FHL book 974.6 X22j 1850.

1850 Connecticut Federal Census, Mortality Schedules **[Microfilm & Digital Capture],** from the state's original copy at the Connecticut State Library, Hartford, CT. Filmed by the Genealogical Society of Utah, 1961, 1 roll, FHL film #234536. To access the digital images, see the online FHL catalog page: **www.familysearch.org/search/catalog/759730.**

1850. *Connecticut 1850 Mortality Schedule* **[Printed Index],** edited by Ronald Vern Jackson, et al, published by Accelerated Indexing Systems, Bountiful, UT, 1981, 107 pages, FHL book 974.6 X2.

1851-1992. *Connecticut, District Court Naturalization Indexes* **[Online Database],** indexed at the FamilySearch.org website. Source: National Archives microfilm M2081. Includes card indexes of naturalization petitions in the United States District Courts in Connecticut. This database has 253,215 records. See **www.familysearch.org/search/collection/2141008.**

1852 and 1856 New Haven County, Connecticut Land Ownership Maps **[Microfiche],** from the original maps at the Library of Congress, Geography and Map Division, Washington, DC, filmed by the Library of Congress, Photoduplication Services on 4 microfiche, FHL fiche #6079301 (1 fiche: 1852 New Haven Co) and FHL fiche #6079302 (3 fiche: 1856 New Haven Co).

1852-1928. *Connecticut, Passport and Birth Certificates* **[Online Database],** indexed at Ancestry.com. Source: CT State Library, Hartford.

This diverse database features a wide range of documents, including passports, birth certificates, baptismal certificates, admission of alien forms, employment information cards, and others. The documents come from a number of different countries and are in various languages (including Italian, Polish, and Portuguese). These records were generally indexed by primary person and birth date, but can include birthplace, parents' names, address, or profession. This database has 2,284 records. See https://search.ancestry.com/search/db.aspx?dbid=2276.

1853-1955. See *Naturalization Records, Tolland County, Connecticut, 1853-1945; Naturalization Index, 1853-1955* **[Microfilm & Digital Capture]**, from the original records at the Superior Court in Rockville, CT, and at the National Archives, Waltham, MA. Filmed by the genealogical society of Utah, 1983-2008, 11 rolls, beginning with FHL film #1319928 (Naturalization Index, Abbey-Hall, G., 1853-1955). To access the digital images, see the online FHL catalog page: www.familysearch.org/search/catalog/595040.

1853-1914 Declarations of Intention, Tolland County, Connecticut **[Microfilm & Digital Capture]**, from the originals at the Superior Court, Rockville, CT. Indexes are found within each volume. Filmed by the Genealogical Society of Utah, 1983, 2 rolls, FHL film #1319927 (Declarations of Intention, 1853-1906), and FHL film #1319930 (Declarations of Intention, 1906-1914). To access the digital images, see the online FHL catalog page: www.familysearch.org/search/catalog/595137.

 1853 see **"Tax, Redding, 1853,"** **[Printed Article]**, in *Connecticut Nutmegger*, Vol. 17, No. 3 (Dec 1984).

1854 New London County, Connecticut Land Ownership Maps **[Microfiche]**, from the original maps at the Library of Congress, Geography and Map Division, Washington, DC, filmed by the Library of Congress, Photoduplication Services on 2 microfiche, FHL fiche #6079303 (2 fiche: 1854 New London Co).

1855 Naturalizations, Windham County, Connecticut **[Microfilm & Digital Capture]**, from the originals at the Superior County, Putnam, CT. Filmed by the Genealogical Society of Utah, 1 roll, FHL film #1278199.To access the digital images, see the online FHL catalog page: www.familysearch.org/search/catalog/598942.

1855-1906 Naturalizations, Windham County, Connecticut **[Microfilm & Digital Capture]**, from the originals at the Superior Court, Putnam, CT. Includes indexes within each volume. Filmed by the Genealogical Society of Utah, 1983, 2 rolls, FHL film #1378199 (Naturalizations, 1855-1888), and FHL film #1378200 (Naturalizations, 1888-1906). To access the digital images, see the online FHL catalog page: www.familysearch.org/search/catalog/598899.

1855-1906 Declarations of Intentions, Windham County, Connecticut **[Microfilm & Digital Capture]**, from the originals at the Superior Court, Putnam, CT. Includes indexes within each volume. Filmed by the Genealogical Society of Utah, 1983, 2 rolls, FHL film #1378200 (Declarations of Intentions, 1855-1892), and FHL film #1378201 (Declarations of Intentions, 1892-1906). To access the digital images, see the online FHL catalog page: www.familysearch.org/search/catalog/598949.

1855-1875. See **"Connecticut Born, NY State Census, 1855, 1865, 1875,"** **[Printed Article]**, in *Stamford Genealogical Society Bulletin*, Vol. 10, No. 1 (Sep 1967).

1855-1924. *New London (Connecticut) City Directories* **[Microfilm]**, by various publishers, filmed by Research Publications, Woodbridge, CT, 1980-1984, 5 microfiche, 14 rolls of 35mm microfilm, beginning with FHL fiche #6044248 (1855-1856 Directory). For a complete list of fiche/roll numbers and contents of each, see the online FHL catalog page for this title: www.familysearch.org/search/catalog/534747.

1855 and 1884 Hartford County, Connecticut Land Ownership Maps **[Microfiche]**, from the original maps at the Library of Congress, Geography and Map Division, Washington, DC, filmed by the Library of Congress, Photoduplication Services on 5 microfiche, FHL fiche #6079297 (3 fiche: 1855 Hartford Co) and FHL fiche #6079298 (2 fiche: 1884 Hartford Co).

1856 Windham County, Connecticut Land Ownership Map **[Microfiche]**, from the original maps at the Library of Congress, Geography and Map Division, Washington, DC, filmed by the Library of Congress, Photoduplication Services on 3 microfiche, FHL fiche #6079305 (3 fiche: 1857 Windham Co).

1856-1905 Naturalization Books, New London County, Connecticut [Microfilm & Digital Capture], from the original records at the Town Hall, Norwich, CT. Indexes are found within each volume. Filmed by the Genealogical Society of Utah, 1983, 2 rolls, FHL film #131942 (petitions, 1856-1864), and FHL film #1319743 (petitions, 1856-1905). To access the digital images, see the online FHL catalog page: www.familysearch.org/search/catalog/593486.

1856 and 1858 Fairfield County, Connecticut Land Ownership Maps [Microfiche], from the original maps at the Library of Congress, Geography and Map Division, Washington, DC, filmed by the Library of Congress, Photoduplication Services on 6 microfiches, FHL fiche #6079295 (3 fiche: 1856 Fairfield Co) and FHL fiche #6079296 (3 fiche: 1858 Fairfield Co).

1857 Tolland County, Connecticut Land Ownership Map [Microfiche], from the original maps at the Library of Congress, Geography and Map Division, Washington, DC, filmed by the Library of Congress, Photoduplication Services on 2 microfiche, FHL fiche #6079304 (2 fiche: 1857 Tolland Co).

1859 Litchfield County, Connecticut Land Ownership Map [Microfiche], from the original maps at the Library of Congress, Geography and Map Division, Washington, DC, filmed by the Library of Congress, Photoduplication Services on 2 microfiche, FHL fiche #6079299 (2 fiche: 1859 Litchfield Co).

1859 Middlesex County, Connecticut Land Ownership Map [Microfiche], from the original maps at the Library of Congress, Geography and Map Division, Washington, DC, filmed by the Library of Congress, Photoduplication Services on 2 microfiche, FHL fiche #6079300 (2 fiche: 1859 Middlesex Co).

1859-1980s. Connecticut City Directories [Online Database], indexed at the Ancestry.com website. Directory collection at the New England Historic Genealogical Society, Boston, MA. This database is a collection of city directories for various years and cities in Connecticut. Generally a city directory will contain an alphabetical list of its citizens, listing the names of the heads of households, their addresses, and occupational information. Sometimes the wife's name will be listed in parentheses or italics following the husbands. To see what cities and years are currently available, view the *Browse this Collection* feature. Begin by selecting a city of interest. A quick check of

the towns indicated the earliest directory was for Hartford in 1859. A few directories spanned into the 1980s. This database has 666,326 records. See https://search.ancestry.com/search/db.aspx?dbid=8777.

1860. Connecticut, 1860 Federal Census: Population Schedules [Microfilm & Digital Capture], from the originals at the National Archives, Washington, DC. Filmed twice by the National Archives, 1950 & 1967, 26 rolls total, beginning with FHL film #803073 (Connecticut: 2nd filming, Fairfield Co, et al) and FHL film #3060 (1st filming, Fairfield, et al). The 2nd filming has one page per frame, while the 1st filming has two pages per frame (and much more difficult to read). To access the digital images, see the online FHL catalog page: www.familysearch.org/search/catalog/704548.

1860. Connecticut 1860 Census Index [Printed Index], edited by Ronald Vern Jackson, published by Accelerated Indexing Systems, Bountiful, UT 1978, 682 pages, FHL book 974.6 X22j 1860.

1860 Connecticut Census Index: Heads of Households and other Surnames in Households Index, compiled by Bryan Lee Dilts, published by Index Publishing, Salt Lake City, UT, 1985, FHL book 974.6 X22d 1860.

1860 Connecticut Federal Census, Mortality Schedules [Microfilm & Digital Capture], from the state's original copy at the Connecticut State Library, Hartford, CT. Filmed by the Genealogical Society of Utah, 1961, 1 roll, FHL film #234536. To access the digital images, see the online FHL catalog page: www.familysearch.org/search/catalog/759738,

1861-1862 City Directory, Hartford, Connecticut [Online Database], originally indexed at the Distant Cousin.com site. For an archived database, see https://web.archive.org/web/20160327224820/http://distantcousin.com/Directories/CT/Hartford/1861_62/

1861-1865. Index to Compiled Service Records of Volunteer Union Soldiers Who Served in Organizations From the State of Connecticut [Microfilm & Digital Capture], from the original records at the National Archives. Filmed by the National Archives, Series M535, 1964, 17 rolls, beginning with FHL film #821909 (Index: A – Bem.). To access the digital images of certain rolls, see the online FHL catalog page: www.familysearch.org/search/catalog/319031.

1862-1866. *Internal Revenue Assessment Lists for Connecticut* **[Microfilm & Digital Capture],** from the original records at the National Archives, Washington, DC. District 1 contains Hartford and Tolland counties; District 2: Middlesex and New Haven counties; District 3: New London and Windham counties; and District 4: Fairfield and Litchfield counties. Filmed by the National Archives, series M758, 1968, 23 rolls, beginning with FHL film #1534625. To access the digital images, see the online FHL catalog page:
www.familysearch.org/search/catalog/577864.

1870. *Connecticut, 1870 Federal Census: Population Schedules* **[Microfilm & Digital Capture],** from the originals at the National Archives, Washington, DC. Filmed twice by the National Archives, 1962 & 1968, 30 rolls total, beginning with FHL film #545595 (Connecticut: 2nd filming, Fairfield Co, et al) and FHL film #295390 (1st filming, Fairfield, et al). The 2nd filming has one page per frame, while the 1st filming has two pages per frame (and much more difficult to read). To access the digital images, see the online FHL catalog page:
www.familysearch.org/search/catalog/698888.

1870. *Connecticut 1870 Census Index* **[Printed Index],** edited by Raeone Christensen Steuart, published by Heritage Quest, 2000, 2 vols., FHL book 974.6 X22c 1870.

1870 Connecticut Federal Census, Mortality Schedules **[Microfilm & Digital Capture],** from the state's original copy at the Connecticut State Library, Hartford, CT. Filmed by the Genealogical Society of Utah, 1961, 1 roll, FHL film #234536. To access the digital images, see the online FHL catalog page:
www.familysearch.org/search/catalog/41227.

1870-1871 Residential Directory, New London, Connecticut [Online Database], originally indexed at the DistantCousin.com website. For an archived database, see
https://web.archive.org/web/20150905090739/http://distantcousin.com/Directories/CT/NewLondon/1870_71 /

1872-1945. See *Naturalization Records, New London County, Connecticut, 1872-1906, 1909-1945* **[Microfilm & Digital Capture],** from the original records at the Town Hall in Norwich, CT, and at the National Archives in Waltham, MA. Includes index. Filmed by the Genealogical Society of Utah, 1983-2008, 27 rolls, beginning with FHL film #1319743

(Declarations of Intention, 1872-1906. To access the digital images, see the online FHL catalog page:
www.familysearch.org/search/catalog/593501.

1875-1906 Declarations of Intentions, New London County, Connecticut **[Microfilm & Digital Capture],** from the originals at the Town Hall, Norwich, CT. Filmed by the Genealogical Society of Utah, 1983, 2 rolls, FHL film #1319741 (Declarations of Intentions, 1875-1888), and FHL film #1319742 (Declarations of Intentions, 1888-1906). To access the digital images, see the online FHL catalog page:
www.familysearch.org/search/catalog/592572.

1876-1906 Index To Naturalization Petitions, Hartford County, Connecticut **[Microfilm & Digital Capture],** from the original records now located at the National Archives, Waltham, MA. Filmed by the Genealogical Society of Utah, 2003, 2 rolls, FHL film #2369652 (A to Johanson, Frederick), and FHL film #2369653 (Johanson, Frederick to Z). To access the digital images, see the online FHL catalog page:
www.familysearch.org/search/catalog/1154415.

1876-1906 Index to Declarations of Intention; Declarations of Intention, Hartford County, Connecticut **[Microfilm & Digital Capture],** from the original records now located at the National Archives, Waltham, MA. The "first papers" filed in the process of becoming a naturalized citizen of the United States, the Declarations of Intentions often give detail information about the applicant's birth origins, arrival in America, and much more personal information. Filmed by the Genealogical Society of Utah, 1983, 1 roll, FHL film #1320430. To access the digital images, see the online FHL catalog page:
www.familysearch.org/search/catalog/570101.

1880. *Connecticut, 1880 Federal Census: Soundex and Population Schedules* **[Microfilm & Digital Capture[,** from the originals at the National Archives, Washington, DC (in 1970), now located at the DAR Library, Washington, DC. Filmed by the National Archives, 1970, 42 rolls, beginning with FHL film #445488 (Soundex: A100-B246), and FHL film #1254094 (Fairfield Co). To access the digital images (Soundex only), see the online FHL catalog page:
www.familysearch.org/search/catalog/670374.

1880 Connecticut Federal Census, Mortality Schedules **[Microfilm & Digital Capture],** from the state's original copy at the Connecticut State Library, Hartford, CT. Filmed by the Genealogical Society of Utah, 1961, 1 roll, FHL film #234537. To access the digital images, see the online FHL catalog page:
www.familysearch.org/search/catalog/229789.

1882-1891. *Middletown, Connecticut Directories* **[Online Database],** indexed at the Ancestry.com website. This database is a collection of eight directories for the city originally published between 1882 and 1891. It is a listing of city residents in those years. In addition to providing the resident's name, it provides their address and occupational information. It includes the names of over 50,500 people, mostly heads of households. See https://search.ancestry.com/search/db.aspx?dbid=4687.

1883-1932 *Coroner's Records, Windham County, Connecticut* **[Microfilm & Digital Capture],** from the original records at the Connecticut State Archives, Hartford, CT. Indexes are found within each volume. Filmed by the Genealogical Society of Utah, 1988, 5 rolls, beginning with FHL film #1602848 (Coroner's Records, 1883-1889). To access the digital images, see the online FHL catalog page: www.familysearch.org/search/catalog/531000.

1883-1932 *Coroner's Records, New Haven County, Connecticut* **[Microfilm & Digital Capture],** from the original records at the Connecticut State Archives, Hartford, CT. Indexes are found within each volume. Filmed by the Genealogical Society of Utah, 1988-1989, 20 rolls, beginning with FHL film #1602852 (Coroner's Records, 1883-1887). To access the digital images, see the online FHL catalog page: www.familysearch.org/search/catalog/531400.

1883-1932 *Coroner's Records, New London County, Connecticut* **[Microfilm & Digital Capture],** from the original records at the Connecticut State Archives, Hartford, CT. Indexes are found within each volume. Filmed by the Genealogical Society of Utah, 1988, 8 rolls, beginning with FHL film #1579179 (Coroner's Records, 1883-1896). To access the digital images, see the online FHL catalog page: www.familysearch.org/search/catalog/530463.

1883-1934 *Directories of Tolland County Towns and Villages* **[Microfilm],** by various publishers, including Rockville, Tolland, Vernon, Coventry, Ellington, Stafford Springs, Somers, Willington, Bolton, and Manchester. Filmed by Research Publications, Woodbridge, CT, 1992, 3 rolls, beginning with FHL film #2156522 (1883 Rockville, Tolland, Vernon, Coventry, Ellington, Willington, and Bolton). For a complete list of roll numbers and contents of each roll, see the online FHL catalog page for this title: www.familysearch.org/search/catalog/968557.

1883-1932 *Coroner's Records, Hartford County, Connecticut* **[Microfilm & Digital Capture],** from the original records at the Connecticut State Archives, Hartford, CT. Indexes are found within each volume. Filmed by the Genealogical Society of Utah, 1988, 17 rolls, beginning with FHL film #1602529 (Coroner's Records, 1883-1891). To access the digital images, see the online FHL catalog page: www.familysearch.org/search/catalog/530850.

1883-1934 *Coroner's Records, Litchfield County, Connecticut* **[Microfilm & Digital Capture],** from the original records at the Connecticut State Archives, Hartford, CT. Indexes are found within each volume. Filmed by the Genealogical Society of Utah, 1988, 6 rolls, beginning with FHL film #1579556 (Coroner's Records, 1883-1897). To access the digital images, see the online FHL catalog page: www.familysearch.org/search/catalog/530489.

1883-1942 *Coroner's Records, Tolland County, Connecticut* **[Microfilm & Digital Capture],** from the original records at the Connecticut State Archives, Hartford, CT. Indexes are found within each volume. Filmed by the Genealogical Society of Utah, 1988, 3 rolls, beginning with FHL film #1602846 (Coroner's Records, 1883-1889). To access the digital images, see the online FHL catalog page: www.familysearch.org/search/catalog/530997.

1884 *City Directory, Hartford, Connecticut* **[Online Database],** indexed at the USGenWeb site for Hartford Co CT. See http://files.usgwarchives.net/ct/statewide/history/gaz1884a.txt.

1884-1934 *Willimantic (Connecticut) City Directories* **[Microfilm],** from original records located at various libraries and societies. The FHL Library has: 1884-1900, 1902-1903,1905-1921, 1923-1924, 1926-1930,1932,and 1934. Filmed by Research Publications, Woodbridge, CT, 1999, 6 rolls, beginning with FHL film #2258297 (1884-1885). For a complete list of roll numbers and contents of each roll, see the online FHL catalog page for this title: www.familysearch.org/search/catalog/1023393.

1885-1890 *Danbury, Connecticut Directories,* **Online Database],** indexed at the Ancestry.com website. This database is a collection of six directories for the city originally published between 1886 and 1890. It is a listing of city residents in those years. In addition to providing the resident's name, it provides their address and occupational information. It includes the names of over 41,400 people, mostly heads of households. See https://search.ancestry.com/search/db.aspx?dbid=4673.

1887-1889 *Norwalk, Connecticut Directories* **[Online Database],** indexed at the Ancestry.com website. This database is a transcription of city directories originally published in 1887, 1889, and 1891. In addition to providing the residents' names, it provides their addresses and occupational information. The database includes more than 18,800 names, mostly heads of household. See https://search.ancestry.com/search/db.aspx?dbid=5218.

1887-1891 *Ansonia, Connecticut Directories* **[Online Database],** indexed at the Ancestry.com website. This database is a collection of four directories for the city originally published between 1888 and 1891. It is a listing of city residents in those years. In addition to providing the resident's name, it provides their address and occupational information. It includes the names of over 35,900 people, mostly heads of households. See https://search.ancestry.com/search/db.aspx?dbid=4704.

1887-1891 *Norwich, Connecticut Directories* **[Online Database],** indexed at the Ancestry.com website. This database is a transcription of city directories originally published in 1887, 1888, 1889, 1890 and 1891. In addition to providing the resident's name, it provides their address and occupational information. It includes the names of over 49,000 people, mostly heads of households. See https://search.ancestry.com/search/db.aspx?dbid=4733.

1887-1892 *Stamford, Connecticut Directories* **[Online Database],** indexed at the Ancestry.com website. This database is a transcription of city directories originally published in 1887, 1889 and 1891. In addition to providing the resident's name, it provides their address and occupational information. It includes over 17,300 names, mostly heads of households. See https://search.ancestry.com/search/db.aspx?dbid=5178.

1888-1892 *New London, Connecticut Directories* **[Online Database],** indexed at the Ancestry.com website. This database is a transcription of city directories originally published in 1888, 1890, 1891 and 1892. It includes over 25,200 names, mostly heads of households. See https://search.ancestry.com/search/db.aspx?dbid=5050.

1888-1893 *New Britain, Connecticut Directories* **[Online Database],** indexed at the Ancestry.com website. This database is a transcription of city directories originally published in 1888, 1889, 1891, 1892 and 1893. In addition to providing the resident's name, it provides their address and occupational information. It includes over 40,800 names, mostly heads of households. See https://search.ancestry.com/search/db.aspx?dbid=4853.

1889-1891 *Derby, Connecticut Directories* **[Online Database],** indexed at the Ancestry.com website. This database is a transcription of city directories originally published in 1889 and 1890. In addition to providing the resident's name, it provides their address and occupational information. It includes over 9,400 names, mostly heads of households. See https://search.ancestry.com/search/db.aspx?dbid=4839.

1889-1891 *Waterbury, Connecticut Directories* **[Online Database],** indexed at the Ancestry.com website. This database is a transcription of city directories originally published in 1889, 1890 and 1891. It includes over 47,600 names, mostly heads of households. See https://search.ancestry.com/search/db.aspx?dbid=5057.

1889-1892 *Bristol, Connecticut Directories* **[Online Database],** indexed at the Ancestry.com website. This database is a collection of seventeen directories for the three cities of Bristol, Plainville, and Terryville between 1882 and 1893. It includes the names of over 23,800 people, mostly heads of households. Archived: https://web.archive.org/web/20140917062949/https://search.ancestry.com/search/db.aspx?dbid=4411.

1889-1892 *Rockville, Connecticut Directories* **[Online Database],** indexed at the Ancestry.com website. This database is a transcription of city directories originally published in 1889, 1890 and 1891. In addition to providing the resident's name, it provides their address and occupational information. It includes over 24,400 names, mostly heads of households. See https://search.ancestry.com/search/db.aspx?dbid=5148.

1889-1894 *Winsted, Connecticut Directories* **[Online Database],** indexed at the Ancestry.com website. This database is a transcription of city directories originally published in 1889, 1890, 1891, 1892 and 1893. It includes over 27,500 names, mostly heads of households. See https://search.ancestry.com/search/db.aspx?dbid=5041.

1890 Colchester Directory, New London County, Connecticut [Online Database], indexed at the USGenWeb site for New London Co CT. See http://files.usgwarchives.net/ct/newlondn/history/direct ories/business/colchest139gms.txt.

1890 *Southington, Connecticut Directory* [Online Database], indexed at the Ancestry.com website. This database is a transcription of a city directory originally published in 1890. In addition to providing the resident's name, it provides their address and occupational information. It includes over 2,275 names, mostly heads of households. See https://search.ancestry.com/search/db.aspx?dbid=4971.

1890-1891. See *Bridgeport, Connecticut Directories, 1890-1891* [Online Database], indexed at the FamilySearch.org website. This database is a transcription of city directories originally published in 1890 and 1891. In addition to providing the resident's name, it provides their address and occupational information. It includes over 44,700 names, mostly heads of households. See https://search.ancestry.com/search/db.aspx?dbid=5123.

1891. *Who's Who in Connecticut* [Microfilm & Digital Capture], from the original book by Ward E. Duffy, published by Lewis Publishing Co., New York City, 1933, 302 pages. Filmed by W.C. Cox Co., Tucson, AZ, 1975, 1 roll, FHL film #1000147. To access the digital images, see the online FHL catalog page: www.familysearch.org/search/catalog/748268.

1884. *Ye Names & Ages of all ye Old Folks in Every Hamlet, City and Town in ye State of Connecticut, Now Living: With ye Sketches of Twenty Living Centenarians* [Book, Microfilm & Digital Version], from the original book by Frederick H. Nash, published by Prince, Lee & Co., New Haven, CT, 52 pages. Filmed by the Genealogical Society of Utah, 1955, 1 roll, FHL film #3668. To access the digital version, see the online FHL catalog page: www.familysearch.org/search/catalog/80529.

1894 City Directory, New Haven, Connecticut [Online Database], originally indexed at the DistantCousin.com website. Archived database: https://web.archive.org/web/20151029052547/http://dista ntcousin.com/Directories/CT/NewHaven/1894/

1897-1968. Connecticut Marriage Records [Online Database], an index published by the Connecticut State Library. Access via Ancestry.com: www.ancestry.com/search/collections/webctmarriages. - Or, access directly from the CT State Library: www.ctatatelibrarydata.org/marriage-records.

1898-1899. *Roster of Connecticut Volunteers Who Served in the War Between the United States and Spain* [Microfilm & Digital Capture], from the original publication of the Connecticut Adjutant General's Office, printed by Case Lockwood & Brainard, Hartford, CT, 1899, 42 pages, Filmed for the FHL by the Library of Congress Photoduplication Service, 1 roll, FHL film #1404252. To access the digital images, see the online FHL catalog: www.familysearch.org/search/catalog/3307513.

1898-1904. See *Record of Service of Connecticut Men in the Army, Navy and Marine Corps of the United States in the Spanish-American War, Philippine Insurrection and China Relief Expedition, From April 21, 1898 to July 4, 1904* [Printed Book], compiled by the Connecticut Adjutant General's Office, printed by Case, Lockwood & Brainard, Hartford, CT, 1919, 222 pages, FHL book 974.6 M2co.

1898-1904. *Connecticut Servicemen, Spanish American War* [Online Database], indexed at the FamilySearch.org website. Original data: *Records of Service of Connecticut Men in the Army, Navy, and Marine Corps of the United States in the Spanish-American War...* This database lists the men who served from Connecticut in the war, the Philippine Insurrection and the China Relief Expedition between 21 April 1898 and 4 July 1904. Records include: Name, Rank, Residence of induction, and Birthplace. This database has 3,840 records. See https://search.ancestry.com/search/db.aspx?dbid=3803.

1900. *Connecticut, 1900 Federal Census: Soundex and Population Schedules* [Microfilm & Digital Capture[, from the originals at the National Archives, Washington, DC. Filmed by the National Archives, 197?, 129 rolls, beginning with FHL film #1242468 (Soundex: A000-A352), and FHL film #1240131 (Fairfield Co). To access the digital images of certain rolls, see the online FHL catalog page: www.familysearch.org/search/catalog/647847.

1901. *Connecticut, Adjutant-General Report* [Online Database], indexed at the Ancestry.com website. Original data: *State of Connecticut Public Document No. 6, Report of the Adjutant-General, State of*

Connecticut, to the Commander-in-Chief, For the Year ended September 30, 1901. Bridgeport, CT, USA: The Marigold-Foster Printing Company, 1901. This database includes the Official Register (which provides the name, organization, residence, rank, date of rank, P.O. address, age, birthplace, and service of every member of the Connecticut National Guard); and the Abstract of Muster Rolls C.N.G. for Nov. and Dec. 1900. This database has 352 pages. See **https://search.ancestry.com/search/db.aspx?dbid=6416.**

1904-1911. *Connecticut, School Age Certificates* **[Online Database],** indexed at the Ancestry.com website. Original data: Connecticut School Age Certificate Stub Volumes, 1903–1912. Connecticut State Department of Education, Record Group 10. CT State Library, Hartford. These records relate to the oversight of child laborers, with certificates for children over 14 as proof of age. The ticket stubs may include a date, town, child's name, date, and place of birth, first names of the mother and father, and evidence provided as proof of age. This database has 10,813 records. See **https://search.ancestry.com/search/db.aspx?dbid=3029.**

1905-1929 Hartford Directories [Microfilm], by Research Publications, Woodbridge, CT. FHL copies and areas include:
- **1905-1906:** Hartford suburban directory for Bloomfield, Glastonbury, Newington, West Hartford, Wethersfield, East Windsor, South Windsor, Windsor and Windsor Locks, Conn. Film #2308491 Item 1.
- **1911-1912:** Hartford suburban directory for Bloomfield, East Windsor, Farmington, Glastonbury, Newington, South Windsor, West Hartford, Wethersfield, Windsor, and Windsor Locks, film #2308491, Item 2.
- **1913:** Hartford, Connecticut little suburban directory for the towns of Canton, Granby, Rocky Hill and Simsbury Film #2308491, Item 3.
- **1913-1914:** Hartford suburban directory for Bloomfield, East Windsor, Farmington, Glastonbury, Newington, South Windsor, West Hartford, Wethersfield, Windsor, and Windsor Locks, film #2308492, Item 1.
- **1915:** Hartford, Connecticut, little suburban directory for the towns of Avon, Canton, East Granby, Granby and Simsbury, film #2308492, Item 2.
- **1915-1916:** Hartford suburban directory for Bloomfield, East Windsor, Farmington, Glastonbury, Newington, South Windsor, West Hartford, Wethersfield, Windsor, and Windsor Locks, film #2308492, Item 3.
- **1918-1919:** Hartford suburban directory for Bloomfield, East Windsor, Farmington, Glastonbury, Newington, South Glastonbury, South Windsor, Unionville, Wethersfield and Windsor, film # 2308492, Item 4.
- **1927:** Hartford suburban (Connecticut) directory for Avon, Bloomfield, Farmington, Glastonbury, Newington, South Windsor, Wethersfield, film #2308493, Item 1.
- **1929:** Manning's Hartford suburban (Connecticut) directory for Bloomfield, Farmington, Glastonbury, Newington, South Windsor, Wethersfield, film #2308493, Item 2.

1905-1945. *Naturalization Records, Litchfield County, Connecticut* **[Microfilm & Digital Capture],** from the original records now located at the National Archives, Waltham, MA. Includes index. Filmed by the Genealogical Society of Utah, 2008, 17 rolls, beginning with FHL film #2431899 (Vol. 1, petition No. 1, 1906 – petition No. 250, 1911). To access the digital images, see the online FHL catalog page: **www.familysearch.org/search/catalog/1495438.**

1906-1945. *Naturalization Records, Windham County, Connecticut* **[Microfilm & Digital Capture],** from the original records at the Superior Court, Putnam, CT. Includes index. Filmed by the Genealogical Society of Utah, 1983-2008, 12 rolls, beginning with FHL film #2346082 (Declarations, 1906-1913). To access the digital images, see the online FHL catalog page: **www.familysearch.org/search/catalog/598966.**

1907 City Directory, Stamford, Connecticut **[Online Database],** indexed at the OldDirectorySearch.com site. See **http://olddirectorysearch.com/Stamford__Connecticut_1907/index.html.**

1910. *Connecticut, 1910 Federal Census: Soundex and Population Schedules* **[Microfilm & Digital Capture[,** from the originals at the National Archives, Washington, DC. Filmed by the National Archives, 197?, 18 rolls, beginning with FHL film #1374140 (Fairfield Co). To access the digital images, see the online FHL catalog page: **www.familysearch.org/search/catalog/648326.**

1910. *Connecticut 1910 Census Index* **[Printed Index],** compiled and published by Heritage Quest, North Salt Lake, UT, 2001, 4 vols., FHL book 974.6 X22c index v.1-4. Also on CD-ROM, see FHL CD No. 386.

1913-1928 Directories for Windham County Towns and Villages [Microfilm], by Research Publications, Woodridge, CT, including Danielson, Attawaugan, Brooklyn, Connecticut Mills, East Brooklyn, Center, Balouville, Dayville, Killingly, East Killingly, Elmville, Pineville, River View. Filmed by Research Publications, New Haven. See FHL film #2308484.

1913-1928 Directories, Connecticut River Valley [Microfilm], of city directories by DeWitt White Co., Publishers, and others. Includes the following years and areas:

- **1913-14:** The Connecticut River Valley (south of Middletown) directory, containing Centerbrook, Chester, Clinton, Cobalt, Deep River, East Haddam, East Hampton, East River, Essex, Guilford, Haddam, Higganum, Ivoryton, Lyme, Madison, Middlefield, Middle Haddam, Moodus, Niantic, Saybrook, Shailerville, Westbrook. Film #2308483 Item 2.
- **1918-1919:** Connecticut River Valley and Shore Line Directory, containing Centerbrook, Chester, Clinton, Cobalt, Deep River, Durham, East Haddam, East Hampton, East River, Essex, Flanders, Guilford, Haddam, Higganum, Ivoryton, Lyme, Madison, Middlefield, Middle Haddam, Moodus, Niantic, Saybrook, Shailerville, Westbrook Union Publishing Co., publishers. Film #2308483 Item 3.
- **1924:** Connecticut River Valley and Shore Line directory, containing Centerbrook, Chester, Clinton, Cobalt, Deep River, Durham, East Haddam, East Hampton, East River, Essex, Flanders, Guilford, Haddam, Higganum, Ivoryton, Lyme, Madison, Middlefield, Middle Haddam, Moodus, Niantic, Saybrook, Shailerville, Westbrook ... Frank P. Morse, publisher. FHL Film #2308483 Item 4.
- **1928:** Dunham's Southern Connecticut Valley and Shore Line directory, covering the towns of Chester, Clinton, Durham, East Haddam, East Hampton, East Lyme, Essex, Guilford, Haddam, Killingworth, Lyme, Madison, Middlefield, Old Lyme, Old Saybrook, Saybrook, and Westbrook, Conn., including villages of Centerbrook, Cobalt, Deep River, East River, Flanders, Higganum, Ivoryton, Middle Haddam, Moodus, Niantic, Shailerville, and Tylerville, compiled and published by Charles H. Dunham. FHL film #2308483 Item 5.

1915-1926 Estate Record Card Index [Microfilm & Digital Capture], from the original records at the Connecticut State Archives, Hartford, CT. Records are arranged alphabetically by name of deceased, with coverage for all towns of Connecticut. Each card contains name of deceased, residence, date of death, probate district, value of estate, tax information, etc. Filmed by the Genealogical Society of Utah, 1989. 19 rolls, starting with film #1503783 (Aaronson, A – Barrows, M.). To access the digital images, see the online FHL catalog page: **www.familysearch.org/search/catalog/598656.**

1917 Connecticut Military Census [Printed Article], see "1917 Connecticut State Military Census," in *Stamford Genealogical Society Bulletin*, Vol. 22, No. 3 (Feb 1980); and "1917 Military Census, World War I - Connecticut," in *Connecticut Maple Leaf*, Vol. 8, No. 2 (Winter 1997).

1917. *Connecticut, Military Census* [Online Database], indexed at the Ancestry.com website. Original data: Connecticut Military Census of 1917. CT State Library, Hartford. The Connecticut "Military Census" was taken in 1917–1918 at the direction of the General Assembly with an eye to assessing manpower available for war and other resources in the state. The census included surveys on agriculture, factories, and even automobiles, but the forms included here are questionnaires filled out by men ages 16 and over. The census was much more than a simple name count, and these questionnaires asked for details in a number of areas: Name, Post office address, Trade or profession, Age, Marital status, Number of dependents, Citizenship, Military service, and Physical disability. This database has 442,226 records. See **https://search.ancestry.com/search/db.aspx?dbid=2277.**

1917 Connecticut, World War I, Military Census of Nurses [Online Database], indexed and digitized at FamilySearch.org. Source: CT State Library, Hartford. See **www.familysearch.org/search/collection/3007513.**

1917-1918. *Connecticut, World War I Selective Service Draft Registration Cards* [Microfilm & Digital Capture], from the original draft registration cards located at the National Archives in East Point, Georgia, microfilmed by the National Archives, 1987-1988. The draft cards are arranged alphabetically by state, then alphabetically by county or city, and then alphabetically by surname of the registrants. Includes name of registrant, address, date of birth, age, race, citizenship status, birthplace, occupation, place of employment, dependent relative, marital status, father's birthplace, name, and address of nearest relative. The Cards are in rough alphabetical order. The FHL has 68 rolls of film, beginning with

FHL film #1561876. To access the digital images, see the online FHL catalog page: www.familysearch.org/search/catalog/746970.

1917-1920. *Connecticut Service Records: Men and Women in the Armed Forces of the United States During World War I* **[Printed Book],** by the Connecticut Adjutant General's Office, Includes Index. 3 vols. Contents: Vol. 1: Andover-Hartford; Vol. 2, Hartford-Plainfield; and Vol. 3: Plainfield-Woodstock. FHL book 974.6 M2cag v.1-3.

1919-1920. *Connecticut, Military Questionnaires, 1919-1920* **[Online Database],** indexed at the Ancestry.com website. Original data: *Connecticut WWI Military Questionnaires, 1919–1920.* CT State Library, Hartford. This database contains a collection of questionnaires filled out by Connecticut soldiers (or their families) who served in World War I. The questionnaires included a page of personal information followed by the respondent's war record with comments and sometimes a photograph. Each record may include: Name, Birth date and place, Citizenship, Church, Father's name and birth country, Mother's name and birth country, Spouse, Children (names, birth dates and places), Occupation prior to and following service, Employer, Current address, Residence prior to service, Date and place of induction, Unit, rank, branch of service, Service history (training, transfers, promotions, engagements, wounds, etc.), and Comments and personal experiences. This database has 13,418 records. See https://search.ancestry.com/search/db.aspx?dbid=2278.

1920. *Connecticut, 1920 Federal Census: Soundex and Population Schedules* **[Microfilm & Digital Capture[,** from the originals at the National Archives, Washington, DC. Filmed by the National Archives, 197?, 137 rolls, beginning with FHL film #1823803 (Soundex: A000-A352), and FHL film #1820174 (Fairfield Co). To access the digital images (Population Schedules only), see the online FHL catalog page: www.familysearch.org/search/catalog/559402.

1920. See **"Eastford, Admission of Electors, Roll, 1920,"** **[Printed Article].** Names listed in *Eastford Historical Society Quarterly,* Vol. 17, No. 3 (Sep 1995).

1924. *Connecticut State Register, 1924 Government & Military Records* **[Online Database],** indexed at Ancestry.com. The information in this database was compiled from the book, *State of Connecticut Register and Manual 1924* compiled by The Secretary (of State), Published by the State, Hartford, 1924. This book contains a listing of employees of the State of Connecticut for the year of 1924. Also includes military and state commissions. This database has 31,741 records. See https://search.ancestry.com/search/db.aspx?dbid=5663.

1926-1992. *Indexes to Naturalization Petitions for United States District Courts, Connecticut, 1926-1992 (Hartford)* **[Microfilm & Digital Capture],** from the original records now located at the National Archives, Waltham, MA. Lists name, volume, and page numbers. Some cards lists name, address, date of admission, petition number, name of court, and signature. The records are listed in alphabetical order by surname, Filmed by the Genealogical Society of Utah, 2004, 21 rolls, beginning with FHL film #2370728 (Aamodt, Ingeborg – Kolar, Michael). To access the digital images, see the online FHL catalog page: www.familysearch.org/search/catalog/1171116.
- **NOTE**: Use this catalog page to access the U.S. District Courts databases.

1929-1959. See *Passenger and Crew Lists of Vessels (February 1929-1959) Arriving at Bridgeport, Groton, Hartford, New Haven, and New London, Connecticut: National Archives Microfilm Publication, M1320* **[Microfilm & Digital Capture],** from original records at the National Archives, Washington, DC. From introduction: "Most of the records are of alien crew members of vessels; however, some alien and U.S. citizen passengers of vessels and airplanes, and some U.S. citizen crew members of airplanes are included. Filmed by the National Archives, series M1320, 13 rolls, beginning with FHL film #2312540 (Vessels arriving at Bridgeport, New Haven and New London, 1929-1941…). To access the digital images, see the online FHL catalog page: www.familysearch.org/search/catalog/1125757.

1930. *Connecticut 1930 Federal Census: Population Schedules* **[Microfilm & Digital Capture],** from the original records at the National Archives, Washington, DC. Filmed by the National Archives, 197?, 33 rolls, beginning with FHL film #2339989 (Fairfield Co). To access the digital images, see the online FHL catalog page: www.familysearch.org/search/catalog/1034484.

1930 & 1940. See *The Greater Hartford Directory* **[Printed Book],** includes Hartford, East Hartford, West Hartford, Wethersfield, Windsor, Bloomfield, and Newington, Hartford Printing Co., FHL books cataloged as 974.62 E4ph.

1931-1972 Manchester Directories **[Printed Books],** published New Haven, Price & Lee. FHL has 1931, 1970, & 1972. FHL books cataloged as 974.62/M1 E4p.

1931-1979 Directories **[Microfilm],** includes Torrington, Winsted, Litchfield, Norfolk, Goshen Directory: Combining Five Distinct Directories: Governmental Directory, Buyers' Directory, Alphabetical Directory, Numerical Directory, Classified Directory, 1931, 1967, 1973, 1976, and 1979. Originally published New Haven: Price & Lee, 1931. Filmed by the Genealogical Society of Utah, 1985, 2 rolls, FHL film #1425529 & 1425513.

1931-1979 Directories **[Printed Books],** includes Middletown, Portland Directory, New Haven, Price & Lee, 1931, includes index. FHL book 974.66 E4p.

1931-1980 Directories **[Printed Books],** includes Ansonia, Derby, Shelton, Seymour Directory: Combining Five Distinct Directories: Governmental Directory, Buyers Directory, Alphabetical Directory, Numerical Directory, Classified Directory, 1931, 1968, 1973-74, 1975-1976, 1980. Originally published New Haven: Price & Lee, 1931 -. FHL book 974.67 E3pa.

1940. *Connecticut, 1940 Federal Census: Population Schedules* **[Digital Capture].** After microfilming, Congress allowed the Census Bureau to destroy the originals to free up space for WWII-related files. Digitizing of the 1940 census schedules microfilm images was done for the National Archives and made public on April 2, 2012. To access the digital images, see the online FHL catalog:
www.familysearch.org/search/catalog/2057745.

1940 Federal Census Finding Aids **[Online Database].** The National Archives prepared a special website online with a detailed description of the 1940 federal census. Included at the site are descriptions of location finding aids, such as Enumeration District maps, Geographic Descriptions of Census Enumeration Districts, and a list of 1940 City Directories available at the National Archives. See
www.archives.gov/research/census/1940/general-info.html#questions.

1940-1945 Connecticut, World War II Draft Registration Cards **[Online Database],** digitized and indexed at FamilySearch.org. Source: National Archives, Records of the Selective Service System, 1926 - 1975, RG 147. See
www.familysearch.org/search/collection/2695954.

1942. *Connecticut Selective Service System Registration Cards (World War II), Fourth Registration* **[Microfilm & Digital Capture],** from the original records at the National Archives, Waltham, MA. These cards represent older men, ages 45 to 65 in April 1942, that were registered for the draft. They had birth dates between 28 April 1877 and 16 Feb 1897. The cards list a name, place of residence, age, date and place of birth, employer's name and address, and name and address of a person who will always know where they are located. The cards are arranged in alphabetical order by surname under each local draft board number. Filmed by the National Archives, 2002-2003, Series M1962, 72 rolls, beginning with FHL film #2281702 (Abalan, George – Thomas, Henry George (Local board 1A, Hartford Co). To access the digital images, see the online FHL catalog page:
www.familysearch.org/search/catalog/1120081.

1949-2012. *Connecticut Death Index* **[Online Database],** a searchable index to the official Connecticut death index created by the Connecticut Department of Health, located at the Ancestry.com website. The index contains over 1.4 million entries, with the name of the decedent, sex, race, death date, death place, place of residence, age, marital status at death, and more. Information from this database will allow a researcher to obtain a copy of a death certificate from the appropriate Connecticut office (State or Town) where the original is stored today. This database has 1,727,562 records. See
http://search.ancestry.com/search/db.aspx?dbid=4124.
- An earlier database (1949-2001), is available at the FamilySearch.org website. See
www.familysearch.org/search/collection/1946874.

1957-1962. *Hartford, Connecticut, Passenger and Crew Lists* **[Online Database],** indexed at the Ancestry.com website. Source: National Archives microfilm A3768. These passenger and crew lists from both ships and aircraft were recorded on a variety of forms that were then turned over to the Immigration and Naturalization Service. Index records include Name of the vessel and arrival date, Ports of departure and arrival (as well as future destinations on a ship's itinerary), Shipmaster, Full name (passenger/crew), Age, Gender, Physical description, Military rank (if any), Occupation, Birthplace, Citizen of what country, and Residence. For military transports, the next of kin, relationships. Later manifests include visa or passport numbers. This database has 4,064 records. See https://search.ancestry.com/search/db.aspx?dbid=9111.

1959-2012 Connecticut Marriage Index **[Online Database],** a searchable index to the official Connecticut marriage index created by the Connecticut Department of Health, located at the Ancestry.com website. The index contains the place of marriage, bride and groom's full name, age, race, nativity, and residence; state file number, marriage date, and the name of the person who performed the ceremony. This database has 2,446,650 records. See http://search.ancestry.com/search/db.aspx?dbid=7158. - This database is also available at the FamilySearch.org website. See www.familysearch.org/search/collection/1936542.

1968-1997. *Connecticut Divorce Index* **[Online Database],** a searchable index to the official Connecticut divorce index created by the Connecticut Department of Health, located at Ancestry.com.

Information may vary from year to year, but generally, each record contains: 1) Certificate Number, 2) Husband's Name, 3) Husband's birth date and state of birth, 4) Husband's race, 5) No. of marriages for Husband, 6) Husband's education, 7) Wife's name, 8) Wife's birth date and state of birth, 9) No. of marriages for wife, 10) Wife's education, 11) State of marriage, 12) Date of marriage, 13) Date of separation, 14) Children under 18, 15) Plaintiff, 16) Town of residence of plaintiff, 17) Custody of children, 18) Decree date, 19) type of decree and to whom granted, 20) Grounds for divorce, 21) Superior Court, 22) Court docket number. This database has 644,037 records. See http://search.ancestry.com/search/db.aspx?dbid=1706. -- This database is also available at the FamilySearch.org website. See www.familysearch.org/search/collection/1967742.

1988–Current. *Connecticut Newspaper Obituaries* **[Online Database].** Digitized and indexed at the GenealogyBank.com website. One search screen for obituaries published in all of the following city newspapers: Ansonia, Derby, Seymour, Bethany, Orange, Woodbridge, Bridgeport, Bristol, Cheshire, Danbury, Darien, Easton, Fairfield, Glastonbury, Greenwich, Hamden, Hamden, North Haven, Hartford, Kensington, Manchester, Meriden, Middlefield, Middletown, Milford, Monroe, Mystic, New Britain, New Canaan, New Haven, New London, New Milford, Newtown, Norwalk, Norwich, Orange, Oxford, Redding, Ridgefield, Shelton, Southbury, Southington, Stamford, Stratford, Torrington, Trumbull, Waterbury, Watertown, West Hartford, Weston, Weston-Easton, Westport, and Wilton. See www.genealogybank.com/gbnk/obituaries/explore/USA/Connecticut/.

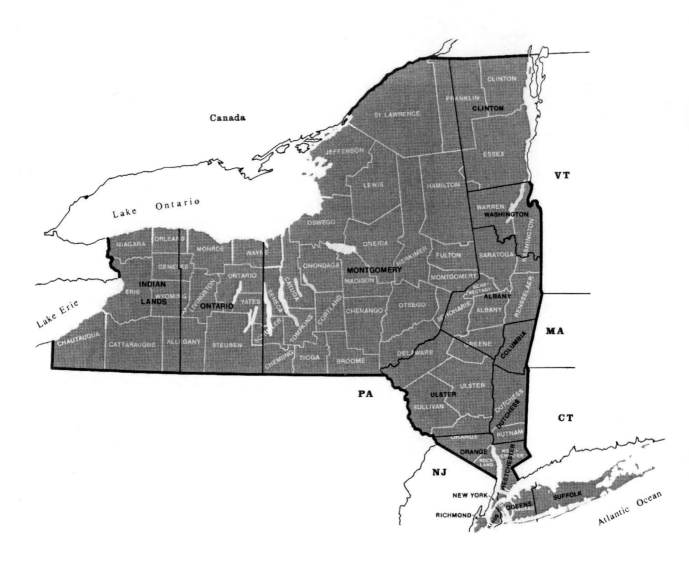

New York • Aug 1790. The 15 counties of New York at the time of the 1790 Federal Census are shown in black. The current 62 counties of New York are shown in white. **Map Source:** Page 236, *Map Guide to the U.S. Federal Censuses, 1790-1920*, by William Thorndale and William Dollarhide.

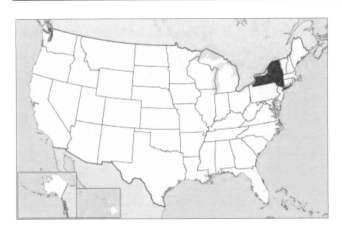

Historical Timeline of New York, 1497-1788

1497. Giovanni Caboto, an Italian sponsored by English King Henry VII, explored the Atlantic coast of North America. He claimed the area for the English King, who changed his name to John Cabot in honor of the event.

1524. Giovanni da Verrazano explored the Middle Atlantic region. An Italian hired by the King of France, he sailed past the present New Jersey coast, entered New York Bay, and saw the Hudson River, then headed north towards present Maine.

1558. Elizabeth I became Queen of England. The earliest explorations of North America took place during her 45-year reign, the Elizabethan Era, or "Golden Age."

1606. Two joint stock companies were founded, both with royal charters issued by King James I for the purpose of establishing colonies in North America. The Virginia Company of London was given a land grant between Latitude 34° (Cape Fear) and Latitude 41° (Long Island Sound). The Virginia Company of Plymouth was founded with a similar charter, between Latitude 38° (Potomac River) and Latitude 45° (St. John River).

1607. May. Led by John Smith and his cousin, Bartholomew Gosnold, the London Company established the first permanent English settlement in North America – the Jamestown Colony.

1609. Frenchman Samuel de Champlain explored the upstate New York area, after dropping down from the St. Lawrence River. He claimed the region as part of New France and managed to name several places after himself.

1609. Henry Hudson was an Englishman sailing for the Dutch East India Company, with instructions to find a shorter route to China. His first northern voyage was blocked by ice floes, so he turned west, stopping at several places later identified (by Latitude-Longitude from his ships log) as the Grand Banks of Newfoundland, Nova Scotia, Cape Cod, Chesapeake Bay, Delaware Bay, and the Hudson River. Unlike Champlain, Hudson did not give names to any of his stops, because he considered them all as reminders of his failure to find the Northwest Passage. The Hudson River seemed like the most likely candidate for the way to China, so Hudson navigated up the river as far as present Albany before giving up. His Dutch sponsors named the river for him upon his return.

1613. A Dutch trading post was set up on lower Manhattan Island. The Dutch discovered that a string of beads would buy just about anything from the Indians.

1624. Fort Orange was established by the Dutch. It was the first permanent white settlement in the New York region, located on the Hudson River, just south of present-day Albany.

1626. Dutchman Peter Minuit purchased Manhattan from the Indians for about $24.00 worth of beads and baubles (according to my 1958 High School history book). The value of the purchased land has increased a little due to inflation.

1664. The Dutch colony of New Netherland became controlled by the English after Gov. Peter Stuyvesant surrendered following a naval blockade. The English also took control of New Jersey from the Dutch.

1664. New York. King Charles II granted to his brother, James, the Duke of York, the following: "…main land between the two rivers there, called or known by the several names of Conecticut or Hudsons river... and all the lands from the west side of Connecticut, to the east side of Delaware Bay." The area was named New York for the first time.

1669. French nobleman Rene-Robert Cavelier (Sieur de La Salle), explored the Niagara region. He later floated down the entire length of the Illinois and Mississippi Rivers, claiming everything he saw for France.

1673. New York and Delaware. Dutch military forces took back New York, New Jersey, and Delaware from the English.

1674. The **Treaty of Westminster** ended hostilities between the English and Dutch and officially returned all Dutch colonies in America to the English. This ended the official Dutch presence in North America – but many of the Dutch settlements continued under English rule, particularly along the Hudson River of New York, and around Bergen in East Jersey.

1707. During the reign of Queen Anne, the **United Kingdom of Great Britain** was established after the Union with Scotland Act passed the English Parliament in 1706; and the Union with England Act passed the Parliament of Scotland in 1707. The English Colonies were now the British Colonies.

1763. Treaty of Paris. The French and Indian War ended. Great Britain gained control of all lands previously held by France east of the Mississippi River, which became the dividing line between British North America and Spanish lands. King George III declared the "Proclamation Line of 1763," as a way of rewarding the Indians who had helped Britain against the French. The proclamation established an Indian Reserve that stretched from the Appalachian Mountain Range to the Mississippi River.

1765. New York City hosted a conference dealing with the Stamp Act, recently imposed on the British Colonies by Parliament. The conference was the first cooperative effort by the colonies to resist "Intolerable Acts" imposed by the British.

1768. Treaty of Fort Stanwix. An adjustment to the Proclamation Line of 1763 took place in New York. The British government, led by Sir William Johnson, met with representatives of the Six Nations (the Iroquois) at Fort Stanwix (now Rome, NY). A new "Line of Property" was drawn, separating British Territory from Indian Territory. The new line extended the earlier proclamation line much further to the west.

From Fort Stanwix, the division line ran to Fort Pitt (now Pittsburgh) and down the Ohio River to the Tennessee River, then into the present Tennessee region. The Fort Stanwix treaty line effectively ceded most of present West Virginia and Kentucky to the British Colony of Virginia, and a sizeable area of western New York was opened for white settlement for the first time.

1776-1783. New York in the Revolutionary War. The 1777 Battle of Saratoga in New York was a major victory by the Americans; a decisive battle of the war that led the French to believe the Americans could win the war. The subsequent French alliance was to become the key to the American victory at the final battle of Yorktown in 1781. The 1783 Treaty of Paris ended the war, and the United States of America was officially recognized as an independent nation by Britain, France, and Spain.

1788. Jul. 26. **New York** ratified the U.S. Constitution and became the 11th state. Albany was the state capital.

About New York's State Censuses

The array of state census records for New York are more numerous and more complete than most other states. A few states have had more census years with territorial or state censuses, but none with the large populations of New York, and for virtually every one of the 62 counties of New York.

- For the purpose of apportionment of the New York State Assembly, the legislature authorized censuses for 1795, 1801, 1807, 1814, and 1821, but none of these early "electoral censuses" included the names of inhabitants.

- More formalized state censuses for New York began with an act in 1825, "An act to provide for taking future enumerations of the inhabitants of this state, and for procuring useful statistical tables." Under that act, state censuses were taken in 1825, 1835, 1845, 1855, 1865 and 1875; then one in 1892, followed by 1905, 1915, and the last one in 1925. In 1930, the state began using the federal decennial census population figures for apportioning the State Assembly.

- As part of the 1825 state census Act, each New York county was charged with taking the state census for their area. And, the Office of the County Clerk was named as the final repository for the original manuscripts, with instructions to "carefully preserve the tables." Two sets of the state census tables were recorded, the original set remained in the county, and

a copy was sent to the state's census office in Albany.
- Long before there was a NY State Archives, the NY State Library was the main repository for archival documents, including the state copies of the NY State Censuses.
- The importance of the "carefully preserve" provision was dramatically fulfilled after a disastrous fire in the NY State Library in March 1911. The state copies of all state censuses, 1825-1905, were reduced to ashes. The extant census manuscripts for that period we read today on microfilm or online databases, came from the original county copies held in each of the 62 counties of New York. For 1915 and 1925, most county copies exist, as well as the state copies.

About New York's Federal Censuses

A spin-off benefit of the "carefully preserve" provision of the 1825 law was that the county clerks were also keepers of their federal census schedules – there are more surviving county copies of federal censuses in New York than any other state. Beginning with 1790, the federal copies, those sent to Washington, DC, are complete for all NY counties through 1940, with the exception of the lost 1890 federal census for all states. But, only in New York are there 30 counties holding 105 county copies of original federal census schedules. (Michigan has ten counties, the next highest number of any state). Each of the NY county copies were microfilmed and digitized along with their state census originals. Thus, they can be compared with the federal copies for accuracy, i.e., missing names, different spellings, etc.

About the First Book on New York Censuses

New York State Censuses & Substitutes, by William Dollarhide, an annotated bibliography of state censuses, census substitutes, and selected name lists in 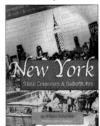 print, microform, or online. The book includes county boundary maps, 1683-1915; and state census extraction forms, 1825-1925. The identification of state censuses and substitutes is for statewide lists, and for each of New York's 62 counties. Publ. Genealogical Publishing Co, Baltimore, 2006, 250 pages, FHL book 974.7X23d. In comparison with this present work, it should be noted

that the 2006 book has state censuses and substitutes for each of the 62 New York counties in great detail. This New York Chapter is more a review of statewide resources and features updates to the 1825-1925 New York State Census databases now online.

Genealogy Resources at the New York State Archives

Dozens of online databases available at Ancestry.com or FamilySearch.org originated from the New York State Archives collections. Details about the types of records in each category can be viewed at the NY State Archives Genealogy Resources webpage. See **www.archives.nysed.gov/research/res_topics_genealogy.shtml.**

Bibliography
New York Censuses & Substitutes

1613-1674. *Genealogical and Biographical Directory to Persons in New Netherland: From 1613 to 1674* **[Printed Book],** prepared by David M. Riker, published by Higginson Book Company, Salem, MA, 1999, 4 vols. Includes bibliography, see FHL book 974.7 D24r. See also *Supplement to the 1999 Directory to Persons in New Netherland from 1613 to 1674,* by David M. Riker, published by Higginson Book Co., Salem, MA, 2004, 456 pages.

1629-1971. *New York Probate Records* **[Online Database],** digitized at the FamilySearch.org website. Images from probate records in various county Surrogate Courts in New York. Most records end in the 1920s with some indexes continuing to the year 1971.This database has 14,045,639 images. See **https://familysearch.org/search/collection/1920234.**

1629-1784. *New York Marriages* **[Online Database],** indexed at the Ancestry.com website. Source: NY State Archives. Includes names of brides and grooms, date of marriage, place of marriage, and often more information. This database has 19,477 records. See **http://search.ancestry.com/search/db.aspx?dbid=4205.**

1629-2000s. See *New York GenWeb Archives* **[Online Database].** The NYGenWeb site offers free genealogical databases with searchable name lists, which may include Bibles, Biographies, Cemeteries,

Censuses, Court, Death, Deeds, Directories, Histories, Marriages, Military, Newspapers, Obituaries, Photos, Schools, Tax Lists, Wills, and more. See **http://usgwarchives.net/ny/nyfiles.htm.**

1629-2000s. *Linkpendium – New York: Family History & Genealogy, Census, Birth, Marriage, Death Vita Records & More* **[Online Databases].** Linkpendium is a genealogical portal site, with links to local databases. Currently listed are selected sites for New York: Statewide resources Selected sites (933), Albany County (1,865), Allegany County (1,162), and 60 more counties. See **www.linkpendium.com/ny-genealogy.**

1630-1975. *New York Land Records* **[Online Database],** digitized at the FamilySearch.org website. County courthouse records. Land and property records from the New York Land Office and county courthouses. The records include land grants, patents, deeds, and mortgages. This collection includes all counties except Franklin, Nassau, and Queens. This database has 8,129,310 images. See **https://familysearch.org/search/collection/2078654**

1630s-1784. See *New York Marriages Previous to 1784: A Reprint of the Original Edition of 1860 with Additions and Corrections Including: Supplementary List of Marriage Licenses; New York Marriage Licenses, - originally - Names of Persons for whom Marriage Licenses were Issued* **[Printed Book],** by the Secretary of the Province of New York, pervious to 1784. Original printed by order of Gideon J. Tucker, Secretary of State. Albany, Weed, Parsons and Company, 1860. Reprinted with additional material by Genealogical Publishing Co., Baltimore, MD, 1968, 618 pages. FHL book 974.7 V28n 1968.

1634-1887. *Documents Relative to the Colonial History of the State of New York: Procured in Holland, England, and France, by John Romeyn Brodhead, agent* **[Printed Book],** edited E. B. O'Callaghan, 15 vols., published by Weed, Parsons & Company, Albany, NY, 1853-1887. Contents: Vols. 1-2, Holland documents, 1856-58; Vols. 3-8, Land documents, 1853-57. Vols. 9-10, Paris documents. 1855-58; Vol. 11, General Index to the documents; Vol. 12, History of the Dutch and Swedish settlements on the Delaware River, 1877; Vol. 13, History and settlements of the towns along the Hudson and Mohawk rivers (with the exception of Albany), from 1630 to 1881; Vol. 14, History of the early colonial settlements principally on Long Island, 1883; Vol. 15,

New York State Archives (vol. 1) New York in the revolution. Prepared under the direction of the Board of Regents, by Berthold Fernow, 1887. See FHL book 974.7 H2d v.1-15. For access to a digital version of all 15 vols., see the online FHL catalog page for this title. See **https://familysearch.org/search/catalog/196658.**

1640-1962. *New York Births and Christenings* **[Online Database],** indexed at the FamilySearch.org website. Name index to birth, baptism, and christening records from microfilm at the Family History Library. This database has 1,367,988 records. See **https://familysearch.org/search/collection/1680842.**

1649-1912. *Patents of the State of New York* **[Microfilm & Digital Capture],** from the original records of the New York Secretary of State, now located at the New York State Archives, Albany, NY. Includes indexes to colonial patents and the manuscript patents. Filmed by the Genealogical Society of Utah, 1973, 60 rolls, beginning with FHL film #947096 (Colonial patent card index, ca. 1637-1775 (location and tract) Albany Co. - Queens Co.). To access the digital images, see the online FHL catalog page: **https://familysearch.org/search/catalog/629503.**

1657-1950. *Encyclopedia of American Quaker Genealogy* **[Printed Book & Online Database],** by William Wade Hinshaw, Thomas Worth Marshall, editor and compiler. FHL has series published Edwards Brothers, Ann Arbor, MI, 1936-1950, 6 vols. The *Encyclopedia* provides abstracts of Quaker meeting records, including names, births, marriages, deaths, transfers, and miscellaneous details about the members of the Society of Friends. New York meetings are covered in volume 3: "Items of genealogical value from records of all meetings of all grades ever organized in New York City and on Long Island (1657 to the present)." FHL book 973 D2he vol. 1-6. To view the fully indexed and digitized version at Ancestry.com, see **www.ancestry.com/search/collections/encycloquakergen**

1659-1999. *New York, Wills and Probate Records* **[Online Database],** indexed at the Ancestry.com website. In most cases, the details found in probates include the names and residences of beneficiaries and their relationship to the decedent. An inventory of the estate assets may reveal personal details about the deceased's occupation and lifestyle. This database has 2,954,587 records. See **http://search.ancestry.com/search/db.aspx?dbid=8800**

1660-1954 New York, Church Records [Online Database], a FamilySearch database digitized and indexed at FamilySerach.org. They are from different denominations located in several counties in New York, see
www.familysearch.org/search/collection/2787817.

1663-1772. *The Documentary History of the State of New York* [Printed Book, Microfilm & Digital Version], by E. B. O'Callaghan, 4 vols., 4,350 pages, publ. 1849, Weed, Parsons & Co., Public Printers, Albany, NY. FHL book 974.7E7am. Also on FHL film #590446; another filming, FHL film #896504. This landmark history contains transcriptions of early New York censuses, rate lists, lists of early settlers, and militia rolls, but is poorly indexed. To access the digital version, see the online FHL catalog page: www.familysearch.org/search/catalog/199371.
- See also, *Lists of Inhabitants of Colonial New York: Excerpted From The Documentary History of the State of New York by Edmund Bailey O'Callaghan* [Printed Index], indexed by Rosanne Conway, published by Genealogical Publishing Co., Inc., 1979, 351 pages, FHL book 974.7 D4L. The Conway index also on 5 microfiche, FHL fiche #6046723, and includes censuses and name lists for Albany, Dutchess, Gloucester (now Vermont), Orange, Ulster, New York, Kings, Suffolk counties; plus lists for Palatines, Quakers, Moravians, and Vermont Sufferers.

1664-1775. *New York Colonial Muster Rolls: Report of the State Historian of the State of New York* [Printed Book], originally published by Wynkoop Hallenbeck Crawford Co., Albany & New York, 1897-1898, reprint by Genealogical Publishing Co., Inc., Baltimore, 2000, 2 vols. In addition to names, the lists often give a person's age and place of birth. Contents: vol. 1: Appendix H. muster rolls of a century, from 1664 to 1760; vol. 2: Appendix M. colonial muster rolls, completion of the work of publishing all rolls deposited in the state capitol, up to the outbreak of the War of the Revolution. FHL book 974.7 M2nyc v. 1-2.

1666-1775. *Index to Estate Inventories, New York County* [Online Database], indexed at the Genealogy Trails website. See
http://genealogytrails.com/ny/newyork/estateinventories.html.

1675-1920. *New York, Genealogical Records* [Online Database], indexed at Ancestry.com. Source: The Genealogical Research Library, Brampton, Ontario, Canada. This database is a comprehensive index of more than 600,000 individuals who are found in various New York records between 1675 and 1920. This database has 797,866 records. See
http://search.ancestry.com/search/db.aspx?dbid=7831.

"1684 Freeholders, Albany County, New York" [Printed Article], in *New York Genealogical & Biographical Society Record*, Vol. 3, page 71.

1686-1980. *New York Marriages* [Online Database], indexed at the FamilySearch.org website. Name index to marriage records from microfilm at the Family History Library. This database has 767,083 records. See https://familysearch.org/search/collection/1680847.

1693 Civil List of the Province of New-Yorke [Online Database], a "list of all the officers employed in the Province of New-Yorke in America the 20th of April 1693, and of their salaries." From T*he Documentary History of the State of New York,* Albany, 1849. Name list at the DunhamWilcox.net website. See
http://dunhamwilcox.net/ny/ny_civil_1693.htm.

"1697 Inhabitants, City of Albany, Albany County, New York" [Printed Article], in *The CAPITAL,* Vol. 9, No. 2 (1994) through Vol. 10, No. 1 (1995).

"1698 Fordham Census (now Bronx County)" [Printed Article], in *New York Genealogical and Biographical Record,* Vol. 38, No. 3 (Jul 1907).

1700. *List of the Officers of the Militia of the Province of New Yorke* [Online Database], from the *Documentary History of the State of New York,* Albany, 1849. Name list at the DunhamWilcox.net website. See
http://dunhamwilcox.net/ny/ny_army_1700.htm.

1700s. *Revised Master Index to the New York State Daughters of the American Revolution Genealogical Records Volumes* [Printed Book], prepared by the General Peter Gansevoort Chapter, DAR, Albany, New York. Indexed by Mrs. Jean D. Worden. Arranged in alphabetical order by surname. Contents: vol. 1. Bible records index; cemetery, church & town records index; family history index; vol. 2: Every name index to the Revolutionary War soldiers' graves. FHL book 974.7 D22w v. 1-2.

1700s-2017 New York, Wills and Deeds [Online Database], a FamilySearch database. Includes an index and images of wills and deeds from various counties in New York. See www.familysearch.org/search/collection/2739057.

1703 Census of New York City, NY [Online Database], names listed at the USGenWeb Archives site for New York. See http://files.usgwarchives.net/ny//newyork/census/1703/1703-nyc.txt.

1704-1930 U.S. Newspaper Extractions from the Northeast [Online Database], This collection contains marriage and death details extracted from various newspapers from Massachusetts, Connecticut, and New York. Details may include names, event dates, ages, family relationships, and other facts of interest. This database has 833,843 records, see www.ancestry.com/search/collections/newspaperextractions.

1704-1995 New York, Church and Civil Marriages [Online Database], digitized and indexed database from the New York Municipal Archives, various county clerk offices, Western New York Library Resource Council and St. Francis Xavier Catholic Church, New York. See www.familysearch.org/search/collection/2373836.

1720. See *Census 1720 of Freeholders of City and County of Albany, New York* [Online Database], indexed at the USGenWeb Archives site for New York: http://files.usgwarchives.net/ny//albany/census/cens1720.txt.

1723-2009 New York, Yates County, Swann Vital Records Collection [Online Database], index and images for the Swann Vital Records Collection from the Yates County History Center in Penn Yan, New York, comprising birth, marriage, and death information for the first white settlers of what is now Yates County, their descendants, and those connected with Yates County and surrounding areas. The predominant source is newspaper obituaries and marriage announcements, and the earliest source is family bibles, family registers, marriage certificates, and clergyman marriage registers. The collection is named for Frank L. Swann (1894-1987), who was the Yates County Historian from 1956 to 1980. See www.familysearch.org/search/collection/1880619.

1726-1783. Genealogical Data From Colonial New York Newspapers: A Consolidation of Articles from the New York Genealogical and Biographical Record [Printed Book], compiled by Kenneth Scott, published by Genealogical Publishing Co., Inc., Baltimore, MD, 1977, 278 pages. Material extracted from the *New York Gazette*, 1726-1744; *the New York Weekly Journal,* 1733-1751; the *New York Mercury*, 1752-1768; and the *New York Gazette* and the *Weekly Mercury*, 1768-1783; published in various volumes of the *New York Genealogical and Biographical Record* from Oct. 1964 to Oct. 1976. Includes index. FHL book 974.71 D28s.

"1730-1769 Patentees, Albany County, New York" [Printed Article], in The CAPITAL, Vol. 8, No. 3 through Vol. 8, No. 4.

"1756 Stockade Inhabitants, City of Albany, Albany County, New York" [Printed Article], in *The CAPITAL*, Vol. 1, No. 3 (Fall 1986).

1774-1776. *Inhabitants of New York* [Printed Book], by Thomas B. Wilson, published by Genealogical Publishing Co., Inc., Baltimore, MD, 1993, 358 pages. Includes New York, Queens, and Suffolk Counties. FHL book 974.7 X4w.

1775-1949 New York and Vicinity, United Methodist Church Records [Online Database], Original data: Manuscripts and Archives Division of the New York Public Library; Methodist Episcopal Church Records in New York City and vicinity. Materials include baptism registers, marriage registers, death registers, membership certificates and registers, minutes of meetings, church financial records, lists of seminary students and teachers, and more. This database has 499,925 records, see www.ancestry.com/search/collections/unitedmethodnypl.

1777-1834. *10,000 Vital Records of Eastern New York* [Online Database], indexed at the Ancestry.cm website. Source: book, same title, by Fred Q. Bowman, 1987. Archived at https://web.archive.org/web/20181209115614/http://search.ancestry.com/search/db.aspx?dbid=49003.

1785-1950. *New York, Queens County Probate Records* [Online Database], digitized at the FamilySearch.org website. Images of probate records and proceedings from the Queens County Surrogate's Court in Jamaica, New York. No index yet. Browse the volume/title for account books, administrations, mixed proceedings, wills, probates, and an occasional index book for a number of years. This database has 2,938,523 images. See https://familysearch.org/search/collection/1916211.

1787-1938. *New York, Orange County Probate Records* **[Online Database],** digitized at the FamilySearch.org website. Images of probate records and estate files from the Orange County Surrogate's Court in Goshen, New York. No index yet. Browse the records for **Estates**/years; **Wills**/years; and **Petitions for administration**/years. This database has 1,418,123 images. See https://familysearch.org/search/collection/1918465.

"1788 Tax List, Harpers Field, Delaware County, New York" [Printed Article], in *The MOHAWK,* Vol. 9, No. 3 through Vol. 10, No. 1 (1993)

1789-1835. *Holland Land Company Records.* **[Microfilm & Digital Capture],** from the original records by Biels Microfilm Corp., 1982. Also known as the Van Eeghen Collection, housed at the Municipal Archives of Amsterdam, Netherlands. Beginning in 1798, Dutch banking interests purchased over 3.3 million acres of land in western New York, covering the modern counties of Allegany, Wyoming, Genesee, Orleans, Cattaraugus, Chautauqua, Erie, and Niagara. The Holland Land Company Archives includes actual investment reports, land purchase negotiations, warrants, patents, titles, land sales ledgers, copies of land contracts, mortgages, deeds, evaluations of delinquent settlers homesteads, financial records, tax assessments and payments, legal, financial and banking records, a large variety of maps, miscellaneous documents of United States government concerns, and a wealth of correspondence between the settlers, the agents and the Dutch proprietors in three languages. For more detailed information concerning the films in this collection, refer to the Inventory of the Archives of the Holland Land Company, which is included on the introduction film to this collection. 202 rolls of film, beginning with FHL film #1421412 (Inventory of the Archives). To access the digital images, see the online FHL catalog page: https://familysearch.org/search/catalog/20454.

1790-1890 *New York, Compiled Census and Census Substitutes Index* **[Online Database],** this is one of the first census databases acquired from Accelerated Indexing to launch Ancestry.com online in 1999. It is still useful as a means of comparing different databases

for the same census years for common errors in spelling, omissions, etc. See www.ancestry.com/search/collections/nycen.

1791-1980. *New York, County Naturalization Records* **[Online Database],** indexed at the FamilySearch.org website. Card index to naturalization records from county courthouses in New York. The records may include declarations of intent, petitions, indexes, and final papers. This database has 541,771 records. See https://familysearch.org/search/collection/1999177.

1792-1906. *New York Naturalization Index (Soundex)* **[Online Database],** indexed at the FamilySearch.org website. Source: National Archives microfilm series M1674. This is an index to photocopies of naturalization documents filed in twelve courts in New York from 1792 to 1906. This database has 744,919 records. See https://familysearch.org/search/collection/2043782.

1793 Freeholders, City of Hudson, Columbia County, New York' [Printed Article], in *The COLUMBIA,* Vol. 14, No. 1 through Vol. 14, No. 3.

1794-1906. *New York, Petitions for Naturalization* **[Online Database],** indexed at the Ancestry.com website. Source: National Archives. Includes: Given name and surname, Court where petitioned, Birth date or age, Nationality, Arrival port, Arrival date, A reference to the location of the original record. This database has 1,202,522 records. See http://search.ancestry.com/search/db.aspx?dbid=2280.

1795-1949. *New York, New York City Municipal Deaths* **[Online Database],** indexed at the FamilySearch.org website. Index to New York municipal death records. The records come from the five-borough city. The time period varies by borough (county): New York City (Manhattan) 1795-1949, Bronx 1898-1948, Brooklyn 1847-1949, Queens 1898-1949, and Richmond 1898-1949. This database has 6,192,370 records. See https://familysearch.org/search/collection/2240477.

1795-1952. *New York Deaths and Burials* **[Online Database],** indexed at the FamilySearch.org website. Name index to death and burial records from microfilm at the Family History Library. This database has 249,927 records. See https://familysearch.org/search/collection/1680846.

"1798 Federal Direct Tax" [Printed Articles], Transcriptions of various name list were published in the *New York Genealogical and Biographical Record,* Vol. 113 (1982).

1799-1804. "New York State Tax Records 1799-1804: A Newly-Available Resource for Genealogists" [Printed Article], in *The NYG&B Newsletter*, Vol. 1 (1990), p 5.

1799-1804. *New York Tax Assessment Rolls of Real and Personal Estates* **[Online Database],** indexed at the Ancestry.com website. Source: NY State Archives. The tax lists include the name of the "possessor," a description of the real estate (e.g., farm, house, land), value of real estate, value of personal property, and the amount taxed. This database has 452,016 records. See http://search.ancestry.com/search/db.aspx?dbid=6771.

1800-1965 *New York, Cemetery Abstracts* **[Online Database],** abstracts from cemeteries in New York state. Compiled by the Eastern States Mission of the Church of Jesus Christ of Latter-day Saints. See www.familysearch.org/search/collection/2552111.

1801-1880. *New York, Marriage Newspaper Extracts (Barber Collection)* **[Online Database],** indexed at the Ancestry.com website. Marriages taken from the *Brooklyn Eagle,* and from the *New York Evening Post*, compiled by Gertrude A. Barber. This database has 53,006 records. See http://search.ancestry.com/search/db.aspx?dbid=8936.

1801-1890. *New York, Death Newspaper Extracts (Barber Collection)* **[Online Database],** indexed at the Ancestry.com website. Source: Deaths taken from the *Brooklyn Eagle,* and deaths taken from the *New York Evening Post,* compiled by Gertrude A. Barber. This database has 164,088 records. See http://search.ancestry.com/search/db.aspx?dbid=8920.

1804-1835. *Pioneer History of the Holland Purchase of Western New York, Embracing Some Account of the Ancient Remains: A Brief History of Our Immediate Predecessors, the Confederated Iroquois, Their system of Government, Wars, Etc., a Synopsis of Colonial History, Some Notices of the Border Wars of the Revolution* **[Printed Book, Microfilm & Digital Capture],** by O. Turner, originally published by Jewett, Thomas & Co., Buffalo, 1849, 2 vols., 666 pages; reprinted by Heritage Books, Bowie, MD, 1991.

Contains lists of names of the land purchasers from the Holland Land Company. FHL book 974.79 H2t. v.1-2. To access the digital images, see the online FHL catalog page: www.familysearch.org/search/catalog/301990.

- See also *Complete Name Index to Pioneer History of the Holland purchase of Western New York by O. Turner, 1849 and 1850* **[Book, Microfilm & Digital Version],** compiled by LaVerne C. Cooley, microfilm of original published by the author, Batavia, NY, 1946, 42 pages. Filmed by the Genealogical Society of Utah, 1971, 1 roll, FHL film #871562. Another filming, FHL film 808352. To access the digital version, see the online FHL catalog page: www.familysearch.org/search/catalog/302956.

1804-1835 Western New York Land Transactions Extracted From the Archives of the Holland Land Company **[Printed Book],** by Karen E. Livsey, Vol. 1, published by Genealogical Publishing Co., Inc., Baltimore, 1991; and *1825-1835 Western New York Land Transactions, vol. 2.,* 1996. Vol. 1 covers the first 25 years of the land tables. Vol. 2 covers the remaining 11 years before the Holland Land company ceased operations in western New York. The land tables are reproduced in the same order as found in the Holland Land Company Records, then a complete name index is included, providing a census substitute for a large area of New York. FHL book 974.7 R28L 1804-1824; and 974.7 R28L 1825-1835.

"1807 Census of Electors, Chautauqua County" [Printed Article], in *Chautauqua Genealogist*, Vol. 14, No. 2 (May 1991).

"1808 Census, Town of Taghkanic" [Printed Article], in *The COLUMBIA*, Vol. 8 (No. 3 (1992) and Vol. 8, No. 4 (1992).

1809-1850. *10,000 Vital Records of Western New York* **[Online Database],** indexed at the Ancestry.cm website. Source: book, same title, by Fred Q. Bowman, 1985. Archived at https://web.archive.org/web/20160722055934/http://search.ancestry.com/search/db.aspx?dbid=49004.

1812-1815. *New York, War of 1812 Payroll Abstracts for New York State Militia* **[Online Database],** indexed at the Ancestry.com website. Source: NY State Archives. Each abstract card includes the name of the soldier or sailor, rank, military organization, date ranges and amounts of payments, and remarks. This database has 95,494 records. See http://search.ancestry.com/search/db.aspx?dbid=5370.

1813-1850. *10,000 Vital Records of Central New York* **[Online Database],** indexed at the Ancestry.cm website. Source: book, same title, by Fred Q. Bowman, 1986. Archived at https://web.archive.org/web/20181209115913/http://search.ancestry.com/search/db.aspx?dbid=49002.

1820-1846. *New York, New York, Index to Passenger Lists* **[Online Database],** indexed at the FamilySearch.org website. Source: National Archives microfilm series M261. This is a digitized card index to early passenger lists of vessels arriving in New York Harbor. This database has 526,400 records. See https://familysearch.org/search/collection/1919703.

1820-1850. *New York, Passenger, and Immigration Lists* **[Online Database],** indexed at the Ancestry.com website. National Archives microfilm series M237. Each record may include: Gender, Birthplace, Age, Occupation, Country of origin, Port of departure, Port of arrival, Date of arrival and Destination, Name of ship (often the type of ship is noted as well). This database has 1,650,952 records. See http://search.ancestry.com/search/db.aspx?dbid=7485.

1820-1957 *New York, Passenger Lists* **[Online Database],** digitized and indexed at the Ancestry.com website. Source: National Archives microfilm series M237, T715, A3461, A3417, and A3426. This database is an index to the passenger lists of ships arriving from foreign ports at the port of New York from 1820-1957. In addition, the names found in the index are linked to actual images of the passenger lists. This database has 82,920,650 records. See http://search.ancestry.com/search/db.aspx?dbid=7488.

1820-1891. *New York Passenger Lists* **[Online Database],** indexed at the FamilySearch.org website. Source: National Archives microfilm series M237. Passenger lists for over 13 million immigrants arriving in New York City from 1820 through 1891. This database has 13,463,708 records. See https://familysearch.org/search/collection/1849782.

1824-1941. New York, Southern District Index to Petitions for Naturalization [Online Database], indexed at the FamilySearch.org website. Source: National Archives microfilm series M1676. This is an index to petitions for naturalization filed in the U.S.

District and U.S. Circuit Courts of the Southern District of New York, located in New York City. This database has 462,441 records. See https://familysearch.org/search/collection/1840501.

1824-1946. New York, Southern District, U.S District Court Naturalization Records [Online Database], digitized at the FamilySearch.org website. National Archives microfilm series M1972. Naturalization records for the U.S. District Court, Southern District which sat in New York, New York. The records from 1824-1906 have volume numbers. Records from 1906-1946 have certificate numbers. This database has 2,187,206 images. See https://familysearch.org/search/collection/2060123.

1824-1962 New York, Church and Civil Deaths **[Online Database],** from the New York Municipal Archives, New York. This database has 42,384 record, see **www.familysearch.org/search/collection/2373798.**

1825-1848. *New York Alien Residents* **[Printed Book],** compiled by Kenneth Scott and Rosanne Conway, published by Genealogical Publishing Co., Inc., Baltimore, MD, 1978, 122 pages. Depositions created under "An Act to enable resident Aliens to take and hold Real Estate and for other purposes." Passed New York legislature on 21 April 1825. Covers four volumes out of fifty-four volumes of depositions located at the New York State Library. Consists of an alphabetical list of aliens listing area of residence, date of real estate deposition, and sometimes the country or area of immigration. FHL book 974.7 R2s.

"1825 New York State Census, Town of Ellicottville, Cattaraugus County" [Printed Article], name list in *Tree Talks,* Vol. 37, No. 4 (Dec 1997).

1828. *Quaker Census of 1828: Members of the New York Yearly Meeting, the Religious Society of Friends (in New York, Ontario, Vermont, Connecticut, Massachusetts, and Quebec) at the Time of the Separation of 1828* **[Printed Book, Microfilm & Digital Capture],** compiled by Loren Fay, published by Kinship Books, Rhinebeck, NY, 1989, FHL 974.7 K2fL. The original of this census can be found on film at the FHL with the title, *A List of the Members of the New York Yearly Meeting at the Time of the Separation, 1828.* Included are the names of those Quakers who participated in the Hicksite separation, see FHL film #17363. To access the digital images, see the online FHL catalog page: **www.familysearch.org/search/catalog/126749.**

1829-1940. *New York, New York City Marriage Records* **[Online Database],** indexed at the FamilySearch.org website. Source: NYC Municipal Archives. Index to marriage records from New York City including Manhattan, Brooklyn, Bronx, Queens, and Richmond boroughs. This database has 1,740,063 records. See **https://familysearch.org/search/collection/2143225.**

1830-1916. *Wills Index, Cattaraugus County, New York* **[Online Database],** indexed at the USGenWeb Archives site. See **www.usgwarchives.net/ny/cattaraugus/wills/willstoc.htm.**

1830-1920. *New York, Census of Inmates in Almshouses and Poorhouses* **[Online Database],** indexed at the Ancestry.com website. Each record may include name, age, date of admission and discharge, sex, color, marital status, birthplace, last residence, length of time in the U.S. and in the state, port of entry, and naturalization details. This database has 249,430 records. See **http://search.ancestry.com/search/db.aspx?dbid=1083.**

1835-1855. *Index to Marriages and Deaths in the New York Herald, Vol. 1* **[Online Database],** indexed at the Ancestry.com website. Source: book, same title, by James P. Maher, 2004. This database has 38,000 deaths and 14,000 marriage records. See **http://search.ancestry.com/search/db.aspx?dbid=49239.**

"1836 Tax Assessments, Ellington, Chautauqua County" [Printed Article], in *Chautauqua Genealogist,* Vol. 21, No. 1 (Feb 1998).

"1845 New York State Census, Town of Genesee, Allegany County" [Printed Article], in *Western New York Genealogical Society Journal,* Vol. 14, No. 2 (Sep 1987).

"1845 New York State Census, Westfield, Chautauqua County" [Printed Article], name list in *Chautauqua Genealogist*, Vol. 20, No. 4 (Nov 1997).

"1845 New York State Census, Stockton, Chautauqua County" [Printed Article], name list in *Chautauqua Genealogist*, Vol. 12, No. 4 (Aug 1989).

1846-1909. *New York, New York City Births* **[Online Database],** indexed at the FamilySearch.org website. Source: NYC Municipal Archives. Index to birth records from New York City including Manhattan,

Brooklyn, Bronx, Queens, and Richmond boroughs. This database has 2,795,113 records. See **https://familysearch.org/search/collection/2240282.**

1846-1851. *New York, Irish Immigrant Arrival Records* **[Online Database],** indexed at the Ancestry.com website. Source: Famine Irish Entry Project. Each record may contain: Surname, Given Name, Age, Gender, Literacy, Native Country, Residence, Destination, Transit Type, Compartment, Port of Embarkation, Ship, Number of Passengers on the ship, Arrival Date, and Occupation. This database has 602,753 records. See **http://search.ancestry.com/search/db.aspx?dbid=5969.**

1847-1936. See *New York, County Marriages, 1847-1848; 1908-1936* **[Online Database],** indexed at the FamilySearch.org website. Name index and images of New York county marriage records. New York state began requiring marriage records for each county in 1908. The collection does not include New York City nor its boroughs. This database has 1,363,318 records. See **https://familysearch.org/search/collection/1618491.**

1850-1880 U.S. Census Non-Population Schedules, New York **[Online Database].** Original data: Nonpopulation Census Schedules for New York, 1850-1880. Microfilm. New York State Library, Documents and Digital Collections, Albany, New York. Non-population schedules contained in this database include agriculture, industry/manufacturers, social statistics, and supplemental schedules. This database has 957,876 records, see **www.ancestry.com/search/collections/nynonpopcensus.**

1850-1880 New York, U.S. Census Mortality Schedules **[Online Database],** indexed at Ancestry.com. Part of the U.S. Federal Censuses from 1850-1880 included a mortality schedule enumerating the individuals who had died in the previous year. Because each of the censuses from 1850-1880 began on June 1, "previous year" refers to the 12 months preceding June 1, or June 1 (of the previous year) to May 31 (of the census year). Questions asked in the mortality schedules: Deceased's name, Sex, Age, Color (White, black, mulatto), Whether widowed, Place of birth (state, territory, or country), Month in which the death occurred, Profession, occupation, or trade, Disease or cause of death, Number of days ill, Parents' birthplaces (added in 1870), Place where disease was contracted and how long the deceased was a resident of the area (added in 1880). This database has 263,880 records, see **www.ancestry.com/search/collections/nymortality.**

1852-1956 New York, Death Index [Online Database], indexed at Ancestry.com. Original data: NY State Death Index, New York Department of Health, Albany, NY. This collection consists of indices of deaths from the state of New York. Details vary but may include the following information for the deceased: name, death date, death city, age at death, gender, certificate number, Death records from Albany, Buffalo, and Yonkers were held locally until 1914. Records from Buffalo and Albany have been added, but deaths from Yonkers do not appear in the collection. Similarly, records from New York City were also maintained separately. Indices to New York City death records may be found in the following collections: *New York, New York, Death Index, 1862-1948;* and *New York, New York, Death Index, 1949-1965.* This database has 5,578,445 records, see **www.ancestry.com/search/collections/nystatedeathindex.**

1855. *New York State Census, 1855* [Online Database], digitized and indexed at the FamilySearch.org website. Source: County original copies on microfilm. Population schedule form includes: Dwelling numbered in order of visitation; material of which dwelling is built; value; family numbered in order of visitation; every name; age, sex and color (black or mulatto); relation to head of family; place of birth (county of New York State, other state or foreign country); married; widowed; years resident in this city or town; profession, trade or occupation; native and naturalized voters; aliens; colored not taxed; over 21 who cannot read and write; owners of land; deaf, dumb, blind, insane or idiotic. Missing counties: Clinton, Dutchess, Genesee, Hamilton, Putnam, Queens, St. Lawrence, Seneca, Suffolk, Tompkins, Westchester, and Wyoming counties. This database has 2,818,214 records. See **https://familysearch.org/search/collection/1937366.**

1855. *New York, State Census, 1855* [Online Database], indexed at the Ancestry.com website. Source: Same as the 1855 database at FamilySearch.org. This database has 2,740,414 records. See **http://search.ancestry.com/search/db.aspx?dbid=7181.**

"1855 New York State Census, Town of Clinton" [Printed Article], in *The CAPITAL,* Vol. 4, No. 2 (1989).

1856-1863. *Index to Marriages and Deaths in the New York Herald, Vol. 1* [Online Database], indexed at the Ancestry.com website. Source: book, same title, by James P. Maher, 2004. This database has 97,000 deaths and 27,000 marriage records. See **http://search.ancestry.com/search/db.aspx?dbid=49240.**

1861-1865. *New York, Civil War Service Records of Union Soldiers* [Online Database], indexed at the FamilySearch.org website. The records include a jacket-envelope for each soldier, labeled with his name, his rank, and the unit in which he served. The jacket-envelope typically contains card abstracts of entries relating to the soldier as found in original muster rolls, returns, rosters, payrolls, appointment books, hospital registers, prison registers and rolls, parole rolls, inspection reports; and the originals of any papers relating solely to the particular soldier. For each military unit, the service records are arranged alphabetically by the soldier's surname. This database has 60,000 records. See **https://familysearch.org/search/collection/1932388.**

1861-1865. *New York, Town Clerks' Registers of Men Who Served in the Civil War* [Online Database], digitized and indexed at the Ancestry.com website. Source: NY State Archives. Each record may include: Surname, State, county, town, Birth date, Residence, Rank, Regiment, Length of enlistment, Place of enlistment, and Discharge date. In some cases, the database may include Parents' names, Previous occupation, Death date, Cause of death, Place of burial, and Bounty paid. This database has 149,901 records: **http://search.ancestry.com/search/db.aspx?dbid=1964.**

1861-1865. *New York, Registers of Officers and Enlisted Men Mustered into Federal Service* [Online Database], indexed at the Ancestry.com website. Source: NY State Archives. Details may include: name, age, and color, residence, place of birth, age at time of death (where applicable), marital status, trade or occupation, voter and citizenship status, literacy, regiment first entered, date originally entered service, manner of separation from service (discharged, resigned, etc.), and much more information. This database has 138,896 records. See **http://search.ancestry.com/search/db.aspx?dbid=5434.**

1861-1900. *New York, Civil War Muster Roll Abstracts* [Online Database], indexed at the Ancestry.com website. Source: NY State Archives. Records may contain: Name, Date of enlistment, Age, Place of enlistment, Grade, Company, Regiment,

Reason for leaving, promotions, Wounds, and Physical appearance. This database has 520,120 records. See http://search.ancestry.com/search/db.aspx?dbid=1965.

1862-1948 New York, New York, Extracted Death Index [Online Database], indexed at the Ancestry.com website. The inclusive dates of deaths are different for each of the boroughs. This database has 4,716,858 records. See http://search.ancestry.com/search/db.aspx?dbid=9131.

1865. *New York State Census, 1865* [Online Database], digitized and indexed at the FamilySearch.org website. Population schedules include: Dwelling numbered in order of visitation; material of which dwelling is built; value; family numbered in order of visitation; every name (including that of anyone absent in army or navy); age, sex and color (white, black or mulatto); relation to head of family; place of birth (county of New York State, other state or foreign country); parent of how many children; number of times married; whether now married, widowed or single; profession, trade or occupation; usual place of employment; native and naturalized voters; aliens; colored not taxed; owners of land; over 21 who cannot read and write; deaf and dumb, blind, insane or idiotic; servicemen (lists those now or formerly in the army or navy of the United States). Missing counties: Allegany, Clinton, Franklin, Genesee, Hamilton, New York, Oswego, Putnam, Queens, Seneca, St. Lawrence, Sullivan, Westchester, and Wyoming counties. This database has 2,623,218 records. See https://familysearch.org/search/collection/1491284.

1865. *New York, State Census, 1865* [Online Database], indexed at the Ancestry.com website. Same as the 1865 database at FamilySearch.org. This database has 2,569,140 records. See http://search.ancestry.com/search/db.aspx?dbid=7218.

1865-1957. *New York, Eastern District Naturalization Petitions, Index* [Online Database], indexed at the FamilySearch.org website. Card index to approximately 650,000 naturalization petitions that were filed in the United States District Court for the Eastern District of New York from 1865 to 1957. The cards within each group are arranged alphabetically by the name of the person naturalized. This database has 675,035 records. See https://familysearch.org/search/collection/1840491.

1866-1897 New York, New York, Department of Health, Manhattan Birth Index Cards [Online Database], Birth index cards for the borough of Manhattan in New York City, New York for the years 1866-1897. Microfilm of original records located in the Municipal Archives, New York. This database has 14,365 records, see www.familysearch.org/search/collection/3154699.

1866-1923. *New York, Kings County Estate Files* [Online Database], indexed at the FamilySearch.org website. Source: Surrogate Court, Brooklyn. The files may include lists of heirs, oaths of executors, reports of witnesses, forms about guardians, etc. This database has 168,543 records. See https://familysearch.org/search/collection/1466356.

1866-1937 New York, New York, Extracted Marriage Index [Online Database], indexed at the Ancestry.com website. Source NYC Dept of Records. The inclusive dates of marriages are different for each of the boroughs. This database has 5,065,035 records. http://search.ancestry.com/search/db.aspx?dbid=9105.

1866-1967 New York, Staten Island, Moravian Cemetery, Interment Records [Online Database], includes interment records and index of the originals at the United Brethren Church. This database has 29,081 records, see www.familysearch.org/search/collection/3092749.

1875. *New York State Census, 1875* [Online Database], indexed at the FamilySearch.org website. Source: County copies of state censuses on microfilm. Population schedules include: Dwelling numbered in order of visitation; material of which dwelling is built; value; family numbered in order of visitation; every name; age, sex and color (white, black, mulatto or Indian); relation to head of family; place of birth (county of New York State, other state or foreign country); whether now married, widowed or single; profession, trade or occupation; usual place of employment (those who cannot read and write; and deaf and dumb, blind, insane or idiotic. Missing counties: Chemung, Clinton, Hamilton, New York (Manhattan), Niagara, Putnam, Queens, Seneca, St. Lawrence, Suffolk, and Westchester. This database has 3,125,090 records. See https://familysearch.org/search/collection/1918735.

1875. See *New York, State Census, 1875* [Online Database], indexed at the Ancestry.com website. Same as the 1875 database at FamilySearch.org. This database has 3,122,735 records. See http://search.ancestry.com/search/db.aspx?dbid=7250.

1878-1909 New York, New York, Extracted Birth Index [Online Database], indexed at the Ancestry.com website. The inclusive dates of deaths are different for each of the boroughs. This database has 2,271,164 records. See http://search.ancestry.com/search/db.aspx?dbid=9089.

1880-1956 New York, State Death Index [Online Database], Index and images of New York deaths registered between 1880 and 1956. Images provided by Reclaim the Records. This database has 4,749,222 records, see www.familysearch.org/search/collection/2803479.

1881-1942 New York State, Birth Index [Online Database], indexed at Ancestry.com. Original data: New York State Birth Index, New York State Department of Health, Albany, NY. The records may include the following information: Name, Birth Date, Birth Place, Gender, and State Certificate Number. This database has 4,831,375 records, see www.ancestry.com/search/collections/nystatebirthindex.

1881-1967 New York State, Marriage Index [Online Database], indexed at Ancestry.com. Original data: New York State Marriage Index, New York State Department of Health, Albany, NY. The collection contains only indexes to records, but the certificate number can be used to order a copy of the original certificate. This database has 8,054,307 records, see www.ancestry.com/search/collections/nystatemarriageindex.

1892. *New York State Census, 1892* [Online Database], digitized and indexed at the FamilySearch.org website. Source: County copies on microfilm at the NY State Library. Population schedule includes: 1) name, 2) sex, 3) age, 4) color, 5) country of birth, 6) citizen or alien, and 7) occupation. Missing counties: Chenango, Columbia, Franklin, Fulton, Jefferson, Livingston, New York (the Bronx and Manhattan), Oneida, Orange, Putnam, Rensselaer, Richmond, Schuyler, Seneca, St. Lawrence, Suffolk, Sullivan, Ulster, Westchester, and Wyoming counties. This database has 3,766,108 records. See https://familysearch.org/search/collection/1529100. For the Ancestry.com version, see http://search.ancestry.com/search/db.aspx?dbid=3212.

NOTE: New York conducted decennial state censuses on the 5's, 1825 through 1875. Due to political disagreements, the NY State Assembly was unable to authorize a census for 1885. The 1892 was the only census year that skipped the 5's sequence, and supplanted both the 1885 and 1895 years. New York returned to the 5's sequence thereafter with their censuses of 1905, 1915, and their last state census taken in 1925.

1882-1944. *New York, Naturalization Records* **[Online Database],** indexed at the Ancestry.com website. National Archives microfilm series M1972. The naturalization records may contain: Name of individual, Native country, Date of naturalization, Residence, Occupation, Birth date, Date and place of arrival, and Children's names. This database has 1,097,300 records. See http://search.ancestry.com/search/db.aspx?dbid=2499

1887-1921. *New York, New York, Soundex to Passenger and Crew Lists* **[Online Database],** indexed at the FamilySearch.org website. Source: National Archives microfilm series A3485. This collection contains a Soundex index to Passenger and crew Lists for vessels arriving in New York Harbor. This database has 5,800 records. See https://familysearch.org/search/collection/2443349.

1889. *New York Times, Obituaries & Marriage Notices* **[Online Database],** indexed at the Ancestry.com website. Source: *NY Times, Obituaries & Marriage Notices, 1889,* by Sherri Bobish, publ. 2001. This database has about 12,000 names. See http://search.ancestry.com/search/db.aspx?dbid=5662.

1890. *New York City Police Census, 1890* **[Online Database],** indexed at the Ancestry.com website. Source: FHL microfilm, extracted by Howard Jensen and Kristi Brown, 2001. The 1890 Police Census was conducted after the 1890 federal census for NYC was questioned for its completeness. Taken by policemen on their beats, the census proved to have 13 percent more residents than the federal census. The 1890 federal census was lost in a fire in Washington, DC in 1921, so this Police Census is a perfect substitute. This database has 51,556 records. See http://search.ancestry.com/search/db.aspx?dbid=3519.
- See also the FamilySearch version: *1890 New York, New York City, Police Census* **[Online Database]** with 1,479,855 records (no explanation why the two database have such a huge difference in numbers), see www.familysearch.org/search/collection/2381996.

1890. *New York City Directory, 1890* **[Online Database],** indexed at the Ancestry.com website. Source: Ancestry's 1890 Census Substitutes Compilation. This database has 384,407 records. Archived at https://web.archive.org/web/20160512065218/http://search.ancestry.com/search/db.aspx?dbid=3605.

1892. *New York, State Census, 1892* **[Online Database],** indexed at the Ancestry.com website. Same as the 1892 database at FamilySearch.org. This database has 3,754,629 records. See http://search.ancestry.com/search/db.aspx?dbid=3212.

1892-1924. *New York Passenger Arrival Lists (Ellis Island)* **[Online Database],** indexed at the FamilySearch.org website. Source: Ellis Island database. Name index to lists of nearly 25 million people (not just immigrants) who arrived at Ellis Island, Port of New York, 1892-1924. In addition, includes a link to images of arrival lists at the Statue of Liberty-Ellis Island Web site. This database has 24,414,218 records. See https://familysearch.org/search/collection/1368704.

"1896 Fenton School Tax Records, Broome County, New York" [Printed Article], in *Cohocton Journal,* Vol. 27, No. 2 (Apr 1999).

1898-1902. *New York, Spanish-American War Military and Naval Service Records, 1898-1902* **[Online Database],** indexed at the Ancestry.com website. Source: NY State Archives. Details on the cards can include: soldier's name, rank, company, and regiment at enlistment, enlistment date and place, residence at time of enlistment, names of organizations served in, ranks held during service, engagements, wounds received, date, cause, and rank held at separation from service, birthplace, age at enlistment, occupation, physical description, remarks.
This database has 56,974 records. See http://search.ancestry.com/search/db.aspx?dbid=5351.

1900-1935. *New York City Directories* **[Online Database],** indexed at the FamilySearch.org website. The title should be "City Directories from over 60 Cities of the State of New York." Source: Collection on microfilm at the New England Historic Genealogical Society, Boston. This database requires a search in the Browse this Collection search box for the locality and the year of the publication. This database has 49,324 records. See http://search.ancestry.com/search/db.aspx?dbid=8773.

1902-1956. New York, Northern Arrival Manifests [Online Database], indexed at the FamilySearch.org website. This collection comprises two record sets from the National Archives: Manifests of alien arrivals at Buffalo, Lewiston, Niagara Falls, and Rochester, New York, 1902-1954 (NARA M1480) and Soundex card manifests of alien and citizen arrivals at Hogansburg, Malone, Morristown, Nyando, Ogdensburg, Rooseveltown, and Waddington, New York, July 1929-April 1956 (NARA M1482). These card manifests, arranged in Soundex order, document over 1,000,000 arrivals. See https://familysearch.org/search/collection/1876434.

1905. *New York State Census, 1905* **[Online Database],** indexed at the FamilySearch.org website. Source: County originals on microfilm. The population schedule includes an address; name; relation to head of family; color, sex and age; place of birth (U.S. or foreign country); number of years in United States; citizen or alien; occupation; and inmates of institutions (residence at time of admission). This database has 7,513,232 records. See https://familysearch.org/search/collection/1463113.

1905. *New York, State Census, 1905* **[Online Database],** indexed at the Ancestry.com website. Same as the 1905 database at FamilySearch.org. This database has 7,213,631 records. See http://search.ancestry.com/search/db.aspx?dbid=7364.

1906-1942. New York Book Indexes to Passenger Lists [Online Database], digitized at the FamilySearch.org website. Source: National Archives microfilm series T612. This is a collection of images of book indexes to passenger manifests for vessels arriving at New York Harbor. This database has 748,065 records. See https://familysearch.org/search/collection/2299396.

1906-1948. See *New York, New York Guard Service Cards, 1906-1918, 1940-1948* **[Online Database],** digitized and indexed at the Ancestry.com website. Source: NY State Archives. This database contains service record cards for veterans of the New York Guard for both the WWI and WWII eras. This database has 286,117 records. See http://search.ancestry.com/search/db.aspx?dbid=6081.

1906-1954. *New York Records of the State National Guard* **[Online Database],** digitized and indexed at the FamilySearch.org website. Index and images of National Guard service cards from the New York State Archives. This database has 724,527 records. See https://familysearch.org/search/collection/2329262.

1907-1966. *New York, Western District, Naturalization Index* **[Online Database],** indexed at the FamilySearch.org website. Source: National Archives microfilm series M1677. This is a digitized card index to petitions for naturalization recorded in Buffalo and Rochester, New York. This database has 89,554 records. See https://familysearch.org/search/collection/1854307.

1907-2018 New York, New York, Marriage License Indexes **[Online Database],** records from 1907 to 1951 present indexes of marriage licenses issued by the New York City Clerk and are accompanied by images. Note that the bride and groom appear on separate images, listed alphabetically according to surname. These records may contain name of the bride or groom, marriage license date, page number, volume number, marriage license number, The marriage licenses, affidavits, and certificates themselves are not available online at this time; these abstracts were created with limited information for filing purposes. Records from 1950 to 2018 are presented index only and also represent an index of marriage licenses. These records may contain the following information: name of bride and groom, marriage license date, marriage license place, marriage license number, Note: For select marriage events between 1950-1953, marriage licenses may be listed twice, with and without image. This database has 15,554,761 records, see www.ancestry.com/search/collections/nycmarriageindex.

1909-1957. See **New York, New York Passenger and Crew Lists, 1909, 1925-1957 [Online Database],** indexed at the FamilySearch.org website. Source: National Archives microfilm series T715. Passenger arrivals to New York Harbor. This database has 29,488,850 records. See https://familysearch.org/search/collection/1923888.

1910-1965 New York, New York, Birth Index **[Online Database],** digitized and indexed at Ancestry.com. Original data: New York City Department of Health, courtesy of www.vitalsearch-worldwide.com. Digital Images. Within these images, you can expect to find a variety of information, including: Name, Date of Birth, Borough in which they were born, This database has 7,864,162 records, see www.ancestry.com/search/collections/vsnybirths.

1914-1919. See *New York, Abstracts of World War I Military Service, 1917-1919* **[Online Database],** indexed at the Ancestry.com website. Source: NY State Archives. This collection includes index cards listing details abstracted from federal military service records for Army officers, enlisted men, sailors, Marines, and nurses who enlisted or were drafted in New York, beginning in 1914. This database has 514,859 records. See http://search.ancestry.com/search/db.aspx?dbid=3030.

1914-1931. New York, Bronx Probate Estate Files [Online Database], digitized at the FamilySearch.org website. Name indexes and images of estate files. The files may include lists of heirs, oaths of administrators, reports of witnesses, forms about guardians, etc. This database has 771,828 images. See https://familysearch.org/search/collection/1856428.

1915. *New York State Census, 1915* **[Online Database],** indexed at the FamilySearch.org website. Source: NY State Archives. The population schedule includes an address, name; relation to head of family; color, sex and age; place of birth (U.S. or foreign country); number of years in United States; citizen or alien; if naturalized, when and where; occupation, inmates of institutions (residence at time of admission); and infants under one year. This database has 9,742,867 records. See https://familysearch.org/search/collection/1937454.

1915. *New York, State Census, 1915* **[Online Database],** indexed at the Ancestry.com website. Same as the 1915 database at FamilySearch.org. This database has 9,756,993 records. See http://search.ancestry.com/search/db.aspx?dbid=2703.

1917-1918. *Biographies from Who's Who in New York* **[Online Database],** indexed at the GenealogyTrails.com website. See http://genealogytrails.com/ny/newyork/bios_index.html.

1917-1919 New York, Abstracts of World War I Military Service **[Online Database],** digitized and indexed at Ancestry.com. New York sent more soldiers to fight in World War I than any other state in the Union. In fact, New Yorkers represented more than 10 percent of U.S. troops. This collection includes cards listing details abstracted from federal military service records for Army officers, enlisted men, sailors, Marines, and nurses who enlisted or were drafted in New York. The majority of the records begin in 1914 and continue through 1919. The cards include the following details: name, serial/service number, race, place and date of enlistment or induction, place of birth, age or date of birth, service organization(s) with assignment dates and transfers, rank (grade) with date of appointment engagements, whether wounded in action, how badly and date, overseas service dates, discharge/separation date and information, and degree of disability at discharge. This database has 514,859 records, see www.ancestry.com/search/collections/nyabstractswwi.

1917-1954. *New York, New York National Guard Service Cards* **[Online Database],** indexed at the Ancestry.com website. Source: NY State Archives.

Each record may include name, address, date of enlistment, company, and regiment. This database has 254,183 records. See http://search.ancestry.com/search/db.aspx?dbid=60808.

1917-1957. *New York, New York, Index to Alien Crewmen Who Were Discharged or Who Deserted* **[Online Database],** digitized and indexed at the FamilySearch.org website. Source: National Archives microfilm series A3417. This is a digitized card index to the passenger lists on microfilm series T715. This database has 1,270,298 records. See https://familysearch.org/search/collection/2467808.

1917-1966. *New York, Southern District Naturalization Index* **[Online Database],** indexed at the FamilySearch.org website. Source: National Archives microfilm series M1675. This is a collection of digitized card indexes for Declarations of Intention recorded in New York City. This database has 560,546 records. See https://familysearch.org/search/collection/1840493.

1917-1974. *New York State, Passenger and Crew Lists* **[Online Database],** indexed at the Ancestry.com website. Source: National Archives: *Selected Passenger and Crew Lists and Manifest*. Contained in this database are passenger arrival and departure lists, and crew arrival and departure lists for vessels that were filed in Buffalo, New York, 1945–1974, Oswego, 1917–1972, Rochester, New York, 1944-1958, and Sodus Point, New York, 1945-1957. This database has 1,807,152 records. See http://search.ancestry.com/search/db.aspx?dbid=1277.

1924 New York, New York, Voter List **[Online Database],** Original data: New York City Municipal Archive, New York. Lists are organized by borough (Bronx, Brooklyn, Manhattan, Queens, or Staten Island). From there, records are broken down by Assembly District, and from there, by Election District, street, and finally, house, or dwelling number. Voter registers are great records to use as census substitutes, since they will usually contain the names of heads of households, as well as other adults living in the same dwelling between census years. See www.ancestry.com/search/collections/1924nycvoters.

1925. *New York State Census, 1925* **[Online Database],** indexed at the FamilySearch.org website. Source: NY State Archives. The population schedule includes an address, name; relation to head of family; color, sex, and age; place of birth (U.S. or foreign country); number of years in United States; citizen or alien; if naturalized, when and where; occupation, inmates of institutions (residence at time of admission); and infants under one year. This database has 11,117,922 records. See https://familysearch.org/search/collection/1937489.

1925. *New York, State Census, 1925* **[Online Database],** indexed at the Ancestry.com website. Same as the 1925 database at FamilySearch.org. This database has 11,117,985 records. See http://search.ancestry.com/search/db.aspx?dbid=2704.

1940-1945. *New York, WWII Enlisted Men Cards* **[Online Database],** indexed at the Ancestry.com website. Source: New York State Military Museum. This database contains a service card file for New York National Guard enlisted men and noncommissioned officers activated for federal service during World War II. In federal service, the men were organized as the 27th Infantry Division. The unit was federalized in October 1940 and mustered out of service in late 1945. The cards list an individual's name, home address, date of birth, place of birth, New York State service history (enlistment dates, etc.), U.S. service history (enlistments dates, etc.). This database has 29,428 records. See http://search.ancestry.com/search/db.aspx?dbid=2341.

1941-1945. *World War II Enlistments, Bronx County, New York* **[Online Database],** indexed at the USGenWeb Archives site for New York. See www.usgwarchives.net/ny/bronx/military/militarytoc.htm.

1948-1972 New York, Ogdensburg Passenger and Crew Lists **[Online Database],** This collection contains Passenger and Crew Lists of Vessels Arriving at (1948-1972) and Departing From (1960-1968) Ogdensburg, New York. The records are arranged in chronological order. The arrival lists mostly contain crew members. It corresponds with NARA publication A3409 and was filmed at the NARA facility in Washington D.C. This database has 4,565 records, see www.familysearch.org/search/collection/2427236.

1949-1965 New York, New York, Death Index **[Online Database],** digitized and indexed at Ancestry.com. Original data: New York City Department of Health, courtesy of www.vitalsearch-worldwide.com. Digital Images. Within these images, you can expect to find a variety of information, including: Name, Age at Death, Date of Death, Death Certificate Number, Borough in which they died. This database has 1,883,314 records: www.ancestry.com/search/collections/nydeathindexlate.

1950-1995 New York, City Marriage Licenses Index **[Online Database],** from the originals at the New York City Clerk's Office, filmed by Reclaim the Records: The NYC Marriage Index. This database has 3,124,586 records, see www.familysearch.org/search/collection/2727138.

1954-1956 New York Rouses Point and Waddington Crew Lists **[Online Database],** this collection contains Crew Lists of Vessels Arriving at Rouses Point and Waddington, New York, 1954-1956. The records may include name of vessel, ports of departure and arrival; date of arrival; and the following information about each crew member: full name, citizenship, position in crew and identification number. These records correspond with NARA publication A3449 and were filmed at the NARA facility in College Park, Maryland. This database has 4,158 records, see www.familysearch.org/search/collection/2443343.

1957-1963. *New York State Health Department, Genealogical Research Death Index* **[Online Database],** indexed at FamilySearch.org. Source: NY Dept of Health. Index to death records from the state of New York, excluding New York City. This database has 590,658 records. See https://familysearch.org/search/collection/2285574.
- See also *New York State, Death Index, 1957-1968* **[Online Database],** indexed at Ancestry.com. This database has 1,242,391 records, see www.ancestry.com/search/collections/newyorkstatedeathindex.

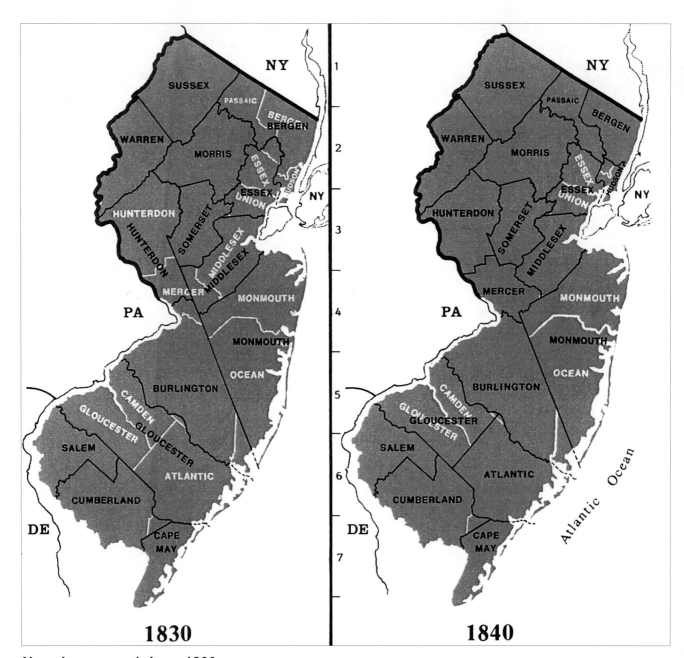

1830   **1840**

New Jersey • 1 June 1830. Shown in black on the left-hand map are the 14 counties of New Jersey at the time of the 1830 Federal Census. New Jersey's 21 current counties, where different, are in white. New Jersey's first four Federal Censuses, 1790-1820, were lost. The only difference in county boundaries between the years 1790 and 1830 was the addition of Warren County, taken from Sussex in 1824.

New Jersey • 1 June 1840. The right-hand map shows the 18 counties of New Jersey at the time of the 1840 Federal Census. Counties formed after 1840: Camden County, taken from Gloucester in 1844; Ocean County, taken from Monmouth in 1850; and Union County, taken from Essex in 1857.

New Jersey
Censuses & Substitute Name Lists

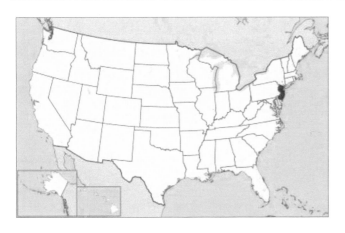

Historical Timeline of New Jersey, 1497-1788

1497. Giovanni Caboto, an Italian sponsored by English King Henry VII, explored the Atlantic coast of North America. He claimed the area for the English King, who changed his name to John Cabot in honor of the event.

1524. Giovanni da Verrazano explored the Middle Atlantic region. An Italian hired by the King of France, he sailed past the present New Jersey coast, entered New York bay, then headed north towards present Maine.

1558. Elizabeth I became Queen of England. The earliest explorations of North America took place during her 45-year reign, the Elizabethan Era, or "Golden Age."

1606. Two joint stock companies were founded, both with royal charters issued by King James I for the purpose of establishing colonies in North America. The Virginia Company of London was given a land grant between Latitude 34° (Cape Fear) and Latitude 41° (Long Island Sound). The Virginia Company of Plymouth was founded with a similar charter, between Latitude 38° (Potomac River) and Latitude 45° (St. John River).

1607. May. Led by John Smith and his cousin, Bartholomew Gosnold, the London Company established the first permanent English settlement in North America – the Jamestown Colony.

1608. English Capt. John Smith of the Jamestown Colony, explored Chesapeake Bay. He was probably looking for crab cakes.

1609. New York. Samuel de Champlain explored the upstate New York area, after dropping down from the St. Lawrence River. He claimed the region as part of New France and managed to name several places after himself.

1609. Delaware. Henry Hudson, an Englishman sailing for the Dutch East India Company, discovered Delaware Bay and River. A year later, Captain Samuel Argall, an English sea captain, named the bay and river after Thomas West, Baron De La Warr, governor of Virginia.

1613. New York. A Dutch trading post was set up on lower Manhattan Island. The Dutch discovered that a string of beads would buy just about anything from the Indians.

1638. Delaware. Dutchman Peter Minuet led a group of Swedes to the Delaware and established Fort Christiana (now Wilmington), the first permanent settlement on the Delaware and the founding of the New Sweden Colony.

1651. Delaware. Peter Stuyvesant, Dutch governor of New Netherland, built Fort Casimir (now New Castle) just a few miles south of Fort Christina on the Delaware, but the Swedes were not pleased with the Dutch intrusion.

1654. Delaware. The Swedes captured Fort Casimir and renamed it Fort Trinity. A year later the Dutch defeated the Swedes, ending the New Sweden colony, and Delaware became part of New Netherland. But, several Swedish communities continued.

1660. New Jersey. Bergen was established by the Dutch, the first permanent town in present New Jersey.

1664. New York and New Jersey. The Dutch colony of New Netherland became controlled by the English after Gov. Peter Stuyvesant surrendered to the English following a naval blockade. The English also took control of New Jersey from the Dutch. King Charles II granted to his brother, James, the Duke of York, the following: "…main land between the two rivers there, called or known by the several names of Conecticut or Hudsons river… and all the lands from the west side of Connecticut, to the east side of Delaware Bay." The area was named New York for the first time.

1664. Delaware. Sir Robert Carr drove the Dutch off the Delaware and claimed the land for James, Duke of York. Delaware then became an English colony.

1665-1674. New Jersey. In 1665, James, Duke of York, granted to Sir George Carteret and Lord Berkley of Stratton, a part of the New York colony between the Hudson River and the Delaware River. In 1674, Berkley sold his share to the Quakers. Carteret's original portion was then named East New Jersey, and the Quaker's portion was named West New Jersey.

1674. The Treaty of Westminster ended hostilities between the English and Dutch and officially returned all Dutch colonies in America to the English. This ended the official Dutch presence in North America – but many of the Dutch settlements continued under English rule, particularly along the Hudson River of New York, and East Jersey.

1676. West New Jersey. Still in England, William Penn was heavily involved in the transportation of Quakers to the West Jersey Colony. He was a trustee in the colony's establishment and was responsible for drawing up the first set of laws. They would become the basis for the Great Experiment he envisioned for Pennsylvania a few years later.

1681. Pennsylvania. William Penn was granted land in North America by Charles II to establish the colony of Pennsylvania. He arrived in October 1682 on the ship *Welcome*. He visited Philadelphia, just laid out as the capital city, and soon after his arrival, summoned a General Assembly, called for uniting Delaware with Pennsylvania, and created the first three Pennsylvania counties of Bucks, Chester, and Philadelphia.

1682. Delaware. James, the Duke of York, transferred control of the Delaware Colony to English Quaker William Penn.

1702. New Jersey. East and West Jersey were combined into one colony. The two Proprietors appointed a governor for the Province of New Jersey, but with continued land sales by both East New Jersey and West New Jersey. Thereafter, the two land offices remained intact under the administration of Land Commissions, for the purpose of selling land to individuals. Both commissions still exist today.

1707. During the reign of Queen Anne, the **United Kingdom of Great Britain** was established after the Union with Scotland Act passed the English Parliament in 1706; and the Union with England Act passed the Parliament of Scotland in 1707. The English Colonies were now the British Colonies.

1755. French and Indian War. Gen. Edward Braddock led an expedition through Maryland and Pennsylvania to the west, building Braddock's Road, the first overland route from Maryland to the Ohio River, but French-led Indians defeated Braddock's forces near Fort Duquesne (now Pittsburgh). The original trace of Braddock's road was blazed by a 21-year old George Washington.

1763. Treaty of Paris. The French and Indian War ended. Great Britain gained control of all lands previously held by France east of the Mississippi River, which became the dividing line between British North America and Spanish lands west of the Mississippi.

1776-1783. Revolutionary War. The 1783 Treaty of Paris ended the war, and the United States of America was officially recognized as an independent nation by Britain, France, and Spain.

1787. Dec. 12. **New Jersey** became the 3rd state to join the Union just a few hours after Pennsylvania.

New Jersey's State Censuses, Federal Censuses, and Ratable Lists

NJ State Censuses: For the purpose of apportionment of its General Assembly, New Jersey began taking state censuses in 1855. They continued every ten years thereafter until the last one in 1915. The 1855 and

1865 censuses have some missing counties but cover most of the state. The worst losses are for the 1875 census, which has just three counties with name lists. The 1885 through 1915 censuses are complete for all counties. All of the extant census originals were microfilmed by the NJ State Archives and copies are available elsewhere, including the FHL library in Salt Lake City. The available state censuses were digitized and indexed by both FamilySearch.org and Ancestry.com under their sharing agreements. Looking at each database will tell you who did the indexing and who did the digitizing. In addition, Ancestry.com has an 1875 name list online for Sussex County only. And, the NJ State Archives has a searchable online index for the 1885 State Census for Passaic County and Atlantic city.

NJ Federal Censuses: The first four censuses of 1790, 1800, 1810, 1820; and 1890 were all lost (the most census losses of any state). Beginning with the 1830, they are complete for all counties through 1940, with the exception of the lost 1890 federal census for all states. The 1950 census name lists will open to the public in 2022.

NJ Ratable Lists. From the 1700s through the 1800s, numerous tax lists were prepared at the county level in New Jersey. A person named in one of these assessment lists of county residents was called a "ratable." Many of the original Ratable Lists are now at the NJ state archives. After the NJ Federal and State Censuses, the NJ Ratable Lists probably provide the next best chance of finding a lost ancestor in New Jersey.

New Jersey State Archives

Genealogical and Colonial Records. There are many original records with value to genealogists at the New Jersey State Archives. The list of genealogical resources includes state censuses, ratable lists, vital records, deeds, wills, probates, orphans, and militia. For more specific details, see
www.nj.gov/state/archives/catsestat01.html.

Searchable Online Databases are categorized under Birth, Marriage, and Deaths; Land, Probate, and Court; and Military & Wartime:

Birth, Marriage, and Death Records:
- **Colonial Marriage Bonds**, ca. 1666-1799
  11,533 marriage bonds
- **Marriage Records,** May 1848 - May 1878
  146,111 marriage records

- **Death Records,** June 1878 - June 1894
  Over 450,000 death records (Data entry ongoing)

Land, Probate and Court Records:
- **Early Land Records**, ca. 1650-1801
  22,979 land records, over 59,300 names
  (Data entry ongoing)
- **Supreme Court Case Files**, 1704-1844
  54,912 case files, over 188,400 names
  (Data entry ongoing)
- **Legal Name Changes**, 1847-1947
  12,253 name changes, 46,008 names
- **1885 State Census** - Passaic County and Atlantic City. 69,302 names

Military and Wartime Records:
- **Revolutionary War Damage Claims**, 1776-1782
  2,662 claims, 7,435 names
- **Civil War Service Records**, 1861-1865
  82,471 names
- **Civil War Payment Vouchers**, 1861-1865
  15,770 vouchers, 113,736 names
- **World War I Deaths**
  3,427 names (9,310 scanned images)
  Descriptive cards, photographs and correspondence
- **New Jersey National Guard Photographs**
  1,316 images

For more information about Searchable Databases, Research Request Forms, and more, see
https://web.archive.org/web/20170614221453/https://wwwnet1.state.nj.us/DOS/Admin/ArchivesDBPortal/index.aspx.

Bibliography
New Jersey Censuses & Substitutes

1630-1923 History of Bergen County, New Jersey **[Online Database],** indexed at the Ancestry.com website. Source: Book, same title, by Frances Augusta Johnson Westervelt, publ. 1923. This database has 1,202 pages, see
http://search.ancestry.com/search/db.aspx?dbid=13763.

1630-1924 History of the Municipalities of Hudson County, New Jersey **[Online Database],** indexed at the Ancestry.com website. Source: Book, same title, by Daniel Van Winkle, publ. 1924. Full text page images with an OCR index. This database has 1,200 pages, see
http://search.ancestry.com/search/db.aspx?dbid=13801.

1631-1782 New Jersey, Published Archives Series [Online Database], indexed at the Ancestry.com website. This database contains 27 volumes from the New Jersey Archives series: *Calendar of Records in the Office of the Secretary of State* (1664–1703; 1 volume). These include records of land sales, deeds, arrest warrants, letters of administration, powers of attorney, inventories of estates, licenses, commissions, orders declaring cohabitation and unlawful marriage, indentures, and other documents. *Documents Relating to the Colonial History of the State* (1631–1776; 10 volumes). These include letters and correspondence, minutes, accounts, petitions, indentures, affidavits, memoranda, and other documents. *Journal of Governor and Council* (1682–1775; 6 volumes).The journal contains minutes from meetings and actions of New Jersey's governor and provincial council. *Newspaper Extracts* (1704–1782; 16 volumes). These include mention of military matters, political and editorial comments and letters, announcements of property sales, runaway soldiers and slaves, reports on court proceedings, "names of Tories of New Jersey, whose property had been confiscated and was to be sold," naval engagements, eulogies, "announcements of horse breeders," "the loss of lottery tickets," legislative appointments, and other items. Many of the volumes have indexes at the back. See http://search.ancestry.com/search/db.aspx?dbid=2175.

1631-1825 Ship Passenger Lists, New York and New Jersey [Printed Book], compiled and indexed by Carl Boyer, III, Newhall, CA: publ. by C. Boyer, 1978, 333 pages. Contains reprints of passenger lists named in Lancour's Bibliography of Ship Passenger Lists. See FHL book 973 W3.

1631-2000s. New Jersey GenWeb Archives [Online Database]. The NJGenWeb site offers free genealogical databases with searchable name lists, which may include Bibles, Biographies, Cemeteries, Censuses, Court, Death, Deeds, Directories, Histories, Marriages, Military, Newspapers, Obituaries, Photos, Schools, Tax Lists, Wills, and more. See http://usgwarchives.net/nj/njfiles.htm.

1631-2000s. Linkpendium – New Jersey: Family History & Genealogy, Census, Birth, Marriage, Death Vita Records & More [Online Databases]. Linkpendium is a genealogical portal site, with links to local databases. Currently listed are selected sites for New Jersey: Statewide resources Selected sites (656), Atlantic County (522), Bergen County (922), Burlington County (670), Camden County (516), Cape May County (347), Cumberland County (456), Essex County (1,294), Gloucester County (410), Hudson County (737), Hunterdon County (617), Mercer County (887), Middlesex County (711), Monmouth County (861), Morris County (761), Ocean County (401), Passaic County (649), Salem County (393), Somerset County (513), Sussex County (559), Union County (703), and Warren County (501). See www.linkpendium.com/nj-genealogy.

1660-1775. *General Index to the Documents Relating to the Colonial History of the State of New Jersey* [Printed Book], prepared by Frederick W. Ricord, originally published Newark, NJ, 1888, reprint by Genealogical Research Society of New Orleans, 1994, 198 pages. See FHL book 974.9 H22r.

1660-1777. *Early Settlers of Bergen County* [Online Database], an excellent review, and names of the first land owners of the area, starting with grants of land made by Governor Carteret.. Includes many of the descendants of the original settlers. See https://sites.google.com/site/bergencogenweb/home/history/early-settlers-of-bergen-county.

1660-1856. *Index to Deeds, Surveys and Commissions. Originals and Indexes from all West Jersey and East Jersey Counties* [Microfilm & Digital Capture], an index to the original records of the Department of State, now at the New Jersey State Archives. Includes Grantee-Grantor indexes for all New Jersey counties, which can serve as a better list of residents in an area than a heads of household census. See FHL film #539948. To access the digital images, see the online FHL catalog page: www.familysearch.org/search/catalog/136219.

1660-1931 New Jersey, Births and Christenings Index [Online Database], indexed at the Ancestry.com website. FamilySearch extractions from microfilm at the Family History Library, Salt Lake City, UT. Each record may include name, gender, race, birthplace, birth date, christening, place, christening date, death date, age at death, father's name, age, birthplace, mother's name, age, birthplace, paternal grandparents, maternal grandparents, and FHL film number. This database has 4,513481 records. See http://search.ancestry.com/search/db.aspx?dbid=2539.

1660-1980 New Jersey Births and Christenings [Online Database], indexed at the FamilySearch.org website. Name index to birth, baptism and christening records from microfilm at the Family History Library,

Salt Lake City, UT. This database has 1,148,023 records. See https://familysearch.org/search/collection/1675383.

1664-1920 History of Middlesex County, New Jersey [Online Database], indexed at the Ancestry.com website. Source: Book, same title, by John P. Wall, publ. 1921. The original book, with full text page images and an OCR index. This database has 1,173 pages.
http://search.ancestry.com/search/db.aspx?dbid=15468.

1666. Documents Relating to the Colonial History of the State of New Jersey, vol. 1, pp 15-16, N.J. Archives [from Grants and Concessions, p.669] Indian Deed for Elizabethtown Grant [Online Database], text at the USGenWeb Archives site for New Jersey. See
http://files.usgwarchives.net/nj/statewide/history/new_je2.txt

1666-1924 Municipalities of Essex County, New Jersey [Online Database], indexed at the Ancestry.com website. Source: Book, same title, publ. Lewis Historical Publishing Co., 1925. Full text page images with an OCR index. This database has 1,542 records. See
http://search.ancestry.com/search/db.aspx?dbid=13845.

1670-1760 Calendar of New Jersey Wills [Online Database], indexed at the Ancestry.com website. Source: NJ Historical Society, Calendar of New Jersey Wills, Administrations, etc, 1901. This database has 32,291 records. See
http://search.ancestry.com/search/db.aspx?dbid=4723.

1670-1817 New Jersey, Abstract of Wills [Online Database], indexed at the Ancestry.com website. NJ Archives, Published Archives series. Abstracts capture and summarize the main points of a will and can include details such as dates, names, place of residence, spouse, family members, date proved, executors, the value of an inventory made of the estate, and descriptions of real estate and bequests. Documents abstracted may also include inventories and records related to administrations and guardianships. This database has 34,004 records. See
http://search.ancestry.com/search/db.aspx?dbid=2793.

1670-1980 New Jersey Births [Online Database], indexed at the FamilySearch.org website. Source: NJ State Archives. Each record includes, at least, the name of child, date of birth, place of birth, and parents' names. This database has 1,052,607 records. See
https://familysearch.org/search/collection/2365245.

1670-1980 New Jersey Marriages [Online Database], indexed at the FamilySearch.org website. Index to selected marriage records located at the New Jersey State Library and to marriage card indexes created by the Gloucester County Historical Society, the Salem County Historical Society and the Genealogical Society of Pennsylvania. This database has 581,963 records. See
https://familysearch.org/search/collection/2365247.

1670-1988 New Jersey Deaths [Online Database], indexed at the FamilySearch.org website. Source: NJ State Archives. Each record may include the name of the deceased, date of death, place of death, gender, and may list parents' names. This database has 641,690 records. See
https://familysearch.org/search/collection/2365246.

1675-1970 New Jersey, Church Records [Online Database], indexed at the FamilySearch.org website. Source: FamilySearch microfilm extractions from local historical societies and universities. Includes church records from various denominations in New Jersey. The record content and time period varies by denomination and locality and may include any of the following: Event dates and places (birth, baptism, marriage, death or burial), Names of parents, children, other family members, and witnesses, ages, residence, and previous residences This database has 1,144 records. See
https://familysearch.org/search/collection/2106099.

"1677 Assessment Lists, Settlers of Delaware Shores, Salem County" [Printed Article], in *Genealogical Magazine of New Jersey*, Vol. 13, No. 1 (Jan 1938).

1677-1678. See Burlington County, NJ History Early Settlement of the County [Online Database], indexed at the GenealogyTrails website. See
http://genealogytrails.com/njer/burlington/early_settlement.html.

1678-1980 New Jersey Probate Records [Online Database], digitized at the FamilySearch.org website. Images of probate records from various court houses in New Jersey. Most records end in 1920 but some counties have records up to the year 1980. Browse the records by county and record type. No index yet. This database has 1,913,824 images. See
https://familysearch.org/search/collection/2018330.

1678-1985 New Jersey Marriages [Online Database], indexed at the FamilySearch.org website. Name index to marriage records from microfilm at the Family

History Library, Salt Lake City, UT. This database has 324,149 records. See https://familysearch.org/search/collection/1675446.

1679-1929. *A history of Trenton, Two Hundred and Fifty Years of a Notable Town With Links in Four Centuries* **[Online Database],** indexed at the Ancestry.com website. Full text image pages with an OCR index. This database has 1,131 pages. See http://search.ancestry.com/search/db.aspx?dbid=15104.

1680-1709 The Burlington Court Book: A Record of Quaker Jurisprudence in West New Jersey **[Online Database],** indexed at the FamilySearch.org website. Source: Book, same title, publ. American Historical Association, Washington, DC, 1944. Full text image pages with an OCR index. This database has 428 pages: http://search.ancestry.com/search/db.aspx?dbid=13867.

1680-1787. *A Collection of Memorials Concerning Divers Deceased Ministers and Others of the People called Quakers: in Pennsylvania, New Jersey, and Parts Adjacent, From Nearly the First Settlement to 1787...* **[Printed Book],** publ. W. Alexander and Son, York, PA, 1824, 351 pages, FHL book 974.K2q. Also on microfilm, see FHL film #928506.

1682-1956 New Jersey County Marriages **[Online Database],** indexed at the FamilySearch.org website. Source: FamilySearch extractions from county microfilms at the Family History Library. All New Jersey counties represented. At the catalog webpage, click on "Learn More" to see the coverage and years for each county. This database has 300,071 records: https://familysearch.org/search/collection/1803976.

1683-1802 New Jersey Marriage Records **[Online Database],** indexed at the Ancestry.com website. Source: NJ State Archives. Entries list name, residence, spouse name, year, month, and day. This database has 26,952 records. See http://search.ancestry.com/search/db.aspx?dbid=2794.

1683-1883. See *History of the Counties of Gloucester, Salem, and Cumberland, New Jersey: With Biographical Sketches of their Prominent Citizens* **[Online Database],** indexed at the Ancestry.com website. Full text image pages with an OCR index. This database has 873 pages. See http://search.ancestry.com/search/db.aspx?dbid=15008.

1683-1890. See *A History of Monmouth and Ocean Counties, Embracing a Genealogical Record of Earliest Settlers in Monmouth, and Ocean Counties* **[Online Database],** indexed at the Ancestry.com website. Source: Book, same title, by Edwin Salter, publ. 1890. Full text image pages with an OCR index. This database has 542 pages. See http://search.ancestry.com/search/db.aspx?dbid=15434.

1683-1926. See *Northwestern New Jersey: A History of Somerset, Morris, Hunterdon, Warren and Sussex counties* **[Online Database],** indexed at the Ancestry.com website. Source: Book, same title, publ. Lewis Historical Publishing Co., 1927. Full text page images with an OCR index. This database has 1,920 pages. See http://search.ancestry.com/search/db.aspx?dbid=13781.

"1684 Assessment List, Burlington County" [Printed Article], in *Pennsylvania Magazine of History and Biography*, Vol. 15, No. 3 (Jul 1891).

1684-1895 New Jersey Marriages **[Online Database],** indexed at the Ancestry.com website. Source: Jordan Dodd, Liahona Research, from microfilmed records at the Family History Library, Salt Lake City, UT. Includes marriage records for Warren County, Atlantic, Bergen, Cape May, Cumberland, Gloucester, Salem, Sussex, Hunterdon, and Somerset counties. Each record provides spouses' names, marriage date, and county of residence. This database has 48,711 records: http://search.ancestry.com/search/db.aspx?dbid=4480.

"1687 Tax List of the Lower Division, Gloucester County" [Printed Article], in *Genealogical Magazine of New Jersey*, Vol. 13, No. 1 (Jan 1938).

1689-1801 Bergen County, New Jersey Deed Records **[Printed Book],** by John David Davis, publ. Heritage Books, Bowie, MD, 1995, 412 pages, FHL book974.921 R28d. To access a digital version of this book, see the online FHL catalog page for this title. See https://familysearch.org/search/catalog/755150.

"1693 Census, New Sweden, Wiacaco Congregation" **[Printed Article],** in *Swedish American Genealogist,* Vol. 9, No. 3 (Sep 1989)

1700-1889 Bergen County, New Jersey Marriage Records **[Online Database],** indexed at the Ancestry.com website. Source: extractions from the original marriage returns from ministers and justices of the peace. Copied at the Bergen County Courthouse, Hackensack, NJ. This database has 118 pages. See http://search.ancestry.com/search/db.aspx?dbid=13869. - See also *Index of Bergen County Marriages* [Online Database], prepared by the Red Mill Chapter, DAR , Maywood, NJ. See http://search.ancestry.com/search/db.aspx?dbid=14255.

"1704 Census, Cape May County" [Printed Article], in *Cape May County Magazine of History and Genealogy,* Vol. 2, No. 4 (Jun 1942).

1708-1985 *Pennsylvania and New Jersey, Church and Town Records* [Online Database], indexed at the Ancestry.com website. Source: Historical Society of Pennsylvania. The documents in this database are mostly Protestant church records from congregations in Pennsylvania and New Jersey, but there are also some for locations in the neighboring states of Maryland, Delaware, and Virginia. In addition to church records, sources also include funeral homes, cemeteries, newspapers, historical societies, and personal records. They include a wide variety of records, such as lists of church officers, communion lists, marriages, registers of members, registers of elders, deacons, etc., baptisms, confirmations, burials, probationers, histories, receipts, agreements, other miscellaneous items, and newspaper extracts. The documents list millions of names, and many contain details on vital events such as births, marriages, and deaths. In them, you may find names, birth dates, marriage dates, spouse's name, parents' names, and places where an event (baptism, marriage, death, burial, etc.) took place. This database has 10,934,014 records. See http://search.ancestry.com/search/db.aspx?dbid=2451.

"1709 Census, Northampton" [Printed Article], in *American Genealogist*, Vol. 1, No. 5 (Jul 1899) and in New Jersey Historical Society Proceedings, Vol. 4, No. 1 (1849).

1710-1913. *A History of Morris County, New Jersey, Embracing Upwards of Two Centuries* [Online Database], indexed at the Ancestry.com website. Source: Book, same title, publ. Lewis Publishing Co., 1914. Full text image pages with an OCR index. This database has 1,138 pages: http://search.ancestry.com/search/db.aspx?dbid=15331.

1720-1988 *New Jersey Deaths and Burials* [Online Database], indexed at the FamilySearch.org website. Name index to death and burial records from microfilm at the Family History Library, Salt Lake City, UT. This database has 449,612 records. See https://familysearch.org/search/collection/1675445.

"1722 Heads of Families, Maidenhead" [Printed Article], in *Hunterdon Historical Newsletter*, Vol. 13, No. 2 (Spring 1977).

"1735 Tax List, Franklin, Somerset County" [Printed Article], in *Our Home: A Monthly Magazine,* Vol. 1, No. 8 (Oct 1873).

"1735, 1745 Rate List, Franklin Township, Hunterdon County" [Printed Article], in *Genealogical Magazine of New Jersey,* Vol. 42, No. 3 (Sep 1967).

"1739 Tax List, Gloucester County" [Printed Article], in *Gloucester County Historical Society Bulletin,* Vol. 5, No. 5 (Sep 1956).

1739-1991 *New Jersey, Wills and Probate Records* [Online Database], indexed at the Ancestry.com website. Source: Ancestry extractions from New Jersey county and district courts. In most cases, the details found in probates include the names and residences of beneficiaries and their relationship to the decedent. An inventory of the estate assets may reveal personal details about the deceased's occupation and lifestyle. There may also be references to debts, deeds, and other documents related to the settling of the estate. This database has 469,752 records. See http://search.ancestry.com/search/db.aspx?dbid=8796.

"1745 Census, Lower Penns Neck" [Printed Article], in *Genealogical Magazine of New Jersey,* Vol. 52, No. 1 (Jan 1977).

1749-1986 *New Jersey, County Naturalization Records* [Online Database], digitized at the FamilySearch.org website. Naturalization records and their index books from county courthouses in New Jersey. Browse the images by county, year, index books, declarations of intention books, or petitions books. This database has 791,233 images. See https://familysearch.org/search/collection/2057433.

1748, 1755 *Land Records, Monmouth County, New Jersey* [Microfilm], from the originals at the NJ State Library. These are freeholders' lists. Names are arranged in alphabetical order. Filmed by the Genealogical Society of Utah, 1979, 1 roll, FHL film #1024666. To see if this microfilm was digitized yet, see the online FHL catalog: www.familysearch.org/search/catalog/17867.

1749-1986. *New Jersey, County Naturalization Records* **[Online Database]**, digitized at the Ancestry.com website. Source: FamilySearch extractions from county records on microfilm at the Family History Library, Salt Lake City, UT. Records may include petitions for citizenship, certificates, and other related documents. This database has 786,130 images. Browse the images by county. There are county indexes to most record books. See **http://search.ancestry.com/search/db.aspx?dbid=60084**.

"1750 Freeholders List, Middlesex County" **[Printed Article],** in *New Jersey Historical Society Proceedings,* Vol. 13, No. 2 (1894).

"1751 Ratables, Lower Precinct, Cape May County" [Printed Article], in *Genealogical Magazine of New Jersey,* Vol. 14, No. 2 (Apr 1939).

"1751 Ratables, Maurice River Precinct, Cumberland County" [Printed Article], in *Genealogical Magazine of New Jersey,* Vol. 14, No. 2 (Apr 1939).

"1755 Freeholders List, Essex County" [Printed Article], in *New Jersey Historical Society Proceedings,* Vol. 13, No. 1 (1894).

1755. See *Land Records, Essex County, New Jersey* **[Microfilm],** from the originals at the NJ State Library. Includes the names of freeholders, names arranged in alphabetical order. Filmed by the Genealogical Society of Utah, 1979, 1 roll, FHL film #1024666.

"1761 Middletown Assessment" [Printed Article], in *Monmouth Connection*, Vol. 13, No. 2 and Vol. 13, No. 5 (May 2002).

"1768 Ratables, Lower Precinct, Cape May County" [Printed Article], in *Genealogical Magazine of New Jersey,* Vol. 14, No. 3 (Jul 1939).

1768-1846. *County Tax Lists (Ratables)* **[Microfilm & Digital Capture],** from a typescript index to the originals at the NJ State Archives, Trenton, NJ. This is an index to   tax lists for all New Jersey counties. Filmed by the Genealogical Society of Utah, 1972, 1 roll, FHL film #913174. To access the digital images, see the online FHL catalog page: **www.familysearch.org/search/catalog/96527**.

1772-1890. See *New Jersey, Compiled Census and Census Substitutes Index* **[Online Database],** indexed at Ancestry.com. Originally edited by Ronald Jackson,

Accelerated Indexing, Salt Lake City, UT. This collection contains the following indexes: 1772-1822 Tax Lists Index; 1800 Cumberland County Federal Census Index; 1824-1832 Bergen County - Paterson City; 1830 Federal Census Index; 1840 Federal Census Index; 1840 Pensioners List; 1850 Federal Census Index; 1850 Slave Schedule; 1860 Federal Census Index; 1870 Federal Census Index; 1890 Veterans Schedule; Early Census Index. This database has 807,660 records. See **http://search.ancestry.com/search/db.aspx?dbid=3562**.

1776-1993. *New Jersey Newspaper Archives* **[Online Databases],** digitized and indexed newspapers at the GenealogyBank website for the following cities: Aberdeen, Absecon, Bridgeton, Burlington, Camden, Egg harbor City, Elizabethtown, Elwood, Jersey City, May's Landing, Morristown, New Brunswick, Newark, Rahway, Salem, Trenton, Vineland, and Woodbury. See **www.genealogybank.com/explore/newspapers/all/usa/new -jersey**.

1776-1979 New Jersey, Essex County, Superintendent of Soldiers' Burials **[Online Database].** Source: NJ State Archives, Trenton. Includes grave registration records arranged alphabetically by the veteran's name. The microfilm of the original record is in the Essex County Records Building in Newark, New Jersey. This database has 37,435 records, see **www.familysearch.org/search/collection/3235409**.

"1777 Tax List, Gloucester County" [Printed Article], in *Gloucester County Historical Society Bulletin,* Vol. 4, No. 8 (Jun 1955).

"1784 Census, Gloucester County, New Jersey" [Printed Articles]. Name lists by towns or townships, published serially in *Gloucester County Historical Society Bulletin*, in the following issues:
- Unnamed Area, in Vol. 20, No. 6 (Dec 1986) and Vol. 20, No. 7 (Mar 1987), and Vol. 8, No. 3 (Mar 1962).
- Newton, in Vol. 20, No. 2 (Dec 1985) and Vol. 20, 3 (Mar 1986).
- Lower Township, in Vol. 19, No. 8 (Jun 1985) through Vol. 20, No. 1 (Sep 1985).
- Upper Township, in, Vol. 19, No. 3 (Mar 1984).
- Deptford, in Vol. 19, No. 5 (Sep 1984) and Vol. 19, No. 6 (Dec 1984).
- Middle Township, in Vol. 19, No. 3 (Mar 1984) & Vol. 19, No. 4 (Jun 1984).

1778-1822. *Tax Ratables, Bergen County, New Jersey* **[Microfilm & Digital Capture],** from the originals at the NJ Public Record Office, Trenton, NJ. Contains tax ratables of old Bergan County. Includes townships of Bergen (now Hudson Co.), Franklin (area now partly in Bergen Co. and partly in Passaic Co.), Hackensack (area in Bergen Co.), Harrington (area now in Bergen Co.), New Barbadoes (area now in Bergen Co.), Pompton (area now in Passaic Co.), Saddle River (area now partly in Bergen Co. and partly in Passaic Co.), and abstracts for the county. Filmed by the Genealogical Society of Utah, 1971, 2 rolls, FHL film #865462 (Bergen – New Barbadoes, 1778-1822); and FHL film #865463 (Pompton – Saddle River, 1778-1822). To access the digital images, see the online FHL catalog page:
www.familysearch.org/search/catalog/80686.

1778-1822. *Tax Ratables, Burlington County, New Jersey* **[Microfilm & Digital Capture],** from the originals at the NJ State Library. Contains tax ratables of old Burlington County. Includes townships of Burlington (now Burlington township and Burlington city), Chester (area now in Burlington Co.), Chesterfield (Chesterfield and Bordentown townships), Evesham (area now in southwestern Burlington Co.), Little Egg Harbor (area now partly in Washington and Bass River townships, Burlington Co. and partly in Little Egg Harbor township, Ocean Co.), Mansfield (Florence and Mansfield townships), New Hanover (New Hanover and North Hanover townships), Northampton (area now in Burlington Co.), Nottingham (now Hamilton township, Mercer Co.), Springfield (same area), Washington (area now in southeastern Burlington Co.), Willingboro (Willingboro, Delanco, Edgewater Park, and Levittown townships), and abstracts for the county. Filmed by the NJ State Library, 1971, 4 rolls, FHL film #865464 (Burlington – Chesterfield, 1778-1822); FHL film #865465 (Evesham – New Hanover, 1778-1822); FHL film #865466 (Northampton – Washington, 1778-1822); and FHL film #865467 (Willingboro – Abstract, 1778-1822). To access the digital images, see the online FHL catalog page:
www.familysearch.org/search/catalog/80673.

1778-1822. *Tax Ratables, Essex County, New Jersey* **[Microfilm & Digital Capture],** from the originals at the NJ State Library. Contains tax ratables of old Essex County. Includes townships of Acquackanonk (area now in Passaic Co.), Bloomfield (area in Essex Co.), Caldwell (area now in Essex Co.), Connecticut Farms (area now in Union Co.), Elizabeth (area now in Union Co.), Livingston (area in Essex Co.), Newark (now in Newark city), New Providence (area now in western Union Co.), Orange (area now in Essex Co.), Rahway (area now in Union Co.), Springfield (area now partly in Essex Co., and partly in Union Co.), Union (area now in Union Co.), Westfield (area now in Union Co.). Filmed by the NJ State Library, 3 rolls, FHL film #865470 (Acquackanonk – Elizabeth, 1778-1822); FHL film #865471 (Livingston – Rahway, 1778-1822); and FHL film #865472 (Springfield – Westfield, 1778-1822). To access the digital images, see the online FHL catalog page:
www.familysearch.org/search/catalog/80661.

1778-1822. Tax Ratables, Gloucester County, New Jersey [Microfilm & Digital Capture], from the original records at the New Jersey State Library, Trenton, NJ. Contains tax ratables of old Gloucester County. Includes townships of Deptford (area in Gloucester co.), Egg Harbor (area now in Atlantic Co.), Gloucester (area now in Camden Co.), Great Egg Harbor (area now in Atlantic Co.), Greenwich (area in Gloucester Co.), Newton (area now in Camden Co.), Waterford (area now in Camden Co.), Weymouth (area now in Atlantic Co.), Woolwich (area in Gloucester Co.), and abstracts for the county. Filmed by NJ State Library, 1971, 2 rolls, FHL film #865473 (Deptford – Great Egg Harbor, 1778-1822); and FHL film #865474 (Greenwich – Abstracts of County, 1778-1822). To access the digital images, see the online FHL catalog page: **www.familysearch.org/search/catalog/80653.**

1778-1822. *Tax Ratables, Middlesex Count, New Jersey* **[Microfilm & Digital Capture],** from the original records at the New Jersey Public Record Office, Trenton, NJ. Contains tax ratables of old Middlesex County. Includes townships of East Windsor (area now partly in Mercer Co., and partly in Middlesex Co.), New Brunswick (area in Middlesex Co.), North Brunswick (area in Middlesex Co.), Perth Amboy (area now part of Perth Amboy City), Piscataway (area in northwest Middlesex Co.), South Amboy (area in southeast Middlesex Co.), South Brunswick (area in southwest Middlesex Co.), West Windsor (area now in Mercer Co.), Windsor (area now in Mercer Co.), Woodbridge (area in northeast Middlesex Co.), and abstracts of the county. Filmed by the NJ State Library, 3 rolls, FHL film #865476 (East Windsor – Piscataway, 1778-1822); FHL film #865477 (South Amboy – Windsor, 1778-1822); and FHL film #865478 (Woodbridge – Abstracts of County, 1778-

1822). To access the digital images, see the online FHL catalog page:
www.familysearch.org/search/catalog/80677.

1785-1799. See *Index To Middlesex County Deeds* **[Printed Book],** compiled by the New Jersey Information Service, Kendall Park, NJ, 1992, 26 pages, FHL book 974.9 A1 No. 114.

1785-1906. *Intestates and Others from the Orphans Court Books of Monmouth Co., N.J.* **[Online Database],** indexed at the Ancestry.com website. Source: Book, same title, by Judith B. Cronk, publ. 2002. Full text page images with an OCR index. This database has 242 pages. See
http://search.ancestry.com/search/db.aspx?dbid=49201

1790-1900. *New Jersey Biographical Card Index* **[Microfilm & Digital Capture],** from the original card index at the New Jersey Historical Society, Newark, NJ. The card index relates to Trinity (Episcopal) Church of Newark, NJ and notes baptisms, marriages, deaths, burials, and more. Filmed by the Genealogical Society of Utah, 2000, 25 rolls, beginning with FHL film #2137273 (Explanation of cards and symbols used; Aaronson, Ezra B to Arder, Adam). To access the digital images, see the online FHL catalog page:
https://familysearch.org/search/catalog/961103.

1791-1795. *Compiled Records of the Middlesex County, New Jersey Militia* **[Online Database],** indexed at the Ancestry.com website. Source: Book, same title, by Russell K. Dutcher, publ. 1996. The rosters are arranged by militia company and give, first, the names of the officers, then the non-commissioned officers, and last the privates. In all, some four thousand persons are listed. Preceding the roster itself is a collection of more than a score of genealogical and biographical sketches of the Middlesex militia officer corps. Following the 1791-1795 rosters are additional rosters of some 2,000 Middlesex militiamen who served during the Revolution, as well as a number of tombstone inscriptions pertaining to Revolutionary War soldiers buried in cemeteries in Middlesex County. Still other rosters describe Middlesex veterans of the War of 1812, usually indicating the individual's rank, branch of service, and date of enlistment. This database has about 4,000 records. See
http://search.ancestry.com/search/db.aspx?dbid=49042.

1798-1971. *New Jersey, Deaths and Burials Index* **[Online Database],** indexed at the Ancestry.com website. Source: FamilySearch extractions from microfilm. Each record may include name, birth date, birthplace, age, occupation, race, marital status, gender, residence, street address, date of death, place of death, date of burial, place of burial, cemetery, father's name and birthplace, mother's name and birthplace, spouse, and FHL film number. This database has 1,122,330 records. See
http://search.ancestry.com/search/db.aspx?dbid=2540.

1800-1877. *The Biographical Encyclopedia of New Jersey of the Nineteenth Century* **[Digitized Book],** by Charles Robson, publ. Galaxy Pub. Co, Philadelphia, 1877. A digital version of this book is available online at the FHL catalog page for this title. See
https://familysearch.org/search/catalog/2537012.

1800-1877. *Births and Deaths Noted in the Biographical Encyclopedia of New Jersey* **[Printed Book],** compiled by Elizabeth Hayward, publ. 1954, 47 pages, FHL book 974.9 D32h. Also on microfilm, see FHL film #962404.

1800-1877. *An Index to Soldiers and Patriots Mentioned in the Biographical Encyclopedia of New Jersey (1877)* **[Microfiche],** compiled by Elizabeth Hayward, publ. 1949, FHL microfiche #6045840.

1800-1877. *Marriages Noted in the Biographical Encyclopedia of New Jersey* **[Microfilm & Digital Version],** compiled by Elizabeth Hayward, publ. 1953, 51 pages, FHL film #824079. To view a digital version of this book, see the online FHL catalog page for this title. See
https://familysearch.org/search/catalog/217277.

1800-1970. *New Jersey, United Methodist Church Records* **[Online Database],** indexed at the Ancestry.com website. This collection includes baptism, marriage, burial, and membership records from churches in the Greater New Jersey United Methodist Church Commission on Archives and History. Most records are from churches that have been closed. This database has 721,232 records. See
http://search.ancestry.com/search/db.aspx?dbid=61176.

1800-1980. *A New Jersey Biographical Index: Covering Some 100,000 Biographies and Associated Portraits in 237 New Jersey Cyclopedias, Histories, Yearbooks, Periodicals, and other Collective Biographical Sources Published to about 1980* **[CD-ROM],** compiled by Donald A. Sinclair, publ. by

Genealogical Publishing Co, Baltimore, 1993, part of Family Tree Maker's Family Archives, No. 190. The 100,000 biographies recorded by Mr. Sinclair, were extracted from no fewer than 2,000 individual publications. The subject of each entry in the Index is identified by his full name and his years of birth and death. Following the subject's name, his biography is cited in abbreviated form, the publication in which it appears, with volume and page numbers, designated by a code which is displayed with the list of sources at the front of the book. See FHL book 974.9 D32s (CD-ROM No. 9 pt. 190).

1804-1830. *Index of Wills, Office of Secretary of State, State of New Jersey* **[Online Database],** indexed at the Ancestry.com website. Source: Index of Wills, 1804-1830, Secretary of State, 1901. See **http://search.ancestry.com/search/db.aspx?dbid=13896**.

1813. See *New Jersey Revolutionary War Pensioners for 1813* **[Online Database],** indexed at the GenealogyTrails website. See **http://genealogytrails.com/njer/military/1813revwarpensioners.html**.

1821-2003. *New Jersey, Calvary United Methodist Church Records* **[Online Database],** digitized at the FamilySearch.org website. Church records of the Calvary United Methodist Church (formerly known as Calvary Methodist Episcopal Church) in Keyport, New Jersey. Browse the images by register book and year. No index yet. This database has 2,631 images. See **https://familysearch.org/search/collection/1929560**.

1827-1832. *Census of Paterson, New Jersey* **[Online Database],** indexed at the Ancestry.com website. Source: Original records compiled by Samuel Fisher, pastor of the First Presbyterian Church of Patterson. Includes Census of Paterson, 1825, 1827, 1829, and 1832. This database has 142 pages. See **http://search.ancestry.com/search/db.aspx?dbid=11223**.

1830-1921. *New Jersey, Middlesex County Probate Records* **[Online Database],** digitized at the FamilySearch.org website. Probate records (bound volumes) from the Middlesex County Surrogate Court in New Brunswick, New Jersey. Browse the images by type of record, vol. and years. No index yet. This database has 16,566 images. See **https://familysearch.org/search/collection/1973535**.

1837-1910. *Camden County, New Jersey Marriages* **[Online Database],** indexed at the Ancestry.com website. Source: Book, same title, by Stanley H. Craig, publ. 1932. Each index record includes Name, Wife, and Date. This database has 4,109 records. See **http://search.ancestry.com/search/db.aspx?dbid=3725**.

1840 Census Pensioners of New Jersey **[Online Database],** indexed at the GenealogyTrails website: **http://genealogytrails.com/njer/1840censusofpensioners.html**.

1849-1984 *New Jersey, Jersey City, Holy Name Cemetery, Card Index of Interment* **[Online Database].** Digitized and indexed at FamilySearch.org. Source: Archdiocese of Newark, NJ. This database has 42,736 records, see **www.familysearch.org/search/collection/3016198**.

1851-1852. *Kirkbride's New Jersey Business Directory, General Register and Advertising Medium* **[Microfiche],** by Stacy B. Kirkbride, filmed by Research Publications, Woodbridge, CT, 1980, 6 microfiche, FHL fiche #6044247.

1855. *New Jersey, 1855 State Census* **[Online Database],** digitized and indexed at the FamilySearch.org website. Source: NJ State Archives microfilm. Census image contents: Name of head of household and number of males and females in each household by category: white, colored, native, foreign and children ages 5 to 16. The returns for Pequanac Township in Morris County also list the names of the wife and children in each household. Per NJ State Archives: "No records exist for the following counties: Burlington, Cape May, Mercer, Middlesex, Ocean and Salem. Several others are incomplete." Browse the images by county/township. This database has 76,013 records, see **https://familysearch.org/search/collection/2469955**. For the Ancestry.com version, see **www.ancestry.com/search/collections/njcensus1855**.

1862. *Card Index to Civil War Soldiers' Graves (New Jersey)* **[Microfilm & Digital Capture],** from the original card index at the New Jersey Historical Society, Newark, NJ. Filmed by the Genealogical Society of Utah, 2000, 2 rolls, FHL #2137754 (A-P) and FHL film #2137755 (P-Z). To access the digital images, see the online FHL catalog page: **www.familysearch.org/search/catalog/966738**.

1865. *New Jersey, 1865 State Census* **[Online Database],** digitized and indexed at the FamilySearch.org website. Source: NJ State Archives microfilm. Archives microfilm. Census image contents: Name of head of household and number of males and females in each household by category: white, colored, native, foreign and children ages 5 to 16. For some places, the name of each person in the household is listed, or at least the name of the adults. Per NJ State Archives: "No records exist for the following counties: Cape May, Mercer, Morris, Ocean, Somerset and Warren. Several others are incomplete." Browse the images by county/township. This database has 76,013 records, see
https://familysearch.org/search/collection/2475024.
- For the Ancestry.com version, see
www.ancestry.com/search/collections/njcensus1865.

1875. *New Jersey, 1875 State Census (Sussex County Only)* **[Online Database],** digitized and indexed at Ancestry.com. The 1875 census was taken in all New Jersey counties; however, only images and records from Sussex county are available. Information listed includes: Name of individual, Gender, Age, Nationality and/or Race, Birth Place, County of enumeration, Locality/town of enumeration, Parentage, and Occupation. This database has 18,660 records, see
www.ancestry.com/search/collections/njcensus1875.

1878-1945 New Jersey Naturalization Records **[Online Database],** Digitized and indexed at Ancestry.com. Source: National Archives microfilm series M2123. Includes petitions and other documents related to the naturalization process. This database has 151,283 records, see
www.ancestry.com/search/collections/newjerseynats.

1890 Census Substitute **[Online Database],** indexed at the Ancestry.com website. This is Ancestry's collection of city directories and other name lists about the time of the lost 1890 census. Includes databases for all states. New Jersey City Directories: **Burlington,** 1890-1891; **Camden,** 1887-1891; **Elizabeth,** 1883-1891; **Jersey City,** 1891-1893; **Morristown,** 1887-1888, 1890-1891; **Newark,** 1890-1891; **Orange,** 1887-1890; and **Patterson,** 1890-1893. See
http://search.ancestry.com/search/group/1890Census.

1885. *New Jersey, 1885 State Census* **[Online Database],** digitized and indexed at FamilySearch.org. Source: NJ State Archives microfilm. The 1885 is complete for all counties. Census image contents:

Name of each member of a household, sex, race, age (in categories, under 5, 5-20, 20-60, and over 60), native or foreign born (indicating Irish, German, and Other). This database has 1,294,279 index records. See
https://familysearch.org/search/collection/1803972.
- For the Ancestry.com version, see
www.ancestry.com/search/collections/njcensus1885.

1885. *New Jersey, 1885 State Census Index – Passaic County and Atlantic City* **[Online Index],** searchable index at the New Jersey State Archives website. This database has 69,302 names, see **https://wwwnet-dos.state.nj.us/DOS_ArchivesDBPortal/index.aspx.**

1895. *New Jersey, 1895 State Census* **[Online Database],** digitized and indexed at the Ancestry.com website. Source: New Jersey State Archives microfilm. This digitized index covers all New Jersey counties. Information listed includes: Name of individual, Gender, Race, County of enumeration, and Locality/town of enumeration. This database has 1,560,521 index records. See
http://search.ancestry.com/search/db.aspx?dbid=1054.
- For the Ancestry.com version, see
www.ancestry.com/search/collections/njstatecen.

1901-1903 New Jersey Birth Index **[Online Database],** indexed at FamilySearch.org. This collection contains the New Jersey Birth Index, 1901-1903 acquired by Reclaim the Records and donated to FamilySearch for publishing the images. This database has 120,948 records, see
www.familysearch.org/search/collection/2843408.

1901-2017 New Jersey Marriage Index **[Online Database],** indexed at Ancestry.com. Source: NJ State Archives, Trenton, NJ. The database can be searched, or the images can be browsed by bride or groom, then year range, then surname. The index consists of the following details: Name of bride or groom, Spouse's name, Marriage year, and Marriage location. A record number is available for ordering a copy of the marriage certificate from the NJ State Archives. This database has 11,090,394 records, see
www.ancestry.com/search/collections/njmarriageindexes.

1901-2017 New Jersey Death Index **[Online Database],** indexed at Ancestry.com. Source: NJ Sate Archives, Trenton, NJ. The database can be searched, or the images for records from 1901-2000 can be browsed by year. The index consists of the following details: Name, Age, and Death year. A record number is available for ordering a copy of the death certificate from the NJ State Archives. This database has 5,083,478 records, see www.ancestry.com/search/collections/njdeathindex.

1905. *New Jersey, 1895 State Census* **[Online Database],** digitized and indexed at the FamilySearch.org website. Source: NJ State Archives microfilm. The 1905 is complete for all counties. This digitized index contains the following information for each person: Name, Age, Estimated birth year, Sex, Relationship to head of household, Family number, Film number, DGS number, Image number, City, town, or village, County, Township, ward, or district. This database has 2,146,861 index records. See https://familysearch.org/search/collection/1928107.
- For the Ancestry.com version, see www.ancestry.com/search/collections/njcensus1905.

1915. *New Jersey, 1915 State Census* **[Online Database],** digitized and indexed at the FamilySearch.org website. Source: NJ State Archives microfilm. The 1915 is complete for all counties. This digitized index contains the following information for each person: Name, Age, Estimated birth year, Sex, Relationship to head of household, Family number, Film number, DGS number, Image number, City, town, or village, County, Township, ward, or district. This database has 2,785,409 index records. See https://familysearch.org/search/collection/2061544.
- For the Ancestry.com version, see www.ancestry.com/search/collections/njcensus1915.

1930-1938 New Jersey Bride Index **[Online Database],** digitized and indexed at FamilySearch.org. This collection contains the New Jersey Bride Index, 1930-1938 acquired by Reclaim the Records and donated to FamilySearch for publishing of images. Digital images of the originals are held by Reclaim the Records in Mill Valley, California. This database has 241,227 records, see www.familysearch.org/search/collection/2842740.

1956-1964. New Jersey, Passenger and Crew Lists [Online Database], indexed at the Ancestry.com website. Source: National Archives, Selected Crew Lists and Manifests. This database is an index to manifests of aliens arriving in Newark, New Jersey by air. The type of information that is generally contained in this database includes: Name, Nationality, Gender, Age on Arrival, and Date of Arrival. Other information that can be found on the images includes US address, passport, visa, and other immigration documentation information; place and date of birth; destination and baggage information. This database has 559,403 records. See http://search.ancestry.com/search/db.aspx?dbid=9125.

1990-Current. *New Jersey Newspaper Obituaries* **[Online Database],** digitized and indexed newspaper obituaries at the GenealogyBank website. Included are obituaries found in newspapers from Absecon-Pleasantville, Andover-Stanhope-Newton, Atlantic City, and 90 more New Jersey cities. See the list of cities at www.genealogybank.com/explore/obituaries/all/usa/new-jersey.

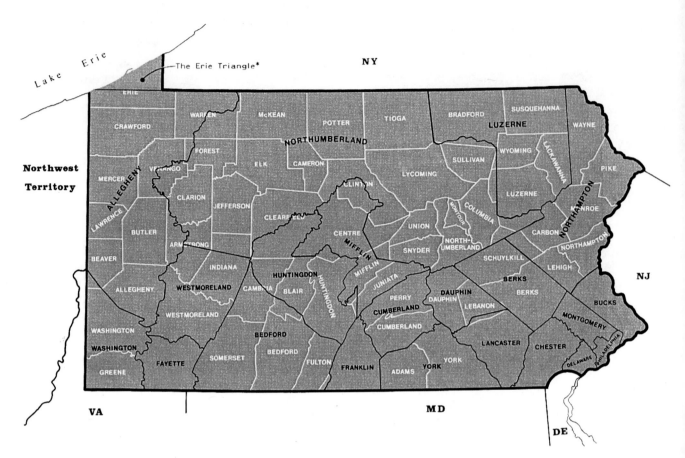

Pennsylvania ● **Aug 1790.** The 21 counties of Pennsylvania at the time of the 1790 Federal Census are shown in black. The current 67 counties of Pennsylvania are shown in white. *Notes: Although the federal government sold the Erie Triangle to Pennsylvania by patent in 1792, Pennsylvania had purchased the land from Indians in 1789. The Triangle was added to Allegheny County in 1792. **Map Source:** Page 289, *Map Guide to the U.S. Federal Censuses, 1790-1920*, by William Thorndale and William Dollarhide.

Pennsylvania
Censuses & Substitute Name Lists

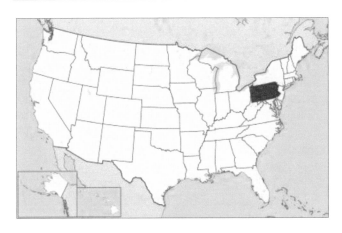

Historical Timeline for Pennsylvania, 1497 1787

1497. Giovanni Caboto, an Italian sponsored by English King Henry VII, explored the Atlantic coast of North America. He claimed the area for the English King, who changed his name to John Cabot in honor of the event.

1524. Giovanni da Verrazano explored the Middle Atlantic region. An Italian hired by the King of France, he sailed past the present New Jersey coast, entered New York bay, and reached the Hudson River, then headed north towards present Maine.

1606. Two joint stock companies were founded, both with royal charters issued by King James I for the purpose of establishing colonies in North America. The Virginia Company of London was given a land grant between Latitude 34° (Cape Fear) and Latitude 41° (Long Island Sound). The Virginia Company of Plymouth was founded with a similar charter, between Latitude 38° (Potomac River) and Latitude 45° (St. John River).

1607. May. Led by John Smith and his cousin, Bartholomew Gosnold, the London Company established the first permanent English settlement in North America – the Jamestown Colony.

1609. Delaware. Henry Hudson, an Englishman sailing for the Dutch East India Company, discovered Delaware Bay and River. A year later, Captain Samuel Argall, an English sea captain, named the bay and river after Thomas West, Baron De La Warr, governor of Virginia.

1638. Delaware. Dutchman Peter Minuet led a group of Swedes to the Delaware and established Fort Christiana (now Wilmington), the first permanent settlement on the Delaware and the founding of the New Sweden Colony.

1651. Delaware. Peter Stuyvesant, Dutch governor of New Netherland, built Fort Casimir (now New Castle) just a few miles south of Fort Christina on the Delaware, but the Swedes were not pleased with the Dutch intrusion.

1654. Delaware. The Swedes captured Fort Casimir and renamed it Fort Trinity. A year later the Dutch defeated the Swedes, ending the New Sweden colony, and Delaware became part of New Netherland. But, several Swedish communities continued.

1664. New York and New Jersey. The Dutch colony of New Netherland became controlled by the English after Gov. Peter Stuyvesant surrendered to the British following a naval blockade. The English also took control of New Jersey from the Dutch.

1664. New York. King Charles II granted to his brother, James, the Duke of York, the following: "…main land between the two rivers there, called or known by the several names of Conecticut or Hudsons river… and all the lands from the west side of Connecticut, to the east side of Delaware Bay." The area was named New York for the first time.

1664. Delaware. Sir Robert Carr drove the Dutch off the Delaware and claimed the land for James, Duke of York. Delaware then became an English colony.

1665-1674. New Jersey. In 1665, James, Duke of York, granted to Sir George Carteret and Lord Berkley of Stratton, a part of the New York colony between the Hudson River and the Delaware River. In 1674, Berkley sold his share to the Quakers. Carteret's original portion was then named East New Jersey, and the Quaker's portion was named West New Jersey.

1674. The Treaty of Westminster ended hostilities between the English and Dutch and officially returned all Dutch colonies in America to the English. This ended the official Dutch presence in North America – but many of the Dutch settlements continued under English rule, particularly along the Hudson River of New York, and East Jersey.

1676. West New Jersey. Still in England, William Penn was heavily involved in the transportation of Quakers to the West Jersey Colony. He was a trustee in the colony's establishment and was responsible for drawing up the first set of laws. They would become the basis for the Great Experiment he envisioned for Pennsylvania a few years later.

1681. Pennsylvania. Charles II granted to William Penn a land charter to repay a debt owed to William's father, Admiral William Penn. This was the largest English land grant to an individual, and William Penn became the sole owner and proprietor, with allegiance to England. Penn's charter specified that the colony was bounded on the "…South by a Circle drawn at twelve miles distance from New Castle … unto the beginning of the fortieth degree of Northern Latitude…" Later surveys revealed that the town of New Castle in fact lay several miles south of the 40th Parallel. Maryland's 1632 charter had specified that their northern boundary was the 40th parallel, and after Penn's grant in 1681, a 25-mile strip of land from the Delaware River to the Appalachian Mountains was claimed by both colonies. Neither Pennsylvania nor Maryland had settlements in the cross-claimed area until many years later, and the boundary remained in dispute for nearly 80 years.

1682. Delaware. The area of present Delaware was transferred from the Duke of York, proprietor of New York to William Penn, proprietor of Pennsylvania. The area became known as the "Lower Counties on the Delaware."

1702. New Jersey. East and West Jersey were combined into one colony again. The two Proprietors appointed a governor for the Province of New Jersey, but with continued land sales by both East New Jersey and West New Jersey. Thereafter, the two land offices remained intact under the administration of Land Commissions, for the purpose of selling land to individuals. Both commissions still exist today.

1707. During the reign of Queen Anne, the **United Kingdom of Great Britain** was established after the *Union with Scotland Act* passed the English Parliament in 1706; and the *Union with England Act* passed the Parliament of Scotland in 1707. The English colonies were now British colonies.

1730-1732. Cresap's War. In the royal grants of both colonies, the 40th Parallel was mentioned as the northern boundary of 1632 Maryland and the southern boundary of 1681 Pennsylvania. But Pennsylvania's grant language incorrectly placed the headwaters of the Chesapeake Bay as the assumed position of the 40th Parallel, which was actually 25 miles further north. Maryland maintained its claim to the 40th Parallel, even though their claim would have put the city of Philadelphia in Maryland, not Pennsylvania. As early as 1718, shiploads of transplanted Ulster Scots / Scots-Irish, arrived in Philadelphia, and almost immediately headed into the Pennsylvania wilderness. They were joined by Palatine Germans (Pennsylvania Dutch), who were the first to settle in the Lancaster area. By 1725, both groups reached the Susquehanna River, which became a barrier to further western settlement. In that year, the Maryland colony issued a land grant to Thomas Johnson, who operated a ferry at Peach Bottom. In 1730, Wight's Ferry and a land office was established by the Pennsylvania colony to facilitate settlement across the river. When the colony of Maryland heard of Wight's Ferry, Lord Baltimore authorized Thomas Cresap of Maryland to open a ferry and land office at Blue Rock. Fights broke out between workers of the competing ferries. The battles of the "war" were mostly in court, and in 1732, Charles Calvert, 5th Baron Baltimore, signed a provisional agreement with William Penn's sons, which drew a compromise line between the Pennsylvania claim and the original Maryland claim. He later reneged, saying the document he signed was not correct. The Maryland and Pennsylvania settlers continued to battle each other over jurisdiction in the areas of present Harford Co MD and York Co PA. The compromise line was not finally agreed to until 1760, when King George III ordered Lord Baltimore (the 6th) to formally accept the 1732 agreement of his father. The line was not surveyed and marked on the ground until 1764.

1755. Braddock's Road. During the French and Indian War, a wagon road was constructed to advance British military forces against the French. Based on a 1753 trail blazed by 21-year old Major George Washington of the Virginia Militia, a road was ordered by British General Edward Braddock. The road was constructed in 1755, from a point on the Potomac River near Georgetown, Maryland, to Fort Cumberland, then into Pennsylvania, and on to Fort Duquesne, now Pittsburgh. This was the first wagon road to cross the Appalachian Mountains. After the war, the roadway was mostly abandoned, but after the formation of the United States, it became known as the **Cumberland Road**, and was part of the primary route for migrations between Baltimore and the Ohio River where the first public land sales took place. The route today is the same as US Hwy 40 / I-70.

1758. Gen. John Forbes, the new British commander, built **Forbes Road** through Pennsylvania, took possession of Ft. Duquesne, and renamed it Ft. Pitt, as the British forced the French out of the western wilderness. Forbes Road was close to the line of I-76 (Pennsylvania Turnpike) and U.S. Hwy 30 into Pittsburgh.

1763. The **Treaty of Paris** ended the French and Indian War (in Europe and Canada: the Seven Years War). France ceded virtually all of its North American claims to Spain (west of the Mississippi) and to Britain (east of the Mississippi). Soon after, King George III declared the "Proclamation Line of 1763," as a way of rewarding the Indians who had helped Britain against the French. The proclamation established an Indian Reserve that stretched from the Appalachian Mountain Range to the Mississippi River.

1764. Pennsylvania and Maryland. After years of arguments between the Penn Family and the Calvert Family, Charles Mason and Jeremiah Dixon surveyed the Maryland-Pennsylvania boundary, which became known as the "Mason-Dixon Line." The line was the same as the compromise agreement made between the Penns and Calverts in 1760. It became the dividing line between the northern and southern British colonies, later, U.S. States. Along the length of the Mason-Dixon Line, stone monuments were erected every five miles, each with the engraved coat of arms of the Penn Family on the PA side of the stone, the arms of the Calvert family on the MD side.

1768. Treaty of Fort Stanwix. A new "Line of Property" was drawn, separating British Territory from Indian Territory. From Fort Stanwix (present Rome, NY), the division line ran to Fort Pitt (now Pittsburgh)

and down the Ohio River to the Tennessee River. In the Fort Stanwix treaty, the Six Nations (Iroquois) ceded lands in western New York and northwestern Pennsylvania. The treaty also ceded nearly all of present West Virginia and Kentucky to the British Colony of Virginia.

1775. Delaware. The three Lower Counties broke away from Pennsylvania. They declared their independence from Great Britain, adopted a constitution, and became the "Delaware State," the first of all the colonies to call themselves a state.

1776-1783. Revolutionary War. The 1783 Treaty of Paris ended the war, and the United States of America was officially recognized as an independent nation by Britain, France, and Spain.

1787. Dec. 7. **Delaware** ratified the U.S. Constitution and became the 1st state in the Union.

1787. Dec. 12. **Pennsylvania** was the 2nd state to ratify the Constitution and join the Union.

1787. Dec. 12. **New Jersey** became the 3rd state to join the Union just a few hours after Pennsylvania.

Online Databases of the Pennsylvania State Archives – ARIAS

The **Archives Records Information System** (ARIAS) is the online platform for the Pennsylvania State Archives. The system was designed to facilitate citizen access to archival records created by all branches and levels of Pennsylvania State Government. Original records now part of the ARIAS collection were first microfilmed, and the images later digitized for presentation on the Web. Currently, about 1,500,000 records are accessible in ARIAS, and the PA State Archives plans to make additional records available in the near future. Specific records of interest to genealogists include the following:

- PA National Guard Veteran's Card File, 1867-1921
- Civil War Veterans' Card File
- Revolutionary War Military Abstract Card File
- World War I Service Medal Application Cards
- Spanish American War Veterans' Card File of United States Volunteers
- Mexican Border Campaign Veterans' Card File
- Militia Officers' Index Cards, 1775-1800

To explore the historical records through ARIAS, see **www.digitalarchives.state.pa.us.**

Bibliography
Pennsylvania Censuses & Substitutes

1680-1700s. *English Colonies in America* **[Printed Book & Digital Version],** by John Andrew Doyle, publ. H. Holt, New York, 1889-1907, 5 vols., FHL book 973 H2d. To view a digital version of this book, see the online FHL catalog page for this title. See **https://familysearch.org/search/catalog/100297.**

1680-1776. *The Colonial Clergy of the Middle Colonies: New York, New Jersey, and Pennsylvania* **[Printed Book],** by Frederick Lewis Weis, originally published by American Antiquarian Society, 1957; reprinted by Genealogical Publishing Co., Inc., Baltimore, 1978, 184 pages. From intro: "The history of the towns of the British Colonies in North America during the colonial period was in large measure that of their churches, and the history of these churches was largely that of their clergy. The ministers of that period were the leaders in theology, law, medicine, education, and to a considerable degree, in politics and Indian warfare. Often they were the only educated persons in a community." FHL book 973 D3wf.

1680-1783. *Scots in the Mid-Atlantic Colonies* **[Printed Book],** by David Dobson, published by Genealogical Publishing Co., Inc., Baltimore, 2002, 150 pages; and *Scots in the Mid-Atlantic States, 1783-1883,* 150 pages. Both books name about 3,000 Scots immigrants to the mid-Atlantic region, before and after the Revolutionary War. Both books provide a series of sketches conveying such information as the immigrant's place and date of birth and death, occupation, date of arrival and place of settlement in the U.S., and names of spouse and children. The most informative source of vital data on Scots who settled abroad is the birth, marriage, and death columns of local newspapers. These compilations depend heavily on such sources, together with certain documentary sources in the National Archives of Scotland, as well as a few other sources both printed and manuscript. These are two volumes in Dobson's regional immigration series, which includes *Directory of Scots in the Carolinas*, *Scots on the Chesapeake*, *Scots in Georgia and the Deep South*, and *Scots in New England.*

1680-1800. *The Ministry and Churches of all Denominations in the Middle Colonies From the First Settlements Until the Year 1800* **[Unpublished Manuscript],** by Edward T. Corwin. This manuscript was prepared by ecclesiastical historian Edward T. Corwin and sent after his death in 1914 to A.J.F. Van Laer, Archivist and Dutch translator with the New York State Library. The manuscript consists of two parts. Part I. "Minutes of all Denominations in the Middle Colonies, before the year 1800," is an alphabetical list of clergy giving their denominations, location, dates of birth and death (when known) and of residence in each community, and frequently a citation to a biographical sketch. Part II. "Churches of All Denominations in the Middle Colonies, before the Year 1800," lists churches alphabetically by community, giving their denomination, year established (if known), and the names and dates of pastors. The states or colonies included in this manuscript are New York, Pennsylvania, Delaware, New Jersey, Maryland, and Virginia. The manuscript is located at the New York State Library in Albany. To access the NYSL Excelsior catalog, see **http://nysl.nysed.gov.** Click on "all libraries," to reach the "search the library catalog" box. Enter the keywords "Middle Colonies Corwin" to find this exact reference. Information about obtaining a copy of the Corwin manuscript is available at the same site.

1680-1880. *Pennsylvania Vital Records* **[Online Database],** digitized and indexed at the Ancestry.com website. From the 3-vol. set, *Pennsylvania Vital Records* (from *The Pennsylvania Genealogical Magazine* and *The Pennsylvania Magazine of History and Biography),* publ. Genealogical Publishing Co, Baltimore, 1983-2009. The vital records that appear here in a total of some 150 articles derive from a mixture of church registers, court records, records of local officials and justices, ministers' records, newspapers, and gravestone inscriptions. They represent a cross-section of the population of early Pennsylvania, providing one of the largest bodies of published source material.
For Vol. 1, See
http://search.ancestry.com/search/db.aspx?dbid=48382.
For Vol. 2, See
http://search.ancestry.com/search/db.aspx?dbid=48383.
For Vol. 3, See
http://search.ancestry.com/search/db.aspx?dbid=48607.

1680-1900s Grantee-Grantor Indexes to Deeds, Pennsylvania Counties [Microfilm & Digital Capture]. Indexes to land sellers (grantors) and buyers (grantees) exist for every Pennsylvania county. All of Pennsylvania's county deed indexes were microfilmed by the Genealogical Society of Utah in the 1970s. Most were digitized by 2019. These name lists are a better overview of the heads of households for a county than a pre-1850 census. To find a particular Pennsylvania county's deed index, visit the FamilySearch catalog: **https://familysearch.org/search/catalog.**
- At the "Place" box, type the county name, Select the desired county, then click on "Search," to see a long list of categories available for the county selected. Note the category, "Land and Property," which is where one will find the deed indexes for a county. The deed transcripts often contain sources of genealogical links that may be found nowhere else. All Pennsylvania land was surveyed under the Metes and Bounds survey system which originated in England. Land descriptions used the lay of the land and can be rather long and convoluted with irregular shapes and references to trees, barns, etc., that no longer exist. To save having to write long metes and bounds descriptions over and over again, the clerks often referred to the original patent for the land being sold, naming the first land holder, subsequent land owners, and in the process, giving father-to-son relationships for several generations.
- As an example of one county, the Armstrong County deeds microfilm is entitled **Deeds, 1805-1891; Deed Index, 1805-1941,** has 52 rolls of film, and begins with FHL film #857226 (Grantor Index v. A 1805-1941). At the FHL catalog webpage, you will learn that this entire 52-roll series has been digitized. One can access the digital images for each roll. To access the Armstrong County digital images, see the online FHL catalog page: **www.familysearch.org/search/catalog/223823.**

1680-1900s. *Pennsylvania Biographical Dictionary: People of all Times and all Places Who Have Been Important to the History and Life of the State* [Printed Book], published by American Historical Publications, Wilmington, DE, 1989, 446 pages, includes index. See FHL book 974.8 D3p.

1680-1938. Encyclopedia of American Quaker Genealogy. Vol. II: (New Jersey and Pennsylvania Monthly Meetings) [Printed Book, Microfilm & Digital Capture], compiled by William Wade Hinshaw, originally published 1938, republished by Genealogical Published Co., Inc., Baltimore, 1994,

1,126 pages. The second volume of the Great Encyclopedia is complete for the New Jersey and Pennsylvania monthly meetings which were part of the Philadelphia Yearly Meeting. It includes all records of genealogical value, both Orthodox and Hicksite, known to be in existence for the meetings from the last quarter of the seventeenth century down to the time the work was originally published in 1938. The records are of two principal classes: (1) births and deaths and (2) minutes and marriages, and they are arranged in alphabetical order, by family name, under their corresponding monthly meeting. The marriages are arranged by the names of both brides and grooms. Also provided are abstracts of Quaker certificates of removal, which enable genealogists to trace Quaker ancestors from one monthly meeting to another. Also available on microfilm, see FHL film # 432600-432601. To access the digital images, see the online FHL catalog page: **www.familysearch.org/search/catalog/185431.**
- **NOTE:** Vol. 4 pt. 2 (Ohio) is on FHL film #432604, indicated as digitized. However, the other 12 rolls of this series are still in process for digitizing.

1681-1838. *Encyclopedia of American Quaker Genealogy, Vol. 2: New Jersey and Pennsylvania Monthly Meetings* [Online Database], indexed at the Ancestry.com website. The Society of Friends (Quakers) were opposed to civil marriage ceremonies, and unless a couple were married within the meeting, they could not continue as members. The huge number of "marriages out of union" are noted in the monthly meeting records, and often give the wife's maiden name as well her new married name, so a genealogical connection can be made to her Quaker parents, grandparents, etc. The recording of births and deaths was also universal, and whole family groups might be listed in the record books. Another important record was when a member of one meeting wanted to move to another meeting. Such transfers were recorded, and the moving persons were given a letter attesting to their membership in good standing, which would be presented to the new meeting house for admission. Thus, it is possible to trace the movements of whole families from one state to another. This database has records. See **http://search.ancestry.com/search/db.aspx?dbid=48130.**

1680-2000s. See *Pennsylvania GenWeb Archives* [Online Database]. The PAGenWeb site offers free genealogical databases with searchable name lists, which may include Bibles, Biographies, Cemeteries, Censuses, Court, Death, Deeds, Directories, Histories, Marriages, Military, Newspapers, Obituaries, Photos, Schools, Tax Lists, Wills, and more. See **http://usgwarchives.net/pa/pafiles.htm.**

1680-2000s. *Linkpendium – Pennsylvania: Family History & Genealogy, Census, Birth, Marriage, Death Vita Records & More* **[Online Databases].** Linkpendium is a genealogical portal site, with links to local databases. Currently listed are selected sites for Pennsylvania: Statewide resources Selected sites (925), Adams County (603), Allegheny County (3,318), and 65 more counties. See **www.linkpendium.com/pa-genealogy.**

1680-2015 *Pennsylvania, Historical Society of Pennsylvania Card Catalog* **[Online Database],** digitized at the FamilySearch.org website. Images of the card catalog in the reference room of the Historical Society of Pennsylvania. This is an alphabetized card index categorized within the following subgroups: Afro-Americana Broadsides, Afro-Americana Manuscripts, Afro-Americana Prints, Broadsides, Family History, Graphics, Library Company Of Philadelphia Manuscripts (LCP), Manuscripts, Music, and Newspapers. This database has 946,124 images. See **https://familysearch.org/search/collection/2524622.**

1681-1950. *Pennsylvania Civil Marriages* **[Online Database],** indexed at the FamilySearch.org website. Index and images of various city and county marriage records, many from Philadelphia. This database has 241,745 records. See **https://familysearch.org/search/collection/2466357.**

1682-1950. *Index to Names of Land Purchasers.* **[Microfilm & Digital Capture],** from the original records located at the Bureau of Land Records, Harrisburg, PA, filmed by the Genealogical Society of Utah, 1976. The FHL cataloged these records as *Warrant Register, 1682-1950.* A warrant register is an index to the land surveys, warrants, and patents issued by the Proprietorship and Commonwealth of Pennsylvania to individuals. The resulting name list of land buyers is a valuable census substitute, naming up to 90% of the adult, white, male population of Pennsylvania. Locating a name of an ancestor in the warrant registers will connect the person to an exact land description for a certain parcel of land. Any subsequent sale of the same land would be recorded (as a deed) in the courthouse of the county wherein the land was located. Subsequent genealogical research can begin at that point for further evidence of a family in a

particular county. The real value of the warrant registers is that they can lead a family historian to the later county deed records, where the hidden genealogical treasures may lie. The Pennsylvania warrant registers are organized by survey districts (usually one county) as follows:
- Warrant registers, Vol. 1-3: Adams, York, Allegheny, Armstrong, Cambria, Fayette, Greene, Indiana, and Somerset counties, FHL film #1003194.
- Warrant registers, Vol. 4-7: Beaver, Butler, Crawford, Erie, Lawrence, Mercer, Venango, Warren, Bedford, Berks, Schuylkill, Blair, and Clarion counties, FHL film #1003195.
- Warrant registers Vol. 8-12: Bradford, Columbia, Montour, Sullivan, Susquehanna, Tioga, Wyoming, Cameron, Clearfield, Elk, Forest, Jefferson, Lycoming, McKean, Potter, Carbon, Lackawanna, Luzerne, Monroe, Centre, Clinton, and Huntingdon counties, FHL film #1003196.
- Warrant registers, Vol. 13-16: Dauphin, Lebanon, Franklin, Fulton, Juniata, Mifflin, Perry, Snyder, and Union counties, Northumberland lottery, Baynton and Wharton survey, Cumberland and Lancaster counties, FHL film #1003197.
- Warrant registers, Vol. 17-20: Northampton, Northumberland, Philadelphia, Chester, Bucks, Montgomery, Delaware, Wayne, Pike, and Lehigh counties, FHL film #1003198.
- Warrant registers, Vol. 21: Westmoreland and Washington counties, FHL film #1003199.

To access the digital images, see the online FHL catalog page: **www.familysearch.org/search/catalog/23738.**

1683-1993. *Pennsylvania Wills and Probate Records* **[Online Database],** digitized and indexed at the Ancestry.com website. Source: PA county, district, and probate courts. In most cases, the details found in probates include the names and residences of beneficiaries and their relationship to the decedent. An inventory of the estate assets may reveal personal details about the deceased's occupation and lifestyle. There may also be references to debts, deeds, and other documents related to the settling of the estate. This database has 1,926,283 records. See **http://search.ancestry.com/search/db.aspx?dbid=8802.**

1682-1976. *Pennsylvania, Church Records* **[Online Database],** digitized and indexed at FamilySearch. Includes images and index to selected marriage records from various churches. This database has 101,989 records, see **www.familysearch.org/search/collection/2466360.**

1683-1994. *Pennsylvania Probate Records* **[Online Database],** digitized at the FamilySearch.org website. This collection includes probate records created in

Pennsylvania counties. The records include wills, estate records and indexes. In most cases, the details found in probates include the names and residences of beneficiaries and their relationship to the decedent. An inventory of the estate assets may reveal personal details about the deceased's occupation and lifestyle. There may also be references to debts, deeds, and other documents related to the settling of the estate. This database has 3,200,560 images. There is no complete digitized index yet. But, images of the index books are included for each county. Browse through the records, first by county, then by any included index books for estates, wills, etc. See https://familysearch.org/search/collection/1999196.

1700-1821. *Pennsylvania, Marriage Records* **[Online Database],** digitized and indexed at the Ancestry.com website. This database contains marriage records from four volumes of the published *Pennsylvania Archives.* Each marriage item includes the name of the groom, bride, and dates and place of marriage. This database has 78,410 records. See http://search.ancestry.com/search/db.aspx?dbid=2383.

1700-1800s. See **"Delivering the Goods: The Country Storekeeper and Inland Commerce in the Mid-Atlantic" [Printed Article],** in The *Pennsylvania Magazine of History and Biography,* Vol. 129, No. 1 (Jan 2005).

1700-1900s, *Immigrants to the Middle Colonies: A Consolidation of Ship Passenger Lists and Associated Data From the New York Genealogical and Biographical Record* **[Printed Book],** edited by Michael Tepper, published by Genealogical Publishing Co., Inc., 1978, 190 pages. See FHL book 973 W3te.

1700-1900s. *Genealogical Miscellanea of Pennsylvania Families: With Related Records from New Jersey, Maryland, Delaware, New York* **[Printed Book],** researched and compiled into this book by Mildred Corson Williams, published at Danboro, PA, 1983, 569 pages. One of the better lists of the earliest families of the Middle Colonies. See FHL book 974.8 D2w.

1700-1914. *Encyclopedia of Pennsylvania Biography* **[Printed Book, Microfilm & Digital Version],** by John W. Jordan, publ. Lewis Historical Pub., New York, 1914, 32 volumes. The biographies cover all eras, but the main focus is 19th and early 20th century. FHL book 974.8 D3. Also on microfilm. Filmed by the Genealogical Society of Utah, 1989. 4 rolls, FHL film #1697289, 1320892, 1320852, 1698080, and 1320892. All 32 volumes of the *Encyclopedia of Pennsylvania Biography* was indexed in **Index to the Encyclopedia of Pennsylvania Biography, Volumes I-XXXII,** compiled by Frederic A. Godcharles; Index to Volumes XXI-XXXII compiled by Walter D. Stock publ. Clearfield, Baltimore, MD, 1996, 277 pages. From preface: "A cumulative index to volumes 1-20 containing about 16,000 names was published in 1932. A cumulative index to volumes 21-32 containing about 26,000 names was compiled in 1994 at the Free Library of Philadelphia." See FHL book 974.D3e. To access the digital versions, see the online FHL catalog page: **www.familysearch.org/search/catalog/209588.**

1705-1868. *Pennsylvania in the 1700's: An Index to Who Was There and Where* **[Printed Book & Microfilm],** by Donna Beers, Published Warrensburg, MO, 1998, 119 pages. Information extracted: name, age when given, event, date, source, and page number. See FHL book 974.8 H22b. Sources from which information was found:

- Lancaster Co., PA 1771 Census from Series 3, Vol. 17 of the Published PA Archives.
- PA Soldiers in the Provincial Service 1746-1759.
- The PA militia in 1777, by Hannah Benner Roach.
- Berks Co. PA births 1705-1800, by Jeffrey J. Howell.
- Berks Co. PA land warrants 1730-1868, by Howell & Paul.
- Bucks Co. PA land warrants 1730-1868.
- Chester Co. PA land warrants 1730-1868.
- East District PA land warrants 1730-1868.
- Lancaster Co. PA land warrants 1730-1868.
- Philadelphia Co. PA land warrants 1730-1868.
- Northampton Co. PA land warrants 1730-1868.
- Berks Co. PA land warrants 1730-1868.
- Bucks Co. PA deed book 5, 1713-1731.
- Bucks Co. PA Wills & Admin. Index 1684-1850.
- Cumberland Co. PA Marriages 1761-1812.
- History of Big Spring Presbyterian Church, Cumberland Co. PA.
- Encyclopedia American Quaker Genealogy Vol. II PA (Phil. MM Bucks Co.; Falls MM Bucks Co.).
- Quaker Arrivals at Philadelphia 1682-1750 by Albert Cook Myers 1971.
- An Index to the Will Books and Intestate Records of Lancaster Co. PA 1729-1850, by Eleanore Jane Fulton & Barbara Kendig Mylin 1981.
- Lancaster Co. PA Tax Lists 1751-1756-1757-1758 by Dr. Albert H Gerberich 1933.
- Index to the 1718-1727 Tax Records of Chester Co. Relating to Areas Later Part of Lancaster Co. PA by Gary T. Hawbaker.

1669-2013. *Pennsylvania and New Jersey, Church and Town Records* **[Online Database],** digitized and indexed at the Ancestry.com website. Source: Historical Society of Pennsylvania. The documents in this database are mostly Protestant church records from congregations in Pennsylvania and New Jersey, but there are also some for locations in the neighboring states of Maryland, Delaware, and Virginia. In addition to church records, sources also include funeral homes, cemeteries, newspapers, historical societies, and personal records. They include a wide variety of records, such as lists of church officers, communion lists, marriages, registers of members, registers of elders, deacons, etc., baptisms, confirmations, burials, probationers, histories, receipts, agreements, other miscellaneous items, and newspaper extracts. The documents list millions of names, and many contain details on vital events such as births, marriages, and deaths. In them, you may find names, birth dates, marriage dates, spouse's name, parents' names, and places where an event (baptism, marriage, death, burial, etc.) took place. This database has 14,243,547 records. www.ancestry.com/search/collections/pachurchtownrecords.

1709-1940. *Pennsylvania Marriages* **[Online Database],** indexed at the FamilySearch.org website. Name index to marriage records from microfilm at the Family History Library. This database has 476,245 records. See https://familysearch.org/search/collection/1681011.

1709-1950. *Pennsylvania Births and Christenings* **[Online Database],** indexed at the FamilySearch.org website. Name index to birth, baptism, and christening records from microfilm at the Family History Library. This database has 951,480 records. See https://familysearch.org/search/collection/1681005.

1719-1996. *Pennsylvania Newspaper Archives* **[Online Databases],** digitized and indexed newspapers at the GenealogyBank website for the following cities: Allentown, Bedford, Brownsville, Bustleton, Carlisle, Chambersburg, Chestnut Hill, Doylestown, Easton, Erie, Germantown, Gettysburg Greensburg Harrisburg Hazleton, Kittanning, Lancaster, Lebanon, Montrose, Newtown, Philadelphia, Pittsburgh, Reading, Scranton, Shippensburg, State College, Sunbury, Tunkhannock, Washington, Waynesboro, West Chester, and Wilkes-Barre. See www.genealogybank.com/explore/newspapers/all/usa/pennsylvania.

1730-1850. *Loosening the Bonds: Mid-Atlantic Farm Women* **[Printed Book],** by Joan M. Jensen, publ. Yale University Press, New Haven, CT, 1986, 271 pages, FHL book 973 H2je. To view a digital version of this book, see the online FHL catalog page for this title. See https://familysearch.org/search/catalog/548909.

1730-1779. *Pennsylvania, Lutheran Baptisms and Marriages* **[Online Database],** indexed at the Ancestry.com website. This database is a collection of Lutheran Church baptism and marriage records from southeastern Pennsylvania between 1730 and 1779. The records were kept largely by Rev. John Casper Stoever. Baptism records, in addition to providing the location and date, include the child's name, parents' names, birth date, and names of sponsors. Marriage records include the names of both spouses, and marriage location. It contains the names of over 6,000 people. See http://search.ancestry.com/search/db.aspx?dbid=4640.

1733-1858. *Warrantees of Land for Philadelphia County, Pennsylvania* **[Online Database],** indexed at the USGenWeb archives site for Pennsylvania.
For Surnames A-K, see http://files.usgwarchives.net/pa/philadelphia/land/warrantees1.txt.
For Surnames L-Z, see http://files.usgwarchives.net/pa/philadelphia/land/warrantees2.txt.

1733-1952. *Pennsylvania, Land Warrants and Applications* **[Online Database],** indexed at the Ancestry.com website. Source: PA State Archives. Land warrants contain descriptions of the land, information about boundaries, landmarks, previous owners, tenants, the amount of money paid, etc. Warrant applications contain less information than full warrants, which may contain maps and other information about the property. This database has 176,771 records. See http://search.ancestry.com/search/db.aspx?dbid=2350.

1740-1773. *Pennsylvania Naturalizations* **[Online Database],** indexed at the Ancestry.com website. This database is a listing of persons naturalized in the colony between 1740 and 1773. Compiled from records in the Pennsylvania Archives, each record contains the individual's name, location of naturalization, and date.

It contains the names of over 3,700 persons. See http://search.ancestry.com/search/db.aspx?dbid=4259.

1740-1900. See *Pennsylvania, 1740-1900* [CD-ROM], originally published Broderbund, 1998, part of Family Tree Maker's Archives. (FHL CD: County and Family Histories, No. 193). Contains images of pages of the following books:

- History of Beaver County, PA: And its Centennial Celebration, by Joseph H. Bausman (vols. 1-2).
- History of Butler County, Pennsylvania (vols. 1-2).
- Commemorative Biographical Record of Central Pennsylvania: Including the Counties of Centre, Clearfield, Jefferson, and Clarion.
- History of Erie County, Pennsylvania.
- History of Luzerne County, Pennsylvania: With Biographical Selections, H.C. Bradsby, editor.
- Byram-Crawford and Allied Families Genealogy, by Eunice Bryam Roberts.
- Bibliography of Pennsylvania History: Second Edition of Writings on Pennsylvania history, a Bibliography, compiled by Norman B. Wilkinson.
- The descendants of John Cadwallader of Wales, Horsham and Warminster, by Anna H. Baker.
- Family Record and Biography, compiled by Leander James McCormick.
- Chester (and its vicinity), Delaware County in Pennsylvania: With Genealogical Sketches of Some Old Families, by John Hill Martin.
- Monnet family genealogy: An Emphasis of a Noble Huguenot Heritage, by Orra Eugene Monnette.
- Pennsylvania Archives (vols. 2, 9).
- A Pennsylvania Pioneer: Biographical Sketch With a Report of the Executive Committee.
- The Strassburger Family and Allied Families of Pennsylvania: Being the Ancestry of Jacob Andrew Strassburger, Esquire, of Montgomery County, Pennsylvania, by his son Ralph Beaver Strassburger.

1747-2007. *Pennsylvania, Carbon County, City of Jim Thorpe, Cemetery Records* [Online Database], digitized and indexed at FamilySearch.org. This database has 17,417 records, see www.familysearch.org/search/collection/1447492.

1750-1940. *Lancaster, Pennsylvania, Mennonite Vital Records* [Online Database], digitized and indexed at the Ancestry.com website. Source: Lancaster Mennonite Historical Society. This is a digitized version of a card file maintained by the Mennonite Historical Society. Each card contains names, family relationships, birth dates and places, death dates and places, and marriage dates and places. Links to 2 or 3 generations is possible for virtually every record. This database has 922,365 records. See http://search.ancestry.com/search/db.aspx?dbid=60592.

1755. *Military and Political Affairs in the Middle Colonies in 1755: The Effect of Braddock's Defeat, and Party Dissensions in Maryland and Pennsylvania* [Printed Book & Digital Version], by Daniel Dulany, reprinted from a journal article, no date. To access the digital version, see the online FHL catalog: https://familysearch.org/search/catalog/1764138.

1759 Warrants and Surveys of the Province of Pennsylvania Including the Three Lower Counties [Printed Book, Microfilm & Digital Version], compiled by Allen Winberg and Thomas E. Slattery under the directory of Charles E. Hughes, Jr., 1965 edition published by Department Records, Philadelphia. The Provincial Assembly representing the people of Pennsylvania was in conflict with the sons of William Penn who were the Proprietaries of the Province of Pennsylvania. Records of Warrants under the control of the Proprietaries and which ordered surveys to be made were not public records. This created confusion over property rights and boundaries. In 1759 the Assembly passed a law for recording warrants and surveys. The Proprietaries in 1760 brought the law before King George III who vetoed it. In the meantime, the warrants were transcribed and made public. This is an index of names recorded in the warrants in the present-day Pennsylvania counties of Berks, Bucks, Chester, Cumberland, Lancaster, Northampton, Philadelphia, and York; and the three counties Kent, Newcastle, and Sussex making up Delaware. FHL has a reprint by The Bookmark, Knightstown, IN, 1975, 91 pages. See FHL book 974.8 R2w. To access the digital version, see the online FHL catalog page: www.familysearch.org/search/catalog/249920.

1760-1790s Pennsylvania Tax Lists [CD ROM]. The published Pennsylvania Archives consists of 136 volumes of early Pennsylvania government records, grouped into ten series. Volumes 11-22 of the Third Series contain tax lists from the 1760s to the early 1790s. These lists were transcribed and compiled from original tax lists for their permanent preservation in the late 1880s, and several have been published separate from the PA Archives series. The years and type of tax vary from county to county, but in all cases, the names of tax payers are listed by township and most include the number of acres, horses and cattle owned by each taxpayer. Of special note is the Land Return Tax of 1783 for Westmoreland and of 1784 for Bucks and Bedford counties, along with the List of Inhabitants for York County in 1783. These lists contain names of all inhabitants and can serve as a complete census substitute for those counties. The importance of these tax lists from the Pennsylvania Archives series has seen several publications released. Most recently, for example, Retrospect Publishing of Alexandria, Virginia released a CD-ROM, *Volumes 11-22 of the Third Series,* a digitized textual reproduction in which every word is indexed for finding surnames or places. An earlier publication was *Returns of Taxables for the Counties of Bedford (1773 to 1784), Huntingdon (1788), Westmoreland (1783, 1786), Fayette (1785, 1786), Allegheny (1791), Washington (1786), A Census of Bedford (1784) and Westmoreland (1783)* **[Microfilm & Digital Version],** from the original book edited by William Henry Egle, State Archivist, published Harrisburg, PA, by W.S. Ray, 1897, 782 pages, as part of *Pennsylvania archives,* third series, vol. 22. Filmed by the Genealogical Society of Utah, 1966, 1 roll, FHL film #432614. To access the digital version of Vol. 22, see the online FHL catalog page: **www.familysearch.org/search/catalog/313183.**

1768-1801. *Pennsylvania, Tax and Exonerations* **[Online Database],** indexed at the Ancestry.com website. This database contains exoneration (exemption) returns and diverse tax lists from the colonial and early federal eras of Pennsylvania. Included are supply taxes, 18-penny taxes, liquor taxes, carriage and billiard table taxes, and others. Records from the 18 counties are included:
Details may include, name, residence, occupation, land owned, Negroes owned, tax rate, and whether a man was a single freeman. This database has 1,035,593 records. See **http://search.ancestry.com/search/db.aspx?dbid=2497.**

1772-1890. *Pennsylvania, Compiled Census and Census Substitutes* **[Online Database],** indexed at the Ancestry.com website. Originally edited by Ronald Jackson, Accelerated Indexing Systems, Salt Lake City, UT. This collection contains the following indexes: 1772 Tax List (Northampton County); 1790 Federal Census Index; 1800 Federal Census Index; 1810 Federal Census Index; 1820 Federal Census Index; 1830 Federal Census Index; 1840 Federal Census Index; 1840 Pensioners List; 1842 Chester County Census Index; 1850 Federal Census Index;

1857 Chester County Census Index; 1860 Federal Census Index; 1870 Federal Census Index; 1890 Naval Veterans Schedule; Early Census Records. This database has 75,474 records. See **http://search.ancestry.com/search/db.aspx?dbid=3570.**

1775-1783. *Pennsylvania, Revolutionary War Battalions and Militia Index* **[Online Database],** indexed at the Ancestry.com website. Source: Historical Society of PA. This database contains an index to Pennsylvania in the War of the Revolution, 4 volumes. These books include rosters, muster rolls, histories, diaries, and other documents listing Pennsylvanian troops. The cards in this database list names, sometimes rank, and a volume and page reference to the source volume. This database has 46,763 records. See **http://search.ancestry.com/search/db.aspx?dbid=2591.**

1776-1790. *Election Returns* **[Microfilm & Digital Capture],** from the originals at the PA Historical and Museum Commission, Harrisburg, PA. Filmed by the Commission, 1978, 4 rolls, FHL has the following:
• Election returns: Allegheny County, 1788-1790. Bedford County, 1776-1790; Berks County, 1776-1790; Bucks County, 1776-1790, FHL film #1759094.
• Election returns: Chester County, 1776-1790 & Cumberland County, 1776-1790; Dauphin County, 1785-1790; Delaware County, 1789-1790; Fayette County, 1784-1790; Franklin County, 1784-1790. Huntingdon County, 1787-1790; Lancaster County, 1776-1790; Lebanon County, 1784 Luzerne County, 1787-1790. FHL film #1759095.
• Election returns: Mifflin County, 1789-1790. Montgomery County, 1789-1790; Northampton County, 1776-1790; Northumberland County, 1776-1790. Philadelphia County, 1776-1790; Philadelphia City, 1781-1788; Washington County, 1781-1790. Westmoreland County, 1776-1788, FHL film #1759096.
• Election returns: Westmoreland County, 1789; York County, 1777-1790, FHL film #1759097.
To access the digital images, see the online FHL catalog page: **www.familysearch.org/search/catalog/685513.**

1777-2012. *Pennsylvania, Veterans Burial Cards* **[Online Database],** indexed at the Ancestry.com website. Source: PA State Archives. Information in this database: Surname, Branch of service, Dates of service, Birth date, Death date, Cemetery/Interment name and location, County, Residence at time of death, and War served. This database has 1,160,879 records. See **http://search.ancestry.com/search/db.aspx?dbid=1967.**

1779-1863. *Pennsylvania, Septennial Census* **[Online Database],** indexed at the Ancestry.com website. Source: PA Historical and Museum Commission. Beginning in 1779, the state undertook enumerations of inhabitants every seven years for tax purposes and to determine representation in state government. These counts are called the septennial censuses. The septennial censuses listed all state residents who were eligible to be taxed. Early records might provide only name, county, and township. Women did not typically appear, though some are listed as "Widow" with their late husband's name. As the years went on, the forms collected additional data, and you may find ages, occupations, and gender recorded, as well as women's first names. This database has 391,167 records. See http://search.ancestry.com/search/db.aspx?dbid=2702.

1780. *Pennsylvania in 1780: A Statewide Index of circa 1780 Pennsylvania Tax Lists* **[Printed Book],** compiled by John D. and E. Diane Stemmons, published by Southwest Pennsylvania Genealogical Services, Laughlintown, PA, 1978, 217 pages. Includes the counties of Bedford, Berks, Bucks, Chester, Cumberland, Lancaster, Northampton, Northumberland, Philadelphia, Westmoreland, and York. See FHL book 974.8 R42.

1791. *Allegheny County, Pennsylvania, Return of Taxables, 1791* **[Online Database],** indexed at the GenealogyTrails website. See http://genealogytrails.com/penn/allegheny/allegpa_1791 taxables.html.

1791-1861. *Pennsylvania, Philadelphia, Seamen's Proofs of Citizenship* **[Online Database],** digitized at the FamilySearch.org website. Source: National Archives microfilm series M1880. Proofs of Citizenship used to apply for seamen's certificates for the Port of Philadelphia, Pennsylvania, 1792-1861. This database has 67,977 images. See https://familysearch.org/search/collection/2290427.

1794-1908. *Pennsylvania, Naturalization Records from Supreme and District Courts* **[Online Database],** indexed at the Ancestry.com website. Source: PA Historical and Museum Commission. Includes petitions, declarations, and certificates. This database has 19,698 records. See http://search.ancestry.com/search/db.aspx?dbid=2393.

1795-1930. *Pennsylvania, Naturalization Records from Circuit and District Courts* **[Online Database],** indexed at the Ancestry.com website. Source: National Archives microfilm series M1522. Includes petitions, declarations, and certificates. This database has 417,869 records. See http://search.ancestry.com/search/db.aspx?dbid=2717.

1795-1931. *Pennsylvania, Eastern District Petitions for Naturalization* **[Online Database],** digitized at the FamilySearch.org website. Source: National Archives microfilm series M1522. The information typically includes the name of the individual, petition number, declaration number, birthdate, date of petition or declaration, and occasionally other pieces of information: name variations, marriage information, etc. The card index to this series was digitized and indexed for the period 1795-1952 (NARA M1248). This database has 326,903 images. See https://familysearch.org/search/collection/1913395.

1795-1952. *Pennsylvania, Eastern District Naturalization Indexes* **[Online Database],** indexed at the FamilySearch.org website. Source: National Archives microfilm series M1248. Soundex card indexes to naturalization petitions and declarations of intention from the U.S. Circuit and District Courts for the Eastern District of Pennsylvania. This database has 231,641 records. See https://familysearch.org/search/collection/1937344.

1798. *United States Direct Tax of 1798, Tax Lists for the State of Pennsylvania* **[Microfilm & Digital Capture],** from the original records at the National Archives, Washington, DC. Filmed by the National Archives, series M0372, 24 rolls. Name lists organized as follows:
- Philadelphia City, FHL film #351594- 351595.
- Philadelphia County, FHL film #351596-351598.
- Lancaster County, FHL film #351599.
- Chester (part) and Delaware counties, FHL film #351600.
- Bucks County, FHL film #351601.
- Montgomery County, FHL film #351602.
- Berks County, FHL film #351603.
- Dauphin County, FHL film #351604.
- Northampton and Wayne counties, FHL film #351605.
- Luzerne County, FHL film #351606.
- York County, 351607-351609.
- Cumberland County, FHL film #351610.
- Huntingdon and Somerset counties, FHL film #351614.

- Franklin County, FHL film #351611.
- Northumberland, Lycoming, and Mifflin counties, FHL film #351612.
- Bedford County, FHL film #351613.
- Westmoreland County, FHL film #351615.
- Fayette County, FHL film #351616.
- Green, Washington, and Allegheny counties, FHL film #351617.

To access the digital images, see the online FHL catalog page: www.familysearch.org/search/catalog/290639.

1798-1828. *Pennsylvania Landing Reports of Aliens* **[Online Database]**, digitized at the FamilySearch.org website. Source: National Archives microfilm series M1639. Reports of aliens arriving in the Eastern District of Pennsylvania, 1798-1828. Information in these records typically includes the name of the immigrant, place of birth, date of birth, age upon arrival, port of departure, port of arrival, and date of arrival. Browse through 1,270 pages of yearly reports, each starting with an index. This database has 636 images. See https://familysearch.org/search/collection/1908383.

1800-1882. *Pennsylvania, Philadelphia Passenger Lists* **[Online Database]**, indexed at the FamilySearch.org website. Source: National Archives microfilm series M425, *Passenger Lists of Vessels Arriving at Philadelphia, Pennsylvania, 1800-1882.* This database has 489,494 records. See https://familysearch.org/search/collection/1908535.

1800-1906. *Pennsylvania, Philadelphia Passenger Lists Index* **[Online Database]**, indexed at the FamilySearch.org website. Source: National Archives microfilm series M360. *Index to Passenger List of Vessels Arriving at Philadelphia, Pennsylvania, 1800-1906.* This database has 530,556 records. See https://familysearch.org/search/collection/2173965.

1800-1935. *Pennsylvania, Huntingdon County, Delayed Birth Records* **[Online Database]**, digitized and indexed at FamilySearch. Digital images of the originals are held by the Huntingdon County Register & Recorder in Huntingdon, PA. This database has 4,921 records, see www.familysearch.org/search/collection/3157976.

1803-1915. *Pennsylvania, Philadelphia City Death Certificates* **[Online Database]**, indexed at the FamilySearch.org website. Source: Philadelphia City Archives. This collection has several types of records: 1) Death certificate 2) Death register 3) Return of Death with a hospital certificate, physician's certificate, and

an undertaker's certificate, and 4) Transit Permit with the permit to move a body and an undertaker's certificate concerning the move. The records give the name of the deceased plus the date and place of death and/or burial. The records may also give the date and place of birth, names of parents and spouse, cause of death, and other information. This database has 2,442,468 records. See https://familysearch.org/search/collection/1320976.

1812-1813 Pittsburgh and Vicinity Directory & 1819 Pittsburgh Directory **[Online Database]**, indexed at the PA Genealogy Trails website. See http://genealogytrails.com/penn/allegheny/allegpa_cityd irectory.html.

1812-1814. See *Pennsylvania, Volunteers in the War of 1812* **[Online Database]**, indexed at the Ancestry.com website. Source: PA State Archives. this database is a listing of soldiers who volunteered to fight the British during the War of 1812. Each volunteer is listed with the county from which he came and the year in which he enlisted. In addition to this information, the list is organized by rank and position. This database has 18,666 records. See http://search.ancestry.com/search/db.aspx?dbid=3325.

1845-1960. *Pennsylvania, Pittsburgh, Allegheny Cemetery Records* **[Online Database]**, digitized and indexed at FamilySearch.org. This collection includes an internment card index, internment register, and day books for the Allegheny Cemetery in Pittsburgh. The card index is for the internment register and the plot books. Microfilms of the originals are held at the Allegheny Cemetery in Pittsburgh, PA. This database has197,218 records, see www.familysearch.org/search/collection/3155912.

1852-1854. *Pennsylvania Births* **[Online Database]**, indexed at the Ancestry.com website. Source: PA State Archives. Includes registers of birth from 39 Pennsylvania counties, with names, dates, and other details. This database has 4,803 records. See http://search.ancestry.com/search/db.aspx?dbid=2349.

1852-1854. *Pennsylvania Marriages* **[Online Database]**, digitized and indexed at the Ancestry.com website. Source: PA State Archives. Includes registers of marriage from 49 Pennsylvania counties, with names of parties, date, and place of marriage. This database has 9,368 records. See http://search.ancestry.com/search/db.aspx?dbid=2486.

1852-1854. *Pennsylvania Deaths* [Online Database], digitized and indexed at the Ancestry.com website. Source: PA State Archives. Includes registers of death from 49 Pennsylvania counties, with name of deceased, date and place of death, and more information. This database has 6,144 records. See http://search.ancestry.com/search/db.aspx?dbid=2487.

1860-1869. *Pennsylvania, Civil War Muster Rolls* [Online Database], indexed at the Ancestry.com website. Source: PA Historical & Museum Commission. This collection includes muster out rolls, arranged by regiment and thereunder by company. They list the soldier's name, age, rank, unit, regiment, and company; the date, place, and person who mustered him in; the period of enlistment; and the name of the commanding officer. This database has 324,444 records. See http://search.ancestry.com/search/db.aspx?dbid=9040.

1860-1906. *Pennsylvania, Philadelphia City Births* [Online Database], digitized and indexed at the FamilySearch.org website. This collection is a name index and images of birth registers from the Board of Health in the city of Philadelphia. It includes birth returns filed by physicians, midwives and area hospitals or other facilities. This database has 1,022,168 records. See https://familysearch.org/search/collection/1951739.

1861-1865. *Colonels in Blue: Union Army Colonels of the Civil War: The Mid-Atlantic States – Pennsylvania, New Jersey, Maryland, Delaware and the District of Columbia* [Printed Book], by Roger D. Hunt, publ. Stackpole Books, Mechanicsburg, PA, 2007, 250 pages, FHL book 973 M2hcb. To view a digital version of this book, see the online FHL catalog page for this title. See https://familysearch.org/search/catalog/1921541.

1865-1936. *Pennsylvania, Grand Army of the Republic Membership Records* [Online Database], indexed at the FamilySearch.org website. Source PA Historical and Museum Commission. Includes membership records of the Pennsylvania Department Grand Army of the Republic, an organization of Union army and navy veterans of the Civil War. The descriptive books include town of residence, military unit, date of enlistment, date of discharge, age, and birthplace. This database has 14,100 records. See https://familysearch.org/search/collection/2207723.

1866-1879. *Pennsylvania, War of 1812 Pensions* [Online Database], indexed at the Ancestry.com website. The pension files in this database typically contain either of the following types of notarized documents: **Applications of Soldiers.** These were submitted by veterans and provide the veteran's name, signature, residence, ranks, military units, commanding officers, periods of service, and approximate dates of enlistments and honorable discharges. **Applications of Widows.** These were submitted by wives of deceased veterans and generally contain information similar to that found on the Applications of Soldiers. Marriage dates and husbands' death dates are often included starting in the 1870s. A few applications also provide ages and the veteran's place of death. This database has 19,369 records. See http://search.ancestry.com/search/db.aspx?dbid=2394.

1870-1905. *Pennsylvania, Pittsburgh City Deaths* [Online Database], indexed at the FamilySearch.org website. Includes death registrations for the city of Pittsburgh from the Allegheny County Courthouse. The records are arranged in numbered bound volumes and are by year, month, and year. This database has 164,487 records. See https://familysearch.org/search/collection/1810412.

1877-1886. *Pennsylvania Index, Volume 1* [Printed Book & Digital Version], an index to Vols. 1-10 of the Pennsylvania Magazine of History and Biography, publ. Historical Society of Pennsylvania, 1877-1886. See FHL book 974.8 B2pm v.1-10 index. To access the digital images, see the online FHL catalog: https://familysearch.org/search/catalog/7468.

1883-1945. *Pennsylvania, Philadelphia Passenger Lists* [Online Database], indexed at the FamilySearch.org website. Source: National Archives microfilm series T840, *Passenger Lists of Vessels Arriving at Philadelphia, Pennsylvania, 1883-1945.* This database has 1,176,253 records. See https://familysearch.org/search/collection/1921481.

1883-1948. *Pennsylvania, Philadelphia Passenger List Index Cards* [Online Database], indexed at the FamilySearch.org website. Source: National Archives microfilm series T526. This is a Soundex card index to Philadelphia passenger lists from 1 Jan 1883 through 28 Jun 1948. Each card contains the given name, family name, place of birth, age, gender, occupation, nationality, last permanent residence, destination, name & address of relative or friend, port & date of entry, name of ship, and the volume, page, and line number in the passenger lists. The cards are filed according to the Soundex number associated with each family name and then by given names. This database has 1,153,207 records. See **https://familysearch.org/search/collection/1921483**.

1885-1889. *Pennsylvania, Records of Marriages* **[Online Database],** indexed at the Ancestry.com website. Source: PA State Archives. Entries can include the following details: name of groom, occupation, residence, place of birth, age, color, date of marriage, name of bride, residence, place of birth, age, color, and county where license was obtained. This database has 37,562 records. See **http://search.ancestry.com/search/db.aspx?dbid=2489**.

1885-1950. *Pennsylvania, County Marriages* **[Online Database],** indexed at the FamilySearch.org website. This collection includes civil marriage records created in Pennsylvania counties. The records include registers, affidavits, and marriage licenses. In some instances, divorce records are recorded with marriages. This database has 2,246,248 records. See **https://familysearch.org/search/collection/1589502**.

1885-1951. *Pennsylvania, Philadelphia Marriage Indexes* **[Online Database],** indexed at the FamilySearch.org website. Source: Philadelphia City Hall. Marriage indexes are arranged by the names of brides and grooms with the year of the marriage and the license number. The surname of the spouse is shown in parentheses. Use the license numbers listed in this index to find copies of the marriage license records. Marriage license records for years 1885-1915 are available on microfilm at the Family History Library and Family History Centers. Marriage license records for years 1916-1951 are available at the City Hall, Philadelphia, PA. This database has 1,830,468 records. See **https://familysearch.org/search/collection/1388247**.

1895-1980. *Genealogies of Pennsylvania Families from the Pennsylvania Genealogical Magazine* **[Online Database],** indexed at the Ancestry.com website. This is a 3-vol. index of every family history article published in *The Pennsylvania Magazine* from its founding in 1895 through 1980.
For Volume 1: Arnold-Hertzel, see
http://search.ancestry.com/search/db.aspx?dbid=48375.
For Volume 2: Hinman-Sotcher, see
http://search.ancestry.com/search/db.aspx?dbid=48376.
For Volume 3: Stauffer-Zerbe, see
http://search.ancestry.com/search/db.aspx?dbid=48604.

1887-1979. Pennsylvania, Berks County, Reading, Charles Evans Cemetery and Crematory Burial Record [Online Database], digitized and indexed at FamilySearch.org. This collection includes permit books, burial cards, and diagram cards. Burial cards and diagram cards are an index to the permit books. Burial cards list the name of the deceased, lot owner, lot number, lot section, age at death (year, month, day). (On the cards where birth and death dates are indicated - this information supplied by the funeral director. The cemetery then determined from this information the year, month, and day of the age of the deceased). Diagram cards list lot number and section along with a diagram of the lot and persons interred there on. Microfilm of the original records is located in the Charles Evens Cemetery and Crematory. This database has 101,654 records, see
www.familysearch.org/search/collection/3241365.

1898-1934. *Pennsylvania, Spanish War Compensation* **[Online Database],** indexed at the Ancestry.com website. This database contains applications for compensation for soldiers from Pennsylvania who served in the conflicts around the turn of the century. This database has 34,097 records. See
http://search.ancestry.com/search/db.aspx?dbid=2392.

1900-1923. *Pennsylvania, Philadelphia Case Files of Chinese Immigrants, 1900-1923* **[Online Database],** digitized at the FamilySearch.org website.
Source: National Archives microfilm series M1144. Browse through 60,096 images, which includes an Index to Chinese Case Files, and an Index to ship names appearing case files. See
https://familysearch.org/search/collection/1888682.

1902 Roster of Children in the Soldiers' Orphan Schools: PA **[Online Database],** indexed at the USGenWeb site for Pennsylvania.
For A-J Counties, see
http://files.usgwarchives.net/pa/1pa/xmisc/orphansa-j.txt.
For L-Y Counties, see
http://files.usgwarchives.net/pa/1pa/xmisc/orphansl-y.txt.

1906-1911. *Pennsylvania, Birth Certificates* **[Online Database],** digitized and indexed at the Ancestry.com website. Source: PA Dept of Health. Title should say "Certificates," as this database includes full images and index to birth certificates, 1906-1908. Details include a child's name, birth date, gender, multiple birth, and legitimacy, father's name, race, age, residence, birth-

…continued on page 220

Form No. 1 ⬛—10   MAY 23 1950   COMMONWEALTH OF PENNSYLVANIA   40326
WORLD WAR II VETERANS' COMPENSATION BUREAU

APPLICATION FOR WORLD WAR II COMPENSATION—TO BE USED BY HONORABLY DISCHARGED VETERAN OR PERSON STILL IN SERVICE

IMPORTANT—Before Filling Out This Form Study it Carefully.
Read and Follow Instructions—Print Plainly in Ink or Use Typewriter. DO NOT
Use Pencil—All Signatures Must Be in Ink.

Applicant Must Not Write
In Sp... MAY 16 1950

Date Application Was Filed

1—Name of Applicant.

AAGESEN   JOHN   J.P.
Last   First   Middle or Initial

Batch Control Number
30170

2—Address to Which CHECK and MAIL is to be Sent.   51

3135 MAGEE AVE, PhiLA 24, PA.
House No. St. R. D. P. O. Box   City or Town   County   State

Active Domestic Service
Months $ 19 o
Days   17 $
Amount Due $

3—Date and Place of Birth.

AUG 29, 1925   PHILADELPHIA, PA.
Month Day Year   City or Town   County   State

4—Name Under Which Applicant Served In World War II.

SAME NAME
Last   First   Middle or Initial

Active Foreign Service
Months $
Days $
Amount Due $

5—Date of Beginning and Date of Ending of Each Period of Service Between December 7, 1941
and March 2, 1946 (Both Dates Inclusive) During Which Applicant Was In DOMESTIC
SERVICE.

AuGusT 17, 1944   181-17"

Date of Beginning   Date of Ending

Total Amt. Due $ 19 o
Audited By   Keister
Service Computed By

6—Date of Beginning and Date of Ending of Each Period of Service Between December 7, 1941
and March 2, 1946 (Both Dates Inclusive) During Which Applicant Was In FOREIGN SERVICE.

61N

Date of Beginning   Date of Ending

Amounts Extended By

Approved For Payment
Date   JUL 2 1950
For A. G.
For Aud. G.
For S. ...
Application Disapproved

7—Date and Place Applicant Entered Active Service.

8   17   44   CAMP PEARY - VIRGINIA
Month Day Year   Place

By

8—Service or Serial Numbers Assigned To Applicant.

Service No's.   980 73 18

Serial No's.

9—Date and Place Where Applicant Was Separated From Active Service.

MAY   19   1946   BAINBRIDGE   MD.
Month Day Year   Place

10—Is Applicant Now Serving In Armed Forces On Active Duty?   Yes _____   No _____
If Answer Is YES—Be Sure To Have Certificate Executed And Filed With Application—See Instruction Sheet.

11—Mark "X" Above Name To Indicate Sex And Branch of Service.

X   X   SEABEES
Male   Female   Army   Navy   Marine Corps   Coast Guard   Other—Describe

12—Applicant's Residence At Time of Entry Into Active Service.

155 E. WESTMORELAND - ST.   PhiLA   34   PENNA.
House No.   Street   R. D.   P. O. Box   City or Town   County   State

13—Applicant Was Registered Under Selective Service As Follows.

No 38   Philadelphia 34 Penna
Draft Board No.   City or Town   County   State

1950-1966. See *Pennsylvania, Veteran Compensation Application Files, WWII, 1950-1956* [Online Database], indexed at the Ancestry.com website. Source: PA State Archives. Following World War II, the Commonwealth of Pennsylvania paid honorably discharged veterans and those still in service a bonus compensation. Applications for Compensation asked the following: Name (and name under which veteran served), Address, Date and place of birth, Service dates, Service/serial numbers, Whether on active duty at the time of application, Gender and branch of service, Residence at the time of entry to service, Draft board if drafted, Amount of compensation, Name and address of beneficiaries, Naval stations or posts, Signature and date. This database has 1,193,450 records. See http://search.ancestry.com/search/db.aspx?dbid=3147.

place, and occupation; mother's maiden name, race, age, residence, birthplace, and occupation. This database has 3,932,398 records. See **www.ancestry.com/search/collections/general-60484.**

1906-1963. *Pennsylvania, Death Certificates* **[Online Database],** digitized and indexed at the Ancestry.com website. Source: PA Dept of Health. Includes full images and index to death certificates. Each record contains the following: name and residence of the decedent, city and county of death, gender and race, marital status, age and date of birth, occupation, place of birth, parents' names and birthplaces, date of death, dates attended by physician, cause of death, attending physician and address, length of stay in hospital or institution or length of residency for transients or recent arrivals, place of burial or removal, date of burial, undertaker name and address, and name and address of informant. This database has 22,483,673 records. See **http://search.ancestry.com/search/db.aspx?dbid=5164.**

1906-1990 Pennsylvania, Allegheny, Pittsburgh, Naturalization Card File Index **[Online Database]**, a digitized card index at FamilySearch.org. Source: National Archives, US District Court Records. The names in this collection are not always in strict alphabetical order. Microfilm originals of these records are in the clerk's office of the U.S. District Court in Pittsburgh. This database has 116,726 records, see **www.familysearch.org/search/collection/3037614.**

1908 & 1911. *Pennsylvania, Philadelphia, Board of Health Birth Return Records* **[Online Database],** digitized and indexed at FamilySearch.org. Birth return records for the years 1908 & 1911, filed by the attending physician, midwife, or hospital for the city of Philadelphia. This database has 9,198 records, see

1910-1968. *Pennsylvania, Order Sons of Italy in America, Enrollment and Death Benefit Records* **[Online Database],** indexed at the Ancestry.com website. Records typically include names and death dates. Enrollment cards may also list Address, date of birth, registration/enrollment date, marital status, spouse's name, and spouse's death date, Some records are in Italian. This database has 68,726 records. See **http://search.ancestry.com/search/db.aspx?dbid=1793.**

1914-2007. *Pennsylvania, Schuylkill County, Schuylkill Haven, Funeral Home Obituary Cards* **[Online Database],** digitized and indexed at FamilySearch.org. Digital images of originals housed at the Ebling & Stabingas Funeral Home, Inc., in Schuylkill Haven, PA. This database has 957 records, see **www.familysearch.org/search/collection/3021637.**

1917-1948. See *Pennsylvania, WWI Veterans Service and Compensation Files, 1917-1919, 1934-1948* **[Online Database],** indexed at the Ancestry.com website. This collection consists of folders containing service statement cards, compensation applications, and war service record survey questionnaires filled out by World War I veterans. This database has 706,549 records. See **http://search.ancestry.com/search/db.aspx?dbid=60884.**

1917-1978. *Pennsylvania, Order Sons of Italy in America, Mortuary Fund Claims* **[Online Database],** indexed at the Ancestry.com website. This database has 24,459 records. See **http://search.ancestry.com/search/db.aspx?dbid=1773.**

1920-1980. *Pennsylvania, Oliver H. Bair Funeral Records Indexes* **[Online Database],** digitized and indexed at the Ancestry.com website. Source: Historical Society of PA. This a digitized card index to the funerals by the Oliver Bair Company funeral homes in the Philadelphia area. Each card may include names of people being charged for the funeral, addresses, family members and indications of family relationships (niece, widow, son, etc.), and dates and place of death and burial. This database has 235,771 records. See **http://search.ancestry.com/search/db.aspx?dbid=2414.**

1947-2010. *Pennsylvania Obituary and Marriage Collection* **[Online Database],** digitized at the FamilySearch.org website. Includes newspaper clippings collected by the Old Buncombe County, North Carolina Genealogical Society. This database has 122,063 images. See **https://familysearch.org/search/collection/2282148.**

1952-1957. *Pennsylvania, Crew Lists arriving at Erie* **[Online Database],** indexed at the FamilySearch.org website. Source: National Archives microfilm series A3459. The records contain full name, citizenship, position in crew, whether discharged at the port of arrival, and other information for each crew member. This database has 41,164 records. See **https://familysearch.org/search/collection/2427900.**

1977-2010. *Pennsylvania Obituaries* [Online Database], indexed at the FamilySearch.org website. Obituary newspaper clippings for Pennsylvania collected by the Old Buncombe County, North Carolina Genealogical Society. This database has 99,894 records. See https://familysearch.org/search/collection/2287449.

1981-Current. *Pennsylvania Newspaper Obituaries* [Online Database], digitized and indexed newspaper obituaries at the GenealogyBank website. Included are obituaries found in newspaper from 139 Pennsylvania cities. For the list, see www.genealogybank.com/explore/obituaries/all/usa/pennsylvania.

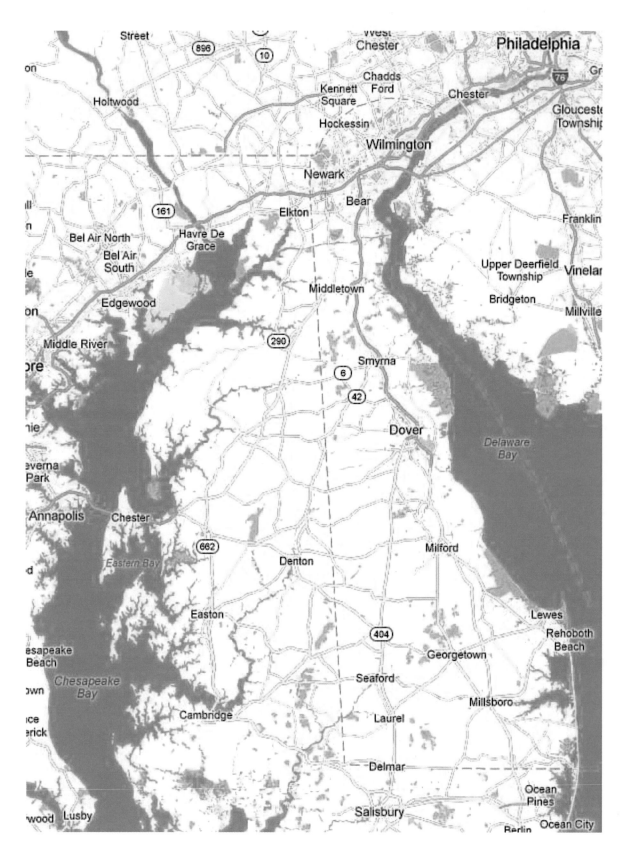

Delaware and Surroundings (from Google Maps).
For a map of 1790 Maryland and Delaware, see Vol. 2, page 18.

Delaware
Censuses & Substitute Name Lists

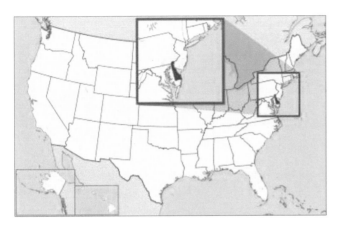

Historical Timeline for Delaware, 1497-1787

1497-1498. English Exploration. Italian explorer Giovanni Caboto is commonly held to be the first European to visit North America, landing in 1497 on the island now called Newfoundland. In 1498, the ships log and published reports from his second trip to North America seem to confirm that he had visited the coast of present New Jersey, Delaware, Maryland, Virginia, North Carolina, South Carolina, and Georgia. He was commissioned by the English King, Henry VII, who anglicized his name to John Cabot. His discoveries became the basis for England's universal claim to all of North America thereafter.

1524. French Exploration. Giovanni da Verrazano, an Italian sailing for King Francis I of France, sailed past Delaware Bay, but did not note the event. He then kept moving north up the present New Jersey coast, entered present New York harbor, then headed north to become the first European to visit present Connecticut, Rhode Island, Massachusetts, and Maine.

1603. England. James I (James VI of Scotland since 1566), became King of England, the first monarch to rule both England and Scotland. He was also the first English King to publicly assert that he was blessed with "the divine right of Kings," meaning he was the voice of God on earth, at least in England and Scotland.

Although James I was most remembered for commissioning a Bible translation, during his reign, the first permanent English colonies of North America were established in Virginia and New England.

1606. James I chartered two joint stock companies for the purpose of settlement in North America. The two companies, called the "Virginia Company of London" and the "Virginia Company of Plymouth" were granted territory from present North Carolina to Maine, with the Long Island Sound as the approximate dividing line.

1607. May. The first permanent English settlement of Jamestown was founded on the James River, a few miles from its mouth on Chesapeake Bay. Over the next few months, English Capt. John Smith (of Jamestown) explored much of Chesapeake Bay, and up the Atlantic coast as far north as present Maine.

1607. Englishman Henry Hudson sailed in search of a northwest passage to Asia. He sailed into present New York harbor and later lent his name to the river there.

1609. Henry Hudson, sailing for the Dutch East India Company, discovered what was to become known as Delaware Bay.

1610. Delaware Bay and River. Samuel Argall, an English sea captain who led a supply mission to Jamestown, named the bay and river after Thomas West, the 3rd Baron De La Warr, and the first governor of the Virginia Colony.

1625. England. Charles I became King of England, Scotland, and Ireland. Charles believed in the same principles his father, James I had espoused, i.e., that as King, he was the infallible interpreter of God's will on earth. Soon after taking office, Charles began to note a large number of non-conformists among his subjects. Along with his Archbishop, William Laud, the King began a campaign to purge his church of the largest group of non-conformists, the so-called Puritans, a militant Calvinist religious sect attempting to purify the Church of England. Unfortunately, Charles I took on a job that led to civil war in England as well as the loss of his head. But his campaign can be credited as the main cause for the founding of the Massachusetts Bay Colony in New England.

1631. Dutch colonists settled Zwaanendael, site of present-day Lewes, Delaware. After a year of constant Indian attacks, the colonists were all wiped out.

1632. The Maryland Charter was granted to Cecilius Calvert, 2nd Lord Baltimore, by King Charles I.

1638. Peter Minuet led a group of Swedes to the Delaware and established Fort Christina (now Wilmington), the first permanent settlement on the Delaware and the founding of the New Sweden Colony.

1651. Peter Stuyvesant, Dutch governor of New Netherland, built Fort Casimir (now New Castle) just a few miles south of Fort Christina on the Delaware, but the Swedes were not pleased with the Dutch intrusion.

1654. The Swedes captured Fort Casimir and renamed it Fort Trinity.

1655. The Dutch overran the Swedes, captured Fort Trinity and Fort Christina, and ended the New Sweden colony. The Swedish settlements on the Delaware then became part of New Netherland under Governor Peter Stuyvesant. But Stuyvesant permitted the Swedish communities to continue as a "Swedish Nation" and to be governed by a court of their choosing. They were also allowed to be free to practice their religion, organize their own militia, retain their land holdings, and continue trading with the native people. The independent Swedish communities continued under the Dutch until 1682, when William Penn was granted the area of present Delaware by the Duke of York.

1660. England. Charles II was restored to the throne as King of England, Scotland, and Ireland. He had lived in exile after the execution of his father, Charles I. In 1649, the Scots had proclaimed Charles the king of Scotland. But the Puritan leader Oliver Cromwell defeated his army in 1651, and Charles fled to France. After Cromwell died in 1658, the English people became increasingly dissatisfied with the government that Cromwell had established. In 1660, Parliament invited Charles to return and declared him king. He

ruled until his death in 1685, and during his reign, the English colonials forced out the remaining pockets of Atlantic settlements made earlier by the Dutch, Swedes, Danes, and French. Charles II saw the Atlantic colonies as a source of trade and commerce, supported development, and granted several more charters for settlement (including one to William Penn in 1681). All of the English colonies thrived as a result.

1664. Sir Robert Carr successfully drove the Dutch off the Delaware and claimed the land for James, Duke of York. Delaware then became an English colony for the first time.

1673. Dutch military forces took back New York and Delaware from the English.

1674. Delaware. The English took back control of the Delaware colony.

1674. The Treaty of Westminster ended hostilities between the English and Dutch and officially returned all Dutch colonies in America to the English. This ended the official Dutch presence in North America – but many of the Dutch settlements continued under English rule, particularly along the Connecticut River, Hudson River, Delaware river, and East Jersey,

1676. New York Royal Grant. Charles II granted to his brother, James, the Duke of York, the following: *"...main land between the two rivers there, called or known by the several names of Conecticut or Hudsons river... and all the lands from the west side of the Conecticut, to the east side of Delaware Bay."* Immediately after the grant, James renamed the area known as New Netherland as the Province of New York.

1681. Pennsylvania. William Penn was granted land in North America by Charles II and established the proprietary colony of Pennsylvania. He arrived in October 1682 on the ship *Welcome*, visited Philadelphia, just laid out as the capital city, and soon after his arrival, summoned a General Assembly, called for uniting Delaware with Pennsylvania, and created the first three Pennsylvania counties of Bucks, Chester, and Philadelphia.

1682. Delaware Colony. James, The Duke of York, transferred ownership of the Delaware Colony to English Quaker William Penn. The "Lower Counties on Delaware" remained part of Pennsylvania until their declaration of independence in 1775.

1685-1688 England. After the death of Charles II in 1685, who died without issue, his brother, the Duke of York, became King James II. Parliament was suspicious of his religious beliefs, thought he was too tolerant with Catholics, and he was disposed in 1688, in what was later called the *Glorious Revolution.* His Protestant daughter, Mary, was placed on the throne, and James fled to France, where he lived out his life and died in 1701.

1688. American colonies that had been given considerable religious tolerance before the Glorious Revolution in England, were now forced to purge Catholics from political office. The colony impacted the most by the edict was Maryland, founded by the Catholic Calvert family. Maryland and the rest of the colonies were required to remove any Catholics from any county or provincial public office.

1689. England. Mary, daughter of James II, had married her first cousin, William of Orange, the sovereign of Holland. They were both staunch and outspoken Protestants. In keeping with the anti-Catholic mind-set of the time, Parliament invited the two of them to become joint monarchs of England in 1689. During the reign of William III and Mary II, the American colonies grew rapidly, and the triangular trade route between the English Colonies, the Caribbean, and England was established, making the American colonies more productive, while the introduction of African slaves to the American colonies proliferated. After Mary II died in 1694, William III ruled England alone until his death in 1702. William and Mary were childless, and were succeeded by Mary's younger sister, Anne.

1702. Pennsylvania's three lower counties (New Castle, Kent, and Sussex) gained a separate Assembly from the three upper counties (Bucks, Chester, and Philadelphia), but both regions were ultimately administered by the proprietor, William Penn, who appointed a Governor shared by both regions.

1702-1714. England-Great Britain. Anne, sister of Mary II was crowned Queen of England in 1702. She gave birth to several children, none of whom lived more than a few days. It was during her reign in 1707, that England and Scotland merged to become the

United Kingdom of Great Britain. (The English Colonies now became the British Colonies). Queen Anne died in 1714. And Parliament, still overly concerned about any possible Catholic replacement, determined that her closest (Protestant) heir was a German from Hanover.

1714. Great Britain. George I was the first of the House of Hanover to rule Great Britain, but a monarch who had little interest in living there. He took "British Holidays," from time to time, but he never learned to speak English.

1727 Great Britain. George II became King of England, Scotland & Ireland, and during his 33-year reign, more than 200,000 so-called "Scots-Irish" left for the American colonies from the borderlands of England and Scotland and from Northern Ireland. The Scots-Irish were the largest group of British immigrants to America prior to the Revolutionary War. They outnumbered (by about 3 to 1) the combined total of the other British immigrant groups, i.e., the Puritans, Quakers, and Royalists / Cavaliers.

1760. Great Britain. George III was crowned King of England. He was the English Monarch who lost the British Colonies. He is credited with first sowing the seeds of revolution in his American colonies, when he issued the "Proclamation Line of 1763," a line which set aside an Indian Reserve from the Appalachian Mountains to the Mississippi River.

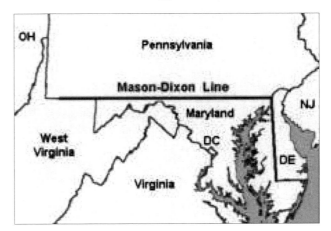

1764. Mason-Dixon Line. The Calvert Family and the Penn Family engaged surveyors Charles Mason and Jeremiah Dixon to mark the Maryland boundary with Pennsylvania (including the Lower Counties on Delaware). The "Mason-Dixon Line" soon became the unofficial dividing line between the colonies/states of the North and the South (Dixie).

1775. Delaware. The three Lower Counties on Delaware broke away from Pennsylvania. They adopted a constitution and became the "Delaware State," the first of all the colonies to call themselves a state, and one of the thirteen to sign the Declaration of Independence.

1783. The 1783 Treaty of Paris ended the Revolutionary War, and the United States of America was officially recognized as an independent nation by Britain, France, and Spain.

1787. Dec. 7. As the first of the original thirteen colonies to ratify the U.S. Constitution, **Delaware** became the first state in the Union.

Delaware Censuses and Name Lists Taken by the Swedes, Dutch, British, and Americans

1631-1664. Swedish and Dutch Colonial Era:
Settlements by the Swedes and Dutch along the Delaware were in constant turmoil. Few name lists of the inhabitants of the first settlements have survived. The earliest name lists were the 1644 and 1647 New Sweden Censuses.

1664-1682. English Colonial Era:
In 1664, the English had taken control of the Delaware settlements, but lost control to the Dutch again in 1673. The English returned again in 1674, and Delaware remained an independent English colony until 1682. The tax lists for New Castle County in 1676 and 1677 were the earliest names lists for the era.

1682-1775. The "Lower Counties on Delaware" Era.
After the transfer to William Penn by the Duke of York in 1682, Delaware remained part of the Pennsylvania colony until it declared its independence in 1775. The earliest recorded name lists from this era are part of the Delaware Vital Records collection, 1680-1934; as well as county rent rolls from the early 1680s.

1775-1787. The "Delaware State" Era:
Delaware maintained its independence from Pennsylvania during the Revolutionary War, and by virtue of the recognition of its delegates to the Continental Congress, Delaware

gained status as one of the original thirteen colonies. Numerous name lists exist for this era, including colonial records specific to Delaware vital records and tax lists.

1787-Current. The State of Delaware Era:
Delaware has never taken a state-sponsored census. Aside from the loss of the 1790 and 1890 federal censuses, all other federal censuses for Delaware are complete and extant. There are several national name lists for the entire U.S. that may include Delaware residents. These national lists are not all shown here in the Delaware section, so a researcher should check the *U.S. Census Substitutes* chapter (Vol. 5). Examples of national name lists include Military Rosters, Army, Navy, and Widow's Pensions, Find a Grave, and the Social Security Death Index.

Bibliography
Delaware Censuses & Substitutes

1638-1664. Histories of the Dutch and Swedish Colonies in Delaware [Printed Books], See 1) *Det Började vid Delaware: om Svenska Hembygder i Amerika* [Printed Book], a history of the Swedish Colony "New Sweden" in Delaware from about 1638 to the 1900s. Includes details on the Swedish customs and traditions in America during the colonial period and today. Published Stockholm: Riksförbundet för Hembygdsvård, 1986, 168 pages, FHL book 975.1 H2, and see 2) *The Colony of New Sweden: A Factual Overview* [Printed Book], by Bill Albensi, an account of the Swedes in the area of Wilmington, Delaware, published by Nopoly Press, Wilmington, 1987, 32 pages, FHL book 975.1 A1 No. 6, and see 3) *Annals of the Swedes on the Delaware: From Their First Settlement in 1638, to the Present Time* [Printed Book], by Jehu Curtis Clay, published by H.L. Hooker & Co., Philadelphia, 1858, 179 pages, FHL 974 F2s, and see 4) *The Dutch & Swedes on the Delaware, 1638-1664,* by Christopher Ward, published by University of Pennsylvania, Philadelphia, 1930, 398 pages, FHL book 974 F2d.

1638-1634. *Swedish Settlements on the Delaware, Vol. 1 & Vol. 2* [Online Database], digitized and OCR index at the Ancestry.com website. Source: *The Swedish Settlements on the Delaware,* by Amandus

Johnson, originally publ. 1911, Philadelphia; reprinted Genealogical Pub. Co., 1969. This database has 475 and 414 pages. For Vol. 1, see https://search.ancestry.com/search/db.aspx?dbid=48465. For Vol. 2, see https://search.ancestry.com/search/db.aspx?dbid=48466.

1638-1684. See *Swedes on the Delaware* [Online Database], digitized and OCR indexed at the Ancestry.com website. Source: *The Swedes on the Delaware,* by Amandus Johnson, publ. Philadelphia, 1927. This database has 391 pages. See https://search.ancestry.com/search/db.aspx?dbid=6343.

1638-1888 Index to Delaware History [Printed Book]. The definitive work is *History of Delaware* by J. Thomas Scharf, publ. 1888. The index to the names mentioned in this 3-vol., 1,100-page history comprises an excellent census substitute of Delaware residents. See FHL book 975.1 H22s v.1-3. Also on microfiche: film #6088424-6088426.

1638–1900s. *Delaware Statewide and County Records* [Online Databases], including cemetery records, histories, military records, and obituaries, indexed at the Delaware RootsWeb website. For Delaware statewide records, see www.rootsweb.ancestry.com/~usgenweb/de/de-state.htm.
- For Kent County records, see www.rootsweb.ancestry.com/~usgenweb/de/kent/index.htm. For New Castle County records, see www.rootsweb.ancestry.com/~usgenweb/de/newcastle/index.htm.
- For Sussex County records, see www.rootsweb.ancestry.com/~usgenweb/de/sussex/index.htm.

1638-2000s. *Delaware Collections at MyHeritage* [Online Database], over 100 databases can be searched at the "Search all Delaware Collections" search/browse screen at the MyHeritage website. Databases include censuses, family histories, town histories, military rosters, and more. A search can be done for a name, place, year, or keyword. See www.myheritage.com/records/Delaware/all-records.

1638-2000s. See *Delaware USGenWeb Archives* [Online Database], extensive collection of indexed records by **DE Statewide** (History, Military Records, Obituaries); **New Castle County** (Cemetery, Census, Church, History, Military, Obituaries, Tax Records, Vital Records, and Wills and Probates), **Kent County** (Cemeteries, Census, Court, History, Land Records, Military Records, Tax Records, Vital Records, and Wills and Probates); and **Sussex County** (Bible Records, Biographies, Cemeteries, Census, Church, Court, History, Land Records, Military Records, Obituaries, Tax Records, Vital Records, and Wills and Probate Records). See www.usgwarchives.net/de/index.htm.

1638-2000s. See *Linkpendium, Delaware: Family History & Genealogy, Census, Birth, Marriage, Death Vital Records & More* [Online Databases]. Linkpendium is a portal to genealogical resources on the Internet, organized by Delaware Statewide Resources (465); Independent Cities, Kent County (437); New Castle County (781), and Sussex County (513). See www.linkpendium.com/de-genealogy.

1638-2000s. See Newspapers.com by Ancestry – Clippings [Online Database]. This is an index to obituaries in the largest newspaper archive on the Internet. The index is available to Ancestry subscribers or to anyone for an initial search. To look at a particular record requires a membership. At the main Newspapers.com screen, do a search for a state or country of interest, then narrow the search further by a name of a person, place of residence, or a time period. This database has over 262 million obits and death notices, see www.newspapers.com.

1640-1953. See *Deed Books of New Castle County, Delaware, 1673-1886, 1952-1953; General Index, 1640-1920* [Microfilm & Digital Capture], from the originals at the New Castle County Courthouse, Wilmington, DE. Filmed by the Genealogical Society of Utah, 1949, 132 rolls, beginning with FHL film #6610 (Grantor Index A-N 1640-1873). To access the digital images, see the online FHL catalog page: www.familysearch.org/search/catalog/333475.

"1644 New Sweden Census" [Printed Article], in *Swedish Colonial News,* Vol. 1, No. 9 (Spring 1994), and **"1647 Census of New Sweden"** [Printed Article], in *Swedish Colonial News,* Vol. 1, No. 15, Spring 1997, two examples of articles in the *Swedish Colonial News,* a publication of the Swedish Colonial Society, Philadelphia, PA, founded in 1909, the oldest Swedish historical organization in the U.S., the periodical includes information on genealogy, history, and projects of the society contributing to the "preservation of the Swedish heritage in colonial America." Current and past issues of the *Swedish Colonial News* are available online. See www.colonialswedes.org/AboutSCS/History.html.

1646-1679. *Duke of York Record: Being an Authorized Transcript From the Official Archives of the State of Delaware, and Comprising the Letters, Patents, Permits, Commissions, Surveys, Plats, and Confirmations by the Duke of York and Other High Officials, From 1646 to 1649, With Revised Index* **[Printed Book],** Original published Wilmington, DE., by Sunday Star Printing Co., n.d., FHL has reprinted copy by Family Line Publications, Westminster, MD, 1988, 199 pages, includes index. See FHL book 975.1R2o.

1648-1800. *Sussex County, Delaware: Marriage References* **[Printed Book],** by F. Edward Wright. Includes index. Published by Colonial Roots, Lewes, DE, 2010, 300 pages, FHL book 975.17 V2w.

1650-1974. *Delaware Vital Records* **[Online Database],** digitized and indexed at the FamilySearch.org website. Source: FHL microfilm of DE Public Archives records. The collection includes birth, marriage, death, bible, and cemetery records spanning various year ranges. Each index record includes: Name, Event type, and Event date. The card image may have more information. This database has 836,573 records. See www.familysearch.org/search/collection/1447341.

1665-1799. See *Colonial Delaware Wills and Estates to 1880: An Index* **[Printed Index],** by Donald O. Virdin, published by Heritage Books, Bowie, MD, 1994, 194 pages, FHL book 975.1 P22v.

1665-1697. *Early Delaware Census Records* **[Printed Index],** Ronald V. Jackson, ed., published by Accelerated Indexing, Bountiful, UT, 1977. See FHL book 975.1 X2. As was typical for many of the Jackson indexes, the source for these "census records" was not given.

1671 Census of the Delaware **[Printed Book],** by Peter Stebbins Craig. From page 1: "The document is endorsed, in the hand of Matthias Nicolls, then Secretary of Governor Francis Lovelace, as 'A list of Inhabitants of the Delaware' and dated 1671. It names 165 heads of households from Matinicum (Burlington) Island [Burlington County, New Jersey] on the north and New Castle on the south." Published by the Genealogical Society of Pennsylvania, Philadelphia, 1999, 102 pages, FHL book 974.X2c.

1671-1769. *New Castle County Land Warrants and Surveys* **[Microfilm & Digital Capture],** from originals at the New Castle County Courthouse, Wilmington, DE. Filmed by the Genealogical Society of Utah, 1949, 2 rolls, FHL film #6614-6615. To access the digital images, see the online FHL catalog page: www.familysearch.org/search/catalog/45825.
- See also *New Castle County Land Warrants and Surveys; Index Cards to Land Warrants and Surveys* **[Microfilm & Digital Capture],** from the original records at the Hall of Records, Dover, DE. Filmed by the Genealogical Society of Utah, 1949, 3 rolls, FHL film #6617 (Index cards), FHL film #6537-6538 (File folders, A1-W3). To access the digital images, see the online FHL catalog page: www.familysearch.org/search/catalog/37601.

1674-1851. *Governor's Register, State of Delaware: Appointments and Other Transactions by Executives of the State from 1674-1851* **[Microfilm & Online Database],** from the original published by the Public Archives Commission of Delaware, 1926, 570 pages. Includes index. Filmed by the Genealogical Society of Utah, 1986, 1 roll, FHL film #1321087.
- This database is also online at Ancestry.com with the title, *Delaware Governor's Register, 1674-1851* **[Online Database].** It includes mainly appointments made by the governor and other state executives. However, it also includes proclamations, letters, land patents, and other official transactions made by the governor, with over 4,000 names mentioned in the database at least once. See https://search.ancestry.com/search/db.aspx?dbid=6473.

"1676 Taxables, New Castle County" **[Printed Article],** in *Pennsylvania Magazine of History and Biography,* Vol. 1 (No. 1, Jan 1895).

1676-1971. *Delaware, Wills and Probate Records* [Online Database], digitized and indexed at the Ancestry.com website. Source: Extracts from Delaware County, District, and Probate Courts. The records include Wills, Letters of Administration, Inventories, Distribution and Accounting, Bonds, and Guardianships. Each index record includes: Name, Probate date, Probate place, Inferred death year, Inferred death place, and Item description. The document image will have much more information. This database has 134.894 records. See https://search.ancestry.com/search/db.aspx?dbid=9044.

1677-1947. *Delaware, Land Records* [Online Database], digitized and indexed at the Ancestry.com website. Source: DE Archives land grants and deed records of the three counties (New Castle, Kent, Sussex) from the county recorder of deeds in each. Most Delaware land had been granted by the time of statehood, so in the years following the Revolutionary War, deeds recording the transfer of lands between private parties were transcribed into the registers of the county recorder of deeds. The records include the names of the grantor (party or parties releasing the land) and grantee (the party or parties purchasing the land), as well as the names of neighbors whose land borders the property, previous owners, and witnesses. The amount of the payment, the dates the deed was written and recorded, and counties and states of residence can be found, as will the terms of the deed and any necessary dower releases. The index record has only the Name, Residence date, and Residence place for a person. The document image will have much more information. This database has 1,983,276 records. See https://search.ancestry.com/search/db.aspx?dbid=61025.

"1677 Taxables, New Castle County, Delaware" [Printed Article], in *Pennsylvania Magazine of History and Biography*, Vol. 3, No. 3 (Jul 1879).

1680-1800. *New Castle County, Delaware: Marriage References & Family Relationships* [Printed Book], by F. Edward Wright. Includes index. Published by Colonial Roots, Lewes, DE, 2011, 461 pages, FHL book 975.11 V2w.

1680-1800. *Calendar of Sussex County, Delaware Probate Records* [Printed Book], compiled by Leon DeValinger, State Archivist. Includes index. Published by the archives, 1964, 310 pages, FHL book 975.17 P23c.

1680-1800. *Sussex County, Delaware Wills and Administrations: An Index* [Printed Book], by Raymond B. Clark, Jr., published by the author, St. Michaels, MD, 1985, 42 pages, FHL book 975.1 A1 No. 17.

1680-1800. *Sussex County, Delaware Probate Records* [Online Database], indexed at the Ancestry.com website. Original data: *Calendar of Sussex County, Delaware Probate Records, 1680-1800.* Georgetown, DE: Public Archives Commission, 1964. This database is a collection of some probate records and will abstracts from the county between 1680 and 1800. Arranged in chronological order, the records provide the individual's name, date of will, names of heirs, executor, and witnesses. It can also reveal the probate date and reference information including will book title, volume, and page number. Containing the names of over 10,000 persons. See https://search.ancestry.com/search/db.aspx?dbid=4295.

1680-1800. *Calendar of Kent County, Delaware Probate Records* [Online Database], digitized and OCR indexed at the Ancestry.com website. Original data: De Valinger, Leon,. *Calendar of Kent County, Delaware probate records, 1680-1800.* Dover, Del.: Public Archives Commission, State of Delaware, 1944. This database has 689 pages. See https://search.ancestry.com/search/db.aspx?dbid=25765.

1680-1699. *Court Records of Sussex County* [Microfilm & Digital Capture], from the original records at the Hall of Records, Dover, DE. Contains proceedings of the Levy Court, County Court, Court of Common Pleas, Orphans' Court, Court of Quarter Sessions, and special courts. Records include appointments, commissions and bonds of officials, records of bridges and roads, taxation, wills, land grants, deeds, births, marriages, apprentice indentures, bounties, etc. Filmed by the archives, 1979, 1 roll, FHL film #475648. To access the digital images, see the online FHL catalog page: www.familysearch.org/search/catalog/57992.

1680-1934. *Index Cards of Delaware Marriages, Baptisms, Births and Deaths* [Microfilm & Digital Capture Database]. Filmed by the Genealogical Society of Utah, 1949, microfilm of original index (typescript) at the Delaware State Archives in Dover. Contains an alphabetical listing of names from primary and secondary sources, such as Bibles, church records,

marriage bonds and licenses, newspapers, probate records, magazines, and *Sketch of Ecclesiastical Affairs in New Castle, Delaware, and History of Immanuel Church* by Thomas Holcomb. Delaware required official recording of vital statistics in 1913; record collections prior to 1913 are considered incomplete. 18 rolls, beginning with FHL film #6416. To access the digital images, see the online FHL catalog page: **www.familysearch.org/search/catalog/294868**.
- This index is available online with the title, *Delaware Vital Record Index Cards, 1680-1934* [Online Database], digitized at the FamilySearch.org website. Includes the Delaware State Archives index cards from the FHL microfilm. This database has 134,797 card images, arranged in alphabetical order: **www.familysearch.org/search/collection/1922410**.

1680-1962. *Delaware, Vital Records* [Online Database], digitized at the FamilySearch.org website. This is a collection of various vital records from the Delaware Public Archives. The collection includes birth, marriage, death, bible, and cemetery records spanning various year ranges. This database has 1,497,613 images. See **www.familysearch.org/search/collection/1447341**.

1680-1978. *Delaware Orphan Court Records* [Online Database], digitized at the FamilySearch.org website. Source: DE Public Archives, Dover. The Orphan Court deals with guardianship of minors, real estate left intestate, partition of real estate, and appeals from the Register of Wills. Browse through the images, organized by County, Record Type, Date Range, and Volume. This database has 130,650 images. See **www.familysearch.org/search/collection/2094183**.

1681-1713. *Colonial Delaware Records* [Printed Book], compiled by Bruce A. Bendler, published by Family Line Publications, Westminster, MD, 1990, 84 pages, includes index. Contains Kent County rent roll 1681-1688; Sussex County rent roll 1681-1688; 1693 tax assessment list of New Castle County; 1693 tax assessment list of Kent County. 1693 tax assessment list of Sussex County; Kent County, quitrents, c1701-1713; and Sussex County quitrents, 1702-1713. See FHL book 975.1 R2b.

1681-1789. *Land Records of Sussex County, Delaware* [Printed Book], abstracts of original records at the Sussex County Courthouse, Georgetown, DE. This 12- volume series has had several contributors: Mary Marshall Brewer, for the periods 1681-1725,

1693-1805, 1753-1763, 1763-1769; Johnita P. Malone, 1722-1731, 1732-1743; F. Edward Wright, indexed by Charlotte Meldrum, 1769-1782; Elaine Hastings Mason & F. Edward Wright, 1782-1789; and Judith K. Ardine, 1789-1792.

1682-1759 *Warrants and Surveys of the Province of Pennsylvania: Transcribed From the Records of the Surveyor General's and Proprietary's Secretary's offices by John Hughes, Recorder of Warrants and Surveys Under the Act of Assembly July 7, 1759; With a Guide to the Books and Index, an Historical Background and a Copy of the Act,* [Microfilm & Digital Capture], compiled by Charles E. Hughes, Jr., city archivist; Thomas E. Slattery, archival examiner. Microfilm of original published: Philadelphia: Dept. of Records, 1957, original manuscripts (9 volumes) in the Dept. of Records, City Archives, Philadelphia. Vol. 3, 4, 5, 7 & 8 include records for New Castle, Kent, and Sussex counties, Delaware, including an identification of the first land grants of Delaware. See FHL film #981096-981097. (See an official recap of these records made public in "1759 Warrants and Surveys" below). To access the digital images, see the online FHL catalog page: **www.familysearch.org/search/catalog/341183**.

1682-1800. *New Castle County, Delaware, Wills and Estates, an Index* [Printed Booklet], compiled by Donald Odell Virdin. Index shows the name of the deceased, the year the will or estate was probated, and the volume and page reference of the will. Published by Raymond B. Clark, 1982, 20 pages, FHL book 975.1 A1 No. 9.

1682-1800. *New Castle County, Delaware Wills* [Online Database], indexed at the Ancestry.com website. Original data: *A Calendar of Delaware Wills, New Castle County, 1682-1800.* Wilmington, DE: 1911. This database is a collection of will abstracts from New Castle County, Delaware between 1682 and 1800. Each record provides the individual's name, date the will was created, and date it was filed. Most entries also provide names of witnesses and family members who received a portion of the person's estate. It contains nearly 1700 entries and about 7000 names: **https://search.ancestry.com/search/db.aspx?dbid=4245**.

1682-1949. *Deed Records of Sussex County, Delaware, 1693-1886; General Index, 1682-1949* [Microfilm & Digital Capture], from the original records at the Sussex County Courthouse, Georgetown, DE. Filmed by the Genealogical Society of Utah, 1948,

62 rolls, beginning with FHL film #2188693 (Index, 1682-1844). To access the digital images, see the online FHL catalog page: www.familysearch.org/search/catalog/296734.

1683-1894. *Delaware, Marriages and Marriage Licenses* **[Online Database],** indexed at the FamilySearch.org website. Source: FHL microfilm of records at the DE Public Archives, Dover. This is an index to selected church marriages and licenses. Each index record includes: Name, Event type, Event date, Event place, Gender, Spouse's name, Spouse's gender, and FHL film number. This database has 5,490 records. See www.familysearch.org/search/collection/2340271.

1683-1947. *Delaware, Wills and Administrations* **[Online Database],** digitized at the Ancestry.com website. This is an image-only database with probate records from Kent, New Castle, and Sussex counties, Delaware. Use the *Browse this Collection* feature to select a county and volume. The volumes are lettered/numbered for an inclusive date range. There are about 3,000 pages of original documents for each county. See https://search.ancestry.com/search/db.aspx?dbid=2369.

"1684 Colonial Delaware Census, Kent County" [Printed Article], see "Census, 1684," in *Maryland and Delaware Genealogist*, Vol. 27, No. 1 (Jan 1986).

"1685 Landholders, Sussex County, Delaware" [Printed Article], in *Genealogical Society of Pennsylvania Publications*, Vol. 40, No. 3 (Spring 1998).

"1686 Colonial Delaware Census, Kent County" [Printed Article], see "Census, 1686," in *Delaware Genealogical Society Journal*, Vol. 3, No. 3 (Apr 1986).

"1688 Colonial Delaware Census, Kent County" [Printed Article]. A 1688 census listing for Kent County was published in *The Pennsylvania Genealogical Magazine*, Vol. 37 (1991), which appears more complete than the earlier list, "1688 Kent County Census," in *Delaware Genealogical Journal*, Vol. 3 (1986).

1693 Tax List, Province of Pennsylvania, and the Three Lower Counties **[Printed Abstracts & Index],** abstracted and indexed by Adams Apple Press,

Bedminster, PA, 64 pages, includes index. Contains Philadelphia County, Bucks County, and Chester County in Pennsylvania; New Castle, Kent, and Sussex counties in Delaware. See FHL book 974. A1 No. 643.

"1693 Tax List, New Castle, Delaware" [Printed Article], in *Genealogical Researcher's Record Round-Up*, Vol. 6, No. 2 (1973) through Vol. 6, No. 4 (1973).

1693 Tax Assessments, New Castle County, Delaware, Part 1 **[Online Database],** indexed at the USGenWeb site for New Castle Co DE. See http://files.usgwarchives.net/de/newcastle/tax/nc1693.txt.

1693 Tax Assessments, New Castle County, Delaware, Part 2 **[Online Database],** indexed at the USGenWeb site for New Castle Co DE. See http://files.usgwarchives.net/de/newcastle/tax/1693nc2.txt.

"1693 Census, Swedes on the Delaware" [Printed Article]. Name list in *Swedish American Genealogist*, Vol. 9, No. 3 (Sep 1989) through Vol. 12, No. 1 (Mar 1992).

1693 Tax Assessments, Kent County, Delaware **[Online Database],** indexed at the USGenWeb site for Kent Co DE. See http://files.usgwarchives.net/de/kent/tax/kent1693.txt.

1693 Tax Assessments, Sussex County, Delaware **[Online Database],** indexed at the USGenWeb site for Sussex Co DE. See http://files.usgwarchives.net/de/sussex/tax/s1693.txt.

"1693 Provincial Delaware Tax Lists" [Printed Article]. Name lists in *The Pennsylvania Genealogical Magazine* Vol. 37, No. 1 (1991).

1696-1697 Tax Records, New Castle County, Delaware **[Online Database],** indexed at the USGenWeb site for New Castle Co DE. See http://files.usgwarchives.net/de/newcastle/tax/nc1697.txt.

1697-1886. *Delaware, Baptisms* **[Online Database],** indexed at the FamilySearch.org website. Source: DE Public Archives and Records of the Holy Trinity Old Swedes Church, Wilmington, DE. This is an index to selected church records in Delaware, mostly from the city of Wilmington. Each index record includes: Name, Event type, Event date, Event place, Gender, Birth date, Father's name, and Mother's name. This database has 6,816 records. See www.familysearch.org/search/collection/2339318.

1707-1939. Delaware, Church Records [Online Database], digitized and indexed at FamilySearch.org. Source: Delaware Bureau of Archives and Records Management, Dover, DE. Includes Church vital records from different denominations and several counties in Delaware. This database has 75,282 records, see www.familysearch.org/search/collection/2787818.

1710-1896. *Delaware Births and Christenings* [Online Database], indexed at the FamilySearch.org website, a name index to birth, baptism, and christening records from the state of Delaware, originally microfilmed by the Genealogical Society of Utah for the Family History Library in Salt Lake City, Utah. The database contains 21,662 records. See www.familysearch.org/search/collection/1674747.

1713-1919 Delaware Marriages **[Online Database],** indexed of the FamilySearch.org website, a name index to marriage records from the state of Delaware, microfilm records at the Family History Library. This database contains 4,424 records. See www.familysearch.org/search/collection/1674782.

"1726 Tax List, Kent County, Delaware" [Printed Article], in *Maryland and Delaware Genealogist*, Vol. 27, No. 4 (Oct 1986); Vol. 28, No. 1 (Jan 1987); and Vol. 28, No. 2 (Spring 1987).

1726-1850. *Tax Lists of Kent County, Delaware* [Microfilm & Digital Capture], from the original records at the Kent County Courthouse, Dover, DE. Filmed by the Genealogical Society of Utah, 1949, 17 rolls, beginning with FHL film #6494 (Tax Lists, 1726-1777). For a complete list of roll numbers and contents of each roll, see the online FHL catalog page for this title: To access the digital images, see the online FHL catalog page: www.familysearch.org/search/catalog/35124.

1728-1802. *Orphan's Court Dockets and Minute Dockets, Sussex County, Delaware* [Microfilm & Digital Capture], from the original records at the Hall of Records, Dover, DE. Filmed by the Genealogical Society of Utah, 1948, 1 roll, FHL film #6688. To access the digital images, see the online FHL catalog page: www.familysearch.org/search/catalog/43210.

1729-1853. *Delaware Marriages and Deaths From Newspapers* [Printed Book], edited by Mary Fallon Richards and John C. Richards, published by Family Line Publications, Westminster, MD, 1997, 279 pages, FHL book 975.1 V28d.

1730-1760. *Some Records of Sussex County, Delaware* [Online Database], digitized and OCR indexed at the Ancestry.com website. Original data: Turner, C. H. B.. *Some records of Sussex County, Delaware.* Philadelphia: Allen, Lane & Scott, 1909. Includes Court Records, Ecclesiastical Records, St. Peters Vestry Book Records, Miscellaneous Records, and Bible Records. The book has an index as well. The time period was derived from a statement in the Preface, "..from the time of the dispute between Lords Baltimore and Penn…" which began in 1730 and ended in 1760. There may be records herein before or after those dates. This database has 403 pages. See https://search.ancestry.com/search/db.aspx?dbid=23326.

1734-1776. *Land Warrants and Surveys of Sussex County, Delaware, Books A1-W6; Index Cards of Sussex County Land Warrants and Surveys* [Microfilm & Digital Capture], from the originals at the Sussex County Courthouse, Georgetown, DE. Filmed by the Genealogical Society of Utah, 1948, 7 rolls, FHL film #6691 (Index cards). To access the digital images, see the online FHL catalog page: www.familysearch.org/search/catalog/50154.

1738-1853. *Tax Lists, New Castle County, Delaware* [Microfilm & Digital Capture], from originals at the Hall of Records, Dover, DE. Alphabetically arranged by surname. Filmed by the Genealogical Society of Utah, 1949, 6 rolls, beginning with FHL film #6531 (vol. 1-17, 1738-1790). To access the digital images, see the online FHL catalog page: www.familysearch.org/search/catalog/37404.

1744-1802. *Marriage License Bonds, New Castle County, Delaware* [Microfilm & Digital Capture], from an original manuscript in Dover, DE. Contents: Includes selected families from the original records, vol. 1: 1744-1789; vol. 2: 1790-1794; vol. 3: 1795-1802, miscellaneous church records of selected families, miscellaneous cemetery records of selected families. Filmed by the Genealogical Society of Utah, 1949, 1 roll, FHL film #6301. To access the digital images, see the online FHL catalog page: www.familysearch.org/search/catalog/14130.

1744-1836. *A List of Marriage License Bonds, so far as They Have Been Preserved in New Castle County, Delaware* [Microfilm & Digital Capture], from a manuscript at the Historical Society of Pennsylvania, Philadelphia, PA. Includes index. Includes a few marriages from other counties in Delaware. Filmed by the Genealogical Society of Utah, 1965, 1 roll, FHL film #441415. To access the digital images, see the online FHL catalog page: www.familysearch.org/search/catalog/338677.

1744-1912. *Delaware Marriage Records* **[Online database],** digitized and indexed at the Ancestry.com website. This database comprises a significant portion of early marriages for the state. This collection was compiled by and is located at the Delaware Public Archives. It was created in part to provide marriage information for years prior to when the Office of Vital Statistics started collecting them in 1913. Records contained in the collection include: Marriage bonds, Marriage certificates, Marriage returns, Governor's authorization for marriage, Certification by Justices of the Peace for marriage, Church records, and Family Bibles. Information contained in this database includes, 1) Names of bride and groom, 2) Ages of bride and groom, 3) Marriage, bond, or other record date, and 4) Marriage place. This database has 297,479 records. See http://search.ancestry.com/search/db.aspx?dbid=1508.

1750-1886. *Delaware Church Deaths* **[Online Database],** indexed at the FamilySearch.org website. Source: FHL microfilm from the DE Public Archives, Dover. This is an index to Delaware church records, mostly from the city of Wilmington. Each index record includes: Name, Event type, Event date, Event place, Gender, Birth year, Death age, Father's name, and Mother's name. This database has 1,848 records. See www.familysearch.org/search/collection/2340266.

1750-1954. *Delaware, Marriage Records* **[Online Database],** digitized and indexed at the Ancestry.com website. Source: DE Bureau of Vital Statistics records at the DE Public Archives, Dover. This collection consists of county marriage records from the three counties in Delaware. Details vary but may include the following information for both the bride and groom: Name, Age at marriage, Marriage date, Marriage place, and Parents' names. The document images may have more information. This database has 649,981 records: https://search.ancestry.com/search/db.aspx?dbid=61368.

"1755 Tax List, Kent County, Delaware" [Printed Article]. Name list published serially in *Maryland and*

Delaware Genealogist, Vol. 29, No. 1 (Winter 1988), through Vol. 29, No. 4 (Fall 1988).

1759 Warrants and Surveys of the Province of Pennsylvania Including the Three Lower Counties **[Printed Book & Digital Version],** compiled by Allen Winberg and Thomas E. Slattery under the directory of Charles E. Hughes, Jr., 1965 edition published by Department of Records, Philadelphia. The Provincial Assembly representing the people of Pennsylvania was in conflict with the sons of William Penn who were the Proprietaries of the Province of Pennsylvania. Records of Warrants under the control of the Proprietaries and which ordered surveys to be made were not public records. This created confusion over property rights and boundaries. In 1759 the Assembly passed a law for recording warrants and surveys. The Proprietaries in 1760 brought the law before the King who vetoed it. In the meantime, the warrants were transcribed and made public. This is an index of names recorded in the warrants in the present-day Pennsylvania counties of Berks, Bucks, Chester, Cumberland, Lancaster, Northampton, Philadelphia, and York; and the three counties Kent, Newcastle, and Sussex making up Delaware. FHL has a reprint by The Bookmark, Knightstown, IN, 1975, 91 pages. See FHL book 974.8 R2w. To access the digital version, see the online FHL catalog page: www.familysearch.org/search/catalog/249920.

1767-1850. *Tax Lists of Sussex County, Delaware* **[Microfilm & Digital Capture],** from the original records at the Hall of Records, Dover, DE. Names are shown in alphabetical order within the Hundreds. Filmed by the Genealogical Society of Utah, 1948, 5 rolls, beginning with FHL film #6674 (Tax Lists, #1-30). To access the digital images, see the online FHL catalog page: www.familysearch.org/search/catalog/53423.

"1779 Delaware, Kent County Tax List" [Printed Article], see "Duck Creek Hundred Levy and Taxes for 1779," in *Maryland and Delaware Genealogist*, Vol. 16, No. 4 (Fall 1985).

1782 Colonial Delaware Census **[Printed Books].** Manuscripts survive for a colonial census taken for Brandywine, Christiana, and St. Georgia's hundreds in

New Castle County; Duck Creek and Little Creek hundreds in Kent County; and Lewes Town Hundred in Sussex County. Two versions of the name lists have been published: _**1782 Delaware Tax Assessment and Census**_, compiled by Ralph D. Nelson, et al, published by the Delaware Genealogical Society, Wilmington, DE, 1994, 404 pages. See FHL book 975.1 X2; and _**The Reconstructed Delaware State Census of 1782**_, Harold B. Hancock, ed., (Delaware Genealogical Society, Wilmington, DE, 1983), 233 pages. See FHL book 975.1 X2.

"1785 Tax List for Kenton Hundred, Kent County, Delaware" [Printed Article], in _Maryland and Delaware Genealogist_, Vol. 5, No. 3 (Jul 1964) and No. 4 (Oct 1964).

1785-1922. _**Delaware Newspaper Archives**_ **[Online Database]**, digitized and indexed at the GenealogyBank.com website. One search screen for names and keywords in the following city newspapers: Clayton, Delaware City, Dover, Georgetown, Holly Oak, Laurel, Middletown, Milford, New Castle, Newark, Newport, Odessa, Smyrna, and Wilmington. See www.genealogybank.com/gbnk/newspapers/explore/US A/Delaware.

1786-1795. _**Delaware Newspaper Abstracts**_ **[Printed Book]**, by F. E. Wright, published by Family Line Publications, Silver Spring, MD, 1984, 78 pages, FHL book 975.1 B3w.

**1790 Reconstructed Delaware Census** **[Printed Book]**. A reconstructed name list aimed at replacing the lost 1790 federal census was compiled by Leon DeValinger, Jr. from tax lists, land records, and other local sources, and published serially in the _National Genealogical Society Quarterly_, later as NGS Special Publication No. 10: _Reconstructed 1790 Census of Delaware_, 1954, 83 pages. See FHL book 975.1 X2.

1790-1890. _**Delaware, Compiled Census and Census Substitutes Index**_ **[Online Database]**, indexed at the Ancestry.com website. Source: Accelerated Indexing Systems, 1999. This collection contains the following Delaware indexes: 1790 Federal Census Index (Reconstructed); 1800 Federal Census; 1810 Federal Census Index; 1820 Federal Census Index; 1830 Federal Census Index; 1840 Federal Census Index; 1840 Pensioners List; 1850 Federal Census Index; 1860 Federal Census Index; 1860 Slave Schedules; 1870

Federal Census Index; and 1890 Veterans Schedule. This database has 1,951 records. See https://search.ancestry.com/search/db.aspx?dbid=3539.

1795-1932 _**Naturalization Records**_ **[Microfilm & Digital Capture]**, from the originals at the National Archives, Philadelphia Branch. Includes an Index to Naturalization Petitions for the U.S. Circuit Court, 1795-1911, and the U.S. District Court, 1795-1928, for the District of Delaware; 1795-1928 Naturalizations Petitions of the U.S. District and Circuit Courts for the District of Delaware, 1795-1930. Some volumes are indexed separately. Filmed by the Genealogical Society of Utah, 1990, 27 rolls, beginning with FHL film #1704294 (Indexes). To access the digital images, see the online FHL catalog page: www.familysearch.org/search/catalog/591379.

1796-1959. _**Delaware Naturalization Records**_ **[Online Database]**, digitized and indexed at the Ancestry.com website. The naturalization records may include, 1) Name of individual, 2) Native country, 3) Date of naturalization, 4) Residence, 5) Occupation, 6) Birth date, 7) Date and place of arrival, and 8) Children's names. This database has 8,110 records, see http://search.ancestry.com/search/db.aspx?dbid=1927.

1796-1958. _**Delaware, County Naturalization Records**_ **[Online Database]**, digitized at the FamilySearch.org website. Includes naturalization records and digitized indexes from county courthouses in Delaware. The record content and time period vary by county. This database has 9,209 images. See www.familysearch.org/search/collection/2057672.

1796-1906. _**Naturalization Papers, A-Z, for New Castle County, Delaware**_ **[Microfilm & Digital Capture]**, from the handwritten copies from the Hall of Records in Dover, DE. From catalog notes: Alphabetically arranged. The records are copies of the original records at the Historical Society of Delaware. Includes loose papers of petitions, intentions, and final papers. Filmed by the Genealogical Society of Utah, 1949, 1 roll, FHL film #6529. This microfilm roll #6529 also includes, _**Naturalization Papers, A-Z, for Kent County, Delaware;**_ as well as _**Naturalization Papers, A-Z, for Sussex County, Delaware.**_ To access the digital images, see the online FHL catalog page: www.familysearch.org/search/catalog/37369.

1796-1959. _**Delaware, Naturalization Records**_ **[Online Database]**, digitized and indexed at the Ancestry.com website. Source: DE State Archives, Dover. The records include Petitions, Declarations, and Certificates. Each index record includes: Name, Birth location, Naturalization date, Record type, Court type, Court location, and Content year range. The document image has more information. This database has 8,110 records. See https://search.ancestry.com/search/db.aspx?dbid=1927.

1798-1906. *Naturalization Records, New Castle County, Delaware* **[Microfilm & Digital Capture],** from original records at the Delaware Public Archives, Dover, DE. From introduction: "This group of records consists of two separate series of volumes documenting the naturalization of foreign-born immigrants. The first series, known as First Papers, records the Declaration of Intent to apply for citizenship. There are nine volumes which cover the period 1832-1906. The second series or Final Papers is simply the finalization of the process, the court-approved naturalization itself. This series consists of nine volumes covering 1798-1906. There are very few entries prior to 1832. In 1906 the naturalization function was transferred to Federal District Courts." Filmed by the archives, 1999, 4 rolls, beginning with FHL film #2188047 (First Papers, 1832-1858). To access the digital images, see the online FHL catalog page: www.familysearch.org/search/catalog/1045785.

1800-1840 Delaware Federal Censuses **[Microfilm & Digital Capture],** from the originals at the National Archives, Washington, DC. Filmed as one series, 1800-1840, 8 rolls total, beginning with FHL film #6413 (entire state). This is another source to see the digital images of the census originals, see the online FHL catalog page: www.familysearch.org/search/catalog/745483.

"1800 Tax List, Dover, Kent County, Delaware" **[Printed Article],** in *Delaware Genealogical Society Journal,* Vol. 8, No. 4 (Oct 1996).

"1800 Road Tax, New Castle, Delaware" **[Printed Article].** Names of taxpayers listed in *Maryland and Delaware Genealogist,* Vol. 26, No. 1 (Jan 1985).

"1800 Tax List, Pencader, New Castle County, Delaware" **[Printed Article],** in *Delaware Genealogical Society Journal,* Vol. 8, No. 4 (Oct 1996).

1800-1818. See *Sussex County, Delaware Land Deeds* **[Printed Book],** abstracted by Leslie and Neil Keddie. Includes indexes in each volume. This 18-volume series includes abstracts of all deeds recorded from 1800 through 1818. For the FHL book number volumes, and the contents of each volume, see the online FHL catalog page for this title: www.familysearch.org/search/catalog/1337460.

1800-1932. *Delaware Birth Records* **[Online Database],** digitized and indexed at the Ancestry.com website. This data collection contains birth records from Delaware from 1800 to 1908. However, there are some records that extend up to 1932. These come from records available on microfilm at the Delaware Public Archives. Information listed in a birth record generally includes: 1) Name of child, 2) Gender, 3) Birth date, 4) Birthplace, and 5) Parents' names. This database contains 446,507 records. See http://search.ancestry.com/search/db.aspx?dbid=1672.

1803-1804. *Kent County, New Castle County, and Kent County, Delaware, Tax Assessment, Sept. 1803-Mar. 1804* **[Microfiche],** from original records at the Hall of Records, Dover, DE. Filmed by the Bureau of Archives & Records, 1979, FHL fiche #6332567 (Introduction, 1 fiche), FHL fiche #6332594 (Kent Co, 13 fiche); FHL fiche #6332567 (New Castle Co, 27 fiche): and FHL fiche #6332601 (Sussex Co, 14 fiche).

1806-1933. *Delaware Marriage Records* **[Online Database],** digitized and indexed at the Ancestry.com website, this database contains marriage records from Delaware from 1806 to 1933. However, there are some records that extend up to 1935. These come from records available on microfilm at the Delaware Public Archives. Information listed in a marriage record generally includes: 1) Names of spouses, 2) Gender, 3) Age, 4) Birth date, 5) Parents' names, 6) Marriage date, and 7) Marriage place. This database has 296,986 records. See http://search.ancestry.com/search/db.aspx?dbid=1673.

"1807 Road Tax, New Castle, Delaware" **[Printed Article].** Names of taxpayers in *Maryland and Delaware Genealogist, Vol. 26, No. 2 (Apr 1985).*

1810 Delaware Federal Census Index **[Printed Index],** edited by Ronald Vern Jackson, et al, published by Accelerated Indexing Systems, Bountiful, UT, 1976, 26 pages., FHL book 975.1 X2pa 1810.

1810 Delaware Federal Census Index, A-Z **[Printed Index],** edited and published by Heritage Quest, Bountiful, UT, 2000, 73 pages, FHL book 975.1 X22/dh.

1811-1933 Delaware Death Records **[Online Database],** digitized and indexed at the Ancestry.com website, This database contains death records from Delaware from 1811-1933. These come from records available on microfilm at the Delaware Public Archives. Information listed in a death record generally includes, 1) Name of deceased, 2) Gender, 3) Age, 4) Death date, 5) Birth date, 6) Spouse's name, and 7) Parents' names. This database has 236,320 records. http://search.ancestry.com/search/db.aspx?dbid=1674.

1815-1955. *Delaware Deaths and Burials* **[Online Database],** digitized and indexed at the FamilySearch.org website, a name index to records from the state of Delaware, originally compiled by the FamilySearch.org site, the database contains 1,490 records. See www.familysearch.org/search/collection/1674781.

1816-1817. *New Castle County Tax Assessment Records* **[Microfiche],** from the original records at the Hall of Records, Dover, DE. Filmed by the Bureau of Archives and Records, Dover, DE, 1978, 27 microfiche, FHL fiche #6332663 (Contents), through fiche #6332680 (White Clay Creek Hundred error list, 1816).

1816-1817. *Tax Assessments of New Castle County, Delaware* **[Printed Book],** abstracted by Karen M. Ackerman. Includes indexes. Published by Family Line Publications, Silver Spring, MD, 1986, 219 pages, FHL book 975.11 R4a.

1820 *Delaware Federal Census Index* **[Printed Index],** edited by Ronald Vern Jackson, et al, published by Accelerated Indexing Systems, Bountiful, UT, 1974, 27 pages., FHL book 975.1 X22j 1820.

1827-1831. *Delaware Advertiser, Genealogical Extracts* **[Printed Book],** by Margaret Mendenhall Frazier, published by Carl Boyer, Newhall, CA, 1987, 266 pages, FHL book 975.1 B3f.

1830 Delaware Federal Census Index **[Printed Index],** edited by Ronald Vern Jackson, et al, published by Accelerated Indexing Systems, Bountiful, UT, 1977, 32 pages., FHL book 975.1 X2p 1830.

1835 Delaware Pensioners **[Online Database],** digitized and indexed at the Ancestry.com website. This database identifies many Delaware soldiers who were covered under various pension acts in the early 1800s. Most entries list name of soldier, rank, area of military service, and other important information. See http://search.ancestry.com/Places/US/Delaware/Default.aspx.

1840 Delaware Federal Census **Index [Printed Index],** edited by Ronald Vern Jackson, et al, published by Accelerated Indexing Systems, Bountiful, UT, 1977, 32 pages., FHL book 975.1 X2p 1840.

1847-1954. *Delaware, Wilmington Vital Records* **[Online Database],** digitized and indexed at the FamilySearch.org website. Includes an index and images of birth, marriage, and death records from Wilmington, New Castle County, Delaware. The birth records end in the year 1919. Each index record includes: Name, Event type, Event date, Event place, Gender, Father's name, Mother's name, and page. The registers images may have more information. The database has 193,469 records. See www.familysearch.org/search/collection/1921755.

1850. *Delaware, 1850 Federal Census: Population Schedules* **[Microfilm & Digital Capture],** from the originals at the National Archives, Washington, DC. Filmed by the National Archives, 1964, 4 rolls, beginning with FHL film #6436 (Kent County). To access the digital images, see the online FHL catalog page: www.familysearch.org/search/catalog/744473.

1850 Delaware Federal Census Index **[Printed Index],** edited by Ronald Vern Jackson, et al, published by Accelerated Indexing Systems, Bountiful, UT, 1977, 83 pages., FHL book 975.1 X2p.

1850. *Index to the 1850 Census of Delaware* **[Printed Index],** compiled by Virginia L. Olmsted, published by Genealogical Publishing Co., Baltimore,1977, 370 pages, FHL book 975.1 X22o 1850.

1850-1860 Delaware Slave Schedules **[Printed Index],** edited by Ronald Vern Jackson, et al, published by Accelerated Indexing Systems, Bountiful, UT.

1850-1860 Delaware Agricultural Census **[Printed Book],** transcribed and compiled by Linda L. Green, includes index, published by L.L. Green, Woodbridge, VA, 2004, 281 pages, FHL book 975.1 X2g.

1850-1870 Delaware Social Statistics Schedules **[Microfilm & Digital Capture],** from the state's original copies at the Delaware State Archives, Dover, DE, under the title, *United States Census of Delaware, Social Statistics Schedules, 1850-1870,* filmed by the Delaware Div. of Historical and Cultural Affairs, 1971, 1 roll, FHL film #1421306. Another filming, FHL film # 1549980. To access the digital images, see the online FHL catalog page: **www.familysearch.org/search/catalog/451417.**

1850-1880 Delaware Agriculture and Industry Schedules **[Microfilm],** from the state's original copies at the Delaware State Archives, Dover, DE, under the title, *United States Census of Delaware, Agriculture and Industry Schedules, 1850-1880,* filmed by the Public Archives Commission, Dover, DE, 1963, 2 rolls, FHL film #1421304 (Agriculture schedules) and FHL film #1421305 (Agriculture and Industry schedules).

1850-1880 Delaware Mortality Schedules **[Microfilm & Digital Capture],** from the state's original copies at the Delaware State Archives, Dover, DE, under the title, *United States Census of Delaware; Persons Who Died During the [Census] Year, 1850-1880,* Lists names of individuals who died during the year ending 1 Jun of the census years 1850-1870 and during the year ending 31 May 1880. Filmed by the Public Archives Commission, Dover, DE, FHL film #1421306. Another copy filmed as #1549980. To access the digital images, see the online FHL catalog page: **www.familysearch.org/search/catalog/451397.**

1852-1853. *New Castle County, Delaware, Tax Assessment* **[Microfiche],** from the originals at the Hall of Records, Dover, DE. Filmed by the Bureau of Archives & Records, 1979, 30 microfiches, FHL fiche #6332612 (Introduction) through fiche #6332631 (General list – all hundreds).

1855-1910 Delaware Death Records **[Microfilm & Digital Capture],** from the originals at the Hall of Records, Dover, DE. Filmed by the Genealogical Society of Utah, 1949, 50 rolls, beginning with FHL film #6360 (Deaths 1855, 1860, 1861-1880). To access the digital images, see the online FHL catalog page: **www.familysearch.org/search/catalog/786107.**

1855-1961. *Delaware Death Records* **[Online Database],** digitized and indexed at the FamilySearch.org website, a name index, and images of records from the Delaware Bureau of Vital Statistics, Dover, DE, originally microfilmed by the Genealogical Society of Utah for the Family History Library in Salt Lake City, Utah. The database contains 238,920 records. See **www.familysearch.org/search/collection/1520546.**

1859-1860 Delaware State Directory **[Microfiche],** from the original published as *Boyd's Delaware State Directory,* by Research Publications, Woodbridge, CT, 1980, "…containing the names of all persons in business on their own account, also the censers, manufacturing statistics, and names of the inhabitants of Wilmington city," by William H. Wilmington and Andrew Boyd. See FHL fiche #6043859.

1860. *Delaware, 1860 Federal Census: Population Schedules* **[Microfilm & Digital Capture],** from the originals at the National Archives, Washington, DC. Filmed twice by the National Archives, 1950, 1967, 7 rolls total, beginning with FHL film #803095 (2nd, Kent County), and FHL film #6435 (1st, entire state). To access the digital images, see the FHL catalog page: **www.familysearch.org/search/catalog/704564.**

1860 Delaware Federal Census Index **[Printed Index],** edited by Ronald Vern Jackson, et al, published by Accelerated Indexing Systems, Bountiful, UT, 1977, 377 pages., FHL book 975.1 X2de 1860.

1860 Delaware Federal Census Index: Heads of Households and Other Surnames in Household Index **[Printed Index],** compiled by Bryan Lee Dilts, published by Index Publishing, Salt Lake City, UT, 1984, 154 pages, FHL book 975.1 X22d 1860.

1861-1865. *Index to Compiled Service Records of Volunteer Union Soldiers Who Served in Organizations from the State of Delaware* **[Microfilm],** from the originals at the National Archives, Washington, DC, filmed by the National Archives, 1964, series M537, 4 rolls, beginning with FHL film #881617 (Index, A-D). For a complete list of roll numbers and contents of each roll, see the online FHL catalog page for this title: **www.familysearch.org/search/catalog/313512.**

1861-1865. *Delaware, Civil War Service Records of Union Soldiers, 1861-1865* **[Online Database],** digitized and indexed at the FamilySearch.org website. The records include a jacket-envelope for each soldier, labeled with his name, rank, and the unit in which he served. The jacket-envelope typically contains card abstracts of entries relating to the soldier as found in

original muster rolls, returns, rosters, payrolls, appointment books, hospital registers, prison registers and rolls, parole rolls, inspection reports and the originals of any papers relating solely to the particular soldier. Index courtesy of Fold3. This database has 179,813 records. See
www.familysearch.org/search/collection/1932394.

1861-1865. *United States Civil War Soldiers Index* **[Online Database],** an index to soldiers who served in the Civil War, culled from 6.3 million soldier records in the General Index Cards to the Compiled Military Service Records in the National Archives. This index was a joint project of the U.S. National Park Service, the Federation of Genealogical Societies (FGS), and the Genealogical Society of Utah (GSU). Each record provides the full name of the soldier, state, regiment, whether Union or Confederate, the company, the soldier's rank, sometimes alternate names, the NARA publication, and roll numbers. It is possible to search for Delaware regiments and see complete rosters of the soldiers. See
https://familysearch.org/search/collection/1910717.

1861-1865. *Soldiers and Sailors Database* **[Online Database],** indexed at the National Park Service website. This is the original database containing information about the men who served in the Union and Confederate armies during the Civil War. Other information on the site includes histories of Union and Confederate regiments, links to descriptions of significant battles, and selected lists of prisoner-of-war records and cemetery records, which will be amended over time. This database has 6.3 million records. 16,223 Delaware troops (all Union) are identified by name and regiment. See
www.nps.gov/civilwar/soldiers-and-sailors-database.htm.

1861-1913. *Delaware Birth Records, Certificates and Returns* **[Microfilm & Digital Capture],** from the originals at the Hall of Records, Dover, DE. The records are quarterly returns and alphabetically arranged. Filmed by the Genealogical Society of Utah, 1949, 37 rolls, beginning with FHL film #6323 (Births 18661-1879). To access the digital images, see the online FHL catalog page:
www.familysearch.org/search/catalog/294972.

1861-1922. *Delaware State Birth Records* **[Online Database],** digitized and indexed at the FamilySearch.org website, a name index to birth records from the Delaware Bureau of Vital Statistics

on FHL microfilm. This database contains 121,234 records. See
www.familysearch.org/search/collection/1534607.

1861-1933. *Delaware Death Records* **[Online Database],** digitized and indexed at the Ancestry.com website. Source: DE Vital Recds, DE Public Archives, Dover. This database contains death records from Delaware from 1861-1933. These come from records available on microfilm at the Delaware Public Archives. Information listed in a death record generally includes: Name of deceased, Gender, Age, Death date, Birth date, Spouse's name, and Parents' names. The document image may have more information. This database has 517,401 records. See
https://search.ancestry.com/search/db.aspx?dbid=1674.

1862-1866. *Internal Revenue Assessment Lists for Delaware* **[Microfilm & Digital Capture],** from the original records at the National Archives, Washington, DC, 1988, series M759, 8 rolls, beginning with FHL film #1578436 (annual lists 1862, monthly lists Sep 1862-Apr 1863). To access the digital images, see the online FHL catalog page:
www.familysearch.org/search/catalog/574311.

1862-1959 Delaware City Directories. See *U.S. City Directories, 1822-1995* **[Online Database],** indexed at the Ancestry.com website. See each directory title page image for the full title and publication information. This collection is one of the largest single databases on the Internet, with a total of 1.56 billion names, all indexed from scanned images of the city directory book pages. All states are represented except Alaska, and there are directories for **Dover** (1879-), **Various Delaware cities** (1874-), and **Wilmington** (1862-1959). For a complete list of cities/counties with directories, use Ancestry's *Browse this Collection* feature to choose a state, choose a city, and choose a directory year available. This database has 1,560,284,702 records. See
https://search.ancestry.com/search/db.aspx?dbid=2469.

"1862-1872 Delaware Income & Manufacturers Tax" [Printed Article]. Name list in *Delaware History*, Vol. 14, No. 4 (Oct 1971).

1865-1872. *Maryland and Delaware, Freedman's Bureau Field Office Records* [Online Database], indexed at the FamilySearch.org website. Source: National Archives microfilm M1906. The Bureau of

Refugees, Freedmen, and Abandoned Lands (often called the Freedmen's Bureau) was created in 1865 at the end of the American Civil War to supervise relief efforts including education, health care, food and clothing, refugee camps, legalization of marriages, employment, labor contracts, and securing back pay, bounty payments and pensions. These records include letters and endorsements sent and received, account books, applications for rations, applications for relief, court records, labor contracts, registers of bounty claimants, registers of complaints, registers of contracts, registers of disbursements, registers of freedmen issued rations, registers of patients, reports, rosters of officers and employees, special and general orders and circulars received, special orders and circulars issued, records relating to claims, court trials, property restoration, and homesteads. This database has 36,376 records. See **www.familysearch.org/search/collection/1989156.**

1866-1894. *Mortgage Records of Sussex County, Delaware* **[Microfilm & Digital Capture],** from the original records at the Hall of Records, Dover, DE. Filmed by the archives, 1950, 7 rolls, beginning with FHL film #2188583 (Mortgage Records, 1866-1870). To access the digital images, see the online FHL catalog page: **www.familysearch.org/search/catalog/1126915.**

1870. *Delaware, 1870 Federal Census: Population Schedules* **[Microfilm & Digital Capture],** from the originals at the National Archives, Washington, DC. Filmed twice by the National Archives, 1962, 1968, 5 rolls total, beginning with FHL film #545618 (2nd filming, Kent County) and FHL film #295399 (1st filming, entire state). To access the digital images, see the online FHL catalog page: **www.familysearch.org/search/catalog/698890.**

1870 Delaware Federal Census Index: Heads of Households and Other Surnames in Household Index **[Printed Index],** compiled by Bryan Lee Dilts, published by Index Publishing, Salt Lake City, UT, 1984, 153 pages, FHL book 975.1 X22d 1870.

1870 Delaware Federal Census Index **[Printed Index],** edited by Ronald Vern Jackson, et al, published by Accelerated Indexing Systems, Bountiful, UT, 1987, 171 pages., FHL book 975.1 X22j 1870.

1870 Delaware Federal Census Index, A-Z **[Printed Index],** edited by Raeone Christensen Steuart, published by Heritage Quest, Bountiful, UT, 1998, 273 pages, FHL book 975.1 X22s 1870.

1870 Delaware Mortality Schedules **[Printed Index],** edited by Ronald Vern Jackson, published by Accelerated Indexing Systems, Bountiful, UT, 1981, 44 pages, FHL book 975.1 X2j 1870.

1873-1900. *The Banks Compilation of Birth Data of Men with Links to New Castle County, Delaware (Including the City of Wilmington) Who Were Born 1873-1900: As Found in the World War I Civilian Registration Cards* **[Printed Book],** abstracted by Raymond H. Banks. Includes name (alphabetical by surname), birth date and place (or other information), ethnic group, county or city draft board, and state. Published by the author, Salt Lake City, UT, 1996, 592 pages, FHL book 975.11 M2b.

1876-2012. *Wilmington, Delaware, Catholic Diocese Cemeteries Index* **[Online Database],** indexed at the Ancestry.com website. This is a shared database with the Catholic Diocese of Wilmington website. Each index record includes: Name, Birth date, Age at death, Death date, Cemetery, Burial place, Publication title, and a link to the Catholic Diocese of Wilmington website. This database has 73,262 records. See **https://search.ancestry.com/search/db.aspx?dbid=70648.**

1880. *Delaware, 1880 Federal Census: Soundex and Population Schedules* **[Microfilm & Digital Capture],** from the originals at the National Archives, Washington, DC (in 1970), now located at the Hall of Records, Dover, DE. Filmed by the National Archives, 1970, 14 rolls, beginning with FHL film #445519 (Soundex: A 130-B263), and FHL film #1254116 (Population schedules: Kent County). To access the digital images (Population Schedules), see the online FHL catalog page: **www.familysearch.org/search/catalog/670378.**

1880 Delaware Mortality Schedules **[Printed Index],** edited by Ronald Vern Jackson, published by Accelerated Indexing Systems, Bountiful, UT, 1981, 61 pages, FHL book 975.1 X2j 1880.

1880. *United States Census of Delaware, Supplemental Schedules for the Defective, Dependent, and Delinquent Classes, 1880* **[Microfilm & Digital Capture],** from the state's copies of originals at the Hall of Records, Dover, DE. Includes schedules for the insane, idiots, deaf-mutes, blind, homeless children, inhabitants in prison, pauper, and indigent inhabitants. Filmed by the Delaware Div. of Historical and Cultural Affairs, 1971, 1 roll, FHL film #1421306. To access the digital images, see the online FHL catalog page:
www.familysearch.org/search/catalog/451428.

1900. *Delaware, 1900 Federal Census: Soundex and Population Schedules* **[Microfilm & Digital Capture],** from the originals at the National Archives, Washington, DC. Filmed by the National Archives, c1970, 26 rolls, beginning with FHL film #1242574 (Soundex: A 000-B416), and FHL film #1240153 (Population schedules: Kent County). To access the digital images (Population Schedules), see the online FHL catalog page:
www.familysearch.org/search/catalog/647875.

1910. *Delaware, 1910 Federal Census: Population Schedules* **[Microfilm & Digital Capture],** from the originals at the National Archives, Washington, DC. Filmed by the National Archives, c1970, 4 rolls, beginning with FHL film #1374158 (Kent County). To access the digital images, see the online FHL catalog page: **www.familysearch.org/search/catalog/647824.**

1910. *Delaware 1910 Census Index* **[Printed Index],** compiled and published by Heritage Quest, North Salt Lake, UT, 2001, 464 pages, FHL book 975.1 X22d 1910.

1910-1955 Death Records **[Microfilm & Digital Capture],** from the originals at the Hall of Records, Dover, DE. Filmed by International Microfilmers, 1973, 75 rolls, beginning with FHL film #1944030 (Death records, 1910). To access the digital images, see the online FHL catalog page:
www.familysearch.org/search/catalog/784075.

1913-1954. *Delaware Marriage Records, 1913-1954* **[Online Database],** digitized and indexed at the FamilySearch.org website, a name index to records from the Delaware Bureau of Archives and Records

Management, Dover, DE, from FHL microfilm, the database contains 112,894 records. See
www.familysearch.org/search/collection/1609795.

1917-1918 WWI Civilian Draft Registration Cards, Kent County, Delaware **[Online Database],** indexed in several alpha groups at the RootsWeb site for Delaware, Kent Co. See
www.rootsweb.ancestry.com/~usgenweb/de/kent/index.htm.

1917-1918 WWI Civilian Draft Registration Cards, New Castle County, Delaware **[Online Database],** indexed in several alpha groups at the RootsWeb site for Delaware, New Castle Co. See
www.rootsweb.ancestry.com/~usgenweb/de/newcastle/index.htm.

1917-1918 WWI Civilian Draft Registration Cards, Sussex County, Delaware **[Online Database],** indexed in several alpha groups at the RootsWeb site for Delaware, Sussex Co. See
www.rootsweb.ancestry.com/~usgenweb/de/sussex/index.htm.

1917-1919. *Delaware, World War I Servicemen Records* **[Online Database],** digitized and indexed at FamilySearch. Captured by the Delaware Public Archives, Dover, DE. This database has 2,559 records, see **www.familysearch.org/search/collection/2858132.**

1919-1922. *Registration of Deaths Out of City (Wilmington, Delaware)* **[Microfilm & Digital Capture],** from the originals at the Delaware Public Archives, Dover, DE. Filmed by the archives, 1999,1 roll, FHL film #2409755. To access the digital images, see the online FHL catalog page:
www.familysearch.org/search/catalog/1348296.

1919-1924. *Registration of Deaths, New Castle County, Delaware, 1919-1924* **[Microfilm & Digital Capture],** from the originals at the Delaware Public Archives, Dover, DE. Filmed by the archives, 1999, 1 roll, FHL film #2409755. To access the digital images, see the online FHL catalog page:
www.familysearch.org/search/catalog/1348298.

1920. *Delaware, 1920 Federal Census: Soundex and Population Schedules* **[Microfilm & Digital Capture],** from the originals at the National Archives,

Washington, DC. Filmed by the National Archives, c1970, 25 rolls, beginning with FHL film #1823914 (Soundex: A 120-B416), and FHL film #1820201 (Population schedules: Kent County). To access the digital images (Population Schedules), see the online FHL catalog page:
www.familysearch.org/search/catalog/567627.

1930. *Delaware, 1930 Federal Census: Population Schedules* **[Microfilm & Digital Capture],** from the originals at the National Archives, Washington, DC. Filmed by the National Archives, c1970, 6 rolls, beginning with FHL film #2340021 (Kent County). To access the digital images, see the online FHL catalog page: www.familysearch.org/search/catalog/1034485.

1940. Delaware, 1940 Federal Census: Population Schedules [Digital Capture], digitized images from the microfilm of original records held by the Bureau of the Census in the 1940s. After microfilming, Congress allowed the Census Bureau to destroy the originals to free up space for WWII-related files. Digitizing of the 1940 census schedules microfilm images was done for the National Archives and made public on April 2, 2012. To access the digital images, see the online FHL catalog page:
www.familysearch.org/search/catalog/2057746.

1940 Federal Census Finding Aids **[Online Database].** The National Archives has prepared a special website online with details about the 1940 federal census. Included at the site are description of location finding aids, such as Enumeration District Maps, Geographic Descriptions of Census Enumeration Districts, and a list of 1940 City Directories available at the National Archives The finding aids are all linked to other National Archives sites. The National Archives website also has a link to 1940 Search Engines using Stephen P. Morse's "One-Step" system for finding a 1940 E.D. or street address conversion. See
www.archives.gov/research/census/1940/general-info.html#questions.

1940-1945. *Delaware, World War II Draft Registration Cards* **[Online Database],** digitized and indexed at FamilySearch. Name index and images of draft registration cards of men who registered during World War II with the exception of the fourth registration. This collection is part of National Archives Record Group 147, Records of the Selective Service System, 1940. Images courtesy of Ancestry.com. The event place is the residence of the registrant. This database has 73,213 records, see **www.familysearch.org/search/collection/2515880.**

1991-Current. *Delaware Newspaper Obituaries* **[Online Database].** Digitized and indexed at the GenealogyBank.com website. One search screen for obituaries published in all of the following city newspapers: Dover, Georgetown, Harrington, Hockessin, Lewes, Middletown, Milford, Newark Seaford, and Smyrna. See **www.genealogybank.com/explore/obituaries/all/usa/delaware.**

U.S. Territories
Censuses & Substitute Name Lists

The U.S. currently has a total of sixteen territories, eleven of which are islands administered by the U.S. Interior Department's Fish and Wildlife System. Five territories are well populated places with various levels of self-government.

Classification of U.S. Territories

Incorporated Organized Territories were those of the United States that were *Incorporated* (part of the United States proper) and *Organized* (having a government authorized by an Organic Act passed by Congress, including a territorial legislature, territorial governor, and a basic judicial system). Within an Organized Territory, residents are under protection of the U.S. Constitution (Bill of Rights, citizenship, trial by jury, et al). The first such territory was the Territory Northwest of the River Ohio, created in 1787. The last were the territories of Alaska and Hawaii prior to their statehood in 1959. There are currently no U.S. territories in this classification.

Incorporated Unorganized Territories are those that are part of the United States proper but have no organized government. There is one territory of the U.S. in this classification: Palmyra Atoll, considered part of the United States proper due to its former status under the Kingdom of Hawaii at the time of the Hawaiian Annexation to the U.S.

Unincorporated Organized Territories are those that are not incorporated into the United States proper but have an organized government. There are currently five (5) territories of the U.S. in this classification: Puerto Rico, U.S. Virgin Islands, Guam, Northern Mariana Islands and American Samoa. Technically, American Samoa is not an Organized Territory, but yet it has all of the elements of one, including an elected governor and legislature, and non-voting member of congress. From 1903 to 1979, there was an Unincorporated Organized Territory of the U.S. called the Panama Canal Zone.

Unincorporated Unorganized Territories are those not in the United States proper and have no organization.

There are currently ten islands in this classification: Baker Island, Howland Island, Jarvis Island, Johnston Atoll, Kingman Reef, Wake Island, Midway Atoll, Navassa Island, Serranilla Bank, and Baja Nuevo Bank.

Commonwealth Territory is a type of Organized Territory of the United States that has an adopted Constitution of self-government that cannot be overturned or modified by Congress without the approval of the Commonwealth. Currently, there are two organized territories of the United States with Commonwealth status: Puerto Rico and the Northern Mariana Islands. (There was a U.S. Commonwealth of the Philippines from 1934 to 1946).

Uninhabited Territories. Regardless of their classification as U.S. Territories, there are currently uninhabited territories as part of the United States. Some current territories were inhabited at one time but are now uninhabited.

Former Territories. For this review of censuses and substitutes available, the former U.S. territories of the Panama Canal Zone and the Philippines have been added to the current list of inhabited territories.

1856 Guano Island Act. The first overseas possessions or "insular areas" of the U.S. began in 1856, when the United States Congress enacted the Guano Islands Act. U.S. Citizens were allowed to legally discover and mine the guano deposits of seabirds, a highly prized source of saltpeter for gunpowder, as well as its use as an agricultural fertilizer. The President of the United States was authorized to take possession of any unclaimed islands and allowed to use the military to protect such interests. Over the years, more than 100 islands were claimed under the Guano Island Act by the U.S., including islands, islets, atolls, shoals, or reefs, mostly in the Pacific Ocean, but a few were in the Caribbean Sea. All of the remaining eleven possessions are currently territories administered by the Fish and Wildlife Service of the U.S. Department of the Interior. Most are designated wildlife refuges and (with a few exceptions) have no permanent residents.

Puerto Rico and U.S. Virgin Islands (from Google Maps)

Part 1 of this review includes the current inhabited territories of the United States within the Caribbean Region: the Commonwealth of Puerto Rico and the U.S. Virgin Islands. Also in this region is the former territory of the Panama Canal Zone, 1903-1979. Databases that are part of a combined Caribbean-West Indies focus are listed first.

Bibliography
Caribbean Region
Censuses & Substitutes

1590-1928. *Caribbean Births and Baptisms* **[Online Database],** indexed at the FamilySearch.org website. Source: FamilySearch extractions from microfilm collections at the Family History Library, Salt Lake City, UT. This is an index to selected birth and baptismal records from various localities in the Caribbean. The year range in the collection title represents the years covered by the majority of the records; however, some records may be from earlier or later years. This collection does not include images of the original records. This database has 5,831 records. See **https://familysearch.org/search/collection/1804229**.

1590-1928. *Caribbean, Select Births and Baptisms* **[Online Database],** indexed at the Ancestry.com website. Source: FamilySearch extractions. See **http://search.ancestry.com/search/db.aspx?dbid=60245**.

1590-2015. *The Caribbean GenWeb Project* **[Online Database].** See **www.rootsweb.ancestry.com/~caribgw/cgw_archive/index.html**. Online databases at this site include:
British Virgin Islands:
- Wesleyan Methodist Church 1815-1933
- Society of Friends (Quakers) 1740-1760
- St. George's Episcopal 1862-1934, Marriages 1862-1866
Puerto Rico:
- 1910 Census of Leguisamo, Mayagüez
U.S. Virgin Islands:
- List of Landowners of the 1841 St. John Census
- List of Colonists of Danish W.I. 1678

- List of Lutheran Clergy
- Land Lister (tax records) 1672-1680
- Land Lister (tax records) 1686-1693
- St. Croix 1841 Census, Part 1
- List of Shareholders of the Danish West India Company, Part 1
- List of Shareholders of the Danish West India Company, Part 2
- List of Shareholders of the Danish West India Company, Part 3
- List of Shareholders of the Danish West India Company, Part 4

1590-2015. *Caribbean Family History* **[Online Database],** online research databases are available for Burials, Ministers, Quakers, Slave Compensations, Tombstone, and more. To review the research databases, see **www.caribbeanfamilyhistory.org**.

1590-2015. *CARSURDEX – Caribbean Surname Index* **[Online Database].** Description from the website: "The Caribbean Surname Index is basically a Discussion Forum containing surname, location, and other 'Boards' where registered users may post their relevant information and hope for a response from other family members searching on the Internet. This Index is 'spidered' regularly by all of the search engines, including Google, so information placed here will show up when other people conduct a search. There are also general discussion Boards where registered users may throw out general or specific questions which others may respond to... discussion is very much encouraged here." See **www.candoo.com/surnames/index.php**.

1590-2015. *Caribbean Genealogy Records – GenealogyInTime Magazine* **[Online Database].** This is an online genealogy magazine with useful search engines, listings of the latest genealogy records, in-depth articles and other helpful resources. For the Caribbean Genealogy Records page, see **www.genealogyintime.com/records/Caribbean-genealogy-records.html**.

1591-1905. *Caribbean, Select Marriages* **[Online Database],** indexed at the Ancestry.com website. Source: FamilySearch extractions. This database has 198,132 records. See http://search.ancestry.com/search/db.aspx?dbid=60247.

1611-1707. *The Original Scots Colonists of Early America. Caribbean Supplement* **[Online Database],** indexed at the Ancestry.com website. Source: Book, same title, by David Dobson, publ. 1999. This database has 158 pages. See http://search.ancestry.com/search/db.aspx?dbid=48522.

1730-1807. *Slave Ship Sailors and Their Captive Cargoes* **[Printed Book],** by Emma Christopher, publ. Cambridge University Press, New York, 2006, 241 pages, FHL book 306.362 C466s.

1739-2015. *Online Resources, Caribbean Genealogy Library* **[Online Database],** a website of the Caribbean Genealogy Library, Island of St. Thomas, U.S. Virgin Islands. Online databases include Danish Archives Documents Online, Danish West Indies Era Passenger Lists, U.S. National Archives Documents, Jewish Families of the Caribbean, Family History Library Resources, Moravian Church Resources, Dr. Aimery Caron Manuscripts, Maria Smith Cemetery Database, Virgin Islands Exodus: 1917 Identity Cards, and Miscellaneous Online Resources. See http://cgl.vi/pages/online.html.

1790-1906. *Caribbean Deaths and Burials* **[Online Database],** indexed at the FamilySearch.org website. Source: FamilySearch extractions from microfilm collections at the Family History Library, Salt Lake City, UT. This is an Index to selected death and burial records from various localities in the Caribbean. The year range in the collection title represents the years covered by the majority of the records; however, some records may be from earlier or later years. This collection does not include images of the original records. See https://familysearch.org/search/collection/1809321.

1790-1906. *Caribbean, Select Deaths and Burials* **[Online Database],** indexed at the Ancestry.com website. Source: FamilySearch extractions. This database has 7,539 records. See http://search.ancestry.com/search/db.aspx?dbid=60246.

The Commonwealth of Puerto Rico is an Unincorporated Organized Territory of the United States, by far the largest U.S. Territory, with an estimated 2021 population of 3.3 million people. Puerto Rico is an archipelago that includes the main island of Puerto Rico and a few smaller islands, such as Isla de Mona, Isla de Culebra, and Isla de Vieques. The north shore of the main island faces the Atlantic Ocean, the south shore faces the Caribbean Sea. The capital is San Juan, a city of nearly 400,000 people.

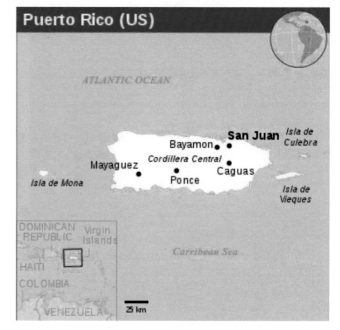

Historical Timeline for Puerto Rico, 1493-1952

Spanish Era - 1493-1898:

1493. Christopher Columbus, an Italian sailing for Spain discovered an island he named San Juan Bautista on his second voyage to the New World. Juan Ponce de Leon, a "Gentleman Volunteer," was a member of Columbus' crew.

1508. Ponce de Leon founded the first Spanish settlement on the island of San Juan Bautista. He later became the first Spanish governor of the island, which merchants and other visitors began referring to as Puerto Rico (Rich Port).

1595. Queen Elizabeth I sent Sir Francis Drake to capture treasure from a wrecked Spanish galleon stored at La Fortaleza, Puerto Rico. Drake failed and returned to England. Unlike the Spanish, the English had no colonies in the New World yet, and preyed on any Spanish ships in the Caribbean, looking for Spanish gold.

1598. Sir George Clifford attacked Puerto Rico with an English fleet. He sacked San Juan, but soon after his food supply spoiled and 400 of his men died of dysentery. The survivors burned San Juan and sailed away. Back in Spain, the King reacted to the event by sending a fleet of new immigrants to Puerto Rico to reinforce the colony. After new Puerto Rico fortifications were installed, English, French, or Dutch raiders were never successful again in causing serious harm to the people of Puerto Rico.

1598-1898. Although often coveted by other Europeans, Puerto Rico was heavily fortified against attacks from the outsiders, and remained under control of Spain for another 300 years.

American Era - 1898-Present:

1898. Puerto Rico was ceded by Spain to the United States as part of the Treaty of Paris ending the Spanish-American War. A military governor was in charge of the transition from Spanish to American rule.

1900. The U.S. Congress installed a civilian government in Puerto Rico, with strict control over island affairs. A territorial governor was appointed by the President of the United States.

1917. The **Jones Act** separated the Executive, Judicial, and Legislative branches of Puerto Rican government, provided U.S. citizenship to the residents, and created a locally elected bicameral legislature.

1948. Munoz Marin was the first elected governor by popular vote. He served for four terms.

1952. Puerto Rico became a Commonwealth Territory, with its own constitution, elected governor, elected legislature, and one elected representative to the U.S. House of Representatives (who can introduce legislation and vote in committees but cannot vote on the floor of the full House).

Bibliography
Puerto Rico Censuses & Substitutes

The Spanish government took censuses of Puerto Rico in 1765, 1775, 1800, 1815, 1832, 1846, and 1857, but most of the name lists from these reports have not survived. Microfilmed/digitized versions of surviving census reports from the period 1801-1859 are shown in the bibliography below. The Puerto Rico censuses of 1860, 1877, and 1887 were included in the regular Spanish censuses. The reports from the censuses were published but any original name lists, if they exist, are located at the Seville Archives.

The first American census taken in Puerto Rico was in 1899 and included population and agriculture schedules. The published report of the 1899 special census includes statistics from the 1860, 1877, and 1887 Spanish Censuses, but the 1899 name lists were not published.

Puerto Rico was included in all U.S. Federal Censuses from 1900 through 2010. A special census was taken for Puerto Rico in 1935 and included population and agriculture schedules. Censuses and substitutes available are listed below:

1645-1969. *Puerto Rico, Catholic Church Records* **[Online Database],** indexed at the FamilySearch.org website. Source: Paróquias Católicas, Puerto Rico (Catholic Church parishes, Puerto Rico). This is an image-only database of Catholic Church records created by parishes in Puerto Rico. These records include baptisms, confirmations, parish censuses, marriages, deaths, and indexes. Browse through the images, organized by the municipalities of Aguadilla, Bayamón, Carolina, Cataño, Cayey, Dorado, Guaynabo, Loíza, Luquillo, Río Piedras, San Francisco, San Juan, Santurce, Toa Alta, Toa Baja, Trujillo Alto, Trujillo Bajo, and Vieques. This database has 191,547 images. See **https://familysearch.org/search/collection/1807092**.

1800-1900. *Catálogo de Extranjeros Residentes en Puerto Rico en el Siglo XIX (Alphabetical Surname Listing of Resident Foreigners in Puerto Rico in the 19th Century)* **[Printed Book],** by Estela Cifre de Loubriel, publ. Ediciones de la Universidad de Puerto Rico, 1962, 190 pages, FHL book 972.95 W2c. Also on microfilm, FHL film #9224457.

1800-1950. *Cárceles (Jails)* **[Microfilm & Digital Capture],** from the originals at the Puerto Rico Departamento de Justicia, San Juan, PR. Includes Registers of deaths of prisoners and correspondence between wardens of the different prisons regarding the prisoners. Filmed by the Genealogical Society of Utah, 1988, 55 rolls, beginning with FHL film #1506929 (Confinados fallecidos Caja 151-153, 1800-1900). To access the digital images, see the online FHL catalog page: **https://familysearch.org/search/catalog/612954**.

1801-1859. *Censo y Riqueza* **[Microfilm & Digital Capture],** from the originals at the Archivo General de Puerto Rico, San Juan, PR. Includes Puerto Rico population and land censuses, filmed by the Genealogical Society of Utah, 1987, 2 rolls, as follows:

- Censo y riqueza Caja 11 1801-1820 Varios pueblos Caja 12 1812-1822 Adjuntas, Añasco, Arecibo, Barranquitas, Bayamón Camuy, Ciales, Cidra, Coamo, Culebra, Juana Díaz, Juncos, Fajardo, Gurao, Guayama, Guaynabo, Humacao, Isabela, Las Piedras, Loiza, Luquillo. FHL film #1389438. Items 4-13.
- Censo y riqueza Caja 12 (cont) 1812-1822 Maricao, Manati, Maunabo, Mayagüez, Naguabo, Patillas, Peñuelas, Ponce, Quebradillas, Río Piedras, Rincón, Sabana Grande, San Germán, Toa Alta, Trujillo, Utuado, Vega Alta, Vega Baja, FHL film #1389438 Items 14-22.
- Censo y riqueza Caja 12 (cont) 1812-1822 Yabucoa, Yauco, Varios pueblos Caja 13 1812-1822 Varios pueblos. FHL film #1389438 Items 23-25.
- Censo y riqueza Caja 14 1836-1839 Varios pueblos Caja 15 1841-1850 Varios pueblos Caja 16 1858-1859 Varios pueblos. FHL film #1389439 Items 1-3.

To access the digital images, see the online FHL catalog page: **www.familysearch.org/search/catalog/607211**.

1811-1874. Matrimonios (Marriages) [Microfilm & Digital Capture], Nineteenth-century Puerto Rican marriage records; documents in the Gobernadores Españoles collection of the Puerto Rico General Archive in San Juan. Filmed by the Genealogical Society of Utah, 1987, 2 rolls, FHL film #1389445 (Proclamas Caja 143, 1811-1839), and FHL film #138446 (Cajas 144-145, 1821-1874). To access the digital images, see the online FHL catalog page: **www.familysearch.org/search/catalog/607335**.

1868-2000s. *Linkpendium – Puerto Rico: Family History & Genealogy, Census, Birth, Marriage, Death, Vital Records & More* **[Online Databases].** Linkpendium is a genealogical portal site with links to Territory and Municipio databases. Currently listed are selected sites for Puerto Rico territory-wide resources (99), and the Municipios of Adjuntas (25), Aguada (23), Aguadilla (32), Aguas Buenas (20), Aibonito (26), Añasco (22), Arecibo (33), Arroyo (22), Barceloneta (21), Barranquitas (22), Barros (4), Bayamón (29), Cabo Rojo (26), Caguas (30), Camuy (22), Canóvanas (12), Carolina (22), Cataño (21), Cayey (27), Ceiba (23), Ciales (24), Cidra (23), Coamo (24), Comerío (23), Corozal (22), Culebra (26), Dorado (23), Fajardo (30), Florida (9), Guánica (22), Guayama (24), Guayanilla (29), Guaynabo (22), Gurabo (20), Hatillo (21), Hormigueros (21), Humacao (29),. Isabela (27), Jayuya (21), Juana Díaz (21), Juncos (22), Lajas (22), Lares (28), Las Marías (20), Las Piedras (21), Loíza (21), Luquillo (21), Manatí (26), Maricao (23), Maunabo (22), Mayagüez (35), Moca (25), Morovis (20), Naguabo (23), Naranjito (19), Orocovis (21), Patillas (22), Peñuelas (20), Ponce (44), Quebradillas Municipio (23), Río Grande Municipio (20), Rincón (23), Rio Piedras (13), Sabana Grande (22), Salinas (23), San Germán (29), San Juan (59), San Lorenzo (29), San Sebastián (25), Santa Isabel (23), Toa Alta (21), Toa Baja (24), Trujillo Alto (20), Utuado (22), Vega Alta (20), Vega Baja (24), Vieques (30), Villalba (21), Yabucoa (21), and Yauco Municipio (34). See **www.linkpendium.com/pr-genealogy**.

1899. *Report on the Census of Puerto Rico* **[Printed Book & Digital Version],** the official report of the census taken after the 1898 Treaty of Paris ending the Spanish-American War and the U.S. acquired Puerto Rico. The book gives details/statistics of the population and agriculture. There are no name lists. The report also includes statistics from the 1860, 1877, and 1887 Spanish Censuses as a base of comparison with the 1899 totals. To access the digital version, see the online FHL catalog page: **www.familysearch.org/search/catalog/232914**.

1805-2001. *Puerto Rico, Civil Registration* **[Online Database],** indexed at the FamilySearch.org website. Source: Oficinas del ciudad, Puerto Rico (city offices, Puerto Rico). This is a database of Births, marriages, deaths, indexes and other records created by civil registration offices in Puerto Rico. Some records may date prior to 1885 as a few municipalities began civil registration before that date. Some of these records have been indexed and are searchable as part of this collection. Additional indexed records will be published as they become available. Browse through the images, organized by municipalities, Adjuntas through Yauco. This database has 4,581,756 images: https://familysearch.org/search/collection/1682798.

1815-1845. *Puerto Rico Records of Foreign Residents* **[Online Database],** indexed at the FamilySearch.org website. Source: National Archives microfilm series T1170. This is an image only database with requests by foreigners for permission to reside in Puerto Rico, some correspondence, lists of foreigners residing in Puerto Rico, and a few copies of final naturalization papers. During this time period Puerto Rico belonged to Spain. Puerto Rico was ceded to the United States in 1898. Browse through images, organized by name range, A to Z. This database has 18,857 records. See https://familysearch.org/search/collection/1919700.

1815-1845. *Puerto Rico, Records of Foreigners (in Spanish)* **[Online Database],** digitized at the Ancestry.com website. Source: National Archives microfilm series T1170, Records of the Spanish Government of Puerto Rico. This is an image-only database with requests made by foreigners to reside in Puerto Rico. Browse the images, organized by the first letter of a subject's surname. The documents in this collection consist of "cartas de domicilio", lists of foreigners residing in various towns in the island, various correspondence, and some copies of the final naturalization papers ("cartas de naturalizacion.") Immigrants to Puerto Rico were given free land and paid no taxes for a period of 5 years, after which they could either become Spanish subjects or return to their homelands. An approved request to reside on the island usually contains the following information: name of immigrant, names of members of his immediate family, country and town of origin, proof of his being of good moral character and a Catholic, amount of capital he was bringing into the country, name of town he planned to live in, and his trade or profession. Most of this material is dated after 1815, when foreign immigration was permitted in Puerto Rico for the first time. Records earlier than 1815 consist mostly of letters from local authorities informing the central government of the arrival of foreigners. The records are in Spanish. This database has 18,857 records. See http://search.ancestry.com/search/db.aspx?dbid=3027.

1816-1837. Emigrados [Microfilm & Digital Capture], digitized at FamilySearch.org. Includes Nineteenth-century Puerto Rican emigration records; documents in the "Gobernadores Españoles" collection of the Puerto Rico General Archive. To access the digital images, see the online FHL catalog page: www.familysearch.org/search/catalog/607158.

1867-1876. Registro de Esclavos [Microfilm & Digital Capture], Slave Registers of Puerto Rico, 1867-1873, 10 rolls, To access the digital images, see the online FHL catalog page: www.familysearch.org/search/catalog/612874.

1872. *Puerto Rico, Registro Central de Esclavos (Register of Slaves),* **[Online Database],** indexed at the Ancestry.com website. Source: National Archives microfilm series T1121, Records of the Spanish Government of Puerto Rico. This database contains a register of slaves in Puerto Rico in 1872. The history of slavery in Puerto Rico goes back to the 1500s. An 1870 law led to the creation of a central register of slaves in the country, and this database contains images of the 1872 register, the "Registro central de esclavos." There are now eight volumes of this register, which cover geographical departments 1, 2, and 4 through 6. Slaves are listed under the department and thereunder the municipality in which they resided. These records may include: Name, Age, Gender, Country of origin, Residence, Parents' names, Marital status, Trade, Physical description, and master's name. Slaves often had only a given name rather that both a given and a surname. Slavery was abolished in Puerto Rico in 1873. These records are in Spanish. This database has 20,058 records. See http://search.ancestry.com/search/db.aspx?dbid=2774.

1885-2001. *Puerto Rico, Civil Registrations* **[Online Database],** indexed at the Ancestry.com website. Source: Digital images by FamilySearch and Departamento de Salud de Puerto Rico, San Juan, PR. Civil registration in Puerto Rico began in 1885. Prior to that, registrations of vital events were kept by the Catholic Church, which was the predominant religion. This collection includes registrations of births, marriages, and deaths in Puerto Rico, which at the start of civil registration was a colony of Spain and after the Spanish-American War in 1898, a possession of the U.S. Civil registration typically took place within a few days of the event, although the gap was sometimes longer. Birth records generally include: Name of the registrant (who may be the father), Age, Marital status, Occupation, Origin, Residence; Date, time, and place of birth, Name of the child and legitimacy; Names of parents, their age, marital status, occupation, origins, and residence; Grandparents' names, origins, and whether deceased; Date and place of registration. Marriage records can include: Groom's name, age, race, marital status, occupation, residence, and origin; Bride's name, age, race, marital status, occupation, residence, and origin; Names of both sets of parents, origins, age, race, occupation, residence; Name and age of person giving consent (usually bride's father); Date and place of the declaration, Date and place of the marriage, Names of witnesses, marital status, occupation, origins, and residence. Death records may contain the following details: Medical certificate, Name of the deceased (married women's death records may be registered with her married name or maiden name), Decedent's age, marital status, residence, and race; Date and time of death; Cause of death; Informant's name and relationship to the decedent. Death declaration, Informant's name, age, marital status, occupation, origins, residence, and relationship to the deceased; Decedent's name, origin, age, race, marital status, occupation, residence, date, time, place, and cause of death; Parents of the decedent and their origins; Grandparents of the decedent; Burial place and date, and Place of registration. See http://search.ancestry.com/search/db.aspx?dbid=9100.

1900. *Military and Naval, 1900 Federal Census: Soundex and Population Schedules* **[Microfilm & Digital Capture],** from the originals at the Census Bureau. After microfilming in the 1940s, Congress permitted the Census Bureau to destroy the originals to make room for World War II records. Puerto Rico military and naval posts only are included in this series. Filmed by the Census Bureau, ca1943, series T1081, 37 rolls, beginning with FHL film #1249622 (Soundex: A000 thru A565); and FHL film #1241839 (Vol. 1). To access the digital images, see the online FHL catalog page: https://familysearch.org/search/catalog/655325.

1901-1962. *Puerto Rico, Passenger and Crew Lists* **[Online Database],** indexed at the Ancestry.com website. Source: National Archives microfilm, Selected Crew List and Manifests. This database is an index to manifests of aliens arriving at various ports in Puerto Rico. Records included in this collection include arrivals by both ship and air. The type of information that is generally contained in this database includes: Name, Nationality, Gender, Age on Arrival, and Date of Arrival. Other information that can be found on the images includes U.S. address; Passport, visa, and other immigration documentation information; Place and date of birth; Destination and baggage information. This database has 2,378,523 records. See http://search.ancestry.com/search/db.aspx?dbid=2257.

1903-1985. Puerto Rico, Naturalization Records [Microfilm & Digital Capture]. Digital images of originals held by the National Archives, New York City. Includes Index to Petitions and Declarations of Intention for Citizenship. The microfilm is not available for circulation. To access the digital images, see the online FHL catalog page: www.familysearch.org/search/catalog/2831399.
- See also, *Declaraciones de naturalización, 1899-1900* [Microfilm & Digital Capture], a Spanish language version of the Naturalization database. See www.familysearch.org/search/catalog/607228.

1910. *Puerto Rico, 1910 Federal Census: Population Schedules* **[Microfilm & Digital Capture],** from the originals at the Census Bureau. After microfilming in the 1940s, Congress permitted the Census Bureau to destroy the originals to make room for World War II records. Filmed by the Census Bureau, ca1943, series T624, 28 rolls, beginning with FHL film #13757769 (Population schedules: Adjuntas, Culebra, Aguada, and Aguas Buenas Co). For a complete list of roll numbers and contents of each roll, and a link to the digitized images for each roll, see the online FHL catalog page for this title. See https://familysearch.org/search/catalog/646844.

1920. *Puerto Rico, 1920 Federal Census: Soundex and Population Schedules* **[Microfilm & Digital Capture],** from the originals at the Census Bureau. Filmed by the Census Bureau, ca1943, series M1601, 198 rolls, beginning with FHL film #1831494 (Soundex: A000 thru A153), and FHL film #1822043 (Population schedules: Municipio Adjuntas, Arroyo, and Aguado). To access the digital images, see the online FHL catalog page: https://familysearch.org/search/catalog/558353.

1930. *Puerto Rico, 1930 Federal Census: Population Schedules* **[Microfilm & Digital Capture],** from the originals at the Census Bureau. After microfilming in the 1940s, Congress permitted the Census Bureau to destroy the originals to make room for World War II records. Filmed by the Census Bureau, ca1943, series T626, 30 rolls, beginning with FHL film #2342373 (Population schedules: Adjuntas, Arroyo, Aguada, and Aguas Buenas municipalities). For a complete list of roll numbers and contents of each roll, and a link to the digital images of each roll, see the online FHL catalog page for this title. See https://familysearch.org/search/catalog/1037614.

1935. *Puerto Rico, Special Censuses, Agricultural Schedules, 1935 (in Spanish)* **[Digital Capture & Online Database],** indexed at the Ancestry.com website. Source: National Archives microfilm series M1882 These schedules recorded statistics on farms, plantations, and market gardens, listing the names of owners, agents, and managers. The type of statistics recorded included the total acreage of land, the value of the farm, machinery and livestock, staples (wool, cotton, grain, etc.) produced, and the value of animals slaughtered, etc. see
http://search.ancestry.com/search/db.aspx?dbid=3033.

1935-1936. *Puerto Rico, Social and Population Schedules* **[Online Database],** digitized and indexed at FamilySearch.org. Source: Social and Population Schedules of the 1935 Special Census of Puerto Rico, National Archives microfilm series M1881. On December 1, 1935, the census in this database was taken, although the compilation of the census carried into 1936. This database includes both an index and images of the census schedules. The records are in Spanish. Enumerators recorded the following details: Municipalidad (municipality) Barrio (district), Nombre de la institución (name of institution), Ciudad o pueblo (city or town), Enumerado por mi este dia (enumeration date), Lugar de residencia (place of residence), Nombre (name), Parentesco de esta persona con el jefe de la familia (relationship to the head of the family), Sexo (sex), Color (color), Edad (age), Condición matrimonial (marital status), Natividad (nativity), Ciudadanía (citizenship), and Ocupación e industria (occupation and industry). The FHL holds 82 rolls of microfilm, used to digitize the images of the 1935 Puerto Rico Census. But microfilm is not circulated. To access the digital images for each roll, see the online FHL catalog page:
www.familysearch.org/search/catalog/2829708.
- The FamilySearch images database was indexed but full access is awaiting review. Meanwhile, both the Images & Index is available at Ancestry.com, see http://search.ancestry.com/search/db.aspx?dbid=2404.

1940. *Puerto Rico, 1940 Federal Census: Population Schedules* **[Digital Capture],** from the National Archives microfilm. After microfilming in the 1940s, Congress permitted the Census Bureau to destroy the originals to make room for World War II records. Filmed by the Census Bureau, ca1943, 51 rolls, beginning with FHL Film/DGS #5462242 (Puerto Rico, Bayamon Municipality). The 1940 census was

released to the public in 2012 as a digital version only. The microfilm is available only in the FHL catalog for reviewing the roll content – their reserve microfilm set is stored at Granite Mountain Vault in Utah. To access the digital images, see the online FHL catalog:
https://familysearch.org/search/catalog/2057785.

1949. *Guía Telefónica, Porto Rico: Edición de 1949* **[Microfilm],** from the original book by the Porto Rico Telephone Co, filmed by the Genealogical Society of Utah, 1990, 1 roll, FHL film #1224503.

1962. *Polk's San Juan, Area Metropolitana de San Juan, Puerto Rico City Directory, 1962* **[Printed Book],** includes all communities in the San Juan metropolitan area. Publ. R. L. Polk & Co, Kansas City, MO, 1962, FHL book 972.951/S1 E4p.

U.S. Virgin Islands
Caribbean Region

The U.S. Virgin Islands is an Unincorporated Organized Territory of the U.S. From 1733 to 1917, it was the Danish West Indies (DWI) of the Kingdom of Denmark-Norway. Purchased by the United States in 1917, it was renamed the Virgin Islands of the United States to indicate a separation from the British Virgin Islands. Its nearest neighbors are Puerto Rico and the British Virgin Islands. The official language is English. The population in 2010 was 106,405. Charlotte Amalie is the capital.
- The U.S. Virgin Islands were organized under the 1954 Organic Act of the Virgin Islands.
- From 1954 to 1970, governors were appointed by the President of the United States.

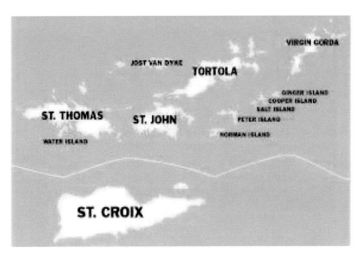

- In 1970, the Organic Act was amended to provide for an elected governor.
- U.S.V.I. also elects one representative to the U.S. House of Representatives (who can introduce legislation and vote in committees but cannot vote on the floor of the full House).
- Since 1954, U.S.V.I. has held five constitutional conventions with the intent to become a Commonwealth Territory of the United States. The U.S. Congress has rejected all five proposed constitutions, the last one during the Obama Administration in 2010.

Bibliography
Virgin Islands Censuses & Substitutes

Censuses of the Danish West Indies were taken at approximately 5-year intervals from 1835 to 1860, and then at approximately 10-year intervals until 1911. The population figures were published in the Statistisk Meddeleser of Denmark. Census name lists available 1835-1911 are included below.

The United States took a special census in 1917, the same year the Virgin Islands became part of the U.S. Since 1924, the U.S. Virgin Islands have participated in the national reporting of vital statistics and are included annually in vital statistics publications of the United States.

1671-1848. *Danish West Indies Chancery Records and Index to Wills* **[Printed Book],** by Gary Thomas Horlacher, publ. Salt Lake City, UT, 1999, 121 pages, FHL book 972.977 P2h.

1672-1860. *Records Relating to the Danish West Indies* **[Microfilm & Digital Capture],** from the originals at the National Archives, Washington, D.C. Contains sentences, transfers of property, resolutions, wills, minutes, land registers, contracts, sales and transfers of sugar to New York from the Danish West Indies (St. Thomas, St. Croix and St. Johns Islands). Filmed by the National Archives, 1971, 19 rolls, beginning with FHL film #847533 (General records of the Danish West Indies, 1672-1703). To access the digital images, see the online FHL catalog page: **https://familysearch.org/search/catalog/101169**.

1672-1917. *U.S. Virgin Islands, Danish West Indies Slave Records (in Danish)* **[Online Database],** indexed at the Ancestry.com website. Source: National Archives microfilm series M1883. During Danish rule, officials kept many records, including the slave-related records found in this database. They include the following: Case papers concerning contested slave ownership, Emancipation records, Registers of free men, women, and children of color; Lists of baptisms, marriages, and burials; Lists of slave owners and former slaves; Mortgages and loans; Slave lists and censuses; Records of Royal Blacks, Compensation agreements, and Courts martial records: **www.ancestry.com/search/collections/danishwestindies slaverecs.**

1676-1946. *A Brief History of Estate Charlotte Amalie on St. Thomas in the United States Virgin Islands* **[Printed Book],** by David Whitney Knight. From back cover: "Estate Charlotte Amalie lies within the heart of the inland valley that most St. Thomians still commonly refer to as 'country'. While a large portion of the estate's land remains in pasture or bush, commercial development, such as the Tutu Park Mall and the Time Center Building, are changing the face of what was once St. Thomas' foremost rural population center." Publ. Little Nordside Press, St. Thomas, VI, 1997, 31 pages, FHL book 972.9722 R2k.

1688. See *The 1688 Census of The Danish West Indies: Portrait of a Colony in Crisis* **[Printed Book],** from original records by the Governor of Danish West Indies, transcribed by Gary T. Horlacher, edited by David W. Knight, publ. Little Nordside Press, St. Thomas, VI, 1998, 26 pages, FHL book 972.9722 X2h.

1717-1814. *St. Thomas & St. John, West Indies Index to Probate Records* **[Printed Book],** by Lolly Prime and Gary T. Horlacher. Transcribed and translated from a card index in the National Archives of Denmark, Copenhagen. Publ. 1997, 117 pages, FHL book 972.972 P2.

1739-1974. *Frederick Evangelical Lutheran Church (Charlotte Amalie, St. Thomas, U.S. Virgin Islands* **[Microfilm & Digital Capture],** Text in Danish and English. Includes ministerial and administrative records of the Frederick Evangelical Lutheran Church, established in 1739 on St. Thomas Island, Danish West Indies, later the Virgin Islands of the United States. The islands of St. Thomas, St. Croix, and St. John constituted a Danish colony from 1754 till 1917, when the United States purchased them from Denmark. To access the digital images, see the online FHL catalog page: www.familysearch.org/search/catalog/449911.

1744-1925. *Church Records, Dutch Reformed Church, St. Thomas* [Microfilm & Digital Capture], Includes members who left the island before 1744 Members dismissed before 1744 Register of persons confirmed, 1828-1925 Register of members, 1828-1882 Index. To access the digital images, see the online FHL catalog page:
www.familysearch.org/search/catalog/450116.

1765-2010. *Virgin Islands U.S. Church Records* [Online Database], digitized and indexed at the FamilySearch.org website. Source: FamilySearch images and extractions from Virgin Islands parish records. This database includes miscellaneous records created by the Anglican, Dutch Reformed, and Lutheran Churches in the U.S. Virgin Islands. Some of these records have been indexed and are searchable as part of this collection. Additional indexed records and images will be published as they become available. Browse through the images, organized by Island, City or Town, and Denomination or Parish. This database has 10,633 images. See
https://familysearch.org/search/collection/1883386.
- For the Ancestry.com version, see
www.ancestry.com/search/collections/fs1virginislandsuschurchrecs.

1765-2010. *Linkpendium – Virgin Islands: Family History & Genealogy, Census, Birth, Marriage, Death, Vital Records & More* [Online Databases]. Linkpendium is a genealogical portal site with links to territory and island databases. Currently listed are selected sites for Virgin Islands territory-wide resources (60), Saint Croix (44), Saint John (21), Saint Thomas (36), and Water Island (2). See
www.linkpendium.com/vi-genealogy.

1765-2010. *Virgin Islands USGenWeb Archives* [Online Database]. The VI GenWeb site offers free genealogical databases with searchable territory-wide name lists and for all Virgin Islands locations. Databases may include Bibles, Biographies, Cemeteries, Censuses, Court Records, Deaths, Deeds, Directories, Histories, Marriages, Military, Newspapers, Obituaries, Photos, Schools, Tax Lists, Wills, and more. See
www.us-census.org/virginislands.

1772-1821. *St. Croix, U.S. Virgin Islands, Slave Plantation and Town Head Tax Lists* [Online Database], indexed at the Ancestry.com website. Source: Virgin Islands Social History Associates, Frederiksted, VI. This database contains images of plantation and town head tax lists from the island of St. Croix in the Danish West Indies. Head tax lists were generally compiled on a yearly basis for every plantation or slave-owning property. These lists were used for tax purposes and listed the name of each person, both slave and free, who lived on the estate. For slaves, usually only their first name was listed. However, since the movement of slaves was restricted, you can usually find individuals living on the same estates or plantations for several years. Some of these records have been indexed and are searchable by name. The rest of the images are available for browsing by year range and year. This database has 30,400 records:
www.ancestry.com/search/collections/virginislandstaxlists.

1778-1970. Catholic Church Records, Cathedral Church of Saints Peter and Paul (St. Thomas) [Microfilm & Digital Capture]. Includes Baptisms, Marriages, Burials. There are often separate registers for whites and free persons of color. Some registers are indexed. Filmed by the Public Library of St. Thomas, 1972-1973, 19 rolls, beginning with FHL film #1520619 (Registers, 1778- 1815). To access the digital images, see the online FHL catalog page:
www.familysearch.org/search/catalog/449814.

1779-1921. *St. Croix, U.S. Virgin Islands, Slave and Free People Records* [Online Database], indexed at the Ancestry.com website. Source: Virgin Islands History Associates, Fredericksted, U.S. Virgin Islands, St. Croix Records. St. Croix in the Danish West Indies was the home to Carib, Arawak, Dutch, French, British, and Spanish settlers before the island was bought by the Danish in 1733. Sugar was its chief industry into the 19th century, and slaves were imported to provide labor for the island's plantations. Slavery ended in 1848, and St. Croix was purchased by the United States in 1916, to become part of the U.S. Virgin Islands. The diversity of records in this database reflects some of St. Croix's diverse history, with records for both free and enslaved people, including the following: Slave lists, Vaccination journals, Appraisals, Censuses, Free men of color, Militia rolls, Manumissions and emancipation records, Tax lists, Civil death and burial records (possibly marriage as well), Immigrant lists, Plantation inventories (include details on enslaved individuals), School lists, Lists of people who have moved, Pensioners lists, Property sold, Immigrant records (arrivals, departures, passenger lists), and Slave purchases. Information varies by document type. See www.ancestry.com/search/collections/vistcroixrecords.

1780-1841. *Catholic Church Records, Holy Cross Parish (Christiansted, St. Croix Island, Virgin Islands)* [Microfilm & Digital Capture], includes Baptisms & Christenings. Filmed by the St. Thomas Public Library, 1974, 1 roll, FHL film #1520638. To access the digital images, see the online FHL catalog page: www.familysearch.org/search/catalog/621014.

1785-1979. *Church Records, All Saints Episcopal Church (St. Thomas, Virgin Islands)* [Microfilm & Digital Capture], from registers of baptisms, confirmations, marriages, and deaths. Includes related pastoral documents and historical records. Filmed by the Bureau of Libraries, Museums, and Archaeological Services, 1979, 7 rolls, beginning with FHL film #1520652 (Baptisms 1823-1920). To access the digital images, see the online FHL catalog page: https://familysearch.org/search/catalog/449915.

1786-1954. *Jewish Birth Records, St. Thomas (Island), U.S. Virgin Islands* [Microfilm & Digital Capture], of the original manuscript, compiled by Enid M. Baa, located at the Hebrew Union College Archives, Cincinnati, OH. Cards are arranged by year, containing brief information about Jews in the Virgin Islands. Filmed by the college archives, 1975, 1 roll, FHL film #1001639. To access the digital images, see the online FHL catalog page: www.familysearch.org/search/catalog/23485.

1788-1925. *Church Records, Holy Trinity Evangelical Lutheran Church (Frederiksted, St. Croix Island, Virgin Islands)* [Microfilm & Digital Capture], includes church registers of baptisms, marriages, confirmations, and burials. Filmed by the St. Thomas Public Library, 1974, 3 rolls, FHL film #1520659-61.To access the digital images, see the online FHL catalog page: www.familysearch.org/search/catalog/621530.

1800-1848. *Testamenter Konfirmerede Gennem Overøvrigheden (Probate Records), 1800-1848* [Microfilm], from the originals at the Rigsarkivet, København. Contains wills approved through the Chancery Office of Denmark, Iceland and the West Indies. Filmed for the Genealogical Society of Utah, 1964, 85 rolls, beginning with FHL film #394868

(1800 Register). For a complete list of roll numbers and contents of each roll, see the online FHL catalog page for this title. See https://familysearch.org/search/catalog/505598.

1815-1832. *St. Croix, U.S. Virgin Islands, Free Colored Censuses* [Online Database], indexed at the Ancestry.com website. Source: National Archives microfilm series M1883; index by Virgin Islands Social History Associates, Frederiksted, VI. This database contains registers listing free black men, women, and children residing on St. Croix between 1815 and 1832. During the Danish rule of the Virgin Islands, Danish officials kept voluminous records, including the freedom charters and registers of free black men, women, and children found in this database. These registers may include: Name, Residence year, Location, Gender, Age, Birth date, Birthplace, Mother's name, Father's name, Race, Religion, Baptism / confirmation details, Marital status, Occupation, Physical condition, Spouse, Children, Household, Relatives, Means of freedom, Length of time in St. Croix, Militia service, And 1816 census number. Records are in Danish; however, VISHA has extracted an index of details in English. This database has 5,672 records. See www.ancestry.com/search/collections/stcroixfreecensuses.

1835-1911. *U.S. Virgin Islands Censuses (Danish Period)* [Online Database], digitized and indexed at the Ancestry.com website. Source: Virgin Islands Social History Associates, Fredericksted, U.S. Virgin Islands. This database contains censuses for the island of St. Croix in the Danish West Indies (today the U.S. Virgin Islands). The censuses are for the years 1835, 1841, 1846, 1850, 1855, 1857, 1860, 1870, 1880, 1890, 1901, and 1911. Information may include: Name, Household number, Status – free or slave, Gender, Age, Birth date or estimated birth year, Religion and when baptized, Marital status, Number of children alive, Occupation, Relationship to head of household, Birthplace or place of origin, Residence, Property owner, Slave owner, and Enumeration date. This database has 227,958 records. See www.ancestry.com/search/collections/virginislandcensus.

1841-1911. *Census Records (Danish West Indies)* [Microfilm & Digital Capture], from the original records at the Rentekammeret (Vestindien), Denmark. Filmed for the Genealogical Society of Utah, 1965, 71 rolls, beginning with FHL film #39199 (St. Croix

Island Rural districts). To access the digital images, see the online FHL catalog page: https://familysearch.org/search/catalog/596977.

1846-1901. *Church Records, Lord God of Sabaoth Evangelical Lutheran Church (Christiansted, St. Croix Island)* **[Microfilm & Digital Capture],** includes letters to the Wardens of the Church, Colonial council materials, voting lists, baptisms, confirmations, marriages, burials, et al. Filmed by the St. Thomas Public Library, 1974, 2 rolls, FHL film #1520662-3/To access the digital images, see the online FHL catalog page: www.familysearch.org/search/catalog/621561.

1885-1962. *U.S. Virgin Islands, Passenger Lists* **[Online Database],** indexed at the Ancestry.com website. Source: National Archives microfilm. These passenger and crew lists from both ships and aircraft were recorded on a variety of forms that were then turned over to the Immigration and Naturalization Service. Details requested on the forms varied, but they typically include: Name of the vessel and arrival date, Ports of departure and arrival (as well as future destinations on a ship's itinerary), Dates of departure and arrival, Shipmaster, Full name, Age, Gender, Physical description, Military rank (if any), Occupation, Birthplace, Citizen of what country, and Residence. For military transports, you may find the next of kin, relationships, and address listed as well. Later manifests may include visa or passport numbers. This database has 888,528 records. See www.ancestry.com/search/collections/passcrewusvi.

1906-1947. *U.S. Virgin Islands, Passenger Arrivals Index* **[Online Database],** indexed at the Ancestry.com website. Source: National Archives microfilm series A3404. This database is an index to the passenger lists of ships arriving from foreign ports at the port of St. Thomas, in the U.S. Virgin Islands from 1906-1948. In addition, the names found in the index are linked to actual images of the passenger lists, copied from the National Archives and Records Administration (NARA) microfilm lists. Information contained in the index includes: Given name, Surname, Age, Gender, Arrival date, Port of arrival, Port of departure, and Ship name, This database has 68,443 records. See www.ancestry.com/search/collections/passengerarrivalsvirginislands.

1917. Census of the Virgin Islands of the United States, November 1, 1917 [Printed Book & Digital Version], publ. U.S. Census Bureau, 200 pages. The census bureau has the full text available as a PDF file, see www.census.gov/history/pdf/1917usvi.pdf.

1918. *U.S. Virgin Islands, Applications for Travel Identification Cards* **[Online Database],** digitized and indexed at the Ancestry.com website. Source: National Archives, *Records of the Government of the Virgin Islands, 1672-1950.* The U.S. acquired the Virgin Islands at the onset of World War I in Europe, with the transfer being completed in March 1917. With travel restrictions in place during World War I, identification as U.S. citizen by right of birth in the Virgin Islands was necessary to travel to the United States. This collection includes applications for travel identification cards made during 1918. Applications included a letter to the Government Secretary with the following information: Name (and signature), Photograph, Date and place of birth, Expected ship of departure and date, Reason for visit (often including addresses of relatives), Address in U.S. Virgin Islands, Occupation, Age, Complexion, Hair, Height, Marks, and Date. On the page image following the application, you'll typically find proof of birth, which is often a baptismal or birth record. This database has 182 pages. See www.ancestry.com/search/collections/usvirginislandsidcards.

1920. *Virgin Islands, 1920 Federal Census: Soundex and Population Schedules* **[Microfilm & Digital Capture],** from the originals of the Census Bureau. After microfilming, Congress permitted the Census Bureau to destroy the originals to make room for WWII records. Filmed by the Census Bureau, ca1943, series M1604, 4 rolls, beginning with FHL film #1831662 (Soundex: A000 thru A156), and FHL film #1822076 (Population schedules: St. Croix. To access the digital images, see the online FHL catalog page: https://familysearch.org/search/catalog/558360.

1930. *Virgin Islands, 1930 Federal Census: Population Schedules* **[Microfilm & Digital Capture],** from the originals of the Census Bureau. After microfilming, Congress permitted the Census Bureau to destroy the originals to make room for WWII records. Filmed by the Census Bureau, ca 1943, 1 roll, FHL film #2342402 (All VI islands). To access the digital images, see the online FHL catalog page: https://familysearch.org/search/catalog/1037616.

1940. *Virgin Islands, 1940 Federal Census: Population Schedules* **[Digital Capture],** from the National Archives microfilm. After microfilming in the 1940s, Congress permitted the Census Bureau to destroy the originals to make room for World War II records. Filmed by the Census Bureau, ca1943, 1 roll, FHL Film/DGS #5461827 (U.S. Virgin Islands). The 1940 census was released to the public in 2012 as a digital version only. The FHL has the microfilm, but it is available only for reviewing the roll content. The FHL reserve microfilm is stored at their Granite Mountain Vault in Utah. For a complete list of roll numbers and contents of To access the digital images, see the online FHL catalog page:
https://familysearch.org/search/catalog/2057795.

1940-1947. *Virgin Islands, World War II Draft Registration Cards* **[Digital Capture],** from the originals at the National Personnel Records Center, St. Louis, MO. Digital capture by the Genealogical Society of Utah, 2016, from 7 rolls of film, beginning with FHL Film/DGS #101503995 (WWII Draft Registration Cards, Virgin Islands, Jackson, Alfredo – McShell, Stanley). For a complete list of roll numbers and contents of each roll, and a link to the digital images for each roll, see the online FHL catalog page for this title:
https://familysearch.org/search/catalog/4092293.

Panama Canal Zone
1903-1979
Caribbean Region

The Panama Canal Zone was an Unincorporated Organized Territory of the U.S., centered on the Panama Canal and surrounded by the Republic of Panama. From 1903 to 1979, the zone consisted of the canal and an area generally extending five miles on each side of the canal. The territory was controlled by the United States, which had built the canal and financed its construction. The Canal Zone was abolished as part of the Torrijos-Carter Treaty of 1977. The jurisdiction of the Canal Zone was formally surrendered to Panama in 1979. and turned over to Panama completely on the last day of 1999.

Historical Timeline:
- In the early 1900s, attempts to negotiate an arrangement with Columbia for a canal zone had failed.
- A convenient Panamanian Revolution ensued, which led to a declaration of independence from Columbia by a new Republic of Panama in 1903.

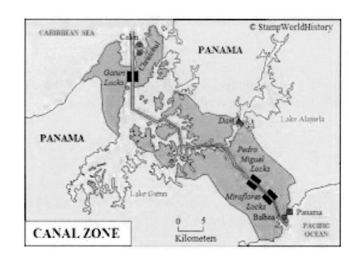

- The U.S. immediately recognized the new Republic and consummated an agreement with Panama that created the Isthmus Canal Zone. In that zone, the U.S. would build a canal, then administer, fortify, and defend it "in perpetuity."
- Construction of the canal began in 1904 and the first ship passed through the canal in 1914.
- During the construction period, the Canal Zone was governed by the Isthmian Canal Commission, under the supervision of the U.S. Secretary of War.
- In 1914, the commission was eliminated, and the canal was governed directly under the Secretary of War (later the Secretary of the Army).
- After an Act of Congress in 1951, the Secretary of the Army appointed a Panama Canal Company board of directors, led by an appointed Governor of the Panama Canal Zone. The governorship was usually given to a retired senior Army officer of the U.S. Army Corps of Engineers.
- For the period 1903-1979, record copies of Canal Zone births, marriages, deaths, divorces, etc. were transferred to the Civilian Records section of the National Archives in St. Louis, MO.

Bibliography
Panama Canal Zone
Censuses & Substitutes

There is no accurate population information for the Panama Canal Zone prior to its acquisition by the United States in 1903. The Republic of Panama did not take its first national census until 1913, although the area of Panama was included in the Columbian census of 1870. The only local census of the Canal Zone was taken in 1912 by the Department of Civil

Administration of the Isthmian Canal Commission. The Canal Zone was included in the regular decennial federal censuses, 1910 through 1970. Vital statistics were reported to the CZ Governor by the health department. Published censuses and substitutes specific to the Canal Zone are listed below:

1904-1914. "Looking for an Ancestor in the Panama Canal Zone, 1904-1914" [Online Article], by Robert Ellis, in *Prologue Magazine* (National Archives, Washington, D.C.), Fall 2007, Vol. 39, No. 3. The complete text of the article is online and gives excellent information about the extent of records of the Panama Canal Zone, particularly court records now located at the National Archives. See **www.archives.gov/publications/prologue/2007/fall/panama.html**.

1904-1979. *Vital Records (Birth and Death): Obtaining Former Panama Canal Zone Documentation* **[Online Database].** This is a website of the Panama Embassy of the United States, U.S. Citizen Services. From the site: "Since December 1, 1999, vital records formerly issued by the Panama Canal Commission are being issued by the Department of State in Washington, D.C. Vital records for births and deaths in the former Panama Canal Zone are available for the period between February 26, 1904 and September 30, 1979. To obtain a copy of one of these documents, write to..." See the full info page for details. Archived at **https://web.archive.org/web/20161026045700/https://panama.usembassy.gov/mobile//obtaining_former_panama_canal_zone_documentation.html**.

1905-1937. *United States, Panama Canal Zone, Employment Records and Sailing Lists, 1905-1937* **[Online Database],** digitized and indexed at the FamilySearch.org website. Source: National Archives, Civilian Personnel Records Center, St. Louis, MO. Includes an index and images of employee records (service history cards), sailing lists of contract laborers, and employee identification records (metal check cards and applications). This database has 144,925 images: **https://familysearch.org/search/collection/2193241**.

1906-1991. *Panama Canal Zone, Gorgas Hospital Mortuary Records, 1906-1991* **[Online Database],** indexed at the Ancestry.com website. Source: National Archives, College Park, MD. Dr. William Crawford Gorgas served as the Surgeon General of the U.S. Army from 1914 to 1918 and is best known for stopping the spread of yellow fever and malaria. His contributions to this work played a significant role in the building and completion of the Panama Canal, as less lives of workers on the Canal were lost due to these diseases. Because of Dr. Gorgas's medical contributions to the area, Ancon Hospital, the U.S. government hospital located in the Canal Zone near Panama City, was renamed Gorgas Hospital in 1928. This database is a necrology (list of the recently deceased) and partial index to the Gorgas Hospital Mortuary registers. These registers contain information on over 26,000 U.S. military personnel, employees of the Panama Canal Commission, and Canal Zone civilians who were processed in this mortuary between 1906 and 1991. Information contained in this index may include: Name of deceased, Age at time of death, Race (Black, brown, negro, white, yellow, etc.), Sex (Male or female), Nationality, Status (usually the individual's occupation or trade), Employer, Death date, Death place (this could be a city, country, ship, or other locality), Received date (date the body was received at the mortuary for processing), Burial place (this could be a city, country, cemetery, or other locality), Burial date (date the body was interned or transferred from the mortuary), Cremation (date or location of body's cremation), Cremains (the disposition of the cremation remains), Register (the register number that is used to access the paper records of the registry), Marker (the number of the marker or gravestone under which the individual is buried), Section (the section number of the cemetery where the individual is buried), Cemetery Row (the row within the section in the cemetery where the individual is buried), Grave (the grave number in the cemetery in which the individual is buried), Cost (the cost charged for processing the individual in the mortuary), and Remarks. This database has 26,202 records. See **http://search.ancestry.com/search/db.aspx?dbid=8848**.

1906-1991. *United States, Panama Canal Zone, Index to the Gorgas Hospital Mortuary Registers, 1906-1991* **[Online Database],** indexed at the FamilySearch.org website. Source: National Archives, College Park, MD. This database is a partial index to the mortuary's registers of military personnel, canal employees and canal zone civilians processed through the Gorgas Hospital Mortuary. See **https://familysearch.org/search/collection/2127918**.

1911. *The Makers of the Panama Canal* **[Microfilm],** of the original book publ. F.E. Jackson & Son, New York, 1911, 410 pages. Includes a collection of short biographical sketches of the Americans, Panamanians, and men of other nationalities who were instrumental in the construction of the Panama Canal. Filmed by the Genealogical Society of Utah, 1 roll, FHL film #1421865.

1912. See *Census of the Canal Zone, February 1, 1912,* Publ. Isthmian Canal Commission, Mount Hope, C.Z., I.C.C. Press, Quartermaster's Department, 1912, 58 pp. This is the published report and name list of 62,000 military personnel and civilian workers residing in the Canal Zone in 1912. WorldCat shows 35 libraries holding a copy of this title, see
www.worldcat.org/title/census-of-the-canal-zone-february-1-1912/oclc/951477.

1920. *Canal Zone, 1920 Federal Census: Soundex and Population Schedules* **[Microfilm & Digital Capture],** from the originals of the Census Bureau. After microfilming, Congress permitted the Census Bureau to destroy the originals to make room for WWII records. Filmed by the Census Bureau, ca1943, series M1599, 4 rolls, beginning with FHL film #1831473 (Soundex: A000 thru H246), and FHL film #1822042 (Population schedules: Canal Zone, EDs 1-8 Civilian, Military and Naval Forces). To access the digital images, see the online FHL catalog page:
https://familysearch.org/search/catalog/558347.

1930. *Panama Canal and Consular Services, 1930 Federal Census: Population Schedules* **[Microfilm & Digital Capture],** from the originals of the Census Bureau. After microfilming, Congress permitted the Census Bureau to destroy the originals to make room

for WWII records. Filmed by the Census Bureau, ca1943, 2 rolls, FHL film #2342372 (Population schedules, Balboa & Cristobal districts, Canal Zone); and FHL film #2342364 (Population schedules, Consular Services). To access the digital images, see the online FHL catalog page:
https://familysearch.org/search/catalog/1037606.

1940. *Panama Canal, 1940 Federal Census: Population Schedules* **[Digital Capture],** from the National Archives microfilm. After microfilming in the 1940s, Congress permitted the Census Bureau to destroy the originals to make room for World War II records. Filmed by the Census Bureau, ca1943, 1 roll, FHL Film/DGS #5461826 (Panama Canal Zone, Balboa Township & Cristobal Township). The 1940 census was released to the public in 2012 as a digital version only. The FHL has the microfilm, but it is available only for reviewing the roll content. The FHL reserve microfilm is stored at their Granite Mountain Vault in Utah. To access the digital images, see the online FHL catalog page:
https://familysearch.org/search/catalog/2057783.

1947-1951. *Annual Genealogical Report, Canal Zone* **[Microfilm],** from the LDS manuscript, original published: Washington, D.C.: Smithsonian Institution Press, 1968. xiii, 119 pages. This is a combined LDS mission report for Mexico, the Canal Zone, and Guatemala. Includes marriages, births, confirmations, blessings, baptisms, ordinations, deaths and members emigrated 1947-1951. Filmed by the Genealogical Society of Utah, 1953, 1 roll, FHL film #38824.

Pacific Region

Guam, Northern Mariana Islands, American Samoa & The Philippines

Part 2 of this review is for the current inhabited territories of the United States within the Pacific Region. Included are the Territory of Guam, the Commonwealth of the Northern Mariana Islands, and American Samoa. Also in this region is the former U.S. Commonwealth of the Philippines. For each territory, a brief introduction describes the territory's location and some jurisdictional history related to the territory's government.

Listed first are databases for the small territories of Midway Atoll and Wake Island; and the other Pacific territories included as part of a combined Pacific Region focus.

Bibliography
Pacific Region
Censuses & Substitutes

1881. *Persons Born in the Pacific Region Included in the 1881 British Census* **[Printed Book],** by Christine Liava'a. From intro: "This booklet contains all the entries of persons born in the Pacific area contained in the 1881 British census, published under license from Her Majesty's Stationery Office. Each entry is given in its household, showing other persons living at the same address. The entries are sorted in country order, but an index of the individuals is also provided, giving a page reference." Countries include: Cook Islands, Fiji, Loyalty Islands, New Hebrides, Samoa, Tahiti, Tonga. Includes index. Publ. 2002, 33 pages, FHL book 996 X2p.

1900-1950s. *Midway Island History.* In 1903, the first Trans-Pacific telephone cable stretched from San Francisco to Honolulu to Midway to Guam to the Philippines. Midway Island, at the half-way point, had a Commercial Pacific Cable Company station that was in place for many years. The Midway station employed several telephone operators who provided a live telephone voice connection as a relay between other stations between San Francisco and Manila. The names of many workers and military personnel who were

residents of Midway Atoll have been recorded and made available at a special website. For more information, history, photos, and name lists, see **www.midway-island.com**.

1907. *The Cyclopedia of Fiji, Samoa, Tonga, Tahiti and the Cook Islands* **[Online Database],** indexed at the Ancestry.com website. Source: Book, same title, publ. Gould Genealogy and History, Ridgehaven, South Australia 2007. Contains information on the founding and progress of each of these island groups in the South Pacific, as well as biographical information. Includes entries on an area's history, culture, geography, industries, as well as hundreds of illustrations, including portraits that go along with biographies. See **http://search.ancestry.com/search/db.aspx?dbid=60660**.

1910 Federal Census. See *Midway Island, Enumerated as part of Honolulu County, Hawaii Territory* **[Online Database],** indexed at the FamilySearch.org website. Midway Atoll, some 1,300 miles northwest of the main Hawaiian Islands, is part of the Hawaiian Archipelago (but not part of the State of Hawaii). For convenience, Midway Island was added to the 1910 Honolulu County name lists as ED 135. See **https://familysearch.org/search/collection/1727033**.
- Search for Residence Place = Midway Island.

1920 Federal Census. See *Midway Island, Enumerated as part of Honolulu County, Hawaii Territory* **[Online Database],** indexed at the FamilySearch.org website (and others). For convenience, Midway Island was added to the Honolulu County name lists as ED 135. See **https://familysearch.org/search/collection/1488411**.
Search for Residence Place = Midway Island.

1930 Federal Census. See *Midway Island, Enumerated as part of Honolulu County, Hawaii Territory* **[Online Database],** indexed at the FamilySearch.org website (and others). For conven-

ience, Midway Island was added to the Honolulu County name lists as ED 2-146. The names of the cable company's telephone operators and maintenance workers dominate the list of residents of Midway Island in 1930. See
https://familysearch.org/search/collection/1810731.
- Search for Residence Place = Midway Island.

1940 Federal Census. See *Midway Island, Johnston Island, and other Islands of the Pacific Enumerated as part of Honolulu County, Hawaii Territory* [**Online Database**], indexed at the FamilySearch.org website (and others). Midway Atoll, some 1,300 miles from the main Hawaiian Islands, is part of the Hawaiian Archipelago (but not part of the State of Hawaii). For convenience, Midway and several more Pacific Islands were added to the Honolulu County name lists. Certain islands were named but have a note on the census page such as "Kingman Reef, no population in April 1940." See **https://familysearch.org/1940census**.
- Search for State = Hawaii. County = Honolulu.

✓ **NOTE:** Page 42 of the Census Bureau's *Population of States and Counties of the United States, 1790-1990* states: "Honolulu County, officially the City and County of Honolulu, comprises Oahu and the small islands northwest of Kauai and Niihau extending from Nihoa to Kure. Prior to 1959 Palmyra, located about 1,000 miles south of the Hawaiian Island chain, also was included."

1941-1945. *History of the Defenders of the Philippines, Guam, and Wake Islands* [**Printed Book & Digital Version**], by Edward Jackfert, Andrew Miller, and Bill Schiller. Includes index. Includes stories and pictures of defenders and captors. Illustrations and portraits on lining papers. Publ. Turner Pub. Co., 1991, 1998, 2 vols., FHL book 973 M2hi v.1-2. For access to a digital version of the two volumes, see the online FHL catalog page: **https://familysearch.org/search/catalog/823964**.

1941-1945. *Japanese Prisoners From Wake Island, Guam and Cavitie* [**Online Database**], a project of Geni, this website includes the names of about 200 of the known 1,600 prisoners (450 military, 1,150 civilians), who were transported to POW camps in China and Japan. Some history of the war in the Pacific and the battle of Wake is also a good read. See **www.geni.com/projects/Japanese-prisoners-from-Wake-Island-Guam-and-Cavitie/914**.

1965. *A Pacific Bibliography: Printed Matter Relating to the Native Peoples of Polynesia, Melanesia, and Micronesia* [**Printed Book**], by Clyde Romer Hughes Taylor, publ. Clarendon Press, Oxford, England, 1965, 692 pages, FHL book 990 A3t.

Territory of Guam
Pacific Region

The Territory of Guam is an Unincorporated Organized Territory of the United States with an established civilian government. As part of the Spanish East Indies, the Island of Guam was ceded by Spain to the United States in 1898, part of the Treaty of Paris ending the Spanish-American War. Located in the western Pacific Ocean, Guam is the largest and southernmost of the Mariana Islands, and at 210 square miles, the largest island in Micronesia. Guam's population in 2015 was 161,785 people. Agana (Hagåtña) is the capital, the largest city is Dededo. Gaum's nearest neighbors are the Northern Mariana Islands, Palau, the Federated States of Micronesia, and Papua New Guinea. Several status referendums were held in Guam over the years, all supporting U.S. Commonwealth status. Guam has an elected governor and legislature, and a person born in Guam is a citizen of the United States. In spite of this, the U.N. has Guam listed as a "Non-Self-Governing Territory," deemed subject to the decolonization process.

Military Rule Era

1898-1950. Guam was under the authority of the U.S. Navy, with an appointed military governor.

Civilian Rule Era

1950. The Guam Organic Act made the island an organized territory of the U.S. with a governor appointed by the President of the United States.

1968. The Guam Organic Act was amended to provide for an elected governor, 15 elected senators, and one elected representative to the U.S. House of Representatives (who can introduce legislation and vote in committees but cannot vote on the floor of the full House). Guam residents can vote on U.S. presidential candidates in primary elections, but not in a General Election for U.S. President.

Bibliography
Territory of Guam
Censuses & Substitutes

1700s – 2000s. *A Complete History of Guam* **[Printed Book & Digital Version],** by Paul Carano and Pedro C. Sanchez, publ. Charles Tuttle, Rutland, VT, 1964, 452 pages. To access the digital version, see the online FHL catalog page:
www.familysearch.org/search/catalog/75315.

1712-2000. *Guam Judicial, Land, Obituaries, and Census Records* **[Online Database],** digitized and indexed at the FamilySearch.org website. Source: University of Guam, UOG Station Mangilao, Guam. This collection consists of images of the Guam Spanish Census, 1896-1897, Judicial Records, 1712-1935, Land Records, 1890-1902, and Obituaries, 1896-2000. The original records are now located at the Micronesia Area Research Center University of Guam. Only the obituaries are currently included in the index for this collection. Browse through the images, organized by Record Type, and Year Range. This database has 92,039 images. See
https://familysearch.org/search/collection/1392581.

1712-1935. *Guam, English and Spanish Judicial Records* **[Microfilm & Digital Capture],** part of the larger Guam Judicial, Land, et al, above. This is the images of the Judicial records (on about 200 rolls of film, organized by year). To access the digital images, see the online FHL catalog page:
www.familysearch.org/search/catalog/1497830.

1890-1906. *Guam, Spanish Land Records* **[Microfilm & Digital Capture],** part of the larger Guam Judicial, Land, et al. This is the images of the Spanish era land records. To access the digital images, see the online FHL catalog page:
www.familysearch.org/search/catalog/1497832.

1896-1897. *Guam, Spanish Census* **[Microfilm & Digital Capture],** part of the larger Guam Judicial, Land, et al, above. This is the images of the Spanish Census taken for Guam. To access the digital images, see the online FHL catalog page:
www.familysearch.org/search/catalog/1497835.

1897-2000. *Guam, Population Cards* **[Digital Images],** of originals held by the University of Guam Richard Flores Taitano Micronesia Area Research Center, Mangilao. To access the digital images, see the online FHL catalog page:
www.familysearch.org/search/catalog/2778239.

1898-1964. *Guam Land Records* **[Online Database],** digitized at the FamilySearch.org website. Source: Department of Land Management, Tamuning, Guam. This is an image-only database of miscellaneous land records from the Department of Land Management, Hagåtña, Guam. This collection is being published as images become available. Browse through the images, organized by the municipalities of Agana, Agat, Asan, Barrigada, Dededo, Inarajan, Machanao, Merizo, New Agana, New Agat, Piti, Santa Rita, Sinajana, Sumay, Talofofo, Umatac, Yigo, and Yona. This database has 288,918 images. See
https://familysearch.org/search/collection/1392585.
- Another version of this database is available at the Ancestry.com website. See
http://search.ancestry.com/search/db.aspx?dbid=61154.

1909-1921. *Index to the Guam News Letter* **[Printed Book],** compiled by Elaine S. Moore, publ. Nieves M. Flores Memorial Library, Guam, 1974, 189 pages, FHL book 996.7 B22. Also on microfiche, FHL fiche #6067036 (3 fiche).

1920. *Guam, 1920 Federal Census: Soundex and Population Schedules* **[Microfilm & Digital Capture],** from the originals of the Census Bureau. After microfilming, Congress permitted the Census Bureau to destroy the originals to make room for WWII records. Filmed by the Census Bureau, ca1943, series M1605, 2 rolls, beginning with FHL film #1831659

(Soundex: A000 thru Z520), and FHL film #1822032 (Population schedules: Guam). To access the digital images, see the online FHL catalog page: https://familysearch.org/search/catalog/558354.

1924-1941. See *Index to the Guam Recorder: March 1924-November 1941* **[Printed Book],** publ. Guam Public Library, ca1941, 181 pages, From intro: *"The Guam Recorder* was the major source of new information concerning the activities of the Naval Government of Guam, the Naval Station, and other news information of both local and international concern." See FHL book 996.7 B22g index. Also on microfiche, FHL fiche #6067037 (3 fiche).

1930. *American Samoa and Guam, 1930 Federal Census: Population Schedules* **[Microfilm & Digital Capture],** from the originals of the Census Bureau. After microfilming, Congress permitted the Census Bureau to destroy the originals to make room for WWII records. Filmed by the Census Bureau, ca1943, 1 roll, FHL film #2342363 (Population schedules, American Samoa & Guam). To access the digital images, see the online FHL catalog page: https://familysearch.org/search/catalog/1037568.

1940. *Guam, 1940 Federal Census: Population Schedules* **[Digital Capture],** from the National Archives microfilm. After microfilming in the 1940s, Congress permitted the Census Bureau to destroy the originals to make room for World War II records. Filmed by the Census Bureau, ca1943, 1 roll, FHL Film/DGS #5462183 (Guam: Agana, Agat, Asan, Barrigada, Dededo, Inarajan, Machanao, Merizo, Piti, Sinajana, Sumay, Talofofo, Umatac, Yigo, and Yona). The 1940 census was released to the public in 2012 as a digital version only. To access the digital images, see the online FHL catalog: https://familysearch.org/search/catalog/2057750

1947-1952. *Guam Passenger and Crew Lists* **[Online Database],** indexed at the FamilySearch.org website. Source: National Archives microfilm series M1778. This is an image-only database with typescript passenger and crew lists of Vessels Departing the Trust Territory of the Pacific Islands for Arrival at Guam, 1947-1952, and Related Records. Most of the passengers and crew were Rotanese, Saipanese, Tinianese although there were some U.S. citizens and Guamanians. Browse through the images, organized by year. This database has 663 images. See https://familysearch.org/search/collection/2301291.

1948-1963. *Agana, Guam, U.S., Passenger and Crew Lists of Arriving Vessels and Airplanes* **[Online Database],** indexed at the Ancestry.com website. Source: National Archives, Washington, DC. These passenger and crew lists from both ships and aircraft were recorded on a variety of forms that were then turned over to the Immigration and Naturalization Service. Details may include: Name of the vessel and arrival date, Ports of departure and arrival (as well as future destinations on a ship's itinerary), Dates of departure and arrival, Shipmaster, Full name, Age, Gender, Physical description, Military rank (if any), Occupation, Birthplace, Citizen of what country, and Residence. This database has 520,378 records. See http://search.ancestry.com/search/db.aspx?dbid=5309.

Commonwealth of the
Northern Mariana Islands
Pacific Region

Since 1978, the Commonwealth of Northern Mariana Islands has been an Unincorporated Organized territory of the United States, consisting of 15 islands in the northwestern Pacific Ocean. Of the total of about 55,000 residents, most of the population lives on the islands of Saipan, Tinian, or Rota, while the other

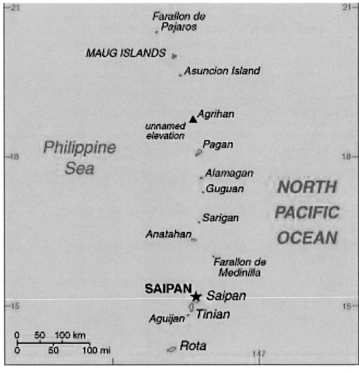

islands are sparsely populated. The administrative center is Capitol Hill, a village of northwestern Saipan Island. However, the city of Saipan is considered the capital because the island is governed as a single municipality.

- At the 1898 Treaty of Paris ending the Spanish-American War, the southernmost island of the Marianas (Guam), was ceded to the U.S. by Spain.

- In 1899, Spain sold the remaining northern part of the Marianas to Germany. The Germans administered the islands as part of its colony of German New Guinea, but with minimal development.

- Early in World War I, Japan declared war on Germany and invaded the northern Marianas. In 1919, the South Pacific Mandate by the League of Nations gave Japan all of Germany's colonial islands, and Japan continued to rule over the Marianas (except Guam) until they were captured by the Americans during World War II.

- After World War II, the Northern Marianas were administered by the United States as a United Nations Trust Territory of the Pacific Islands.

- In four different referendums (1958, 1961, 1963, and 1969), the Northern Marianas voted in favor of joining again with their separated island neighbor of Guam, already an organized territory of the U.S. But Guam rejected the reunification offers in their own referendum of 1969.

- 1975-1978. The people of the Northern Marianas decided not to seek independence, but instead to seek a commonwealth of union as a separate territory of the United States. In 1977, a referendum proposing territorial status with the U.S. was approved by the Northern Marianas voters as well as the United Nations. A new government and constitution came into effect in 1978.

- Now a Commonwealth Territory of the U.S. The Northern Marianas has a constitution, an elected governor, elected legislature, and one elected representative to the U.S. House of Representatives (who can introduce legislation and vote in committees but cannot vote on the floor of the full House).

Bibliography
Northern Mariana Islands
Censuses & Substitutes

By 1668, the Spanish possession of the Philippines incorporated several more islands in the region, including the Marinas. All of the recorded documents naming the early inhabitants of the Marianas are today located in the Manila archives, as the Marianas were a province of the Philippines during most of the Spanish era. Censuses and substitute name lists specific to the Marianas are listed below:

1700s-2000s. See T*he Native Culture of the Mariana Islands* **[Printed Book & Digital Version],** by Laura Thompson, publ. Kraus Reprint Co, New York, NY, 48 pages. To access the digital images, see the online FHL catalog page:
www.familysearch.org/search/catalog/119539.

1718-1898. *Marianas, Varias Provincias, Islas Marianas (Various Municipal and Provincial Documents of the Mariana Islands), 1718-1898* **[Microfilm & Digital Capture],** from the originals at the Record Management and Archives Office, Manila, Philippines. Text in Spanish. Includes calendars (called indexes on the rolls). The calendars are typewritten cards which list folio number and the inclusive years of the book. They do not list the book number. Filmed by the Genealogical Society of Utah, 1990-1991, 32 rolls, beginning with FHL film #1681270 (1718-1822 (1776-1895). To access the digital images, see the online FHL catalog page:
https://familysearch.org/search/catalog/623823.

1795-1898. *Escuelas y Maestros (School Teachers), Isla Marianas Filipinas* **[Microfilm & Digital Capture],** from the manuscripts at the Record Management and Archives Office, Manila, Philippines. Includes school records including correspondence and reports. Contains some applications, personnel files and baptismal and death certificates of teachers. Filmed by the Genealogical Society of Utah, 1990, 2 rolls, FHL film #1627612 (1795-1898, 1861-1898) and FHL film #1627613 (1861-1898 cont.). To access the digital images, see the online FHL catalog page:
www.familysearch.org/search/catalog/386538.

1830-1885. *Terrenos, Islas Marianas Filipinas, (Land Records in the Mariana Islands), 1830-1885* **[Microfilm & Digital Capture],** from the original manuscript at the Record Management and Archives Office, Manila, Philippines. The Mariana Islands were formerly a province of the Philippines under Spanish rule. Filmed by the Genealogical Society of Utah, 1990, 1 roll, FHL film #1627430. To access the digital images, see the online FHL catalog page:
www.familysearch.org/search/catalog/621254.

1876-1898. *Prestaciones Personales* **[Microfilm & Digital Capture],** from manuscripts in the Record Management and Archives Office, National Library, Metropolitan Manila, Philippines. Text in Spanish. Includes tax records listing those responsible for service in public works related projects. Contains

records for the Mariana Islands. Includes some death certificates. To access the digital images, see the online FHL catalog page:
www.familysearch.org/search/catalog/500029.

1885-1945. *Nan'yō: The Rise and Fall of the Japanese in Micronesia 1885-1945* **[Printed Book],** by Mark R. Peattie, publ. University of Hawaii Press, Honolulu, 1988, 382 pages, FHL book 990 B4p No. 4.

1886-1914. *The Germans in Micronesia* **[Microfilm & Digital Capture],** from a typescript by Sherman Lee Pompey, 36 pages, filmed by the Genealogical Society of Utah, 1977, 1 roll, FHL film #795720. To access the digital images, see the online FHL catalog page:
www.familysearch.org/search/catalog/647956.

1887-1889. *The Mariana Islands* **[Printed Book],** by Antoine-Alfred Marche and Robert D. Craig, English translation by Sylvia E. Cheng of "Rapport général sur une mission aux Iles Mariannes" by Antoine-Alfred Marche (1844-1898), French explorer, ethnographer, and scientist – a report to the Paris Museum on his extended mission to the Marianas, 1887-1889. Translation publ. Micronesian Area Research Center, 1982, 52 pages, FHL book 996.7 H6m.

1889-1892. *Padrones de Chinos Islas Marianas Filipinas (Census Records of the Chinese in the Mariana Islands)* **[Microfilm],** from the manuscripts in the Bureau of Records Management, National Library, Manila. The Mariana Islands were formerly a province of the Philippines under Spanish rule. Filmed by the Genealogical Society of Utah, 1978, 1 roll, FHL film #1210553.

1891-1898. *Cedulas (Identification Cards), Islas Marianas Filipinas* **[Microfilm & Digital Capture],** from the originals at the Bureau of Records Management, Manila, Philippines. Filmed by the Genealogical Society of Utah, 1992, 1 roll, FHL film #2180491. To access the digital images, see the online FHL catalog page:
www.familysearch.org/search/catalog/956132.

1903. *Die Neuen Deutschen Erwerbungen in der Südsee: Die Karolinen, Marianen und Samoan-Inseln (Description of the German Colonies in the Caroline Islands, Mariana Islands, and Samoa Islands.* **[Microfilm],** from the original book publ. Dr. Seele & Co., Leipzig, 1903. Filmed by the Genealogical Society of Utah, 1992, 1 roll, FHL film #795976.

1947-1952. *U.S., Applications for Authorization for Inter-Island Travel (Northern Marianas* **[Online Database],** indexed at the Ancestry.com website. Source: National Archives microfilm series A3972,

Applications for Authorization for Inter-Island Travel Certificates by Residents of the Northern Marianas Islands. Details on the applications for authorization for inter-island travel varied, but they typically include: Name of the vessel and arrival date, Full name, Age, Gender, and Race and/or nationality. Applicants authorized to travel during this time period were primarily residents of the Northern Marianas Islands, Saipan District, Trust Territory of the Pacific Islands. This database has 5,404 records. See
http://search.ancestry.com/search/db.aspx?dbid=60500.

American Samoa
Pacific Region

In 1899, Germany and the U.S. divided the Samoan Islands into Eastern Samoa (American) and Western Samoa (German). The eastern island group became a territory of the U.S. in 1900. It was officially named American Samoa in 1917. The population is at about 55,000. The capital is Pago Pago.

- American Samoa is an Unincorporated Unorganized Territory of the United States, but with a unique territorial organization that recognizes the President of the United States as its Head of State. Since 1951, the U.S. Secretary of the Interior has held the delegated power of the President. The territory has an elected governor and an elected legislature. Under the rules for classifying U.S. Territories, American Samoa's unique organization keeps it from being an official Organized

Territory of the United States. And as a result, American Samoa is the only inhabited territory of the United States in which native-born residents are not automatically citizens of the U.S. They are American Nationals, and can travel in the U.S. without a passport, but citizenship has to be applied for by petition for naturalization.

- **Swains Island**, originally acquired by the U.S. as part of the Guano Island Act in 1860, was added to

American Samoa in 1925. The island's coconut tree plantation was harvested, and the island ruled by a proprietorship owned by a single American family (the Jennings Family). They ruled from 1856 to 1925 without any outside authority. Descendants of the original Jennings Family still own the island. The 2010 federal census for American Samoa reported a total of 17 permanent residents living on Swains Island.

Bibliography
American Samoa
Censuses & Substitutes

1805-1910. *Samoa, Select Baptisms* **[Online Database],** digitized and indexed at Ancestry.com. Source: FamilySearch. See **www.ancestry.com/search/collections/60141.**

1850-1972. *Birth Certificates* **[Microfilm & Digital Capture],** from the originals at the High Court, Pago Pago, AS. Some text in Samoan. Includes some delayed registrations. Filmed by the Genealogical Society of Utah, 1974, 46 rolls, beginning with FHL film #1083394 (Birth certificates, 1850-1906). To access the digital images, see the online FHL catalog page: **https://familysearch.org/search/catalog/554705.**

1863-1940. *Samoa Baptisms* **[Online Database],** indexed at the FamilySearch.org website. Source: FamilySearch extractions from records at the Family Library Center. Index to selected Samoa baptisms. Only a few localities are included, and the time period varies by locality. This database has 28,013 records. See **https://familysearch.org/search/collection/1584966.**

1888-1951. *Record of Members (LDS)* **[Microfilm],** from the originals at the LDS Church Historian's Office, Salt Lake City, UT. Includes membership and historical records from various units of the Tutuila District/Conference of the Samoan Mission. Filmed by the Genealogical Society of Utah, 1953-1954, 2 rolls, FHL film #128899 & #128903.

1895-1970. *Samoa, Select Burials* **[Online Database],** digitized and indexed at Ancestry.com. Source: Family Search. See **www.ancestry.com/search/collections/60142.**

1900-1912. *Marriage Registers* **[Microfilm & Digital Capture],** from the originals at the High Court, Pago Pago, AS. Includes indexes. Includes some late registration of marriages. Filmed by the Genealogical

Society of Utah, 1974, 1 roll, FHL #1083947. To access the digital images, see the online FHL catalog page: **www.familysearch.org/search/catalog/556346.**

1900-1928. *Register of Births* **[Microfilm & Digital Capture],** from the originals at the High Court, Pago Pago, AS. Arranged in columns: Name, Sex, Residence, District, When Born, Father, Mother, When Filed. Filmed by the Genealogical Society of Utah, 1974, 1 roll, FHL film #1083867. To access the digital images, see the online FHL catalog page: **www.familysearch.org/search/catalog/556324.**

1900-1928. *Cemetery Records* **[Microfilm & Digital Capture],** from the originals at the San Francisco Federal Records Center, San Bruno, CA. Filmed by the Genealogical Society of Utah, 1975, 1 roll, FHL film #1084801. To access the digital images, see the online FHL catalog page: **www.familysearch.org/search/catalog/556551.**

1900-1938. *Registers of Deaths* **[Microfilm & Digital Capture],** from the originals at the High Court, Pago Pago, AS. Includes indexes. Filmed by the Genealogical Society of Utah, 1974, 1 roll, FHL film #1083946. To access the digital images, see the online FHL catalog page: **www.familysearch.org/search/catalog/556343.**

1900-1945. *Census Returns, American Samoa* **[Microfilm & Digital Capture],** from the originals now located at the Federal Records Center, San Bruno, CA. These are Samoan censuses conducted by the High Court of Samoa, based on the roll contents, for the years 1900-1901, 1903, 1908-1909, 1912, 1916, 1920, 1922, 1923, 1926, and 1945. The printed forms for each census year are printed in the Samoan language, labeled "Amerika Samoa." These original census name lists were filmed by the Genealogical Society of Utah, 1975, 4 rolls, beginning with FHL film #1084778. To access the digital images, see the online FHL catalog page: **https://familysearch.org/search/catalog/583600.**

1900-1956. *Village Affairs, American Samoa* **[Microfilm & Digital Capture],** from the originals at the Federal Records Center, San Bruno, CA. Filmed by the Genealogical Society of Utah, 1975, 3 rolls, as follows:
- Native officials, 1900-1956 [names, office, district, date of appointment, county, residence], FHL film #1084783.
- Petitions and reports, 1924-1950 Village policeman, 1950 Applications for government positions, 1934 Petitions to governor, 1902-1933 (dates mixed), FHL film #1084784.

• Petitions, 1905-1913 (dates mixed), FHL film #1084785.
To access the digital images, see the online FHL catalog page:
www.familysearch.org/search/catalog/583611.

1900-1965. *Divorce Proceedings, American Samoa* **[Microfilm]**, from the originals at the Federal Records Center, San Bruno, CA. Some text in Samoan. Filmed by the Genealogical Society of Utah, 1973-1975, 27 rolls, beginning with FHL film #1084655 (1900-1906). For a complete list of roll numbers and contents of each roll, see the online FHL catalog page for this title. See **https://familysearch.org/search/catalog/556591**.

1900-1968. *Marriage Licenses and Certificates* **[Microfilm & Digital Capture]**, from the originals at the High Court, Pago Pago, AS. Some text in Samoan. Filmed by the Genealogical Society of Utah, 1974, 27 rolls, beginning with FHL film #1083521 (Marriage licenses and certificates, 1900-1910). To access the digital images, see the online FHL catalog page: **https://familysearch.org/search/catalog/554731**.

1900-1972. *Death Certificates* **[Microfilm & Digital Capture]**, from the originals at the High Court, Pago Pago, AS. Some text in Samoan. Filmed by the Genealogical Society of Utah, 1974, 11 rolls, beginning with FHL film #1083510 (Death certificates, 1900-1904). To access the digital images, see the online FHL catalog page: **https://familysearch.org/search/catalog/554725**.

1900-1974. *Civil Cases for American Samoa* **[Microfilm & Digital Capture]**, from the originals at the High Court, Pago Pago, AS. Filmed by the Genealogical Society of UT, 1973-1974, beginning with FHL film #1084050 (Civil cases 1907-1908, 1905-1906, 1900-1902 & Civil docket 1900-1902; 1912-1916). To access the digital images, see the online FHL catalog page: **https://familysearch.org/search/catalog/583585**.

1901-1973. *Land Claims for American Samoa* **[Microfilm & Digital Capture]**, from the originals at the High Court, Pago Pago, AS. Some text in Samoan. Filmed by the Genealogical Society of Utah, 1974, 17 rolls, beginning with FHL film #1084050 (Index to Land Claims, 1906-1918). To access the digital images, see the online FHL catalog page: **https://familysearch.org/search/catalog/557657**.

1902-1961. *Probate Records (American Samoa)* **[Microfilm & Digital Capture]**, from the originals at the Federal Records Center, San Bruno, CA. Filmed by the Genealogical Society of Utah, 1975, 2 rolls, FHL film #1084787 (Probate cases, No. 1-7); and FHL film #1084788 (Probate cases, No. 7 [cont], Wills, 1906-1961). To access the digital images, see the online FHL catalog page: **www.familysearch.org/search/catalog/583626**.

1903-1952. *Court Records, American Samoa* **[Microfilm & Digital Capture]**, from the originals at the High Court, Pago Pago, AS. Includes Pardons and paroles, 1914-1952; Commitments to prison, 1904-1931; Misc. court records, 1918-1944 Niue; Island court proceedings, 1923-1924; and Village court records, 1933-1938. Filmed by the Genealogical Society of Utah, 1975, 1 roll, FHL film #1084791. To access the digital images, see the online FHL catalog page: **www.familysearch.org/search/catalog/583640**.

1904-1925. *Contracts (Native Agreements), American Samoa* **[Microfilm & Digital Capture]**, from the originals at the Federal Records Center, San Bruno, CA. Filmed by the Genealogical Society of Utah, 1975, 1 roll, FHL film #1084792. To access the digital images, see the online FHL catalog page: **www.familysearch.org/search/catalog/556568**.

1906-1965. *Miscellaneous Records Pertaining to Vital Statistics* **[Microfilm & Digital Capture]**, from the originals at the San Francisco Federal Records Center, San Bruno, CA. Some text in Samoan. Contents: Birth & death certificates (mostly duplicate copies; includes correspondence, late registration of births and deaths), 1906-1944; Marriage permits, 1936-1965; Affidavits of deaths, births, name changes, etc., 1948-1956; and Correspondence, 1952. Filmed by the Genealogical Society of Utah, 1975, 1 roll, FHL film #1084801. To access the digital images, see the online FHL catalog page: **www.familysearch.org/search/catalog/556549**.

1918-1965. *American Samoa, Passenger Lists and Travel Documents* **[Online Database]**, digitized and indexed at the FamilySearch.org website. Source: National Archives, Washington, D.C. This database has passenger lists, passports and travel permits, letters of identity, affidavits of birth, visas and visa requests, and naturalization petitions from American Samoa. This database has 6,563 images. See **https://familysearch.org/search/collection/2355804**.

1920. *American Samoa, 1920 Federal Census: Soundex and Population Schedules* **[Microfilm & Digital Capture]**, from the originals of the Census Bureau. After microfilming, Congress permitted the Census Bureau to destroy the originals to make room

for WWII records. Filmed by the Census Bureau, ca1943, series M1605, 3 rolls, beginning with FHL film #1831660 (Soundex: A000 thru P100), and FHL film #1822032 (Population schedules: Samoa: Manua District, Eastern District of Tutuila, and Western District of Tutuila). To access the digital images, see the online FHL catalog page:
https://familysearch.org/search/catalog/558363.

1921-1937. See *School Census, 1921; School Registers, 1937 (American Samoa)* **[Microfilm & Digital Capture],** from the originals at the Federal Records Center, San Bruno, CA. Filmed by the Genealogical Society of Utah, 1975, 1 roll, FHL film #1084782. To access the digital images, see the online FHL catalog page:
www.familysearch.org/search/catalog/583606.

1922-1966. *Adoption Proceedings, American Samoa* **[Microfilm & Digital Capture],** from the originals at the High Court, Pago Pago, AS. Includes indexes. Filmed by the Genealogical Society of Utah, 1974, 4 rolls, beginning with FHL film #1083312. To access the digital images, see the online FHL catalog page:
https://familysearch.org/search/catalog/557651.

1930. *American Samoa and Guam, 1930 Federal Census: Population Schedules* **[Microfilm & Digital Capture],** from the originals of the Census Bureau. After microfilming, Congress permitted the Census Bureau to destroy the originals to make room for WWII records. Filmed by the Census Bureau, ca1943, 1 roll, FHL film #2342363 (Population schedules, American Samoa & Guam). To access the digital images, see the online FHL catalog page:
https://familysearch.org/search/catalog/1037568.

1940. *American Samoa, 1940 Federal Census: Population Schedules* **[Digital Capture],** from the National Archives microfilm. To access the digital images, see the online FHL catalog:
https://familysearch.org/search/catalog/2052181.

1941-1962. *Insanity Records, American Samoa* **[Microfilm & Digital Capture],** from the originals at the Federal Records Center, San Bruno, CA. Filmed by the AS Dept of Health. FHL has 1 roll, FHL film #1084790. To access the digital images, see the online FHL catalog page:
www.familysearch.org/search/catalog/583637.

1946-1953. *War Damage Claims, American Samoa* **[Microfilm & Digital Capture],** from the originals at the Federal Records Center, San Bruno, CA. Some text

in Samoan. Applications for settlements of claims against the United States government for damages caused by the U.S. Marines, 1942-1944, on the Island of Tutuila, American Samoa. Includes affidavits and other supporting documents. Arranged by number (or by village). Filmed by the Genealogical Society of Utah, 1975, 8 rolls, beginning with FHL film #1084793 (No. 1-16). To access the digital images, see the online FHL catalog page:
https://familysearch.org/search/catalog/556557.

1951. *Temporary Telephone Directory of American Samoa, July 1, 1951* **[Microfiche],** publisher not noted. Filmed by the Genealogical Society of Utah, 1 fiche, FHL fiche #6067003.

1962-1971. *Adoption Records, American Samoa* **[Microfilm & Digital Capture],** from the originals at the High Court, Pago Pago, AS. Filmed by the Genealogical Society of Utah, 1974, 1 roll, FHL film #1083949. To access the digital images, see the online FHL catalog page:
www.familysearch.org/search/catalog/556397.

1962-1972. *Affidavits of Delayed Registration of Births* **[Microfilm & Digital Capture],** from the originals at the High Court, Pago Pago, American Samoa. Text in English and Samoan. Includes some indexes. Filmed by the Genealogical Society of Utah, 1974, 16 rolls, beginning with FHL film #1083868 (1962-1963). To access the digital images, see the online FHL catalog page:
https://familysearch.org/search/catalog/556327.

1965. *Index to Divorces, American Samoa* **[Microfilm & Digital Capture],** from the originals at the High Court, Pago Pago, AS. Filmed by the Genealogical Society of Utah, 1 roll, FHL film #1084050. To access the digital images, see the online FHL catalog page:
www.familysearch.org/search/catalog/583575.

1968-1970. *Divorces, American Samoa* **[Microfilm & Digital Capture],** from the originals at the High Court, Pago Pago, AS. Includes indexes. Filmed by the Genealogical Society of Utah, 1974, 1 roll, FHL film #1083948. To access the digital images, see the online FHL catalog page:
www.familysearch.org/search/catalog/556349.

1973 Telephone Directory, American Samoa **[Printed Book],** by the Transpac Corporation, Pago Pago, AS, 1973, FHL book 996.13 E4a.

The Philippines
1902-1946
Pacific Region

As part of the 1898 Treaty of Paris ending the Spanish-American War, the U.S. purchased the Philippine Islands from Spain.

- The Philippines struggle for independence had begun in 1896 and with the help of the U.S. Navy, Spain was defeated and removed from power.

- After learning that the U.S. had no intention of allowing an immediate independent nation, the Philippine rebels shifted their attacks previously directed at the Spanish to the American victors. The Filipino-American War ensued, 1899-1902.

- The Americans defeated the Rebels, and in 1902, the Philippine Organic Act established the Philippine Commission, a body appointed by the President of the U.S. to provide legislative and limited executive powers in the Philippines. An appointed Governor-General of the Philippines led the Philippines Commission. The first to hold that office was William Howard Taft, who served until 1904, and who became President of the United States in 1909.

- In 1907, two chambers of a new Philippines legislature were established, with the Philippines Commission acting as the Upper House and an elected Philippine Assembly as the Lower House.

- In 1916, the Jones Act ended the Philippine Commission, replacing it with an elected Philippine Senate as the Upper House.

- In 1934, the Commonwealth of the Philippines was created, an Unincorporated Organized Territory of the United States. The Commonwealth was established with a constitution outlining a process and timeline to become an independent nation. The process was interrupted by World War II, including an occupation by the Japanese; but the Republic of the Philippines finally became an independent nation in 1946.

Bibliography
The Philippines
Censuses & Substitutes

Philippines Censuses: Although part of the U.S. from 1898 to 1946, the Philippine natives were never included in any of the decennial U.S. federal censuses. A special census was conducted in 1903 by the Philippines Commission, but only the printed report of the census statistics is extant. The U.S. Census Bureau conducted censuses of American Military and Naval personnel stationed in Insular Areas of the U.S., including the Philippines, in 1900, 1910, and 1920. Census substitutes included in the bibliography span the years of the Spanish era into the American era:

1615-1982. *Philippines, Lingayen-Dagupan Catholic Archdiocese Parish Registers* **[Online Database],** indexed at the FamilySearch.org website. Source: Parroquias, Archidiócesis de Lingayen-Dagupan, Pangasinan (parishes, Lingayen-Dagupan Archdiocese, Pangasinan). Indexes to baptisms, marriages, and burials from the Catholic Church parish registers of the Archdiocese of Lingayen-Dagupan covering the years 1615-1982. Currently this collection is for records from 13 of 35 parishes. Additional records will be added as they are completed. This database has 219,587 records. See https://familysearch.org/search/collection/1646454.

1642-1994. *Philippines Births and Baptisms* **[Online Database],** indexed at the FamilySearch.org website. Source: FamilySearch extractions from records at the Family History Library, Salt Lake City, UT. Index to selected Philippines births and baptisms. Only a few localities are included, and the time period varies by locality. This database has 328,442 records. See https://familysearch.org/search/collection/1500711.

1642-1994. *Philippines, Select Births and Baptisms* **[Online Database],** indexed at the Ancestry.com website. Source: FamilySearch extractions. This database has 953,205 records. See http://search.ancestry.com/search/db.aspx?dbid=60123.

1659-1894. Indexes to Capellania [Microfilm & Digital Capture], Chaplaincy calendars of parish trusts, from the originals at the Record Management and Archives, Manila. Filmed by the Genealogical Society of Utah, 1991, 1 roll. To access the digital images, see the online FHL catalog page: www.familysearch.org/search/catalog/438687.

1706-1898. *Index to Bautismos* [Microfilm & Digital Capture], includes card indexes of baptisms recorded in the civil registry offices throughout the Philippines. This database is included in the Philippines Civil Registration (Spanish Period). Filmed by the Genealogical Society of Utah, 1991, 3 rolls, to access the digital images, see the online FHL catalog page: www.familysearch.org/search/catalog/439175.

1706-1911. *Philippines Civil Registration (Spanish Period)* [Online Database], digitized at the FamilySearch.org website. Source: Records Management and Archive Office, Ermita, Manila. This is an image-only database with civil registration of births, marriages, and deaths during the Spanish Period of the Philippines. Prior to about 1815 there are only death records. Browse through the images, organized by Province, Municipality, Record Type, and Year Range. This database has 206,828 images. See https://familysearch.org/search/collection/1935452.

1716-1977. *Philippines, Camarines Sur, Roman Catholic Archdiocese of Caceres, Parish Registers* [Online Database], digitized at the FamilySearch.org website. Source: Parroquias Católicas, archdiocesano de Caceres, Camarines (Catholic Church parishes, Caceres Archdiocese, Camarines). This is an image-only database with baptisms, marriages, deaths, and some confirmations and parish census records of the Roman Catholic Archdiocese of Caceres, Camarines Sur, Philippines. This database has 136,616 images. See https://familysearch.org/search/collection/1457939.

1723-1957 *Philippines Marriages* [Online Database], indexed at the FamilySearch.org website. Source: FamilySearch extractions from the Family History Library, Salt Lake City, UT. Index to selected Philippines marriages. Only a few localities are included, and the time period varies by locality. The year range represents most of the records. A few records may be earlier or later. This database has 822,739 records. See https://familysearch.org/search/collection/1500713.

1723-1957. *Philippines, Select Marriages* [Online Database], indexed at the Ancestry.com website. Source: FamilySearch extractions. This database has 4,583,573 records. See http://search.ancestry.com/search/db.aspx?dbid=60130.

1726-1957. *Philippines, Select Deaths and Burials* [Online Database], indexed at the Ancestry.com website. Source: FamilySearch extractions. This database has 5,082,073 records. See http://search.ancestry.com/search/db.aspx?dbid=60128. - For the FamilySearch version, see www.familysearch.org/search/catalog/1500714.

1726-1957. *Philippines Deaths and Burials* [Online Database], indexed at the FamilySearch.org website. Source: FamilySearch Extractions from records at the Family History Library, Salt Lake City, UT. Index to selected Philippines deaths and burials. Only a few localities are included, and the time period varies by locality. This database has 5,128,622 records. See https://familysearch.org/search/collection/1500714.

1755-1976. *Philippines, Negros Occidental, Roman Catholic Diocese of Bacolod, Parish Registers* [Online Database], digitized at the FamilySearch.org website. Source: Catholic Church parishes, Diocese of Bacolod, Bacolod City. This is an image-only database with church records containing baptisms, confirmations, marriages, deaths, parish censuses, diocesan orders and decrees for some parishes in the Roman Catholic Diocese of Bacolod, Philippines. Original records are located in the various parish archives of the diocese. Browse through the images, organized by Municipality, Parish, Record Type, and Year Range. This database has 168,111 images. See https://familysearch.org/search/collection/2157100.

1759-1901. *Chinos II* [Microfilm & Digital Capture], from originals at the Record management Office, National Library, Metropolitan Manila, Philippines. Text in Spanish. The database includes censuses, passports, passenger lists and other documents regarding the Chinese in the Philippines. The rolls of film are organized by year, but no details about contents of each roll. To access the digital images, see the online FHL catalog page: www.familysearch.org/search/catalog/610932.

1801-1984. *Philippines, La Union, Diocese of San Fernando de La Union* [Online Database], digitized at the FamilySearch.org website. Source: Diocese of

San Fernando de La Union, San Fernando City. This is an image-only database with Church records including baptisms, marriages, deaths, and confirmations from the Diocese of San Fernando de La Union. Browse through the images, organized by Municipality, Parish, Record Type, and Year Range. This database has 33,723 images. See
https://familysearch.org/search/collection/2071967.

1805-1897. *Padrones de Chinos* **[Microfilm & Digital Capture],** from the original manuscripts in the Bureau of Records Management, National Library Bldg., Manila, Philippines. Includes records of Chinese in several Filmed by the Genealogical Society of Utah, 1978, 4 rolls. The database was included with Philippines, Civil Registrations (Spanish Period). To access the digital images, see the online FHL catalog page: www.familysearch.org/search/catalog/90856.

1818-1978. *Philippines, Biliran, Diocese of Naval Parish Registers* **[Online Database],** digitized at the FamilySearch.org website. Source: Diócesis de Naval (Naval Diocese, Naval). This is an image-only database with parish registers. Browse through the images, organized by Municipality, Record Type, and Year Range. This database has 42,440 images. See
https://familysearch.org/search/collection/2322258.

1838-1936. *Philippines Court Records* **[Online Database],** digitized at the FamilySearch.org website. Source: Record Management and Archives Office. National Library, Metropolitan Manila. This is an image-only database with records from various provinces of the Philippines mostly dating from the Spanish Period. These records contain land records, guardianships, wills, powers of attorney and other legal documents. This database has 522,632 records.
https://familysearch.org/search/collection/2094274.

1848-1898. *Estado Numerico de Defunciones* **[Microfilm & Digital Capture],** includes enumeration of deaths by province and municipality in each province in the Spanish Philippines. Filmed by the Genealogical Society of Utah, 1993, 3 rolls. This database was included in the *Philippines, Civil Registrations (Spanish Period).* To access the digital images, see the online FHL catalog page:
www.familysearch.org/search/catalog/829373.

1888-1986. *Philippines Civil Registration (Local)* **[Online Database],** indexed at the FamilySearch.org website. Source: National Census and Statistics Office, Manila. This collection comprises marriage and death certificates from local civil registry offices throughout the Philippines Records are not available for all localities and the coverage varies by locality. This database has 80,235 records. See
https://familysearch.org/search/collection/1410394.

1899-1984. *Philippines, Manila, Civil Registration* **[Online Database],** digitized and indexed at the FamilySearch.org website. Source: Civil Registry Office, City Hall of Manila. Includes images of births, marriages, and deaths and some indexes thereof. Some folders of images are not arranged chronologically and/or sequentially. This collection is partially indexed. The index currently covers birth certificates 1900 to 1980. Browse through the images, organized by Record Type, and Date Range. This database has 5,857,674 images. See
https://familysearch.org/search/collection/1686086.

1842-1984. *Philippines, Eastern Samar, Roman Catholic Diocese of Borongan, Parish Registers* **[Online Database],** digitized at the FamilySearch.org website. Source: Diocese of Borongan Offices, Borongan. This is an image-only database with parish registers of births, marriages, deaths, and confirmations Browse through the images, organized by Province, Parish, Record Type, and Date Range. This database has 57,624 images.
https://familysearch.org/search/collection/2379876.

1849-1856. *Indexes to Mesadas Eclesiasticas* **[Microfilm & Digital Capture],** calendars of records dealing with monthly masses administered throughout he Philippines. Filmed by the Genealogical Society of Utah, 1991, 1 roll. To access the digital images, see the online FHL catalog page:
www.familysearch.org/search/catalog/438595.

1860-1983. *Philippines, Northern Samar, Roman Catholic Diocese of Catarman, Church Records* **[Online Database],** digitized at the FamilySearch.org website. Source: Diocesan Catholic Center Catarman, Catarman, Northern Samar. This is an image-only database with church records containing births, confirmation, marriages, and deaths. Browse through the images, organized by Parish, Record Type, and Year Range. This database has 81,107 images. See
https://familysearch.org/search/collection/2328692.

1900. *Military and Naval (Including Philippines), 1900 Federal Census: Soundex and Population Schedules* **[Microfilm & Digital Capture],** from the originals of the Census Bureau. After microfilming, Congress permitted the Census Bureau to destroy the originals to make room for WWII records. Filmed by the Census Bureau, ca1943, series T1081, 37 rolls, beginning with FHL film #1241838.. To access the digital images (Population Schedules), see the online FHL catalog page: https://familysearch.org/search/catalog/655325.

1902-1945. *Philippines Civil Registration (Archives Division)* **[Online Database],** digitized at the FamilySearch.org website. Source: Archives Division, Bureau of Records Management, Manila. This is an image-only database copies of birth, marriage and death certificates from the Archives Division of the Bureau of Records Management. Includes many localities throughout the Philippines primarily from 1922 to 1932. This database has 185,883 records. See https://familysearch.org/search/collection/2018411.

1903. *Census of the Philippine Islands: Taken Under the Direction of the Philippine Commission in the Year 1903* **[Printed Book & Digital Version],** publ. U.S. Census Bureau, Washington, D.C., 1905. 4 vols. Contents: Vol. 1: Geography, history and population; Vol. 2: Population; Vol. 3: Mortality, defective classes, education, families and dwellings; Vol. 4: Agriculture, social and industrial statistics. These volumes do not include individual names. See FHL book 959.9 X2u v.1-4. Also on microfilm, FHL film #795716 (Vols. 1-2), and FHL film #795713 (Vols. 3-4). To access the digital images, see www.familysearch.org/search/catalog/102416.

1910. *Military and Naval (Including Philippines), 1910 Federal Census: Population Schedules* **[Microfilm & Digital Capture],** from the originals of the Census Bureau. After microfilming, Congress permitted the Census Bureau to destroy the originals to make room for WWII records. Filmed by the Census Bureau, 1 roll, FHL film #1375797. To access the digital images, see the online FHL catalog page https://familysearch.org/search/catalog/651352.

1920. See *Military and Naval (Including Philippines), 1920 Federal Census: Soundex and Population Schedules* **[Microfilm & Digital Capture],** from the originals of the Census Bureau. After microfilming, Congress permitted the Census Bureau to destroy the originals to make room for WWII records. Filmed by the Census Bureau, ca1943, series M1600, 20 rolls, beginning with FHL film #1831476 (Soundex: A000 thru B366), and FHL film #1822040 (Population schedules: U.S. Military Forces). To access the digital images, see the online FHL catalog page: https://familysearch.org/search/catalog/558350.

1937-1941. See *Philippines, Jewish Refugees, 1937-1941* **[Online Database],** indexed at the Ancestry.com website. Source: JewishGen.org. One destination for Jews trying to escape Nazi oppression was the Philippines. This database lists the names of people who received visas to enter the Philippines. This database has 1,318 records. See http://search.ancestry.com/search/db.aspx?dbid=6603.

1945-1981. See *Philippines, Pangasinan, Civil Registration* **[Online Database],** digitized at the FamilySearch.org website. Source: Office of the Civil Registrar-General, National Census and Statistics Office, Santa Mesa, Manila. This image-only database includes national civil registration of births, marriages and deaths from the Province of Pangasinan, Philippines This database has 151,466 images. See https://familysearch.org/search/collection/1989160.

1945-1984. See *Philippines Civil Registration (National)* **[Online Database],** indexed at the FamilySearch.org website. Collection of vital records from various localities in the Philippines. This database has 312,009 records. See https://familysearch.org/search/collection/1852584